George Ireland

George Ireland read history at Oxford University and afterwards was called to the Bar. Over the last fifteen years he has written and edited several thousand short biographies for the obituaries column of the *Daily Telegraph*. He is a contributor to the new *Dictionary of National Biography* and has previously written (as ghost) *A Gilt-Edged Life*, the memoirs of Edmund de Rothschild.

Plutocrats

A Rothschild Inheritance

GEORGE IRELAND

JOHN MURRAY

First published in Great Britain in 2007 by John Murray (Publishers)
An Hachette Livre UK company

First published in paperback in 2008

2

A CIP catalogue record for this title is available from the British Library

ISBN 978-0-7195-6558-8

Typeset in Bembo by M Rules

Printed and bound by Clays Ltd, St Ives plc

John Murray policy is to use papers that are natural, renewable and
recyclable products and made from wood grown in sustainable forests.
The logging and manufacturing processes are expected to conform to
the environmental regulations of the country of origin.

John Murray (Publishers)
338 Euston Road
London NW1 3BH

www.johnmurray.co.uk

To David and Patience Ireland

Contents

Illustrations

The author and publishers would like to thank the following for permission to reproduce illustrations: Plates 1 and 16, Private Collection, London; 5, the Savile Club; 17 and 18, The Earl and Countess of Rosebery. Plate 2 is taken from Hugo's *Illustrated Itinerary of the Ward of Bishopsgate*; plate 4 is from Wheatley's *Round about Piccadilly and Pall Mall*; plate 22 is from Cohen's *Lady de Rothschild and her daughters 1821–1931*. All other images are reproduced courtesy of The Rothschild Archive.

Acknowledgements

I should like to express my gratitude to all those who have encouraged, guided or assisted me in various ways with this book: among others, Roderick Barman, Mathew Claridge, Paul Goulet, Beatrice Gray, Victor Gray, Michael Hall, Jay Iliff, David Ireland, Patience Ireland, Essaka Joshua, Caroline Knox, Caroline Lucas-Tooth, Joslyn McDiarmid, Alidad Mahloudji, Sarah Jane Miller, Richard Onslow, James Owen, Elaine Penn, Georgia Powell, Edmund de Rothschild, Lionel de Rothschild, Barbra Ruperto, Richard Schofield, Caroline Shaw, Ulrike Vogel, Gordon Wise, Samantha Wyndham, Harlan Zimmerman, Mordechai Zucker, the staff of N. M. Rothschild & Sons Limited and the staff of the London Library.

My particular thanks are due to the director of The Rothschild Archive, Melanie Aspey, who has shown unwavering patience and generosity in sharing her knowledge, and all of whose suggestions have proved invaluable.

I owe a considerable debt to the findings of Professor Niall Ferguson in his book *The World's Banker: The History of the House of Rothschild* (1998), on which I have relied for financial figures and conclusions and for other details.

For his undertaking to compile an index, I am most grateful to Douglas Matthews. For their comments on the manuscript, I thank Melanie Aspey, Roland Philipps, Caroline Westmore and, above all, Howard Davies.

Mayer Amschel Rothschild 1744–1812
m. 1770
Gudle Schnapper 1753–1849

Jeannette 1771–1859
m. 1795
Benedict Moses Worms 1772–1824

Amschel Mayer 1773–1855
m. 1796
Eva Hanau 1779–1848

Salomon Mayer 1774–1855
m. 1800
Caroline Stern 1782–1854

Anselm Salomon 1803–74
m. 1826
Charlotte 1807–59

Betty 1805–86
m. 1824
James Mayer 1792–1868

Mayer Anselm Léon 1827–8
Caroline Julie Anselme 1830–1907
m. 1850
Adolphe Carl 1833–1900
Hannah Mathilde 1832–1924
m. 1849
Wilhelm Carl 1828–1901
Sara Louise 1834–1924
m. 1858
Barone Raimondo Franchetti 1829–1905
Nathaniel Mayer 1836–1905
Ferdinand James Anselm 1839–98
m. 1865
Evelina 1839–66
Salomon Albert Anselm 1844–1911
m. 1876
Bettina Caroline 1858–92
Alice Charlotte 1847–1922

Leonora 1837–1911
m. 1857
Mayer Alphonse 1827–1905
Evelina 1839–66
m. 1865
Ferdinand James Anselm 1839–98
Nathaniel Mayer, 1st Lord Rothschild 1840–1915
m. 1867
Emma Louisa 1844–1935
Alfred Charles 1842–1918

Charlotte 1807–59
m. 1826
Anselm Salomon 1803–74

Lionel Nathan 1808–79
m. 1836
Charlotte 1819–84

Leopold 1845–1917
m. 1881
Marie Perugia 1862–1937
Constance 1843–1931
m. 1877
Cyril Flower, Lord Battersea 1843–1907
Annie Henriette 1844–1926
m. 1871
Hon. Eliot Constantine Yorke 1843–78
Nathalie 1843

Nathan Mayer 1777–1836
m. 1806
Hannah Barent Cohen 1783–1850

Anthony Nathan 1810–76
m. 1840
Louisa Montefiore 1821–1910

Nathaniel 1812–70
m. 1842
Charlotte 1825–99

Hannah Mayer 1815–64
m. 1839
Hon. Henry FitzRoy 1807–59

Isabella 1781–1861
m. 1802
Bernhard Juda Sichel 1780–1862

Mayer Amschel 1818–74
m. 1850
Juliana Cohen 1831–77

Nathan James Edouard 1844–81
m. 1871
Laura Thérèse 1847–1931

Babette 1784–1869
m. 1808
Siegmund Leopold Beyfus 1786–1845

Louisa 1820–94

Mayer Albert 1846–50

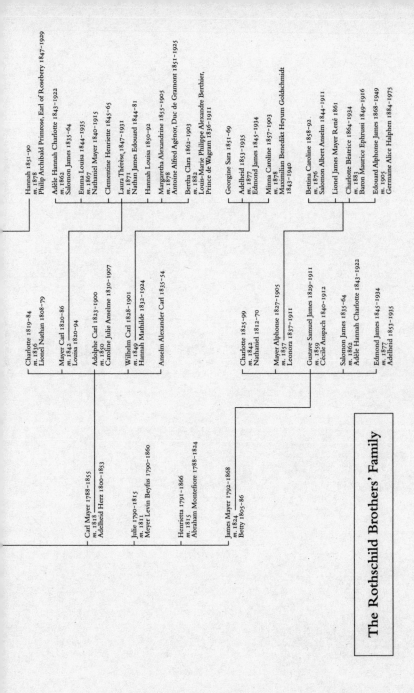

The Rothschild Brothers' Family

Prologue

IN THE EARLY 1840s the English author William Howitt took his wife and young family to live in Germany for three years. The town he selected for their residence was Heidelberg, a convenient base, it seemed to him, from which he might visit other parts of the country in preparation for his book *The Rural and Social Life of Germany*, and a place where his children might attend good schools. It was also to be a place to which he could return from his tours to unwind, to go for walks and to enjoy the company of family and friends. The landscape in which Heidelberg was set – with 'its lovely river, its charming valleys, its wide and open forests' – had a strong appeal for Howitt; and as a town much frequented by the English, Heidelberg presented good opportunities for mixing with his fellow countrymen.

After some initial bad luck with lodgings, the Howitts settled into a house with a garden from which the woods and the mountains were within easy reach. They made friends with some English residents, the children got on well at school, and Howitt and his wife undertook various excursions to gather information for the book. 'In the boundless refreshments of nature, and the society of our few English friends,' Howitt wrote of the period at Heidelberg, 'we had all that we wanted.' Yet once he had completed his German survey Howitt had some searing criticisms to offer of small-town German life. He conceded that Heidelberg itself had served its purpose, had 'tolerably answered' his requirements; but the local inhabitants, in contrast to the country round about, came in for censure.

In *German Experiences*, a small book that followed on from the publication of his *Rural and Social Life*, Howitt declared Heidelberg to be 'perhaps the most wretched, as to the general tone and quality of its society, of all the little [German] University towns'; and he wished his readers to know that he was not alone in this opinion, that he had met 'a good many English of high character who have spent some time in that place, but scarcely with an exception have they left it with disappointment and disgust'. Even a German – 'a celebrated German' – had written to him that of all the university towns in Germany, Heidelberg was 'the most notorious for its frivolity, conceit and impertinence to strangers'.[1]

Colouring William Howitt's recollection of the town above all, though, was the tragic fact that one of his children had died there – as a result, he believed, of medical misconduct. During one of their longer absences on tour, the Howitts placed their children in a local boarding school. It was an establishment they knew, and one at which they had every reason to expect that, for a few months, their children would be well looked after. Friends of the family kept an eye on the children, and all went well until one of the Howitt boys fell ill. The precise nature of the illness is unclear, but at an early stage the boy was moved to the school sick-room and placed under the care of Maximilian Chelius, professor of surgery at Heidelberg University.

Friends visited the boy regularly, and received assurances that his case was a trivial one, 'totally without danger'; but as weeks turned to months, they and the Howitts became increasingly anxious, not least because they could obtain no statement from Chelius himself. After three months had passed, worrying reports from their friends prompted the Howitts to ask an English doctor from a nearby town to examine the boy. It was only then, Howitt recalled, that 'the consequences of long neglect were discovered to be most frightful; and, in fact, fatal'.

Conditions in the sick-room had been bleak; too often the child had been left for long periods alone; but it was the conduct of Chelius that Howitt most bitterly resented. Following the English doctor's visit, Chelius had blithely pronounced not only that the case was a 'most serious one, but [that he] could also foretell accurately how it would terminate!' More staggering still, in Howitt's view, was that 'knowing, as it thus proved, the real state of the case, at its worst stage', Chelius promptly left Heidelberg for four days without making any arrangements for another doctor to attend to the child.[2]

At their wits' end, the Howitts now wrote to consult the best doctors in London, among them Charles Aston Key, a senior surgeon at Guy's Hospital. But it was to be of no avail: to a man, the London doctors 'at once declared that the neglect of the German surgeons in the early stage of the mischief had proved fatal. *Then* it might by active and judicious treatment have been checked – *now* it was impossible, which time only too fully confirmed.'

I

The Importance of the Individual

I T WAS LATE April 1836, and still no firm date had been fixed for his wedding. Never content to be in Frankfurt for long, Lionel waited anxiously for news that his father and mother had started out on the road from London. He whiled away the days in going to his uncle's bank in the Fahrgasse, reading his post, writing his letters, visiting his fiancée and her family, and dining with his sister, his grandmother, his uncles, his aunts and his cousins at their houses in the town.

On 1 May, having learned from his brother Nat in London that their parents' departure for Frankfurt had been delayed, Lionel wrote in the sincere hope that Nat would 'not have to communicate again such information but that we shall soon hear of their being on the road. You can have no idea how disagreeable it is to receive such letters, when one is waiting with such impatience for their arrival, and then to hear of the departure being postponed. I hope that no further disappointment will take place.'[1]

Then twenty-seven years of age, Lionel was the eldest son of Nathan and Hannah Rothschild; the relations in Frankfurt were all on his father's side of the family; his fiancée was one of his first cousins. Nathan was the most famous banker in Europe, and his name was synonymous with great wealth. He and his four brothers – at their banks in London, Frankfurt, Paris, Vienna and Naples – together constituted the most powerful force that had ever been known in the world's money markets. They were all to gather in Frankfurt for Lionel's wedding.

It was in Frankfurt that Nathan and his brothers had grown up, in a house in the Jewish ghetto where their father, Mayer Amschel Rothschild, had begun the family business and had lived until his death in 1812, and where their ageing mother Gutle still resided. The eldest of Lionel's uncles, Amschel, ran the bank and resided in Frankfurt; his uncles Salomon and Carl, of Vienna and Naples, returned regularly to the houses they kept there. Charlotte, Lionel's fiancée, was the sixteen-year-old daughter of Carl (known usually to his English kinsmen as Charles), who had already arrived in Frankfurt for his daughter's wedding.

A fortnight after writing to Nat, Lionel was still corresponding with his mother in London. 'In answer to your question, whether it is not requisite to acquaint our family of my marriage,' he wrote on 15 May, 'I must say I do not think it necessary to write to them. You will most likely call upon them before your departure and might say that the day is not yet fixed, which is really the case, but that the wedding will take place in the month of June and that the greater the number of friends present, the merrier & the more agreeable the party.'[2]

The words 'our family' here referred to Lionel's relations through his mother. English by birth, Hannah was the daughter of a prosperous Jewish merchant in the City of London named Levi Barent Cohen, who came from Holland. Neither her father nor mother was still alive, but most of Hannah's numerous siblings and their progeny lived in and around London. Her sister Judith was the wife of Moses Montefiore, the Jewish philanthropist and upholder of Jewish rights around the world, who in earlier days had been a business associate of Nathan's. Moses' brother Abraham had married Nathan's younger sister Henrietta.

On 18 May Lionel wrote to Nat that the 'ladies are pretty well occupied in making preparations for the arrival of the illustrious visitors and are having their houses & gardens washed and cleaned so as to have everything in apple pie order'. The ladies included Lionel's eldest sister, another Charlotte ('Chilly' in the family circle), who was married to Salomon's son Anselm and lived in Frankfurt. Hannah Mayer, the middle of Lionel's three sisters, twenty-one years old and yet to marry, was also staying in Frankfurt at the time. Among the illustrious visitors expected, besides the bridegroom's parents, was Lionel's youngest uncle James, who had established the Rothschild bank in Paris.[3]

Feeling the need for some exercise, and perhaps to escape as the women made their preparations, Lionel went out with his gun to shoot rabbits; he was 'not very fortunate but had a nice pleasant walk and enjoyed the fresh air'.

A few days later, James left Paris for Frankfurt. In his absence, Lionel's brother Anthony — 'Billy' to his brothers and, at twenty-six, the closest to Lionel in age — had been left to take care of matters at James's bank in the rue Laffitte.

By the end of the month, still without the desired news of his parents' departure from London, Lionel was bored and restless. 'We are living as quietly as people can,' he wrote to Anthony on 1 June. 'Yesterday Uncle Anselm [Amschel] gave a diplomatic dinner which you know are not very amusing; this is the only time [we] have been out of the house . . . I have nothing more to write to you my dear Billy. I can only assure you that I am most heartily glad that the day for my quitting beautiful ffort will very soon be here.'[4]

In fact, on 1 June Nathan and Hannah, travelling with their youngest daughter Louisa, had already reached Calais. From there, Hannah wrote to Nat (then twenty-three), who had been left in charge of Nathan's bank at New Court in the City, asking him to arrange for confectionaries from Gunter's, the renowned London pastry-cooks, as well as some grapes, to be forwarded to Frankfurt.[5]

Two days later, Hannah was writing to Nat from Brussels: 'I hope dear Nat that you do not feel very much the worse for being without us all and that you like your parties at Lady Lansdowne's and the Duke's. Pray write to us all about them and not only about consols and Spanish [stock].'[6]

In Brussels, Nathan and Hannah met the Rothschild party from Paris – James, his wife Betty and their children, as well as Caroline, the wife of Salomon. Accompanying the Paris party was the composer Gioacchino Rossini, a friend of the family whose presence, the fifteen-year-old Louisa predicted, would 'add to the gaiety of the party'. As for Rossini himself, he wrote to a friend that the 'entire purpose' of his trip was 'to attend at Frankfurt the marriage of Lionel Rotschildt [sic], my very dear friend'.[7]

On 4 June, still in Brussels, Hannah informed Nat: 'Everything goes on very well as yet and I hope will continue so. Papa called on the King who asked us to dinner tomorrow. The Duchess of Gloucester is here. As we take our departure in the morning we cannot accept the invitation.'[8]

Making for Frankfurt from another direction was Lionel's youngest brother, Mayer ('Muffy'), with his German tutor Fritz Schlemmer. The pair had set out from Leipzig, where Mayer, aged seventeen, was studying at the university.

On 5 June, the day of his parents' departure from Brussels, in advance of James's party, Lionel wrote to Anthony in Paris: 'We have received yesterday and today your letters addressed to our good parents, so that you must suppose them already here, which I cannot have the pleasure of confirming to you. Tomorrow no doubt we shall be able to have that satisfaction . . . Muffy arrived yesterday and looks very well . . . I hope you do not mind the bother of being alone and that everything goes on well and to your wishes . . .'[9]

Two days running, on 7 and 8 June, Lionel drove to Mainz in the hope of being able to greet his parents there and escort them to Frankfurt; but twice he returned disappointed. 'Here as you may easily suppose we have been doing nothing but waiting for them, which is very unpleasant as you can easily conceive. Uncle Salomon & Anselm [Salomon's son] arrived from Vienna and are very well. Joe [Montefiore, a first cousin] and Muffy are gone to Coblenz to meet them.'

Nathan and Hannah finally reached Frankfurt late in the evening of 9 June. 'Our good parents arrived here very late the night before last, after having been several days longer on the road than we had expected,' Lionel told Nat two days later. 'I should have informed you of their arrival yesterday, but no post left . . .'[10]

Unfortunately, Lionel went on, 'Papa has a most terrible boil on his bottom and suffers very much from it. He has not yet been able to leave his bed and has a great deal of pain. The movement of the carriage inflamed it, so that he requires now double rest. We are in hopes it will be better in a day or two and that there will be no occasion to put off the wedding.' That they had been 'rather long on the road', Hannah explained more delicately in a letter to Nat, was because 'Papa has again a visit from his most unpleasant visitor, a disagreeable boil in a most inconvenient place [which] annoys him considerably particularly in sitting down.'[11]

Nathan was susceptible to boils, and despite his discomfort there was no special cause for alarm. Four years earlier, Charles Aston Key, the surgeon at Guy's whose opinion would one day be sought by William Howitt, had recommended that Nathan's boils 'be forwarded by poultice' and that his 'constitution should be supported by the quinine which I have prescribed and one or two glasses of wine'. The development of the boils, Key considered, would be sufficient to 'terminate Mr Rothschild's ailments'.[12]

For the time being, Nathan took to his room at the Römische Kaiser hotel. 'Papa has not yet left his bed,' Lionel told Nat a day or two later, 'his boil has not yet come to a head and gives him a great deal of pain. I am afraid it will last a few days longer. It quite disturbs our family party and makes us all dull.' Hannah, striking a more cheerful note, reported to Nat that she and Nathan had seen their future daughter-in-law and had found her 'beautiful as members [of the family] have already said and her manner agreeable'. Hannah had been pleased, too, to find that Charlotte was 'simple and amiable in her manner, not having shown any affectation'.[13]

On 13 June Lionel's impression was that his father was 'much better', though Nathan was still in considerable pain. He had been attended by local doctors, but his family had decided to call in Professor Chelius from Heidelberg – and what everyone had thought was a boil unluckily turned out to be a large abscess, which Chelius had proceeded to drain by making two openings. Nathan, consequently, had been under the knife – a dangerous as well as distressing procedure in the days before antiseptic surgery or anaesthetics.

'Yesterday they were afraid of being obliged to enlarge the second wound,' Lionel informed Anthony, 'as there was a large lump which did not appear to have any connexion with those that had already been cut, but since then it made its way into the large opening; it has been running famously and no other operation, it is expected, will be necessary. Professor Chelius arrived this morning and found both wounds in a much more forward state than he had imagined, in fact he is quite satisfied with the way they are going on and assured us that only time is requisite to see Papa quite restored.'[14]

James and his party from Paris had arrived on 12 June, and the wedding was now fixed for the 15th. Nathan was adamant that the ceremony must not be postponed and that, as Lionel relayed to his brothers, 'if he is not able to go out of the room, we shall have the ceremony here in the Inn – where I am now writing'.

Remembering his circle in London, Lionel hoped that on the day of his marriage Nat would 'give a good dinner to our most intimate friends . . . Pray remember me to [my uncles] Ben [Cohen], Isaac [Cohen] & [my cousin] George [Samuel] and excuse me for not writing . . .' Not forgetting the three dozen men who were employed at New Court at that time, he went on: 'Pray let the clerks have a good dinner, and get all drunk or if they like the Thames I think they might make a party at Greenwich. If some of them are too proud, let them make two parties and take their better halves with [them].'[15]

On 13 June, the bride-to-be's seventeenth birthday, her mother Adelheid gave a ball, though Charlotte herself stayed away. 'Papa is better today than he has been,' Hannah wrote to Anthony the next day, 'and I hope will be able tomorrow to enjoy the celebration of the Wedding. Every part of the family excel themselves for our comfort in all respects and things go on perfectly amicably. The Bride is very much agitated at all this, and could not make her appearance at a Ball her Mama gave last night; I went there for a short time, Papa not being there things were not so agreeable but every thing was very grand.'[16]

One member of the wedding party who was understandably less affected by Nathan's misery than the Rothschilds was Rossini. Felix Mendelssohn – whom the Rothschilds also knew – happened to be in Frankfurt at the time, and unexpectedly bumped into Rossini on the street. Afterwards, he wrote to his mother that Rossini had kept him 'laughing incessantly the whole time'.

On learning that Mendelssohn was in Frankfurt, the Rothschilds invited him to join them at the wedding celebrations, but he declined. He was not, he explained to his mother, 'in the vein or humour at present for balls or any other festivities'. Yet at the same time, he said, 'these people [the Rothschilds] really cause me much pleasure, and their splendour and luxury, and the universal respect with which the citizens here [in Frankfurt] are forced to regard them all (though they would naturally assault them if they dared) is a real source of exultation, for it is all owing entirely to their own industry, good fortune, and abilities'.[17]

As Nathan wished, the wedding went ahead as arranged. 'We have just come back from the ceremony,' Lionel wrote to his absent brothers on 15 June, '& I am very happy to have the pleasure of informing you that everything passed off perfectly well. Papa was well enough to come there; as his complaint is only one that gives pain, it required but little resolution of which you know Papa has enough. The ceremony lasted half an hour and was very solemn, a small temple having been built on purpose and by candlelight. Afterwards a small breakfast for the religious gents and now the ladies are preparing for the dinner which is to take place at 6 o'clock. We then go to Wilhelmsbad and shall be absent but a short time as we remain here a few days before we return. The ceremony went off uncommonly well as Papa was there and our family circle was complete.'[18]

Mayer's tutor reported to Nat that Nathan was 'present at the wedding & with jokes of every kind tried to shorten the long speech of the worthy rabbi & to cheer up those present'.[19]

For Hannah, though, the occasion had been overshadowed by Nathan's condition. 'It was a great pity,' she confided to Nat the next day, 'that I could not give you a lively account of the festivities which were so elegantly prepared for the celebration of the Wedding, the enjoyment of which has been so entirely destroyed by the indisposition of Papa. I hope and think from appearances that he will soon, please God, be relieved from the excessive pain he has endured. It is an abscess which is rather obstinate in forming and coming to a head . . . thank God there is no danger, but the pain and inconvenience it brings is most distressing and precludes us from participating in any thing . . .

'Yesterday morning he took courage at 6 o'clock . . . to get up and walk to Charlotte's [Chilly's] which he effected tolerably and afterwards dressed – and went to [Uncle] Charles's to be present at the celebration of the ceremony and I am happy to say it went off very well, but on his return he was seized with the excessive pain which usually comes on about 2 o'clock and lasts for six hours.'[20]

After a dinner for eighty at the bride's parents', the newly married couple left in a 'splendid travelling carriage with 4 post horses' for Wilhelmsbad. There they spent the night and the next day, returning to Frankfurt the following evening. 'As Papa was so unwell,' Lionel explained to his brothers, 'we did not like remaining away longer than necessary.'[21]

In Paris, Anthony was not so concerned. 'I have the pleasure of enclosing all the letters from Frankfort,' he wrote to Nat. 'You will perceive that Papa has had a bad boil on his bottom. I am very pleased that every thing is going on so well at ffort . . . I gave a grand dinner yesterday to celebrate the wedding. I was a little too tipsy to think at 12 o'clock of Lionel.'[22]

As it happened, the night at Wilhelmsbad had not been an unqualified success, as Anthony later reported heartily to Nat: 'Poor Rabbi [Lionel] could not take his Wife's Maidenhead. The fright brought on the flowers. Poor fellow – he will be obliged to cool his passion for a few days.' The bridegroom himself was unruffled: 'I can only say,' Lionel said of his new wife, 'that she is a most beautiful person in every respect.'[23]

On the morning of 17 June, Nathan obtained some relief when his abscess was cut open once more. 'Papa I am happy to say is much better,' Lionel reported. 'I think in a few days he will be quite well. He has suffered a good deal, but is now thank God in good spirits.' Five days later, it seemed as if Nathan was on the mend. 'Papa I am happy to say is going on very well and in a few days will, I hope, be able to get up,' Lionel informed Anthony and Nat. 'He is still very weak and does not like to talk much, so that we have not been able to say anything about business affairs . . .'[24]

Nathan and Hannah had by now left the Römische Kaiser to stay in greater privacy with Chilly and Anselm in their house on Neue Mainzer Strasse. 'Charlotte's house is extremely pretty,' Hannah wrote approvingly to Anthony. 'The apartments are commodious and well arranged and [there are] a great many nice things in them.' To Nat she wrote of his sister's 'beautiful residence filled with curiosities' and of visits from the newly married couple.[25]

'Lionel frequently comes in and his young wife with him,' she recounted. 'I hope and think with the blessing of God, they may be a very happy couple. Her beauty has been highly spoken of and you will shortly see her I hope and be a personal judge of her good qualities . . . By the bye, Lionel wishes for a large family; she already complains of feeling a little sickness – and I must tell you this is a symptom.' It was perhaps the fact that her daughter Chilly was seven months pregnant that put the latter idea into Hannah's head; Lionel's wife did not give birth to their first child until August the next year.[26]

By 26 June, nine days after the latest operation on Nathan's abscess, the treatment seemed to be working. 'Papa, thank God, is going on very well and is in much better spirits,' Lionel assured his brothers. 'His boil continues discharging uncommonly. I cannot say when he will be able to get about, but we hope in a few days to see him out of bed.'[27]

Writing to Nat, Hannah Mayer reported that Nathan was satisfied with Professor Chelius, 'who has a great reputation & whose directions Papa attends'. Although, she went on, Chelius 'does not flatter us that Papa will be quite recovered for some weeks . . . he assures us there is not the *slightest* degree of *danger* & that one must be patient'.[28]

With these assurances, Henrietta Montefiore and her son Joe left Frankfurt on 26 June; Hannah's elder brother from London, Solomon Cohen, set out on the return journey to England; and James and Betty, with Caroline, made plans for a brief visit to take the waters at Bad Kreuznach, a short distance from Frankfurt. 'Lionel & his Bride look very well & happy,' Hannah Mayer observed in a letter to Nat. 'They talk of leaving in about a fortnight.'[29]

Writing from Chilly's house, Hannah Mayer described her daily round to Nat – from which it is easy to see why members of the family felt the need to get out of Frankfurt, if only briefly, in the stifling summer heat. 'You can well imagine my dear Nat that we are none of us much inclined for gaiety,' she wrote. 'Mamma does not quit Papa's side for an hour, & with the exception of dreadful long tedious dinners every day we do not leave the house. Indeed, the weather is so extremely hot that we are better there than driving about in the town. Louisa & I take German & embroidery lessons which occupy our mornings. We then dress for dinner, which important meal generally takes two to three hours, & in the evening take a drive or meet all together here.'

Louisa, too, found the dinners an endurance; she asked Nat to picture her seated at the table between her grandmother Gutle and her aunt Eva, Amschel's wife, being 'stuffed so full as scarcely to be able to breathe'.[30]

As the end of June neared, Lionel told his brothers that their father was 'more comfortable than for some time', though it would be 'some time before he is able to travel'. Having had 'the second wound enlarged' on 30 June, Nathan 'found himself much easier . . . There are some little swellings of matter between the two wounds which have diminished considerably since the opening.'[31]

Chelius's plan, as Lionel understood it, was to keep the two wounds open so as to 'draw all the matter out' and thus prevent another abscess from forming. 'Papa suffers now & then very considerably being obliged to remain in the same position, and the Boils being in such a sensitive place. I do not think that he will be able to leave quite so soon as you wish but you must endeavour to write pleasant letters and to make him comfortable and to let him receive agreeable accounts.'

On 1 July, in a letter jointly to Anthony and Nat, Hannah wrote: 'The gatherings and the swellings have so rapidly succeeded each other that we cannot speak with certainty about them but at present things have united in one which is much better placed than hitherto and which now begins to discharge itself very well . . . Dear Nat I hope you have no trouble in domestic affairs. Papa is quite pleased and satisfied with your management and all you do; regularity and attention is all which can be required.'[32]

On 7 July Chelius arrived from Heidelberg again, and deemed it necessary to perform a further operation. 'The Boil was very deeply placed and had been running abundantly, so as to have occasioned a mortification of the fibres, which were obliged to be taken out,' Lionel reported. 'It was a painful operation but has perfectly succeeded. All the doctors are satisfied with the turn it is taking and have every hope of a speedy recovery. There is another small Boil lower down, which will require a similar operation, but this is of much less importance than the former and will not give so much pain.'[33]

Two days later one of the wounds required opening again. 'Papa underwent the operation with the greatest possible courage and all the time made jokes. The wound was larger than the first as the Boil was most terribly deep and must have been very painful. The Doctors think that he will be within a very short [time] able to set out on his way home.' Nathan had asked Lionel to tell Anthony and Nat 'that he is quite satisfied with you both'.[34]

On 11 July, Lionel reported that Nathan's boils were 'going on as well as they can. The first is very far advanced: every morning and evening large pieces of dead fibres come out, there is hardly any more in it. The second is not quite so far advanced; till now it has only discharged matter, but tomorrow they expect that something else will make its appearance. All the doctors are satisfied with the manner in which they are going on, but they cannot fix any period when they think with the least certainty that he may be able to leave. His health in every other respect is perfectly good, and he bears with very great patience his confinement & pains.'[35]

Stoical as the patient was, though, and despite his medical team's expressed satisfaction with his progress, a sense of uneasiness was beginning to take hold. When suffering from boils in the past, Nathan had recovered in eight to ten days; now almost a month had elapsed.

On 2 July, Fritz Schlemmer, used to helping Hannah with her correspondence, had been instructed to write to Nat to request him to consult both Charles Aston Key, now senior surgeon at Guy's, and Benjamin Travers, formerly a lecturer on surgery at St Thomas's and a doctor who had attended Nathan for many years. The hope was that their joint experience of Nathan's past ailments might enable them to advise the German doctors of the treatment to which the patient would be most likely to respond. As the days passed, it was further resolved to ask Travers to travel to Frankfurt in person.[36]

'We have received with pleasure Mr Travers's letter informing us of his willingness to pay us a visit,' Lionel wrote to his brothers on 12 July. 'We accept his offer and beg you my dearest Nat to lose [no] time in sending him off. We hope that by that time Papa will be so much better as not to be in want of his kind services, but as this disease has lasted so long, it is quite impossible to say anything for certain. So we think you would be pleasing Papa if you will send him to us without loss of time. We have the best advice and have full confidence in the Doctors, but in an old friend like Mr Travers Papa would have still more confidence and would be more at ease.

'The Doctors say that they are satisfied with the manner in which the Boils are going on and that nothing new had formed itself. The first wound is much better than it has been all the time. Yesterday a very large piece of the dead fibres was extracted and according to appearances, there do not seem [to be] any more in that one. The second Boil was not so far advanced when the operation was performed, and as it was deeper than the first, the pieces of hard matter and fibres have been slower in making their appearance . . . We hope to have better accounts for tomorrow. In the mean time you will do well to send Travers with the Rotterdam Steamer and to let him come as soon as he can.'[37]

On 14 July, Nathan was subjected to further surgery. 'Papa's health is going on as well as can be expected,' Lionel resignedly reported. 'The second wound was enlarged this morning. There was a hard lump that could not make its way through without a fresh opening. The operation was very painful as the hardness was uncommonly deeply placed . . .

'We are in hopes that today's operation will be the last and that we soon shall be able to inform you of Papa's recovery. We are happy to say that nothing new has come, but until the wounds begin to heal nothing can be relied upon . . . Papa is a little cross in not receiving letters from any of his London relations & friends. You would do well to give them a hint.'[38]

In a separate letter to Nat, Lionel relayed the doctors' assurances that 'everything is going on well and much better than they expected.' 'Papa begs you,' he continued, 'to send 100 Bottles of Soda Water, 20 Bottles of Lavender Water and a chest of good oranges . . . by the best and most expeditious conveyance, not minding the expense.' The next day, he asked Nat 'to enquire [in London] if there are not to be had travelling beds for invalids' and to 'send us a description of one'.[39]

Another two days passed and Lionel felt that his father was making tolerably good progress: 'Papa, I am happy to say, is going on well. He still suffers a great deal of pain from the immense wounds, which they do not allow to heal, but, thank God, nothing new is coming.'[40] On the 20th Nathan was still suffering 'a good deal from the large wounds, as they take some time to get clean, and there are several pieces of fibres which have not come out yet so that patience and time are requisite, and being in bed so long makes him uneasy and a little cross.' By the 21st Lionel found his father 'a little better today than he was yesterday. He does not suffer quite so much and is not so cross. The doctors say that the wounds are going on well.'[41]

The next day, none the less, Lionel wrote of his sense of relief on learning that Nat 'had immediately attended to my letter' and was 'on the point of sending off Travers'. 'Today,' he went on, 'the professor arrived from Heidelberg, but as he has so much to do he cannot remain long. Whilst he is here, Papa is very quiet and goes on well, but when he is not here, he . . . agitates himself. These last three days he has been uneasy, which is not to be wondered at after a confinement of six weeks. This has prevented his wounds from improving and has made him suffer again a little pain, but he is now tranquil and I hope will remain so. The professor expected to [have] found him better, but he ascribes it only [to his] having agitated himself too much and thank [God] has perceived nothing new.'[42]

Anxiety escalated on 24 July when Nathan became feverish. 'My letter of yesterday by way of Paris will have informed you of the uneasy state we were in on account of Papa's health,' Lionel wrote to Nat the next day. 'Today I am happy to say that there is a slight improvement, but very satisfactory accounts I cannot give. His agitated state brought on a fever, which yesterday evening was violent. Today, thank God, this fever has a little diminished and his wounds have again begun to run; a fresh hardness has shown itself, which must be opened . . . We hope that Travers will arrive tonight and that tomorrow we shall have better news. Yesterday evening Papa was in danger; thank God he is today a little better . . . We must hope & pray that the severest moments are over and that he will now continue improving. I shall not fail to write to you the exact truth. We must have confidence in the Almighty, who has always protected us, and I have no doubt but all will go to our satisfaction.'[43]

Mayer and Fritz Schlemmer, who had returned briefly to Leipzig, now hurried back to Frankfurt, and by the time Benjamin Travers arrived on 26 July, Lionel was conferring earnestly about business with his mother. 'My dear Nat,' he wrote that day, 'I did not like to mention in my other letter to whom you can give the procuration. Mamma thinks it requisite that two persons should sign particularly as it is for another person that you give the procuration – Mamma mentioned Ben [Cohen] and J[ohn] Helbert [her sister Adeline's husband]. We leave this to you to act as you like. We send you also two procurations – one in blank & the other for BC. Fill these in as you like . . . We beg you to make use of the procuration that we send only in case you can not do without it.'[44]

On 27 July, Nathan was so poorly that, when lucid, he signed a new will. Moses and Judith Montefiore arrived in Frankfurt the following day.

'We arrived there in time to see him alive,' Moses wrote in his diary, 'but death was fast approaching. At four o'clock on the same day his brother, Anselm, asked him to say prayers, which he did, and all present joined him; he then kissed his wife and said "good night" quite distinctly. At five he breathed his last, and passed away without the slightest struggle. I was with him the whole time, and remained in the room an hour after all the others had left it. I had thus the melancholy satisfaction of paying the last respects to his remains . . . He was a good friend to me and my dear Judith in our early life . . . Hannah did not leave him for a moment during his illness, and remained in the room for some time after his death, returning there again the same evening.'[45]

Six days later in London, *The Times* reported that the 'intelligence of Mr Rothschild's death, which arrived this morning, has occupied attention here to the exclusion of all other topics. The event was indeed firmly believed yesterday to have taken place, and it appears now that the communication was made from Boulogne yesterday morning by pigeon, and that it reached the City in the course of the afternoon. It was made in three words only – "Il est mort," the simplicity of the announcement being not inappropriate to the importance of the individual.'[46]

The story of the pigeon bearing the news of Nathan's death to England is one of the most famous and frequently retold of all tales connected with the Rothschild family. Another version recounts how a carrier pigeon, disabled by a gunshot wound, was caught near Brighton, and that beneath the shoulder feathers of the bird's left wing was discovered a small note inscribed with the words 'Il est mort', followed by a number of (Hebrew) 'hieroglyphics'.[47]

Such incidents were not unknown:–when strange signs were observed on the wings of a pigeon shot by Lord Portman's keeper in 1848, it was thought that they might relate to money market intelligence and the wings were forwarded to New Court for scrutiny. Yet carrier pigeon, disabled or otherwise, was not the means by which in 1836 the news of Nathan's death reached London first of all.[48]

At the time of the Napoleonic wars, Nathan had set up the most effi-cient courier service in Europe. In early March 1815, as Moses Montefiore was later to recall, Nathan thus became the first man in London to learn that Napoleon had escaped from Elba and landed near Cannes on 1 March. The news came by courier because it was 'too precious to be entrusted to the usual pigeon-post'. So in 1836, within an hour of Nathan's death a courier was despatched from Frankfurt to London with the news. Bundled into an express stagecoach bound for Calais, Fritz Schlemmer paused briefly in Brussels, then pressed on 'without a moment lost' for England to break the news at New Court – and no one there, he was clear, had yet heard of 'the catastrophe' when he arrived.[49]

'Government securities of all descriptions,' *The Times* continued, 'but more particularly those of the foreign markets, have been falling in value during the week, in anticipation of this event, but its confirmation has had a contrary effect, probably on account of the understanding there is that his business, under the management of his sons will go on as usual.' The news of Nathan's death had been announced on the Royal Exchange – or 'Change' as it was invariably known – on Wednesday 3 August; for more than a quarter of a century, Nathan's regular presence there had made him seem almost a part of its structure.

Three days after Nathan's death, Hannah and her family began to make their way home with the body. They arrived in London by boat on Thursday 4 August, and accompanied the large oak coffin to New Court. On 6 August a lithograph was published showing a silhouette of Nathan standing with his back to his favourite pillar on Change – 'The Shadow of a Great Man'. On Sunday, a short item in the *Observer* announced his death. 'The rise of his fortune is all within the present century,' the writer explained. 'Although he had never acquired a correct knowledge of the English language, and consequently expressed himself in a strange sort of diction, yet it was impossible to be with him for ten minutes and not to perceive that his understanding was sagacious, clear, and sound. His death is one of the most important events for the City, and perhaps for Europe, which has occurred for a very long time.'[50]

The funeral took place on Monday 8 August. 'At a few minutes past one o'clock the remains were removed [from New Court] in a hearse drawn by six horses, which drew slowly into King William-street, at the head of thirty-six mourning, and forty-one private carriages; among the latter of which were those of the Austrian, Russian, Prussian, Neapolitan, and Portuguese Ambassadors . . . the Lord Mayor, Sheriffs and many of the Aldermen of the City of London. In the first coach next to the hearse, were the four sons of the deceased as chief mourners; and in the other mourning coaches that followed were the relatives and friends of the family.'

From King William Street, the funeral procession moved into Cornhill, 'where the crowds were so great that it was with some difficulty the police could make a sufficient space for it to pass. On reaching Whitechapel Church, the children belonging to the Jews' Orphan School in Bell-lane, and to the [Jews'] Free School and Jews' Hospital in Mile End-road, joined the procession, which continued to move slowly until the hearse drew up at the north entrance of the burial-ground belonging to the Great German Synagogue in Duke's-place.

'Mr Aarons, the minister of the burial-ground, performed the Hebrew service, and Dr Solomon Herschell [sic, Hirschel], the High Priest or Rabbi, delivered in the English language a most feeling and eloquent address . . . The body was then removed towards the grave . . . The four sons, in performing the last melancholy ceremony of throwing three handfuls of earth into the grave, were very much affected. The friends of the deceased, among whom were Mr Montefiore his brother-in-law . . . went through a similar ceremony, after which the grave was filled in.'[51]

Moses Montefiore recorded how he had 'remained at the burial ground above an hour after the mourners had left, and saw the grave of my kind and truly lamented friend arched over, filled up, and a large slab of Yorkshire stone placed upon it. Thus have I witnessed all that was mortal of my dear friend consigned to the earth; his spirit the Almighty, in His great mercy, has taken to a better world, there to enjoy in glorious eternity the reward of his charitable actions.'[52]

In the will he had signed in Frankfurt, Nathan named his four sons – Lionel, Anthony, Nat and Mayer – as 'heirs in chief' of all his real and personal estate. 'It is my fervent and sincere wish that these my four sons should always act together in union and peace,' the will continues, 'and that they should continue to carry on, subject to the observance of the existing agreements with my brothers, the banking-house established by me in London, under my name.

'My beloved wife Hannah (born Cohen) is always to co-operate with my four beloved sons on all important occasions, and to have a voice in all deliberations: moreover, it is my special wish, that my sons shall not engage in any transactions of moment, without having previously asked her maternal advice; and that all my children, sons as well as daughters, shall always treat her with sincere affection, true attachment, and the greatest respect; as she (who during a series of years, has aided me in prosperity and adversity, like an affectionate, faithful and loving wife) in so high a degree deserves.'[53]

In the aftermath of these events, none of Nathan's immediate family gives any hint of dissatisfaction with Professor Chelius's handling of Nathan's case. Although the pattern of Chelius's conduct – the repeated assurances that all would be well, the continual absences from the patient's bedside – might with hindsight have appeared unprofessional, as it was to strike William Howitt, the Rothschilds are silent on the subject. Indeed, in the years ahead they would occasionally consult Chelius again. When Amschel fell ill in Frankfurt in 1841, the professor was summoned from Heidelberg; Salomon's wife Caroline considered consulting Chelius about her eyes; and later on in life both Nat and Mayer thought Chelius's opinion worth knowing.[54]

Yet it seems unlikely that after their father's death they did not hear and ponder the 'suggestion in circulation' that reached the ears of the anonymous author of Nathan's obituary in the *Gentleman's Magazine* in September 1836. The rumour was 'that better surgical assistance than that which was to be found on the spot might have saved him'. But, as Nathan's obituarist hurriedly went on to remark: 'Professor Chelius, of Heidelberg, who attended him throughout his illness day and night, is a man too celebrated and too well known to require any observations. Mr Travers's attendance was principally desired on account of his long acquaintance with, and knowledge of, the constitution of the deceased.'[55]

Unfortunately, there is no record of what Benjamin Travers thought either – though there does survive a letter that he wrote to one of Nathan's sons, probably Lionel, nearly three years after Nathan's death. In the letter, Travers explains that all attempts to procure from Germany 'a Copy of the Case of your late excellent Father, as drawn up at my earnest request by Dr Chelius of Heidelberg' have failed. 'If either the original or a duplicate is in [the] possession of Madame de Rothschild [Hannah] or your family,' Travers continues, 'I should be greatly obliged by the loan of it for a few days, when it shall be carefully returned . . . It is scarcely necessary to add that it is solely with a professional view that I am anxious to have it . . . the case was one of deep & unusual interest in itself, so considered. Begging you to believe that I have abstained from motives of delicacy from sooner applying to you, & that I am now compelled to trouble you reluctantly . . .'[56]

That no such medical report appears to have been preserved among the very extensive Rothschild family papers might suggest that it was never made available – that Chelius, or his assistants, did not care to submit the case to the scrutiny of Benjamin Travers or anyone else. However, aside from the Howitt family's harrowing experience of Chelius in Heidelberg some years later, and ignoring the spectre of medical neglect, it has since been suggested that the persistent refusal of Nathan's abscess to heal, even without modern antibiotics, might indicate that Nathan was suffering from diabetes, and that death was the result of septicaemia.[57]

2

Dinner at Upton

LONG AFTER HIS professional association with Nathan and the Rothschild family had ceased, Fritz Schlemmer reflected on his remarkable employer. He did so in a private memoir, which eventually came to light among the papers of a Miss Lili Schlemmer in Germany in 1926, and which since then has lain largely neglected.[1]

It is in this memoir that the former tutor tells of his race to London with the news of Nathan's death. There is nothing to suggest that the memoir was written for the benefit of anyone but Schlemmer himself; and since he, perhaps more than any other non-family member, had had the opportunity to observe Nathan *en famille* over a period of years at close quarters – and with shrewdness (he had trained as a lawyer in Hanau) – the memoir possesses a distinct and commanding quality.

By the summer of 1836, Fritz Schlemmer had lived and taken his meals with Nathan and his family in London, and during spells on the Continent, for the best part of a decade. He had been responsible for Nat's education as well as Mayer's. Not only had his duties been those of a tutor; as well as helping Hannah with her letters, and with her German, he had also assisted Nathan with some of his most confidential business correspondence.

During a period of hectic business dealings with Spain, Nathan had sent Schlemmer off to learn Spanish – after which he did not hesitate to wake him up in the middle of the night to translate a courier's despatch. When Prince Talleyrand caught sight of Schlemmer at a dinner in London given by the Spanish ambassador (the Prince had been dining at the Rothschilds' the night before), he ostentatiously led the tutor off into a corner for a word, tantalising the assembled company.

It is thus, so far as it is possible to tell, a man with neither grievances nor secret agenda who, in a memoir he wrote for himself, set down his impressions of a world-famous figure whom he had known and liked, for whom he had worked, and in the midst of whose family he had lived for several years. Furthermore, he was someone to whom, from the earliest days of his employment, Nathan had talked and reminisced in a relaxed and unaffected way.

'Ever since he was a young man,' Schlemmer wrote of Nathan, 'he had worked with the object of making progress by work, application and honesty. This object he pursued almost to the exclusion of everything else throughout his life. But it would be a mistake to believe that he saw the great wealth that came to him as means of procuring pleasures . . . For himself and for his family he needed relatively little money. Luxury held no attraction for him. The work in itself, to take in at a glance and to exploit the business world in which he moved, [to feel] the pride in surpassing what others achieved – to prove that his perception was more penetrating than that of other financiers, as if he were playing a game of chess – [that was] the driving impulse in his being. Honest and benevolent by nature, he only ever grew angry if a rival used his friends or co-religionists against his interests.'[2]

Nathan's achievement was astounding, though he had not exactly come up from nowhere. His father, Mayer Amschel Rothschild, had from modest beginnings as a dealer in coins, medals and *objets d'art*, become one of eighteenth-century Frankfurt's leading merchants and financiers. His success owed much to his skilful management, as court agent, of the financial affairs of the immensely rich Landgrave William IX of Hesse-Kassel, the sovereign prince whose mercenaries were a source of huge income, as well as the inspiration for that terrifying Hessian trooper, the Headless Horseman, of Washington Irving's tale *The Legend of Sleepy Hollow*.

In due course, Mayer Amschel's five sons (each of whom bore Mayer as a second name) joined him in his thriving business. Of the five, Nathan, the third son, was the most able, and after Mayer Amschel's death in 1812 – the year of Napoleon's disastrous invasion of Russia – he was for the rest of his life recognised within the family as the 'general in command' of operations. James, Nathan's junior by fifteen years, was to show ability of a very high order, too.[3]

More than a decade before Mayer Amschel's demise, Nathan had left Frankfurt for England. An entry register of aliens records his arrival at Yarmouth, accompanied by his father's bookkeeper, Seligman Geisenheimer, on or before 26 May 1800, and his request for permission to proceed to London.[4]

Born in 1777, Nathan was thus a man in his early twenties when he landed at Yarmouth. By 1804, when he was granted letters patent of denization (the equivalent to naturalisation), he had decided to put down his roots in England. Subsequently, he married Hannah, established the City firm that later became N. M. Rothschild & Sons, the merchant bank, at New Court, St Swithin's Lane, and made his fortune.

The story of his path to riches was a subject of endless fascination for his contemporaries; it became 'as popular a story as the legend of Alfred burning the cakes, or of William Tell transfixing the apple on his son's head'. This was all the more so after 1848, when a contemporaneous record of Nathan's own account of his early years, given to the assembled company at a private dinner he had attended in February 1834, was published by John Murray.[5]

The setting for this revelation was Ham House, and the record was made by one of Nathan's fellow guests, a man of the utmost probity whom Nathan knew. No other record of the occasion, or of any comparable disclosure by Nathan, has ever come to light, and consequently the dinner at Ham House has become, as one authority has rightly observed, 'an episode, which every memorialist, biographer and historian of Nathan Mayer Rothschild recounts'.

The Ham House in question was not, as sometimes has been supposed, the Jacobean mansion on the banks of the Thames near Richmond, but rather Ham House at Upton, in the parish of West Ham, not far from Stratford, in Essex. The mystery of Nathan's presence at the Thames-side Ham House, which at the time of the dinner belonged to the elderly Countess of Dysart, to whom Nathan had no known connection, is no mystery at all: he was dining somewhere else altogether. To place the famous dinner in its context is, therefore, of some interest.[6]

Ham House at Upton was the home of Samuel Gurney, the leading bill broker in the City of London of that era and a man prominent in the Society of Friends – the Quakers. An associate of Nathan's in the City, Sam Gurney, too, had made a fortune – he was sometimes even dubbed the 'Quaker Rothschild' – and the two men, and their families, were friends.

Cementing the friendship had been a shared desire for the lifting of the restrictions to which Jews and Quakers in England had long been subjected because of their religious beliefs. One of Nathan's granddaughters, recalling her family's association with the Gurneys, later explained that 'owing to religious principles on both sides, they suffered from the same political disabilities'; but the disabilities extended well beyond the exclusion from seats in Parliament she had in mind.[7]

While Nathan and Sam succeeded triumphantly in the worlds of commerce and finance, the fact that neither of them belonged to the Church of England had precluded them from many other fields of action. Religious requirements would have made it impossible for them to obtain a degree from Oxford or Cambridge, thus ruling out a career in the professions; and until the repeal, thanks to Lord John Russell's exertions, of the Test and Corporation Acts in 1828, all officials – government and municipal, civil and military – were required, on taking office, to receive the Sacrament according to the forms of the Church of England.

Other restrictions applied to the Jews specifically. Barred from the Freedom of the City of London until 1831, for example, Jews were forbidden to engage in retail trade within the City's boundaries. Until the repeal in 1846 of *De Judaismo*, a thirteenth-century statute from the reign of Edward I, it was arguable that Jews could not even own freehold land. But the age, of course, was one of the most glaring inequalities, not only where faith was concerned.[8]

'You may knock down Nathan Rothschild, though he is a very rich man,' declared *The Black Book* in 1835, in its catalogue of national abuses, 'or a worshipful alderman, or even a right honourable lord mayor, and the justices will only charge you a few shillings for the liberty you have taken; but if you knock down a peer, though he is ever so insolent, it is almost as bad as murder.' Sitting in judgment, a peer was not required to give his verdict upon oath, like anyone else, but only upon his honour, 'just as if a peer alone had *honour* and all others were base perfidious slaves, from whom truth could only be extorted when they had been forced into the presence of their Creator'.[9]

Where faith was concerned, oaths posed peculiar difficulties for people of conscience whose religious beliefs did not chime with those of Canterbury. While oaths were formulated so as to be suitable only for members of the Church of England, and so excluded Roman Catholics and Dissenters, no Jew would swear a Christian oath and no Quaker would swear an oath of any kind at all. In the seventeenth century, Quakers had been jailed in large numbers for refusing their persecutors' provocative demands to swear the Oath of Allegiance.[10]

Naturally, there had grown up a sense of solidarity among groups whose members were thus excluded from mainstream areas of life. Joseph Avis, a Quaker carpenter who in 1699 was engaged to construct a synagogue, declined to accept any payment for the work in excess of his costs; and during the early years of the Regency, the board of synagogue Deputies, the Jews' national representative body, elected a deputation 'to wait upon some respectable Quaker to ascertain the sentiments of the Society of Friends on a pending Bill in Parliament referring to the rights of marriage, baptism, and burial'.[11]

As Nathan Rothschild and Sam Gurney rose to prominence in their respective communities, they were drawn into the leadership of the movement for equality under the law for non-Anglicans with members of the Established Church; and they saw some advances. Following the parliamentary repeals of 1828, the signing of a declaration was substituted for the sacramental test; and five years later, when in 1833 the Quaker Joseph Pease was elected to a seat in the Commons, the House resolved to allow him to make an affirmation in lieu of an oath, on the grounds that Quakers were by then entitled to do so in courts of law.

The Jews, however, derived no benefit whatever from the 1828 repeals. Thanks to the intervention of Edward Copleston, Bishop of Llandaff, a last-minute House of Lords' amendment to the Bill for the Repeal of the Tests obliged anyone signing the new declaration on accepting public office 'solemnly and sincerely to testify and declare upon the true faith of a Christian'.

Beyond the law and Parliament, there was prejudice, too, and a persistent irritant to Nathan was the difficulty that Jews experienced in obtaining insurance, especially fire insurance. So in 1824 Nathan and his brother-in-law Moses Montefiore had joined forces with Sam Gurney – and with Francis Baring, a partner in Baring Brothers, and John Irving, a City merchant and an MP – to become founder presidents of the Alliance British and Foreign Life and Fire Assurance Company. Among the founder directors of the company was Timothy Curtis, who was later to become a Governor of the Bank of England (1837-9).

The final spur to the incorporation of the Alliance is said to have been the refusal by the Guardian insurance company to employ another of Montefiore's brothers-in-law, Benjamin Gompertz – mathematician, Fellow of the Royal Society and acknowledged expert on questions of mortality and probability – as an actuary, on grounds of his being a Jew. 'Vat, not take you because of your religion!' Nathan is alleged to have exclaimed. 'Mein Gott! Den I vil make a bigger office for you den any of dem.'[12]

As Gompertz was now appointed actuary to the Alliance, one of Gurney's brothers-in-law, Thomas Fowell Buxton, a liberal Anglican, agreed to be one of the company's auditors. As an MP, Buxton subsequently introduced the Bill into the House of Commons that led to the lifting of Lloyd's monopoly of marine insurance, so paving the way for Nathan and his associates to establish the Alliance Marine Insurance Company as well. In its early years the Alliance was run chiefly by Moses Montefiore and Sam Gurney, initially from a room made available at New Court.[13]

After 1828, Nathan and Moses devoted time and effort to the campaign for specifically Jewish emancipation – even if some of the humbler among their co-religionists did not share their concern. When asked to subscribe to the emancipation campaign, one Whitechapel Jew retorted: 'If Rothschild wants to get emancipated, let Rothschild pay for it.'[14]

From without Judaism it was men such as Sam Gurney and Fowell Buxton, together with agitators for the rights of Roman Catholics, who supported the Jewish cause. In 1829, the year when Daniel O'Connell's defeat of Vesey Fitzgerald in the Clare election led to the Catholic Relief Bill, forcing Catholic Emancipation on the government in London, Moses Montefiore recorded that he had 'met a number of gentlemen interested in the emancipation of the Jews'. Among them were the Catholics O'Connell and The O'Gorman Mahon; Isaac Lyon Goldsmid, a wealthy Jewish broker (whom Nathan never liked); and Sam Gurney and Fowell Buxton.[15]

Later in the year, Moses attended a dinner given by Goldsmid to meet, among others, the liberal Lords Lansdowne, Suffield and Auckland and, again, O'Connell, The O'Gorman Mahon and Fowell Buxton. 'The O'Gorman,' Moses found, 'was very sociable; he wished to see the Portuguese Synagogue, also to have the opportunity of presenting the Jews' petition to Parliament.' The Marquess of Lansdowne was a former Chancellor of the Exchequer and Home Secretary.[16]

In January 1830, Moses went to a synagogue meeting to hear the legal opinion of Stephen Lushington, MP – lawyer, parliamentary reformer and anti-slavery campaigner – on the present state of civil disabilities of the Jews: 'It was resolved to petition Parliament for the removal of the said disabilities, and to request Messrs N. M. Rothschild, I. L. Goldsmid, and Moses Montefiore to see the Duke of Wellington on the subject.'

Later that year, a Bill for removing the political disabilities of the Jews was for the first time introduced into the Commons by Robert Grant, MP for Inverness. Grant was associated with that group of evangelical philanthropists, reformers and anti-slavers known as the Clapham Sect, and with his brother Charles (later Lord Glenelg) had taken a keen interest in the cause of Jewish emancipation. But despite the support of Lord John Russell – and of Thomas Babington Macaulay, son of the Claphamite Zachary Macaulay, in his maiden speech – Grant's Bill was thrown out.

Nathan then also became associated with the chief enterprise of Fowell Buxton's career: Buxton's leadership of the campaign in Parliament, as William Wilberforce's successor, to obtain the abolition of slavery throughout the British Empire. The culmination of the campaign came with the

Royal Assent to the Bill for abolition in August 1833 – in consequence of which Nathan was engaged by the government to raise a £15 million West India Loan to compensate the slaves' former owners.[17]

So when Nathan was invited to Ham House at Upton, it was only natural that Buxton, who went there often, should be asked to join the party, together with his eldest son Edward, just down from Cambridge.

Ham House was a few miles' drive east from the City, and had been the Gurney family home since 1812, when Sam had acquired the house and its small estate from his father-in-law. In an earlier time, the property had belonged to the Quaker botanist and physician Dr John Fothergill, of whom Benjamin Franklin said he could hardly conceive that a worthier man ever lived. Fothergill had created a botanical garden at Ham that in its heyday was second only to Kew, and the remnants of which – trees in particular – were still to be seen.[18]

Nathan went there accompanied by Anthony, Hannah Mayer and Louisa. The house that met their eyes as they came up the drive was, in the estimation of Augustus Hare, 'an unpretending dwelling . . . its many chimneys sending up their wreaths of curling smoke'. 'There was not an approach to grandeur, or even stateliness in the mansion. It was just such a place as a weary traveller would feel a longing to enter, sure of comfort within its walls . . .' The drawing room was 'furnished with the simple elegance characterising the homes of Friends'; the dining room was 'neither too large nor dreary, nor too small and cramped'.[19]

The Rothschilds should have felt very much at home: the Gurneys were a close-knit clan, happiest when 'surrounded . . . by troops of near relations, with whom they lived on terms of the utmost fellowship and intimacy, and who dropped in daily at the family dinner-hour'. One frequent visitor to Ham House was Sam's elder sister Betsey – that 'alp amongst women' Elizabeth Fry, Quaker preacher and penal reformer, who had a house at Upton, too.[20]

The Gurneys continued to use the Quaker 'thee' and 'thou' in conversation and in correspondence, and they were serious-minded people. Sam's brother Joseph John, a Minister in the Society of Friends as well as a partner of Gurney's Bank in Norwich, recalled dining in Hampstead with his sister Louisa, who was married to the banker and anti-slavery campaigner Samuel Hoare (Hoare, Barnett were bankers to the Alliance).[21]

'At dinner we had an interesting party,' Joseph John wrote afterwards, '[John Bird] Sumner, Bishop of Chester, Dr [Stephen] Lushington, [Fowell] Buxton, and my sister Elizabeth Fry. The conversation turned to the subject of capital punishment. Lushington in the warmest terms expressed his abhorrence of the system. After dinner a brisk discussion arose on the religious conditions of the Long Parliament.' Bishop Sumner later succeeded William Howley as Archbishop of Canterbury.

Brisk discussion was very much Nathan's style, though in conversation he could be a good deal less earnest than some of his Quaker friends. After he had dined as the guest of Wilhelm von Humboldt, the Prussian Minister in London (and the brother of Alexander, the scientist and explorer), his host described an incident that had taken place in the course of the evening.

'Yesterday Rothschild dined with me,' Humboldt reported to his wife. 'He is quite crude and uneducated, but he has a great deal of intelligence and a positive genius for money. He scored off Major Martins beautifully once or twice. M. was dining with me too and kept on praising everything French. He was being fatuously sentimental about the horrors of war and the large numbers who had been killed. "Well," said R., "if they had not all died, Major, you would probably still be a drummer." You ought to have seen Martins' face.'[22]

At Ham House, Nathan entertained the assembled company to a well-paced account of his early days in business – which Fowell Buxton recounted in a letter to his daughter the next day.

We dined yesterday at Ham House to meet the Rothschilds, and very amusing it was. He (Rothschild) told us his life and adventures. He was the third son of the banker at Frankfort. 'There was not,' he said, 'room enough for all of us in that city. I dealt in English goods. One great trader came here, who had the market to himself: he was quite the great man, and did us a favour if he sold us goods. Somehow I offended him, and he refused to show me his patterns. This was on a Tuesday; I said to my father, 'I will go to England.' I could speak nothing but German. On the Thursday I started; the nearer I got to England, the cheaper the goods were. As soon as I got to Manchester, I laid out all my money, things were so cheap; and I made a good profit. I soon found that there were three profits – the raw material, the dyeing and the manufacturing. I said to the manufacturer, 'I will supply you with material and dye, and you supply me with manufactured goods.' So I got three profits instead of one, and I could sell goods cheaper than anybody. In a short time I made my 20,000*l*. into 60,000*l*. My success all turned on one maxim. I said, I can do what another man can, and so I am a match for the man with the patterns, and for all the rest of them! Another advantage I had. I was an off-hand man. I made a bargain at once. When I was settled in London, the East India Company had 800,000 lbs of gold to sell. I went to the sale and bought it all. I knew the Duke of Wellington must have it. I had bought a great many of his bills at a discount. The Government sent for me, and said they must have it. When they got it, they did not know how to get it to Portugal. I undertook all that, and I sent it through France; and that was the best business I ever did.'

Another maxim on which he seemed to place great reliance, was, never to have anything to do with an unlucky place or an unlucky man. 'I have seen,' he said, 'many clever men, very clever men, who had not shoes to their feet. I never act with them; they cannot get on themselves; and if they cannot do good to themselves, how can they do good to me?' By aid of these maxims he has acquired three millions of money . . . I forgot to say, that soon after M. Rothschild came to England, Bonaparte invaded Germany; 'The Prince of Hesse Cassel,' said Rothschild, 'gave my father his money; there was no time to be lost; he sent it to me. I had 600,000l. arrive unexpectedly by the post; and I put it to such good use, that the prince made me a present of all his wine and his linen.'

'I hope,' said —— [blank], 'that your children are not too fond of money and business, to the exclusion of more important things. I am sure you would not wish that.' Rothschild: 'I am sure I should wish that. I wish them to give mind, and soul, and heart, and body, and everything to business; that is the way to be happy. It requires a great deal of boldness, and a great deal of caution to make a great fortune; and when you have got it, it requires ten times as much wit to keep it. If I were to listen to all the projects proposed to me, I should ruin myself very soon. Stick to one business, young man,' said he to Edward; 'stick to your brewery, and you may be the great brewer of London. Be a brewer, and a banker, and a merchant, and a manufacturer, and you will soon be in the Gazette.'[23]

Whether the 'three millions of money' that Buxton mentions was a figure given by Nathan himself is unclear, but it has been calculated that by the time of his death Nathan was worth approximately £3.5 million – equivalent to something like £2 billion today – and that this made him richer, in terms of net wealth, than anyone else in Britain, then the richest country in the world. All the more remarkable, as Joseph Barrow Montefiore, one of Moses' first cousins, pointed out, was that Nathan was 'not the rich man he is usually said to have been in his early London days. I remember my father once asking him why he didn't keep his carriage, and he said he would when he had £25,000 of his own.'[24]

One stage of his progress that Nathan omitted from his story concerned his earliest days in London. In 1800, the year of his arrival at Yarmouth, he had an address at No. 37 Cornhill and was in contact, on behalf of his father, with the bankers Harman, Hoare & Co., of Frederick Place, Old Jewry. The firm was then in the hands of John Harman, in partnership with his son Jeremiah, who was also a director (and later, from 1816 to 1818, Governor) of the Bank of England. When, twenty-five years later, it seemed that a run on the Bank's gold reserves might result in a suspension of cash payments, Jeremiah was still a director – and Nathan was sufficiently influential to be able to avert a national crisis by shipping great quantities of gold coin to the Bank's vaults from France.[25]

Another of Nathan's early contacts in London was Levi Barent Cohen, to whom Nathan carried letters of introduction. A prosperous linen merchant, when Cohen had arrived from Holland thirty years before, he had been armed with an introduction to his uncle by marriage George Goldsmid, the brother of I. L. Goldsmid's father Asher, and of Benjamin and Abraham Goldsmid, the dominant financiers in the City of the late eighteenth and early nineteenth centuries.[26]

By the time Nathan arrived in England, Levi Cohen was one of the most respected, and respectable, members of the Jewish community in the capital. He was the father of a large family – Hannah was the third of his six daughters – and lived with his family at No. 11 Angel Court, Throgmorton Street, in the City. The family solicitor, Edwin Dawes, had his brass plate up at No. 9, and in later life recounted the following episode to the historian Lucien Wolf:

'When Nathan Rothschild was courting Hannah Cohen, his future father-in-law one day asked him for the name of his solicitor so that the settlements might be put in order. It happened that Rothschild had no regular solicitor, but he remembered having seen on the door-post of an adjoining house in Angel Court the inscription "Edwin Dawes, Attorney", and with his usual self-possession he gave that name to Mr Levi Cohen. "That is very fortunate," answered Mr Cohen, "for Mr Dawes happens to be my own solicitor." Nathan Rothschild at once walked round to No. 9, and interviewed Mr Dawes. "I am going to marry Levi Cohen's daughter, Hannah," he said in his slap-dash way, "and I want you to draw up the settlements on my behalf." No introduction could have been more satisfactory. Mr Dawes was delighted to act for a gentleman who had found such favour in Levi Cohen's eyes, and Mr Cohen himself was not less gratified to know that his future son-in-law, to whom some suspicion of recklessness then attached, was in the hands of so prudent an adviser.'[27]

According to J. B. Montefiore, 'old Levi Barent Cohen was very shy about giving him [Nathan] his daughter Hannah. He insisted on being assured that his intended son-in-law was worth £10,000, and he got little Herz, the broker – Puckel Herz, they called him – to examine the future millionaire's books.' At the time of their marriage on 22 October 1806, Nathan was twenty-nine, Hannah twenty-three.[28]

Levi Cohen settled £3,248 14s 6d in 3 per cent consolidated bank annuities on his daughter – a generous sum when one considers, for instance, that nearly thirty years later, in 1844, on her marriage to an acquaintance of the Rothschilds, Lady Augusta Somerset received a marriage settlement of £7,000, paying interest at 5 per cent, from her father the Duke of Beaufort.[29]

Once married, Nathan and Hannah set off for Manchester, where Nathan was still engaged in the business of exporting textiles to the Continent. There was then only a small Jewish community in the town, small enough, until 1806, for an upstairs room in Garden Street, Withy Grove, to serve as a synagogue. Yet for a cloth merchant, there was no more promising place on earth.[30]

'Every part of the cotton trade, from the importation of the raw material to its completion by the weaver, the bleacher, the dyer, and the calico printer, is carried on in this town and parish,' a Georgian commentator declared. 'But it is not to the local manufacturers of the town or county that the trade of this place is confined; woollens, linens, and stuffs are brought here, as to a general depository, and a foreign merchant or an English dealer may in this place replenish his stock with all the products of the great manufacturing districts of the kingdom.'[31]

By what means Nathan conveyed his bride to Manchester we do not know. A well-off couple would probably have travelled post, hiring horses to draw their own carriage, or hiring post-chaise and horses, from stage to stage at posting houses in the towns en route. The fastest means of making the journey, on the other hand, was by the mail coach – at an average speed of eight and a half miles an hour.

The Manchester Mail left the inn yard of the Swan with Two Necks – colloquially 'The Necks' or 'The Wonderful Bird' – in Lad Lane, Gresham Street, every weekday evening at 7.30 p.m.; it stopped briefly at the General Post Office in Lombard Street, and arrived at the Bridgewater Arms in Manchester High Street at 6 p.m. the next day. It was from outside the GPO in Lombard Street that the lines of beribboned, laurel-decked mail coaches admired by Thomas de Quincey would hurtle off round the country, 'like fire racing along a train of gunpowder', with tidings of the Allies' victories over Napoleon.

Alternative to the mail, there were privately owned stagecoaches. Moses Montefiore, bound for Kent during his honeymoon in 1812, left London by stagecoach for Chatham. Services to Manchester were provided by the *Defiance*, running daily between The Necks and the Bridgewater Arms, and the *Telegraph*, which followed the mail route but ran between the White Horse Inn, Fetter Lane, and the Mosley Arms in Market Street,

Manchester. Manchester's chief mail contractor, Alexander Patterson, conducted his business from the Bridgewater Arms, where Nathan used to go for tea and muffins.[32]

By 1804, Nathan had premises in Brown Street, in the town's commercial district, and a residence in Downing Street, Ardwick – a suburb that was 'chiefly occupied by the merchants of the town . . . particularly distinguished by the neatness and elegance of its buildings'. Later, Nathan traded as 'Rothschild Brothers, merchants, 5 Lloyd Street', and moved to a 'spacious, modern, and well-built' house in Mosley Street, a fashionable development.[33]

'Mosley-street contains many capital houses,' wrote Joseph Aston in *A Picture of Manchester* (1816), 'and if it had fortunately been a few yards wider than it is, would have been one of the best streets in the north of England.' Adjoining the house Nathan had a 'large and commodious' warehouse in Back Mosley Street. ('Mosley' was in reference to the family of Sir Oswald Mosley, Bt, lord of the manor of Manchester.)[34]

Embarking on married life in Manchester, Nathan and Hannah acquired some new furnishings. An invoice dated 7 November 1806, for furniture and packing cases supplied to Nathan by John Fildes, a cabinetmaker of Lamb's Conduit Street in Holborn, refers to ten mahogany chairs with morocco covers, a matching chaise longue, a work table, two card tables, some footstools, fire-screens, curtain rods and mirrors. Nathan and Hannah's first child, Charlotte (Chilly), was born in Manchester on 10 August 1807.[35]

Nathan dealt with suppliers in other Lancashire towns besides Manchester, as well as in Leeds, Glasgow and Paisley; and he made regular trips to the Continent. While he shipped cloth to his father in Frankfurt, he also had customers for textiles in London, Amsterdam, Rotterdam, Paris, Lyons, Nancy, Metz, Hamburg, Leipzig, Strasbourg and Salzburg. During his absences from Manchester, Hannah ran the office: business letters were directed to her; she dealt with orders and signed cheques on behalf of the firm.[36]

The young couple, however, were not destined to remain in Manchester for long. In 1808, for reasons that are not altogether clear – the difficulty of moving English goods abroad during the French blockade and the death of Hannah's father were most probably contributing factors – Nathan began to shift his business, as so many have done before and since, from commerce to finance, and to transfer his affairs to London, to No. 12 Great St Helens, off Bishopsgate Street in the City. Pickford's, the carriers, undertook the house removal, by canal boat.

A letter dated 3 August 1808 from Peter Fawcett, a Manchester dyer, testifies to Nathan's transformation: it is addressed to 'N. M. Rothschild, Esqr., Banker, London'. Two days after Lionel's birth in London on 22 November 1808, Peter Fawcett wrote again, to congratulate Nathan 'most heartily on the birth of a son and heir, to inherit a handsome fortune which will some time hereafter fall to his lot'. Anthony was born at home in London on 29 May 1810.[37]

Writing in 1814, the Reverend Joseph Nightingale described Great St Helens as a 'handsome open place'. Access to the enclave, and to the parish church of St Helen, was via an ancient gateway on Bishopsgate. No. 1 Great St Helens provided the entrance to the surviving portion of medieval Crosby Hall, while several of the other houses, including Nos. 3 and 4 and Nos. 11 and 12, were in origin Elizabethan.[38]

According to the clergyman-antiquary Thomas Hugo, writing later in the century, No. 12, the Rothschilds' address, was 'a house of red brick, ornamented with pilasters of the same material. Over one of the windows is a tablet, ornamented with a cornice, and intended probably for the insertion of a date, or the initials of the owner; though if so the purpose has not been carried out. The character of the doorways is rather later; but I feel little hesitation in attributing this plain but truly artistic design to that master of beauty Inigo Jones.'[39]

London's Jewish population, which in 1808 numbered around 16,000 individuals (representing two thirds of all English Jews), had long been concentrated in and around this area of the City. Jews of Portuguese and Spanish origin – the congregation known as *Sephardim* – worshipped at a synagogue in Bevis Marks, while the more numerous *Ashkenazim* – Jews from western and central Europe – had three main places of worship: the New Synagogue in Great St Helens, the Hambro Synagogue in Church Row, Fenchurch Street, and – oldest of the three – the Great Synagogue in Duke's Place. After Charles Wesley, brother of John, had visited the Great Synagogue in 1770, he declared that he 'never before saw a Jewish congregation behave so decently. Indeed, the place itself is so solemn, that it might strike an awe upon those who have any thought of God.'[40]

At a meeting between representatives of the three Ashkenazi synagogues of London in 1804, it was resolved that 'no Synagogue should accept as member any individual who was member of another'. The Cohens and the Rothschilds belonged to the congregation of the Great Synagogue.[41]

'This synagogue of the German Jews,' enthused Joseph Nightingale, 'in consequence of a legacy left for that purpose by a lady of immense property was rebuilt in 1790, in a very superb and handsome manner. This

edifice is of brick, with a roof supported by massy stone pillars, and is decorated with the utmost magnificence. Seven modern highly finished brass
branches, of peculiarly excellent workmanship, are suspended from the
ceiling. The whole building is well worthy of inspection, and the Christian
visitor is always treated with civility and respect. So that, on a Friday
evening, at the commencement of the Jewish Sabbath, the chanting is
very solemn and impressive, and the whole of the religious economy of this
congregation is under the superintendence of the Rev. Solomon Hirschel,
the presiding Rabbi.'[42]

The office of rabbi of the Great Synagogue held by Dr Hirschel – who
was to deliver the address at Nathan's funeral – was combined with that of
Chief Rabbi, ecclesiastical head of the Ashkenazi congregation in Britain.

Hannah's father was a warden (*Parnas*) of the Great Synagogue, and
after his death was succeeded by her eldest brother, Joseph – who was to be
remembered in the family as 'a big man with a florid complexion,
emphatic and somewhat dictatorial'. In April 1809, the year of King
George III's golden jubilee, Joseph Cohen, with fellow wardens Moses
Samuel and Asher Goldsmid, welcomed three of the King's sons – the
Dukes of Cumberland, Cambridge and Sussex – to a Friday evening
service at the synagogue.[43]

So impressed by his visit was the liberal-minded Duke of Sussex that he
became not only a keen student of Hebrew and, in 1813, patron of the
Jews' Hospital, but a champion of Jewish emancipation too; the Duke of
Cambridge, when Viceroy of Hanover (1816-37), emancipated that kingdom's Jews. By the time Nathan became a warden of the Great Synagogue
in 1818, he had been a seat-holder there for more than a decade.[44]

It was in 1810 that Nathan moved his family and business once more,
from Great St Helens to more spacious premises in New Court, in the very
heart of the City, close to Mansion House, Lombard Street and the Bank
of England. Opposite the Bank of England was the recently founded
London Stock Exchange, at premises in Capel Court since 1802; and at a
stone's throw there was the Royal Exchange (Change), bounded by
Threadneedle Street to the north and by Cornhill to the south, which
served as the centre for international business.

Foreign stocks were still bought and sold on Change, rather than in
Capel Court, and it was on Change that the leading men of the London
money market conducted their operations. When prices were fluctuating
and Change was 'full of bustling and rumours', it was said that men from
the Stock Exchange 'with eyes like basilisks, and faces lined and surfaced
like an asparagus bed ere the plants come up' could be seen 'darting in at

the north door of the Royal Exchange, bounding towards the chief priests of Mammon'.[45]

The house that Nathan had taken was No. 2 New Court, an unpretentious, red brick building, constructed over three floors, with attics and a basement. It was large enough for him to use the ground floor for business and still to have plenty of room upstairs to accommodate a growing family. Built for a City merchant, the house had a small warehouse alongside for the storage of goods; its ground floor was known as 'the shop'. According to Lucien Wolf's researches, the annual rental was valued at £96, 'on which in those happy days rates were levied at the rate of 2d in the £'. Lacking a mews in New Court, when he had need of one Nathan rented a nearby coach house and stable from a solicitor named George Crocker, of Cross Street, Finsbury Square.[46]

Two other houses in New Court became vacant at about the same time: No. 3, the largest, was taken by an insurance broker named William Masson; No. 4, which faced the Rothschilds' house across the small court, was occupied by Benjamin Travers, then a young surgeon retained by the East India Company.[47] After Hannah's younger sister, Judith, had in 1812 married Moses Montefiore, she and Moses (who belonged to the Sephardic branch of Jewry) took over No. 4 from Travers. Yet to dedicate his life to the welfare of Jews around the world, Moses was a partner, with his brother Abraham, in a firm of City brokers.

Nathan was already making a name for himself in the City. Having in 1809 secured authorisation to buy British bonds with the interest earned by the Elector of Hesse-Kassel's holdings, over the next four years he bought securities worth more than the Elector's £600,000 that had arrived 'unexpectedly by the post'. Then in 1814 came his big chance – his engagement by J. C. Herries, the Commissary-in-Chief (responsible for army pay and supply), to procure and deliver the coin necessary to finance the last phase of Wellington's campaign on the Continent, the final push from liberated Spain into France.[48]

In January 1814 Herries was authorised to engage Nathan by the Prime Minister, the Earl of Liverpool, and the Chancellor of the Exchequer, Nicholas Vansittart (later Lord Bexley), and to allow him a commission of 2½ per cent on the sums delivered. Nathan was then given added responsibility for delivering the subsidies that Britain was providing to her less solvent allies – principally Russia, Prussia and Austria, and King Louis XVIII and his exiled court at Ghent.

With the help of his brothers and other agents on the Continent in what was in large part a smuggling operation, Nathan accomplished his mission with speed and efficiency at a critical time for the Allies. 'I do not know,' Lord Liverpool confided in 1815 to Viscount Castlereagh, the Foreign Secretary, 'what we should have done without him last year.'[49]

The commissions Nathan earned from the operations made him a rich man. Nor were his partners disgruntled. In early 1815, Amschel wrote from Frankfurt: 'I remember what our father, peace with him, told me on his death-bed. "Amschel keep your brothers together and you will become the richest people in Germany!" This is almost true.'[50] That year Nathan's account with the British government totalled close on £10 million, and the Rothschilds became sterling millionaires. In 1816, James was 'quite ready to believe that we have enough money to last us all our life. But we are still young and we want to work. And [as] much for the sake of our prestige as Jews as for any other reason.'[51]

The reputation that Nathan gained as a result of the success of the operations, and the contacts that he and his brothers made in the process, for example with the Austrian statesman Prince Metternich, were to prove of enormous and longstanding worth to their business. Furthermore, the courier service that Nathan set up to help accomplish his task – so well organised that he was to be the first in London to learn not only of Napoleon's escape from Elba, but also of Wellington's victory at Waterloo – would in after years frequently provide him and his brothers with political and market intelligence comfortably ahead of their rivals.

In that pre-telegraph, pre-railway age, Nathan's agents at the Channel ports had vessels ready to carry despatches at a moment's notice, while post boys on either side of the Channel waited to race off on horseback to deliver them. Cross-Channel packet captains and stagecoach guards could expect to be rewarded for carrying Nathan's messages with all possible speed. In addition, there were pigeon men, with carrier pigeons ready to fly between Paris, Boulogne and London; usually, the birds would be released in flocks of eight to a dozen at a time, so spreading the risk posed by marksmen and hawks.[52]

The sequel to Moses Montefiore's account of the arrival at New Court, in March 1815, of the courier bearing the news that Napoleon had escaped from Elba and landed near Cannes – news 'too precious to be entrusted to the usual pigeon-post' – well illustrates the value to Nathan of the confidential advance intelligence that his courier service provided.

Having handed the courier, a Frenchman, a packet of despatches for him to take on his return journey, 'Mr Rothschild asked him, as he filled a stirrup-cup, if he knew what news he had brought. The man answered "No". "Napoleon has escaped from Elba and is now in France," announced Mr Rothschild. For a moment the man looked incredulous. Then, waving his glass, he shouted *"Vive l'Empereur!"* and enthusiastically tossed off a bumper.' As the courier left, Nathan turned to Moses and said: 'If that is the temper of the French I foresee we shall have some trouble yet.' He then gave Moses instructions as to what sales to effect on the Stock Exchange, before hurrying off to convey the news to Lord Liverpool.[53]

On 18 June 1815, the day of Waterloo, James Gallatin, son of the American envoy Albert Gallatin, recorded in his London diary: 'Great anxiety. Consols have fallen terribly. I have never seen greater depression; everybody one sees seems frightened. A rumour today that a battle had been fought and that the Duke of Wellington was crushed; tonight that is contradicted. One cannot believe anything. They say Monsieur Rothschild has mounted couriers from Brussels to Ostend and a fast clipper ready to sail the moment something is decisive one way or the other.'[54]

According to a source close to John Wilson Croker – Louis Jennings, the editor of Croker's papers – once the Rothschild courier had conveyed the tidings of Wellington's victory to New Court, having paused only to break the news to Louis XVIII at Brussels on the way, Nathan sent the man (again a Frenchman) straight on to Lord Liverpool, who at first doubted the truth of the news. The story goes that when, in answer to questions put by Croker, who was Secretary to the Admiralty, the courier described how at Brussels the French King had received him in his dressing-gown, and how on learning the news he had embraced the courier and kissed him, on both cheeks, Croker pronounced the news to be genuine.[55]

Nathan and Hannah's third son, Nathaniel (Nat), had by then been born on 2 July 1812. Perhaps in thanks for the safe delivery of another child, that year – the year of Charles Dickens' birth – Hannah founded a society for the relief of poor Jewish women and their newborn infants, the Ladies' Benevolent Institution. The society provided a suit of clothes for the mother, two for the child, a pair of sheets, five shillings a week for a fortnight and further assistance if necessary. Later, Hannah was to provide a complete suit of clothes annually for each pupil – 600 boys and 300 girls – of the Jews' Free School in Bell Lane, Spitalfields.[56]

Hannah Mayer Rothschild was born on 10 March 1815, ten days before Napoleon entered the Tuileries palace, from which Louis XVIII had fled for Ghent the day before. The year 1815 also saw the Rothschild and Montefiore families become further connected by marriage: Moses' brother Abraham married, as his second wife, Nathan's youngest sister Henrietta. Having previously married a Christian (who soon afterwards died), Abraham had for a time been all but disowned by his orthodox family. Of Henrietta, a granddaughter was later to remark that she 'never became quite English . . . and never lost her German accent', and that she 'had a great fund of the racy old Jewish humour, which made her conversation most entertaining'.[57]

Mayer was born to Nathan and Hannah on 29 June 1818; Louisa was born on 6 July 1820, the year of George IV's accession.

Nathan was an affectionate and adored parent who enjoyed the company of his children. Years later, an acquaintance recalled the occasion 'when like the renowned King of France, you let your beloved children make their equestrian exercises on your back'. Nathan was a good brother too: in 1814 his nephew Solomon Worms came from Germany to live at New Court; and in 1815 Nathan was much affected by the death of his sister Julie. 'I feel my spirits very depressed indeed and by no means able to attend to business as I could wish,' he told his brother Carl. 'The melancholy communication of the death of my sister has entirely unhinged my mind and [I] have done but little business to day on that account.'[58]

A fleeting impression of the quiet domestic life at New Court in the early years of the Rothschilds' residence there may be caught from Judith Montefiore's diary for 1812. 'We passed the evening at my dear sister Hannah's, who is always happy to see us, and I am ever glad so,' Judith wrote two days after her marriage to Moses. 'How many pleasant days have I spent there without company, but that of my dear sister Rothschild and a friend, which I have found far superior to the gayest circles.' In the evenings they played whist, or a card game called Commerce.[59]

Hannah was a devoted and thoughtful wife. When once, away from home, she learned that Nathan had a 'cold in his eyes', she wrote to urge him to 'let Mr Travers prescribe for you' and to 'beg that you put on your slippers when you get out of bed; the season is getting changeable and you must take care not to get cold'.[60]

Nathan and his brothers wrote to one another daily, in German written in Hebrew script (*Judendeutsch*). Never shy of bullying or criticising his brothers – even his father – in his own letters, Nathan routinely read theirs to him after dinner. 'I am reading through your letters not just once but maybe a hundred times,' he wrote testily in 1816. 'You will imagine that yourself. After dinner, I have nothing to do. I do not read books, I do not play cards, I do not go to the theatre. My only pleasure is business and in this way I read Amschel's, Salomon's, Jacob's [James's], and Carl's letters.'[61]

Yet Nathan and Hannah were not an unsociable couple. Less orthodox than Moses Montefiore, or than Nathan's family in Frankfurt, they were also less restricted in their social activities; while they drew the line at pork, they seem not to have kept strictly *kosher*. But unfortunately there is no account of any social entertainment that can with certainty be placed at New Court in the decade from 1810 – although it is very tempting to identify Nathan with the 'Mr R' who at some point in the period 1810-13 welcomed a visitor from Germany to a sumptuous dinner at his home in London.[62]

The unnamed guest, who in the anonymous memoir of his visit permits the reader to know that he is a Prussian Baron, had travelled part of the way to England in the company of 'Lady P' and her husband, an English couple from Frankfurt, and in London he was provided with an introduction to 'Mr L', the envoy of the Elector of Hesse-Kassel. In his description of the splendid and varied fare spread before him in Mr R's dining room, no dish of pork is recalled.

> I made also a visit to Mr R, to whom I had already written from Harwich, and was received with the utmost politeness and attention. Soon after, he sent me an invitation to dinner, which I could not but accept, though our abodes are nearly four miles distant from each other . . . I met a select party in the drawing-room, the windows of which were hung with gold brocade. Soon after, dinner was announced, and an excellent one it was. Viands and made-dishes were, according to custom, served up at once; so that the table looked like the counter of a restaurateur. Excellent salmon, roast beef, roast veal, fowls, partridges, hares, woodcocks, pastry, sauces, preserves, vegetables, pickles, and a hundred other things, constituted such an abundance, that every one present could choose whatever he liked to feast upon, about which he was always asked by the gentleman of the house, who had taken the head of the table. I myself hesitated not a moment at paying my addresses to Sirloin, for so they call the honest roast beef, and was accordingly helped to a nice bit . . .
>
> As soon as the cloth was removed, a choice dessert made its appearance, consisting of delicious fruits, both foreign and domestic, and confectionary; and in its train came a number of bottles with different sorts of wine, which in their silver stands were pushed from one gentleman to another so many times that in the end they were found to have travelled a couple of miles round.[63]

In February 1812, one of Hannah's brothers-in-law, Samuel Moses Samuel (the son of Moses Samuel), a City merchant who traded with Portugal, supplied Nathan with twenty-six and a half dozen bottles of Port (1804 vintage), ten dozen of mature Madeira, and a further whole pipe of Madeira.[64]

A decade later, in 1822, the Vicomte de Chateaubriand, serving as Louis XVIII's ambassador to England, dined as a guest of the Marquess of Londonderry and was entertained by the Lord Mayor of London on his barge; he also 'dined in the East End of the town with Mr Rothschild of London . . . The roast-beef equalled that of the Tower of London in state-liness; the fish were so long that one could not see their tails; ladies, whom I met there and nowhere else, sang like Abigail.'[65]

Most visitors to No. 2 New Court, of course, went there to see Nathan on business. Among them, in June 1818, was the budding diplomat Woodbine Parish, who in 1813–14, when he had been working for the Commissary-in-Chief, J. C. Herries, had met Nathan almost every day. Preparations were now in hand for the Congress at Aix-la-Chapelle, the meeting of the Allies to determine, among other things, whether the time had come to withdraw their armies from France. Britain was to be repre-sented at the Congress by Lord Castlereagh, whose party was going to require banking facilities at Aix. It had been reported that one of Nathan's brothers was already there, attending to some business of the King of Prussia, so Parish, who was to be a member of Castlereagh's suite at the Congress, was instructed to call on Nathan for assistance. Afterwards, he described his encounter in a letter he wrote to his father:

'I went to see him in the City and was very kindly received by him as an old acquaintance, all the more welcome of course as coming from Lord Castlereagh. Upon explaining my errand he at once said there would be no difficulty in his brother giving us whatever money we wanted, and sat down to write to him to that effect, asking, however, for how much he should give us a letter of credit. I said I could not specify any amount, that he had better tell him to let us have whatever money we wanted. No, he said, I must state a sum, £5,000 or £10,000 or what?

'On my repeating that I had no idea myself how much would be required, he said, "Well, let me see, who is going? I know there will be Lord and Lady Castlereagh, Mr Planta, you, Mr Chad, Lord Clanwilliam, Lord Francis Conyngham, and others who may, or may not, be of the party."

'"Well," he said, "there will be so many masters, and so many servants, so many horses and carriages, there will be the house and lodgings for the attachés, travelling expenses, entertainments, etc, you will all be there a month or six weeks, you will want £5,000 to £10,000, so I will give you a letter of credit for £10,000, and that will be more than you can spend." He then wrote a few lines to his brother, which he handed to me open to read, and then burst out laughing at my face on finding it was written in Hebrew!

'Business over he rang the bell and ordered coffee, which was brought in by a servant in gorgeous livery, upon a splendid silver salver, with all its appurtenances of the same, strikingly contrasting with his own appearance, "en déshabillé" in an old dressing-gown, with his black silk breeches loose and unbuttoned at the knee, his ordinary costume in the Counting House, as I was told, but cutting a very different figure to his appearance on Change, as I have seen him with all eyes upon him.

'What struck me very much was his correct information as to the details of our party and his knowledge of the persons likely to compose it, some of whose names I believe had not even transpired at the Foreign Office . . .

'He is certainly a marvellous man in his way, and by the establishment of his family connections in every capital in Europe, has obtained an influence such as no one ever had before, over all the money markets of the world. His transactions seem to be unlimited, and his wealth is said to be untold . . .'[66]

During that same year, 1818, when Prussia desired to raise a loan, Wilhelm von Humboldt could only advise his government in Berlin to approach New Court. 'Rothschild,' he explained, 'is now easily the most enterprising businessman in this country. He is moreover a man upon whom one can rely, and with whom the Government here does considerable business. He is also, as far as I know, just, exceedingly honest, and intelligent. On the other hand, I must add that if business is to be given to him to carry, it will be necessary to fall in with his ideas, for he has acquired the independent habit of mind developed by riches and a fairly long sojourn in this country, and he is now engaged in such a constant number of financial transactions that it will not greatly affect him if one of them fails to come his way. He wants to take over the whole loan himself; on this point he is likely to be exceedingly firm, and he has asked in advance that the Prussian Consul here, against whom he is prejudiced, shall not be allowed to interfere in the matter in any way.'[67]

The £5 million Prussian loan that Nathan subsequently issued set a new trend in foreign loans: for the first time, dividends were payable in London rather than abroad, and in sterling rather than in a foreign currency that was subject to exchange rate fluctuations. The loan was a success and in 1822, by issuing further loans for Prussia, Russia and the Bourbon government of Naples, Nathan became the leading contractor in the foreign loan market.[68]

There were, of course, the smaller clients too, and their interests were not neglected. When, for example, Catherine Hussey, a wealthy widow to whom Nathan had provided letters of credit and recommendation, was swindled out of £50,000, Nathan was ready to assist in efforts to track down the money, and the Irish fraudster, on the Continent. Not long before her death in 1817, Madame de Staël, the literary daughter of Louis XVI's finance minister Jacques Necker, regretted that she had not placed 'all her monetary affairs in the hands of Monsieur Rothschild of London'.[69]

In 1820 the composer Louis Spohr, soon to be appointed conductor of the court orchestra of Hesse-Kassel, called on Nathan with a letter of recommendation from Rothschild's in Frankfurt and a letter of credit from another Frankfurt firm. He was, he recounted, 'exceedingly amused' by a scene at New Court: 'After Rothschild had taken both letters from me and glanced hastily over them, he said to me in a more subdued tone of voice: "I have just read (pointing to the *Times*) that you managed your business very efficiently. But I understand nothing of music; this is my music (slapping his purse), they understand that on the exchange!" Upon which, with a nod of the head, he terminated the audience.'[70]

Rather grandly, Spohr recorded that during his stay in London he twice declined Hannah's invitations to dine: 'Madame Rothschild invited me to dinner; but I did not go, although she repeated the invitation.' He was, however, prepared to concede that the 'letter of recommendation to Rothschild was not wholly useless, for he took a whole box at my benefit concert'. The concert took place on the day of Queen Caroline's tumultuous entry to London on her return from Italy.

Whether Nathan himself made use of the box that night we do not know, but he may well have done. Despite his protestations to the contrary, he seems to have enjoyed music and did sometimes go to the theatre. 'Last night we were at the Opera & saw your favourite Taglioni dance,' his daughter Chilly later wrote to him from Paris. 'At all her beautiful steps, we wished you were there to applaud her.' Marie Taglioni was the first dancer to have flowers thrown to her on the stage of the Opera in Paris; Lady Blessington described her style of dancing as 'totally new . . . she seems to float and bound like a sylph across the stage'.[71]

To men in the City, Nathan was most familiar as a figure on Change, where twice a week, on Tuesdays and Fridays, he went to conduct his business in foreign bills. It was a place little changed since Thomas Addison had found 'secret satisfaction as an Englishman to see so rich an assembly of countrymen and foreigners making this metropolis a kind of emporium for the whole earth' – a place where he had found himself 'jostled by a body of Armenians' or 'lost in a crowd of Jews or Dutchmen, sometimes Danes, Swedes or Frenchmen'.[72]

At ground level in the central courtyard of Change, each particular market had its own pitch or 'walk' – East India Walk, Virginia Walk, Jamaica Walk, Canary Walk, Italian Walk and so on. Around the edge of the court ran a colonnade, in the south-east corner of which, between Spanish and Portugal walks, was Jews' Walk, and it was there that Nathan would take up his position, invariably standing on the same spot with his back to the same column.[73]

As merchants came up to him there, observed a contributor to the *Gentleman's Magazine*, Nathan 'never hesitated for a moment in fixing the rate, either as a drawer or a taker, on any part of the world; and his memory was so retentive, that, notwithstanding the immense transactions into which he entered on every foreign post day, and that he never took a note of them, he could dictate the whole on his return home with perfect exactness to his clerks. His liberality of dealing was another conspicuous feature of these operations, and many merchants whose bills were objected to elsewhere found ready assistance from him, and his judgement was proved by the very small amount of loss which he incurred in consequence of such liberality.'[74]

3

Stamford Hill

V IGNETTES OF HANNAH are comparatively scarce, but Nathan's brothers were from the first struck by her self-possession and poise. According to one of her granddaughters, she was a 'far-seeing and clever woman', 'authoritative and somewhat masterful', one who 'managed all members of her family, even when they had attained to man's estate. She was striking in appearance, with very beautiful blue eyes, a fine brow, and a straight Grecian nose.'[1]

An entry in Moses Montefiore's diary for 1829 (by which time he and Judith had moved from New Court) confirms that there was a resolute aspect to his sister-in-law's nature. 'Judith and self took a ride to see Hannah Rothschild and her husband,' Moses recorded. 'We had a long conversation on the subject of liberty for the Jews. He said he would shortly go to the Lord Chancellor and consult him on the matter. Hannah said if he did not, she would. The spirit manifested here by Mrs Rothschild, and the brief but impressive language she used, reminded me most strikingly of her sister, Mrs Montefiore.'[2]

Hannah and Judith were two of Levi Cohen's six daughters. By his first wife, Fanny (who came from Amsterdam), Levi had had two sons, Joseph, the future Warden of the Great Synagogue, and Solomon, and also a daughter, named Fanny. Widowed by 1780, Levi then married his late wife's sister Lydia, who bore him nine more children, eight of whom survived to adulthood: Barent, Esther, Hannah, Judith, Benjamin (Ben), Isaac, Jessie (or Jesse) and Adeline.

Two of the children faded from the picture early on. Fanny, on marrying her first cousin Solomon Cohen Wessels in 1797, went to live in Amsterdam. She and her family in due course became the Rothschilds' 'poor relations', forever writing in hopes of financial assistance. Barent Cohen died a bachelor in 1807.

The remainder of the Cohen children married within the Anglo-Jewish community and provided Nathan and Hannah's children with a network of English cousins. Ben married Moses Montefiore's sister Justina; Isaac married Sarah Samuel, a granddaughter of Moses Samuel, Joseph Cohen's co-warden of the Great Synagogue; Jessie married Meyer Davidson, who assisted Nathan in the purchase and delivery of coin to Wellington's troops in the Peninsula; Adeline married John Helbert, a stockbroker whose firm acted for New Court.[3]

The Cohen boys seem to have received a good education. Ben attended a Jewish 'academy' in Cambridge run by Solomon Lyon, a rabbi from Prague who also taught Hebrew to students at the university and to the Duke of Sussex. By the standards of the day, the Cohen girls were well educated too. Judith learned to speak German, Italian and French, and she knew Hebrew. Some mastery of foreign languages was considered essential for everyone in their cosmopolitan circle, as Hannah was to impress on Anthony when he was travelling on the Continent in the 1820s.[4]

'When you are again settled at a place,' she wrote, 'I hope you will have good masters for the French and German languages for according to appearances when so many of your friends are in different countries and the business which please God you will attend to will require that you should possess a good knowledge of as many as you can acquire – and which you will find very essential to know.'[5]

Solomon Cohen's wife, another Hannah, lived to bemoan a grandson's ignorance of any language except English: he was, she remarked, 'an interesting, handsome young man, but can speak no language save his own. It is a great fault in his education, I hope not too late to remedy.'[6]

After their marriage in 1802, Solomon and Hannah Cohen lived at No. 12 Angel Court, next door to Solomon's parents. Solomon's father-in-law Moses Samuel was a cultured man of liberal outlook, a founder of the Society for the Cultivation of the Hebrew Language and Literature. He lived to a great age (at ninety-six he attended Nathan's burial), and was remembered for his oft-repeated comment on the town houses acquired by younger members of his family: 'Palaces, by my God! Palaces!' One of Solomon's brothers-in-law, Phineas Samuel, whose daughter Sarah married Isaac Cohen, published a book in Hebrew when he was only eighteen. Samuel Moses Samuel, Phineas's eldest brother, married Esther Cohen – and their daughter, Henrietta, would marry Nathan's nephew Solomon Worms.[7]

Three of Solomon Cohen's four sons died in infancy or boyhood, but he and his wife took care that their daughters, like Solomon's sisters, received a 'careful and thorough education' appropriate for young ladies, including lessons in music, painting, embroidery and riding. Two of the daughters, Emily and Hannah, went with their Rothschild first cousins,

Hannah Mayer and Louisa, to dancing classes at the school established in London by James Harvey D'Egville, the greatest English ballet master and choreographer of the day.[8]

Hannah Rothschild's education had left her with literary leanings. In the 1830s Lionel would write to her of 'the Duke of Sussex & your other friends of German literature', and among her circle was the novelist Lady Stepney, author of *The New Road to Ruin* (1833) and *The Three Peers* (1840) and earlier works published under the name 'Mrs Manners'. William Jerdan attended 'poor dear Lady Stepney's soirées' and called her 'that innocent being'; when Benjamin Disraeli met her, 'very fantastically dressed', one evening in 1832, Lady Stepney asked his opinion about a Leonardo da Vinci and paid him 'the most ludicrous comments'.[9]

Through Nathan's connection with J. C. Herries, Hannah even came within range of Jane Austen. Herries himself, so Disraeli discovered when seated next to him at dinner, 'turned out quite a literary man – so false are one's impressions'; and when Jane Austen was staying in London with her brother Henry in the autumn of 1815, they went to dine at Herries' house in Cadogan Place. It was, Jane told her sister Cassandra, 'a large family party – clever and accomplished'. Subsequently, Herries' sister Isabella called to see Jane at Henry's house in Hans Place.[10]

A further link to Jane Austen came through Nathan's client Catherine Hussey, the heiress who was defrauded of £50,000. She was the widow of the Reverend John Hussey, younger brother of Edward Hussey, of Scotney Castle, Lamberhurst, in Kent. While the Husseys' youngest sister, Harriet, married an Austen, Edward's son, another Edward (1780–1817), may perhaps be identified with the 'Ed: Hussey' of whom Jane Austen writes to her sister Cassandra in a letter from Godmersham Park, Kent, dated 14 October 1813.[11]

Besides their cultured attainments, Levi Cohen's daughters acquired some knowledge of business – together with a strong sense of the important part it had to play in their lives, and a taste for it. While Hannah was thus equipped to assist Nathan with his business from the start of their married life in Manchester, Judith, five days after her marriage to Moses in June 1812, noted in her diary: 'The Loan being contracted for this morning, my dear husband was induced to attend to business, as he is greatly concerned at such a period, although it is rather unusual to attend to business within seven days after marriage. However, as this is a matter of consequence, he was perfectly right . . . Most probably I shall have a few trifling transactions in the funds merely to amuse. I commenced yesterday by purchasing Consols, by which I have gained a few pounds . . .'[12]

When Judith and her 'dear Monte' finally set off on their honeymoon a few days later, they headed for Kent, where they concluded a brief tour with two nights at the York Hotel in Margate. The era when Londoners would flock to Margate by Thames paddle-steamer had not yet dawned; visitors from London still arrived in sailing vessels called 'hoys', after a voyage, in fair weather, of nine hours. The Montefiores arrived by post-chaise from Deal.[13]

Two small Londoners who were visiting Margate at the same time merited a mention by Judith in her diary: her nephew Lionel, aged three, and niece Chilly, aged four. In the care of someone called Jesse – probably their nurse, possibly their as yet unmarried aunt Jessie Cohen – the children were boarding with a Mrs Brashin in Margate High Street, where their aunt and uncle called to see them. 'They were rejoiced to see us both and looked remarkably well,' Judith recorded on 27 June. 'We left them to be dressed and promised to return and fetch them to walk on the pier. Lionel, who walked with me, pointed out everything remarkable and displayed great observation in one so young.'[14]

On 29 June, having decided to start back for London at midday, Judith and Moses got up early. 'We arose at six, went to bathe, then walked over the sands to Dandelion Gardens, which I was much pleased with, and gave the gardener a trifle to swing us. We both swung at the same time. I am extremely partial to that exercise. We then returned to breakfast. On our way [we] met Charlotte [Chilly] and Lionel, with Jesse, took them home with us to breakfast, which we made a very hearty meal of after bathing and a long and delightful walk. The children left us, and being resolved to see as much of the place as our short stay would allow, we walked out again, but did not go into any of the libraries.'[15]

While Judith never bore any children, Chilly and Lionel's aunt Esther Samuel, their mother's elder sister by a year, had a young family of roughly their age. The son, George, was to become a firm friend. The Samuels lived in London, and at one time also had a house on the Sussex coast; and it is in a letter from Brighton, written in October 1819, that we next catch sight of the young Rothschild children, in the company of their Samuel relations.

'My dear Sister Hannah Mayer & myself bathed in the Sea yesterday,' Chilly informed her mother. 'She bathed as usual very well. The Sea was very warm & consequently the bathing very agreeable. Mayer had a warm bath. I have the pleasure to inform you that my dear little brother's face is considerably better & I do not doubt but that in a day or two it will be perfectly well: in every other respect he is quite well [,] being very lively & his cheeks very rosy. Hannah Mayer is quite well & she sends you & dear Papa many, many kisses with love to you both.

'Henrietta, Cecilia, Amelia & George Samuel drank tea with us [;] we passed a very pleasant Evening [,] My kind Governess exerting herself & doing everything in her power to amuse us & render us comfortable. Miss Andrews [the governess] would have written but she has been so much occupied but particularly this morning being so very uncommonly fine that Miss Andrews & Myself have been out walking during the greatest part of the Morning. She desires to be particularly remembered to you. Hannah Meyer [*sic*] unites with me in love & duty to you & Papa. We are all very well & hope that you are so.'[16]

The next September, Chilly and Miss Andrews were staying by the sea again, this time with Anthony and their Solomon Cohen cousins, though Solomon himself had remained in London. 'I duly received your kind letter of the 26th inst.,' Solomon wrote to his wife, 'by which I obtained the account of your sailing expedition which was rather a rash attempt, but thank God, no ill effects have resulted from it. The nausea of sea sickness is very unpleasant, but the consequences are far from being unhealthy, provided the vomitings are not too violent. I should think it must have relieved Miss Andrews. Pray make my best respects to her, and my kind love to Charlotte [Chilly] Rothschild, Anthony, and likewise to all our dear children . . . Lionel's eye is rather better; he has leeches applied to it . . .'[17]

Solomon's attitude to seasickness seems more curious now than it would have done in the Georgian era. The author of a guide to Margate in 1789 stated that few persons 'in genteel life' travelled in the hoys 'unless recommended by their physicians so to do, in order to experience sea-sickness, which is thought to be very beneficial in some cases'.[18]

Beyond the network of cousins, the Rothschild children's friends and playmates included the young Gurneys at Upton. A family anecdote passed down the generations told of an occasion when as a girl Hannah Mayer was dressed up in Quaker attire by Sam Gurney's daughters and 'introduced in the parlour to their parents as a new addition to the Society of Friends'.[19]

While Nathan's daughters were educated at home – Miss Andrews' place was eventually supplied by a Mlle Mérienne, from Geneva – the boys were in due course sent to school. Lionel, Anthony and Nat went to Maurice Garcia's boarding school for Jewish boys at Peckham, then a village in the country to the south of London.[20]

According to Joseph Barrow Montefiore, Lionel and Anthony thus only narrowly escaped an alarming experience at the hands of Hyman Hurwitz, a learned, but outlandish, Jewish schoolmaster whose Hebrew scholarship was admired by Isaac D'Israeli (father of the future prime minister), and whose Hebrew poetry was translated into English by Samuel Taylor Coleridge. Judith Montefiore enjoyed reading Hurwitz's *Hebrew Stories*.[21]

'I was at school with them [Lionel and Anthony] at Garcia's,' recalled J. B. Montefiore. 'At first I went to Hurwitz's school, at Highgate; but Hurwitz's declined. The parents of the richer pupils objected to Hurwitz, who was a Pole and used to wear a tall Polish hat and stride about the schoolroom with a cane ferociously stuck in his Wellington boots. They got Garcia, who was previously a book-keeper in Barrow and Lousada's counting house, to establish a more select academy at Peckham and there Lionel and Anthony Rothschild were sent.'[22]

At a later stage, the boys' schooling was placed in the hands of a German pastor, the Reverend Dr Schwabe. Lionel, and probably Anthony too, was studying with Dr Schwabe when in 1823 the likeable Miss Andrews wrote a letter to Hannah from Frankfurt, where she had taken Chilly to stay with her relations. As Miss Andrews was writing her letter, the final preparations were being made for Frankfurt's famous Michaelmas fair. By now even Mayer, aged five, had begun school.[23]

'I had yesterday the pleasure of receiving a letter from Lionel for which I thank him, and take it very kindly that he finds time, amidst the numerous pursuits his education necessarily imposes on him to write a few lines to his distant friend. Anthony will I hope follow his example and favour me with an epistle soon. To Nathaniel I really owe an apology for deferring so long to address him . . . I hope my old favourite Mayer is as lively and hearty as ever. I could not suppress a smile on hearing he has been to school at Mrs Hogg's. There seems to be a sort of fatality in the names of his preceptresses. Hannah Mayer has written several nice letters to Charlotte [Chilly]. I hope at her leisure to be favoured with one from her.'

When Hyman Hurwitz had established his school in Highgate in 1799, there had been a Jewish presence in the neighbourhood for at least a century. Affluent London merchants – Christian and Jew – had begun to move there, and to Hampstead, so as to escape the noxious miasma of town. The Thames in those days was little more than an open sewer, stinking in the summer, and the City – London's main residential as well as business quarter – was a maze of narrow streets and lanes, teeming with people and choked up with horse-drawn traffic.[24]

In the first half of the nineteenth century, London was no less dirty, stinking or unhealthy. The smoke from thousands of coal fires added filth to the polluted air; pea-soup fogs would obliterate the city for days at a time. Erik Gustav Geijer, a Swedish visitor to London writing in 1809, found 'houses all alike, all dark and smoke-begrimed' in an 'atmosphere of coal smoke in whose twilight moves an unending multitude of people'. 'London,' he declared, 'is a foggy, smoky hole and fits not badly with the description of the ancients of the place of abode of the god of riches, who dwelt far from the day, down in the earth, dug for treasure and did not ask for light.' Geijer soon found lodgings in the cleaner air of the village of Stoke Newington.[25]

The incessant rumbling of wheels on cobblestones, the shouts of drivers and the cries of street vendors hawking their wares made London a noisy place as well. As an apprentice tea-broker working in St Swithin's Lane, J. B. Montefiore witnessed the commotion caused by the arrival of the mail coach carrying consignments of bullion to New Court, and described how despatch riders bearing intelligence for Nathan 'mounted on ponies, sweltering with foam, with despatch bags dangling from each side of their saddles . . . made the old Lane ring with their clattering hoofs'. It was no wonder that the residents of New Court were as keen as anyone to escape to the fresh air and peace of the country.[26]

In 1817, Moses Montefiore bought Tinley Lodge, a farm near Tonbridge in Kent; later, in 1830, he was to acquire East Cliff Lodge at Ramsgate. But from the earliest days of their marriage he and Judith liked nothing better than to spend a night or two at the Red Lion inn at Smitham Bottom in Surrey.[27] According to their faithful friend and travelling companion, Dr Louis Loewe (who later edited their diaries), Moses and Judith would often go to Smitham Bottom 'on Sunday and remain until the next day, sometimes until the middle of the week'. They would go for long walks over the Surrey hills and 'always found on their return to the little inn, an excellent [kosher] dinner, which their servants had brought with them from London'.[28]

The Montefiores were staying at Smitham Bottom when Lydia Cohen was taken ill on a Saturday in 1818. So as to avoid breaking one of the Commandments by riding in a carriage on the Sabbath, Moses went to London on foot, a walk of five hours. By the time he arrived, his mother-in-law had expired; but Moses must have been heartened by the sentiments she expressed in her will: 'Now, my dear Children, I have a grand point to say and it is my last wish, I hope you will abide by it, as it is for all your good, which is, that I Beg and Pray you do not forget that you are Jews and keep your Religion, and always have in your memory your Father who is in Heaven & take example from him, then I am sure you will all be good, and the Almighty will bless you all, with your children.'[29]

The Montefiores' diaries record that in 1814, the year of the signing of the first Peace of Paris and of the Congress of Vienna (and also the year when the Thames last froze over) Judith and Moses paid frequent visits to a country house that Nathan had taken at Highgate. No further reference, though, is ever made to it, and in the summer of 1814, in a lone surviving letter of Hannah's from that year, the Rothschilds were to be found taking their pleasures in Surrey, at Egham races – *en fête*, as was the capital, to honour the presence of the Allied Sovereigns to whom Nathan had been directing Britain's subsidies.[30]

'London at present is all Gaiety,' Hannah wrote to Nathan's brother James in June. 'What with the visits of the Emperor [of Russia], King [of Prussia] &c there are nothing but grand sights and entertainments. I suppose you [remember] last year when we went to Egham races and feasted so heartily on a Breakfast at Richmond. I assure you I do, from having spent a very pleasant day. Well last week the Races were again and several of the Family and self went. All the Distinguished Foreigners were there of course, the Applause they met with were [sic] indeed great. Thousands and thousands of the most Elegant People in this Country standing on carriages waving and applauding. The English take the greatest pride in their Horses and Carriages which were truly magnificent. You would have particularly admired them. We had a most excellent view of all the Royal Visitors.'[31]

Within two years of the Montefiores' visits to Nathan at Highgate, the Rothschilds had moved into, and out of, another house on the fringes of London, this time at Clapton. A pleasant, country situation, Clapton had been the chosen place of residence of Israel Solomons, a rich East India merchant whose daughter Jessie had married the financier Benjamin Goldsmid (bringing with her a princely dowry of £100,000). A surviving inventory of 'Furniture &c deficient & broken in Mr Boddington's House [at] Clapton late in the occupation of N. Rothschild Esqre' is dated 17 December 1816. The list itemises '1 Green Curtain (piece cut off)', '2 pieces of Carpet' and 'A Japand [sic] shaving pot'.[32]

Then in 1819 Nathan and Hannah found a property they liked in neighbouring Stamford Hill, three to four miles north of the City and just beyond Stoke Newington, where Geijer had found lodgings ten years earlier. Before building a palatial house for himself at Roehampton, Benjamin Goldsmid had owned a 'tasteful and elegant residence' at Stamford Hill.[33]

The house that took the Rothschilds' fancy was about thirty years old. A bill from Dawes & Chatfield, Nathan's solicitors, for work done in April–May 1819 in connection with the title and deeds of the property, refers to the 'purchase made by him [Nathan] of Mr Taylor's House at Stamford Hill'. The vendor was John Taylor, East India merchant and MP, who described himself as a friend of Nicholas Vansittart and whose residence is recorded as 'Stamford Hill House'; earlier occupants included Isaac Barrow Lousada, a broker, and an East India Company director called Colonel Bannerman.[34]

As Sam Gurney found Upton convenient for the City – and as Woodford suited John Harman and his son Jeremiah – so Nathan was able with ease to reach Stamford Hill after a day's work, or even after dining late in town. On Tuesdays and Fridays (foreign post days) he would, so one of Lionel's sons later maintained, often give dinners at New Court – as in 1822 he did for Chateaubriand – which might easily last until midnight.[35]

When the Rothschilds moved up to Stamford Hill the area was still rural, a place of meadows, pasture and market gardens. 'You can come and dine with me at my country house!' Nathan called after Louis Spohr as the composer was leaving New Court in 1820. During the summer months, the local population would be swollen by itinerant haymakers.[36]

Staying in London during the summer of 1829, Felix Mendelssohn was invited one Saturday in July to dine at Stamford Hill, which he described as 'a green village, full of trees, gardens and roses'. 'As we are to breakfast with other acquaintances in the same place on Sunday morning,' he continued, 'we have resolved to stay over-night at the village inn, go into the fields in the morning, and astonish the people by our early appearance.'[37]

Mendelssohn's father Abraham (the son of Moses Mendelssohn, apostle of secular education for the Jews) was a banker in Berlin, and it may well have been the Rothschilds whom Felix was planning to astonish; in June, he had written a scherzo in Chilly's *Livre d'or*, a kind of musical autograph book that she had recently begun. Louis Spohr later wrote in it, too.[38]

Stoke Newington, straddling the London road to Hertford (the local stretch of which served as the village high street), offered the convenience of frequent stagecoach services to the City. In 1820, there were hourly services to Gracechurch Street, and hourly and half-hourly services to Bishopsgate – though by then Nathan had his own carriages, driven for him by Brock, who was to serve as his coachman for eighteen years.[39]

Having retired from D'Israeli & Parkins, Benjamin D'Israeli, City merchant, stockbroker and grandfather of the future prime minister, migrated from No. 5 Great St Helens to No. 7 Church Row (later No. 170 Church Street), Stoke Newington. D'Israeli belonged to the Sephardic branch of Jewry, and Church Street was home to 'quite a Jewish colony'. Such 'removals to the suburbs', as J. B. Montefiore put it, 'gave rise to an interesting function every year. On Hoshana Rabba the wealthy Jews used to drive down to synagogue in their carriages, with powdered footmen and glittering harness, and Bevis Marks would be filled with a crowd to see them.'[40]

There was a Quaker presence in Church Street, too. William Allen, the Quaker chemist and philanthropist, lived there from 1807; he was an early encourager of Fowell Buxton in his philanthropic activities. Before moving to Hampstead, Samuel Hoare, the Quaker banker who married Sam Gurney's sister Louisa (Buxton's sister-in-law), lived in Paradise Row, Church Street, where in the 1820s his brother Jonathan Hoare also owned a house. The young Anna Sewell, a Quaker who would become famous as the author of *Black Beauty*, lived nearby with her mother Mary.[41]

Dissenters of all sorts favoured the neighbourhood. The Reverend Dr Schwabe, the pastor to whom the Rothschild boys' education was entrusted after Garcia's, was a neighbour at Stamford Hill.[42]

Had Lionel and Anthony instead attended the Manor House School, Stoke Newington, run by the Reverend John Bransby, they could have been pupils alongside Edgar Allan Poe, who in his story 'William Wilson' described Stoke Newington as a 'misty-looking village of Old England, where [there] were a vast number of gigantic and gnarled trees, and where all the houses were excessively ancient'. It was far enough from London for Mr Bransby to signal to the boys that he was off for the day by cleaning his gun.[43]

The Rothschilds' house beyond the village had eight acres of land and was to serve as the family's retreat from the metropolis for the best part of the next twenty years. The clean air was one of its foremost attractions, as Hannah explained in a letter to her friend Lady Carmarthen: 'We are still at Stamford Hill. We find this situation more agreeable than in the streets of London; we do not have any benefit from our national friend, the fog – and I must say that I am unkind enough to do all I can to avoid this boast of Old England.'[44] Lady Carmarthen, later Duchess of Leeds, was a daughter of the Baltimore cotton merchant Richard Caton; her sister was married to the Duke of Wellington's eldest brother Richard, the Marquess Wellesley.

Hannah's relations felt as she did about getting out of London. In 1818 Abraham and Henrietta Montefiore had acquired a house at Stamford Hill; Esther Samuel and her husband did so too. Ben Cohen went to live by the Thames at Richmond, where Levi Cohen seems once to have had a house; and Solomon Cohen established his family near Islington, in Grove House, Canonbury Place, from the upstairs windows of which the view towards London was still across open country.[45]

In 1823, Miss Andrews was glad to hear that Hannah's sister Jessie Davidson had 'at length acquired a residence so likely to gratify her constant desire for air and exercise'. And when Judith Montefiore was going through her drawers and found 'some tickets of Mr Fontaine's', she thought she 'might as well make use of them as not, so took a ride on horse-back about two hours'. Fontaine was evidently the owner of a riding school.[46]

Hannah was reminded of the benefits of exercise and fresh air – and of the benefits of sensible eating – when she consulted William Allen's friend William Babington, the doctor and mineralogist, about a digestive complaint. 'What I most depend on,' Babington confided, 'is the regularity of your general management of yourself. I consider you as being very abstemious, & there can be no question but the lighter & more simple your diet, the more regular your exercise & the less confining & burthensome your pursuits, the greater your security for a few years to come.' When Moses Montefiore was elected a Fellow of the Royal Society in 1836, William Babington was one of his supporters.[47]

From the bedrooms of the Rothschilds' new house at Stamford Hill the view was of the garden and fields. Chilly, after she had married and left home, imagined her sister Louisa – her 'dear little Lully' – 'quite delighted to be again at dear Stamford Hill', although 'the weather . . . will prevent your playing about in the garden'. Lionel and Anthony, 'surrounded by their father with every luxury', J. B. Montefiore remembered, had 'a miniature carriage with four white goats to drive about the grounds'.[48]

Gardening was all the rage; on a visit to Blenheim in 1822 the Duke of Wellington and his friend Mrs Arbuthnot found the Duke of Marlborough 'gardening mad'. Nathan joined the Horticultural Society (soon to become the Royal Horticultural Society), and ordered designs for a glasshouse from the architect and designer Thomas Allason, surveyor to the Alliance.[49]

Besides playing in the garden, the Rothschild children had ponies to ride. Nathan bought mounts for them from Scotland – Shetlands to begin with, no doubt – through a Regent Street dealer named Campbell. In 1830, Hannah was glad to hear that Nathan himself had bought a cob – and added that his brother Salomon would like to have one too.[50]

Riding became one of the children's greatest pleasures. Louisa would ask after her pony Billy White; Hannah Mayer once told her father that she had passed a religious holiday in Paris 'as agreeably as can be expected considering we were not able to ride'. Chilly went so far as to declare that riding was 'Lionel's favourite amusement'; and when an old school friend of Lionel's, Richard Sheppard, later wrote to invite him to stay with him in the country for a few days one summer – to 'get into the Stroudwater

Mail Coach & come & visit me in Gloucestershire to talk over old matters' – he assured him that a horse would be 'at your service'.[51]

When Fritz Schlemmer arrived to take up his post at Stamford Hill, he
was almost at once taken by Nat to see over the stables. When Nat proceeded
to ask the new tutor from Germany if he could ride, Schlemmer replied that
he had done so, but that he had never had regular lessons at a riding school.
'We've not learned to ride at a school,' Nat scoffed, 'but out foxhunting.'[52]

All four of the Rothschild boys had tutors at the pre-university stage:
while Nat and Mayer were taken care of by Schlemmer, an Englishman,
John Darby, was engaged for Lionel and Anthony. Except for the fact that
he was a clergyman's son, little is known of John Darby or of his background. Of Fritz Schlemmer, on the other hand, a certain amount can be
gleaned from his memoir and other sources.

He came to the Rothschilds as a result of a recommendation to Nathan's
brother James from Count Alexandre de Laborde, the son of Louis XV's
banker Jean Josephe de Laborde, who had been guillotined in 1794. Before
qualifying as a lawyer in Hanau, Schlemmer had been tutor to Count de
Laborde's son in France. When Lady Blessington encountered the Labordes
in Naples in 1823, she found the count to be a 'clever well-informed man,
fond of literature and science', while his son Léon was 'highly educated and
accomplished'.[53]

From Naples, Léon de Laborde had embarked on an extended trip to
the Middle East, accompanied by his father as far as Cairo, then by Linant
de Bellefonds, the hydraulic engineer, with whom he visited, among other
places, Petra. It was through Léon's drawings, used to illustrate his *Voyage
en Arabie Pétrée* (1830), that Petra was first revealed to a wider world. On his
return, Léon was appointed private secretary to Prince Talleyrand at the
French embassy in London – which might in part explain the friendliness
Talleyrand showed to Fritz Schlemmer. Further to recommend Schlemmer
to Nathan was the fact that he had relations in England whom Nathan
knew – people named Schunk, partners in the firm of merchants Schunk,
Mylius, of Lloyd Street in Manchester.[54]

Notwithstanding Schlemmer's inexperience of riding – for exercise he
boxed and fenced; for relaxation he played the organ – anyone of any substance in England kept horses. Some residents of rural Stamford Hill kept
other livestock too. One of the Rothschilds' neighbours, so Nathan told
Fowell Buxton, was 'a very ill tempered man; he tries to vex me, and has
built a great place for swine, close to my walk. So, when I go out, I hear
first, grunt, grunt, squeak, squeak; but this does me no harm. I am always
in good humour.'[55]

Why the man wished to vex Nathan is not recorded, nor whether the choice of pigs was meant as a special insult. When the banker Thomas Coutts and his wife were subjected to a nuisance at Holly Lodge, their villa at Highgate – which otherwise was 'as perfectly quiet as though it were in the midst of the New Forest, or on Salisbury Plain' – the motive was purely pecuniary.[56] Wishing to make Coutts pay an exorbitant price for a small patch of land that was visible from his drawing-room windows, its owner 'made a point of bringing carts, and all the accessories of farming to be deposited there'. To these were added building materials – heaps of bricks, gravel, lime and sand – and old clothes were hung up in full view. When the Couttses were entertaining guests, sometimes royalty, the man would see to it that the carts 'were left just in the way of the carriages' and that his labourers were as busy and intrusive as possible.[57]

More considerate neighbours of the Rothschilds included James Freshfield, of Abney House, Stoke Newington, with whom in 1825 Nathan and several other local residents joined together to open the Stamford Hill and Stoke Newington dispensary for the poor. Among local tradespeople were the Windus family, whose coach-building business – Windus & Co., of Bishopsgate – enjoyed Rothschild patronage for many years.[58]

Along with the space, the air and the opportunities for exercise and sport, houses out of London offered much greater scope for entertaining. At Richmond, Ben Cohen welcomed the Duke of Sussex to his garden parties. At Canonbury, Solomon Cohen's house was in 1825 the setting for the marriage, performed by Chief Rabbi Hirschel, of Solomon's daughter, Jeannette, to David Salomons, who was later to become a leading light in the movement for Jewish rights. While the ceremony itself was performed under a crimson canopy in the drawing room, the guests – Nathan and Hannah, and Judith and Moses among them – repaired to a large marquee in the garden for the wedding breakfast.[59]

Such events could not conceivably have been staged at New Court. When Prince Hermann von Pückler-Muskau (the model for Count Smorltork in *Pickwick Papers*) called at New Court, he found Nathan in 'a poor obscure-looking place' and had to make his way 'with some difficulty through the little court-yard, blocked up by a wagon laden with bars of silver'. Nathan's standing in the world of finance – as well as his appointment, resulting from his brother Salomon's application to Prince Metternich, as Austrian Consul in London in 1820 – made the house at Stamford Hill invaluable from the point of view of hospitality.[60]

A popular staple of the social round was the musical entertainment.

When Hannah's literary acquaintance Lady Stepney (whose husband, Sir Thomas, was equerry to the Duke of York) was asked by Lady Charlotte Guest (whose mother had made an unfashionable second marriage) how best to 'get into Society', she recommended giving a concert; the plan succeeded. Nathan and Hannah, too, gave concerts, as the pianist and composer Ignaz Moscheles recorded in his diary in the summer of 1821:

'July 11. A grand evening musical party at the Rothschilds', at their country house on Stamford Hill, given to the foreign Ministers present in England on account of the approaching coronation of George IV. I was introduced to most of the Ministers, who, with the old Prince Esterhazy, expressed themselves greatly pleased with my playing. In the intervals vocal solos and quartets were given by English singers. Not at home till four o'clock in the morning.'[61]

Confidant of Salieri and Beethoven, friend and mentor of Mendelssohn, when Moscheles had first been heard in London a month before, at a Philharmonic concert on 11 June, he had been hailed as an equal, as well as a friend, by Clementi and J. B. Cramer. Three days later, on 14 June, he had given a recital for Prince Esterhazy, the Austrian ambassador, at Chandos House, where Nathan and Hannah may have heard him. According to Philipp von Neumann, the Austrian embassy first secretary, Moscheles 'astonished us not only by his extraordinary talent but by his exquisite taste and the novelty of his style of execution'.[62]

In Paris a few months before, Louis Spohr had noted: 'Moscheles has been here a month. He makes a great sensation with his extremely brilliant play, and wins the admiration of both artists and dilettanti . . .' The young Robert Schumann – whom Mayer and Fritz Schlemmer were to encounter in Leipzig – wrote to his mother: 'I work hard, and am getting on famously; in three or four years I hope to be ready for Moscheles . . . I mean to take him for my model in everything.' So Moscheles was a catch for the Rothschilds.[63]

Three years later, Nathan and Hannah landed an even bigger fish. In the summer of 1824 they staged a 'gorgeous evening' at Stamford Hill 'when Rossini and his wife performed, the one playing and the other singing. There was a splendid display on that occasion of gold plate and other dazzling presents given to old Rothschild by the sovereigns of Europe.'[64] Rossini, probably the most admired and courted musician in the world at that time, had come to England with his wife, the singer Isabella Colbran, in December 1823. Six months before he performed at Stamford Hill, the Duke of Devonshire's sister, Lady Granville (a daughter of the renowned Duchess Georgiana), had heard him perform at Brighton. 'On Monday we had Rossini. The King all graciousness to him,' she wrote to the Duke from the Pavilion. 'He sang, which went to our musical hearts, "Otello" and "Figaro", etc . . . I hope to hear more of him, for it is an unspeakable pleasure.'[65]

Like Mendelssohn and Spohr, Rossini inscribed a piece in Chilly's *Livre d'or*, and he gave lessons to Louisa when, aged about thirteen, she was staying in Paris. As Hannah then explained to Nathan: 'Louisa takes lessons of Rosini [*sic*] in singing. He was very pleased with her voice and offered to teach her.' The music master clearly did all that he could to oblige. 'This week,' Louisa told her father, 'I have had some lessons with Rossini in singing, and hope, my dear Papa, to be able to sing you two or three new little songs when I come home. He is very good-natured and always comes at what hour and day I like.'[66]

Lionel got to know the composer well in the 1830s, and would refer to him as 'my friend Rossini' – hence Rossini's presence, as practically the only non-family guest, at Lionel's wedding in Frankfurt in 1836.[67]

While the entertainments at Stamford Hill might be impressive, the house itself was by no means pretentious. Thus it was that Prince Pückler-Muskau found that at Stamford Hill 'the royal banker has bought no ducal residence, but lives in a pretty villa'. The Prince was struck, too, by the family's steadfast adherence to its faith. 'We found some Directors of the East India Company, and several members of his own family and faith, whom I liked very much,' he recorded. 'I extremely respect this family for having the courage to remain Jews.'[68]

The scene on which Fritz Schlemmer first set eyes when he arrived at Stamford Hill on a Sunday afternoon in the 1820s was one of cosy domesticity. Shown into the drawing room, he came upon Nat, seated in front of the open piano, playing the violin, while Hannah and 'two sweet little daughters' – Hannah Mayer and Louisa – were sitting close by, gazing up at the newcomer. Nathan was not at home, but when he came in he collapsed onto a sofa and chatted to the new tutor without ceremony; at the dinner table, as at Ham House, he reminisced.[69]

On Saturdays, the family would be joined by a Mr Levy, 'a little old Jew in a tail-coat, breeches and buckled shoes', who expounded passages from the Hebrew Bible, directing his remarks especially to the younger members of the family. From time to time, there was also a visit from Chief Rabbi Hirschel, who was recalled by Schlemmer as an altogether more august presence – 'a figure from Rembrandt, seven feet tall with a huge hat that he never took off, even when in the house, and a long black frock coat'. It was said that when Dr Hirschel appeared in public, he 'commanded the reverence of the rudest kind that walked the streets; and there were but few who touched not their hats, and made way for "the High Priest of the Jews", as he was familiarly, but erroneously, termed'.[70]

When in 1830 the first volumes of Prince Pückler-Muskau's letters were published in Germany, Chilly read them with great interest. 'Pray dear Mama,' she wrote to Hannah from Frankfurt, 'have you read the second part of Prince Pichler's [sic] work on England? Shall I send it to you? I have left it at Uncle Anselm's [Amschel's] or else I would copy what he writes *about you* as I think you would be gratified by it. *Papa* is the subject of two letters. St[amford] H[ill] house is tolerably accurately described, but New Court still more accurately.'[71]

The passage about Hannah comes at the very end of the Prince's account of his visit to Stamford Hill: 'It shows great prudence in Mr R to have accepted neither title nor order, and thus to have preserved a far more respectable independence. He doubtless owes much to the good advice of his extremely amiable and judicious wife, who excels him in tact and knowledge of the world, though not perhaps in acuteness and talents for business.'

The Prince had the right idea about the titles, though he may not have known the whole story. 'It is really not right for my brother to have refused "the honour of the knighthood",' James had written to Hannah in the summer of 1815, 'for it is a mark of distinction for our [Jewish] nation.' Similarly, after the Austrian Emperor had elevated all five Rothschild brothers to the rank of baron in 1822, Nathan – who that year was promoted from Consul to Consul-General in London – made no use of the title. He was received at Court in London in 1824–5; but unlike his brothers – and indeed unlike his wife and his sons – he continued to be known as Mr Rothschild.[72]

The Prince was quite right in sensing the value to Nathan of his wife's advice, though he perhaps underestimated the extent of her role. As Louisa once said to her father: 'I suppose you are rather impatient to see Mama as you can scarcely be a day without her.' Nor were Nathan's professional advisers in any doubt of Hannah's valuable qualities.[73] Preparing for a review of the partnership agreement between himself and his brothers in 1824, Nathan sought legal advice as to how best to secure the financial interests, under English law, of Hannah and the children in the event of his death. The man he consulted was Lewis Allsopp Lowdham, a Chancery lawyer attached to the Lord Chancellor's office and someone who clearly knew Nathan well.[74]

'Mrs Rothschild,' Lowdham ventured, 'knows so much of your

concerns, & in case of your death so much will devolve upon her, that I sh[oul]d recommend – independently of having the advantage of her advice, which without any unnecessary compliments I think you will find an advantage; she has moreover more time to think than yourself – your talking this matter over with her.'[75]

4

Monarchs of the Golden Bags

IN THE SUMMER of 1824 there was to be a great gathering of the Rothschild family in Frankfurt, the first of its kind for six years. In 1818 they had assembled for the marriage of Nathan's younger brother Carl to Adelheid Herz; now they would meet for the marriage of James to his niece Betty, Salomon's only daughter. This was to be the first in a long series of Rothschild marriages contracted between close family members; Chilly's marriage to Salomon's son Anselm would be next, followed by Lionel's marriage to Charlotte.

These marriages were made, in part at least, because the Rothschild family came increasingly to see itself, and to be seen, as a family apart from, and above, other Jews; on occasion, they even wrote about themselves as the 'Royal Family'. Another consideration, in an era when dowries loomed large, was the desire to keep control of family wealth. Betty's dowry was 1.5 million francs (£60,000), which, in the event of James's predecease and there being no children, it was agreed she would recoup, with an additional 2.25 million francs.[1]

Marriages between close kin were not, in any case, uncommon within small, tenacious faith groups. Isaac Goldsmid married his first cousin Isabel, the younger daughter of his uncle Abraham Goldsmid. Quakers made such marriages too: Sam Gurney's wife was a Gurney on her mother's side; his elder brother John's wife was a Gurney first cousin; his cousin Dick's daughter married her stepmother's brother. Nor was close kinship by any means a deterrent to royal matches: Queen Victoria married her first cousin Prince Albert.

An alliance between uncle and niece was certainly less usual than one between cousins. When, in 1833, a Bill for the emancipation of the Jews was again introduced in the Commons, a splenetic William Cobbett foamed: 'Jew has always been synonymous with *sharper, cheat, rogue*. This has been the case with no other race of mankind. Rothschild married his own niece.' Yet even beyond Jewish circles such marriages were not unknown: in 1806, Count Christian von Bernstorff, later the Prussian

Minister in London and Foreign Minister and an acquaintance of the
Rothschilds, married his niece Elise.

Hannah set out for Frankfurt towards the end of June, in the company
of Lionel, Anthony and Nat. Hannah Mayer and Louisa remained at
Stamford Hill with their father; Mayer was at school. Chilly, accompanied
by Miss Andrews, had already been in Frankfurt for several months, staying with her aunt Caroline, Salomon's wife, and cousin Betty, James's
bride-to-be.

'Mrs de Rothschild [Caroline] & her very amiable daughter have both
written long letters to you,' Miss Andrews had written to assure Hannah.
'Your own dear child also has repeated her assurances of health and welfare.
She is looking remarkably well & is I think grown since we left England,
very considerably. Her Uncle and Aunt continue to evince towards her that
affectionate solicitude which satisfies me [that] their affection for one for
whom I must ever feel a strong attachment, but more especially during her
separation from her anxious, and indulgent Parents, is sincere & ardent.
Betty continues to win the admiration of all who see her; she rises in my
esteem every day.'[2]

Nathan escorted his wife and three sons across the Channel to see them
on their way – now without doubt in their own carriage. Fritz Schlemmer,
having spent the night at Dover after first landing in England, had seen a
magnificent coach and four drawn up outside his inn in the morning, and
was staggered to learn from a servant that it had been sent by the
Rothschilds to collect him.[3]

When Judith and Moses set off for the Continent in 1827, they did so
in a large travelling carriage drawn by four horses. They left London by the
Dover Road early in the morning, breakfasted at Dartford, dined at
Canterbury and arrived at Dover twelve hours later. The carriage went on
board with them and served as their cabin during the crossing. Post-horses
and postilions were hired at intervals for the continuation of the journey on
the Continent.[4] For the passage across the Channel itself, Nathan's agents
at Dover, Lathom, Rice & Co., could obtain berths or vessels for the
crossing, which in fair weather took three hours. When Amschel and
Salomon had visited England in 1819, Nathan instructed his agents 'to have
in readiness the same vessel that brought them over which was found very
convenient and comfortable'.[5]

As Nathan recrossed the Channel and returned to London, Hannah and
the boys, placed in the charge of a courier, set off for Brussels – accompanied, Hannah recorded, by a 'Baroness Langsdorff'. The anonymous
Prussian nobleman who dined in London with 'Mr R' in 1810–13 referred

to 'Mr L', the Elector of Hesse-Kassel's representative in London – a post that by 1824 was occupied by Baron Langsdorf, whose mail the Rothschilds would from time to time forward or hold. Hannah and her party arrived in Brussels on the morning of 28 June.

Whenever Lord Londonderry, Lord Castlereagh's half-brother, passed through Brussels, the city always struck him, he said, 'as being a bad imitation of Paris'. Hannah, likewise, having been for a stroll, wrote to her 'Dear Rothschild' that she found Brussels 'more resembling some parts of Paris than any thing like London'. She saw 'a pretty park, not well kept' and, while impressed by the abundance of fruit and vegetables for sale, decided that neither 'the appearance of the inhabitants nor [the] habitations are very prepossessing'.[6]

The city, then still in Holland, was home to a large English population, attracted there by the low cost of living. Lady Granville, having been to the theatre in Brussels a few months before Hannah's arrival, informed her sister Lady Morpeth that the 'house was chiefly filled with vulgar-looking English, with large French bonnets. As there are six thousand of them at Brussels, this is not wonderful.'[7] Hannah, however, informed Nathan that there were not many English about, and that only one of her compatriots, Sir Coutts Trotter, Bt, had been to call on her. A member of the Coutts family and a partner in the bank, two years earlier Trotter had been one of the two principal mourners at Thomas Coutts' funeral. Forty years later, his grandson and heir, Sir Coutts Lindsay, Bt, was to marry one of Hannah's granddaughters.[8]

At the end of their mother's letter, Lionel, Anthony and Nat each added a postscript. Lionel's was the most grown-up by far. 'Our journey,' he wrote, 'was rather fatiguing, having travelled last night, but now we are quite refreshed again, having remained here all morning and intend to do so to night. We had one particular adventure, which for the moment made us a little frightened when we came to the custom house of the Dutch, the officer wished to open all our trunks, and to look at everything, which made the courier in a passion, and the other men wishing to show their authority, a violent quarrel ensued. The officers were so enraged against our courier that they sent two men with him to the governor of the town, but owing to our cabinet Passports, the courier was dismissed and might if he had liked, have fined the officers. Thus far we have not proceeded in our journey without some trifling adventure. I hope we shall have a letter from you at Frankfurt, with love to all the family . . .'[9]

The route from Brussels to Frankfurt would have taken Hannah and her sons via Liège, Aachen, Cologne, Coblenz and Mainz, where a bridge of boats stretched across the Rhine to Kassel. It was only after crossing the bridge that one entered a pronouncedly German world. An English traveller who did so in 1820 noted that as far as Mainz – not long since occupied by the French – 'francs and Napoleons are more in circulation than the German money; but the toll is demanded on the opposite side in *kreutzers*, a little coin, sixty of which make a florin'. At Mainz, there were still 'French cafés, French restaurateurs, French barbers, French *commissionaires*'; everybody there spoke French, 'bad or good', whereas at Kassel 'only here and there an individual' did so.[10]

Frankfurt was the capital of a small republic, and the seat of the German Diet, made up of representatives from the German states that had emerged, or re-emerged, after the defeat of the French. The city had its own resident diplomatic corps, and then, as now, was a centre of commerce and finance. To either side of the old stone bridge across the Main, the river presented 'a respectable little cluster of shipping . . . a degree of life and bustle which would be more striking to any one than an Englishman familiar with London and Bristol'.[11]

Touring through Germany in 1822, Washington Irving had found Frankfurt to be a 'beautiful town', and the only one that was thriving: 'In most of the German towns, in consequence of the breaking up of the little German principalities and courts during the time of Bonaparte, and the merging of these petty governments into large states, you see continually the traces of former splendour; the ruins of petty aristocracies; old palaces deserted and falling into ruin; or turned into barracks, hospitals, &c. Frankfort, on the contrary, is an independent commercial town; its palaces are built by bankers and merchants, and are continually increasing.'[12]

In one aspect, Frankfurt had made a much less favourable impression on Lady Emma Edgcumbe twenty years earlier. Walking about with her sister and governess, Lady Emma and her companions lost their way; they found themselves, she remembered, '*dans le quartier juif*, from which we were most glad to escape, as we were surrounded, and almost mobbed, by a peculiarly unprepossessing, unpleasing set of people, who seemed inclined to be impertinent'.[13]

Until the French bombardment of the city in the summer of 1796, Frankfurt's Jewish community – which at the time of James's and Betty's wedding accounted for about one seventh of its 50,000-strong population – had been strictly confined to the cramped, overcrowded Judengasse. After the bombardment, and in consequence of the destructive fires that broke out, it would have been impractical for all the Jews to return to the ghetto, even had the authorities wished them to do so.

Goethe's mother, who was in Frankfurt throughout the French assault, later explained to her son that 'no house would have been burnt down if the fatal idea . . . that the French intended to plunder had not got the upper hand. The misfortune arose in the Jews' quarter – for everything had been cleared out there – hardly a living being was left there – and the madness went so far that they placed great padlocks on empty houses. When it took fire, first, no one could get into the bolted-up houses without force; secondly there were no Jews there to put it out; thirdly, in the houses there was naturally not the least preparation.'[14]

It was in the Judengasse, in a tall narrow house without a garden (except for a patch on the roof), that Mayer Amschel and Gutle Rothschild raised their ten children, the youngest of whom, James, was born in 1792. Moreover, they continued to live there, by choice, after 1796, and Gutle was to remain there to the end of her days, aged ninety-five, decades after her husband had died and her sons had married and left for those palaces in the city that were admired by Washington Irving.

Staying in Frankfurt in 1840, during a German tour with his sister Elizabeth Fry, Sam Gurney and his daughter Elizabeth went to visit Gutle in the Judengasse. 'Papa and I called on Mrs Rothschild. The mother to Nathan Rothschild,' Elizabeth recorded. 'She appeared pleased in seeing papa as having been her son's friend. She prefers living in the Jews' street in a miserable house tho' from the immense wealth of the family she might reside in a palace. It was a very interesting sight. She looks very old but gaily attired with artificial flowers gay ribbons &c. We had not time to visit the usual sights of the town but we walked about in the Public Gardens and walked round Baron Rothschild's villa and garden.'[15]

While Nathan and James left Frankfurt altogether, Salomon and his wife Caroline moved out of the Judengasse into the town in 1807; Amschel and Eva acquired an elegant house on the Zeil, and in 1811 another in a semi-rural location to the north of the town, on the road to Bockenheim; Charles and Adelheid, who would always spend long periods in Frankfurt as well as at Naples, found a town house in Neue Mainzer Strasse, a smart residential street.

With Nathan's encouragement, Amschel subsequently bought a large garden adjacent to his country house (a 'pretty villa-like house' in the eyes of one of his young English relations); it was something for which he had always yearned. It was perhaps in Amschel's garden that Sam Gurney and his daughter were to take their stroll in 1840. Certainly, in 1824, it was with Amschel and Eva that Hannah and her children stayed for James's wedding.[16]

Sunday Morning 6 o'clock

Dear Rothschild

In the very early part of the morning before any of the family are up & while I hope you & the dear part of my family who are still at Stamford Hill are enjoying a sound sleep, I embrace this leisure hour to have the pleasure of writing to you. We arrived here as I informed you on Friday & had the inexpressible happiness of finding our dear Charlotte quite well, thank God, & only I think improved in her looks, full of impatience for our arrival & quite delighted at the event.

We stop'd at your brother Amschel's but not finding Charlotte there we desired the post boys to go to your brother Salomon's, where she was. Of course her enquiries about yourself & the children did not cease for a long time. Betty is looking also exceedingly well, & as amiable as ever. Charlotte & her are sincerely attached & are inseparable. We remained some time & had refreshments at Salomon's, & then went to Amschel at whose house we are staying.

That every thing is made as delightful as possible for us it is needless for me to assure you. I should not wish to be so dissatisfied to say a single thing is wanting, not to be highly pleased with our reception. The boys are perfectly at home, & that they should decide to have renewed their visit I am not in the least surprised at. Their favorite Mr Mosa I have had the pleasure to be introduced to. He *adores* the boys. He has tears in his eyes while he is speaking of them. He perfectly answers to the character of a jolly & hearty huntsman.

All the family have been here. They are every one in good health, your mother particularly so, for she [is] considerably stouter & looking in better health than when we were here three years ago. The event for which we are assembled here seems to give her the greatest satisfaction & I assure you she is the most lively of the party. It is a great gratification that a person at her advanced age should have all her faculties so perfect, & to the children as well as to [the] Parent this is certainly one of the greatest blessings a kind Providence bestows. Your absence is very much regretted & it is over & over again repeated by all the party . . . [but] it is not possible to have all our wishes fulfilled. We have much to be satisfied with . . . Mrs Charles Rothschild arrived here likewise on Friday from Naples. I do not know if Charles will be here for the wedding – James's letter does not mention the time when he sets off. He should contrive to put off business on this particular occasion.

Now dear Rothschild I must hope that you will allow me to make some little present to each of your sisters . . . I know your answer; it is do what you like – I shall avail myself of it & do the needful to about 25 to 30 pounds for each of them.

I hope you will be particular in your letters & tell [me] how Hannah Meyer [*sic*] & Louisa are, if they are contented & happy. Does Hannah Meyer make your breakfast, & does sweet Louisa run after you up stairs [?] . . . Mayer I hope is well at school & Allard does not forget to send him a cake on Friday. You are fully employed I am sure with all this additional charge . . . I beg you will remember me very kindly to all the family whom you see. To each member I will write by the first opportunity . . .

Hannah Rothschild[17]

On 5 July Anthony wrote in a short letter to Nathan: 'Yesterday we went out a shooting with Mr Mosa. We had good sport. Lionel killed 2 rabits [*sic*] and Mr M. 2 rabits and a wild duck.' Lionel, now aged fifteen, confirmed this in his letter home, and went on to inform his father: 'Last week I went with Uncle Anselm [Amschel] on Change. It is a very small place & it seemd to me that there was very little business doing, in comparison with that of London. We expect Uncle James to morrow, the marriage is to take place next Sunday. Uncle James & Betty will depart the same evening for Switzerland. I hope Hannah Mayer is as good a girl as ever & keeps the house in good order. Pray give my love to her & Mayer & Louisa.'[18]

A Rothschild wedding in Frankfurt drew together a numerous extended family. Except for Henrietta, Nathan's sisters had all found husbands in the local German Jewish community. Jeannette, the eldest, had married a Worms (their son Solomon had gone to live at New Court); and Isabella, Babette and Julie – whose death in 1815 had so upset Nathan – had all married local men. Consequently, there was a mass of cousins to invite to a family event.

Apart from Nathan, Henrietta was the most notable absentee from the festivities. In the hope of restoring Abraham's failing health – he was suffering from tuberculosis – she had taken him to Italy. After the wedding in Frankfurt, Hannah and Chilly went to Geneva, where the Montefiores were pausing on their way home; but soon afterwards Abraham – by all accounts a handsome as well as a humorous man – died in a hotel at Lyons.[19]

James arrived in Frankfurt on 7 July. 'Yesterday arrived the party from Paris in health & in good spirits,' Hannah reported home the next day. 'The scene at the moment was very animated, all the Family assembled. The Bride a great deal agitated at first but in a few moments quite herself, very much pleased & delighted with the many elegant & exceedingly well chosen presents in jewellery, shawls &c. Every one desired to see them, &

congratulations coming in from every side, both from the Family as well as from strangers . . . Today Salomon, his son [Anselm] & James are gone to pay their respects to Prince Metternich at Joannesburgh [Johannisberg]. I do not think he [Metternich] will be at the wedding on account of the Family being very numerous, & besides the necessity of making different arrangements in the [*kosher*] kitchen for his party. I think he will dine here a day or two after the wedding.'[20]

Chilly added a postscript: 'I have with the greatest pleasure read in my dear Mamma's letters that you & my sisters & Mayer are all very well, but regret to observe the fall of the funds, which I am well aware always has so much influence on your spirits. Here we are all very gay, being quite a congress of the *monarchs of the golden bags* . . . The bridegroom is very gallant and has brought some beautiful presents for his future Lady. I would willingly extend my letter dear Papa, but the badness of my pen would render it impossible for you to decipher it & with united love will only ask you to bless me . . .'[21]

No account of James's wedding has come to light; but staying in Paris some months later Hannah found the newly married couple 'very well, Betty in particular so, looking forward to the event which is to make her a mother, but not preventing her going out'. Betty was expecting her first child, another Charlotte, who one day was to marry her English cousin Nat.[22]

James and Betty began their married life at No. 19 rue d'Artois (rue Laffitte after 1830), a handsome eighteenth-century *hôtel* that had been built for Louis XV's banker Laborde, the grandfather of Fritz Schlemmer's pupil, and which was already serving as James's residence, as well as his counting house.

Performing in Paris at the start of 1821, Moscheles had found that 'music and dinner parties were frequently given by the Prussian and other ambassadors, and the *haute finance*, represented by Lafitte, Rothschild, Fould and others, vied with each other in hospitable and luxurious entertainments'. In October 1821, the Austrian diplomat Philipp von Neumann described 19 rue d'Artois as 'almost absurdly splendid'; it was, he believed, 'the second finest [house] in Paris . . . the furnishing alone cost 800,000 francs [£32,000]'.[23]

Within a short time of her arrival at rue d'Artois, Betty was making an impression as a hostess, as Lady Granville, now the British ambassadress in Paris, noted in December 1824: 'On Saturday we dined at a sumptuous feast at Rothschild's. He has married his niece, a pretty little Jewess, *née coiffée*, a very good thing at Paris, for, just out of her nursery, she does the honours of her house as if she never had done anything else.' Two months later, at 'a ball at Rothschild's on Saturday', Lady Granville found a 'tremendous crowd of Jews, English and French'. Outside in the street, there was a 'line of carriages, in which the Seftons and many others spent two hours'.[24]

One thing that must have cheered the Earl of Sefton and his wife as they waited was the prospect of a feast prepared under the direction of the Rothschilds' *chef de cuisine*, Marie-Antoine ('Antonin') Carême, the most famous chef of his time. Lord Sefton was a discerning gourmet – his own chef, Louis Eustache Ude, who had served his apprenticeship in the kitchens of Louis XVI and later worked for Letitia Bonaparte, Napoleon's mother, made him an object of envy in London – and thanks to Carême, whose former employers included Prince Talleyrand, the Prince Regent and the Tsar of Russia, James had since 1823 maintained a table of unsurpassed splendour.[25]

Several times, the Prince Regent tried to re-engage Carême (whom he had paid £1,000 a year), and one day the Rothschilds would miss him too; after Lord Sefton's death in 1838, Anthony wrote from Paris to ask Nat to enquire about engaging the late Earl's cook for James, 'as we like good dinners in the winter'.[26]

Hannah was accompanied to Paris by Chilly, Lionel, Anthony and Hannah Mayer; she hoped that Nat was making a 'good housekeeper' for his father in her absence. Having taken leave of James and Betty, she and her party set off on the road to Hanover. The journey would again take them to Frankfurt. 'We then, dear Rothschild,' she wrote to Nathan, 'shall proceed to Göttingen & with the blessing of the Almighty [shall] arrange for the boys, that they may be comfortable & make the desired progress, which in their future stages in life may be satisfactory to you & advantages [*sic*] to them.'[27]

Lionel and Anthony were to attend Göttingen University, the reputation of which was then as high, if not higher, than that of any other university in Germany. The young Goethe's cherished hope of beginning his university days at Göttingen had been dashed when his father insisted on Leipzig.[28]

Founded by George II in 1737, the university numbered among its alumni the Duke of Sussex, the Duke of Cumberland, Prince Metternich and the brothers Wilhelm and Alexander von Humboldt. The Duke of Cambridge, who was Viceroy of Hanover from 1816 until the Duke of Cumberland's accession to the throne in 1837, regarded Göttingen

University as the pearl in Hanover's crown.[29] 'A Göttingen chair,' wrote John Russell in the 1820s, 'is the highest reward to which a German *savant* aspires, and to study at Göttingen is the great wish of a German youth . . . The professor is more comfortable, in a pecuniary point of view, and possesses far greater facilities for pushing on his science, than in other universities; the student finds a more gentlemanly tone of manners than elsewhere, and has within his reach better opportunities of studying to good purpose.'[30]

Thirty-six permanent professors catered to the needs of some 1,200 students, more than half of whom were non-natives of Hanover; some students came from as far off as America, attracted by the university's reputation as a forward-looking, liberal institution that offered a broad education and was free of religious restrictions. From a social point of view, it was perhaps also worth noting, along with Russell, that a 'greater proportion' of its students were 'young men of rank, and of respectable or affluent fortune, than elsewhere'.[31]

In the document certifying Lionel's university matriculation, aged sixteen, on 12 May 1825, the freshman is styled 'Lionel de Rothschild, Anglus, philos. stud.' Anthony, now approaching his fifteenth birthday, matriculated on the same day, as did his and Lionel's tutor John Darby, though while the Rothschild brothers were registered in Göttingen's philosophy faculty, Darby, who was described as the son of a clergyman, registered with the faculty of theology.[32]

The nature and extent of the studies that occupied the young men's time is unclear. In the tradition of German scholarship – *Lehrfreiheit* and *Lernfreiheit* – the professors taught what they wished, while the students learned from whichever professors took their fancy. Lionel and Anthony certainly attended lectures and, though registered in the faculty of philosophy, they would have been free to attend any lecture course they chose, provided they paid the relevant professor for it. Political economy, jurisprudence, divinity, medicine, mathematics, mineralogy, astronomy, natural history, Greek and Latin and oriental literature were some of the subjects on offer. When their cousin Charles (Mayer Carl, their uncle Carl's son) went to Göttingen aged seventeen in the 1830s, he studied law, politics, history, philosophy and philology – the professorial chair in the last school being held by Jacob Grimm, now more often remembered, with his brother Wilhelm, for the fairytales.[33]

The university also boasted a magnificent library (the Grimm brothers worked there as librarians), as well as resident fencing and dancing masters. Given the difference in the Rothschild brothers' ages, John Darby no doubt helped to select, or to map out, a course of studies and exercise suited to each.

'I received your few lines with great pleasure,' Anthony wrote to his father in early December 1825, 'and should have answered them when Lionel wrote to you, but I was at a [sic] college when he did, & therefore deferred it till to day. Our time is now so much occupied that we cannot find time to write letters in the week, which if we could, would, I dare say, afford to you & us great pleasure. We are paying the greatest attention to our studies wishing not to loose [sic] any part of our time whilst we are here, and that we shall derive as much advantage from them as you will expect. I never pass any day without doing some sums in arithmetic as you particularly wished. I should like to know your opinion on the free trade of corn. I think that it will not be very advantageous, particularly for the English farmers, & likewise will take much money from the market . . .'[34]

Improvement of Lionel and Anthony's command of German was surely one of the objects of their stay in Hanover, and Lionel, for one, had the benefits of foreign languages clearly in mind. 'I have had the pleasure of receiving yesterday two letters from Göttingen,' Chilly wrote to their mother from Paris, '& rejoice to find that my Brothers are pursuing their studies with such persevering assiduity. Lionel, it appears, has begun Danish in the hope of becoming Consul for that country, & I trust he will not be disappointed.'[35]

Denmark had close dynastic ties to Hesse-Kassel: the Elector William I whom Lionel's grandfather had served, and his brother Charles, Regent of Schleswig-Holstein, were both married to daughters of King Frederick V of Denmark. In 1790, moreover, Charles of Hesse-Kassel's eldest daughter became the wife of the future Danish King Frederick VI. Mayer Amschel had consolidated his standing at the Court of Hesse-Kassel when in 1803 he floated a bond for Denmark and sold it in its entirety to the Elector William I. No mention, however, is ever again made of Lionel's consular aspirations in this direction.

Throughout their time in Göttingen the brothers and their tutor lived in rented accommodation at Judenstrasse 459. A handful of other Englishmen who were lodging nearby included the poet Thomas Lovell Beddoes, then a medical student; William Hamilton, a future diplomat; and Edward Bouverie Pusey, already a keen student of theology and later the initiator of the Church of England's Oxford Movement. Beddoes borrowed copies of the *Literary Gazette* from John Darby; Hamilton, who had been in the same house as Beddoes at Charterhouse and had previously met Lionel and Anthony at Brighton, renewed his acquaintance with the

Rothschilds and borrowed their copies of the *Courier*, the daily newspaper that they had sent to them from England.[36]

In London, the brothers' progress at Göttingen was followed keenly. 'You asked me dear Lionel in a former letter if I would wish to know in what manner you proceed with your studies,' Hannah wrote in early 1826. 'I am sure that your education and progress constitutes one of my most anxious wishes, and to be made acquainted with any thing that relates to it must be most desirable to me.' Some weeks later, 'gratified lately by having your letters very regularly', Hannah assured Anthony how it was 'with much satisfaction' that she had learned of his resolve to carry on studying over a holiday. 'Mr Darby,' Hannah added, 'is happily pleased with your determination, and I think from his expression has your welfare much at heart.'[37]

Hard graft, though, was clearly not all that Hannah had in mind for her sons while they were abroad. In a letter addressed to 'Monsieur le Baron Lionel de Rothschild, à Monsieur Meyers, Juden Strasse, Göttingen', she was 'sorry that you do not avail yourselves of going into society, for I really think it would both amuse and improve you. If you would wish I should write to Mr Darby upon the subject let me know.' Whether or not she did so is not recorded, but from Göttingen Lionel and Anthony could easily visit friends in Frankfurt, among them the family of their uncle Carl's wife Adelheid Herz, Lionel's future mother-in-law.[38]

To Mr Nat Rothschild, Stamford Hill

Frankfurt 2 Jan 1826

My dear Nat

I should have answered your kind letter before, which I received at Göttingen, but the weather this last two days having been so fine I thought I might enjoy it very well in shooting which took up the whole day. We have amused ourselves the last three days better than we did at first; we have [been] out shooting four times. The first twice, the weather was very bad and we had some snow which made it rather uncomfortable. Friday we went to the chase of a gentleman here, and had pretty good sport. Yesterday there was a large party, 41 hares were shot. Every time I have killed two or three hares. Adolph Hertz [*sic*, Adelheid's brother] went out with us. Mr Moser did the same to him as to us when we first shot. He had no shot in his gun, but yet he shot a hare as he says. Aunt Henrietta told me that you have been at the farm with [her son] Joseph. How did you amuse yourself there?

I know you do not care if I trouble you a little with my commissions. I have another which I hope you will be so kind as to execute. The measure of a hat is enclosed in this, which you will have the goodness to send to me at Göttingen. It is for A. Hertz who asked me to write for it. Pray send a good one for the *reputation* of our English hatmakers. I also want a riding whip for his sister Helen, a black one with silver. I leave it to your taste to choose a very handsome one. She told me she would not accept it, but I think she will. I will send you the money with that for the present for Mr Moser which I hope soon to receive. You will do me a favour if you do not speak about them, this not because I think it is wrong but because every person talks so much about such things. We have been several times to the Hertzs' house and have found them as always very kind.

There is nothing new in the family. Mrs Beyfuss [*sic*] had a little girl yesterday. We have just packed up all our things and are going to night in the diligence to Cassel, and then shall hire a coach from that place to Göttingen, where we shall arrive to morrow about 10 o'clock. We are now going out to pay a few visits before we go. Excuse this scrawl as I have written it in great haste. Give my best love to Mamma, to whom I will write from Göttingen, to Papa & all at home.

Your affectionate Brother
Lionel Rothschild[39]

As Lionel and Anthony studied at Göttingen and amused themselves in Frankfurt, in London their father had been staging a rescue operation.

A financial crisis towards the end of 1825 had brought the Bank of England close to suspending cash payments. To avert this, Nathan, acting in concert with James, had shipped enormous quantities of gold sovereigns from Paris to the Bank's vaults in London. 'Had it not been for the most extraordinary exertions, above all on the part of old Rothschild,' the Duke of Wellington reflected some years later, 'the Bank must have stopped payment.'[40]

In the maelstrom resulting from the crisis, some 145 banks went bankrupt, among them Pole, Thornton & Co., a leading City firm which came to grief in December 1825. From the collapse of Pole, Thornton, the junior partner, Henry Sykes Thornton, emerged with credit; it was recognised that he had done all he could in impossible circumstances, and consequently he was invited to join a new bank partnership then being formed – Williams, Deacon & Co.[41]

Thornton's father, also Henry, had with William Wilberforce been one of the Claphamites' most influential leaders, and young Henry's guardians, following his parents' deaths, had been the liberal reformers, Charles and Robert Grant. At Cambridge, where he had been an outstanding mathematical student, Thornton had lived in the same lodgings as his friend Tom Macaulay, who was to speak in favour of Robert Grant's Jewish Disabilities Bill during his maiden speech in the Commons in 1830.

Having rescued the Bank of England, at the end of December Nathan saved Williams, Deacon from failure, before it had even opened its doors. Henry's sister, Marianne, recounted the drama in a letter to Hannah More, the Claphamite writer. Late in the day, Marianne explained, Henry and his partners discovered 'that it was absolutely necessary they should have a very large supply of sovereigns in their House for their country Banks, but such is the scarcity of gold now in London that they could not by any means obtain as much as they wished'.

The partners, she went on, 'were in despair, and separated in the evening, fearing this difficulty would prevent their opening on Monday'. Henry Thornton could see only one solution – 'to get into a post chaise instantly, go during the night to Brighton where John Smith was, knock him up, persuade him to return to town with him, go with Alexander Baring to Rothschild, and those two Princes of the City might induce the Jew King of the City, Rothschild, to give them the money, for he, probably, was the only man in England who could help them having it was suspected, been hoarding up sovereigns for exportation for some time'.[42]

John Smith was a partner of Smith, Payne & Smiths, bankers, together with Hoare, Barnett, to the Alliance. His son, John Abel Smith, had been a contemporary of Henry Thornton's at Cambridge. A friend of the Quaker William Allen and of the socialist Robert Owen (in whose concerns Hannah Rothschild took a friendly interest), John Smith was also a Whig MP. During the struggle to repeal the Test and Corporation Acts in 1827–8 he was to act as Lord John Russell's lieutenant in the Commons; and, like his cousin William Wilberforce, Smith was a staunch opponent of the slave trade.[43] Alexander Baring was senior partner of Baring Brothers, Nathan's principal rivals. He, too, was a Whig MP, though less liberal than Smith; he exasperated Fowell Buxton with his calls for moderation over slave-trade abolition.[44]

Henry Thornton, his sister continued, went down to Brighton and 'found Mr J. Smith, whose kindness is beyond all praise, quite willing to return with him, and by dint of a little persuasion and exhortation the Jew was induced to bring out his gold, first charging 2½ commission, then saying he did it out of public spirit, and lastly begging they would never tell it or he would be besieged night and day. However, Henry and the sovereigns were in Williams's House before hardly anyone knew he had been further than home during the night.' Whether or not Alexander Baring accompanied Smith to see Nathan is not disclosed.[45]

As Nathan was rescuing Williams, Deacon, Hannah – whilst worrying about Hannah Mayer and Mayer, both of whom were recovering from a bout of measles – was organising a house removal. Nathan had taken a lease on a town house in a fashionable part of London.[46]

'I have been exceedingly busy this last fortnight in moving &c &c,' Hannah wrote to her absent sons on 7 January 1826. 'You may well suppose that I have had plenty of business on hand – in arranging at Stamford Hill, being almost every day at New Court & likewise preparing the house at Piccadilly. Papa, myself and Charlotte [Chilly] are going to sleep there for the first time to night. The house is not perfectly finished, and I find it impossible to get things completed until I am there. The house and furniture look exceedingly well, and I am wishing for the time when we are to have you among us, when I do not doubt but you both will be greatly pleased with the arrangements. Now that we are used to the height of the rooms we do not find them inconvenient. The stair case is very much improved, & there is a very pretty Billiard Room and Table which please God on your return you will enjoy.'[47]

The house was No. 107 Piccadilly, overlooking Green Park, and the local society, not to mention the situation, a far cry from New Court. While St Swithin's Lane was home to such figures as Mr J. Berridge, who translated Nathan's will into English, immediately to the east of No. 107 Piccadilly, Coventry House (No. 106) was the town house of the seventh Earl of Coventry. Lord Coventry's mother Maria, wife of the sixth Earl, had been the elder of those celebrated eighteenth-century beauties, the Gunning sisters. No. 105, formerly Barrymore House, belonged to the Marchioness of Hertford, wife of the third Marquess, the Prince Regent's former crony 'Red herrings'.[48]

Lady Hertford ('Mie Mie') was the natural daughter of 'Old Q', the fourth Duke of Queensbury, who had left her No. 105, which became known as Hertford House, as well as No. 84 Piccadilly and much else. Until the Reform Act of 1832, Lord Hertford returned eight MPs from his pocket boroughs – only the Earl of Lonsdale, with nine ('Lowther's Nine-pins'), returned more – and Hertford was the model for the Marquess of Monmouth in Disraeli's novel *Coningsby*: 'His general mien was truly grand, full of a natural nobility, of which no one was more sensible than himself.' J. W. Croker, who is said to have interpreted the Rothschild courier's account of Wellington's victory at Waterloo to Lord Liverpool, and to have been the model for Rigby in *Coningsby*, was Lord Hertford's political adviser.[49]

Known as Lord Yarmouth – and so to some as the 'Yarmouth bloater' – until his father's death in 1822, on coming into his inheritance Lord Hertford had at his disposal a net income of at least £90,000 a year. Having separated from her husband and taken her children to live in Paris, where after 1827 she lived in the former Hôtel de Brancas, on the corner of the rue Laffitte and the Boulevard des Italiens, 'Mie Mie' had made No. 105 available to Lord Hertford, but he preferred to live in Seamore Place, Park Lane, and later at Dorchester House, while maintaining a villa, St Dunstan's, in Regent's Park.[50]

In the summer of 1814, when it was serving as the Pulteney Hotel, No. 105 had accommodated Tsar Alexander and his sister the Grand Duchess of Oldenburg. The Rothschilds' new house had at that time been occupied by Marshal Blücher, the Prussian army commander, who used to sit in an armchair at the top of the steps, smoking a pipe and acknowledging the greetings of passers-by.[51]

Further eastwards along Piccadilly, No. 94, Egremont House, was occupied by the first Marquess of Cholmondeley, then by the Duke of Cambridge (when it became Cambridge House); and there were the great mansions of Devonshire House (the Duke of Devonshire) and Burlington House (Lord George Cavendish). No. 82, Bath House, named for the old Pulteney Earls of Bath, had in 1821 been rebuilt for Alexander Baring in sumptuous style; to Baring's partner Swinton Holland it was the 'Palazzo di Piccadilly', and to William Cobbett 'Scrip Castle'.[52]

The Pulteneys had owned a large part of Mayfair, which on the death of the childless Countess of Bath in 1808 had passed to the ten-year-old Sir Richard Sutton, the second Baronet, to whom the Rothschilds paid half-yearly ground rent of £97 1s 8d. Enormously rich, Sutton was a devotee of field sports – it is said that he spent £300,000 on foxhunting during his lifetime – and he became well known to the younger Rothschilds. Following the Duke of Cambridge's death in 1850, Sutton resided at No. 94 Piccadilly until his death there in 1855, after which Lord and Lady Palmerston took a lease on the house.[53]

To the west of No. 107, standing at the corner of old Park Lane, Gloucester House (No. 137 Piccadilly) was residence of the Duke of Gloucester and his Duchess, the Princess Mary, a daughter of George III; No. 141, at the corner of Hamilton Place, was the town house of that diehard Lord Chancellor, the Earl of Eldon, now well into his third decade on the Woolsack. And beyond a further row of large houses, Robert Adam's original red-brick Apsley

House, yet to be given its facing of Bath stone and Corinthian portico, belonged to the Duke of Wellington. Outside Apsley House, the turnpike straddling the road at London's western limit – making the Duke's residence 'No. 1, London' as well as No. 149 Piccadilly – had only been cleared away the previous October.[54]

If Hannah had any misgivings about moving to a neighbourhood so very different from the City, she might have been consoled by the thought that Judith and Moses had recently left New Court for a new house, in a still unfinished row, in Green Street, Park Lane, and that there their tranquil mode of home life continued.

'This day passed in calm domestic delight,' Judith wrote in her diary one Saturday evening in December 1825. 'Arose at ten, the weather being rainy, which prevented Monte going to the synagogue, having every Saturday but one attended that place of devotion since we have resided in this our new house, which has been from the 11th of October last. Breakfasted in the library, read our prayers, read a story or two of Boccacio.' Later, the Montefiores moved to a house in Park Lane itself, their residence fronting Hyde Park.[55]

Nor did Hannah sever ties with her old City home: she and Nathan retained family apartments at New Court, for use, in particular, when religious considerations made it convenient, if one was not as energetic as Moses, to be within easy walking distance of synagogue. 'This will just arrive as you will be going to New Court for the Holydays,' Lionel wrote to his mother in 1832; Charlotte, in Paris, imagined her parents and siblings 'in delightful New Court feasting on *Motzers* & *Dutch cheese*. I wish I could convey myself among your breakfast party to have a nice slice of smoked Salmon.'[56]

In March 1826, less than three months after the move, Hannah wrote to Anthony: 'We are quite settled at Piccadilly now, and if we were ourselves gay maybe very soon [should] have a very large acquaintance, but . . . Papa [is] very averse to company – however agreeable a little gaiety is at times it is much better to cheque [*sic*] an inclination for this kind of living than to indulge – our Sunday Parties such as the Family and one or two others continue. We find the Billiard Table a great resource. Charlotte, Nat & they all manage to play. We are sadly in want of beaus and I am sure you must be confident that we feel the loss of your society.'[57]

It was not long, though, before they began to lead the kind of social life in Piccadilly that Hannah – apparently more than Nathan – enjoyed. 'Dined with Mr N. M. Rothschild,' Moses noted in his diary on 9 April, 'met there Prince Esterhazy, [the ninth] Duke of St Albans, his brother, and two sisters, Lady Augusta Cotton, a son of Lord Coventry, and the Earl of Lauderdale.'[58]

It may be that the seating plan for dinner called for tact. Fifteen years earlier, Lord Coventry's eldest son George, Viscount Deerhurst, had caused a stir by eloping with the Duke of St Albans' first cousin (the daughter of the sixth Duke), the sixteen-year-old heiress (with £100,000), Lady Mary Beauclerk. George's sister Augusta, Lord Coventry's eldest daughter, was married to Lieutenant-General Sir Willoughby Cotton. Their mother Peggy, the Earl's second wife, did not herself come from an aristocratic background; she was a daughter of Sir Abraham Pitches, brandy merchant, of Streatham.[59] When Moses met Lord Lauderdale on a subsequent occasion at the Rothschild table, together with Charles Grant (Lord Glenelg) and various other 'important personages', he described the assembled company as 'most zealous' for the success of the cause of Jewish emancipation.[60]

After his marriage in 1827, the ninth Duke of St Albans became a Piccadilly neighbour of the Rothschilds; he married the widow of Thomas Coutts, who owned a large house on the corner of Stratton Street. He and his wife, who became more friends than acquaintances of the Rothschilds, were guests at a dinner given in Piccadilly by Nathan and Hannah in 1829; they dined at Stamford Hill, too, and asked the Rothschilds back. 'You may be in London on Wednesday,' the Duke wrote to Hannah in January 1830, 'and if you do not leave it, pray come to us to cut our twelfth cake. All unite in kind remembrance to you and Mr de Rothschild and family.'[61]

If anyone doubted that wealth, used carefully, could unlock doors, they had but to look at the Duchess, who, as Miss Harriot Mellon, had begun adult life on the stage. Before she married her Duke, she was, said Mrs Arbuthnot, 'a memorable example of the power of money. She lived with Mr Coutts many years before his first wife died, was an actress & now, because he has left her his whole fortune, she gives balls and breakfasts & is invited by every body.' As the widowed Mrs Coutts, the first large social gathering Harriot attended after her first husband's death was the christening, in 1824, of Sir Coutts Trotter's grandson and heir Coutts Lindsay, Hannah Mayer's future son-in-law.[62]

It had been through a Jewish family who showed her much kindness during her early days on the stage that the future Duchess had caught her first glimpse of rich living; at a wedding party the family gave, she had observed the women wearing 'a greater profusion of diamonds than she ever saw at Court in after days'. Aged thirty-seven at the time of her marriage to the 79-year-old Thomas Coutts, she was nearly fifty when she married the 26-year-old Duke. In 1830, her annual income from Coutts' was said to be £80,000, while Nathan's annual income during the last five years of his life averaged £87,623.[63]

Within eighteen months Nathan was very much at home in his new house, happy to remain there on his own when his wife and children were away. 'I have very little news to tell you from here,' Hannah wrote to Anthony the next summer. 'London is gay and we are invited to a great many parties but we do not go to many of them as Papa is not fond of late hours. I lent Aunt Esther our house at Stamford Hill for SW [Solomon Worms] and HS [Henrietta Samuel] wedding. It is a great accommodation to them and does not put me to any inconvenience as I am going with your sisters to Paris the day after for a few weeks and Papa is very much attached to Piccadilly.'[64]

Nathan did not allow his dislike of late hours (a dislike that he shared with Harriot St Albans) to interfere with his guests' enjoyment of the hospitality he offered. ' "Rex Judaeorum" gave a magnificent dinner,' Prince Pückler-Muskau recounted in 1827, 'the dessert of which alone, as he told me, cost a hundred pounds. I sat next to a very clever woman, Mrs A[rbuthnot], the friend of the Duke of W[ellington] . . . We had a great exhibition of splendour. The table service was of vermilion and silver; that of the dessert, I think, all gold. Under the portrait of Prince Metternich (a present from the original) in an adjoining room, was a large gold box, perhaps a copy of the Ark of the Covenant. A concert succeeded the dinner, at which Mr Moschelles [sic] played as enchantingly as his wife looked. It was not till two o'clock that I got away to a rout at the Duke of Northumberland's . . .'[65]

Moscheles' wife Charlotte, an accomplished harpist, was the daughter of Adolphus Embden, of Hamburg, who in 1825 – following his daughter's marriage earlier in the year – had come to London with a letter of introduction to Nathan from his cousin David Jacques, a business associate of Nathan's in Hanover.[66]

Moscheles himself performed regularly at Hannah's soirées in the late 1820s. 'Twenty-three sat down to table [at the Rothschilds'],' Moses recorded in 1829. 'Moschelles [sic] came in the evening, played on the piano, and accompanied Miss Rothschild. It was near twelve before the party broke up.'[67]

The 'Miss Rothschild' whom Moscheles accompanied was in all likelihood Hannah Mayer, a musical – and beautiful – girl who had a fine singing voice and also played the harp. The piano on which Moses heard him play was almost certainly a recent acquisition of Hannah's from Erard

Brothers. When, the year before, Hannah had heard Moscheles perform on a new instrument with which Mr Erard had recently presented him, she had decided that she would like to have one too – at a cost of 160 guineas. Both Chilly and Louisa seem subsequently to have acquired pianos from Erards' as well.[68]

Moscheles not only gave recitals at the Rothschilds'; for a time in 1829 he also, as he recalled, 'had the management of Madame de Rothschild's concerts and paid on her account the following sums: Madame Stockhausen, £35 for two evenings; M. de Bériot, £5 for one; M. Mori (violin player), £7 for one; Mlle Pisaroni, £20 for one; Donzelli, £10 for one; Curioni, £10 for one; Schütz and wife, £15 for one; De Begnis, £25 for two; myself £40 for two; making in all £167 – a pretty sum according to our German notions.'[69]

Two years later, when the virtuoso violinist Niccolò Paganini was preparing for his first visit to England, Lionel wrote to Hannah from Paris: 'Paganini will give you a letter. He charges £500 for a night.' Moscheles considered Paganini's avarice 'to border on the fabulous' and there is no evidence that Hannah engaged him.[70]

Another performer at Hannah's after-dinner concerts in Piccadilly in the late 1820s was the Spanish guitarist Trinidad Huerta. Composer as well as performer, Huerta was well regarded by Rossini. As well as playing at Hannah's concerts, he gave music lessons to her sister Judith, and he continued to keep in touch with the family for years afterwards.[71]

Together with the fine music and the magnificent plate, some of it made by Paul Storr, rich fare was served up at the Rothschilds': turtle soup, turkey stuffed with truffles, foie gras and – a real treat – Strasbourg pies, the delicacy made from goose liver and white truffles that Pushkin associated with Talon's French restaurant in St Petersburg. Pineapples – a luxury of those days – might be eaten with other fruit as dessert; and to help wash it all down there was fine wine.[72]

When a wine merchant, Henry Abbott, was asked by Nathan for 'a cask of good Claret' but could find no cask 'of a quality that can be recommended', he offered instead 'a small quantity of about 13 dozen in bottles just received from Bordeaux . . . of the Chateau Margaux vintage and of the year 1822'. They were, said Abbott, 'genuine wines of superior qualities nor will you, I trust, consider them high priced being £5 per dozen'. The wine seems to have been a success: Margaux was to remain a favourite claret of Nathan's family ever after – so much so that when Anthony heard that Château Margaux itself was for sale he hoped that one of his uncles in Paris would buy it, '& then we should always be able to have good wine'.[73]

If a guest of Nathan's had raised his eyes from the magnificent table, taken his nose out of a glass or looked around the room as he listened to the music, however, he would have seen nothing much of an equivalent quality hanging on the walls.

When visiting Nathan at Stamford Hill, Pückler-Muskau had found it 'diverting to hear him explain to us the pictures around his dining-room (all portraits of the sovereigns of Europe, presented through their ministers), and talk of the originals as his very good friends, and, in a certain sense, his equals'. In addition to those pictures, Nathan owned a half-length portrait of Hannah by the fashionable Sir William Beechey (Queen Adelaide and the Duchess of St Albans both sat to him), the charge for which, noted in Beechey's account book, was a rather stiffer than usual £150. Nathan also commissioned a large family group portrait of himself, Hannah and the children – Lionel, Anthony and Nat are restraining a big, frisky dog – by the less well-known W. A. Hobday.[74]

Otherwise, the artist Richard Dighton, forever short of money, found Nathan a reliable and sympathetic patron in a modest way. Besides including a caricature of Nathan, 'A View from the Exchange', in his series of City characters, over a period of more than twenty-five years Dighton executed numerous small watercolour and gouache portraits of family members. Moritz Daniel Oppenheim, from Frankfurt, painted various small portraits in oils of Lionel, Anthony, Nat and other relations on the Continent. But except for portraits Nathan does not seem to have been interested in acquiring pictures – a notion which a tale related by the Reverend Moses Margoliouth in *The History of the Jews in Great Britain* (1851) tends to confirm.[75]

When a Jewish picture dealer named Herrmann, whom Nathan had known in Manchester, moved up to London, he asked Chief Rabbi Hirschel for 'a line of recommendation to Rothschild, with a view to disposing of a couple of most valuable paintings'. Dr Hirschel obliged, and Herrmann went to call on Nathan – who, the story goes, 'seemed startled, when Mr H. asked three hundred pounds for a picture, which was really cheap at that price. "What, three hundred pounds! I cannot afford to spend so much money on pictures. I must buy ponies for my boys, and such like things, which are either useful or profitable, but I cannot throw away money on paintings. However, as the Rabbi has recommended you to me, I will buy a picture for thirty pounds. I do not care what sort of thing it is. I want to make it a present to some one. Choose one from among your collection, for that amount and bring it to me." Thus spoke a man who counted his property by millions!'

Margoliouth includes some curious tales in his *History*, but this one is supported by a surviving letter to Nathan from 'J. D. Herrman, No. 4 Greek Street, Soho Square' dated 11 September 1833:

> Sir, Begging to apologise for having deferred sending you the Painting you did me the honor of ordering of me, by my wish to select a subject not unworthy of your expectation I hereby humbly offer you 'a Landscape by Van Hugtenburgh' trusting that it will meet with your kind approbation. Should I still have been unhappy in my choice, I respectfully sollicit [*sic*] the honor of a visit from Mr Rothschild junr for the purpose of placing any picture in my Collection at his disposal.[76]

The Mr Rothschild junior was most probably Lionel or Anthony – Nat was abroad, Mayer was still only fifteen – and the sons' appreciation of paintings was markedly different from the father's, as began to become apparent in the next stage of Lionel's and Anthony's education on the Continent.

5

Englishmen Abroad

HAVING COMPLETED THEIR studies at Göttingen, on 29 April 1827 Lionel, Anthony and John Darby left Frankfurt at the start of a tour through Saxony and Bohemia that would lead them by stages to Vienna. Lionel kept a 'Journal through Germany', and from its pages emerges as the observant character his aunt Judith had recognised him to be as a small boy at Margate. The older Lionel, though, was not, as the remarks he made to his father about the Frankfurt Exchange in 1824 indicated, easily impressed by what he observed; and he saw no reason, in the pages of his journal at least, to pretend otherwise.[1]

The tour was of a cultural nature, and it is evident that Lionel already felt himself to be something of a connoisseur in matters of taste. Here his points of reference were emphatically English – not so surprising in someone who had been born and brought up in England, but noteworthy in the context of Lionel's unusually cosmopolitan connections and experience. Yet even his father identified closely with England; Chilly once asked her sister Louisa to give her 'best love to Papa', and to 'be so good as to tell him I would write to him a Hebrew letter, but that as he considers himself an Englishman, I think an English letter would give him more pleasure'.[2]

The first leg of the journey from Frankfurt took the three companions northwards towards Eisenach and Gotha, through the fields and orchards once covered by the great beech woods of the Thuringian forest. Travelling in their own carriage, they covered the distance of twenty-six German miles in twenty-four hours, arriving at Gotha, capital of the independent duchy of Saxe-Gotha, in the evening of Monday 30 April. The last part of the drive, through a picturesque range of hills beyond Eisenach, was along a section of road that Lionel judged to be 'as fine as possible being cut through the hills all the way'. Gotha itself, though, did not greatly impress.

'The town is rather dull . . . there are no large or handsome buildings,' Lionel noted. The Duke's palace, two wings of which served as a museum, appeared a 'very plain building'. The cabinet of natural history contained 'not many remarkable things'; the picture gallery was 'small'. But Lionel allowed that the Duke (who was also Prince of Coburg, where he resided) had only recently begun to collect pictures, and that 'if he goes on with that generosity with which he has commenced' – Lionel noted works by Carlo Dolce, Rembrandt, Snyders, Paulus Potter and van Dyck – 'he will soon have a fine collection'. A group of Chinese objects on display, however, were 'only worth the attention of a German who has never been out of his country. In every English house some of them are to be seen.' The charge for looking over the museum – four Prussian dollars – struck Lionel as 'very dear'.

From Gotha they proceeded, via the Prussian town of Erfurt – 'made lively by the quantity of soldiers, which are in every Prussian town' – to Weimar, capital of the Duchy of Saxe-Weimar. Of the personalities Lionel encountered on the way to Vienna, it was two residents of Weimar – the 'German Athens' – who earned the highest place by far in his estimation: Goethe and his patron the Grand Duke.

Frequently described by his contemporaries as the most popular prince in Germany – sometimes as the most popular in Europe – Karl August, Grand Duke of Saxe-Weimar, had during the course of his long and benign reign welcomed as new residents in his small duchy Wieland (his tutor), Herder, Schiller and Goethe. The last, the only survivor of the four by the time of Lionel and Anthony's visit, had become a local attraction, prey to a steady stream of foreign visitors; like Voltaire at Ferney in the 1760s and 1770s – and not unlike Nathan Rothschild in London – Goethe had become a fixture on the European tour.[3]

'Goethe,' wrote Lionel, 'is now considered to be the greatest wonder of Weimar and every stranger is anxious only to get a sight of him; these last few years he has been thought rather rude to strangers, but he is obliged to be so. Formerly he received every person who called upon him. Of course then a very great part of the day was taken up by receiving visits, which was not the most agreeable manner of passing his time. He now receives but few visits, which is not to be wondered at, as he is a very old man, and employs his time in correcting the editions of his works and in thinking of the next world which he before long will see. He does not even pay the Grand Duke visits; he receives one every week from the latter. We had the satisfaction of passing a quarter of an hour with him. He was very polite to us, and gave me a few lines of his handwriting.'

They were fortunate that Goethe put them at their ease. After Louis Spohr and his wife had performed together – he on the violin, she on the harp – at a court concert in Weimar twenty years earlier, the 'two Poet-heroes Goethe and Wieland' came up to them. While Wieland had 'seemed quite charmed . . . and evinced it in his own animated and friendly manner', Goethe 'addressed a few words of praise to us with a dignified coldness of mien'. Moreover, Goethe was no lover of the Jews. When marriage between Jews and Gentiles had been legalised in Frankfurt – a place that Goethe, a native of the city, detested – he had warned: 'This scandalous law will undermine all family sense of morality, intimately associated with religion as it is . . . Who knows whether or not bribery has played a role in all this; who knows whether the all-powerful Rothschilds are behind it?'[4]

That Lionel and Anthony were from England and were accompanied by an English tutor may perhaps in part account for the great man's politeness to his visitors. Although no Anglophile, before going to Leipzig University at sixteen, Goethe had himself had an English tutor, a young man from Leeds named Harry Lupton, and learned enough English to read Dodd's *Beauties of Shakespeare* – a foretaste of the works of that 'heavenly genius' that would so entirely move the soul of Wilhelm Meister, hero of Goethe's autobiographical novel.

The Grand Duke Karl August, Lionel judged, is 'a prince very much loved by all his subjects and deserves it, both on account of his liberality to his subjects and his desire for their happyness [*sic*]'. He 'does everything in his power to make his small town gay and pleasant; every week he gives dinner parties and balls, to which every person who has been introduced to him is invited. They are not like stiff court assemblies, but like private parties, which of course renders them much more pleasant . . . The English are very well received by the Duke and he encourages their stay in his capital in every way possible. They are always at court, and make themselves as free there as at their own houses . . .'

The three travellers left Weimar 'very much pleased with the place and the people but still more so with the Duke himself'. The inhabitants aside, two things that Lionel particularly admired about Weimar were the park at the back of the ducal palace, 'very agreeable, it being very much in the English stile [*sic*]', and the Grand Duke's library with its 'very good collection of prints, principally English'. The Weimar picture collection contained 'many pretty things of the modern school, but that is all'. The Grand Duke's country house, although 'not at all large', the rooms 'not at all elegantly fitted-up', the park 'not so fine as the one in the town', had a hothouse that was 'very well stored with the rarest plants'.

From Weimar, on Thursday 3 May, they drove to Jena – 'the university is not considered one of the best, and is only frequented by those who are obliged to do so' – where they had to choose between two different roads to Leipzig. To take the shorter route, via Naumburg, meant passing through a part of Prussia, where 'one is obliged to be examined', presumably by customs officials. It was rejected in favour of the more rural road through Altenburg, where for Lionel there was nothing worth seeing; 'the peasants in this small country have their costume, which is not one of the most becoming . . . something like some of the Swiss, but much more ugly'.

The party arrived at Leipzig in the middle of one of the city's great bi-annual fairs. Lionel noted with approval the 'very great bustle' of the place, and that he and his companions were 'kindly received by all to whom we had letters'. Unfortunately, though, the King of Saxony's death shortly after their arrival 'put a stop to every amusement . . . 200 poor girls who sang and played in the fair were taken out of their beds & driven out of the town, that on the next day every chance of hearing a note of musik [sic] might be avoided . . .' Leipzig itself, Lionel found a 'very small town for the number of inhabitants, which is about 40 th[ousand], the streets narrow & the houses very high. There is but little in the town worth seeing . . .'

On the outskirts of Leipzig, on the other hand, he was much taken with the city's observatory, though 'they have been so foolish there to adopt their own line of meridean [sic]'. He thought the observatory 'well worth mounting, as one has from the top a very good view of the town and of the country round it. The country is very flat and one can see round the town to an immense distance; the meadows are very fine and are much like those in England . . . In the famous battle of Leipzig, 1813, the late King & his wife the two first days were in this observatory, beholding the two grand armies. The man who then waited upon them now shews the field of battle, and how the ground was possessed by the allied armies and Napoleon.'

Lionel and his party visited three private picture collections in Leipzig, of which Lionel rated the one belonging to a Mr de Speck 'by far the best', noting that the owner 'has had many good opportunities to buy pictures, having commenced making his collection in the French revolution'. Among 'many very good pictures', Lionel saw a 'very pretty head of Carlo Dolce'. Of the two other collections, one had 'many pretty things of modern artists, but nothing very fine', while the other 'is considered by the owner a much finer collection than it really is, and he gives many of [the] pictures out for originals of the first artists, and [they] are not so'. In contrast to his picture collection, Mr de Speck's garden, which was said to be worth a visit, was no good at all – 'a common garden . . . quite void of taste'.

How it came about that the now eighteen-year-old Lionel had developed such a discriminating eye is uncertain; but he would have had good opportunities to look at Old Master paintings in London, even if not in his own home.

In Pall Mall, and later Trafalgar Square, there was the National Gallery, formed around the core of the J. J. Angerstein collection that had been bought for the nation in 1824; and at the British Institution, also in Pall Mall, there were regular loan exhibitions of paintings – Old Masters during the summer and autumn, modern masters in the spring – from the best private collections.[5]

There were collections to be seen in the great town houses too. In May and June, the public were admitted to the Marquess of Westminster's picture gallery at Grosvenor House, and also to Cleveland (later Bridgwater) House to view the outstanding Orléans pictures that the Marquess of Stafford (Lord Granville's elder half-brother) had inherited from the Duke of Bridgwater. After the French Revolution, the Orléans collection had passed briefly through the hands of Jeremiah Harman, Nathan's early banking contact in the City.[6] In the 1840s, Lionel applied for permission to view the Bridgwater and the Westminster pictures on behalf of some friends, though not for himself – so, by then at least, he presumably knew both collections.[7]

There were further private collections at Apsley House, Chesterfield House, Devonshire House and Montague House, while at Lansdowne House there was a noted sculpture gallery and a famous Venus by Canova. Lionel would have had little difficulty in gaining access to see any of these collections on application, and a short carriage drive away, there was the excellent Dulwich College picture gallery – free entry, four times a week.[8]

Beyond Leipzig, having crossed the river Mulda by ferry, Lionel and his companions proceeded along the road connecting Leipzig with Dresden, Bohemia, Silesia and Austria. They arrived at Dresden – 'Germany's Florence' – on the evening of Wednesday 9 May, and remained there for almost a week.

Touring Italy in 1816, Spohr had found that Florence 'does not quite come up to the expectations one forms of it from the description of over-enthusiastic travellers. Dresden is called the German Florence, but is not much honoured by the parallel. The situation of Dresden, as well as the city itself are incomparably finer. The Arno is a dirty, mean-looking river, and is not in the least to be compared to the majestic Elbe. The four bridges which lead over it and connect the two parts of the town are certainly good and substantial, but not so long or so elegant as that of Dresden. Neither has Florence such fine buildings nor such handsome squares as Dresden, and excels it alone in its treasures of art of every kind.'[9]

Lionel was not so sure. 'One is rather disappointed with Dresden,' he confessed. 'Its situation being so very good, one would expect a large imposing city, but it is every thing but that. The only two buildings which make any exterior show are the Catholic church and the bridge, the latter continually crowded with people, but there is so little bustle & life that one would think that the people are not allowed to speak. Dresden is famous for many of its public institutions, to see which is worth the trouble of a long journey, but there are also some which are not worth seeing.'

The library, he conceded, was 'a very good one'; but the collection of antiquities was 'hardly worth noticing', the collection of china 'hardly worth seeing', the natural history and print collections 'not very particular'. The Grüne Gewälb was 'very interesting for ladies who like to see very large diamonds'; the promenades round the town were 'not very good'. The renowned collection of Old Masters in the Zwinger, however, did strike Lionel as being 'really a most beautiful one', 'as fine as any in Germany'. Although the cost of engaging 'the inspector' to point out the best paintings was, at one ducat, 'rather dear', it saved time – and no doubt assisted Lionel in compiling the long list he recorded in his journal.

Outside the town, the trio visited Moritzburg, the palatial hunting and shooting headquarters of the Kings of Saxony. 'In the Thier garten,' Lionel noted, 'many stags are kept, also wild boars which have been caught in the woods, have their tusks taken out and are now fenced in a park. When the King wishes to hunt he has one of these turned loose and lets about 100 English foxhounds after it.'

Leaving Dresden on 15 May, they made a brief tour, in the company of a Mr Douglas, through Saxon Switzerland, ending up with 'two tiresome days', out of season, at the spa town of Töplitz – 'very dull', 'nothing good but the dinners' – from where they drove to Prague. 'We left Töplitz Monday morning 5 o'clock for Prague where we arrived the same day at 6 o'clock,' Lionel recorded. 'We travelled very slowly as we had several times to wait for horses. The road all the way is as dull and uninteresting as possible.' Prague itself seemed scarcely better, though perhaps Lionel's view of it was coloured by the fact that its large Jewish population was 'very much oppressed' and 'obliged to live in one part of the town'.

'There are very few curiosities in Prague,' Lionel began. 'The town itself is well built, the streets broad and the houses large, but there are no fine buildings. The churches are in great number but none are worth seeing; they are decorated with old gaudy antiquities, which are so musty that a clean person would not like only to touch them. The King's palace is very old, the rooms are very bad, and the furniture still worse. The ballroom is very large but not well decorated . . . The church which is quite close to the palace, properly belongs to it, is filled with complete rubbish . . . The theatre is pretty good: the house itself is large and well fitted up. The orchestra is very good, but the actors are middling . . . The environs of Prague are not so good as one would expect from its situation on a large river . . .'

It was perhaps with a feeling of relief that Lionel and his friends left Prague for Vienna on Thursday 23 May. Even then, though, they were 'disappointed in the country, having heard from several people that it was very beautiful, but we found it quite the contrary, very dull and uninteresting'. They reached Vienna at 7 p.m. on Friday 24 May, had supper, and caught the last act at the Italian Opera.

'You must know by our former letters,' Anthony wrote to his mother a day or two later, 'that we arrived here safely on Friday afternoon. We have been expected since a long time, as they wrote from Ffort that we were coming to this town, without mentioning which way we should take . . .' Tired of waiting, no doubt, their uncle Salomon was not in Vienna to welcome them; he had gone to Baden, the small spa town, famous for its sulphur springs, fourteen miles to the south of the city – a place 'overflowing, in summer and autumn, with idleness and disease from the capital'. When the imperial family took up residence at Baden during the summer, fashionable people would 'confine their visits to driving down on Saturday afternoon, going to the ball on Sunday evening, and returning to Vienna on Monday morning'. Riding along the road to Baden on Saturday morning, Lionel and Anthony met their uncle coming along in the other direction, and returned with him to Vienna.[10]

With the Austrian government a Rothschild client, Salomon had set himself up in Vienna in 1821, as representative of the Frankfurt house. He naturally became the member of the family closest to Prince Metternich – who also became a client, often referred to in the family's correspondence as 'Uncle'. As the country's law forbade Jews to buy property in Vienna, Salomon took over the whole of the Hotel zum Römischen Kaiser, the best in the capital. His action is said to have put out the King of Württemberg, who had been a frequent guest at the hotel, and to have inconvenienced Beethoven, who had given recitals there; but Salomon settled in unperturbed, converting the premises for home and business use.[11]

With Vienna, Lionel confessed, both he and Anthony 'were very well pleased' from the start. They found the city's buildings 'very good', even 'built with good taste'; drives in the Prater were 'endless and most beautiful'; there was a 'great bustle' in the town ('I think it is the only German town where there is any'); they 'had no reason to find fault' with the cuisine; the imperial (Spanish) riding school was 'without doubt the finest in Europe'. Only the imperial palace, to Lionel's way of thinking – and, in fairness, to that of some emperors, too – was 'not good enough for such a town. It is very plain from outside and dirty and badly built.'

He and Anthony spent their time as any other visitors might: strolling through the city's streets, museums and galleries and attending the theatre and opera. Of the private picture collections – and it was in paintings by the Old Masters that Lionel's primary interest lay – there were three 'worth noticing', those belonging to the Princes Liechtenstein and Esterhazy, and to the Countess Schönborn.

In Prince Liechtenstein's collection, Lionel listed the 'principal' masters as 'Guido [Reni], Carlo Dolce, L[eonardo] da Vinci, Titian, Domenichino, Wouwerman, Van Dyck, Lucas Cranach', along with many others. 'It cannot be expected,' he went on to warn, though, 'that all are originals which are given out as such, and as [with] most princes, the Lichtensteins [sic] have of course been cheated very much.' As for the gallery of Prince Esterhazy, Lionel considered it inferior to Prince Liechtenstein's – 'full of bad pictures and copies, which the prince has dearly bought for originals'. He ventured that the only picture of Esterhazy's that was 'of any considerable value' was 'one by a Scholar of Rembrandt which is given out as a Rembrandt. It certainly is equal to the best of his master pieces.'

Anthony's reaction to the two princely collections was slightly different from his brother's. Prince Liechtenstein's, he wrote to his mother, was 'much the finest . . . a great many very bad & some of the best masters but very badly arranged', while Esterhazy 'has also some very fine pictures, & a great many very bad, but these are very well arranged'. As Anthony grew older, he was to earn a reputation in the family for his good taste in interior design and arrangement. The drawback of viewing either collection, he felt, was that 'there being so many pictures in the two collections, & the best not being pointed out to us, we were obliged to look at them all which was very tedious'. While Anthony counted 1,600 pictures in the Liechtenstein collection, Lionel counted only 1,200.[12]

The Countess Schönborn's collection was, in contrast to the other two, Lionel thought, 'very small', although it contained 'many pretty things', among them 'the four finest of Rembrandts, also a very pretty Carlo Dolce, a few of Teniers & Van Dyke [sic]'. 'The whole gallery is in three small rooms, but,' Lionel commented approvingly, 'quite large enough for a private person.'

In the various imperial collections, Anthony saw 'some of the finest

Cameos antiques stones &c: there is one Cameo on which is Augustus with his family [which] is considered to be the finest & the 4th largest in the world. It was bought by Rhodolph [sic] 2 for 12,000 ducates [sic], & a great many others. There are 40 of these very large & fine cameos: there is also a very good collection of medals more than 100,000 from the most antient time till the present . . .' It was with just such items that Anthony's grandfather, Mayer Amschel Rothschild, had dealt in his early days.

'The Schatzkammer here,' Anthony continued in his letter to Hannah, 'has many curiosities . . . there are some figures well cut out in Ivory, but it is the most remarkable by the many precious stones, which it possesses & particularly diamants . . . There are the crowns of the kingdom & particularly one of Charles the Great, his sceptor [sic] & some other things. There is also a piece of wood which they said was a piece of the cross, placed there by Maximilian. I do not believe it to be. I know how very superstitious the Emperors of Austria were . . .'

The activities that Lionel and Anthony described in their letters met with their mother's wholehearted approval. 'Vienna,' she wrote to Anthony, 'must be a place of great interest, as it contains so much for a scientific man, and it is exceedingly gratifying to us to perceive that your curiosity is alive to visit every thing worth notice . . . to take advantage of what may be useful is what every person of sense will commend you for and I anticipate the pleasure of soon seeing you and much improved . . .'[13]

A few days later Hannah wrote to assure Anthony that she and his father had 'derived great satisfaction from our correspondence which has during the whole period of your and Lionel's absence been kept up with great spirit and without any relaxation whatever on your part and which I assure you dearest Anthony has given us the greatest satisfaction, convincing us that you feel pleasure in doing that which is agreeable to us, being a very excellent specimen of your future conduct which you may be assured is very interesting to us and as you are now about entering upon some of the busy affairs of this life, occupy our serious consideration and therefore I feel much pleasure in expressing our approbation of what we have so well found to agree with our wishes . . . Your brothers and sisters here are very much grown. Nathaniel in particular is quite a man. I dare say I shall find you and Lionel equally so . . .'[14]

By the end of 1827, Lionel had joined his father at New Court while Anthony, now seventeen, accompanied by the fifteen-year-old Nat, was studying in Strasbourg.

The journey to Strasbourg across eastern France late in the year was bleak, not least on account of the view from the carriage window. 'From Paris to Strasburgh,' John Russell observed, 'even the professed hunter of curiosities would find little to reward his pursuit; and the mere passing traveller, who is hastening to a certain point, finds nothing at all . . . In a well-cultivated part of England, even the winter landscape is not entirely desolate. Every where the smoke of the farm-house rises . . . at every turn one comes across a sportsman and his dog. In France, man seems to be as dead as nature. The traveller looks out over an endless, dreary extent of brown soil, seldom varied by the meanest cottage.'[15]

Another drawback was the poor state of the roads – something that was especially noticeable to anyone accustomed to travelling in England. By the 1820s, thanks to the efforts of Thomas Telford and John McAdam, the main roads in England were not only being realigned and levelled – hills flattened and valleys filled in – but, even more importantly, roads were being given solid, all-weather surfaces. The main road from Paris to Strasbourg, on the other hand, was appalling in the winter, as Chilly found to her displeasure one December.[16]

'What dull weather! What a dull journey!' she protested to Hannah. 'In short how dull & miserable every thing looks. We left Paris Sunday morning; it is today Wednesday, [and] the rain has scarcely ceased one half hour. The days are so very short that we have been obliged to travel day & night. The roads are so terribly bad that we should otherwise never advance, and in all this extent of country that we have traversed it has appeared almost uninhabited, scarcely even a beggar at the carriage door for the most miserable hovel must still appear preferable to the alternate snow & rain which have attended us. I can scarcely [conceive of] any thing less comfortable than travelling in France at this time of year & with this weather. It is enough to give one the spleen.'[17]

Arrival at Strasbourg did little to lift the traveller's spirits either. It was, said Russell, 'an irregular, old-fashioned, heavy-looking town, most inconveniently intersected by muddy streams and canals, and full of soldiers and custom-house officers'; it had 'the double misfortune of being at once a frontier trading town, and an important frontier fortification. The appearance of the inhabitants, and the mixture of tongues, announce at once that the Rhine was not always the boundary of France.' Anthony made a similar observation in a letter to his mother from Strasbourg on 30 December 1827.[18]

'You must know by this time that it is our intention to write twice a week,' he began. 'I will write every Sunday & Nat will write on a Tuesday. We mentioned in our last letter that there were holydays here for 10 days. They will be finished next Wednesday or Thursday, when we shall recommence our studies.' Of the two brothers' twice-weekly letters, only three, all of them from Anthony, seem to have survived. 'You must not think,' Anthony continued, 'that we have been idle all this last week, [though] we have truly not studied as much as usual . . . we have been to two balls since the last week and are going to a soirée to night, therefore I have had time enough to examine the society. I think that here is a great mixture of that German pride & French politeness. There are very few ladies of the first families here that can be called *Ladies*, & if they think themselves so they do not behave so towards strangers. I am not the only person who thinks so but many other people [do too]. The ladies here are not so fine as I expected to find them having heard so much of them: it is seldom that you see a lady with [a] good set of teeth, the water being very bad that most people have a swelling in the neck . . .'[19]

Anthony and Nat lived in rented rooms belonging to a Madame Hepp. There was a Jewish community in Strasbourg – in 1834 an impressive synagogue would be built there – but no details of the society in which the two young men mixed have come to light. 'We have passed our ten days of vacation in studying in the daytime,' Anthony reported home on 6 January 1828, '& have either been to parties or paid visits to our acquaintance in the evening. To morrow all our lessons will begin in the usual way. We are glad to perceive that the Strasbourg pies are so much liked in England. They are famous all over Europe. The patissier told me that he sends a great many to Russia. I sent you also some goose's liver yesterday knowing that it is a favourite dish of Papa. You must not write too often for the liver it being very dear & ought only to be eaten on particular occasions.'[20]

While Anthony's and Nat's studies entailed attendance at classes and lectures, the specific nature of the studies, just as when Anthony was with Lionel at Göttingen, is not disclosed. Nor is any reference made to John Darby or to any other tutor, though it seems unlikely that the two young men were staying in Strasbourg by themselves. As at Göttingen before, a newspaper was sent to them from England every day.

'Our studies go on in the usual way,' Anthony informed his mother on 3 February, 'we follow the lectures regularly at the Academy & I find a great difference between these lectures here & those at Göttingen: this university cannot be compared to that. The professors here are not very celebrated & in most of the faculties except Medicine & Chemistry there is a great want of professors. There is only one professor who lectures on History. If any person wishes to follow a regular course of History he must remain here for 3 or 4 years.'[21]

While Anthony refers to 'this university', strictly speaking there was no such institution in Strasbourg at that time. Goethe completed his studies at Strasbourg University in 1772, but subsequently the foundation was suppressed, as a stronghold of German sentiment, by the authorities of the French Revolution. It would become a university again in 1872, but in the period during which Anthony and Nat were resident in the city the institution that continued in the old university's place was known as the Académie Royale – the 'Academy' to which Anthony refers.

At all events, it seems that Anthony would look back on his time there with pleasure. More than forty years later, at the time of the Franco-Prussian war of 1870, James's eldest son Alphonse wrote from Paris to his cousins in London: 'Anthony's heart must be bleeding, seeing the beautiful Strassbourg cathedral destroyed and the University library, where he spent the best years of his youth.'[22]

At New Court Lionel made such good progress that in the summer of 1828 he was left there in charge, with his uncle Ben Cohen to assist him, while his parents paid a visit to Frankfurt. As Nathan conferred about business with his brothers, he could rest easy about matters at home. 'We have to express our entire satisfaction at your punctuality in writing and your attention to the important concerns of the Counting House, which you may be quite certain affords Papa the greatest pleasure,' Hannah wrote to assure Lionel in August. 'We have been at this place for these four days without any thing particularly new or entertaining taking place,' she continued with less satisfaction. 'I was not allowed to put my desire in practice of going to an Hotel. It appears the custom of having a family, however large, to receive at the house of the established family, could not be done away with; the trouble it gives is to me a great drawback to the recreation of going out.

'Papa and his Brothers with Anselm are almost continually engaged in deliberating upon the arrangement of their concerns, which are held in the Tower in the Garden and are perfectly *secret* . . . Anselm is entirely engaged with the family topics among the Gentlemen . . . Anthony and Nat are here also; they are in temper and manners the same. Nathaniel is very much grown and is the exact height of Papa. I think they will both return [to England] for a short time with us. Anthony will after come to Frankfurt where I most sincerely hope he will be established for his advantage and to the satisfaction of his friends . . .'[23]

In a postscript to Hannah's letter, Nat regretted that Lionel was not with them as well. 'Frankfurt is rather dull,' he went on, 'we have no amusement but shooting. Yesterday we were out with Papa and all his brothers;

however all but Uncle James soon left us and then we had good sport. I shot a roe buck running as fast as it could, and a brace of partridges. We have only been once to see the Herz's; your friend Marian is at Baden, and Mama and all the family find Helen only rather pretty.'

A short time afterwards, Hannah wrote to Lionel again: 'Mrs Charles de Rothschild [Adelheid, *née* Herz] takes great pains to make our stay here pleasant and gives very elegant entertainments. We dined there yesterday and met Mr and Mrs Heine of Hambro [Hamburg] who are very pleased with the manner of your doing business . . . I hope our stay here will not be prolonged much beyond the [Jewish] new year Holydays . . . I hope dearest Lionel you will arrange with the concerns of the counting house so that your services for those two days will not be wanted . . . I beg you to remember me very kindly to Benjamin and tell him Papa and all the family are perfectly satisfied with his attentions, likewise to Esther [Samuel] and all my brothers and sisters. Why do we not hear from Solomon Cohen [?] – tell him there are many enquiries for him.'[24]

By January 1829, Anthony was, as planned, working in Frankfurt under the eye of his uncle Amschel. He was not in the same league as Lionel – did not progress in the same effortless way – but he was eager to learn, none the less. 'According to your request to inform you now and then of your son's progress in the Counting House,' one of the Frankfurt clerks informed Nathan, 'I have the honour to say that I ceaselessly instruct him in all arithmetical problems and am glad to perceive that he has the intellectual grasp and makes good use of what I have to teach him. In due course I shall give the young Baron systematically the knowledge of the art of arithmetic and I shall continue to explain to him arbitration of exchange and all the business curriculum of the Counting House.'[25]

By the time Anthony wrote to his father in July, he seems to have been getting the hang of the business, though he had not learned to write of it clearly. 'With us it goes on very steady,' he reported. 'We have made a little loan for a Prince of Hechingen Hohenlohe for 25,000£ by which we may gain a few £ in profit . . . Uncle Amschel does not wish to part with his Russian Bonds as he likes 5% interest very much. You tell him to propose to the Elector some Dutch 2½% Bonds; he says that he has lost all his courage to offer him so many different foreign Bonds, as he wrote to Sichel to bye [*sic*] some Neapolitan who has not bought more than a few thous. £ thinking they will be lower instead of that they have risen . . .'[26]

The style contrasts markedly with the fluency with which his sister Chilly expressed herself when, at about the same time, she wrote to thank her parents for a present of some money they had sent her. She wrote confidently and with clarity about her financial affairs: 'You will perhaps be surprised Dear Papa, when I tell you Anselm made the whole a present to me, and as I really have more money than I know what to do with, I mean to invest it, and am going to ask your advice dear Papa in what manner, & what security you would think best. The English are much too high; the French are to be converted; the *Maccaroni* [Neapolitan] will not I am afraid last for ever, therefore as I already have 500£ in the Russian I think it best to make a round sum, and if you are also of my opinion dear Papa, I shall be much obliged if you will at the present price invest this amount in these [*sic*] security. I hope dear Papa this is quite like a man of business, & will meet your approbation.'[27]

In late November 1829, at about the time of Lionel's twenty-first birth-day on the 22nd, Anthony's thoughts were turning to England. He was hoping for the chance to leave Frankfurt with a consignment of gold bullion for Paris, and afterwards to cross over the Channel for a brief visit home. 'There is not the least thing new here,' he wrote to his mother. 'We have had some very severe & cold weather . . . Pray give my love to Lionel [.] I hope he has passed an agreeable birthday. I regret very much not being of the party for I dare say you must all have amused yourselves very well. I hope please God if I should remain on the continent till I am 21 then to pass that day in England.'[28]

In fact, Anthony was back in England in early 1830. On his way to see Nathan at Stamford Hill on 1 February, Moses Montefiore met Anthony and Lionel with their father on the road. 'On reaching Newington,' he wrote in his diary, 'I met N. M. Rothschild in his carriage. Lionel and Anthony were with him; the two latter got into my chariot, and I drove with the former to Prince Esterhazy, whither he [Nathan] was proceeding with the intention of conferring with him on the subject of [Jewish] emancipation in Austria.'[29]

While Anthony now settled down to work with his father and Lionel at New Court, Nat, who was to be eighteen in July, was sent abroad again – to travel, to improve his language skills and to learn something of his family's business concerns on the Continent. Mayer's education having been placed for the time being in the hands of Dr Schwabe, Fritz Schlemmer accompanied Nat across the Channel.

After a little more than a week in Paris, the pair travelled south to the Pyrenees, to meet Nat's aunt Betty at the spa town of Bagnères de Luchon. While Betty took the waters, Nat and Schlemmer spent their days going for walks and for rides; one day, on hired ponies, they made the ascent of the Pic du Midi. Léon de Laborde was staying in the neighbourhood, and Schlemmer introduced him to Nat.

In late July they were back on the road once more, travelling in an open carriage-and-pair via the Pont du Gard to Lyons – where a great surprise lay in store for them. Arriving at Lyons in the evening, they found their way blocked by guards at the city's gates, and on enquiry were informed of the cause. 'Your coachman,' a sentry explained sternly, 'is sporting a white cockade. You are to remove it at once and replace it with a tricolour cockade.' The reason for this, the two travellers found out, was that since they had left Bagnères de Luchon, a revolution in Paris had led to the toppling of King Charles X.[30]

In a letter to Nathan of the previous December, Chilly, who was then living with Anselm in Paris, had told Nathan that she 'could not dare enter the field of politicks. It is becoming quite the fashion here as in London, for politicks to be the constant topick of conversation at dinner, & to judge from universal clamour sure never was [a] Ministry more unpopular than the present. Betty & myself paid a visit yesterday to Princess Polignac who was very polite; she invited us to two soirées & seemed in very good humour.'[31] Princess Polignac was the daughter of an English peer, the first Lord Rancliffe; the unpopular Ministry was that of her husband, Prince Jules de Polignac, who had previously been ambassador in London.[32]

Despite the uneasy state of French politics, few had foreseen a revolution. In London, in late February, Charles Greville had noted in his diary: 'Went to Esterhazy's ball; talked to old [Nathan] Rothschild, who was there with his wife and a dandy little Jew son. He says that Polignac's Government will stand by the King's support and Polignac's own courage . . .' James was sufficiently unconcerned to contract for a modest French government loan, and in the summer Nathan sent Lionel to work with him in the rue d'Artois.[33]

As Nat and Fritz Schlemmer were travelling up through France in their open carriage, Lionel, accompanied by his uncle Carl and family, who had been staying in England, crossed over to France on Sunday 25 July.

'I am happy to say,' Lionel wrote to his father from Calais, 'that after a quick passage of only three hours, we arrived quite well in this *nice* place, & are now preparing for a good dinner. No person on board was ill. Immediately I left you I went into the Cabin & did not wake till I was in the Harbour. Uncle Charles & all of them were also very well & desire to be most kindly remembered [to you]. There is nothing new here.' After 'rather a warm journey' to Paris – the country was in the grip of a heat-wave – Lionel found 'all the family in perfect good health'.[34]

It was on the very day of Lionel's arrival in France that Charles X signed the *ordonnances* that so rapidly brought about his fall. Liberty of the press was suspended, the Chamber of Deputies dissolved, and a system of election introduced that was designed to exclude the opposition from power. Countersigned by all the King's ministers, the decrees were published in the *Moniteur* on Monday 26 July, when rowdy groups of protestors began to collect on the Paris streets.

'You can easily imagine our astonishment on our arrival here, to find everything here in such a state,' Lionel wrote home the next day. 'I assure you it is very difficult to give you a just idea of it, it is so different to what an English mind is accustomed, one moment one thinks oneself on the eve of seeing a revolution, the next, that every thing in a short time will be again in order. I have been here so short a time that I can give no opinion, & will only endeavour to inform you of every thing I have heard . . . To day all the newspapers appeared as usual which has created a little noise, before all the newspaper offices there are soldiers & the gens d'armes who have seized all the papers & taken the Editors before the police, this alone is enough to make a disturbance in any free country: all the shops in those streets are of course closed: in the Palais Royal there was a man selling some of these papers. He was immediately seized, some of the Boys & of the common people took his part, but in a few minutes everything was quiet again, the gates in the Palais Royal & the shops are all closed, this circumstance in itself is trifling, but when it comes to London they make a great story of it. Before all the ministers' houses there are also gens d'armes. All these things make people speak, but in the end I do not think it will come to anything very bad . . . To day there is to be a meeting of all the members of the late parliament [;] what they will do, it is not possible to say, but the report is, that they will declare themselves the only & true representatives of the people & without their sanction nothing is legal, that is done by the ministers & that after the 1st Jan no taxes need to be paid . . . this is the opinion of the opposition, who think that we shall see very dreadful times again, but the other party, the ministerial, who have completely the command of the army, think that with force they shall be able to carry everything, the only thing papa is that the King before long will see the Danger.'[35]

Opposition to the King and his government was soon showing itself among the crowds of people who took to the streets. Shops were shut for fear of riots and looting, and at about seven o'clock on Tuesday evening troops were provoked into firing. The crowds dispersed, but the next day they were back; barricades went up and the fighting escalated.[36]

By Thursday 29 July, royal troops had disappeared from the streets and retreated to the palace of Saint-Cloud. On Friday, Lionel scribbled a reassuring note to his parents from the mansion that his uncle Salomon had bought at Suresnes: 'I have only a few minutes to inform you that we are all still at Suresne [*sic*] & perfectly well, without any information that we can rely upon. In the afternoon we hope to have another opportunity of writing, but I send this in case we have none, assuring you that all of us are perfectly well, & completely out of danger.' By Saturday, King Charles X had been overthrown.[37]

'Thank God every thing is now settled, and we are all quiet in Paris,' Lionel wrote with relief on 31 July. 'The Duke of Orleans has been declared Lieutenant General of all France, a completely new Ministry formed, and the Chambers will open, as they ought to have done, on the 3rd of August. The state of Paris at present is really wonderful. The streets are crowded with persons, all laughing and as gay as if they had come from some Dance [;] in the squares & open places all the Garde Nationale & Royal Troops who had delivered up their arms, marching & being cheered by the people [;] in every corner the three colored Flags & every person with a red, Blue & White Cockade.

'In the Boulevards & Streets every hundred yards the fine large Trees [have been] cut down and the pavement taken up & piled up against them & broken doors &c so that nothing can pass. At present they have made through each a small passage, so that one can pass through on foot. These barricades, as they call them, are not only in the principal streets, but in all the small ones, so that it was impossible for the soldiers & artillery to pass any where.

'This week has passed like a dream & even now the very day after all the fighting, one can hardly believe it. The King & all the Ministers have left Paris & will go no person knows where. Yesterday there were at St Cloud with the King more than fifteen thousand men, all of them chosen for their known loyalty. Today the greater part of them have left him, & are returning to Paris without their arms. Never was there a more glorious week for France. The people have behaved in a way that will be admired by every person, and will make them now to be reckoned amongst the first of nations. During all these troubles not one single excess has been committed, the guard national [*sic*] before all the public places, some of them the poorest devils possible, and conducting themselves as well as possible. All Paris is now armed, all the Bankers & first people have entered in the Garde Nationale [;] there exists at present such a spirit that it would require more than the whole French army to retake it. In the Tuilleries

& the Louvre, there has not been so much damage as was expected [;] all the windows & a few pictures have been destroyed, but nothing of any consequence.

'All the Ministers have been named this instant . . . Dupont de l'Eure for Justice, Rigny for Marine, Baron Louis [for] Finance, [the Duc de] Broglie for the interior. All the Bonds &c that were here, we took to Suresne, & were yesterday so afraid of an attack that we had them concealed in the middle of the garden, for in the morning we heard that the Duke of Orleans was to be proclaimed King, and if King Charles 10 had been able to keep all his troops which were then at St Cloud – about 15,000 men – there might have been still a great deal more fighting, but thank God every thing is now over, and I am in great hopes that every thing is settled. Charles the 10 even Wednesday afternoon might have had everything if he would only have restored the charter, sent away his Ministers, and called the Chambers together, but he would not agree, & has now lost every-thing. It will be a good lesson for other govern[men]ts.

'In business I think Monday everything will begin. Today they have done a good deal in Bills. The Exchange & Bank are not yet open. The Rentes will no doubt open very high, but there is no saying. Baron Louis is a very clever financier & will do everything for the credit of the coun-try . . . Today we walked from Suresne & have been about the town, just to see the people & the streets and are now going to dinner, so must wish you every thing that is good . . . My best love to Billy, Louisa & all the family & Hannah Mayer.'[38]

On 7 August the Duc d'Orléans was proclaimed King of the French – not, like his predecessors, King of France and Navarre – and took the name Louis Philippe; and over the next eighteen years he was to make himself most accessible to Lionel's uncle James, and regularly to receive members of the Rothschild family at his Court. 'The Baron paid the King a visit last night,' Nat would write in the 1840s. 'His Majesty was amazingly polite & almost kissed him, so pleased was he.'[39]

Whether Nat and his tutor braved Paris or returned to England after they learned of the July revolution is not clear, but by the beginning of October they were at Coire, in Switzerland, en route for Italy via the Splügen Pass. A week later Nat was writing from Lombardy. 'We intend leaving Milan in a few days & shall proceed to Venice,' he wrote to Chilly in Paris on 9 October. 'It is our plan to visit almost every place in the north of Italy as we have plenty of time for the South . . . & with best love to Rabbi Leib [Lionel] whose hasty epistles I will answer before leaving this place . . .'[40]

The ambitious plan for touring northern Italy was curtailed. 'We hastened on our way to Florence,' Fritz Schlemmer remembered. 'If my companion had made use of this opportunity to learn the language of the country, he would have profited more from his stay.' Yet Nat's overall progress was good: he and his tutor 'spoke to one another first in one language and then in another' and Nat was soon speaking 'very good German and French' though 'only a little Italian'.

From Florence, where Schlemmer introduced Nat to the wonders of Italian Renaissance art, they made for Rome, intending to settle there for a while. They found some roomy apartments in the heart of the city, and agreed to take them for three months. But no sooner had they done so than a despatch arrived from Nathan in London instructing them to leave for Naples without delay – which they duly did, travelling by day and night, to reach Naples in the evening of 2 February 1831.[41]

'Nothing,' Nat surmised, 'can be more picturesque & beautiful than the situation of Naples. The town itself is very fine, & presents a particularly lively appearance to a person who has just quitted Rome.' He and Schlemmer put up at the Hotel Vittoria, the best hotel in town. As the authors of a contemporary vade mecum put it: 'le meilleur des hôtels de Naples est sans aucune comparaison celui de la Vittoria, tenu à Chiaja par M. Martin'.[42]

'According to your desire we left Rome immediately upon the receipt of your letter & arrived here late last evening, after rather a quick journey,' Nat informed Nathan the next day. 'This morning I went to the counting house & read all the letters from Frankfort & Paris. Unfortunately there were none for me giving me directions what to do. However I considered it my best plan to enquire what business had been transacted & also the variations in the prices of gold &c. You may well suppose that in one day I have not been able to learn much, however I hope when I receive your plans I may be of some use . . .'[43]

Nat's uncle Carl had gone to Naples to set up a subsidiary of the Frankfurt house, C. M. de Rothschild e figli, in 1821. Carl and his brothers had decided to do this at the urging of Prince Metternich, in the wake of military intervention by Austria, financed by the Rothschilds, to suppress an uprising against the Bourbon King Ferdinand I, whose Queen was an Austrian Archduchess.

'I have not yet had time to deliver my letters of introduction,' Nat went on. 'I shall do so to morrow & shall try to pump a little news out of some of the great people. I perceive by Uncle Charles's letter that he only intends coming here in the month of May. Pray write to him to come as soon as he can for then it will [be] twenty times as agreeable for me & I shall then be able to do a great deal more good. I m[ust] beg of you dear Papa to w[rite to] me v[ery of]ten & to tell me every thing that you wish me to do for unless you give me good instruction I shall be placed in rather a difficult position. I have no doubt Mr Renevier would have preferred my remaining at Rome. At all events I shall be a cheque [sic] on him; you may depend upon it I will do all I can.'

Renevier seems to have been the managing clerk in the Naples counting house, and to have been rumoured, in Charles's absence, to be harming Rothschild interests. 'I have not yet had the pleasure of receiving a letter from you since my arrival here,' Nat wrote to Nathan on 7 February, 'but do not doubt that Thursday's post will bring me some news from you, which I hope will enable me to understand better my mission. Yesterday the rentes got up about ½%, nothing however was done for the house in them. Mr Renevier told me that he had a bad opinion of them . . . As far as I can judge the business seems to be very irregular here. I never can make out what is going on or what has been done. Perhaps it is my fault & is owing to my want of experience. When your instructions arrive I trust I shall be more capable. There seems to me to be such a loss of time in all the transactions. Yesterday Renevier was waiting at the bank the whole day to make a transfer without effecting it & today he is gone on the same business . . .'[44]

As the days turned into weeks and nothing from Nathan came, Nat began to fret. 'You my dear Rabbi must be aware of the difficulty which I find to be of the slightest service,' he wrote to Lionel on 13 February. 'You know I have not the least experience in business & that I am not either acquainted with the routine of counting house affairs. It is therefore quite out of the question for me to take a leading part in them. I might perhaps have procured some useful information from the Ambassadors or ministers, but unfortunately in all the letters of introduction which Uncle Charles has given me to those grand personages he has always mentioned that I was travelling in Italy for the sake of finishing my education & in company with my *governor*. One can not expect that any body will communicate important news to a young man who has not yet ended his studies & whom one naturally would imagine to take no immediate interest in political matters.'[45]

As the end of February neared, Nat was still without instructions of any kind. For some reason the situation in Naples seems no longer to have been viewed as urgent from London; otherwise, a courier could easily have reached Nat by now. Passing through Naples in April 1830, Charles Greville had noted in his diary: 'Sir Henry Lushington [the British Consul] said at dinner yesterday he had seen at Naples a *Courier* newspaper of that day week, produced by Rothschild and brought by one of his couriers. I came very fast, but was 236 hours on the road, including 20 hours' stoppage. This is 168 hours, which appears incredible, but "gold imp'd [*sic*] by Jews can compass hardest things".'[46]

'I have not yet received any letters from you since my arrival here,' Nat informed Nathan on 26 February. 'I can not at all account for so long a delay for in your last which came to hand at Rome nearly a month ago you promised to write every post . . . Falconnet asked me the other day if it were true that Renevier was going to be married & then to establish a [counting] house in partnership with a Neapolitan. I of course said I knew nothing about it, & then he said it was reported so all over the town . . . Uncle Charles also has not written since the two last post days. I almost begin to suppose he is on his road hither, which I trust may be the case . . .' Falconnet was a prominent Naples businessman with whom the Rothschilds regularly dealt.[47]

Unluckily for the nephew, Charles was not on his way back, and although eventually Nat did begin to receive letters from London, he complained that his hands were tied. 'Your letter of the 22nd of last month came safe to hand this morning,' he wrote to Nathan on 13 March, '& I am very happy to learn that you intend doing a great deal of business with us. Your permission that I may sign every thing at the office is of no use unless you send a procuration, as nothing is allowed to be done without this act of the notary . . .'[48]

Nat's frustration only increased. 'I do not like this place particularly for business,' he complained a few days later. 'Renevier trys [*sic*] as much as he can to prevent my doing the least good. I certainly must say I should have preferred very much making my début in commercial affairs at London.' Local market practices depressed him too: 'You have no idea what a disagreeable place this is to have anything to do in the funds,' he told his father in April. 'Every body speculates, from the grandest nobleman in the land to the lowest shopkeeper, & all in such very small sums.'[49]

In comparison to the aggravations of business in Naples, the social side of life was less trying – though even here Nat had got off to a bad start on his first evening. Among the English community encountered by Lady Blessington during a stay at Naples in 1823, Sir William and Lady Drummond were, she declared, 'conspicuous for their hospitality'. Although Sir William, who had been British Minister at the Court in Naples during the first decade of the century, had died in 1828, it was to his widow's house that Nat was first invited.[50]

'I went last night to Lady Drummond's,' he wrote home on 4 February. 'It was very stupid, quite a stiff diplomatic rout. If one may consider it as a true specimen of Neapolitan Society I shall not be a great frequenter of it.' Things, however, did not turn out so badly, and ten days later he was cheerfully writing to Lionel that the 'society here is very pleasant, every body very polite indeed & invite me very often. There is however a great deal more etiquette than at Rome or Florence. I do not doubt this week I shall get better acquainted with the Ambassadors & then I shall find it pleasanter in company & more useful for information . . .'[51]

An added bonus was that although Charles was absent from Naples, Nat's aunt Adelheid had remained behind, and she naturally entertained her nephew and his 'governor'. According to Schlemmer's recollection, the company at Adelheid's parties consisted largely of foreign visitors, most of them English, and among them was a Mr Auldjo – the alpinist, traveller and writer John Auldjo, who was then in Naples preparing his *Sketches of Vesuvius* (1833). Schlemmer took Auldjo up on an invitation to visit him at his lodgings in Santa Lucia, to inspect a telescope that Auldjo had recently installed in his room, for the purpose, judging by the excellent drawings he made for his book, of viewing the volcano across the bay.

During his visit to Auldjo's lodgings, Schlemmer was introduced to 'a young German artist whom I knew by name but had never met – Felix Mendelssohn-Bartholdy'. Mendelssohn and Schlemmer hit it off, and went on to become good friends, continuing to see one another when they had both returned home to Germany. Indeed, it was through Schlemmer that Mendelssohn met his future wife Cécile Jeanrenaud, who was a cousin of Schlemmer's through the Schunks.[52]

Curiously, the two men can only narrowly have missed meeting one another in the summer of 1829 when Mendelssohn was staying in London. With Moscheles, Mendelssohn had given a performance of his Two Piano Concerto in E, and in June he paid at least one visit to Stamford Hill. Possibly, Schlemmer was then away on holiday with his two young charges. Certainly, at some point in June that year, Moses Montefiore 'gladly accepted for Mrs Montefiore and himself an invitation to make a tour in the Isle of Wight with the Baron and Baroness Anselm de Rothschild, and Messrs Nathaniel and Meyer [*sic*] de Rothschild'.[53]

Whatever the explanation, Schlemmer now took Mendelssohn with him to visit the Neapolitan Rothschilds, where one evening they overheard an English guest – 'une lady anglaise' whose name is not recorded – regaling Nat's aunt with a story about a pianist who had recently moved into the apartments above her own. From what she had heard of his playing, she said, he had a superb technique – but what a shame it was that he knew only one piece, and that he played it all day long. 'We were sitting at another table,' Schlemmer recalled. 'Felix did not let on that he was the culprit responsible and that he was working on a new capriccio.'

Neither Nat nor his companion gives any hint of mixing in Neapolitan society, though it seems unlikely to have been for want of opportunity. After attending a ball in Naples for the Princess of Salerno in January 1828, Judith Montefiore had noted the presence of some five hundred members of the nobility, and the next day a ducal couple paid a call on her. But on the other hand, when James Morrison, the enormously wealthy glovemaker, was staying in Naples in January 1827 and went to a ball given by Falconnet – 'a very splendid affair indeed . . . it proved quite a hit' – he saw how it 'was an awful moment for them – it was their first experience to get the aristocracy to come'. 'There has been hitherto,' Morrison continued, 'a great gulf between the least noble and the greatest merchant and banker. At the Ball of the Nobility, at which we were on Monday, these are rigidly excluded, but of course it never occurred to them to formally exclude a haberdasher and therefore I got in.'[54]

Yet Nat's family was to an extent a case apart. After attending a soirée at the Rothschilds', Morrison observed that Baron Rothschild 'really commands here, both Court, Exchange and fashion'. That Nat reached Naples rather later in the year, and that Charles was absent, were perhaps contributing factors. In January 1834, when Henrietta Montefiore was staying in Naples and Carl was in residence, her experience was more like Judith's. 'This town is quite full with all nations and every one of the fashionables is anxious to show off namely in giving parties to the Royal family,' she wrote to Hannah. 'Also the Court is very gay. Last Saturday was the first party at the palace, Monday is the next [.] They did me the honour to invite me to both . . . My brother Charles will have also their Majesties next Tuesday . . .'[55]

Possibly, as at Lady Drummond's, Nat felt Neapolitan society to be stupid and stiff. As J. B. Richard observed in his guidebook: 'La noblesse de Naples est très-nombreuse; elle a beaucoup d'ostentation; ses équipages sont superbes et très-multupliés, ses habillemens fastueux; ce n'est que soie, que broderie en or ou en argent.' On the other hand, Richard continues: 'La plus grande liberté règne dans cette ville, et les femmes y sont moins réservées que partout ailleurs.' Perhaps Nat felt constrained by his inadequate grasp of Italian.[56]

In March, the approach of Passover gave rise to a new anxiety. 'Lionel mentions in his last letter that it is your wish I shall spend the Passover holydays at Rome,' Nat wrote to Nathan. 'I have not as yet made up my mind what to do with respect to them. If I go to Rome I shall be so terribly bothered with the thousands of poor Jews with which that place abounds . . .'[57]

When, in early 1839, Moses and Judith stayed briefly in Rome, Judith was distressed at the treatment received by the city's Jews at the hands of the Pope. 'How painful! it is to find our people under so many disadvantages here,' she exclaimed in her diary. 'Three thousand five hundred souls are obliged to maintain themselves by shops, and in a confined part of the city. Arts, sciences, mechanism are prohibited. Four times in the year two hundred are obliged to attend a sermon for their conversion. It is said that no proselytes are made, except occasionally from among the most destitute. Leo XII deprived them of the privilege granted by Pius VII of keeping shops out of the Ghetto.'[58]

As Passover approached, Nat opted to stay in Naples. 'I trust by the time this letter comes to hand you will have spent the Passover holydays comfortably,' he wrote to his parents. 'I have got some biscuits & although they [sic] are no persons of our persuasion here, I shall strive to conform to all the rules of this particular feast . . .' His aunt Adelheid appears to have left town, and soon Nat decided that the time had come for him to leave Naples too.[59]

'I hope my dear Papa you intend to write to me to come home soon,' he wrote in mid-April. 'I am really afraid I do no good here, & I am quite sure I should learn the business in a quarter of the time with you . . .' The next day he wrote to Paris to recruit Lionel's support: 'I have frequently written to you [of] my great dislike to Naples which I assure you increases every day. I assure you however I should not mind that at all, but then I am afraid I am of no service & that I should be much better employed in London where I certainly might learn business in about a twentyth [sic] of the time & twenty times as well as here. The doctor [Schlemmer] also is so very uncomfortable. He has nothing in the world to do & sits all day moping at home. Therefore do my dearest Rabbi write to Papa & tell him to let us come home . . .'[60]

Nat's continuing dislike of Naples, and his companion's listlessness, were both perhaps, in part, a reaction to the city's climate in the spring. It affected Anna Jamieson when she was staying there in March 1821. 'I know not whether it be incipient illness,' she wrote in her *Diary of an Ennuyée*, 'or the enervating effects of this soft climate, but I feel unusually weak, and the least exertion or excitement is not only disagreeable but painful.' In 1831 Naples made Mendelssohn feel 'languid, disinclined for everything serious – in fact, apathetic. I lounged about the streets all day with a long face, and would have preferred to stretch myself on the ground, without thinking, or wishing, or doing anything. Then it occurred to me that the principal classes in Naples really live in precisely that way; and that consequently the source of my depression did not originate in me, as I had feared, but in the whole combination of air, climate, etc.'[61]

By 26 April, Nat had thankfully received Nathan's consent to leave: 'According to your permission that I may return home, I shall set off next week, & shall go thro' Paris . . .' In fact he was still in Naples a week later, having resolved to make the most of a few more days in that part of the world. 'To morrow I am going to Paestum which will occupy me about three days,' he informed his father. 'I shall not be able to write to you next post. I intend waiting for your letters of next Saturday & Monday & then I shall bid adieu to Naples. In the hopes of seeing you very soon I beg you my dear Papa to give my best love to Mamma & my brothers & sisters . . .'[62]

Nat eventually reached Paris in early June. 'Your Nathaniel is here with us working at the office and is a very nice boy,' James wrote to Nathan on 4 June. 'If you wish, I will keep him here with me for a year, just like any other apprentice, to enable him to learn how to keep the books in order, and I can guarantee you that, if he is prepared to listen, he will become the most skilful of all . . .'[63]

6

Cult of the Horse

WRITING TO HANNAH prior to Nat's return to England from the Continent in the summer of 1831, Lionel said that he had 'not the least doubt that Mr Schlemmer will make any objections to yr proposals. He is too sensible a man not to know when he is well off. I am sure any arrangement that you make will be accepted by him with pleasure.'[1] In the event, Mayer was returned into the charge of his old tutor, and nothing further is ever heard of Dr Schwabe – except that in 1845 a letter arrived at New Court from W. H. Schwabe, of Throwleigh Rectory, near Exeter, asking for help to gain him appointment as a chaplain in the East India Company, 'having so often heard from my father of your readiness to favor *him*'.[2]

It had been mooted that Mayer might attend University College, London, which had opened, free of religious entrance requirements, in 1828. The idea for a non-sectarian university in the capital had first been put to Isaac Goldsmid by the poet Thomas Campbell. Goldsmid had then enlisted the support of the liberal statesman Henry (later Lord) Brougham, and the two men had brought together a group of influential men to put flesh on the bones of the idea.

Lord John Russell, Lord Auckland, Alexander Baring, Sir James Mackintosh and other prominent, liberal-minded men came together with leading members of the groups excluded from Oxford and Cambridge. The Duke of Norfolk was there for the Roman Catholics; Zachary Macaulay for the Evangelicals; and among several representatives of English Jewry there was Nathan Rothschild. The foundation stone of the new institution was laid by the Duke of Sussex in April 1827, and UCL opened in October the next year. Hyman Hurwitz, whose school Nathan's sons had been spared, was appointed Professor of Hebrew.[3]

Aged sixteen, Nat, nominated by Nathan, became one of the university's earliest entrants in 1828. He spent two years there, studying German, natural philosophy and political economy in his first year, chemistry and political economy in his second. Robert Browning, the poet, was among his fellow students; two of Browning's kinsmen were Rothschild clerks.

The Chair of Political Economy was held by John Ramsay McCulloch, author of the textbook *Principles of Political Economy, with a Sketch of the Rise and Progress of Science* (1825), whom Nat rightly considered to be a 'very clever fellow'. Fritz Schlemmer introduced Mayer to McCulloch's works in the schoolroom at Stamford Hill.[4]

In the case of Mayer, however, the plan to send him to university in London was for some reason abandoned. Although, according to Schlemmer, Hannah would have liked to keep him at home, it was decided instead to prepare him for university in Germany – and one thing he needed to work on was his German. 'I am glad dear Mayer liked his Watch,' Chilly wrote to Hannah from Frankfurt in July 1831. 'Pray dear Mama *make* him write a letter in *German* if he can to Mrs S[alomon] de R, if not in English in his best writing. Uncle Charles's boys write both remarkably well, & I am sure it will be compared. I am particularly desirous he should write nicely.'[5]

Carl and Adelheid had three sons by now – brothers for Lionel's future wife – though only two of them were old enough to write: Mayer Carl, usually known as Charles, and later nicknamed by his cousins 'Carlo Dolce', who was aged eleven and would one day marry Louisa, and Adolphe, or 'Dolly', who was eight. A third son, Wilhelm, known as Willy, was only two; a fourth, Alexander, was to follow.

In general, Mayer, still only thirteen, does not seem to have benefited much at all from his time with Dr Schwabe; on his return to the Stamford Hill schoolroom, according to Fritz Schlemmer, there was 'a good deal of ground to be made up', and now Mayer's curriculum had also to assist him in attaining a new and ambitious goal.

Mulling over the boy's future beyond university, Nathan and Hannah had decided that he should prepare to enter Parliament. To Schlemmer, this seemed quite normal: of any young Englishman from a rich family, he understood, the expectation was that he would one day obtain a seat in the House of Commons – that he would become 'a member of the Chapel of St Stephen and be able to put the letters MP after his name'. Although Jews were still barred from sitting in the Commons on account of the oath, to Fritz Schlemmer Mayer's position appeared no different to that of any other well-heeled young Englishman of the time.[6]

The parents had found cause for hope, no doubt, in the repeal of the Test and Corporation Acts in 1828 and in Catholic Emancipation in 1829 – and more recently from following the parliamentary debates on the Reform Bill. Lionel, certainly, looked forward to seeing a more equitable society established. 'I am very pleased to see that this reform bill has had a little effect upon some of the aristocracy,' he had written from Paris to his mother in April. 'It is a very good thing. Some of the great persons are really insupportable. The great difference that they always made between the different classes will soon be done away with, & the society in England will be more like that here, which is by far more agreeable.'[7]

Other members of the family were less enthusiastic. 'Uncle J begs me most particularly to write his opinion,' a dutiful Lionel explained to his parents. 'He thinks that if the reform bill passes, it will bring the same result as the revolution did here. The King wanted to take away from the people all their rights, which brought the revolution. In England, the King gives the people more than their rights, which will have as bad consequences as the contrary has had.'[8]

A particular concern was the destabilising effect reform might have on the markets – something that was troubling Salomon's wife Caroline when she wrote to Hannah from Suresnes in October: 'Paris is thank God now very quiet, & I hope it will remain so for a long while, and that your reform [bill] will not occasion new changements in the Politick affairs, and make a great variation in the funds . . .'[9]

Chilly hoped simply to see things settled, fearful of where they might otherwise end. 'It appears that in London nothing is spoken of but the grand question of reform,' she wrote to Hannah in December. 'I wish to heaven it were all amicably settled & arranged. From what I hear the country appears to me in a very unsettled state. The late disturbances in France are a bad example. They show that the strength of numbers decides everything. The mob ought never to get the upper hand . . .'[10]

Against this background, and with a future in Parliament to prepare for, Mayer's curriculum now naturally enough incorporated the study of politics – mostly European, since Fritz Schlemmer, as he confessed, knew little of English politics – and of political economy, through the pages of McCulloch's *Principles of Political Economy*. There was also a good deal of history, English and European, 'from the best sources' – Nathan's library shelves were well stocked – and it was proposed that Mayer would go on to study all these subjects in greater depth in Germany.

In the late autumn of 1831, however, Mayer was eager to see something more of his own country and so in November, having been laid up at home for some weeks after injuring his leg in a fall, he was given time off from the schoolroom to make a short excursion with his tutor.[11] From Frankfurt, relieved to learn that 'poor Mayer is quite recovered from his accident', Charlotte wrote to Hannah in early December: 'He must be delighted to have an opportunity of visiting some parts of England, as it is a journey for which he had always expressed so ardent a desire. I don't however think it very probable that I shall receive a description of his tour from his pen [;] this would almost be expecting too much.'[12]

As testament to Mayer's English journey, and as if to confirm his sister's poor opinion of his letter-writing habits, there is but a single first sheet, ending in mid-sentence, of a neatly written letter – lines have been ruled on to the writing paper with a pencil – dated 28 November, that Mayer sent to his 'dear Papa' from Manchester:

'I promised yesterday to write today otherwise I should not do so as I am very tired having seen the spinning machines of Mr Murray & Mr Poolay [Pooley], to which Mr Souchet [Souchay] took us, they were both very polite to us and shewed us all the machinery which is very curious & said they knew you very well when you were here. When we went to Schunk, Mylius et Co. this morning we found your letter of the 24th inst, for which I am very much obliged to you, & called upon Collin & Dufay as you told us. We are going to morrow to Mr Heywood & Lloyd. Mr Schunk took us to the Change & when he had inscribed our names, as it is usual there, a great many people asked us how you were & whether you would not take once a trip to Manchester. Mr Barnes asked if we would one morning go & see his spinning machines [.] He told us all about your old housekeeper & said that she had been dead some time. We also went to your old house at Mosely [sic] Street. Mr Souchay has been very polite to us & asked us to his house whither we are going to night. We stayed at the Bridgewater Arms where you used to take tea & muffins & I believe the people who kept it then have been dead sometime, & the hotel is now kept up in a different place. I hope you will not expect us back quite so soon, as there are many things to see here & in Liverpool. Every person says that the town has very much changed since you were here; there is a new change & I believe Adams-court has been taken down. I will now my dear Papa conclude you have heard . . .'[13]

Aside from the fact of Mayer being Nathan's son, it is possible that Mr Souchay's politeness was due in part to the presence of the tutor. Manchester had continued to attract German merchants (there were at least forty-six there by 1825) and Fritz Schlemmer's Schunk cousins were related to a family named Souchay in Düsseldorf. When Felix Mendelssohn paid a short visit to Manchester in 1847, he did so as the guest of Charles Souchay, partner in business with Martin Schunk, a longstanding and prominent member of Manchester's German merchant community.[14] Mayer was entirely right about the Bridgewater Arms: it was now situated on the corner of Mosley Street and Market Street.

As they thundered by the Bald-Faced Stag at Finchley in the Manchester Mail, Mayer and his tutor might, if sufficiently sharp-eyed, have glimpsed the name of the brewers 'Combe, Delafield & Co.' painted on a board on the front of the inn.[15]

Besides running his Wood Yard brewery, off Long Acre, Harvey Christian Combe (brother-in-law to Joseph Delafield) had served as Lord Mayor of London, and as MP for the City of London from 1776 to 1817, the year before his death. His eldest son, another Harvey, continued with the brewery, and was also for more than twenty years Master of the Old Berkeley foxhounds, which he owned.

For a time, Harvey Combe ran the Old Berkeley (named for the fifth Earl of Berkeley, who had earlier hunted the country) with the help of Stewart Marjoribanks, MP for Hythe in Kent from 1820 to 1847. Stewart, whose parliamentary seat Mayer would one day hold, was the third of five brothers from Berwickshire.[16]

John Marjoribanks, the eldest, was MP for Bute, then Berwickshire, and partner in an Edinburgh bank; as Provost of Edinburgh, he was created a Baronet. The second brother, Campbell, was a director, and twice chairman, of the East India Company. The fourth, Edward, was a partner of Coutts from 1796 until his death, aged ninety-two, in 1868. The fifth, James, joined the Bengal Civil Service.

It seems likely that Nathan would at some stage have encountered the elder Harvey Combe in the City, and his sons certainly became acquainted with the younger Combe; in the 1830s they hunted with his Old Berkeley pack in south Bucks – as did Jane Austen's nephew and biographer, Edward Austen Leigh.[17]

As to the Marjoribanks family, Nathan knew Coutts and its partners well – Sir Coutts Trotter had called on Hannah in Brussels; the Duchess of St Albans owned the largest share in the business – and his links with the East India Company went back to the Napoleonic era. Campbell Marjoribanks was perhaps one of those directors of the Company whom Prince Pückler-Muskau found dining at Stamford Hill. Moreover, Sir John Marjoribanks' youngest son David, a partner in the firm of City stockbrokers Marjoribanks, Capel & Co., had from 1815 worked with Nathan – 'had been in the thick of every thing at that time, with my great & ever trusted Friend, your most excellent and agreeable Father', as he wrote to Lionel more than half a century later – and became a firm friend to Lionel, Anthony and Nat.[18]

After his marriage, in 1834, to an heiress in Berwickshire, David was to change his surname to Robertson, but it was still as Marjoribanks that, a few months after Mayer's visit to Manchester, he wrote the following amiable letter to Nat:

Dulwich, Tuesday morning

My dear Rothschild,

Here is a fine fresh morning & I shall leave other matters, including the Funded Debt of England, in the safe custody of yourself & my friend Mr Anthony & be off to Epsom.

I shall go again tomorrow & if you or you & your Brother Anthony have also a mind to have a day's fun, if you will come down here to Breakfast (this place being in the direct line to Epsom) I can mount one or both of you. You could leave your jig [*sic*] here that you come down in, to go back at night, or I shall be very glad to see you here all night. If you like to try your new Dover purchase you can send it down here tonight & one of you ride it over tomorrow.

There will be some very pretty Racing tomorrow, & a good long ride does a man a great deal of good.

At any rate on Thursday next, unless I hear from you to the contrary, my Brown Mare shall be at your service, & at the back of the great Stand for you at 1 o'clock, but come tomorrow, you will like it,

Ever your &c
D Marjoribanks[19]

David Majorbanks lived at Knight's Hill Cottage, Dulwich, once the residence of Lord Thurlow, the famous Lord Chancellor. Like Stamford Hill, Dulwich was still in the country. Staying there in 1827, John Lawrence, a sporting writer, found that at Knight's Hill Cottage 'every thing shews health, and comfort, and convenience; where one might fancy oneself a hundred or two of miles from London . . . Mr M., with plenty of garden ground for useful and ornamental purposes, has forty or fifty acres of excellent meadow-land for horses or sheep. The air is soft and salubrious, and the views cheerful and pleasant . . . Knight's Hill has plenty of yard room, stabling, and sheds, with good water near at hand, and its proprietor seems to enter into the spirit of the whole with the energy of a true lover of the horse . . .'[20]

Lawrence had gone to inspect Marjoribanks' stallion Richard, to whose portrait the equestrian artist Abraham Cooper (examples of whose work Mayer was later to own) was putting the finishing touches when Lawrence arrived. The horse, Lawrence found, was 'a stout and true runner, honest, and of excellent temper . . . [he] has been very successful this season, and the balance of his account of profit and loss stands boldly on the right side.

Exclusive of his bred stock, I apprehend that Surrey, and Kent, and Middlesex will anon have to thank Richard for some capital hunting, hackney, and coaching stock.'

The era in which Lawrence was writing – the forty years following the Battle of Waterloo – was one of unprecedented interest in all matters connected with the horse. 'One of its most distinctive features,' according to one authority of the period, 'was the cult of the horse which never before or since has played so great a part in the lives of Englishmen of every class, and of which Charles James Apperley, known to fame as Nimrod, and Robert Smith Surtees were the chief chroniclers.' Few were unaffected, and to men such as David Marjoribanks and the Rothschild brothers the close proximity of the country to London offered no end of opportunities for equestrian pursuits of all kinds.[21]

One thing that stuck in Fritz Schlemmer's mind about his first day at Stamford Hill was how Nat had been quick to point out that he and his brothers had learned to ride by foxhunting, not by attending a riding school. In 1834, after meeting Anthony at Ham House, Fowell Buxton reported him to be 'a mighty hunter; and his father lets him buy any horses he likes. He lately applied to the emperor of Morocco, for a first-rate Arab horse. The emperor sent him a magnificent one, but he died as he landed in England. The poor youth said very feelingly "that was the greatest misfortune he ever had suffered"; and I felt strong sympathy with him.'[22] Anthony could hardly have found a more sympathetic ear. 'No Arab ever took a greater delight in horses than Mr Buxton,' Fowell's son Charles remembered. 'He was considered a very good judge, and never hesitated to give any price, in order to render his stud more complete.'[23]

A few months after Anthony had been bemoaning his misfortune over the Arab to Fowell Buxton, Nat commissioned a clerk of his uncle Salomon's in Vienna to find him a good mount. 'My dear Baron!' the man replied, 'I had the pleasure to receive your few lines of 10 inst [May] & must infinitely regret not to have found before now the opportunity of executing your commission. There is not one horse in this moment nor here nor in Hungaria that could satisfy you, but I trust I will get one in a few weeks time, having given my orders to the director of Count Hunyady's studs – the best of the country & as soon as I get the answer, I'll have the pleasure to forward it to you.' (Count Hunyady was a son-in-law of Prince Liechtenstein and a well-known figure at the gaming tables in Paris.)[24]

The life led during the hunting season by one of the Rothschilds' neighbours, and reported by Nimrod after a visit to Surrey in 1823, provides a good illustration of the possibilities that were open to residents of London and the suburbs during the winter in the pre-railway era:

> There is one member of the Surrey Hunt who deserves a place here, as a character which all true sportsmen must admire; and that is Mr Hobson . . . He hunts with three packs of hounds, and wears 'the livery' of each, never missing a day . . . His house is situated at Stamford Hill, five miles north of London . . . whither he never fails to return every night, after hunting, *over London-bridge*, though certain to be in Surrey again the next morning, if there is any hunting to be had. He is a very heavy man, and past the prime of life but he is said to have been at the first turning out of a deer before Lord Derby's [stag] hounds, twenty-seven years ago. His horses lie at Croydon . . . Mr Hobson always comes in his carriage to Croydon, where he generally dines after the sport of the day, and then gets into it again, ready dressed for the drawing-room . . .[25]

More than a decade later, Hobson, aged eighty, was 'still at his post' with the Old Surrey.[26]

Parts of the Old Berkeley country hunted by Harvey Combe were also within easy reach, but the country was so vast that a resident of Stamford Hill who wished to return home in the evening would have had to pick his days with care, and meets were seldom advertised. The whole line of the hunt's country extended from London to Cirencester; there were kennels at Rickmansworth in Hertfordshire, Wheatley in Oxfordshire, Kingston Bagpuize in Berkshire, Cricklade in Wiltshire and Lechlade in Gloucestershire. The nearest 'draw' to London was Scratch Wood, Edgware Bury. Hunting four days a week, with the odd bye day, Master, men, hounds and horses were either hunting or travelling every day of the week.[27]

David Marjoribanks' proposal to Nat and Anthony seems humble by comparison; and the brothers were no doubt keen to fall in with it. Dulwich and Epsom were within easy reach, and thoughts of racing, as well as hunting, were beginning to occupy their minds – first planted there, perhaps, by a mother who had derived such pleasure from attending the races at Egham in 1813–14. During a visit to Paris in December 1831, Nat wrote to Anthony at New Court: 'I am very glad that you had such a good day's hunting & that Frank carried you well. You may buy Martin's little horse if you get him cheap & can chase him away with President . . .'[28]

Frank was a dependable hunter in the stables at Stamford Hill; President was a bay colt that Lionel had bought from Joseph Anderson, the pukka

Piccadilly horse dealer with whom, it was said, 'there is none of that nau-
seous nonsense which assails the ear on your first *entrée* into other yards, but
a plain upright manner of dealing. His horses are of the very *best stamp*, and
though his prices may be high, yet have you the satisfaction of knowing . . .
that the object of your purchase is a sound horse.' On his twenty-first birthday in November 1829, Lionel had received from his father (as each of his
brothers was to receive on the same occasion) a present of £25,000.[29]

As 'Mr Rothschild', Lionel entered President in the St Albans steeplechase of 8 March 1830, an occasion arranged by the trainer Tommy
Coleman and the first organised event of its kind to be held in England.
The idea for the race had arisen in conversation among some Guards officers at the Turf Hotel, St Albans, which Coleman built and ran – and
where you could not only stay, but keep your horses in training, too.
Captain Becher, after whom Becher's Brook in the Grand National course
was to be named, made the Turf Hotel his headquarters. Prince Esterhazy,
the Austrian ambassador, was one of several owners who kept their racehorses at Coleman's training stables there.[30]

Of the fifteen horses that took part in the steeplechase in 1830, eight
were ridden by their owners, though President was ridden for Lionel by
the Waterloo veteran Captain Seymour Blane, an officer in the Third
Regiment of Foot Guards. The race was won by a Captain Macdowall, on
a horse called Wonder. President was not placed, though the name
Rothschild did enter the list of winners elsewhere that year – in Schleswig-
Holstein, whose princely family were frequent guests of Lionel's family in
Frankfurt. At the Augustenburg races in September, the Duke of
Schleswig-Holstein's eight-year-old dark bay mare Madame Rothschild,
ridden by the Duke's son Prince Frederick, won the Christian-August
Cup. 'At the last turn Madame Rothschild let out, passed the whole and
came in by a length and a half.'[31]

When it came to hunting, unlike their southward-looking neighbour
Mr Hobson, the Rothschild brothers – to begin with – favoured the much
closer country to the north of Stamford Hill. As the connection with St
Albans might suggest, they rode to hounds in Hertfordshire, though the
hunt they favoured was the Puckeridge, to the east of the county, rather
than the Hertfordshire Hunt Club to the west.

Hertfordshire was not the best hunting country; indeed, in 1827 it was
described as possibly 'one of the worst hunting countries in England; it is
almost entirely under the plough, and intersected with numerous lanes'.
But it was convenient for Lionel and his brothers and in Hertfordshire they
could enjoy their sport among friends. Fowell Buxton's uncle Sampson

Hanbury, a Quaker brewer, was Master of the Puckeridge from 1799 to 1832; and Sam Gurney's cousin Dick Gurney (who was Sampson Hanbury's uncle as well as his brother-in-law) was an enthusiastic Puckeridge supporter. So, too, was Seymour Blane.[32]

Dick Gurney was 'one of the best known men of the shires', but he used to say that a fourteen-mile run with the Puckeridge was the best run he had ever seen. He weighed nineteen stone (he owned to sixteen), and was described by Whyte-Melville as 'one of the heaviest men I ever saw ride perfectly straight to hounds'.[33]

The man who looked after Gurney's half-dozen hunters and rode second horse for him was Tom Rance, another well-known figure in the hunting world of that era. In 1830, on leaving Gurney's service, Rance served for a time as Lionel's pad-groom, his duties being to attend his master in the field, carry his capacious sandwich case and pick him up when he fell.[34]

Of Sampson Hanbury (who weighed seventeen stone) R. S. Surtees wrote: 'The Squire himself would make an admirable subject for the pen of an Addison or Washington Irving. His low-crowned hat, square-cut coat, flapped waistcoat, big boots and breeches, good-natured smile, a word for everybody, added to his slow and cautious style of riding, and the rat-tailed brown horse that walked in and out of his fences, presented the beau ideal of an old English country gentleman.'[35]

Before the mid-1820s, the hunt – whose kennel Hanbury established at the village of Puckeridge – had been known officially as 'The Hertfordshire', but unofficially as 'Mr Calvert's', having begun, and for many years continued, as a private pack belonging to the Calvert family, whose business was also brewing. Until 1826, Sampson Hanbury was Joint Master of the hunt with John and Nicolson Calvert, and a young cousin of theirs, Harry Calvert, became a friend of the Rothschild brothers.[36]

Harry was the only son of General Sir Harry Calvert, Bt, who at the time of Waterloo was Colonel of the 14th Foot – then known, after a popular malt beverage, as 'Calvert's Entire' (and later, when reduced in size, as 'Calvert's all Butt'). Young Harry succeeded in the baronetcy on his father's death in 1826, and the next year, on the death of a cousin, inherited the ancient Verney estates in Buckinghamshire. He assumed the surname of Verney and as Sir Harry Verney, Bt, was later to encourage the Rothschilds, Mayer in particular, to become landowners in the same county.[37]

Another Hertfordshire connection was the Smith family, children and grandchildren of the banker Abel Smith. It was Abel Smith's sixth son

John, banker and parliamentary supporter of Lord John Russell in the struggle to repeal the Test and Corporation Acts, who had escorted Henry Thornton, in desperate need of gold sovereigns, to see Nathan in 1825.

Abel Smith's fourth son Samuel acquired properties in Puckeridge country, including Sacombe Park, near Ware, which in 1834 passed to his younger son; his elder son married Harry Verney's sister Frances. Abel Smith's third son Robert, who in the 1790s was created a peer as Lord Carrington (and whose eldest son changed his surname from Smith to Carington), acquired large estates in Buckinghamshire.

John Smith's son, John Abel Smith (Henry Thornton's Cambridge contemporary), became a staunch friend of Lionel's; he was to help Lionel in the search for a country property, and used to invite him to Sacombe to shoot. Later, John Abel Smith encouraged Lionel to embark on a political career and, with Lord John Russell, became one of his two most stalwart supporters.[38]

In the age of the horse cult, there was a craze for shooting, too. Lionel and his brothers had shot since their boyhood days with Mr Moser in Frankfurt; Nathan himself occasionally went out with them. The sport was a staple pastime for anyone who had access to land over which to shoot. Preparing to spend a period in the country with her husband, Lady Granville once asked: 'What may Granville shoot – birds, roebucks, neighbours? He must have something to kill.'[39]

Nathan had only a few acres at Stamford Hill; but his friends asked the boys to shoot with them. One such was Lewis Lowdham, the lawyer in the Lord Chancellor's office with whom Nathan dealt over presenting a petition to Parliament for Jewish rights in 1829. 'I shall be kept here by the Special Commission all the Week,' Lowdham wrote to Nathan from Nottingham in 1832. 'My best regards to Mrs Rothschild & *the young Lads*. Tell them I have had no shooting. I hear of nothing but burnings & hanging, so that it wd. not be very pleasant to them, otherwise I shld. be glad to see them.'[40]

In 1834, Nat and Anthony were invited by another of Nathan's friends, Matthias Prime Lucas, alderman and former Lord Mayor of London, to shoot with him at Wateringbury Place, near Maidstone, in Kent. A letter that Nat received from Lucas gives an idea of how such an expedition was to be accomplished, and of the arrangements that it entailed.[41]

'As you have promised me the pleasure of yr compy to take a day or two of Shooting on Monday and Tuesday,' Lucas wrote, 'I write merely to say that we shall expect you and your Brother or friend on Sunday at Dinner at *five*. We have no Coaches pass our Village . . . either to or from London on Sunday, but every other day we have a most excellent Coach which passes our House at hf past 8 every morning [and] gets to the George Inn Boro [Borough] at 12 – leaves the Belle Savauge [Sauvage] Ludgate Hill at ¼ past one, the Geo Inn Boro at hf past one precisely and passes our House at hf past five. I mention this in case you would like to come to morrow – or have Dogs [,] Guns [,] or any thing to send by or [*sic*] servants. We shall be as happy to receive you at Dinner tomorrow as on Sunday and then shall [have] Stables for yr Horses & a Bed for yr Servant all ready – and I will do all I can to insure you two or three days good Sport . . . Pray offer my best regards to my kind and most excellent Friend yr good Father.'

Sport, of course, could combine usefully with other concerns. 'I am going to give a letter of introduction to Count [Anatole] Demidoff,' Lionel wrote to Nathan from Paris in September 1830. 'He leaves here for London tomorrow. He is a very nice young [man], his name is of course known to you; he has at least £60/m [£60,000] a year. Raikes & Co. do his business. I spoke to him about giving us a share, and with a little persuasion I am sure he would do it. He is very fond of Horses & shooting. Anthony can therefore amuse him.'[42]

On a shoot or at the races – perhaps less so in the hunting field – there was always the chance, given the right company, of hearing something useful. James was in no doubt of this in the uncertain period that followed the 1830 revolution in France. 'In the Evening we saw one of the Ministers who was in excellent spirits & was not in the least anxious about England,' Lionel wrote to assure his father in September 1831. 'You can see that they are not very anxious for to day all the Ministers but one are out of town for pleasure, a thing they have not done for a very long time, & the one that is here, is obliged to be, to attend to the Races which take place today. Most of the Ministers are gone out shooting & Uncle James with them, as he hopes to find out plenty of good news to write to you & if any thing particular will send you a courier tonight.'[43]

A year later, Lionel was doing the same as James. 'I had not the pleasure of writing to you yesterday,' he explained to his parents, 'as I accompanied Montalivet & Appony out shooting which in any other time than the present would be very amusing, but now one goes with these great personages to hear what is going on more than for the sake of amusement.' Charles-Camille Bachasson de Montalivet was Louis Philippe's Minister of the Interior; Count Antoine Apponyi was the Austrian ambassador in Paris.[44]

For Anthony and for Nat, furthermore, a combination of sporting and business connections brought a new dimension to their social life in

London: in June 1832 they were both elected members of the Garrick Club, which had been founded the year before in premises until then in use as Probatt's Family Hotel, at 35 King Street, Covent Garden. Proposed by the actor Tyrone Power (great-grandfather of the film actor), Nat was seconded by two stockbrokers, David Marjoribanks' partner, James Capel, and John Durrant, and by Lewis Lowdham. Anthony was proposed by Durrant and seconded by the others. The club's patron was the Duke of Sussex, and its early membership included two future prime ministers, William Lamb (later Lord Melbourne) and Lord John Russell, as well as the Duke of Devonshire.[45]

In late 1832, with Lionel still in Paris and Anthony back in Frankfurt, Nat was working with Nathan at New Court. David Marjoribanks, staying in Leicestershire at Melton Mowbray, the 'headquarters' of foxhunting, now invited Nat to go down by the Leeds Mail to join him for a few days. 'You really must come down here,' he urged his friend. 'If you wish to spend a week or two, that will be equal to months of ordinary Sport & real enjoyment to a man who is fond of Hunting & Riding. It is the quietest, most comfortable Place away from Home that ever I lived at & about the cheapest.'[46]

Marjoribanks obviously did not belong to the wild set of upper-class hooligans led by Lord Waterford who once daubed the walls of Melton, as well as the town's nightwatchmen, with red paint – so inspiring the phrase 'to paint the town red'. 'There are some young chaps, but a very few,' Marjoribanks explained, 'who lead on in other Places a hard life of drinking but those you never see & have nothing to do with. They live in private houses & lodgings. I find by far the pleasantest is to live quietly at the George Inn, just like a private House. You go away at 8 or 9 o'clock in the morning & come home at 6 or 8 in the evening. You see the fellows out Hunting & talk as much to them as you like, but it is better to live quiet & alone, as it avoids drinking, & you cannot hunt every day & drink. You fatten & improve in Health & Condition upon the every day Hunting, but the drinking a man is not up to who rides from 30 to 70 miles a day sometimes.'[47]

Barring accidents, Nat would certainly have enjoyed himself. At Melton there were three great packs of foxhounds on the doorstep – the Quorn, the Cottesmore and the Belvoir – offering the best hunting six days a week. 'We have had some most splendid Sport,' Marjoribanks went on. 'I have been out these last 6 days & have neither had a Fall or lamed a Horse . . . My very kindest regards to your Father & tell him that I will forfeit all the good opinion he may have of me (if he has any) if he lets you come here, if it does not fully bear out the character I have given it, the best place by far you can come to from home . . . Tell [George] Samuel he ought to come.'

Whether or not Nat went to Leicestershire on that occasion is uncertain, but it seems as if one or more of the Rothschild brothers had done so by the opening of the next season. Cottesmore country extends into Lincolnshire, and in mid-October 1833, as the start of foxhunting in November approached, Fritz Schlemmer pictured Anthony getting the dependable hunter Frank fit so as to be 'the best in Lincolnshire and Leicestershire'.[48]

Before that, though, in October 1832, Nat had begun to experiment with staghounds. 'Many thanks for your kind letter,' Anthony wrote to him from Frankfurt, 'which I should have answered before but really I have nothing in the least new worth writing to you. You will have perceived from my letters that I have arrived at this horrid place . . . I generally pass my time [thus:] at 7 o'clock I get up, go out shooting & remain till 3 o'clock when I come home to dinner & from then on play whist till 10 & then I go to bed. Till now I have not seen any girls here & I want something so bad that I do not know what to do . . . It is such a horrid place, nothing to be done . . .

'I was glad to hear that you got the hart. Why did you not go out with the Puckeridge [?] . . . How are all the horses [?] You will be able to amuse yourself a little now [,] particularly as Lionel intends passing some time with you. I almost envy you & only wish that I could have a few good days hunting . . . If Lionel should not be gone send my fur coat . . . & you may also order a new brown hunting coat, the same as I had when I left. Stulz knows . . . Puckeridge buttons if they have any.'[49]

Nimrod, snobbish and clothes-conscious, would definitely have approved of Anthony's – and Nat's – choice of tailor, Stultz & Housley, of Clifford Street, Mayfair. John Stultz had been Beau Brummell's favourite tailor; and vital elements in Nimrod's *beau idéal* of a foxhunting man, 'turned out of the hands of his valet', were the 'exact Stultz-like fit of his coat' and 'his superlatively well-cleaned leather breeches and boots'.[50]

A few days later, this time writing to Lionel, Anthony thought of one or two more things he would like made for him, by Stultz and also by the well-known makers of trousers and breeches, E. W. Anderson, of South Audley Street, of which firm Lionel was also a client.[51] 'I write to Nat to send me my fur coats,' Anthony wrote. 'Will you be so good as to order a new black frock coat of Stulz, and two pairs of black trousers of Anderson

[?] If you have room will you be so good as to bring them with [you] to Paris & send them on to me by Charlotte [?] – one pair of trousers for shoes & the other pair for boots – & tell Nat that I should be much obliged if he would send me my gun as soon as possible. He could send it by the Rotterdam Steamboat to be forwarded to me . . .'[52]

One possible reason for Nat's desertion of the Puckeridge was that Sampson Hanbury's successor as Master, Lord Petre, and his huntsman Sam Hort, were failing to provide the kind of sport – the good long points – that Puckeridge supporters expected. The next season, after all, Anthony himself would be preparing Frank for the shires, apparently with no second thought of the Puckeridge. Conceivably, Lord Petre invited Nat to spend a day with the pack of staghounds that he kept in Essex.[53]

Whatever the reason for Nat's experiment, hunting with staghounds, though frowned upon by the purists, had a twofold advantage over fox-hunting. First, there was no risk of failing to put up the quarry – no risk of a blank day – as the captive deer, shorn of antlers in the case of a stag, was turned out of a cart ('enlarged') at the start of proceedings, and, all being well, recaptured, with a noose or net, at the end and returned to its paddock to run another day. Secondly, an hour or two at least of good, fast riding was almost guaranteed.

It was a combination that appealed strongly to men whose work in the City allowed them only the odd day's sport – a day they did not care to waste in hanging around the covert side. As Nat once said in relation to racing: 'It's good fun when one wins but something like a blank day with the fox hounds when one loses.'[54]

While one sporting writer of the 1830s scorned 'the pursuit of an horn-less wretch turned out of a cart, like a tame pigeon let loose from a trap', staghunting was not for the faint-hearted; the pace could be punishing, the points excessively long. As Philipp von Neumann, the Austrian diplomat, found in 1822, it was 'a very violent exercise and even a dangerous one'. One of the fifth Earl of Berkeley's sons, Grantley, kept a pack of staghounds at Cranford House, to the west of London beyond Isleworth, and when he turned a stag out on Hillingdon Heath, near Uxbridge, in March 1825, the animal was finally taken only after a run of four hours and twenty minutes. 'Out of about two hundred horsemen that started with the deer,' it was reported, 'only six were up when taken . . . We add with regret that four horses died, one of which was Mr Berkeley's famous horse Brutus.'[55]

There were hazards, too, in hunting a stag on the outskirts of London, as Grantley Berkeley – whose brother Augustus took part in the St Albans steeplechase of 1830 – makes clear in his *Reminiscences of a Huntsman*. 'No man went harder than the late Lord Alvanley,' he recalled, 'and no man ever caught more falls . . . One day he had been hunting with me, and we ran over an unfortunate line of country, the stag leaving the legitimate scene of our sports, and, setting his head for Hounslow, Isleworth, Twickenham, and Brentford. Lord Alvanley left us before I had taken the deer, in good time to join his friends in the bay window at White's. They asked him, "What sport?" and he replied, "Devilish good run; but the asparagus beds went awfully heavy, and the glass all through was up to one's hocks . . . They say that garden stuff is ris [sic] since they saw us among 'em."'

On another occasion described by Grantley Berkeley, the stag actually ran into the London streets. He and his brother Moreton 'had stopped the hounds outside the Regent's Park, all but two couple, who went at the flanks of the deer pell-mell into the town . . . Women screamed, children cried, men shouted, and horses shied, as the unwonted animal came down the pavement or swerved from the passengers across the streets.' The chase finally came to an end near Russell Square in Bloomsbury, with the stag 'backing his haunches against the street door' of a house in Montague Street, where he was at last recaptured.[56]

In 1832, Nat had within easy reach of London a choice of several packs of staghounds with which to hunt. Grantley Berkeley had in 1829 sold his hounds to Augustus Sullivan, who built kennels for them at Great Hampden, near Missenden, in Buckinghamshire, hunting them from there three times a week, sometimes across the Vale of Aylesbury. The Derby Hounds, hunting across Surrey and Kent, were still at Croydon; formerly the Earl of Derby's, they were now managed as a subscription pack by Richard Tattersall.[57]

As C. J. Apperley, Nimrod once wrote to Lionel (who read his articles about hunting and had written to him with a hunting enquiry) that although he had 'certainly always placed foxhunting first on our list of sports', in Lord Derby's time he had nevertheless seen 'some excellent runs with the *stag*, and I admit there are many counties in England – Surrey for one – which are much better adapted to staghounds than to fox hunting'.[58]

In Essex, Lord Petre had his staghounds. At West Drayton, Hubert de Burgh kept a pack, which from time to time would visit the Vale of Aylesbury, as did the Royal Buckhounds, from Ascot.[59]

Until 1830, the Mastership of the Buckhounds was for seven years held by the Duke of Wellington's elder brother Lord Maryborough, whose carriage was later seen at Nathan's funeral. The Earl of Chesterfield succeeded him as Master. The Buckhounds' huntsman was Charles Davis, who in

1824 had taken over the post from his father-in-law George Sharpe – who had previously been Sampson Hanbury's huntsman in Hertfordshire. In 1832–3, the Buckhounds had a superb season, including a 'most extraordinary and nearly unprecedented run with the celebrated Ripley deer'.[60]

The astonishing run was described by an eyewitness: 'Starting from Iver Heath, he took us by Denham, Harefield, Pinner, and Edgware, towards Barnet; and, thence bending to the left, went *eight miles below St Albans*, where hounds and horses *being completely done*, we were obliged to leave the deer and take up our quarters for the night. It was not until five days afterwards that the stag was retaken. I should add, that the distance covered in the run was estimated at the lowest computation at *forty miles!*'[61]

In the early 1840s Nat – and his brothers – were certainly hunting with the Buckhounds, but one is left guessing as to which pack, or packs, of staghounds Nat gave his support in the 1832–3 season, which was to be his last in England for two years. There is, though, one reference in 1832 to a horse of Nat's receiving treatment, under the eye of a groom, 'in a good box in Croydon', which would seem to make the Derby Hounds – Philipp von Neumann's choice a decade earlier – a likely contender.[62]

At all events, Nat's new hunting exploits were to earn him the nickname 'Stag', and would spark off a long-lasting enthusiasm for staghunting in his family.

7

A Snuffbox from the Sultan

D URING NAT'S DISMAL time in Naples in the spring of 1831, one
bright spot had been provided by the arrival of two young
Englishmen – 'Cambridge men', though their names are not recorded –
who sailed in to Naples in their yacht. Nat got to know them, paid several
visits to the yacht – described by Fritz Schlemmer as a 'little gem', 'organised scientifically and with the best possible taste' – and he went sailing
with them in the Bay. It transpired that the two men were on their way to
Constantinople, but that while they knew everything they needed to know
about navigation and the stars, they knew nothing of Byzantine history.
Schlemmer did what he could to fill them in, and the pair then sailed away.
No more is heard of them; but it may be that the talk of Constantinople
planted the seed of an idea in Nat's mind.[1]

Two years later, in early April 1833, another English acquaintance of
Nat's from Naples, John Auldjo, having completed the work for his
meticulous *Sketches of Vesuvius*, set sail from Naples in the British naval
vessel *Actaeon*, also bound for Constantinople. On 11 April, *Actaeon*
anchored off Nauplia, which was then serving as the capital of Greece, the
new state, supported by Britain, France and Russia, which following the
destruction of the Turkish fleet at Navarino in 1827 had gained independence from Ottoman rule. When Moses Montefiore arrived in Naples on
his way back from the Holy Land, via Malta, in early 1828, he was carrying despatches from Admiral Sir Edward Codrington, the British
commander at Navarino, for Lord Burghersh, the British Minister in
Florence. In 1829, Codrington dined with Nathan and Hannah in London,
where it is quite possible that Nat met him.[2]

Another passenger in *Actaeon* was Lord Ponsonby, until recently Britain's
envoy in Naples and now en route to take up his new duties as ambassador
to the Porte. In late April, nearing her destination, *Actaeon* was obliged to
lie at anchor for several days in the Dardanelles, awaiting a southerly wind
to carry her on across the Sea of Marmara and up to Constantinople. On
1 May, she at last dropped anchor in the Bosphorus, opposite Therapia, the

village where the British and French embassies were then established. On 4 May, in the afternoon, 'the ambassador landed in state: the yards were manned, and the salute was fired'.[3]

As *Actaeon* was held up in the Dardanelles, Nat once more had his nose to the grindstone in the rue Laffitte. 'My dear Mamma,' he wrote in a post-script to his letter to New Court on 27 April 1833, 'I have nothing in the world to write about or else I should address a separate letter to you. As you are well aware, business & politics occupy us entirely. I have not been yet to the theatres or the opera or to a single party. Next week I hope to be a little gayer. Rossini has written a song for you & will send it in a day or two. You have no idea how he has changed. He is become quite thin & genteel & looks quite young.'[4]

By mid-May, as Hannah was making final preparations in London for a ball she was to give in honour of the Duc d'Orléans, heir to King Louis Philippe, Nat's life in Paris continued humdrum. 'The Exchange for the last two or three days has been exceedingly quiet, & scarcely any business,' he reported. 'Today the 3% [rentes] have fluctuated between 78.20 & 25 cents. Half of the brokers are walking about taking advantage of the fine weather – in fact it is almost too hot to occupy oneself in any manner whatsoever . . . I hope to hear to morrow that your ball was most brilliant & that every body was pleased . . . Here the weather is too hot for dancing.'[5]

Yet despite the slowness of business and the enervating heat, Nat's prospects had begun to look up. He was, he owned, 'much obliged' to his parents for their 'kind permission to go to Constantinople & shall please God avail myself of it. I think it would be a great pity if one of us were not to take advantage of such an opportunity to visit so interesting a country, particularly when such a considerable business renders it necessary that somebody must go. The Greek Loan affair will be brought into the Chamber for certain on Friday & will pass without difficulty, at least all the members assure us that such will be the case.'

Three days later, Nat and Lionel were both 'very much gratified in learning the success which attended your brilliant fête, & have no doubt that it was by far the best ball that has been given this season. Every body here asks us about it & all the friends of the Duke of Orleans are pleased that you should have shown him so much attention . . . We went last night to the opera . . . Lord & Lady Londonderry were in the next box to us [;] her ladyship has got rather stout & looks all the better for her visit to Paris.'[6]

Returning to his own concerns, Nat continued: 'I must now, dear Mamma, say a word about myself. In the first place I must thank you for your kind permission to go to Constantinople. I think it will be a very instructive and agreeable journey & at the same time I hope profitable. Of course it will not be possible for me to leave before the Greek affair has passed the Chamber here, and as it is likely that it will last a week or perhaps a fortnight before that happens, I intend setting off tomorrow night for London & hope to be with you please God on Tuesday night. I shall only be able to pass a few days with you however, as it is quite necessary that I must be in Paris to receive all the instructions about making the payment to the Turkish Government, as the company of bankers who have half share of the loan are likewise interested to the same amount in the payments.'

The Greek affair awaiting approval by the Chamber was the loan of 60 million francs – approximately £2.4 million – that Britain, France and Russia were to guarantee to the new government of Greece. When the Rothschilds' old client Prince Leopold of Saxe-Coburg had declined the Allies' offer of the Greek throne (he was to become King of the Belgians instead), the choice had fallen on Prince Otto of Bavaria, a younger son of King Ludwig I. Subsequently, the fifteen-year-old Otto had been proclaimed King of Greece in Nauplia in 1832, with a council of regency to govern on his behalf until he attained his majority in 1835. Of the loan – for which Nathan successfully contracted – £550,000 was to be paid to Turkey in compensation for ceding the large slice of territory that now constituted the kingdom of Greece.[7]

How it was, exactly, that Nat came to be offered the chance of travelling to Turkey to effect the payment is nowhere explained. Judging by the permission he was thankful to receive from his parents, it can hardly have been their idea. It rather sounds as if he simply volunteered.

The day after the Londonderrys were spotted by Nat at the theatre, they were guests at a 'grand dinner chiefly of English people' given by James and Betty at the rue Laffitte. Hannah had sent venison and pineapples from London; Nat counted twelve men at work in the kitchen beforehand. Lord Londonderry must have been interested to hear of Nat's mission. At an audience in Constantinople in 1840, in a preposterous address to the Sultan, he boasted that during thirty-five years' service to England he had fought 'always for legitimacy against revolutions and rebellious subjects' and that he had 'always deprecated the dismemberment of any part of a great empire'.[8]

He was less scrupulous when contemplating the dismemberment of a friend's household. On 26 May, Lionel reported to his mother: 'Ld. Londonderry was at Boulogne [a château James had bought at Boulogne-sur-Seine] yesterday, and was in raptures with everything. They dined some time ago with us in Paris and were so pleased that they sent the next day to the Cook and all his Aides and to the confectioner and offered to each £50 more a year. The next day when Ld. Londonderry knew that they were all out, he went quite alone, examined everything and offered the other man the same thing. It is very pleasant to have such friends.'[9] Before taking charge of the Rothschild kitchen in 1823, Antonin Carême had worked for Lord Londonderry when, as Lord Stewart, the latter was Ambassador in Vienna. Carême had finally retired in 1830, but it seems as if his replacement was continuing to maintain an enviably high standard of cuisine.[10]

By now Nat had returned to London for a few days – taking with him a selection of hats and dresses chosen by Lionel for their mother and sisters. But by 5 June he was back on French soil, writing a note from the Quillacq Hotel, Calais: 'We have just finished a very good dinner after having had a most excellent passage which only had the effect of giving us good appetites. The custom house people have behaved very well. I have got the carriage thro' without duty & every thing else in good order. Joseph is very pleased & only regrets Piccadilly for one thing, which is being deprived of the sight of the beautiful Miss Cresswell . . . Give my love to Billy & my charming sisters & Muffy & remember me to the Dr . . .'[11]

Joseph was Nat's manservant. When Lionel had been advising his mother about arrangements for Nat's and Fritz Schlemmer's return to London in 1831, he had said: 'About Joseph I will write to you after I have seen him. You know he is no great favorite of mine, but I think he would do better than Robert to look after Anth & Nat's things & Robert might go into the Stables. Whatever you wish I will attend, only be so good to let me know.' Nat, apparently, did not share Lionel's reservations about Joseph, though whether or not he took the man with him all the way to Turkey he does not say. Forty years later, though, he still had a manservant named Joseph.[12]

Having returned to Paris, on 9 June Nat had 'no news whatever except that the Greek loan guarantee passed the chamber of Peers yesterday with a good majority'. Ten days later, on the eve of his departure, Betty gave a small family dance at Boulogne. The property there, Lionel noted, was 'very much improved, the Gardens enlarged, Houses pulled down & built up again'.[13]

Unluckily for Nat, the first leg of his journey took him to Frankfurt, where arrangements connected with his forthcoming mission – in particular the selection of an experienced clerk to go with him – were in the hands of his uncles. There was, though, some compensation: he could stay with his sister Chilly and family in their new house. 'I only wish you were here my dear Mamma,' Nat wrote after a tour of inspection, 'to see how comfortably our good Chilly is established.' By now Chilly had two little daughters, Julie and Mathilde, though her first-born son, Mayer Anselm, had died.[14]

Business life in Frankfurt was slow. 'Here my dear Papa,' Nat reported at the end of June, 'business in stocks is exceedingly slack, only a few trans-actions in the course of the exchange & seldom fluctuations greater than one sixteenth occur . . .' Uncertainty over his travel plans acted as a further drag. 'Altho' Uncle Salomon arrived the day before yesterday & altho' we have had one conversation on the subject,' Nat went on, 'still we have not fixed upon the route which I shall be obliged to take. Probably it will be as I already have written, first to Greece, then to Constantinople & to leave that place so as to spend the winter at Petersburg. It is as yet doubtful whom I shall have for my companion . . . Probably in the course of the week the whole affair will be arranged . . .'[15]

Held up in Frankfurt for the best part of the next three weeks, Nat gave his parents a description of his uneventful routine. 'There is very little amusement now going on in Frankfort,' he wrote on 10 July. 'I pass all the day in the counting house, & in the evening go to the play, & afterwards play a rubber of whist. Charlotte [Chilly] has got a capital French cook & gives us famous good dinners. We dine at 2 & sup at 8 o'clock. This is a very good arrangement as the meals do not interfere with the evenings which one can pass in walking in the promenades if a stupid piece is given at the theatre. You see that one spends one's time in a very innocent manner in this good town. I know pretty well that I am getting famously tired of it & really for a single man I do not think there is a duller place in the world than Frankfort.'[16]

The days there – 'so very quiet & monotonous that a description of one's occupation would amount to nothing' – were briefly enlivened by a visit from Prince Esterhazy, who was on his way to England. 'He looks uncommonly well & asked particularly after you all,' Nat told his parents on 2 July. 'He seems very glad to return to London [;] he starts to morrow night. He dines to day at Uncle Anselm's with a grand party & to morrow quite alone with us at Charlotte's . . .' The dinner that Chilly gave for the Prince, said Nat afterwards, was 'really a feast for the greatest of epicures & friends of gastronomy'.[17]

On 17 July, after a few days away at Schwalbach, Nat confessed that he had 'never expected to remain so long at Frankfort but as the Greek busi-ness goes on so slowly I suppose another month or 6 weeks will elapse before my presence will be necessary in Greece. I do not know as yet who will accompany me . . .' Four days later, however, Lionel, in Paris, had learned that Nat was on his way to meet James and Betty in Switzerland, and that from there he was at last to proceed to Greece. 'As he has told every person that he is going there,' Lionel observed to Anthony, 'it would be foolish now not to go, although the payment to be made to Turkey is much less than first imagined.'[18]

A month later, wending his way south, Nat had reached Aix-en-Savoie. By nature easily discouraged, he was already dissatisfied with his lot, casting around, one senses, for someone else to blame. 'Oh dear Billy what a beastly place your Aix appears to be – such lots of dirt,' he wailed to Anthony. 'I have such a nasty room, I expect to be eaten up by the bugs & fleas, which you will allow is not a pleasant anticipation. I must put up with things as I find them. God knows I do not expect much pleasure from my journey. I must travel to Greece like a courier & when I am there I shall find any thing but sun. Pray dear Billy do not forget me & write very often & very long letters . . .'[19]

Six days later, he was still downcast when he wrote from Milan. 'I expected to have found some letters on my arrival here from you,' he wrote to his parents. 'I was disagreeably disappointed, as not a line have I received for some time from home.' It was as if he were reliving his spell in Naples over again. 'You may easily conceive,' he went on, 'that it is not very pleasant when one is quite alone to be left without a word to find one's way to so distant a country as Greece. However I do not attribute it to neglect, but imagine it is owing to your having addressed your epistles to some other town nearer the place whither I am bound.'[20]

One good thing, Nat conceded, was that he was not going to be alone for much longer. He was expecting the arrival in Milan the next day of the man who had at last been selected to accompany and to assist him on his mission. His uncles Anselm, Salomon and Charles had between them failed to choose a candidate from among at least three of their employees, in Frankfurt and Naples, whose names – Weisweiller, Goldschmidt and Fischer – had been canvassed for the role, and in the end it had been James who found the man. He had engaged a Genevoise named Metzger, whom, fortunately, Nat considered to be 'a clever man & perfectly fit for the situation which he is about to fulfil'.

While awaiting Metzger's arrival, Nat had 'made every possible enquiry as to the road I had better take. I find that I must proceed to Ancona, where once a month a steam boat goes to the Ionian Islands . . . I hope at the latest to be at Napoli in the course of ten days. You may depend upon it my dear Papa I shall lose no time & shall do all in my power to fulfil your wishes.' 'Napoli' was short for Napoli di Romania, the Italian name for Nauplia, capital of the new kingdom of Greece. On 11 September, a Rothschild correspondent in Ancona reported that Nat's steamer had arrived safely at Corfu, and that from there it would proceed to Zante – en route for the Greek capital.[21]

Arriving there in April, John Auldjo had observed a 'lofty sombre cliff, whence a chain of sloping rocks extend to the fortress above Nauplia, the castellated Palamide . . . At the base of the Palamide, rises a second hill, on which is built the town, extending down to the water's edge.' It was the strength of the fortress atop the Palamede (named for Nauplius' son Palamedes), along with the excellence of the harbour and the fact that there was already a town there – 'crazy enough, I allow,' declared another visitor, Adolphus Slade, 'but capable of improvement' – that had recommended Nauplia as a capital.[22]

Some improvements had been made to the town since the arrival of King Otto and the regency council. Auldjo found that 'many respectable houses have been recently erected, several good shops opened, and the streets are much cleaner than might be expected.' Slade, attached to a British naval squadron some months later, noted numerous 'cafés, billiard-rooms, raki shops and other resorts' and some 'tolerable shops' that displayed French and English wares, though 'the Greeks in general seemed more partial to the Turkish mode of arranging and selling'. Another English visitor considered that the 'appearance of the inhabitants, the bustle in the shops, and the general air of cleanliness about the town, made it appear the first and most flourishing city in Greece'.[23]

One drawback to Nauplia at that time was the number of Bavarian troops about the place, pending the organisation of a Greek national army. To Auldjo the Bavarians were 'mean-looking men', and their light blue uniform 'far from imposing'. An even greater drawback was the perpetual threat of malaria from nearby marshland – as Nat and his companion were to discover all too soon.[24]

Nat and Mr Metzger must have reached Nauplia at about the time that their arrival at Corfu was being reported by the correspondent in Ancona. Subsequently, by 19 September, Nat had made sufficient progress with his mission to despatch a courier to New Court 'with the permission of the Regency for Eichthal [a German banker involved in the concern] to deliver to you without delay the bonds of the Greek Loan . . . I hope you will be satisfied that I have exerted myself to my utmost to bring this affair to a happy conclusion.'[25]

With respect to Turkey, matters were progressing smoothly, too. 'As regards the payment of 18 millions of Piastres to be effected for account of the Greek Government to the Turks,' Nat continued, 'I am happy to say I have obtained permission to make the payment & shall in consequence go to Constantinople in about a fortnight. I should probably have proceeded thither sooner, but the Regency intends sending a minister to the Ottoman Court by that time, & wishing him to meet with a good reception they requested [me] to put off my departure for a few days & to sail in the same ship as his Excellency. I have not been able to come to an arrangement as to how they are to be debited for the payment . . .'

On 26 September, having by now been in Nauplia for more than a fortnight, Nat wrote a long letter home to his mother. He was without a companion once more, had received no word from England for five weeks, and was getting anxious. He hoped, he said, that by the next steamer, which was due in a few days' time, he would receive some news. 'In my former letters,' he went on, 'I told you how well I have been received at Napoli. Every body is as polite and kind as possible to me. All the ambassadors, the regency & even the Greek ministers show me more attention than if I were, God knows what. This tends very much to make my sejour at this place pleasant, & really although I am quite alone, I find that time passes rapidly on. I have got very comfortable rooms, am very well off indeed for servants, & have received since my arrival every day invitations for dinner. It is very fortunate that people are so hospitable in this part of the world, for if such were not the case I should now & then be at a loss [to know] how to pass my time.'[26]

The council of regency – Bavarian to a man – governed under the presidency of Count Josef Ludwig von Armansperg, a successful, though unpopular, former finance minister of Bavaria. When Otto came of age in 1835, he would follow the advice of his father, the British government and the Rothschilds – all parties that wished to see Greek finances in capable hands – and appoint Armansperg as his Chancellor. As to the ambassadors in Nauplia, Britain was represented by Edward Dawkins (and later by Sir Edmund Lyons), France by M. Piscatory.

Nat then turned to the subject of Metzger. 'The principal cause of Napoli being a disagreeable place of residence is its extreme unhealthiness; endemic fevers rage during the whole year & if one is at all subject to inflammation, or rheumatism, it is pretty nearly certain that a fever will attack you. It is likewise necessary to be very careful as to what one eats & drinks & excesses must be avoided. There is not a single German with whom I am acquainted who has not experienced the effects of this hot

A View from the Royal Exchange.

Nathan Rothschild, in a caricature by Richard Dighton, 1817. It was on the Royal Exchange, or 'Change', that Nathan conducted his extensive business in foreign bills

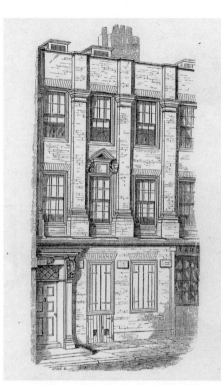

Left: No. 12 Great St Helens, the Rothschilds' first London house

Below: The Great Synagogue, Duke's Place, by Pugin and Rowlandson, 1809. The Cohens and the Rothschilds belonged to this synagogue's congregation

above: Hyde Park Corner in 1820: No. 148 Piccadilly, which later became Lionel's town house, is the northermost of the terrace of three (third lantern from the right)

right: No. 107 Piccadilly (bow front), which took the place of New Court as a family residence in the mid-1820s. Since demolished, it is seen here in a drawing of 1927

THIS PAGE

Top: Family group at the marriage of Anselm and Charlotte (Chilly) in Frankfurt in 1826, by Richard Dighton, with (*left to right*) Carl and Salomon; Chilly and Anselm; Louisa, Nathan, Hannah Mayer and Lionel

Above: Gunnersbury Park, by E. Kretschmar, 1847. Built by Alexander Copland and sold to Nathan in 1835, the house was described as 'well adapted for *the Residence of a Nobleman, Minister of State, or Family of Distinction*'

OPPOSITE PAGE

Top: New Court in 1819: No. 2, to the right of the picture, was occupied by the Rothschilds; No. 4, to the left, by Benjamin Travers, then by Moses and Judith Montefiore

Left: Nathan, Hannah and their children in 1821, by W. A. Hobday, with (*left to right*) Nathan, Mayer, Louisa, Hannah, Chilly, Hannah Mayer, Lionel, Anthony and Nat

Anthony (*left*) and Lionel, by M. D. Oppenheim, *c.*1827. Anthony was 'Billy' to his brothers; Lionel was known as 'Rabbi'

Nat, by M. D. Oppenheim, *c.*1827. Nat earned the nickname 'Stag'

Above: Anselm and Chilly
(at easel) with young family
and the children's nurse in
1838, painted by Chilly.
Their principal home
was in Frankfurt

Right: Mayer, known
as 'Muffy' or 'Tup',
with Mentmore
Towers, the house
designed for him by
Sir Joseph Paxton,
in the distance

In announcing to you, which we do with feelings of the deepest sorrow, the death of our lamented Father, Mr. N. M. ROTHSCHILD, we beg to inform you, that the Business carried on by him will be continued by us, under the Firm of N. M. ROTHSCHILD & SONS, IN EVERY RESPECT AS HERETOFORE, in connexion with the Establishments at Frankfort, Vienna, Paris and Naples.

We request your attention to our respective Signatures at foot.

We are, Gentn

LONDON, 9 August, 1836.

Your obedient Servants,

Lionel Nathan de Rothschild will sign ......

Anthony Nathan de Rothschild will sign ..

Nathaniel Nathan de Rothschild will sign ...

Circular signed by Lionel, Anthony and Nat announcing their intention, following Nathan's death, to continue their father's business as N. M. Rothschild & Sons climate. The Bavarian troops have suffered terribly & some few have died. I am not in the least afraid & hope to remain as well as I have been all along. The person however who accompanied me has not been equally fortunate. The day after our arrival here, he caught the fever, was kept to his bed for a fortnight & is obliged to return home as a longer stay in this country might bring on another attack. He started this morning for Patrass, where there is a chance of his meeting the steamer. If he does, he will arrive in London at the same time as this letter & will be able to give you accounts of me.

'I shall remain here about a fortnight or perhaps three weeks longer, & shall then sail for Constantinople where in all probability I shall pass a couple of months. As you can easily imagine my dear Mamma, it is not very agreeable to remain in so distant a country quite alone. I should therefore be very much obliged if immediately you would let some one come & meet me. I know nobody whom I should like so well to have with me as Mr Schlemmer; as well as being a very pleasant companion, he would be of as much use to me as any one else – but then what will Mayer do? If it were possible to make other arrangements for Mayer for three or four months, for Mr Schlemmer would not be absent longer, I think he would be decidedly the best person. You, my Dear Mamma, are the best judge. At all events I must beg you not to send me a stranger; a person with whom I am not acquainted would not be of the slightest service to me.

'This country is in a very unsettled state; robberies & murders are of daily occurrence. The King had a famous example of it the other day. At the beginning of the week, he started on a tour in the interior. On the very first day, at a few miles from his Capital, he met a man who had been stopped by robbers only an hour before, & had received five wounds in defending his property.'

In Nauplia itself, John Auldjo had observed that the King 'rides out every day without guards, and almost unattended; and strolls upon the public promenade at the hours when the *beau monde* frequent it. His presence, however, excited little attention; and, except by his uniform, the star upon his breast, and the few aides-de-camp who attend him, he would hardly be recognised by a stranger.' Slade recalled that some 'driving and riding were practised on the only road, extending three to four miles; Otho drove his own phaeton, *à l'anglaise*.'[27]

'The society here is pleasant,' Nat continued, 'but of course has the same fault as all little towns – one meets the same people over & over again. The two houses where I generally pass the evening are those of Countess Armansperg & of the French Minister. The former has three very nice daughters, who are really quite an acquisition to this enchanting town. At the Frenchman's I play my rubber at 6 pence a point & am much more amused than if I betted high.'

According to Slade: 'The diplomatists dined each other occasionally; and a weekly *soirée* at Countess Armansperg's collected the fashion and rank of the place. Her daughters were a valuable present to Greece. In manner and accomplishments of course unrivalled, in beauty, too, surpassing the natives, these amiable young ladies, I mean the two eldest, gave their hands afterwards to the brothers Cantacuzene, sons of the prince of that name.'[28]

Six weeks later, Nat finally landed on Turkish soil at Smyrna (Izmir), the cosmopolitan city and chief port of western Anatolia. Why Nat did not sail direct from Nauplia to Constantinople, he does not explain – only that he finally reached the Ottoman capital after 'a tedious & uninteresting journey of 12 days from Smyrna'.[29]

Five years had passed since 'the population of Constantinople lined the shores in wonder, at the appearance of the first steamer (the *Swift*) which had ever passed the Hellespont' in 1828. By the time Nat reached Smyrna, the steamboat *Maria Dorothea* (Austrian-owned, with a French crew) made the journey to the capital in forty hours; but it was not until 1834, the year after Nat's arrival, that a regular steamer service was set up. So Nat, it seems, made the journey to Constantinople by land – and even then at a sedate pace. The lightly laden traveller could cover the distance comfortably in less than a week; but given the length of Nat's absence from home, and the kind of society in which he mixed, he was no doubt encumbered with much luggage.[30]

One of the most useful members of staff at the British consulate in Smyrna – which was situated on the quayside, a stone's throw from the busiest landing place – was John Chamurian, the consulate's dragoman, who could arrange the post-horses necessary for the journey. He did so for Adolphus Slade in 1834, while Slade put up at an inn called the Cloche d'Or before he and his servant Mustapha set out for the capital. Possibly Nat, too, stayed at the Cloche d'Or; we do not know. Slade travelled light, but the mode of travel favoured by an acquaintance, also following the overland route from Smyrna to Constantinople, gives an idea of how a rich man like Nat might go equipped – and of the disadvantages.[31]

Four hours out of Smyrna, having passed over the famous Caravan Bridge on the road to mount Sypelas and the town of Magnesia, Slade – with Mustapha and a packhorse – reached the hamlet of Yatakeuy. There they 'overtook Count Stawelberg, a Russian, who, in a Russian brig of war, had accompanied our squadron from Nauplia, and anchored at Smyrna the same afternoon. Bound also to the Eastern capital, he was paying the penalty of wealth in four heavy-laden sumpter-horses, with the further incumbrances of an Italian valet and cook. He seemed to envy my "light order"; a carpet-bag tied on the back of a led horse. He courteously invited me to join his breakfast, which, consisting of an omelette and cold fowl with French wine, was laid on a white cloth, on a broad stone beside a fountain. How such necessaries diminish the relish of an oriental ride! . . . I declined; knowing the necessity of spare diet on a rapid equestrian journey . . .'[32]

At Magnesia, Slade met the Count again. 'As I was about to start again, after two hours' repose, in came my Russian Count and caravan. He had taken nine hours to perform what occupied me five hours and a-half; a serious difference under broiling sun. He was knocked up; moreover sadly perplexed in consequence of having no medium of communication with his Tartar. Seeing that, and his inclination to push on instanter, the very way to plunge into a fever, I spoke to this said Tartar, and recommended him by no means to leave Magnesia before the morning, if he valued the health of his charge . . .' For Nat, travelling in November, the heat cannot have been such a problem, and it remains a mystery why he should have found the journey – much of it through beautiful country – so dull.[33]

By the time he reached Constantinople – alone, as Schlemmer had not been sent to join him – he had had no news from home for two months. Consequently, he was thrilled to find that several packets of letters were awaiting his arrival; post arrived once a week from Vienna and from St Petersburg. 'I assure you I read your kind & gratifying letters over & over again, and every time with a greater degree of satisfaction,' he told Nathan and Hannah. 'You will perceive my dear Parents by the perusal of my letter to Anthony, how delighted I was to reach at length Constantinople. You will also observe that my journey hither was not of the most agreeable description. However thank God I am now quite comfortable. I have got very nice rooms, have enjoyed very good health & in fact have all that I can possibly desire or expect at such a distance from you.'[34]

Like all other western Europeans visiting or residing in the Ottoman capital – most of them Roman Catholic and generally referred to as 'Franks' – Nat would have lodged in Pera, a district of the city that was both included in the term Constantinople and distinct from it, geographically and culturally. Separated by the Golden Horn, where the wide channel formed by the waters of the Bosphorus makes a natural harbour, Pera stands on the high ground opposite the promontory where Constantine founded his imperial capital – the promontory referred to as either Constantinople or 'Stamboul', on the extremity of which, Seraglio Point, the Ottoman sultans sited the sprawling palace known as Topkapi.

The concentration of Europeans meant that Pera had a very different feel to it. There, Adolphus Slade observed, 'French furnished magazines attract the Turkish ladies, otherwise a stranger might deem himself in any dirty Italian town. Annexed to Constantinople, it is as independent of it as though part of Pekin. A quarter of the Mussulman capital, it exhibits all the paraphernalia of Catholicism, in feasts, processions, burials and masses.' Except when in conflict with Turks, foreign residents of Pera were subject to the laws of their own native states.[35]

Two years before Nat set eyes on it, Pera had been all but reduced to ashes in a devastating fire; 20,000 houses had been lost. By May 1833, though, six months before Nat's arrival, three handsome new streets had been finished and the British Consul-General, John Cartwright, 'perhaps one of the most excellent and kind-hearted individuals ever invested with the consular authority', was dispensing 'generous and unbounded hospitality' from the new house he had built. New Court provided banking services to Cartwright and when Nat's future brother-in-law, Henry FitzRoy, was staying in Constantinople with his brother in December 1838, they 'had a most excellent and jolly dinner and Christmas party at Mr Cartwright's'.[36]

Cartwright, who had lived in Pera for more than a decade, had a well-known servant – another Mustapha – who was sometimes made available to show English visitors the sights. Born a Swiss, Mustapha was said to have been captured by pirates, sold into slavery and converted to Islam. Henry FitzRoy and his brother went sightseeing with Mustapha in 1838, and it is possible that Nat did so in 1833, but in the letters that survive he does not say.[37]

Nor, except for remarking on them with satisfaction, does Nat reveal anything about the rooms he found in Constantinople. Possibly he took apartments, as John Auldjo had done and as Slade was to do, in the lodging-house kept by Giuseppino Vitale, which, in the absence of a decent hotel at that time, was probably the best that Pera had to offer.[38]

It was at Giuseppino Vitale's that Misséri, the multilingual travelling servant immortalised by A. W. Kinglake in *Eothen*, found his master's party rooms; and when Henry FitzRoy arrived in Pera, he 'went to try for rooms at an Englishman's house but found none so came to Madame Giuseppini's where in hot weather all must be comfortable, but in this piercing cold, the absence of stoves is sensibly felt'. When Lord and Lady

Londonderry arrived one night in 1840, on the other hand, a *chaise de poste* was waiting to convey them from their boat to a lodging-house run by one Mlle Joseph; their way was lit only by glimmers of light from the paper lanterns carried by passing Turks.[39]

Aside from the lodging-houses and the presence of the stalwart Consul-General – Slade wrote that to Cartwright 'the Franks of all nations look up as the firm interpreter of their rights, as their chief barrier against the encroachments of the sultan' – the Pera side of the Golden Horn offered the traveller the invaluable resources of Stampa's, 'that emporium of all good condiments, where Adrianople tongues, Yorkshire bacon, Scotch whisky, French cognac, Scotch ale, London porter, English cheese, and Havannah segars [*sic*] may be obtained for a "consideration".' Lord Londonderry noted that in the main street of Pera there were also available 'goods from England, France, America, and Holland, sold by Jew dealers; and all things can be procured, though at extravagant prices'. Stampa's was situated in Galata, the commercial district, established by the Genoese, at the foot of the hill up to Pera. English visitors, of whom there were many – Nat reported that there were 'continually travellers arriving here, but none of distinction, the great proportion are English' – could obtain routine banking facilities at Black & Hardy.[40]

'I was very happy to learn that you were satisfied with the manner in which I have arranged the affair of the Greek bonds,' Nat continued in his letter to London. 'I trust that you received them in due time . . . I have not seen any of the Turkish Ministers as yet. The fashion here of visiting them is to send a dragoman to them to fix the hour & day. Lord Ponsonby has been kind enough to give me his dragoman for this purpose & probably I shall be received with great ceremony by the Reis Effendi [the Minister for Foreign Affairs] in the course of this week.'[41]

John Brabazon Ponsonby was reputed to be the most handsome man of his day; he was the only man whom Harriette Wilson, courtesan and unblushing memoiriste, found genuinely irresistible and never criticised. It was sometimes said that Ponsonby owed his success in diplomacy to the fact that George IV, so as to keep him away from the ladies of his Court (Lady Conyngham in particular), had insisted that he be given high posts abroad for long periods. Lord Augustus Loftus, a fellow diplomatist, nevertheless considered Ponsonby to be a 'shrewd observer, with a sharp insight into character, a man of large views, of a strong and decided will . . . Nothing upset him, nothing disturbed his equanimity.' In 1846 Lord Ponsonby was appointed Ambassador in Vienna, where Nat's cousin George Samuel served as his private secretary.[42]

Since the devastating fire in Pera, anyone who wished to call on Ponsonby at the British embassy – or 'the palace of the British embassy' as it was then termed – had to make the trip to Therapia, a pretty village on the banks of the Bosphorus not far from the mouth of the Black Sea. The French ambassador, Admiral Roussin, was established at Therapia, too, but whereas he and his embassy had the use of a spacious palace and grounds once occupied by Prince Ypsilante, Ponsonby's accommodation was comparatively cramped and had little land. A 'ruinous inconvenient concern' according to Adolphus Slade, the property had been confiscated from an Armenian merchant and presented to the British by the Sultan, who himself had a summer residence at Therapia. The British thought it proper to pay the displaced Armenian rent.[43]

Lord and Lady Ponsonby – the former Lady Elizabeth Villiers, the beautiful youngest daughter of the fourth Earl of Jersey – made the best of it none the less. When Moses Montefiore was in Constantinople in 1840, to secure the Sultan's protection for the Jews in the wake of a horrifying persecution in Damascus (a *cause célèbre* of the day), he and Judith were entertained to a 'sumptuous dinner' at Therapia and found the Ponsonbys 'extremely amiable'. Slade recalled that he 'often enjoyed under his excellency's roof the rare union of eastern hospitality and refined civilisation: *on y trouve le luxe morale et physique*'.[44]

Nat had a choice of transport from Pera to Therapia. In good weather, the best means was by water, by caique or by one of the 'elegant four-oared, or six-oared *piadés* of the Bosphorus'. In stormy conditions in the winter, Slade advised 'sending to Ahmed Aga, the Tartar, for one of his excellent horses. Ride gently down the long street of Pera . . . then gently touch his flanks, and he will carry you the eleven miles within the hour, not counting a halt of ten minutes at the pretty *cafeneh*, by the side of the ravine, two thirds of the distance.' When the Montefiores made the trip it was October; they hired a barouche, which 'owing to the state of the roads was obliged to be drawn by four horses'. The wheels of the barouche, Judith related, 'frequently got into deep ruts which required all the dexterity of an expert and good-tempered coachman to prevent an overturn. We had not to complain of want of exercise.'[45]

The distance from Constantinople, a factor which at times during the winter precluded communication with the city altogether, made Ponsonby reluctant to leave the embassy at other times too – as he was to make clear when replying to Lord Londonderry's request for help in arranging an audience with the Sultan in 1840. 'I cannot present any body to the Sultan,' the ambassador explained, 'without exposing myself to perpetual inconvenience of having to present every body, and to make a journey of twenty miles every day, and spend my whole time in attendance upon visiters [sic] to this place. This is the plain truth, and I tell you frankly . . . I am too constantly occupied to have a moment for even taking the air, much less for so long a journey as from hence to Pera . . .'[46]

Londonderry was beside himself with indignation at Ponsonby's refusal to assist him (the Austrian envoy, resident in Pera, was more obliging); but for Nat the loan of the ambassador's dragoman seems to have been all that was needed for him to arrange interviews with the Sultan's ministers. The dragoman was Frederick Pisani, from a family that claimed kinship with the famous Pisani of Genoa. He was a cultured man as well as a fine linguist; a valuable library of Arabic manuscripts that he had collected went up in flames in the great fire of Pera.[47]

Besides the Reis Effendi, the Sultan's ministers included the Grand Vizier, whose office by 1833 was more or less nominal; the Seraskier Pasha, war minister and commander-in-chief of the Ottoman army; the Capitan Pasha, supreme commander of the navy; the Sader Azam Musteyshari, minister of the interior, as well as ministers of finance and commerce, a master of the mint and various others. The ministers had their offices at the Porte, below Topkapi, in Stamboul, which from the Pera side of the Golden Horn could be reached in a few minutes by boat, or by a ride overland of five to six miles.[48]

In mid-January 1834, Nat reported that he was 'very well satisfied with my sejour in this capital. The difference between it and all the other towns that I have visited is so wonderfully great, that really one can form no idea of it without having seen it. The Turks have likewise paid me great attention. I have been to see nearly all the Ministers, with whom I smoked & drank coffee out of cups about twice as big as a large thimble.'[49]

His multilingual education paid dividends, even with Frederick Pisani at his side. Knowledge of Italian was useful throughout the Levant, while French was the language spoken among the European community and in diplomatic circles. Both languages were useful for conversation with the Sultan's ministers. When, in 1829, Lord Albemarle had an audience with the Grand Vizier, Mohammed Reschid Pasha, they conversed in Italian; when Lord Londonderry later met the Reis Effendi, he found him a 'very agreeable minister, who speaks French admirably, and with whom I wanted no interpreter'.[50]

Lord Londonderry wrote an account of the interview he had with the Foreign Minister one evening, which, in the absence of any such account provided by Nat, serves to give an idea of the proceedings:

The pacha led me through two rooms to a cabinet, in the middle of which was a brass brazier; and four large wax candles, in tall candlesticks, stood on the floor, as is usual in all Turkish apartments. I was then motioned to sit down, and, waiting due time, according to eastern usage, and to produce an imposing effect, I proceeded, as I had been instructed, to ask after his excellency's health; this being always the preface in every Turkish conference. Another great point is, to be extremely slow, and allow great intervals to elapse, not only between every thing you hear and your rejoinder, but also between every subject that is started and the succeeding. His excellency having replied as to his health, and inquired after mine, we discoursed much at length on common topics . . . In about twenty minutes, ten or twelve slaves entered, bearing very long pipes, with yellow tops, and placed before each of us a small box with lighted tinder, in which the end of the pipe reposed. Each of the visitants was offered the pipes in succession . . .

When the cabinet was so full of smoke that one could hardly see, the attendants returned, and carried away the pipes; conversation was resumed, and then more servants entered, bearing in very small cups, placed in an ornamented and costly holder, a few spoonfuls of excellent coffee, already sugared, without cream or milk. The company, just sipping these, returned them, and the servants vanished; shortly afterwards they again advanced with large cut glasses, some filled with red sweetmeat or clear water, and others full of sherbet, perfumed with attar of rose. The latter was particularly good and refreshing . . . After an hour's visit I rose, and, saying every thing I really felt of graciousness and kindness . . . I took my leave, being followed out through the rooms by his excellency.[51]

Apart from his meetings with ministers, Nat had been mixing mostly in European society. 'All the Ambassadors & members of the Corps Dip have been all along exceedingly polite and kind to me,' he assured his mother in January. 'I have likewise joined as much as possible in the society of the merchants [;] there are a few of them who have good houses, as the fire burned them all. I have been to a few dances, but the ladies are seldom very beautiful [;] scarcely any of them can read or write & consequently [are] not very bright in their conversation. The education of a Perote lady consists in the act of dressing herself & making sweetmeats; their idleness is excessive. I dare say that three quarters of them have never been at Constantinople, altho' it only takes ten minutes to be rowed in a boat across [to] the Porte.'[52]

Whether Nat had seen any of the city's sights – with or without Cartwright's servant Mustapha – he does not say, but he had found time to visit the shops:

'I am afraid, my dear Mamma, that I shall not be able to fulfill Papa's commissions to buy gold and silver curiosities. The Turks never use the precious metals for anything but money, and in the ornamenting of guns, pistols, swords, & coet. These last mentioned articles are to be found in great abundance, but I do not think that they would suit Papa. Constantinople is the worst place in the world for old things [;] the frequent fires that occur destroy every antique object. Pipes are to be had very handsome ornamented with diamonds & coet, but tremendously dear. The Turks use very pretty coffee cups, but I understand that they come from Genoa & it would therefore be folly to buy any . . . I shall have the pleasure of sending you . . . in a few days a box containing beautiful attar of roses, some seraglio heads and pastilles, some Papooshes or slippers, and a few Broussa silks and embroidered muslins. I hope that a box I sent some time since containing different things has arrived & that you have found the drapes and scarves to your fancy.'

Nat was also hoping to be granted an even grander interview in Constantinople than he had obtained so far – in preparation for which he must surely have thought wistfully of his tailors Stultz & Housley in London. 'I hope before I leave to have an audience of his Sublime Highness the Sultan,' he reported. 'It is however necessary to go in uniform and unluckily I have not got a presentable one. I ordered a scarlet coat embroidered with gold of an English tailor who is established here & the stupid fellow made it about three inches too small. I have now been obliged to have brass buttons put on my travelling jacket, and embroidered cuffs & collar. I hope to look very smart. At all events it will [be] good enough for Turks. Count Medem, Anthony's friend, has been kind enough to offer me his cocked hat and sword. I trust his Highness will make a present. I shall try & give him a hint.'

Count Paul Medem, a Russian diplomat, was chargé d'affaires at the Russian embassy in London in 1834–5. He was a cousin of Prince Talleyrand's niece, the Duchesse de Dino, who acted as her uncle's hostess at the French embassy in London. When he was chargé d'affaires in Paris in 1839, he was described by Princess Lieven as '*clever*'; but when Moses Montefiore called to see Count Medem at the Russian consulate in Alexandria in 1840, he found him asleep.[53]

Chateaubriand's remark that the Turkish government was 'an absolute despotism, tempered by regicide' was fully justified by the circumstances in which the Sultan whom Nat hoped to meet, Mahmud II, had ascended the throne in 1808. His brother, Mustapha IV – who had been Sultan since the deposition and murder of their cousin Selim III in 1807 – was deposed and strangled. Mahmud was then the last remaining descendant of Othman, the founder of the dynasty.

In 1833, Mahmud was still only forty-eight years old, but he had the looks of an older man. One Friday in May, John Auldjo saw him riding in procession to mosque 'closely wrapped up in a greyish brown cloak, with a collar of diamonds, emeralds, and rubies, arranged in the form of flowers – the richest and most brilliant ornament I ever beheld. Like his officers, he also wore a plain fez . . . It was drawn close over his ears, and down to his large black eyebrows, and his beard hung over the diamond clasp of the cloak. His face is long; his nose, slightly arched, indicates talent and resolution; and his eye is remarkably large, bright, and penetrating . . . The Sultan has the appearance of being about fifty-five years of age; and his blotched face, and red nose, sufficiently indicate a penchant for the bottle: indeed, on the present occasion, he displayed strong symptoms of being in what is called "a state of licquor", as well as in a most particular bad humour. It is reported that he and his sword-bearer get drunk together every day, and that he once forced the Grand Mufti to drink half a bottle of Champagne.'54

Nat had to wait several weeks before receiving his summons to an audience with Mahmud, but in early March 1834 he wrote crowingly to Nathan and Hannah: 'What do you say my dearest Parents to the honor which His Highness was gracious enough to confer on me? You do not know what it is to be received by the Sultan. No person of inferior rank than a minister plenipotentiary can be presented at court. I however consider myself Ambassador Extraord[inary] & Plenip[otentiary] & consequently have a right to the most brilliant reception. The Sultan signified that it was his intention to bestow a mark of his satisfaction, but I do not know whether it is to be a ring, or snuff box, or a grand decoration. I hope the latter. I have already given them to understand that the diamond crescent will be the most acceptable.'55

To some extent Nat was right to be pleased at the attention he was receiving. By March 1841, with the sole exception of the Duke of Devonshire, not one English visitor, noble or otherwise, had been presented to Mahmud or his successor by Lord Ponsonby – including the Earl of Durham, who was Ambassador in St Petersburg at the time of his visit. Others, like Lord Londonderry, had perhaps succeeded in arranging their audiences by other means – as Nat himself presumably had to do with the help of Pisani. At the time, though, so far as he knew, he was 'the first person without diplomatic functions who has had such a mark of attention shown to him. The Turks have wonderful respect for cash & as they have heard a very good report of us, they are very desirous of our connexion. I should not wonder if something good were to present itself at some future period.'[56]

Had someone been on hand to poke fun at Nat, they might have questioned whether the palace authorities actually understood who he was. When Sir Pulteney Malcolm, Admiral of the Mediterranean Fleet, arrived in Constantinople, the Sultan supposed him to rank third in importance in the British Empire, equivalent of the Ottoman navy's Capitan Pasha – and consequently granted him the quite exceptional privilege of touring the harem.[57]

No account of Nat's audience with Mahmud has been preserved, but when Lord Ponsonby himself had been summoned by the Sultan a few months before, he had been received – accompanied by his nephew, a British army officer, and his attaché, Mr Waller – at one of the Sultan's modern, waterside palaces. On being admitted to Mahmud's presence, they had found him seated on a divan in 'an apartment splendidly painted and decorated'. After an exchange of the customary compliments, coffee and pipes were brought in, and the Sultan showed his visitors a portrait of himself on horseback, 'painted by some Sardinian artist. It was a resemblance, but indifferently executed.' The audience lasted an hour.[58]

The 'grand decoration' that Nat hoped to receive was the Order of Glory (Nishan Iftikar), instituted by Mahmud in 1831. When Lord Londonderry went for his audience with Mahmud's successor, he noted that the Foreign Minister and the Sultan's chamberlain were each wearing the 'crescent of diamonds and the rich sword and belt' of that order. In the event, however, Nat's particular wish was not fulfilled, though he was tolerably pleased with the gift he received instead.[59] 'I have had a beautiful present from his highness the Sultan,' he conceded. 'It is a magnificent snuff box all over diamonds, worth about three to four hundred pounds. I have shown it to several people & they have assured me that nobody less than an Ambassador had ever been presented with so valuable a souvenir. I would have very much preferred a decoration & should have got it, had not a friend of mine, whom I will not name, belonging to the Corps Diplomatique, intrigued against me.'[60]

Whether or not Nat was right in scenting treachery in the air, a snuffbox was probably as much as he might reasonably have hoped for. When the Sultan sent Count Nesselrode, Russia's Foreign Minister, his imperial order, M. de Bouteneff, the Russian ambassador to the Porte, received a snuffbox. On the other hand, it was not only ambassadors who received gem-encrusted snuffboxes from the Sultan, as Nat may possibly have known. The artist whose portrait of Mahmud had failed to impress Lord

Ponsonby – a certain Signor Gobbi, an attaché of the Sardinian embassy – was rewarded by the satisfied sitter with a snuffbox set with diamonds.[61]

Some might have thought Nat lucky to get anything at all. Until Mahmud abolished the practice, every new ambassador, far from receiving a present, had been obliged to present the Sultan, as well as the Grand Vizier, Reis Effendi and other ministers, with jewels and snuffboxes to the value of £5,000–6,000.[62]

Having planned to leave Constantinople for St Petersburg in January 1834, Nat was in the event unable to leave until late March, and by then his trip to Russia had been cancelled. The loan arrangements proved hard to conclude, and disaffection with the business set in.[63] 'The contract which I considered as good as ra[tif]ied is null & the Turks have demanded bills of exchange,' Nat explained. 'To morrow I intend giving them bills on London & shall take the receipt as required by the Greek Government. You need not fear about its all being done with the greatest care. I am quite sick & tired of the Turks. You can not form an idea of their shameful double dealing. I regret exceedingly that I ever came here to do business. To morrow I shall settle the affair & shall then take my leave of this detestable place. I am really so tired that I really can not write any more . . .'[64]

His last, undated, letter from Constantinople amounts to one long sigh of relief. 'Thank God I can now say positively that I shall leave to morrow morning this great Capital on my return homewards. You can not have an idea how happy it makes me to think that I shall shortly have the extreme satisfaction of seeing you & my dear brothers & sisters. I intend starting as early as possible to morrow & expect after a ride of 11 or 12 days during which I shall traverse Roumelia & Servia to arrive at Semlin. I shall there have to perform a quarantine of 10 days to cleanse myself from Turkish impurity [possible plague infection] & then three days more will enable me to reach Vienna.

'I am glad to say that I shall not have to perform this tedious journey quite alone. Mr Weisweiller arrived a few days since & will accompany me. You must not fancy that travelling in the East is as convenient as in other countries – all day on horseback & such horses too. I promise you one regrets old Frank.

'I have already bid adieu to all my Constantinopolitan friends & it was really a happy moment. It is almost worthwhile to go abroad & remain for some time away from home to experience the delight of returning.'[65]

Nat returned home via Vienna, on horseback at least as far as Belgrade, then the Ottoman frontier town with Austrian territory, 627 miles from Constantinople. Tartars (Turkish couriers) performed the journey in seven days. From Belgrade, the traveller bound for Vienna crossed the Save to the Serbian town of Semlin (now Zemun). 'The two frontier towns are less than a cannon-shot distant,' Kinglake noted, 'and yet their people hold no communication . . . It is the Plague, and the dread of the Plague . . .' A period of quarantine then followed – Kinglake mentions fourteen days – before the traveller could resume his journey.[66]

On 19 April, Nat despatched a courier from Vienna to London with the news of his safe arrival: 'Uncle Salomon is very well & looks better than ever . . . Give my love to Rabbi Leib & all friends.' He called on Prince Metternich and on Sir Frederick Lamb, Lord Melbourne's younger brother, at the British embassy – Lamb 'communicated no news what-ever' – but he did not mean to make his stay a long one.[67] 'I intend remaining here a few days longer,' he wrote on 22 April. 'I shall probably take my leave on Monday or Tuesday next. I propose going to Frankfurt & thence to Paris, at both of which places my stay will be but very short. I hope at latest to be in London by the first of June. I am quite tired of having nothing to do, & of travelling about.'[68]

He reached Frankfurt during the first week in May and was, he wrote to his parents on 7 May, 'as pleased as possible that I am able to say that by the end of next week I shall be again at home where I trust to meet you & my brothers & sisters in the very best health'.

'There is very little news here, business as quiet as possible,' he went on. 'Uncle Anselm does very little [;] his state of health renders him very nervous & I recommend you very strongly my dear Papa to coax him a little in your letters & by no means scold as it has more effect than you imagine. Charlotte thank God is very well . . . Her little girls are very much grown & Julie is really the dearest & most engaging child that I ever saw. Little Matty likewise begins to chatter & talks about Grand Papa NM & his good lady.'[69]

Nat's trip to Turkey had an unfortunate sequel, though to what extent Nat was to blame for it, if he was to blame for it at all, is hard to say. 'We had yesterday a visit from Ld Granville and from the Greek Minister,' Lionel wrote from Paris to his parents in July. 'They complain terribly about our not paying Nat's Bill [on London]. They say that the Grand Turk has broken off every communication with the Greek Govt, has refused to give the Greeks Passports, and will not let any of their ships leave till the Bill is paid: it has put all the Diplomatic Corps in mouvement [sic] . . .'[70]

8

Gunnersbury Park

———— ∞ ————

'MAMMA THINKS OF leaving Brighton at the beginning of next week as the weather has set in disagreeable & stormy, besides which almost every person is leaving for town.' It was early February 1833, and Hannah Mayer was writing to Lionel in Paris. Her brother was contemplating a short visit to England. 'We hope to see you in Piccadilly,' Hannah Mayer went on. 'I am sure you will be more amused there than at this place . . . Mamma desires me to tell you that she hopes you will come, & at the same time says, she is sure you will be better amused in town. As Parliament is assembled all the gaieties will commence & there is really nothing at all at Brighton worth your while coming down for; but *we all* wish you very much to come & see us in town . . .'[1]

Brighton was the closest Sussex coastal resort to London and, owing to the frequent presence of royalty, the most fashionable. In the winter, King William IV continued his brother's custom of moving his Court to the Pavilion, where he and Queen Adelaide gave dinners and were generally more visible than George IV had been. The King's children by Mrs Jordan would accompany the royal couple, so when the Royal Hunt followed the Court to Brighton to turn out deer on the South Downs, the field sometimes included Lords Adolphus ('Dolly') and Frederick FitzClarence.[2]

For several decades Brighton had been popular in Jewish circles. In an article in the *Morning Post* in 1807 it was remarked that 'the front of *Donaldson's* Library is a complete Stock Exchange. Jews and Gentiles are speculating upon the sport of the day.' Isaac Goldsmid was a frequent visitor to the town; Chief Rabbi Hirschel resided in a house there for a time. In 1824 a small synagogue was opened in Devonshire Place, while the *Brighton Guardian*, launched in 1827, was founded, and for many years edited, by Levy Emanuel Cohen.[3]

While Hannah might take the children to Brighton in the autumn, from Christmas until early February there was a kind of mini-Season there. Nathan would then install his family at the Albion Hotel, and drive down to join them for Saturday and Sunday. When Lionel wished to book rooms at the Albion in 1844, he was informed by the hotel manager 'that the charge for the apartments he wishes viz. a *large & small* sitting room, *2 double*-bedded rooms with *one single* room will be £10 10s 0d per week'. If you did not take your own carriage, a stagecoach could get you down from London in five or six hours – provided you could get a seat in one. Ben Cohen wrote to Nathan at the Albion one Christmas: 'I intended [giving] myself the pleasure of being with you this evening, but could not get a place in *any* of the Stages. I beg to be kindly remembered to Hannah, Lionel, Anthony, Nathnl., Judith & Moses, Henrietta & all friends . . . Wishing you all many happy returns of the season.'[4]

Unlike his brothers the Dukes of Cambridge and Sussex, William IV was not such a friend to the Jews. As Duke of Clarence, he had had a Jewish agent, Abraham Joseph, of Plymouth; but as King he once said to the new Bishop of Ely: 'I do not mean to interfere in any way with your vote in Parliament, except on one subject, *the Jews*, and I trust I may depend on you always voting against them.' Whether or not King William received any of the Rothschilds as his guests at the Pavilion is not known, but it seems unlikely. Anthony did, though, make friends with Dolly FitzClarence, and in 1831 he obtained a ticket for William's Coronation.[5]

'I regret dear Tony your disappointment in not being able to avail yourself of the ticket for the Coronation,' his mother wrote to him. 'Do not call me ill natured when I say that I was gratified in your not going; the reflection of having deprived oneself of a pleasure when it interferes with a duty is a delightful gratification . . .'[6]

The Duchess of St Albans, the leading hostess in Brighton society, certainly did not neglect to invite Rothschilds to her parties and balls. 'The Duchess has a party almost every evening & is very civil to us,' Hannah told Nathan in January 1833.[7] The Duchess's arrival in Brighton, it was said, was 'the signal for a more animated social intercourse; her house was the rendezvous at which introductions were made, parties formed, excursions and festivities planned'. St Albans House was 'the head quarters of social gaiety, and seemed the centre around which all fashion, wit, and pleasure of the place revolved'.[8]

For Hannah, as for others, the Duchess's presence livened things up. 'This will be a very quiet week as the Duchess remains in town till Thursday,' Hannah wrote to Nathan that February of 1833. 'We have a whist table, and much skill is shown.'[9] After a bout of entertaining at St Albans House, when her domestic staff were in need of a rest, the Duchess would move to the Bedford Hotel, where Lionel and his brothers were in later years to take their families to stay.

Beyond their family circle, the Rothschilds do not appear to have sought out the society of their co-religionists in Brighton, but there was no shortage of fine people to see. When Hannah was writing from Stamford Hill of her dislike of 'our national friend, the fog' to Lady Carmarthen, she continued: 'I dare say we shall pay Brighton a visit in a few weeks. If we do go I shall be very happy to have the additional pleasure of visiting your sister there.' The sister, the Marchioness Wellesley, had previously been married to Robert Paterson – whose sister was the first wife of Jerome Bonaparte, Napoleon's youngest brother.[10]

Others in the Rothschilds' circle included the widow of Sir John Trollope, Bt, whose first cousin was the father of the novelist Anthony Trollope, and Thomas Coutts' daughter Sophia, the wife of Sir Francis Burdett, Bt, and the mother of Angela Burdett-Coutts. A Mrs Mitchell whom they knew may perhaps be identified with the lady of that name who, with her husband and daughter (both of whom were known to Mrs Arbuthnot), frequented the company of Lord Hertford. Lord Londonderry dined 'at Mr Mitchell's' in 1825, and in early 1837, during an outbreak of influenza, J. W. Croker wrote to Lord Hertford: 'You have heard also of old Mitchell? Some one at White's said, "I am sorry for poor Mitchell; but it is a kind of consolation to think one will never be obliged to *dine* with him again." '[11]

In February 1833, Hannah Mayer wrote to Lionel: 'We have been to some parties here . . . Lady Trollope & Lady Burdett had each a little dance on the carpet, & Mrs Mitchell . . . had one also to introduce a sister of hers. Mrs Cummings [gave] a party also, which was one of the most pleasant, & I think I have given you an exact account of where we have been to, with the exception of a little dinner party at Sir R[obert] & L[ad]y Macfarlane's. We have generally a few persons to dinner on Saturday or Sunday when Papa is here . . .' From 1837 to 1843 General Sir Robert Macfarlane was Colonel of the 32nd (Cornwall Light Infantry) Regiment of Foot.[12]

Along with social possibilities, Brighton offered a mild coastal climate with good hours of sunshine at a bleak time of year. 'The weather to-day has been most beautiful, which induced us to take a drive towards Worthing, in the carriage & four,' Hannah Mayer wrote to her father in January. 'We met the King, & *the* Duchess, & we all thought that our equipage was quite as neat in every respect to rival with either of these grand personages.' In February, she wrote: 'We received your letters this morning & we hope to see our brother Lionel with you tomorrow. We had expected either Anthony or Nat this afternoon to go to the Duchess's ball this eveng. We hope that all will be well & that we shall have the pleasure of seeing you all as usual to-morrow.'[13]

Louisa, now aged twelve, sent Nathan 'a few lines to you to tell you [how] we past [sic] our time yesterday and to-day. I already told you that we were going to see the Pavilion, which we liked very much. Some of the rooms are very beautiful, among which are the dining room and music room; these are particularly handsome. The drawing rooms, passages & bedrooms are all in Chinese style, and in almost every nook and corner you are startled by a large Chinese figure shaking his head. In the evening we had a little party, consisting of three of the Miss Cummings, Aunt Esther and two of her daughters. We had a round game which lasted till twelve o'clock; do not be startled by this gambling, but I think the most lucky of us won by five shillings . . .'[14]

Besides the society, the sightseeing and the sunshine, Brighton offered the supposed benefits of sea bathing and bracing sea air. 'Ere this reaches the White Cliffs of old Albion, you will, no doubt, have had the pleasure of receiving your dear little ones from the invigorating baths of Brighton,' Miss Andrews had written to Hannah a decade earlier. 'I hope the renovating breezes have had their usual salutary effect upon their rosy cheeks . . .' As the children got older, they would spend as much time as they could out of doors. 'We have been out all day riding & walking,' Hannah Mayer, now seventeen, informed Nathan, '& I assure you we profit as much as possible of our stay here to take much exercise.'[15]

Special treatments, too, were available in Brighton, of which Mayer, now a pimply fourteen-year-old, took advantage. 'I hope you will excuse my not writing this week as often as I should,' he wrote to his father in early February (in somewhat idiosyncratic English), 'but as we all of us writ nearly the same it would be very tedious for you to read mine. Here there is nothing news. Brighton is getting very empty on account of persons leaving for parliament. I have taken several champooing baths which have done me some good and therefore hope to see you to morrow with a pimpless face.'[16]

By the autumn of 1833, Lionel was back in Paris, Nat was on his way to Turkey and Anthony was at New Court. Mayer, now fifteen, was once more given leave from his schoolroom studies for a brief British tour. This time, again in the company of Fritz Schlemmer, he travelled up the eastern side of the country to Scotland.

During his days as a textile merchant, Nathan had travelled to Scotland on business. Later, he seems to have enjoyed dealing with Scotsmen in the City. Mark Boyd, a young Scot who went with his brother to call on Nathan at New Court in the 1820s, was 'received by the great European capitalist very kindly on that and all subsequent occasions. I well remember how heartily he made me laugh. He said, "I like your brother, and I dare-say I shall like you; and I do generally like Scotchmen, but not all of them. Do you know," he said, addressing me, "that Scotchmen and ourselves [the Jews] are just the same? But your brother is a tight hand at a bargain, for when I deal with him in French Rentes I always lose money by him; he is such a screw. I hope to be more fortunate with you." '[17]

Among those to whom Mayer carried letters of introduction was Sir William Marjoribanks, Bt, David's eldest brother, who lived on the family estate at Lees, near Coldstream, in Berwickshire. From there Mayer wrote to his father:

Coldstream, 17 October 1833

My dear Papa,

I had the pleasure of receiving your letter the day before yesterday at York & was very glad to see that you were quite well . . . We have been travelling from place to place since my last & have seen many objects worthy of notice . . . We left Mr Paxton's Monday morning for Brocklesby Hall the seat of Lord Yarborough. It is an old house in the midst of a large park. There was nothing in the house but a few fine pictures. But what pleased me most were his horses & his kennel.

From there we went to Hull where there was nothing to be seen but the docks & the trinity house in which are a great number of curious things brought by different travellers from all parts of the globe. There was a fair there and in the evening we went to the theatre. I never saw such a company of actors as well as the audience. The former not knowing their respective parts, and the latter consisting chiefly of sailors, were as odoriferous as they were vociferous.

The next morning we went to York, where . . . your correspondent behaved to us in as polite a manner as possible. He gave us orders to view the most remarkable objects which that town is full of. By means of this we saw the county gaol & the museum; the former is built on a new principle, & it would be impossible for any person to escape. But that [sic] what struck me the most was the minster. You must remember that part of the building was burnt down about 3 years since. It has been repaired & no vestiges of the fire remain.

From York we came to this place by the mail without stopping anywhere as there is nothing but wild barren heaths the whole way. We are now stay-ing with Sir W. Marjoribanks, who asked us to remain with him a few days. It is on the Scotch side of the river [Tweed] . . . We expect to be at Edinburgh by Monday and to stop Sat[urday] at Selkirk.

With best love to Billy,

Yrs affectionately M.A.R.[18]

Shooting at Mr Paxton's, at Redbourne, in Lincolnshire, so Fritz Schlemmer reported to Anthony, was great fun; he and Mayer only wished that Anthony had been there with them. Mayer had been looked after by an experienced gamekeeper, so Schlemmer had been able to relax. At dinner in the evenings Mayer had been much more confident and talkative than his tutor had expected; he had talked farms and estates to his host, and had also acquitted himself well in conversation with the ladies.[19]

In the stables at Brocklesby, Mayer and his tutor had seen thirty-two beautiful hunters, and in the kennel Lord Yarborough's famous Brocklesby hounds – then one of the pre-eminent packs in the country. In the second half of the eighteenth century, with Hugo Meynell, the first Lord Yarborough had led the way in the science of hound breeding, and in the nineteenth century Brocklesby blood was prized by every kennel in England. The pictures that Mayer saw hanging at Brocklesby Hall may possibly have included George Stubbs's painting of the first Lord Yarborough's 'Ringwood', pride of the Brocklesby kennel and one of the country's most celebrated hounds.[20]

Taking the mail coach from York – where they scouted around for horses to buy, but had no success – Mayer and his tutor would have travelled on by the Great North Road. The down mail (heading northwards) was then timetabled to leave York at 5.34 in the afternoon, reach Berwick-on-Tweed at 8.47 the next morning, and arrive in Edinburgh at 2.23 p.m.[21]

From Morpeth, about ten hours on from York, to Edinburgh, the Great North Road had in 1824 been remade, as straight and as flat as possible, by Thomas Telford. The route between London and Morpeth had at that time also been surveyed, and work on portions of the road between London and York had begun. But in 1825, with the opening of the first railway for passenger traffic, between Stockton and Darlington, the authorities responsible concluded that the days of the road were numbered. Less than a decade later, when Lionel went to Perthshire for the grouse, he made much of the journey by rail.

Mayer's next letter to his father was from Edinburgh.[22]

Edinburgh, 21 October

My dear Papa . . .

Since I had the pleasure of addressing you last, we have been continually travelling in order not to delay arriving at this place, as we were obliged to stay at the hospitable house of Sir Wm. Marjoribanks for two days, from whence I wrote to you . . . I do not think I gave you a description of the persons we met there. They were Sir William, his mother, & brother. They are a very good sort of people and did everything to please us, but after we had talked of every thing relating to China, & India, there was a dearth of conversation, and we thought it better to leave too soon than too late.

Among the excursions we made from their house, was a very pleasant one in the neighbourhood at Noreham [*sic*] Castle. It is quite in ruins but lies on a very fine situation over the river Tweed. The ruins are nothing very extraordinary but the view from there is very pretty. We returned over a suspension bridge which is the first ever made in the country. The next day I went out fishing in the river Tweed. I was very fortunate in my sport, & caught a great number of the finest trout. I wished very much to have sent you some.

We left Coldstream early yesterday morning for this place coming through Kelso and Melrose. Near Kelso are the remains of Dryburgh Abbey. Nothing remains about them but the bare walls and the only thing interesting is the tomb of Sir W. Scott. From thence we went to Melrose, & on our way we saw the abbey . . . the remains are very fine specimens of Gothic architecture. From Melrose we went to Abbotsford the seat of Sir W. Scott, but were unfortunately disappointed in seeing it as the housekeeper had gone away.

We arrived here last night; and this morning we went to your correspondent Sir Wm. Forbes where I drew a bill of 70£, & I dare say this letter of advice will arrive in due time. We are very anxious to proceed to Gordon Castle as soon as possible, as all the persons whom we met tonight at Mr Hay's at dinner told us that we ought to make the best of our time in order not to be too late for the highlands. We shall however be obliged to stay here a day or two longer in order to see the place properly . . .

With best wishes to Mamma, Billy, & my sister . . .

M.A.R.

The Dr desires me to write his best respects to you & will write tomorrow.

The Duchess of St Albans, when still the widowed Mrs Coutts (though accompanied by her future ducal husband and one of his sisters), had stayed with Sir John and Lady Marjoribanks in late 1825. She and her party had travelled from London to Edinburgh in eight carriages, but had made do with three, each drawn by four horses, when they paid a visit to Abbotsford.[23]

Writing to Anthony in 1833, Fritz Schlemmer mentioned that the Dowager Lady Marjoribanks (Sir John's widow) – who spoke with 'a regular Scottish brogue' that Schlemmer found hard to understand – 'knows your Aunt James very well and told us a great deal about Paris'. He also asked Anthony to arrange for two sporting guns to be forwarded to them, care of Sir William Forbes in Edinburgh.[24]

Mayer's letter from Edinburgh was written a year and a month to the day after Sir Walter Scott's death on 21 September 1832. Everyone had been reading Scott since long before he died; he was the most widely read author of his day. When Prince Pückler-Muskau visited Goethe in Weimar in 1826, one of the subjects they discussed was Walter Scott; and when Chilly, having met Scott in Paris that year, pronounced the author's appearance to be less good than his books, she was surely speaking from experience: a catalogue of Nathan's library lists fourteen volumes of Scott's *Novels and Tales*, nine volumes of his *Tales of a Grandfather* and one volume of his complete *Poetical Works*.[25]

Even in those days, though, Scott's work was not without its critics. Staying at Clifton for his health's sake in 1821, Abraham Montefiore wrote to his 'Dear Friends' at New Court and Stamford Hill about Scott's latest novel: 'May have you read the work so much talkd of Kenilworth [?] I hope you are of my way of thinking, that it is a most immoral as well as the most improbable tale [that] ever was told. I cannot see the least merit in it . . . [it] deserves quick condemnation, wch it wd most undoubtedly receive was it not for the name of its author . . .'. When asked by Lady Granville what he thought of Scott's *Heart of Midlothian*, Frederick Lamb, who was reading the book at the time, said it was 'the worst novel I ever read'.[26]

Mayer, on his return to Stamford Hill, recorded his mixed reaction to Scott's *Lay of the Last Minstrel*: 'I read this poem of W. Scotts at Edinburgh [in] October 1833, & had just visited the principal places mentioned in it. I did not much like the plot but there are some very pretty pieces of poetry, particularly the whole of the introduction. The description of Melrose Abbey by moonlight, & of the windows in the 2nd Canto is very pretty.' Of *Marmion*, Mayer went on: 'I like this poem better than the previous one. The plot which is not very interesting at first becomes exceedingly so as it draws to a close. I read this [in] November 1833 directly after I had returned from Scotland.'[27]

Nathan's correspondent bankers in Edinburgh, where Mayer went to draw a bill for £70, had associations with Scott. Sir William Forbes, Bt, a prominent local banker until his death in 1806, is mentioned in Scott's notes to *Marmion*. He was, Scott ventured, 'unequalled, perhaps, in the degree of individual affection entertained for him by his friends, as well as in the general esteem and respect of Scotland at large'. Lady Forbes was a daughter of Sir James Hay, Bt, of Hayston – a connection, perhaps, of the

Mr Hay with whom Mayer and Fritz Schlemmer dined. The Forbes' eldest son, another William, had married Williamina Stuart, on whose affections the young Walter Scott had once set his heart.

Mayer's disappointment at failing to see inside Abbotsford must soon have receded at the prospect of a visit to Gordon Castle, near Fochabers, the seat of 'The Cock of the North' – George Gordon, fifth Duke of Gordon and chief of the clan Gordon. Staunchly conservative, the Duke came of a family noted in the past for its Stuart sympathies; the dukedom was a creation of James II. In 1832, the fifth Duke was one of the twenty-two 'stalwarts' who voted against the third reading of the Reform Bill, when Wellington and the bulk of the opposition abstained.[28]

The Duchess, Elizabeth, twenty-four years her husband's junior, was the only child of a rich East India merchant named Alexander Brodie. On her marriage to the Duke in 1813, she had brought with her £100,000, and on her father's death her resources more than doubled. But it was said of the Duchess that 'her large fortune was the least part of her value: she possessed upright principles, good sense, and she turned out a first-rate woman of business.'[29] Of the Duke's five sisters, one married a Marquess (Cornwallis) and three married Dukes – Richmond, Manchester and Bedford – with all of whose families Mayer and his family later became acquainted.

How it was that Mayer came to be invited to stay at Gordon Castle remains a mystery. Lady William Gordon, widow of the Duke's uncle, was a close neighbour of the Rothschilds in Piccadilly; she lived just across the street from them in Ranger's Lodge, Green Park. Alexander Brodie's involvement in the India trade had perhaps brought him into contact with the Marjoribanks family or with Nathan; or conceivably, as in the case of the old Lady Marjoribanks, there was a connection via James and Betty de Rothschild in Paris.[30]

The Duke's father, the fourth Duke of Gordon – once described as the greatest subject in Britain – had been a great favourite at the Bourbon Court. He used to relate how at the ball at Versailles for the marriage of the Dauphin, the future Louis XVI, in 1770, he was commanded by Louis XV to open the ball with the Dauphine, Marie Antoinette. In 1826, aged eighty-four, he danced with Madame de France.[31]

The Gordon family also had a link to the Jewish community in London. One of the fifth Duke's uncles, the turbulent Lord George Gordon, instigator of the 'No Popery!' riots in London in 1780, created a further stir in 1786 by converting to Judaism. Having learnt about Jewish customs and ceremonies, and to read Hebrew, he was circumcised by a rabbi in Birmingham and subsequently attended the Hambro Synagogue in London.[32]

When, before long, he was committed to Newgate for publishing a libel on Queen Marie Antoinette, Lord George was, so one of his Jewish visitors recalled, 'very regular in his Jewish observances; every morning he was seen with his phylacteries between his eyes, and opposite to his heart. Every Saturday he had public service in his room, by the aid of ten Polish Jews . . . His Saturday's bread was baked according to the manner of the Jews, his wine was Jewish, his meat was Jewish, and he was the best Jew in the congregation of Israel.' He refused to meet Jews without beards, grew his own beard down almost to his waist and declined to uncover his head when appearing in court. He signed his letters 'Israel Bar Abraham G. Gordon' and died in jail in November 1793, aged forty-three.[33]

His ducal nephew gave a warm welcome to Mayer and his tutor at Gordon Castle – the grandest and most aristocratic country house in Britain at which any of Nathan Rothschild's children had yet, so far as is known, been asked to stay. Schlemmer found the Duke to be a cheerful man with a lively sense of humour; having been partly educated in Geneva, he was also fond of French conversation.

The castle was full of guests, whom Mayer and his tutor met when they assembled for dinner, and then afterwards over whisky, and tea, until midnight. During the course of the evening it also emerged that the Duke was fond of music, and that in one of the castle's splendid rooms there was a fine organ. When Schlemmer asked his host if it would be possible to hear the organ, he was informed that no one present could play; so he suggested that he might do so himself. This, he recalled, acted upon the Duke 'like an electric shock'.

Candles were brought into the room and, rather than summon his servants to pump the organ, the Duke manned the bellows himself. Realising that sacred music was not suitable to the spirit of the gathering, Schlemmer proceeded to play a selection of secular items, ending up, as he recalled, with a popular song with the refrain 'Charley come home'. Apparently, this delighted the Duchess – who 'since her youth . . . had been a supporter of the Stuarts and wished to know nothing of the Hanoverians' – and she and all the company joined in the song.

'Thus passed eight wonderful days, spent riding, pheasant shooting, etc' – at the end of which, having by then been away for three weeks, Mayer and his tutor 'hastened back home without stopping, travelling by day and night in a cramped stagecoach'. The up mail from Edinburgh to London was timetabled to make the journey in 45 hours and 39 minutes.[34]

On his return to London, Mayer, it was noticed with approval at home, was 'alert, lively and outgoing'. Hannah, especially, observed the change with pleasure: she found that her 'handsome' son, having been treated on his tour as 'Mr de R, an independent gentleman and not as a pupil on tour with his tutor', had 'grown up'. This, said Fritz Schlemmer, was good for his own self-esteem – but before long the 'routine days of work resumed and with them the usual laziness'.

That Nathan had use neither for titles nor for membership of the landed classes – no desire for social aggrandisement of a conventional kind – put him in a class of his own among the most successful of his City associates. Jeremiah Harman received no title, but the 'pleasure grounds' around his house at Woodford, in Essex, were described as being 'of little less than two miles in extent, and backed by a prospect upon which even the most fastidious eye might have satisfactorily gazed'. Members of the Smith family had acquired estates in Hertfordshire, Sussex and Buckinghamshire; Robert Smith had been raised to the peerage as Lord Carrington. The Barings had progressed along much the same lines, beginning with Francis Baring, contemporary of Nathan's father and the founder of the banking dynasty.[35]

Francis Baring accepted a baronetcy in 1793, and in 1801, having already acquired a manor house and 1,200 acres near Lewisham, paid the Duke of Bedford £150,000 for the Stratton estate in Hampshire. He remodelled the house there at a cost of £25,000, furnished it with a fine collection of paintings and spent £40,000 on planting the grounds. Described by Lord Erskine as 'unquestionably the first merchant in Europe; first in knowledge and talents, and first in character and opulence' (words that might as well have applied to Nathan later on), at the time of his death aged seventy in 1810, Baring was worth £625,000, of which £400,000 was in land. By 1825 the Rothschild bank was ten times the size of Barings, their nearest rivals, and when Nathan died as plain Mr Rothschild in 1836 he was worth nearly six times as much as Sir Francis Baring at the time of his death; and still Nathan had bought no grand country house and estate.[36]

That he was exceptional in this was noted by Benjamin Disraeli in a speech that he made, in praise of the landed interest, in the House of Commons a decade later: 'From the days of Sir Robert Walpole to the present moment, with one solitary exception [Nathan], all those who have now realised huge fortunes in our great seats of industry have deposited the results of their success in the soil of their country . . . Every family which has acquired great wealth has invested that wealth in the purchase of land . . .' Shortly before he died, though, Nathan had dipped his toe into the water.[37]

On 1 July 1835 Hannah received a letter from the office of a Mr Rainy, of Messrs White, Blake, Houseman & Tylee, solicitors, of Essex Street, Strand, informing her that 'Mr Copland's Ex[ecut]ors will accept Mr Rothschild's offer of £17,000 for the purchase of Gunnersbury Park including the Fixtures & Timber'. The property had been advertised for auction in London on 30 June, so it seems as if the auctioneer had failed to find a buyer in the room, and that Nathan secured it for his price after the sale.[38]

Bought to replace the house at Stamford Hill, it was not just another pretty villa with eight acres of land. The agents' particulars describe an 'Elegant and Magnificent Mansion' in the parish of Ealing in Middlesex, recently built by Henry Holland's partner Alexander Copland, 'a gentleman of acknowledged taste, who spared no expense, with a view to substantial durability, convenience, and embellishment'.[39]

Standing on 'a handsome Terrace of considerable elevation', on the site of a house once occupied by Princess Amelia, a daughter of King George II, the new mansion boasted 'internal arrangements, equally adapted to the display of splendid hospitality, or to the supply of every domestic comfort . . . so perfect as to admit of little further improvement. The principal suite of apartments are nearly 100 feet in extent, and are approached through a Hall which has very recently been embellished by a series of alto relievo panels executed from the designs of Flaxman.'

Beyond the house itself – 'conveniently secluded from the more frequented avenues to town' – the facilities included a 'Spacious Conservatory, Ornamental Pleasure Grounds, Luxuriant Plantations and Walks of great variety, Alcoves, Pavilion, with Stone Portico of the Doric order, Grapery, Pinery, and succession Houses'. The view to the south from the Pavilion was to 'Kew Gardens with its lofty Pagoda, Richmond Park and the Surrey Hills'. Further amenities included stabling, coach houses, dairy, laundry, brew-house, ice-well, orchard and kitchen garden. The setting was seventy-five acres of gardens, park and farmland, of which rather more than forty-five acres were freehold, the remainder being held on a lease.

The farmland was an especially desirable feature for the new owners; with Lionel's encouragement, Hannah had been looking for a farm to buy since 1832. Moses and Judith had long ago bought a farm in Kent; Henrietta Montefiore owned one in Sussex, at Worth Park, where Nat and Mayer would go to shoot with their cousin Joe. And the idea of a farm, or of a property with a farm, was clearly something that appealed to Nathan.[40]

Writing from St Leonard's, in Sussex, where she was staying with Hannah in January 1832, Hannah Mayer had reported to Nathan that they had seen 'a very fine estate which belongs to Lord Ashburnham . . . There is a beautiful Park and an enormously pretty dairy which would please you very much.' After inspecting James and Betty's establishment at Boulogne-sur-Seine in September 1833, she told Nathan that her uncle and aunt 'take as much pleasure in superintending a little farm as you would'. On the leasehold land at Gunnersbury, Hannah and Nathan now had a small estate farm, with farmyard, cattle sheds and a piggery.[41]

With a 'Beautiful Park' planted with mature trees and containing 'two fine Sheets of water', one with an ornamental bridge, and situated just off the road between Acton and Ealing, Gunnersbury Park and Mansion, the agents ventured, comprised a property which 'from its superior arrangements and proximity to the Metropolis, being only about Six Miles therefrom, is remarkably well adapted for *The Residence of a Nobleman, Minister of State, or Family of Distinction*'.

Despite the agents' puff, Nathan and Hannah did not consider their new property to be 'so perfect as to admit of little further improvement'. While Thomas Allason was employed to undertake alterations to the house in Piccadilly, Nathan and Hannah engaged the architect Sydney Smirke, whose brother Edward was one of Copland's executors, to undertake an extensive scheme of alterations and improvements to the house at Gunnersbury and to its ancillary buildings.[42] Smirke was producing plans for the Rothschilds by the end of 1835, though the house was not to be ready for occupation for some time. Nevertheless, in *Boyle's Court Guide for January 1836*, Nathan's residences are listed as No. 107 Piccadilly and 'Gunnersbury park, near Acton, Middlesex'.[43]

Clearly Nathan was pleased with his new acquisition. Lying ill in Frankfurt in July 1836, he asked Lionel to find out from Nat 'to whom you send all the good fruit and things from Gunnersbury and how the place looks'. And as Hannah sat at her husband's bedside day after day, her thoughts, too, strayed to their new establishment.[44]

'I long to see Gunnersbury,' she wrote. 'I should like dear Nat that the fruit and other things might be properly disposed of for I should not like the gardener to have uncontrolled power to do what he likes with the things. It would be a bad commencement. I should like plenty of chicken to be reared – the butter might be salted and barrelled and put in tubs it would do for cooking and the fruit preserved . . . Anthony wrote to me [from Paris] that the vases and other marbles were sent. I must also recommend these to your kind care that the clerk of the works places them safe not to get injured.'[45]

Sadly for Nathan, he was never to see Gunnersbury again, and it was not until the summer of 1837 that the house was ready for occupation. When Hannah, to whom Nathan left Gunnersbury in his will, returned to England as a widow and, after burying her dear Rothschild, wished to mourn away from the noise and distractions of Piccadilly, she rented a house at Roehampton. By then the house at Stamford Hill had been sold.

9

Courtship and Marriage

⸺◦◦◦⸺

THE IDEA OF a match between Lionel and Charlotte seems to have begun to take shape – in the minds of some of the Rothschild women, at least – in late 1831. If contemplated before then, Lionel's sister Chilly certainly gave no hint of it when writing to Hannah about her cousin Charlotte's birthday celebrations in Frankfurt that summer. She did not even refer to Charlotte by name.

'These last few days we have been unusually gay,' Chilly wrote. 'Last Monday there was a juvenile ball at Uncle Charles, whose daughter completed her twelfth year. It would have been a very agreeable party, nothing could have been better arranged, but unluckily between 9 & 10 there was an alarm of fire in the street adjoining the Counting house. You can have no idea what an effect the report of fire creates. All our gentlemen left immediately & a general damp was thrown over the whole party.'[1]

In November, Chilly reported to her mother that 'Mrs Charles has I believe given up all idea of going this winter to Naples. Her daughter has improved very much the last few months. She is dark but will I think be much admired . . .' Days later, referring to a hoped-for visit from Lionel and Nat that had come to nothing, she confessed that her regret at not seeing her brothers in Frankfurt had to it an extra dimension: 'I should have been very glad to have seen them, & I want Lionel to make a certain young Lady's acquaintance. I am very curious to know what he will think of her. You dear Mama will say, time enough for these things.'[2]

Henrietta Montefiore addressed the matter more straightforwardly. 'Madame Charles de Rothschild is just as she was six years ago,' she reported to Hannah from Frankfurt some months later. 'Now for her daughter, who is not just the same in figure as she was six years ago, and without saying one word too much in her praise, she is an extremely pretty, well behaved and elegant girl, and I have no doubt if Lionel were to meet her and not knowing who she was that he would make love to her.'[3]

If Lionel and his brothers had any inkling that matchmaking was afoot, they give nothing away in their letters. Anthony, working in Frankfurt during the autumn of 1832, mentioned his Italian cousins' departure in October, but remarked only that 'Mrs Charles with all her family have left here since some days for Naples . . .' When he returned to the subject in a letter to his mother six weeks later, it was only to say how everyone in Frankfurt was 'very sorry that Mrs Charles has left. She used to make one of the best houses; her absence is a very great loss to the society here. She has been imitating Uncle A and has been arranging her house in a very grand style. It will be magnificent when finished.'[4]

There seems to be no further reference at all to their cousin Charlotte in the English family's correspondence until 1834. In March that year, Henrietta's thirteen-year-old daughter, Louisa, mentions Charlotte in a letter to Lionel's sister Louisa, though without making any reference to Lionel himself. Henrietta's son Nathaniel (Joe and Louisa's brother) and her other daughter, another Charlotte, had both been unwell, and the Montefiores were staying in Naples. 'Since Nathaniel is recovered from Scarlatina [scarlet fever],' Louisa wrote, 'we have rode almost every day on horseback as that exercise is very much recommended for Charlotte [Montefiore]. We have got very nice horses. We wished Charlotte R [Rothschild] very much to ride with us but as she is not English her taste is not always the same as ours, and she refused our request . . .'[5]

A month later, in a letter to Hannah from Frankfurt, Chilly asked: 'Were you not rather surprised to hear [of] Lionel's sudden determination of going to Turin? The [business] affair in question is I believe by no means an easy one. I most sincerely hope he will succeed . . . It does not as yet appear certain whether our Neapolitan friends will be able to leave this summer. Do you think Lionel will proceed on to Naples?'[6]

In May, humiliated by his failure in Turin to win appointment for the rue Laffitte to manage a £1 million loan for the Kingdom of Piedmont-Sardinia, Lionel could not face travelling on to Naples.[7] 'You will be a little astonished to see this letter dated from this place,' he wrote to his parents from Paris, 'where I arrived last night rather unexpected, but having been vexed with my Turin Affair I was not in the least disposed to travel about for pleasure. You will, I am afraid, think that I acted wrongly in not proceeding on to Naples, but having commenced by a failure, I did not like risking a second one in the same journey. Uncle Charles will think that I do not much care about paying him a visit, so I intend writing that I only came home to settle my accounts and then shall set off for his beautiful place. In the meantime my dear Parents, I beg you will let me know what you would like me to do. If you think I ought to go to Naples, or to pay you a visit first, which I should like to do, I should then be ready to act completely as you wish.'[8]

In the event, the notion of going to Naples was either abandoned, or the trip was postponed until September. Throughout the remainder of May, June and the first half of July, Lionel continued to write from Paris, after which he seems to have spent a period at home in England; his steady stream of correspondence from Paris resumes in mid–August, but breaks off again in September. Then by 1 October he is writing from Madrid, where he was to remain until the end of June the next year, conducting pro-tracted, and this time successful, negotiations with the Spanish government for control of the country's valuable mercury industry.

No mention of Naples or of the Neapolitan cousins is made for some months to come, and in his letters to Anthony, who had taken his place in Paris, there is no suggestion that Lionel was in any hurry to give up his bachelor life:

'Here there is no society at all,' he wrote to Anthony at the end of November. 'You will be then a little curious to know how I pass my time and what fun I have. In a few lines I can tell you everything. When I first arrived everything was new, but now I am quite a settled inhabitant of Madrid. I breakfast & remain at home till 11 o'clock, then pay visits to all sorts of persons from the Minister down to the Washerwoman who takes charge of my love affairs which, by the bye, are not of much consequence, but are still necessary in a country like this, where nothing else seriously occupies [a] man's thoughts. I then come home about 6 o'clock and have a good dinner, the only good thing we get here . . . I have not had any wonderful adventures in my search after the fair sex, nor have I met with anything worth mentioning. I have also not bought any pictures lately; good things of every description are scarce.'[9]

He attended a bullfight, and he dined with the French and the British envoys in Madrid. 'The whole as you may suppose is disgusting,' he wrote of the bullfight. 'They say it never pleases the first time, but you can have no idea what a popular amusement it is. They take as much interest in it as we English do in a famous horserace or foxhounds.'[10]

The two diplomats – George Villiers, later the fourth Earl of Clarendon, was the British Minister – had been 'as polite as can be. This is the only society that there is. The Spaniards give nothing; they walk about every Evening from 5 to 7 in their Park, which is their greatest amusement. The theatres they say are very bad. Of the Ladies I cannot say much . . . The Spanish Ladies have not much to boast of in their Exterior; of the Interior I cannot yet judge. I know they do not appear very tempting.'

By the time he wrote to Anthony in mid–December, it seems as if Lionel was beginning to take a rather closer interest in the Spanish ladies. He asked Anthony to send him from Paris 'two pair of the very finest white worked stockings for a Lady . . . They can be sent in a letter . .' In February he thanked Anthony for 'the gloves, braces & stockings, which arrived in good order. If another courier leaves, you will oblige me by sending me some more ladies gloves but larger than the others which are too small.'[11]

The Spanish guitarist Trinidad Huerta, who had played at Hannah's concerts in London, was in Madrid at the same time as Lionel. Thirty years later, he recalled how in 1835 he had 'often had the honor of dining with Mr De Rothschild in Madrid that year . . . Every evening I made music at his Hotel & generally was he accompanied by his friend La Casene.' Writing to Mayer from Madrid in 1848 Hannah's nephew Lionel Helbert had a message for Lionel: 'Tell the Baron I saw his old love. She is still goodlooking. Her sister is living with Sartorius.'[12]

When, in March 1835, it was mooted that Anthony might take his elder brother's place in Madrid, Lionel advised him that if he were to do so he would do well to bring with him, in addition to his cook, silver cutlery and table ware, 'as many nice little things for ladies as you can. You will find lots to accept them, little trinkets & all sorts of things. I write to you all this in case you should come, but tell my uncles that I will do whatever they wish if my Parents are of the same opinion.' In the event, Anthony did not go to Madrid, but his brother's bachelor days were now numbered.[13]

'If Uncle Charles is gone to Naples,' Lionel continued, 'it will not be necessary for me to go so soon to Ffurt. Every thing will therefore depend upon the family plans, as I think it makes very little difference for me to go to ffort a few months earlier or later as I have no particular fancy to get married just immediately. A few weeks later or earlier makes no difference without our good parents wish to go to ffort. You must therefore be so good as to settle it amongst yourselves, and whatever is agreed upon I shall be happy to do.' In the event, he left Madrid on 29 June, and subsequently made the journey to Frankfurt.

On 29 September, Hannah wrote to Charlotte that she had learned of 'the recent happy conclusion to an event we have for some time been anticipating', and of 'the very amiable moment you gave your consent to this union with our good Lionel'. 'I will not praise our good Lionel,' she went on, 'only tell you that we have ever found him amiable, with a temper and disposition that cannot fail to promote the happiness of her who has approved of him . . . Your Uncle and I have sent you a Pearl

Necklace begging you to accept of it kindly and to receive it as a token of love . . .'[14]

That Charlotte was still only sixteen may account for the faintly domineering tone of a letter she received from her future mother-in-law in October. 'I am persuaded that you entirely engross Lionel's time and attention,' Hannah wrote. 'I therefore request you to say that I hope he will give a little time to write to us for there are a thousand things which we want his opinion upon and as we cannot have any personal communication with him at present he must not give up corresponding. I shall be happy to learn that you are becoming very intimate with Hannah Mayer [who was staying in Frankfurt]. She is of rather quiet habits, but is a very good girl and I hope you find her amiable.'[15]

Following his engagement, Lionel remained in Frankfurt until shortly after the New Year of 1836, when he set off on his way back to England, via Paris. It was from an inn at Metz, which he had just reached after 'a long cold drive of thirty six hours hardly without leaving the carriage', that he wrote his first letter since quitting Frankfurt to his 'Dearest Beloved Charlotte'. Continuing in a somewhat gothic vein – 'it is now five o'clock in the morning, most terrible weather, the wind making such a noise that I almost fancy the inn haunted' – Lionel maintains an uncharacteristically dramatic pitch:

'Never, never would I have undertaken this journey had it not been necessary to make some preparations for the only person for whom I would make every sacrifice. The few hours I have been away from you and which have appeared an eternity, an age, have passed melancholy, but have been fully occupied with the sweet remembrance of the happy minutes spent together. My consolation, my conviction is that they are the commencement of the many happy days we shall pass together, my expectation, my hopes, have been more than realized; continue Dear Charlotte to have the same sentiments towards [me], and my happiness is insured.'[16]

In his first long letter to Charlotte from Paris, written during the evening of 7 January, his first day there, Lionel continues in the same feverish style. 'Now that I am separated, I only know the meaning of the word, and am only able to judge of my love, of my entirely devoted love for you Dear Charlotte. I wish I were able to express it in words, but I cannot, even in endeavouring to do so my pen has fallen from my hand, and more than an hour has passed thinking of you without having taken it up. You will laugh at me, perhaps not understand me; if so have only compassion, and believe me I am as sincere as a man can be, and only pray that you will think me so . . .'[17]

Charlotte's first letter to Lionel, responding to his letter from Metz, is dated 8 January. 'My heart is palpitating with joyful emotions,' she begins, 'but words are unavailing to depict the sentiments which pervade my soul, and I can but attempt to express the delight your very affectionate letter has inspired [in] me. Nothing charms me so much as to hear that our feelings and sympathies are shared; when separated from our friends, nothing consoles us more of the pains of absence than to learn that the moments passed together are remembered with pleasure. Pray, favour me often with a few words; a single line from you will always be welcomed with heartfelt joy. Occupations, amusements &c are, I know, most detrimental to a correspondence, but the ties which unite us are sacred, and ought to be recognised as superior . . .'[18]

Considering that Charlotte was only sixteen, and that her first language was German, this was an impressive – and successful – debut. But as a daughter of Anthony's would remember, Charlotte was a 'brilliant linguist' – with the assistance, it seems, of an English tutor named Howe.[19]

By 13 January, Lionel had 'passed several long days anxiously and tediously without hearing one word from you Dearest Charlotte, when I received your few lines and was then, for the first time since I have left, rendered happy for a few minutes; but I am now again in my melancholy state. Your letter I have read over & over, and each time have regretted more & more the great distance that now separates us. I was also grieved to see that you still have such an indifferent opinion of me. You talk of amusements, occupations &c; do you think I can have any that I do not enjoy with you Dear Charlotte? I have been invited everywhere, been entreated to join in some parties of amusement with old friends, but have declined; the only manner of passing my time without being annoyed is when I am alone at my hotel, thinking and only thinking of you dearest Charlotte . . .'[20]

Oddly, since he and Charlotte were now engaged, Lionel imagines that her parents would know nothing of his writing: 'Pray remember me most kindly to your brother Charles,' Lionel wrote, 'who is the only person I suppose that will know of your receiving letters from me.' Perhaps such a fantasy added fuel to the sensation of romance. Their correspondence could hardly have remained a secret for long: from the moment of his arrival in Paris, Lionel found himself 'in the midst of curious and inquisitives' and was 'tormented with questions from all sides'.[21]

Spending a quiet evening with Betty and her mother Caroline, 'the only subject of our conversation, as you can easily imagine, was my occupations during my stay at ffort. With what pleasure, I may almost say eloquence, did I speak of them. My answers to all their questions were listened to with pleasure. They had some idea of your perfections, and were really happy in hearing them confirmed in every respect. They perhaps wished to flatter me, but how I rejoiced in knowing that it was only the truth. When they have the pleasure of seeing you they will be more than convinced of it . . .'[22]

When he wrote on 16 January, it was to thank Charlotte for 'the assurance of those sentiments of which I am happy to say I have experienced the proof, and which I shall strive all my life to possess. I can only assure you, Dear Charlotte, that my endeavours will always to be to prove myself worthy of your affection, and to make you acknowledge that I love you as dearly and tenderly as any person can . . . I have had all my little things carefully packed, and was considering all the time with heartbeating [sic] pleasure the day when I shall see them arranged in my little house & criticized by my dear cousin and beloved Charlotte.'[23]

Threatening to undermine Lionel's romantic programme, however, some Frankfurt busybody had planted a seed of doubt in Charlotte's mind. On 17 January, Lionel wondered: 'What interest can a certain person have in doubting my love for you Dear Charlotte, I regret to see such ill natured persons & shall prove to you all my life that every word I have said and say to you, is true. How I wish I could send you my heart and there you would see every word written, but I can only add that every word comes from there, and that you alone Dearest Charlotte possess it . . . I must leave off as the horses are at the door.'[24]

Lionel was then on the point of leaving for London. Five days later, he resumed the correspondence, declaring that he will 'go mad' if he cannot soon explain his feelings in person. But from then on, while his letters continue to contain affirmations and reassurances of his love – and also reproaches if he senses that he is being neglected – the tone overall becomes less theatrical, more practical. Once back in England, Lionel was more his old self.[25]

'I am happy to say that I found my good parents in excellent health & spirits and rejoicing at my good accounts,' he wrote on 22 January, 'how happy they are to see me so attached to you and so fortunate as to have obtained the favors of a person of whom every person speaks in such high terms, and whose acquaintance they are so anxious to make . . . I have seen several houses and have found one that I think will suit . . . The other little things that we shall want will then easily be found.'

Over the next two months, until returning to Frankfurt for the wedding, Lionel continued to look for a house. He ordered two new carriages, commissioned Anthony to enquire in Paris about engaging a cook, bought a pony for Charlotte's brother Dolly, and wondered if he might buy one for Charlotte, too. 'Write to me, Dearest Charlotte, if, on my return to ffort, you will ride on Horse Back. I should be too happy to purchase a horse suitable for you. I should certainly advise you to ride.' It was an activity for which she was never able to work up much enthusiasm.[26]

Anthony found a cook, though not until June, when Lionel was back in Germany. 'I shall send the Cook off to morrow,' he wrote to Nat in London. 'I do not know whether he is a very good cook. I tried him several times & we were all very well satisfied. Rabbi need not make the least compliment for should he not suit he can pack him off.' Luckily, the man passed the test with Nat, too. 'I am glad that you like the Cook,' Anthony wrote later. 'I never liked ours & always thought him a most infernal bad one.'[27]

With her fiancé in London, Charlotte was now and again beset with doubts and fears. Lionel did his best to reassure her. 'Do not think that any attractions or charms of sweet home or anything else can alter my sentiments,' he wrote on 6 February. 'I have given you Dearest Charlotte my heart, and do not wish to have it back, without you are willing to return it to me. Why Dear Charlotte do you say that you are sometimes in doubt as to my constancy and love? Do you judge others by yourself? I know that you have heard many things since my departure, but would have thought you never could have believed any of them. I am so confident in my love for you and in my hopes of rendering you happy that I console myself with the idea of your future love if I do not possess it now.'[28]

He spent the greater part of his days at New Court, and 'the evenings at home, in a quiet family circle, looking at the newspapers, I will not say reading them, for my thoughts can only be occupied with one object, and with that I assure you they are so fully taken up, that I attend to nothing, and am continually being blamed for my being so absent'. Lionel, as his mother wrote to his fiancée on 23 February, 'is impatient to return to you, but things cannot well be done in a hurry'.[29]

A City dinner that Lionel attended at the end of February was 'not a party of pleasure; in fact since my departure from Frankfurt I do not know that word any longer. Never did I pass my time more tiresomely and tediously. Very shortly I shall be preparing for my journey and hope soon to be able to announce to you the day fixed for my departure.'[30]

It was in fact some three weeks before he finally set off, and by then – set to receive £75,000 from Nathan on marrying – he had found and taken 'a very nice small house . . . not very large, but quite newly and elegantly furnished'. The house was No. 10 Hill Street, Berkeley Square, and it was to be the couple's first marital home.[31]

With Nathan dead, Lionel, with Nat to help him, took charge at New Court; and it was his misfortune that he did so just as a period of financial stability was coming to an end. In July 1836, for the first time in nine years, the Bank of England had raised its lending rate (Nathan had in the past been a large-scale borrower); and then from early August there was a steady fall in the price of Consols.[32] 'Personal affairs are quite as precarious as they have been for some time,' Hannah wrote to Mayer from Roehampton. 'We must hope for better times.' But Consols continued to decline and by the end of the year New Court had sustained its first annual loss since the revolutionary year of 1830.[33]

On 31 December 1836, Anthony wrote from Paris to 'wish you all a happy new year and that the next may bring us greater blessings than the last'. But 1837, the year of Queen Victoria's accession, was for the City, and for New Court, a year overcast by a crisis in the American economy.[34] After 1830, Nathan and James had begun to look to the United States, to take an interest in loans to individual States and in the financing of American trade. As Massachusetts, Louisiana, Maryland and other States sought development capital from Europe, offering attractive rates of interest and seeming security with their loan stock, escalating exports of American cotton and tobacco to Europe generated a good business in bills.[35]

New Court dealt in American stock, and participated in the bills business. Then as investor confidence in America waned from mid-1836, American firms soon found themselves unable to remit the huge sums owing to their European creditors. Together with Barings and various other City houses, Rothschilds – who in 1834 had replaced Barings as the United States government's agents in London – were caught out as, one after another, the firms with which they had had dealings ran into trouble.

The peak of the crisis in London came in May–June 1837, though the fall-out from a further American crisis was to bedevil the City in the period 1839–42. Lionel, consequently, had more than enough on his plate at New Court; and, perhaps inevitably, the effects of this were felt at home – by Charlotte. 'Lionel was never with me between the hours of ten in the morning & 6 in the evening,' she later confided to her journal. 'Oh! why did I waste those hours in vain regrets, in tears? Why did I not then ardently & arduously apply [myself] to study, study that would have dried my tears and made my thoughts flow into pleasant & profitable channels?

I could have accomplished much in those days, when if I had no joys, I also had few cares and few domestic duties to fulfil.'[36]

In the months after her marriage and Nathan's death, Charlotte, now 'in the land & city of fogs', was plunged in gloom. She missed 'the bright skies of other climes, the pure exhilarating air of other countries'; she allowed 'the dense atmosphere of the metropolis' to weigh down her spirits, 'which had never been buoyant'; she was 'far away from parents, brothers & friends'; she 'knew no one in this large town save those who were too much engrossed by their own painful feelings & regrets to bestow indulgent thoughts on the stranger, who in the sunniest, brightest hour of her youth had left . . . a happy home endeared by thousands of associations, crowded with pictures of early enjoyment, with dear faces never to be forgotten, to seek a new country, a new home, a home quite silent & untenanted, save by books!'

For a brief period, her spirits were lifted by the arrival, on 25 August 1837, of Leonora, her first child, 'whose birth was happiness so exquisite to me, felicity so perfect, bliss so unexpectedly great, that the moments which followed her appearance in this world of fogs & cares, swept away at once the recollection of past sufferings, of moral anxiety and anguish, of physical pain & fatigue. And I had known both much & long . . .' All too soon, though, the spell was broken, when, so Charlotte maintained, Hannah Mayer made the unfortunate remark that the new baby looked 'like a frog or a toad'. 'It was the first cloud that came upon the sunshine of my happiness,' Charlotte remembered, 'and it caused my tears to flow fast & long.'

Her low spirits were evidently leading to a loss of perspective and sense of proportion. Her mother's reaction to London and to the treatment she received from her relations a year later is in striking contrast. Having returned home, Adelheid wrote to thank Hannah 'repeatedly for the many proofs of real kindness you so amiably bestowed on myself and family during our stay in London and which I shall *never* forget. I consider London the most delightful place that possibly can exist, and do not understand how there can be any comparison made with Paris, which perhaps on account of the social amusements, theatres, etc, etc, may have the preference, but in *no further respect whatever*.'[37]

On 25 August 1839, Leonora's second birthday, the birth of another daughter, Evelina, was, Charlotte later confided, 'attended with infinitely less pain' − but it was 'also followed by less intense joy than Leonora's arrival. Perhaps I was disappointed at not having a son . . .' Lionel appeared to Charlotte to be indifferent to the new baby. 'Her father was not in the room at the time she made her appearance in this world of mingled joys &

cares. He was neither glad nor sore to hear of her arrival, and thought her rather plain than otherwise when he condescended to look at her tiny face. As she was my second child & only a girl, no one thought much of her, and she passed through the earlier months & years of infancy unnoticed except by me.'[38]

Unfortunately, Lionel, with much else to think about, did not record his side of the story. In later life he would sometimes say that he would have liked to have five daughters rather than just two, though it may well be, as Charlotte seems to suggest, that in 1839 he had been hoping for a son. Anthony certainly assumed so. 'I congratulate you with all my heart to [sic] the new comer – & beg of you to make my congratulations to your good lady,' he wrote from Paris on 28 August. 'In these affairs one must take what one can get . . . I hope nevertheless that we shall soon hear the young Lady is quite well – & also your wife . . .'[39]

As well as being preoccupied with the precarious state of affairs in the City and across the Atlantic, Lionel had in 1839 to contend with two other worrying family concerns. The first came early in the year, when James was taken seriously ill in Naples.

Since Nathan's death James had tended to behave – to the intermittent irritation of his nephews in London – rather as the new Rothschild 'general-in-command'. It was not unknown for a letter of his to end with the injunction, 'write an answer immediately', and Lionel once observed to Mayer that James liked 'to poke his nose into everything'.[40] 'You will see that Uncle James has had a very violent attack,' Anthony wrote from Paris in early 1839. 'God grant that he may recover . . . that the next accounts may be better.' Anthony's prayer was to be answered, but it seems as if James came perilously close to death.[41]

Passing through Naples in mid-March, bound for the Holy Land, Moses and Judith saw the patient just as he had begun to recover from what Moses referred to vaguely as 'so dangerous an illness'. James was, Moses reported to Lionel and Nat, 'extremely weak from the severity of the remedies that have been applied. He is only permitted to speak a few words, but his spirits are good & thanks to Heaven there is now no further reason to apprehend danger; his situation during the last week was very critical [;] even his medical attendants did not view without alarm the symptoms of his disorder, and his friends were under the most painful anxiety. Though he has not yet left his bed, he continues daily to improve and is now free from fever . . .'

In a postscript to her sister Hannah, Judith added: 'I had this morning the pleasure of seeing baron James who is thank the Almighty recovering: the few words he was allowed to say tended principally to enquire after yourself and family. He partook of some broth whilst we were in the room, and his good Lady said he had relished a roasted apple previously – but the Doctors recommend care in diet and general living and they hope for his speedy & perfect restoration . . .'[42]

As their father lay ill at Naples, James's young children remained in France, and Hannah and Lionel sent them presents. Alphonse, now twelve, wrote to thank Lionel a thousand times for 'the large and strong dog Beppo'; he thought his new pet very fine and handsome. The breed of the dog is not mentioned, but at about that time Lionel was looking for a Newfoundland. Having been shown one that he considered too small, he was offered another that was 'said to be the largest in London . . . in height one yard less 4 ins to the shoulder . . . The Owner wants 12 Gs for him . . .' Perhaps this was Alphonse's Beppo.[43]

Hot on the heels of James's illness came a second family drama. 'That affair of H.M. makes us all here very uncomfortable,' Anthony wrote from Paris on 23 April. 'We must nevertheless put up with it. I only hope that poor girl that she will be happy . . .'[44] Six days later in London, on 29 April at St George's, Hanover Square, Hannah Mayer married Lord Southampton's younger brother Henry FitzRoy. Nat was the only member of the bride's family to attend the wedding; Hannah escorted her daughter to the church door but went no further.

Hannah Mayer was a beautiful girl, with fair skin, blue eyes and a small, graceful figure. The groom – Oxford educated (Magdalen College) – was a handsome man, well over six feet tall, with thick dark hair and bright blue eyes; aged thirty, he was MP for Lewes and a politician for whom a bright future was predicted. His family was aristocratic on both sides.[45]

Henry's grandfather, on whom the barony of Southampton had been conferred, was a grandson of the second Duke of Grafton; his late mother was a first cousin of Lord Hertford; his uncle, also Henry FitzRoy, had married the Duke of Wellington's only sister Anne. His brother Charles, the third Lord Southampton, a well-known Master of Foxhounds, had married the niece of an earl; his first cousin Georgiana married the future seventh Duke of Beaufort; and Viscount Castlereagh, heir to the third Marquess of Londonderry, was groomsman at his wedding.

Henry, moreover, was a decent man and, although a younger son and not rich (more than a decade later his debts to tradesmen at Oxford had still not been paid), he was by no means an unsuitable choice – except for the fact that he was a Christian, and that on marrying him Hannah Mayer became one too.[46]

While her family in London were sad and perturbed, her uncle James on the Continent was beside himself. Something of *un homme nerveux* at the best of times, when convalescent in Switzerland after his illness James's nerves, according to Anthony, were 'so excessively agitated that the least thing puts him out'. For some time to come, the mere thought of his niece's marriage to a Christian, against her family's wishes, made him boil.[47] 'The fact that Hannah Mayer married made me quite ill and frankly speaking I did not have the courage up until now to write,' he wrote to Nat two months after the wedding. 'She robbed our whole family of its pride . . . You write to me that she has found everything [in her marriage] but religion. But just that means everything. Our luck, our blessings, depend upon it. However, we shall have to forget her and cut her out of our memory . . . We just wish her happiness and in future we shall just look upon the whole matter as if she had never existed for us.'[48]

History does not relate how Hannah Mayer and Henry met, but by the summer of 1838 they had fallen in love. Indeed, by then things had reached such a pitch – marriage was already being talked of – that the Rothschilds asked Henry to go abroad for six months. He agreed, and on his way to Turkey kept a diary, extracts from which, published by his great-grandson almost a century later, make it all but impossible to think that his feelings were anything but genuine.[49]

To Henry, Hannah Mayer was simply Hannah. 'How much every scene in this reminds me of Hannah,' he wrote after seeing a performance of *Norma* in Berlin. 'I have so often turned from a passage that peculiarly pleased me, to try and read the expression on her pretty face as she sat at my side. What would I not now give for one glimpse of that countenance!'[50]

'Give me a small cosy home with Hannah and I never wish again to move,' he wrote a few days later. 'However, here or there would be all equally blessed and happy where she was. We shall certainly be compelled to live on the Continent for cheapness but the worst is I dare scarcely hope that we shall live anywhere together and without her I cannot be happy. Could I but have the offer how happy I should be!' Henry's feelings were reciprocated, though Hannah Mayer was only allowed to write to him once a month. 'Arrived at Vienna where I had the happiness of finding a letter from my beloved Hannah,' Henry wrote on 24 October. 'I read and reread her dear kind letter with a joy I cannot express. Thank God she is not yet changed.'[51]

Henry's reflection that, after marrying, he and Hannah Mayer would have to live on the Continent for cheapness' sake, suggests that he was expecting his future wife to be cut off by her family – and she stood to lose a great deal by marrying in the teeth of their opposition. She had received £12,500 from her father during his lifetime, and a further £12,500 on his death. No one could deprive her of those sums; but under the terms of Nathan's will she was to be denied more than four times as much if she married against the wishes of her immediate family.

In his will Nathan had left Hannah Mayer and her sister Louisa each a stake of £50,000, paying interest at 4 per cent, in their brothers' business, and another £50,000 each, to be invested in the same way, to serve as a dowry. Both sums of £50,000 were to be paid in cash to each daughter on marriage – but if either daughter were to marry 'contrary to the will of her mother and brothers', she was to forfeit the whole of the £100,000, as well as the interest.[52]

In the event, the support Hannah Mayer received on her wedding day from her mother and from Nat shows that she did not exactly marry against the will of her immediate family, and there is no evidence to suggest that she was deprived of her inheritance or dowry. 'As for me,' Nat said later, 'I wd sooner sell the last shirt I had than owe H.M. her money.' Indeed, as things turned out it was Henry's family, not Hannah Mayer's, who seized the opportunity to tighten the purse strings.[53]

Charles Southampton – whom Harriet Arbuthnot considered 'very dull and stupid' and who in the hunting field was noted for his swagger and his use of 'very strong language' – used Henry's marriage to Hannah Mayer as an excuse to cut off his brother's allowance. In this act of mean-spiritedness he is said to have been encouraged by his wife, a 'very pleasing & pretty woman' to outward appearances. Fortunately for Henry, his mother, a Protestant zealot, was no longer alive to stir up any more trouble.[54]

The marriage displeased Hannah Mayer's uncle James from several points of view: 'What sort of example would a girl be for our children who says: "I marry against the wish of my family"?' he asked Nat. 'Why should my children or my children's children follow my wishes if there is no punishment? Now I come to the main point: Religion. In our family we have always tried to keep up the love for, the attachment to the family . . . In this way it was more or less understood from early childhood that the children would never think of marrying outside the family. This way the fortune would stay inside the family . . .'[55]

When Anthony and Mayer visited James and Betty in Switzerland in July, Hannah Mayer's marriage was still very much on their uncle's mind.

'Since I have been here,' Anthony wrote to Nat and Lionel, 'you may naturally think & expect that all their conversation is respecting H.M. I have requested Uncle James as well as Betty to write to you in as friendly terms upon that subject as possible, as I said it would, I am sure, even produce a greater effect than all the quarrelsome letters in the world. Their principal reason & what they wish us to do is not to receive H.M. for the present & which is easily understood. They say a sister is married against the consent of one's family – if after two months you will receive her – what example will it have upon the remainder part of the family – they say will my daughter who sees her cousin who married against the consents of all her family received by them will she marry whom I like – no, she will also fall in love with a Christian & God knows what my boys will also do if they see that H.M. is received.

'That is their reasoning. I recommend you my dear Brothers more for your own sake, and also to endeavour to keep the union up amongst us – not to receive H.M. for the present . . . I am certain that by degrees when it is all forgotten that you will be able to do what you like . . . I have told them that what Mamma intended doing we could not help, as she was Mother & would certainly follow her own feelings. Nevertheless if Mamma were to see H.M. I certainly would recommend her also for the present not to invite H.M. . . .'[56]

In time, of course, the storm blew over. Hannah did not see her daughter for a while, but asked Nat to pass on any news he had of 'an Individual who still so much interests me but who has separated herself from me'. Anthony, on the other hand, paid Hannah Mayer a visit in January 1840, and in July the next year reported from Frankfurt that 'HM & her fitzy' were 'very much pleased' with a visit they were making to Ems, where Hannah Mayer's uncle Amschel was staying at the time. In January 1843, Anthony went down to Badminton for a few days' hunting with the Duke of Beaufort, to whom Henry was connected by marriage.[57]

From Mainz, where they were staying in the summer of 1843, Henry and Hannah Mayer – now with their 'fine fat baby' Arthur – went to spend a day in Frankfurt with Anselm and Chilly. In Paris the next year (now the parents of a 'fine fat little girl', Blanche, as well) they dined with Nat one evening, and another evening with Nat, Louisa and Charles. Four years later, even the once splenetic James was welcoming them to his table for dinner.[58]

10

The Crack Pack

'THERE IS A considerable university at Leipzig. The public institutions
that belong to it are much the same as at every other German university. The professors are all learned but I believe there are none very
celebrated. There is no particular building for the students: they live about
the town as in every other German university.'

This had been Lionel's verdict on Leipzig University when he was pass-
ing through the city on his tour with Anthony and John Darby in 1827. Joe
Montefiore had none the less spent a year there in 1832–3, and it was from
Leipzig University that Mayer broke off his studies to visit Frankfurt with
Fritz Schlemmer in the fateful summer of 1836. By then, according to
Schlemmer, Mayer was 'a big strong man', though 'lazy when it came to
physical exercise'. But in the lecture room and in private classes Mayer
applied himself to studying history, geography, politics, German literature,
algebra and geometry, and also to improving his grasp of German.[1]

Schlemmer had relations in Leipzig and took apartments to share with
his pupil in a building where one of his Schunk uncles resided. Also resident in the building, and quite a bonus, was Felix Mendelssohn, whom
Schlemmer had known since his time at Naples with Nat. Mendelssohn
was now director of the Leipzig Gewandhaus, and in 1835 Ignaz Moscheles
had made the journey from London to appear with him in the first of his
Gewandhaus concerts. 'I took my pupil to introduce him to the latter
[Mendelssohn],' Schlemmer recalled, 'and then to call on Frege. Later I
made a series of interesting acquaintances, among them Clara Wieck with
her father and sister, M. and Mme Schleinitz, Robert Schumann . . . and
several other celebrated musicians.'[2]

Mayer and his tutor dined regularly at the Hotel Bavaria, at a table next
to Mendelssohn and Schumann. In the evenings, Schlemmer remembered,
'we four met up at our lodgings after dinner, where we drank coffee and
played chess. Robert Schumann would often be seated at the grand piano
that I had hired from Wieck's shop.' When Mendelssohn's mother and sister
Fanny came to stay in Leipzig, the four friends all enjoyed themselves

'immensely, but were completely exhausted. The studies also suffered to some degree.'[3]

In a letter from Leipzig written two months before Mayer set off for Frankfurt to meet his parents, Schumann told his sister-in-law: 'Mendelssohn . . . is a god among men, and you ought to know him. David, the leader of the orchestra, is another of my associates; also a certain Dr Schlemmer, the companion of young Rothschild; and Rothschild himself. You will find these three in Leipzig when you come. The doctor will be quite your sort – a man of the world, every inch of him.'[4]

A decade later, Mendelssohn dedicated his Opus 65 organ sonatas to Fritz Schlemmer; and in Mendelssohn's honeymoon diary of 1837 there is a drawing of Schlemmer playing a church organ, with Mendelssohn conducting. Another familiar face in Leipzig was Schlemmer's former pupil Léon de Laborde, who in the summer of 1836 was making a study, in the university library, of early book printing.[5]

In the autumn, Mayer exchanged Leipzig for Heidelberg University – a Heidelberg church is the setting for the drawing of Schlemmer and Mendelssohn – where the pattern of lectures and classes resumed, and where Mayer continued to make steady progress at maths, history, German and other subjects. Neither the place where he and his tutor lodged, nor the style in which they lived there, is recorded. But according to William Howitt, writing in the early 1840s: 'Mr [John] Murray, in his "Handbook", has inserted a passage in regard to the cheapness of Heidelberg . . . He speaks of an Englishman who lived there in 1834, whose annual expenses were only 380*l.*, including horses, carriages, and servants. Every thing, no doubt, was then much cheaper, and such a miracle of living possibly *might* be done then; but it is difficult to credit this story even of that time, except the gentleman was a *single* gentleman.'[6]

In mid-December, Schlemmer wrote to Nat in London to assure him that Mayer would now be well able to deal with German business correspondence when the time came. It was only in French that Mayer's progress was at a standstill, and that, Schlemmer suggested, could easily be remedied by a period spent with the family in Paris. The only thing that troubled Schlemmer was his pupil's reluctance to mix in society; rather than go out in the evenings, Mayer preferred to sit at home with a book. However, in London Mayer's conduct was noted with unqualified approval. 'I allude to your refusal to partake of the parties which are offered to you,' Hannah wrote to him in mid-November. 'Papa's memory deserves to be respected as I am sure you feel it should be.'[7]

*

Lionel and Nat were by now back at New Court; Anthony was again in Paris. As Lionel returned after a day's work in the City to his tearful young wife in Hill Street, Nat made his way out to Roehampton, where Hannah also had her three daughters for company. On 26 October, Chilly, who had returned to London with the party accompanying Nathan's body, gave birth to a healthy son, named Nathaniel Anselm. The boy, his grand-mother noted, surely with no great surprise considering his parentage, bore a 'strong family likeness'.[8]

Nat and Lionel had resolved not to hunt that winter, so for exercise Nat rode daily to New Court and back. 'Your brothers,' Hannah wrote to Mayer from Roehampton in November, 'would rather we were in Town but this would not suit us.'[9]

It was to be more than six months before Hannah returned to Piccadilly (that 'bustling place'), but in the meantime she followed affairs at New Court, as Nathan had intended, with keen interest. 'Now that we are deprived of our best friend,' she explained to Mayer, 'there is more respon-sibility upon ourselves and it requires great care to act well so that at a future period we can look back and be satisfied with what we have done . . .'

In Paris, Solomon Cohen's daughter Jeannette – whose marriage at Canonbury Nathan and Hannah had attended in 1825 – saw Anthony, now twenty-six years old, not long after the New Year of 1837. The strains of recent months had left their mark. 'Anthony still wears his peruke,' Jeannette reported cheerfully to her sister, 'and tells me that he is as grey as my venerable husband and that his shaving has not been of any use.'[10]

Jeannette also reported that she had been to dinner with James and Betty, and from her account it seems that the Paris Rothschilds were out of mourning. 'On Monday last, though I was not very fit to go out,' she went on, 'we dined with the James de Rothschilds. I did not like to absent myself as they had been so obliging as to make the party on purpose for us, and a most sumptuous one it was . . . We were in the state rooms which were all thrown open except the ballroom. It is quite impossible for any sovereign prince to live in a style of greater magnificence . . . The curtains of the different rooms are each of a different coloured silk, fringed and looped with gold and silver, the walls and ceiling decorated by the first artists; in some rooms the former are hung with the same costly materials as the curtains and chairs; and over all there is the most perfect freshness; in London with our smoke they could not remain so. As to the dinner, it was equal to the palace in which it was served. The company which was very brilliant consisted chiefly of English and Americans.'

It was perhaps no surprise that Anthony, whose appetite for rich food was as hearty as his sense of humour, was getting fat, as well as bald, on life with his uncle and aunt. On the first day of a visit to the rue Laffitte some months later, Lionel wrote in haste to Nat that he had found 'all friends quite well. Billy is fat, but not looking very fresh . . . but they all say he is pretty steady, and very attentive to the Counting House.'[11]

In contrast to James and Betty's social programme in Paris, there is no record of the London Rothschilds resuming the social round until August 1837, when Hannah gave a dinner for Count Ludolf, the Neapolitan Minister in London, and his wife. The next month Lionel, Anthony and Nat (Mayer was by now studying, though not for a degree, at Cambridge) went together to the Guildhall to witness Moses Montefiore's swearing-in as a Sheriff for Middlesex and London. Moses' nomination had been proposed by Timothy Curtis, now Governor of the Bank of England, and seconded by Sam Gurney.[12]

In January 1838 Lionel and Charlotte, with Nat and Louisa, attended a dinner given by Moses – who had been knighted by Queen Victoria the previous November – for the Vice-Chancellor; and then in February, several family members, including Hannah, were spotted at a party in Mayfair. The person who caught sight of them was Benjamin Disraeli, recently elected to the Tory benches in the Commons but then still best known as a novelist. Towards the end of her letter from Paris a year before, Jeannette Salomons had asked her sister: 'Have you read *Henrietta Temple*? It was published here at the same time as in London for five francs. It is by the author of *Vivian Grey*, D'Israeli the younger. We do not like it . . .'[13]

According to Rothschild family tradition, it was in 1837 that Disraeli was 'accepted as a friend' by the family; and it seems that this came about as a result of a transaction that mixed politics with finance. A. R. Wagg, of the City stockbrokers Helbert, Wagg and a grandson of John Wagg, who was sole partner in the firm until 1848, recalled that when Disraeli was elected MP for Maidstone in 1837, 'according to the then law of the land, [he] had to invest £500 in British Government Securities. He was so hard up in those days that he had to borrow the money from Rothschilds, and on their instruction we bought the necessary stock.'[14]

The occasion for Disraeli's sighting of the Rothschilds in February 1838 was a musical evening at No. 5 Grafton Street, the town house of Robert Parnther. The Parnthers (or Panthers) were friends of the Duke of Wellington. Mrs Parnther, who played the harp, had had an affair with the Spanish general Don Miguel de Alava, who had fought with the English at Waterloo and served as Wellington's ADC. At the time of the affair, Harriet

Arbuthnot referred to Mrs Parnther as '*La bête féroce*'.[15] In a letter to his sister Sarah, in language reminiscent of Jane Austen's Mr Collins, Disraeli described the event as a 'most recherché concert at Parnther's, where I found all the élite of town'. The Duke of Wellington was there, 'looking very well in his garter, riband, and the golden fleece', together with 'as many stars as in an Arabian story', among them the 'Lansdownes, Salisburys, Stuart de Rothesay, Duke of Beaufort, Douro, Cantaloupe, Fitzroy, Loftus &c., and Mrs W[yndham] L[ewis], who was very proud, evidently, of being there'.[16]

But amongst the glittering company, he reported, 'the most picturesque group was the Rothschilds. The widow still in mourning, two sons, some sisters, and, above all the young bride [Charlotte], or rather wife from Frankfort, universally admired, tall, graceful, dark, and clear, picturesquely dressed, a robe of yellow silk, a hat and feathers, with a sort of *Sévigné* beneath magnificent pearls; quite a Murillo.' If the 'Fitzroy' referred to was Henry FitzRoy, it was perhaps at the Parnthers' party that Hannah Mayer and Henry met. There is no record of the Rothschilds socialising with the Parnthers on any other occasion, which might just suggest that the evening had disagreeable associations for Hannah Mayer's family.

In the summer of 1838, Disraeli attended a party given by the Rothschilds at Gunnersbury, where Hannah was now installed. In the weeks after Victoria's coronation in June, London continued to teem with members of the aristocracy and foreign swells – 'visible every night,' as Disraeli told his sister, 'with their brilliant uniforms and sparkling stars' – and on 18 July a throng of five hundred assembled at Gunnersbury for what Moses Montefiore called a 'splendid fête', and what the reporter of the *Court Gazette* declared to be 'one of the most delightful re-unions of the season'.[17]

Ambassadors, 'Princes of distinction' (Esterhazy, Schwarzenberg and various others from Germany) and Marshal Soult, from France, mingled in a crowd with the Duke of Sussex and his wife Lady Cecilia Underwood (soon to be created Duchess of Inverness), the Duchess of Cambridge (by birth a Princess of Hesse-Kassel), Prince George of Cambridge, the Dukes of Wellington and Devonshire, the Duke and Duchess of Somerset, the Duchess of Richmond, Lords Londonderry, Melbourne and John Russell and 'most of the highest nobility of the land'.[18]

Also present were Lady Charlotte Guest (who had consulted Hannah's friend Lady Stepney as to how best to get into Society) and her ironmaster husband Josiah ('Merthyr'), who was shortly to receive a baronetcy.

Merthyr's partner in the famous Dowlais Iron Works in Wales was Wyndham Lewis, who, like Disraeli, sat in the Commons as a member for Maidstone, and whose wealthy widow, Mary Anne – noticed by Disraeli at the Parnthers' – was to marry Disraeli in 1839.[19]

The party, Moses recorded, 'commenced with a concert, at which several great artists, including Grisi, Lablache, Tamburini, and Rubini performed. This was succeeded by a déjeuner, and in the evening a grand ball was given in a magnificent tent erected for the purpose. The gardens were illuminated with six thousand variegated lamps. The company remained until near midnight, all the guests complimenting the Rothschild family most highly on their taste and hospitality.'[20]

The summer before, Grisi, Lablache, Tamburini and Rubini had been among the 'principal foreign and English singers of the season' engaged to perform before five hundred guests at a fete given by the Duchess of St Albans at Holly Lodge, her villa in Highgate. A description of that occasion – the cost of which was estimated to have been in excess of £2,000 – suggests that Hannah may well have sought the Duchess's advice in planning her own entertainment. The timing of Hannah's fete was fortunate. With the death of her brother Joseph Cohen less than a week later, she might well have had to consider calling the whole thing off.[21]

Disraeli, who became a frequent guest, as well as a friend, of the Rothschilds, almost certainly had Gunnersbury in mind when later conjuring up the Hartmanns' house, Lavender Hill, in *Falconet* (1881) – the title of which might recall the name of the Naples merchant family whom Nat met and with whom New Court dealt. Lavender Hill, Disraeli wrote, was 'a mansion situated in unusually ample grounds for a villa residence and approached through lodges and by roads ingeniously winding . . . [Hartmann Brothers] were bankers to more than one European potentate, and whenever any member of the Royal or Imperial families paid a visit to England they spared one day to be entertained at Lavender Hill with much magnificence; banquets and balls in colossal tents, and all the bowers and groves of Lavender resonant with musicians and illuminated with many lamps of many colours . . .'[22]

Dining at Gunnersbury 'with the widow Rothschild' in January 1840, the Austrian diplomat Philipp von Neumann found that 'the beauty and luxury of this house surpass anything I have seen'.[23]

Situated only a few miles from London, Gunnersbury was ideal for receiving important guests – and clients – in pleasant surroundings; but it was not far enough from London for the country sports that Hannah's sons so loved. Consequently, by the autumn of 1838, Lionel had acquired a property forty miles from London. He had bought a pack of hounds, the Astar Harriers, together with their kennel, at Hastoe, situated in the woods above Tring Park in west Hertfordshire, just over the border from Buckinghamshire.

He bought the pack from a Mr Adamson, who for the next three years, until 1841, stayed on as his agent-cum-manager, helping to recruit new hunt servants (or hound servants as they were known in those days), to find extra stabling for Lionel's and his brothers' hunters, to supervise improvements and alterations to the kennel as they became necessary and so on.

One factor that made Hastoe a promising proposition to Lionel was the advantage of the quick, easy journey down from London by train, the railway having reached Tring in 1837. The rail journey was no more than an hour; the station was a fifteen-minute canter from the hunt kennel.

The Rothschild brothers' acquaintance with Harvey Combe and his Old Berkeley foxhounds, moreover, meant that hunt country around Tring was already known to them, while other factors, such as Nat's taste in hunting and the men whom Lionel had encountered in the St Albans steeplechase of 1830, seem likely also to have played a part in drawing the Rothschilds to the neighbourhood.

In the season of 1834–5, after his return from Constantinople, Nat had resumed staghunting. Writing from Lisbon in the spring of 1835, George Samuel explained, with laboured humour, that the arrival of a letter from Nat in London had 'convinced me that neither Diana nor Venus had led him [Nat] into any difficulties and great had been my solicitude for I knew to how many dangers he might have been exposed in his too ardent pursuit of the Deer and Hart. Heaven defend me from punning . . .'[24]

Some of the most exciting staghunting country of all was in the Vale of Aylesbury, a great tract of wild, open land intersected by wide brooks. The fences were notoriously testing, most being formed of a ditch on the taking-off side, a double hedge of thorn planted on a wide bank, and another ditch beyond – best taken at two jumps, landing between the hedges and leaping from the bank. 'I am very glad that you find Baronet a good Horse,' George Samuel had continued in his letter to Nat from Lisbon, 'I wish I had him here, to shew the Portuguese what jumping is. They here consider a jump of 2 feet wide something awful, and congratulate you on your fortunate escape if you do not fall . . .'

In the mid-1830s, the Vale attracted, at regular intervals, the Royal Buckhounds from Ascot, and also the pack maintained by Hubert de

Burgh at West Drayton, close to Grantley Berkeley's former sporting headquarters at Cranford (which Berkeley had given up on becoming Master of
the Oakley, in Bedfordshire). Despite his aristocratic name, de Burgh was
a grandson of a London merchant named Fysh Coppinger, who had married one Easter de Burgh, assumed her surname, and bought the manor of
West Drayton from Henry Paget, the Earl of Uxbridge. Hubert had inherited West Drayton from his grandmother Easter in 1823.[25]

Having spent a day in the Vale with de Burgh's hounds in February
1837, Nimrod noted that although 'hardly any body knew that Mr De
Burgh's hounds were to be at Aylesbury, as they were not advertised in any
of the papers', none the less 'those who had arrived were all the right sort.
Amongst them were Lords Clanricarde and Suffield, Sir Seymour Blane,
Messrs De Burgh, Learmonth, Vyse, Cosby, and several other well known
riders.'[26]

Of the men Nimrod names, Clanricarde, Blane and Thomas Cosby had
all ridden in the St Albans steeplechase; Seymour Blane (a baronet since his
father's death) had been mounted on Lionel's horse President. Like Cosby,
William Learmonth and Richard Howard Vyse, Blane also hunted with the
Buckhounds – as well as, in his case, with the Puckeridge. Lord Suffield,
who kept his own pack of staghounds in Norfolk and was also for a short
time Master of the Quorn, was the son of one of those liberal peers sympathetic to the cause of Jewish civil rights whom Moses Montefiore met at
dinner with Isaac Goldsmid in 1829.[27]

While Lionel and Nat may have foresworn hunting for the 1836–7
season, there is no reason to suppose that they did not resume in 1837–8.
Thomas Cosby had by then taken over as master of de Burgh's staghounds,
and in March 1838 he took the pack for several days to Aylesbury; having
met at Oving, they 'had a severe run of four hours – took at Thame,
hounds and horses beat'.[28]

As to Harvey Combe, he now confined hunting his Old Berkeley
hounds to south Bucks and west Hertfordshire. Years later, one of
Anthony's daughters recalled that her father and uncles, encouraged by
Hannah, had taken up with the Old Berkeley, 'the kennels being in the
neighbourhood of Tring'.[29] In 1834 Combe had given his original Old
Berkeley pack to the Surrey Union and had then taken 'Squire' George
Osbaldeston's celebrated Pytchley pack, which when sold at Tattersall's in
1840 was to fetch a record price of 6,511 guineas. Lionel was to be among
the buyers of Osbaldeston's hounds, but as early as 1836 Anthony – already,
no doubt, with first-hand experience of the pack – was seeking to buy
hounds from Combe for hunting in France.[30]

A few weeks prior to Nathan's death, and already planning to pass the autumn in Paris, Anthony wrote to Nat in London requesting him to 'be so good as to tell Huffam to ask Comb [*sic*] if he can sell me 6 good dog hounds for hunting this year'. Writing again, he asked Nat to 'tell Huffam to be so good as to try to send me 4 more fox hounds the same as the one he has already sent – I enclose him the name – they say he is the best hound that ever was hunted in France. They have promised me if I should procure them the 4 hounds to have it [*sic*, the hunt?] every Sunday. So dear Stag tell Huffam to procure them for me from Comb.'[31]

Seymour Huffam, an insurance broker at Lloyd's, was a friend of Combe's and acted as a kind of agent, in sporting matters especially, to the Rothschild brothers. Clearly, they liked him: in correspondence Huffam addressed himself to 'Dear Mayer'; and George Samuel, in his letter to Nat from Lisbon, asked to be remembered 'kindly to your Father & Mother and all your Family' and sent his 'best wishes to Uncle Ben [Cohen] & Dr Schlemmer & Seymour Huffam'. Later, they named a horse 'Mr Huffam' in Seymour's honour.[32]

Lionel and Nat were having sport with the harriers at Hastoe by late October 1838. 'My dear Baron Lionel,' wrote Joe Montefiore from Sussex, 'I sent you up a hare yesterday which I hope will give you a good run tomorrow morning. It is the first one that has been caught for some time or you would have had one long before this . . . Our pheasants have not yet recovered from the *fright* they suffered when Nat was here so that it will be better to leave them in repose a little longer, perhaps until the leaf is off the trees.'[33] On a visit to Paris that December, Lionel hoped that in England Nat had 'not quite such cold weather and will be able to have some sport in the Morngs'.[34]

A common custom with harriers at that time was to hunt hare in the morning and afterwards to turn out a bag fox – one previously trapped, or acquired from a dealer (Leadenhall Market was a centre of the trade) or from another hunt country, or even from abroad, and kept at the kennels. It was a custom that Lionel and Nat followed. 'I send you a nice Remittance of 3 live foxes which I hope will arrive quite safe and that they will give you 3 good days hunting,' Anthony wrote from Paris in 1839. 'I am only sorry that I cannot participate of the same pleasure, but it is quite impossible.'[35]

Nat, though, seems to have been inclining more and more to hunting carted deer. In early January 1839 he received a letter on the subject from Joseph Anderson, the Piccadilly horse dealer from whom Lionel had bought President. Anderson hunted with the Buckhounds, and also kept a pack of staghounds for hunting the country on the border of Hertfordshire and Middlesex. 'Pray permit me to ask,' he wrote to Nat, 'whether I am to expect the contribution you so kindly promised for the furtherance of the plan of taking the Hounds to the Aylesbury Country for some Stag-hunting, one meeting having been arranged ostensibly for the convenience of your self & Brother, but from which you were both, unavoidably, absent.'[36]

It is conceivable that Lionel's harriers hunted deer as well as hares and foxes. As a young man, Grantley Berkeley whipped-in to a pack of harriers that 'after hunting occasional bag foxes, hunted occasional fallow deer. We had a beautiful little fallow doe that gave us several good runs, and then we had some red deer.' Whatever the case may have been, when the chance came to take up full-time staghunting under his own steam, Lionel seized it. In 1839, when Sir Charles Shakerley, another stalwart of the Royal Hunt, decided to dispose of the staghounds he kept at Somerford Park in Cheshire, Lionel bought some fifteen couple.[37]

Towards the end of September 1839, the London dealer William Herring, 'Importer of Red and Fallow Deer to Her Majesty', informed Nat that he had 'taken the Deer' – and in November Baron Rothschild's Staghounds were in action. Moreover, Lionel, Anthony, Nat and Mayer were all four together in England that autumn.[38]

On 22 November, Thomas Hart, a farmer at Ascott, near Leighton Buzzard, wrote to Lionel that he had 'heard with much pleasure that your Hounds the other day passed over the Farm I occupy and not having an opportunity of witnessing it, I beg to offer you a field of upwards of forty acres on an elevated spot to uncart your Deer at any time you may please, trusting that your noble example of residing and affording sport in this immediate neighbourhood may be followed by other Gentry.' The next day, another local farmer, Henry Sawyer, wrote that he had 'not the least objection to Mr Rothschild turning his Deer out here next Wednesday'.[39]

In the season of 1839–40 Adamson arranged with a local land agent, John Glenister, for Lionel to take the 'Mansion Stabling' of Tring Park, which then formed a part of the deceased estate of a City businessman named William Kay – and which, more than thirty years later, Lionel was eventually to buy. By the end of November 1839, Nat and Lionel had some half a dozen hunters at Tring, a second horse being almost essential for a day's staghunting. Three of those hunters, Scotsfoot, Paganini and King Charles, were of such a quality that they were still being spoken of forty years later.[40]

In 1840 the Tring Park letting was put on a formal footing. For fifteen shillings a week and the horses' manure, Lionel agreed to take 'the Tring

Park Mansion Stabling and Coach Houses' and 'the Stabling in the Estate Farm Yard' – an arrangement that seems to have given rise to the idea that some years before, in 1833–4, Lionel's father had rented Tring Park from William Kay as a summer residence.[41] The story goes that when, that summer, a dog belonging to one of Nathan's grooms pulled down a deer in the park, Kay threatened not to renew the lease. Associated with the tale of the deer's destruction is a card addressed to Nathan at New Court, bearing the words: 'A Haunch of Venison from Tring Park. Killed July 21st 1834. With Mr Kay's Compliments.' Thus, it has been said, began the Rothschild connection with Tring. Yet the story seems to be the result of a confusion.[42]

Kay was a director of the Alliance, of which Nathan – with Sam Gurney, Moses Montefiore and others – was a president, from its foundation in 1824. By then, Kay was also the owner of Tring Park, while in London he lived at No. 14 Angel Court, Throgmorton Street, a few doors away from Levi Barent Cohen's old home. So Nathan would have known Kay for at least a decade prior to 1834. It is also established that Kay let his country house: in February 1827, Sir George Crewe went to visit his mother 'at "Tring Park", Herts, which she had taken for a few months'. The cold, Sir George recalled, 'became daily more and more intense – the House was old and not well-furnished, the rooms of a lofty and chilling size, the passages long and full of eddies of the merciless wind, which prevailed from the N.E. for nearly three weeks'.[43]

Sir George's mother left Tring not long afterwards, but later in 1827 the house was let to Augusta Smith, whose uncle, Sir Drummond Smith, Bt (Augusta was born a Smith and married a Smith), had at one time owned the estate. After the marriage at Tring, in December 1828, of Augusta's daughter Emma to the Reverend Edward Austen (later Austen Leigh), the nephew and biographer of Jane Austen, the newly-weds lived with Mrs Smith and Emma's five unmarried sisters at Tring Park. While Edward and Emma continued to live there until November 1833 – Edward served as curate to the Vicar of Tring (and had the odd day out with the Old Berkeley) – Augusta Smith remained there until October 1834, thus ruling out Nathan's residence at Tring that summer.[44]

Nor does it seem likely that Nathan would have rented Tring Park at any other time. Until the arrival of the railway in 1837, Tring was a journey of four or five hours from London. Since Nathan already had what he regarded as a country house at Stamford Hill, one might wonder whether he would really have wished to take another one, so much less convenient. It seems doubtful, too, that Kay, with his connection to Nathan in the City, would have threatened, on trivial grounds, not to renew any lease that Nathan, a man of such substance, might have held.

As to the haunch of venison, it was probably no more than a present. When Thomas Coutts and his wife were staying at Brighton in 1817, the Duke of Clarence sent 'an immense haunch of venison to Mrs Coutts, which strangers went to view in the hotel larder'; and when Nathan's brother Amschel was once anxious not to be outdone in entertaining Prince Metternich in Frankfurt, Anthony, who was there at the time, asked for a Rothschild courier to be despatched from London with 'plenty of scarce and good things' including pineapples, grapes, a live turtle and a haunch of venison.[45] Less sensationally, Lewis Lowdham sent Nathan 'a nice little Haunch of Venison for the New Year of 1832' – and on 2 January 1832 Mr Ward, of the Customs at Dover, wrote to thank Nathan for 'a very fine Haunch of Venison received yesterday morning'.[46]

Moreover, while the tale of the groom's dog and the deer appears to be rooted in fact, the incident – or one strikingly similar to it involving dogs kept by John Oliver, Lionel's whipper-in – took place at a later date. In January 1841, John Glenister, the agent handling Tring Park on behalf of Kay's son, Richard Smith Kay, wrote to Lionel: 'There are 2 or 3 Greyhounds kept by Oliver (I am given to understand they are his) and a week or two since they hunted and killed one of the Deer in the Park, which was overlooked upon Oliver paying for it, and promising that the dogs should not be allowed to go into the Park again. But yesterday they killed another Deer, which was put out of sight, no doubt by some of the grooms who were exercising in the Park. I could gain no clue to it, and I desired one of the Policemen, with the Keeper, to search for it, when it was found hidden in the hollow of an old Tree, torn to pieces.

'My only motive for making this communication is to request the favor of your prohibiting the grooms keeping dogs, as it is highly necessary, in some way, to prevent a recurrence of the past, or we shall not be able to keep the Deer in the Park at all, if they are hunted in this manner . . .'[47]

So it seems as if it was Lionel's purchase at Hastoe in 1838, rather than Nathan's supposed residence at Tring in 1834 or at any other time, that marked the start of the Rothschild family's connection with the area – a connection that would eventually lead to their becoming the largest landowners in Buckinghamshire.

Lionel's presence at Hastoe, associated as it soon was with a new pack of staghounds, fully funded by an owner known to have deep pockets, was greeted as a valuable addition to local life, by the landowners as well as the farmers. 'I have seen William Harcourt & made the request you wished,' reported a Guards officer friend of Lionel's, Lieutenant the Hon. Major Henniker. 'He told me to say to you that you were perfectly welcome to hunt over all his estates in that quarter of the world, & that he was glad to hear of your intended project of keeping hounds for the folks of the neighbourhood. He wishes [you] good sport & enjoyment with them . . .' Harcourt owned the Mentmore manor estate.[48]

In March 1840, an encouraging note arrived for Lionel at the kennel from a member of one of Buckinghamshire's prominent landowning families, the Dashwoods of West Wycombe. 'Mr Dashwood presents his compliments to the Baron Rothschild,' the note reads, '& takes leave to express to him the wishes of many persons in the neighbourhood that his hounds should meet again at West Wycombe & if it should not interfere with his fixtures it would be a great accommodation that it should take place on the 30th inst. the day prior to the Steeple Chase at Wycombe.'[49]

Despite this, it has sometimes been suggested that Lionel may have formed Baron Rothschild's Staghounds as an alternative to the 'aristocratic' and 'snobbish' Royal Buckhounds, and that 'social competition' played a role. In particular, a remark with which Nat concluded a letter to his brothers from Paris in November 1840 – 'Good bye for today, mind you ride like Trumps and do not let the Queen's people fancy we are all tailors' – has been taken to indicate frosty, perhaps anti-Jewish, attitudes to the Rothschilds among Royal Hunt supporters. The suspicion, however, is not well supported.[50]

First of all, to own his own pack of hounds was the dream of every sporting man. 'If I were as rich as Mr Darcy,' cries a young Master Lucas in *Pride and Prejudice*, 'I should not care how proud I was. I would keep a pack of foxhounds, and drink a bottle of wine every day.' In 1840 the Rothschilds' friend David Marjoribanks (now Robertson) formed a pack of his own foxhounds in Berwickshire.

Secondly, after 1838 there are no more reports of Thomas Cosby hunting Hubert de Burgh's old pack in the Vale of Aylesbury, so there was room for a new pack of staghounds in the district. Lionel's pack was no more an alternative to the Buckhounds than de Burgh's or Cosby's had been. When the Buckhounds paid a visit to the Vale – generally in November and February, and then only for a week at a time – care was taken to ensure that fixtures did not clash; the two packs would hunt on alternate days, so providing a good programme of sport for both local residents and members of the Royal Hunt Club staying at the White Hart in Aylesbury.

Further, blue blood was never a prerequisite for hunting, even with the

Royal Hunt. Just as Grantley Berkeley's pack of staghounds had among its regular followers Mr Gunter, the famous pastry-cook, so Nimrod, when identifying members of the group depicted in Francis Grant's *Meeting of the Royal Staghounds on Ascot Heath* points out Mr J. Bainbridge, 'a member of the fraternity of merchants – England's pride', and Joseph Anderson, the horse dealer.[51] Bainbridge was noted as 'a very bold horseman' who 'thinks nothing of "a header", as he calls a fall, which is now and then the cause of a broken neck'. It was not background that counted but sportsmanship; a man's position in the hunting field was determined 'by the manner he goes across country'.[52]

Prior to the start of the 1840–41 season, Charles Davis, the Buckhounds' huntsman, volunteered to do what he could to supply Lionel with deer if he should be in want of them. 'C.D.' would, he wrote, be 'very happy to serve the cause of hunting in any way he can'. His brother, the equestrian and sporting artist R. B. Davis, later hoped to paint the Rothschild 'hunt people, horses and hounds'.[53]

It is the word 'tailors' in Nat's remark that has given rise to the suspicion of anti-Semitism, cheap tailoring being a trade with which Jews of the period were closely associated. John Leech, who drew for *Punch* and illustrated many of R. S. Surtees' hunting novels (Leech himself hunted with the Puckeridge), was one who helped to perpetuate this caricature. A cartoon he drew for *Punch* in 1845, *Bubbles of the Year – Cheap Clothing*, shows a fat, hook-nosed Jew puffing away at a cigar as he surveys a workroom of cross-legged skeletons stitching away on the benches.[54]

Surtees' prejudice against Jews, rich ones especially, was even more pronounced than his prejudice against army officers. In *Ask Mamma* there is the avaricious swindler, Sir Moses Mainchance, a Christian convert who, having obtained a baronetcy, abandons commerce and sets up as a country gentleman. In *Plain or Ringlets* there is the 'party of cigar-smoking Israelites' lolling in a barouche at the races 'with their great arms over the side, like half-drunken sailors on a spree', and the Misses Jewissons, 'turning up their oiley hook noses at everything'.[55]

Others undoubtedly harboured such sentiments, though there was, of course, a good deal of hypocrisy. John Leech and his wife would dine with Lionel and Charlotte in the 1860s. When Nimrod – scrupulous in answering Lionel's enquiries, unctuous when requesting a contribution to his retirement fund – contemplated the sale of an idyllic, ancestral country house in 1825, he imagined his heart bleeding when the property fell into the hands of 'some half-bred Englishman – some Dutch-Jew broker'.[56]

Yet such attitudes were probably less widespread in the first two thirds of the nineteenth century than in the last, when Jewish immigration to England substantially increased. By 1830 England's Jewish community, made up of some 27,000–28,000 individuals, still amounted to less than one quarter of one per cent of the country's entire population – a proportion that was unchanged in 1860. Over the same thirty-year period in London, the Jewish community accounted for no more than approximately one per cent of the total population.[57]

Nor, of course, was tailoring a Jewish monopoly. When Baron Rothschild's hounds met at Dinton Castle in 1848, the meet was 'not within five minutes' walk of the railway station' and so was judged by a sporting journalist 'not likely to be patronised by the crowd of cockney dealers and tailors that seem to be the curse of stag-hunting in most countries'. Cockneys aside, one of the most famous tailors of the nineteenth or any other century, Henry Poole, of Savile Row – who made clothes for Mayer – rode to hounds in the Vale in the 1850s.[58] Moreover, in Victorian sporting parlance – and Nat was an avid reader of *Bell's Life* and the *Sporting Magazine* – the term 'tailor' was used of anyone who lacked knowledge, experience and finish: someone who, in the eyes of a sporting expert, was obviously doing everything wrong.[59]

In any case, it is difficult to see why the Rothschilds, who received such crowds of grandees at Gunnersbury, should have been sneered at by the same kind of people in the country. It was not as if they were unwelcome in London clubs. By April 1839, Nat belonged to Crockford's as well as to the Garrick, and Anthony was keen to follow suit. Crockford's boasted a membership of countless peers and princes, the Duke of Wellington, Prince Esterhazy and Prince Talleyrand among them. Lord Sefton's former chef, Ude, was for a time in charge of the kitchen (on a salary of £1,200 a year). 'It was very fine,' a visitor noted just after the club's opening in 1827. 'Supper lavish. It is to be the fashionable gambling resort of the aristocracy.'[60] While Captain R. H. Gronow recalled that Crockford's membership 'included all the celebrities of England', Nat and his brothers also attended dances at Almack's, the exclusive London assembly rooms in King Street, St James's.[61]

One prominent habitué of the Garrick, Crockford's and Almack's – and also of the Royal Hunt Club – whom Anthony and Nat knew was Count Alfred d'Orsay, the dandy-cum-artist (and the dedicatee of Disraeli's novel *Henrietta Temple*) who married the stepdaughter of Lady Blessington, his mistress. Captain Gronow described d'Orsay driving along in his tilbury looking 'like some gorgeous dragon-fly skimming through the air', and it may be that that tilbury belonged to Nat. While he was away in Paris in

1840, Nat lent d'Orsay his London cab and horse, and later Nat ordered a tilbury – built by Tilbury's – to be sent over to him in France.[62]

By May 1840, Nat was also a member of the Windham Club, a gentlemen's club in St James's Square; and in 1841 Mayer was elected to Brooks's, followed by Lionel the next year. Brooks's, in St James's Street, was the principal London club for Whig grandees; Lionel (who also joined the Reform), was proposed by Lord John Russell, as was Anthony, who joined Brooks's in 1853. Besides the political element, Brooks's membership included several of the best-known masters of foxhounds of the nineteenth century – Thomas Assheton Smith, Sir Harry Goodrich, Bt, and Sir Richard Sutton, Bt, who funded his foxhunting with his Mayfair rents.[63]

When the sporting writer 'Will Wimble Junior' imagined a man with '*Will Honeycomb*'s blood' in his veins, the character 'wore a *Stultz* coat, took wonderfully to Rossini, and was accounted a good performer on a Wednesday night in Willis's Rooms [Almack's]; besides being a member of one or two of the exclusive sort of clubs' – all of which fitted the Rothschilds.[64]

But for the unfavourable construction placed on the remark about tailors in his letter, there is no evidence that Nat felt any unease about the Royal Hunt. In a letter he wrote the day before, he hints at nothing at all but his regret at missing a whole week's hunting – 'what capital fun' – in the Vale. The next November, when the Buckhounds were again due to visit the Vale, he assured his brothers that he would 'like exceedingly to be able to avail myself of yr invitation to come over to London immediately. There is nothing I should enjoy more than a meet in the Aylesbury country with the crack pack and her Majesty's . . .'[65]

Nat was long remembered for the brilliant dash he cut, mounted on a hunter called Rouge, in a run with the Buckhounds from Southall to Bushey Heath, and there is nothing to suggest that his brothers felt any less welcome with the Royal Hunt than he did.[66] When the Buckhounds met at Aston Abbotts on 30 November 1841, it was reported that a large field of about a hundred included Lionel – and by no stretch of the imagination did he ride like a tailor. During a run of an hour and five minutes in pursuit of a hind called Beauty, he was one of the 'parties foremost throughout'. It was noted of Lionel that he 'had good hands, and rode like a sportsman'. On 3 December 1841, having met at Hardwick and uncarted a 'good'un' called Sailor, the Buckhounds had a run of 'two hours and a half without a check'. This time, Mayer was noticed: 'Captain Vyse, M. Rothschild, Esq., Messrs Davis, Metcalfe, Oldacre, and about five others only were in at the take – the distance calculated at more than thirty miles.'[67]

Mayer had by then been elected to Brooks's, having been proposed by the eighteenth Earl of Erroll. Lady Erroll – who was described by Lady Granville as 'a domestic, lazy, fat woman' – was a daughter of William IV and Mrs Jordan, and so a sister of Anthony's friend Lord Adolphus FitzClarence, who rode to hounds with the Royal Hunt. Lord Erroll, who was Lord Steward of the Household from 1839 to 1841, had earlier been Master of the Horse to Queen Adelaide. He rode to hounds with Harvey Combe's Old Berkeley pack – and from 1835 to 1839 was Master of the Buckhounds.[68]

11

Town and Country

———◦◦◦———

BY JUNE 1838, Lionel had moved Charlotte and Leonora from the house in Hill Street to what was to become their permanent London home in Piccadilly. After Evelina's birth in August, the family circle was to be increased by Natty, born in November 1840, and then by Alfred in July 1842, and Leopold in November 1845.

The opportunity to move to the new house had come about following the death of Hubert de Burgh's father-in-law, Vice-Admiral John Tollemache. A notice in the *Gentleman's Magazine* had recorded the Admiral's death on 16 July 1837 'at his residence in Piccadilly Terrace', but in *Boyle's Court Guide* his address was given as No. 148 Piccadilly. Both were correct: the Terrace was the row of houses (no longer standing) on the north side of Piccadilly, running from the east side of Apsley House (No. 149) to Hamilton Place, with Hyde Park behind. To add to possible confusion, Nos. 146–148, built in the last quarter of the eighteenth century and the first houses to have gone up in the row – comprising a self-contained terrace within the Terrace – were sometimes referred to as Nos 1–3 Hyde Park Corner.[1]

Hubert de Burgh had married Marianne Tollemache, fifth of the Admiral's eight daughters. Born John Halliday, the Admiral had in 1821 changed his surname in accordance with the will of his mother's childless brother Wilbraham Tollemache, sixth Earl of Dysart, for whom No. 148 had been built between 1775 and 1780. The earldom of Dysart passed to the Admiral's aunt Louisa, who also inherited Ham House, on the Thames near Richmond. Had Nathan been dining there rather than at the Gurneys' Ham House in Essex when in 1834 he related the story of his early years, the aged Louisa Dysart (born in 1745) would have been his hostess.

No. 148 Piccadilly continued to be rated to the Admiral's son, John Tollemache, until 1844, so it seems as if – to begin with – Lionel exchanged 10 Hill Street for the more spacious interiors of a Piccadilly residence without any definite prospect of long-term tenure. In 1842, he none the less obtained estimates from Cubitts for improvements, including alterations to the top of the house that involved adding a storey and installing a new staircase, as well as to the existing 'Attic floor, Chamber floor, Drawing Room floor, Ground floor, [and] Basement'. The alterations to the drawing-room floor were to include a 'new conservatory' (£350), those to the basement 'new offices under the garden' (£1,250). The estimate came in total to £3,220.[2]

Possibly, as with Hill Street, Lionel took No. 148 furnished: in December 1844, John Tollemache wrote to fix a convenient time 'to remove my pictures from 148 Piccadilly'. Moreover, the year before, Lionel seems very nearly to have left No. 148 for another house in Piccadilly. In June 1843, his sister Chilly wrote to congratulate him on his 'new house', while Nat wished him and Charlotte 'every happiness for a long series of years in your new residence'.[3] Away from home that August, Lionel himself wrote to Charlotte: 'Anthony writes that Dawes [the lawyer] was not quite satisfied with the papers about the house in Piccadilly . . . I am glad to see that you have not taken possession of the house; follow Dawes's advice, he is perfectly honest and merits all confidence.' And then six months later Chilly's husband Anselm wrote to Lionel: 'What a curious fellow you are. You buy beautiful pictures & a splendid house & sell it again.'[4] Although the house is not identified, conceivably it was Coventry House, next door to Hannah. Lord Coventry died, predeceased by his eldest son Lord Deerhurst, in May 1843 to be succeeded by his young grandson, and shortly afterwards there was a sale of items from Coventry House, some of which Lionel bought.

In any event, No. 148 was in one of the very best locations in London, in keeping with which the domestic staff was led by a capable butler-cum-valet named Toogood. The housekeeper's name was Mary Cobham. When Lionel and Charlotte moved into their new house, a fair proportion of the local residents already had, and if not would before long form, connections with the Rothschild family.[5]

With the Duke of Wellington at Apsley Hou se on the western side, their next neighbour to the east, at No. 147, was Lady Cockerell, widow of Sir Charles Cockerell, Bt, the East India Company writer who had made a fortune in Bengal before returning to England to set up as a banker and to enter Parliament. Lady Cockerell was a daughter of the first Lord Northwick, and it was her brother, who inherited the peerage, that assembled the vast Northwick collection of paintings and works of art. The Cockerells' daughter Harriet had married Lord Deerhurst, and it was her son who became the ninth Earl of Coventry in 1843.

Next door but one to Lionel and Charlotte, No. 146 Piccadilly was the town house of Sir Edmund Antrobus, Bt – who wrote his address as 'H. P. Corner'. Sir Edmund was a partner, initially with Thomas Coutts and Edward Marjoribanks (David's uncle), in Coutts bank (then Coutts, Marjoribanks & Antrobus). His younger brother, Gibbs, had married Jane Trotter, daughter of Sir Coutts Trotter, Bt, the Coutts' partner who had called on Hannah in Brussels in 1824 and whose grandson, Sir Coutts Lindsay, Bt, would one day become Hannah Mayer's son-in-law. It was at a ball given by Lady Antrobus in the spring of 1835 that the young William Gladstone met and fell in love with Caroline Farquhar, who refused to marry him.

For Queen Victoria's coronation on 28 June 1838 – for which on 27 June the Lord Mayor of London wrote to offer Hannah a spare ticket he had received – Lionel joined with Sir Edmund Antrobus and Lady Cockerell to pay for the erection of a stand in their shared front courtyard from which their friends might view the procession.[6]

No. 145 belonged to the second Marquess of Northampton, who in 1838 succeeded the Duke of Sussex as President of the Royal Society. Lord Northampton's mother was a sister of Augusta Smith, who had lived at Tring Park; his heir, Earl Compton, was observed with Lionel and others at the Newport Pagnell Steeplechase in 1842.

No. 142 served as the town house of the twenty-first Lord Willoughby de Eresby, Joint Hereditary Lord Great Chamberlain, and his wife Clementina, heiress of the Perth Estate in Scotland. Harriet Arbuthnot thought the Willoughbys 'very agreeable people', and they were a couple with whom Lionel, Charlotte and their children were to make friends. When he wrote to Charlotte in August 1843 about the mystery house, Lionel was on his way, with Mayer and their uncle James, for a few days' stalking and grouse shooting on the Willoughby de Eresbys' Drummond Castle estate near Crieff.[7]

Thomas Wentworth Beaumont, a landowner grown prosperous on the sales of rich mineral deposits from his north-country properties, resided at No. 144 Piccadilly. His eldest son (later the first Lord Allendale) was to marry a daughter of that gentleman jockey, staghunter and statesman, the first Marquess of Clanricarde, a figure known to Lionel since the St Albans Steeplechase of 1830. Beaumont, by a curious coincidence, had acquired the lease of No. 144 from Augusta Smith's uncle Sir Drummond Smith, Bt, who, prior to William Kay, had owned Tring Park.

When George Toogood left Lionel's service in 1845 – with a good reference, but with a wife whom Nat described as 'troublesome' – Lionel received applications from butlers previously employed by Lord Denman, the Lord Chief Justice, and Lord Rosebery. Another applicant had worked for Alexander Fullerton and his wife Lady Georgiana, a daughter of Lord and Lady Granville, who had just published her debut novel, *Ellen Middleton* (1844), a tragic tale with a High Church slant that Lord Brougham described as 'rank Popery'.[8]

The exterior of No. 148 appears in nineteenth-century engravings of Hyde Park Corner, but of the interiors inhabited by Lionel and Charlotte prior to rebuilding in the 1860s there is no comparable record. Probably the prevailing flavour was French, as the Prince Regent's taste for the French arts of the seventeenth century continued to infect fashionable society well into the first decade of Victoria's reign. The Rococo revival style known as 'Louis Quatorze' – 'tasteless excrescences, excess of gilding', as Prince Pückler-Muskau put it after visiting Crockford's in 1828 – was a popular recipe for the grand London interior. Louis Quatorze was the style chosen for Benjamin Wyatt's great gallery at Apsley House, and also for Holdernesse House (on which it was estimated that Lord Londonderry spent £100,000) and for Stafford (later Lancaster) House in the Mall.[9]

The London Rothschilds were, of course, familiar with fashionable decor in the land of Louis XIV itself. On the way back to London from Frankfurt during his engagement, Lionel had written to Charlotte from Paris of the decorative works under way in the rue Laffitte, the results of which would impress Jeannette Salomons a year later, but which in 1836 seemed to Lionel somewhat overdone. 'The ground floor will be finished by the end of the month and will rival any palace,' he reported. 'At Paris, a rich man, whether Banker or Prince, can act in the same way, but in every other place such an establishment would appear ridiculous. The first floor, the daily habitation, is nearly as splendid, so much gold that for the first few days one is quite dazzled.'[10]

After dining in Paris one evening a few years later, Nat wrote to his brothers in London: 'We went afterwards to the Opera Comique. It is just finished and quite in the style of Mrs. Salomon's house.' But in spite of such remarks, French-inspired decoration and furnishings allied to Old Master paintings – seventeenth-century Dutch and Flemish (favourite schools of King George IV), with French, Spanish and English elements – is the look most likely to have evolved at No. 148.[11]

Taking a leaf from his mother's book, Lionel had been an admirer of French furniture and porcelain since his early twenties. In 1831 he left some bids at 'a sale of old Furniture & some china vases' in Paris, but, up against strong bidding from English buyers, failed to get what he had wanted. 'I hope another time to be more successful,' he wrote to Hannah. 'I know yr taste for these things, and will try to show you that we agree in this respect. Be so good to let me know if you would like some old inlaid Furniture, a Secretaire or Commode, made in the time of Louis 14th – here these things are quite the rage – or if you would prefer some old sevre [sic] China.'[12] A year later, he succeeded in buying for Hannah 'twelve plates & a very pretty Sevre [sic] vase, which I hope you will like' – and asked if he should wait to send them to England with Prince Esterhazy or 'under the address of any other Ambassador' so as to avoid payment of duty.[13]

When Lionel wrote of 'old inlaid Furniture . . . made in the time of Louis 14th' he meant 'boulle', the furniture decorated with that distinctive form of marquetry, developed at the Court of Louis XIV by André Charles Boulle, in which thin sheet brass and tortoiseshell are employed instead of wood, and with gilt bronze (ormolu) mounts. It was a style of furniture that had been sought by George IV for Carlton House. In late 1820, Mrs Arbuthnot wrote in her journal: 'The King had talked [to the Duke of Wellington] of going to Hanover, but the Duke says there is not much chance of that unless we allow him to take his eating and drinking money, his money for buhl furniture & for buying horses, which we could not think of doing.'[14]

Advancing from boulle, in 1834 Mayer, still only sixteen, and so presumably with his parents' blessing, spent £1,000 on a magnificent ormolu-encrusted eighteenth-century bureau-cabinet that was said to have been made for Augustus the Strong of Saxony. It can now be seen in the Victoria and Albert Museum.[15]

As to paintings, James set a fashion in the family for works by the eighteenth-century French artist Jean-Baptiste Greuze. 'I bought a beautiful Greuze yesterday, dear Billy,' Nat told Anthony in the 1840s, 'two young ladies showing their titties & such pretty ones.'[16]

Lionel had begun to buy pictures by the mid-1830s. Writing to Anthony from Madrid in 1834, he said that he had 'not bought any pictures lately; good things of every description are scarce', and in 1835, shortly before his departure from Spain, he was intending to 'send my large pictures by way of Cadiz and the small ones I shall bring with me'.[17] Unfortunately, he gave no description of those pictures, but by 1838 Lionel had already a reputation in England as a collector of 'fine Paintings', even as someone to whom it seemed worthwhile to offer a whole collection for purchase en bloc.[18] Possibly, John Tollemache's note about his pictures in

1844 was written not because No. 148 had been let furnished for the previous few years, but rather because the pictures had been left there for inspection with a view to sale.

By then, Lionel had been seen to spend large sums on paintings at auction in London. In May 1840, at the sale of Sir Simon Clarke's pictures by Christie's, he bought a Rembrandt that had belonged to George IV for his uncle James (£840); a Murillo, *The Good Shepherd*, for his mother (£3,045, the highest price of the sale), and a Flemish genre scene, *The Industrious Housewife*, by David Teniers (£283 10s). The National Gallery bought the only other Murillo in the sale – *The Infant St John* – for £2,100. Other lots went to Sir Robert Peel, an avid collector of Dutch pictures; Lord Northwick; the Earl of Normanton, and Charles J. Nieuwenhuys, Europe's leading picture dealer.[19]

The Rembrandt that Lionel bought for James was the artist's magnificent self-portrait, *Le Port Drapeau: Rembrandt in the character of a Standard Bearer*. After the sale, though, in a flurry of indecision that might now seem surprising, James first of all asked Anthony to dispose of the painting 'if it could be done to advantage', then on reflection said that he had better keep it 'if you have not bought the Murillo for me', then requested Anthony to try and exchange it for 'the Murillo'. Whether it was Hannah's Murillo that he preferred, or the one bought by the National Gallery – both of them depicting Christian subjects – is unclear. In the end, James kept the Rembrandt.[20]

Furniture, Sèvres porcelain and pictures were not the Rothschild brothers' only areas of interest. In common with the third Marquess of Hertford, who with the Reform Act of 1832 'became disgusted with politics, and devoted his principal attention to buying works of art', they also shared a taste for snuffboxes and armour.[21]

After marrying, Lionel considered disposing of various items he had acquired on the Continent in his bachelor days. 'You told me,' Anthony wrote from Paris, 'that you wished to sell a good many of your things. Let me [know] what you wish to sell – & also whether you wish to sell the Armour . . . [The Duke de] Frias sells all his things next week. Do you wish to have the Shield [?]'[22] A decade later in London, Lionel was invited to inspect 'a splendid suit of armour of the finest description engraved and inlaid with gold' in which the Duke of Norfolk was said to have expressed an interest; and he once sold a very fine suit of armour – a transaction of which he did not care to be reminded afterwards – to Lord Ashburnham. As to snuffboxes, while Nat received his jewel-encrusted gift from the Sultan, in April 1839 Anthony wrote proudly of a 'very handsome Gold Snuff box' that he had bought for himself in Paris for 1,000 francs (£40).[23]

A week or two after Anthony had bought his snuffbox, a report appeared in the British sporting press of the three-day May race meeting at Chantilly – a meeting 'which may now be said to take first rank in France'. The reporter noted the presence each day of the heir to the throne, the Duc d'Orléans, and his brother the Duc de Nemours, Lord Henry Seymour (younger brother of the future fourth Marquess of Hertford), other members of the French Jockey Club 'and a long list of the most *distingué* in the Fashionable and Sporting Circles'.[24]

The Duc d'Orléans and Lord Henry Seymour (the first president of the French Jockey Club in 1833–4) were the leading racehorse owners in France, and in the two-year-old stakes on the first day of the Chantilly meeting, Thursday 16 May, d'Orléans' colt Borodino 'took the lead, and kept it', beating by four lengths Lord Henry's filly Jenny – and a colt called Anatole belonging to 'Baron A. Rothschild'. Anatole (by Royal Oak, a stallion of Lord Henry's) belonged to Anthony, and the Rothschild family's long-lasting association with racing had now commenced.

The next afternoon (Friday), Hannah and Louisa arrived in Paris to stay at Suresnes. Anthony, though no slimmer, was looking better than when Lionel had seen him six months before; on Sunday Louisa reported to Nat that neither 'the bloom on his countenance, nor the embonpoint of his figure' had diminished. 'The gentlemen are gone today to Chantilly, where there are some races,' she went on, 'they much wished us to accompany them, but as the drive is long, and we are not particularly fond of this sort of thing we prefer taking the drive to St Cloud, where the fountains play to-day.'[25]

Anthony was not discouraged. In an article for the *Sporting Magazine* about a month spent at Chantilly in the autumn of 1839, 'A Devonian' informed the journal's readers that 'Mr A. Rothschild has recently built stables for twelve horses at La Morlaix [Morlaye], three miles from Chantilly, and intends taking the field under the *surveillance* of another of the Edwardses.'[26]

Racing was a sport imported from England – the first races at Chantilly took place in 1834 – and many of the people involved in it, trainers and jockeys especially, were English. The 'Edwardses' referred to the numerous sons of James 'Tiny' Edwards, who in the early part of the nineteenth century was the Earl of Chesterfield's trainer. One of the sons, Bill, trained for

George IV in the last years of his reign; another, George, became the Duc d'Orléans' trainer.[27]

Anthony did not, however, as things turned out, engage an Edwards (there were four more brothers), but rather secured the services of Thomas Carter, whose previous employers included Lord Henry Seymour and Henry FitzRoy's brother Lord Southampton. Carter was to prove 'a very good trainer & a very civil fellow'.[28]

While 'A Devonian' was looking over the establishment at La Morlaye, however, Anthony himself was in England, in the throes of finalising an important personal matter, which, in the light of Hannah Mayer's recent marriage to Henry FitzRoy, had caused him some annoyance at the hands of his uncles that summer. Like Lionel in Madrid in the summer of 1835, in the summer of 1839 Anthony felt no particular desire to settle down and marry. 'Billy is very angry that there should be no ladies after his taste,' Mayer had reported to Nat and Lionel from Baden-Baden in July. 'He brought with him an enormous store of bonnets [condoms], but as yet has had no opportunity of using them.'[29]

His uncle Amschel, though, was pressing other plans upon him. 'I spent two days at ffort & never was I more uncomfortable in my life,' Anthony wrote to his brothers in mid-July. 'Uncle A[mschel] was a regular bother, asking me about getting married and writing to Uncle S[alomon] that I only waited till his death to marry a Christian. I told him quite short that if Aunt Henrietta would cash up, that I was ready when he said of course & he would not advise me without Louisa had the same fortune as [her brothers] Joseph and Nathaniel, so I said very well and I believe he wrote to that effect – for later we left much better friends . . .'[30]

In December, Benjamin Disraeli recounted to his sister Sarah how he and his wife had 'dined en famille with Mrs Montefiore to meet Anthony de Rothschild, who is to marry one of the Montefiores, Charlotte'; but in fact Anthony was to marry Henrietta's younger daughter, Louisa, while Charlotte later married her uncle Horatio Montefiore, Moses' and Abraham's brother, in 1847.[31]

Whether Henrietta had really been making difficulties about Louisa's dowry is not recorded; but she could be daunting. Although one of Anthony's daughters was to recall her as having a 'very bright and cheerful nature', Nat once described her as 'the most disagreeable woman ever beheld' and considered it 'very fortunate for us [that] she does not give us very frequently the pleasure of her society'.[32]

A young doctor who accompanied Henrietta and Abraham to Italy in 1824 found her formidable. 'I have never seen anyone more affectionate than she,' he wrote of her from Rome. 'She looks after him [Abraham] almost by herself . . . She does without food and sleep, survives the cold and chill. She tolerates all this with almost superhuman vigour. But if her nature seems scarcely human she does not at all incline to the nature of angels for most of all I think she has got a most unfortunate and accursed power of causing trouble for other people . . . In no way do I need a poetic imagination to conjure up a Medusa and the hair style which she loves to affect is just like snakes.'[33] The doctor, a Quaker whose mother had been a governess to the Gurneys, was Thomas Hodgkin, of Guy's Hospital. In a paper in 1832 he described the malady that bears his name, Hodgkin's Disease, and for many years after his trying trip to Italy he would act as a medical adviser to Moses Montefiore.

After the troublesome summer break with his uncles, Anthony returned to Paris, but in mid-November Chilly's husband Anselm wrote to his cousins in London: 'I hear with pleasure [of] the happy arrival of Baron Anthony [in London] & hope to be able to address to him very soon my most sincere congratulations . . .' A week later, Anselm wrote again: 'We had the pleasure of receiving your letter my dear Lionel & I hope that we shall soon have that of congratulating Squire Billy on his approaching marriage . . .'[34] At some point, it seems, Anthony went down to the Montefiores' country house in Sussex to ask for Louisa's hand. 'It will appear quite strange to me to be at Worth,' Louisa wrote to him the following January, 'as I have not returned there since our short though all important stay there.'[35]

In late November or early December, Chilly, waiting once more to give birth, this time to Ferdinand, wrote to Hannah from Paris that she was 'most happy to be able to commence my letter by congratulating you most sincerely on the happy communication conveyed in your kind letter of this morning of the definitive arrangement for the approaching matrimonial connexions of our good brother Anthony.

'Most sincerely do I hope that these new ties may contribute to his happiness and assure him every felicity attainable in this World. He writes the Wedding is to take place in the Commencement. I trust nothing will occur to prevent our being present. I should like to witness an event decisive I trust of the happiness of one so dear to us all & I should be delighted to have an opportunity of coming to pay you a visit.'[36]

Anthony returned to Paris at the end of December, where he received a very charming letter from his fiancée.

'Whenever I thought of you during your journey (which I can assure you was very often the case),' Louisa wrote to him on 31 December, 'you presented yourself to my mind comfortably stretched on your bed half buried in cloaks and great coats of fur with two cigars in your mouth to make up for lost time. Is this the correct picture? You can have no idea how much we all miss you and how often your name is mentioned among us. I wish you could also have a *tiny* feeling of regret although I do not think it probable considering all the amusement and occupation you will have at Paris . . . I perfectly understand how disagreeable it must be to you to renounce at once the pleasant kind of life you have been leading for so many years and the place in which you have been enjoying yourself (at least I know it would be so to me) for at *best* an uncertain prospect of happiness . . .'[37]

They were married on 30 March 1840; and in early April, Anthony wrote to his brothers that he and Louisa had 'almost decided to go to morrow to Windsor to pass Saturday & Sunday, & Monday morning we shall [go] to Tring at 10½ am. Be so good as to order a good breakfast, as my wife is very anxious to see the stag turned out.'[38]

Contrary to Louisa's expectations, for several years after their marriage she and Anthony lived mostly in Paris, either at the Bristol Hotel or in 'spacious apartments' at their uncle Salomon's house. There were periodic spells in Frankfurt (where the decorative accent of their cousins' houses was also French) and visits to London, but for some years they had no permanent London town house of their own.[39]

However, in 1842 – 'getting sick of Paris . . . & living in a Hotel is a thing which I do not much like' – Anthony was in hopes of acquiring T. W. Beaumont's lease on No. 144 Piccadilly. But it was not to be; instead, he bought a long lease from the Marquess of Westminster on No. 2 Grosvenor Place Houses (19 Grosvenor Place after 1875), the middle one of three substantial stuccoed Italianate houses then being planned by the builder Philip Nowell, to the south of Hyde Park Corner. The view from the upper floors of the house would be of the grounds of Buckingham Palace.[40]

While the new house, with stables and coach house to the rear, was under construction, Anthony and Louisa resided at No. 38 Grosvenor Place, then in the row of houses between Chester Street and Wilton Street. Constance, the first of their two children, was born in London in 1843, followed by Annie in 1844. Aged three, staying in Brighton, Constance met her grandfather's old friend Samuel Gurney, now grown stout and with a 'great shock of white hair'. When Sam picked Constance up and tossed her in his arms, she called out: 'Put me down, you old white bear!'[41]

No. 1 Grosvenor Place Houses, considerably smaller than No. 2, was occupied by the fourth Duke of Cleveland, who in the 1850s married Lady Dalmeny, the widow of the heir to the fourth Earl of Rosebery. The Duchess's two daughters by Lord Dalmeny were to provide playmates for Constance and Annie, while her son, the fifth Earl of Rosebery (the Liberal Prime Minister), was to marry Mayer's only daughter Hannah.[42]

As building work progressed in Grosvenor Place, Anthony, ever anxious when it came to spending, or even investing, his own money, was worried 'that I shall not be able to manage about my house, as I am frightened it will cost me too much tin & trouble – and I see that it will be much better to have it done as plain as possible'. But once the house was finished – Anthony took possession in September 1844 – it was, so Constance recalled, 'carefully decorated by the most capable French artists. It was also exquisitely furnished according to my father's remarkably good taste, well known to all members of the family.'[43]

From Paris, Anthony brought with him his coachman, Gentil, and a French manservant, Déprès, who served as butler, valet and confectioner and whose 'very appearance gave a patent of distinction to the house'. Yet when making preparations for their 'first grand dinner party – our first grand bore' at Grosvenor Place, Anthony's wife was 'nervous and fidgety, principally because the rooms are too smart – much too smart for my taste'; she dreaded being 'made to appear fond of show and glitter'. Afterwards, however, she was gratified to record: 'Our dinner went off pretty well . . . The rooms were much admired but, to my delight, not apparently thought too smart . . .'[44]

Except for their religion and the scale of their wealth, two things in particular still set the London Rothschilds apart from their upper-class acquaintances: they were barred from a seat in either House of Parliament; and they had no country house and estate. They had Gunnersbury and there, by stages, Hannah and then Lionel added substantially to the land-holding, eventually accumulating several hundred acres; but Gunnersbury remained in essence a much grander version of the house at Stamford Hill – a house with grounds in the country, perhaps, but not a country house and estate.

Of their Piccadilly neighbours, the Duke of Wellington had been granted Stratfield Saye, in Berkshire, by a grateful nation; Lord Coventry had inherited Croome Court, near Worcester; Sir Charles Cockerell had bought Sezincote, in Gloucestershire, and had had the house refashioned in the 'hindoo' (Mughal) style; Sir Edmund Antrobus owned the West Amesbury estate – and with it Stonehenge – in Wiltshire; Beaumont owned two country houses; Lord Northampton's principal seat was Castle Ashby, in Northamptonshire; and the Willoughby de Eresbys owned a castle and estate in Lincolnshire (Grimsthorpe) as well as Drummond. John Tollemache (later the first Lord Tollemache) engaged Anthony Salvin to build for him the mock-medieval Peckforton Castle on a hilltop in Cheshire – spending £68,000 on the castle and £280,000 on estate improvements and buildings.[45]

Yet the Rothschilds had begun to take a closer interest in, and to experience more of the country, and of the country-house life of which Mayer had had an early taste at Gordon Castle. In the autumn of 1841, Hannah, accompanied by Louisa and her cousin and now fiancé, Mayer Charles, made a tour – by rail as well as road – of the Midlands, northern England and Scotland, visiting various houses and estates en route; and in letters to Lionel and Mayer in London (Nat was now with Anthony in Paris) Hannah gave her impressions of what she had seen.

Althorp, the Earl Spencer's Northamptonshire seat, was, she found, 'a fine Place, the Park beautifully wooded, the cattle superb . . . the walls very well covered with some excellent paintings'. The Earl Fitzwilliam's colossal house, Wentworth Woodhouse, near Rotherham, was set in 'a very fine Estate . . . Deer and other cattle in abundance, the Drive up to the castle very good'; the 'very lady like Housekeeper' showed Hannah and her party over 'spacious and most comfortable apartments . . . but what is most worthy of notice are the pictures, many of the very first order. There is also an interesting Menagerie and a very good collection of rare birds.'[46]

Derbyshire – and Chatsworth (the Duke of Devonshire's) – made the greatest impression on Hannah of all that she saw. She had passed through the county in earlier days, but had 'lost the recollection of its beauty'. 'I do not know if you have been here before,' she wrote from Matlock, 'but the situation and country being so extremely fine no person who admires fine scenery and beautiful country could possibly regret the time at a place which combines so many advantages of nature.' Of the estates she had seen, Chatsworth took the palm for 'ingenuity and taste' – 'no expense, talent or trouble deficient, the place is beautiful by art and nature in the extreme'. The Duke's new 'conservatory' – Joseph Paxton's Great Stove – was 'marvelous and very scientific'. Charles, she added, was 'very pleased with all he sees, not quite so much with what he eats'.[47]

At Mulgrave Castle, near Whitby, the travellers were the guests of Lord and Lady Normanby, who extended to them 'a most kind reception'. The castle was 'very finely situated' and the 'accommodation excellent, combining the comforts and elegance of a modern residence with that of an ancient building'. When Charles went shooting, Hannah and Louisa drove about the grounds in a pony chaise. Nor could Hannah say enough for her host and hostess: Lady Normanby took 'great pains to make her guests in every way comfortable – she is an accomplished woman'; Lord Normanby was 'very easy in his manners and hospitable'.[48]

In Scotland, they visited Hamilton Palace, 'a Place of great architectural beauty and elegance, some of the first rate Italian pictures and the very celebrated one by Rubens, Daniel in the Lion's Den – our travelling companion Charles was in extacies'. Charles 'had an opportunity to display his talent in languages for the Duke [of Hamilton] held a long conversation with him in Italian'. The standard of hospitality, though, was less good – 'it was rather *dry* as no refreshments were offered'. The Duchess was a younger daughter of William Beckford, though Hannah makes no mention of her presence.[49]

Travelling through Westmorland on the return south, Hannah and her companions, who had now been joined by Mayer, stopped briefly at Lowther Castle, a seat of the first Earl of Lonsdale. The castle was 'large and of fine architecture, nothing very particular to notice excepting some good pictures'. On the other hand, at Lowther the Rothschild party was 'regaled with a good luncheon and a kind reception', and there were several people there whom they knew.[50]

Rather less than two years later, in August 1843, Lionel, with Mayer and their uncle James, visited several well-known country houses on the way to and from the Perthshire grouse moor, and Lionel wrote about them in his letters to Charlotte, who was staying at Gunnersbury. Anthony had been left in charge at New Court.

One of the first houses Lionel saw was one of the most famous of all, though still he was not easily impressed. 'Yesterday morning after we left York we went to Castle Howard – rather a nice place,' he wrote from Thirsk, 'but nothing wonderful, it is in fact just like Blenheim, only much smaller. The country is a little finer and the views more extensive, a few fine pictures – but altogether a place not worth putting oneself out to see.'[51]

The seat of Anthony's future ducal neighbour in London, however, got a much better write-up, as did the Duke of Northumberland's castle at Alnwick, from where Lionel reported to Charlotte: 'All yesterday we saw but one place, the Duke of Cleveland's Raby Castle, a fine hall and the outside very grand. We arrived here [at Alnwick] last night about 12 o'clock and this morning we rose early to see the castle, which is quite worth seeing and astonished the gentlemen with us. It is all in the same style and very complete, so that you could not find fault with anything.'[52]

Holyrood, in Edinburgh, was 'only worth seeing on account of the historical recollections'; Dalkeith Palace, a seat of the Duke of Buccleuch, was 'a mixture of all & everything, bad taste &c'; 'Sir W Scott's place', Abbotsford, was 'interesting on account of the person who lived there more than anything else. The house is nicely arranged with a good many old things & some very good furniture.'[53] Better than Holyrood was the ale at the Douglas Hotel in Edinburgh. James enjoyed it so much that he ordered a hamper of it to be sent to New Court – and left the bill for it unpaid until 1847 (£3 3s 6d including interest).[54]

On the road to Crieff, they visited Lord Rosebery's seat, Dalmeny, and also Hopetoun House. Dalmeny was for Lionel 'one of the nicest places I have ever seen . . . It is situated on one of the most beautiful rivers, the grounds most elegantly laid out, immense large trees in all directions and ships sailing up & down.' Another time, he would have liked to have been asked to Dalmeny to stay, but for some reason thought an invitation unlikely. Compared to Dalmeny, Hopetoun was 'a Louis 14 palace, but did not please us as much as the former'.[55]

From Crieff, they visited the park and gardens of Drummond Castle, where Victoria and Albert had been feted by the Willoughby de Eresbys during their Scottish tour the year before. The Willoughbys were abroad, but the park at Drummond, Lionel told Charlotte, was 'of a more wild & grand description than anything else we have seen till now, immense trees, rocks & the most beautiful green fields and a very large lake in the middle'. Deprived of sport on a wet day, Lionel and his companions returned to the park, and walked in the castle gardens.[56]

They also visited the Marquess of Breadalbane's Perthshire seat, Taymouth Castle, as 'they say his park &c are worth seeing'. James greatly admired the dairy he saw there, and subsequently asked Mayer to have a sketch made of it 'with every detail' so that he could build a copy of it in France. For Lionel the visit to Taymouth was spoilt by the fact that Lady Breadalbane did not invite them to dinner and altogether was 'not very polite'.[57]

As to the sport itself, they stalked – James killed a young stag – and they shot; one day, they bagged twenty-two brace of grouse between them, another day fifteen. The grouse shooting, Lionel explained to Charlotte, was 'different to what we are accustomed to see and particularly to that which our good uncle has at Ferrières, where all the game is driven to him and he has but to fire away. Here we have to walk after the dogs and to seek for game, which is a much greater excitement and at the same time more fatiguing . . . The sport is considerably increased by the beautiful scenery;

as soon as one's attention is taken off the dogs, it is attracted to the beautiful views in all directions.'[58]

Not content with the little farm on his property at Boulogne-sur-Seine, James had since 1829 owned Ferrières, an estate, with château, situated about twenty miles to the east of Paris. It was there that he proposed to build his new dairy. Visiting James and Betty in the summer of 1842, Hannah wrote to Mayer:

'We have been passing a few days at Ferrieres, the shooting place and estate of Uncle James. They are doing a great deal to it; the first view of the place is not imposing because it is flat. 10,000 acres of land are a great many; it is very productive, more so than land is in general in France on account of the soil being moist and rich and brings in a good revenue. I and Louisa accompanied Betty in driving through the woods, which possess many very pretty alleys of trees [which] are very agreeable; there are excellent springs in the place and [it] is an Estate, dear Mayer, which I think you would say is worth having; as James's family are growing up and getting more extensive it will become very useful to him.'[59]

Mayer and his brothers already quite saw the point of owning a country property, in particular as they needed somewhere to stay near Hastoe if they were to make the most of the hunting in the winter – which entailed more than two days' hunting a week, on Mondays and Thursdays, with Baron Rothschild's Staghounds. In late November 1842, when William Selby Lowndes' foxhounds met at Creslow Great Ground in the Vale, the field included 'Messrs Rothschild', who, along with a handful of other local sporting characters, 'rode well up with the pack, and went through the day with great credit'.[60]

It was feasible to go down to Tring for the day – the rail journey from Euston was about an hour – though not ideal to have to do so for two or more meets in a week. 'Follow my advice,' Nat had recommended his brothers in 1840, 'and do not let the opportunity slip of getting out [of stock] at fair prices so that when the season comes we may have a little hunting without sweating and bothering ourselves in the railway carriages.'[61]

In the early days, Lionel made use of the Rose and Crown at Tring, an old coaching inn run by Timothy and Sarah Northwood. In 1840 Sarah Northwood wrote to him to ask for his continued custom, though whether that included his use of rooms for the night is not stated.[62]

By then Lionel had already begun to look for more property in the area. In the spring of 1839, he had instructed Adamson to make enquiries of

William Kay's executors about Tring manor. In August, with the help of
John Abel Smith and a London land agent, he was considering Lord
Chesterfield's 5,000-acre estate at Wing, near Leighton Buzzard; but as
enquiries were under way the estate was sold to someone else – to the City
banker Samuel Jones Loyd, of Jones, Loyd & Co.[63]

Thereafter, with much to do in London, Lionel tended to leave the
search for more property to his brothers. 'I dare say,' wrote one of his correspondents in forlorn hopes of receiving a reply, '[that] between the
Pursuits of the Chase, and the Occupation of the Counting House, you
have no Balance of Time to spare.'[64] Yet the Rothschild brothers were in no
hurry to take on a big house and estate. Writing from Paris, again in 1840,
Nat particularly advised Mayer against assuming the burden of a large
property. 'If it is a very nice place,' he reasoned, 'you might take it for one
year on trial & then engage it for a term if it suits us but to be saddled at
once with a large establishment does not seem to me very agreeable.' To
begin with, a farm would do; their brother-in-law Anselm, who thought
land to be 'always the best investment', began with farms at Frankfurt.[65]

In late April 1840, 'glad to observe you ended the season so brilliantly
and that Tup distinguished himself', Nat urged his brothers 'strongly to
enquire about the farm near Hardwick. If you consider it an eligible purchase, do not hesitate about it. I am quite ready to take my share *or* any
share.' An 'eligible purchase' meant a property that would pay a return, as
Hannah's remark about Ferrières indicates.[66]

'I hope you will induce Leader [a Bucks landowner] to sell his place so
as to make it a fair investment,' Nat wrote again. 'If you can get it to pay
3% int. do not hesitate a moment.' He returned to the theme again,
encouraging his brothers 'to make enquiries as to whether Leader really
intends to dispose of his estates in Bucks. I should like amazingly to lay out
about £25,000 for my own acct in land there & would be satisfied with 3%
int. if I could not get more. I advise you to be active & not let it slip
through your fingers as you did with the Hardwick estate.'[67]

In May 1840, Mayer was informed that Champneys, at Wigginton,
near Tring, was available to let; in July, he and his brothers learned that the
Mursley estate, near Winslow, was coming up for sale; in October,
Anthony arranged with Sir Seymour Blane to look over Moor Place
House, near Great Hadham, with a view to taking it. For the time being,
however, the brothers continued to wait for a better proposition.[68]

When, in May, they were put on notice that the lease on the stables of
Tring Park would not be renewed, Nat airily brushed the matter aside. 'I
do not mind their turning us out of the stables at Tring much,' he declared.

'It is rather inconvenient but our horses could be kept at Aylesbury & those for the kennel at the kennel.' At the most, he said, they would need 'a couple of hacks more to ride over to the [railway] station. That is all the difference.'[69]

Subsequently, Mayer was offered the chance to buy Champneys outright; and Lionel contemplated purchasing Luton, Lord Bute's estate in Bedfordshire. As Anthony dithered over whether or not to buy the Ampthill estate in Bedfordshire, it was sold to the Duke of Bedford. He was also offered a lease on the Pishiobury estate in Hertfordshire, where he was already renting some land, and fleetingly he considered buying an estate at Bromley, in Kent – rejecting it as being too close to London.[70]

However, in September 1842 Mayer took the plunge and bought, for £5,000, from a man named Warner, some farms and cottages in the parishes of Mentmore and Wing, a few miles from Tring. He took over a cottage by the church for himself. Anthony approved of his brother's acquisition: 'I hope old Tup will give us some good shooting on his farms,' he wrote from Paris. 'I am glad he has made such a good purchase . . . I wish he would find me something that would pay me so well.' The Baron's hunt set-up would be moved to Mentmore in 1843–4.[71]

In the meantime Lionel, with Adamson supervising the operation, simply extended the premises at Hastoe. The works being completed there on 23 October 1841, Adamson then took his leave, departing the scene for good – Lionel having agreed to take over a cottage that Adamson had occupied nearby. 'The Baron has not any mansion in the neighbourhood,' a visitor to Hastoe noted in January 1843, 'but attached to it is a snuggish little box, where a man, whom the favors of the Blind Goddess have not rendered too fastidious, may very well condescend to take his ease after a long day's hunting, and enjoy his bright glass of generous Port – your only wine when you are fagged.'[72]

The hunt establishment at Hastoe was laid out with a 'tolerably spacious' yard flanked on two sides by loose boxes and stabling. Beyond, on higher ground, was a further seven-stall stable and two loose boxes fronting the kennel, the latter consisting of two tiled yards, with feeding room, boiling house and 'other usual appurtenances'.

A feature of the stable yard in 1843 was a tame fox, kept in a large wire cage opening out of an old beer barrel. John Harris, a former servant of Hannah's at Gunnersbury, when writing to Lionel for assistance in joining a 'school of industry for the blind' at Bristol, recalled that he had 'often beat up Hares for your Honor when shooting and am the young Man who caught the tame Fox when it was lost'.[73]

Five hundred yards from the kennel were two paddocks, each about an acre and a half in extent, enclosed by high palings, containing the red deer – stags, heviors and hinds – destined to be chased across the Vale. Two stags in 1843, Doddington Laddie, aged five, and Galewood, aged four, came from Lord Ossulston's park at Chillingham Castle in Northumberland. Heir to the Earl of Tankerville, Ossulston had recently given up staghunting; his park keeper, John Cole, who described the deer as 'good runners', sent the animals off by steamer from Berwick to London. The next year, five brace of deer (four stags and six hinds) were obtained from Lord Fitzwilliam's herd at Wentworth Woodhouse; and in 1844 Lionel bought, via the park keeper at Wentworth, for £84, eleven red deer that had belonged to the late Charles Stuart Wortley.[74]

The Huntsman, William Roffey, whose duties included selecting the deer, lived close by the kennel, as did the Whip, Tom Ball, and the Stud-groom, John Oliver, whose dogs pulled down the deer in the park at Tring. Tom Ball, who was known as a superb horseman, had previously whipped-in to Grantley Berkeley (when Master of the Oakley), to Lord Suffield (when Master of the Quorn) and, for the season just prior to his engagement by Lionel, to David Robertson in Berwickshire.

Among the hunters stabled in the lower yard was Swift, a bay horse bought from Anderson of Piccadilly, combining 'speed, courage and every capability that a first-rate hunter should possess, with a perfect knowledge of his business . . . no day too long, no jump too big for him'. In the box next to Swift – whom Bill Roffey had ridden for the staghounds' first four seasons – was Ormsby, a powerful brown horse, a winner of the fiercely competitive Brocklesby Hunt Steeplechase and 'a great favorite with the Baron [Lionel], who generally bestrides him, and whose weight is not easily carried by anything but one of the proper stamp'.

A grey stallion called Lincoln, and Truffle, a black gelding – both hand-some and, according to Roffey, 'as good as they look' – were two of the hunters favoured by Anthony, while King Charles was the mount preferred by Mayer. Squib, a grey gelding regularly ridden by Roffey, was a horse with stamina. By the end of one day in 1842, when the deer had been taken at Oxford after a run from Oving of about twenty-one miles, Squib had carried Roffey for sixty-five miles since setting out for the meet in the morning. Tom Ball's favourite mount was The Unknown, a dark grey six-year-old with a tan muzzle that never refused a jump.

Of the horses stabled in the upper yard, the outstanding hunter was Grouse (originally called Waterloo), Lionel's 'great gun'; a dark brown horse, standing at rather more than sixteen hands, Grouse was considered to be the 'perfection of a crack hunter'. With Ball up, he won the Aylesbury Steeplechase in 1842. 'The Baron, on Grouse or Ormsby,' it was reported in 1843, 'plays his part pretty well on most occasions, and he is no feather-weight. His brothers, likewise, Messrs A. and M. Rothschild, ride well, and occasionally go like beans, being partial to a scurry; and another brother [Nat] . . . is said to be nothing but a top-sawyer.' In 1845 Lionel was riding above 14 stone.[75]

Of the twenty-seven and a half couple of hounds in the kennel in 1842–3, fifteen or so had been acquired from Sir Charles Shakerley, the balance of the pack being made up of drafts from other kennels, Lord Yarborough's, the Duke of Grafton's, Lord Chesterfield's and Thomas Assheton Smith's among them.

Two of the hounds, Blue Bell and Angler, it was judged, 'would not disgrace any kennel in the world'; and from the sale of Squire Osbaldeston's pack there was Falstaff, a son of the famous Furrier. Falstaff was the sire of Lionel's strong, light-coloured hound, Gunnersbury, 'a driving, forcing hound on a scent'. It was said that as Gunnersbury crashed through the double hedges of the Vale, he appeared 'as though he would tear them to pieces'; he was 'as good a hound as ever went out of doors'.[76]

Meets were advertised in the *Northampton Herald* as well as in *Bell's Life*; and besides Lionel, his brothers, George Samuel, Henry FitzRoy and the hunt servants, several local characters are recorded riding to hounds with the Baron's during the hunt's first few seasons.[77]

One such was Mr Hall, of Weedon; mounted on his hunter, The Chummy, he was said to be 'a hard man to beat over any part of the Vale'. Another was Will Golby, of Weedon Hill, 'a stalwart yeoman . . . who pulls down the scale to the tune of nearly 14st. when in the saddle, refuses nothing in his line, and has a shy at all sorts of fences – gates, doubles, or brooks – with more pluck than prudence, occasionally paying somewhat dear for his morning's fun'. A third was George Cooke, of Winslow, whose company at dinner the Rothschilds enjoyed.[78]

From among the local gentry there was William Learmonth, of Wing Cottage, who had hunted with de Burgh's staghounds and also hunted with the Buckhounds; he was a 'very natty man' who wore black boots and whose hat sat 'very much on the back of his head'. There was also Tom Crommelin, a 'very neat man' who wore an eye-glass and lived with his friend Mr Sheddon at Hastoe; and there was 'Squeaker' Lee, who practised as a solicitor in Lincoln's Inn Fields.[79]

Like Learmonth, Captain Richard Howard Vyse, of Stoke in Bucks and Boughton in Northants, was another regular with the Baron's who had hunted with de Burgh's and who also hunted with the Buckhounds. He was a younger son of Colonel (later Major-General) Richard Howard Vyse, the soldier-cum-Egyptologist whose explosive charge blew a large piece off the Sphinx at Giza during the search for a secret chamber in 1837. Major Richard Gilpin, of Hockliffe Grange, near Leighton Buzzard, at whose house the Duke of Bedford's harriers sometimes met, was a stalwart of the Baron's from the start, and also helped Lionel to arrange meets.[80]

The Cloth was represented by the Reverend Christopher ('Kit') Erle, the Rector of Hardwick, a well-endowed living in the gift of New College, Oxford. When, at a dinner, the Bishop of Oxford once informed Erle (whose curate took all the church services) that he objected to his clergy riding to hounds, Erle replied that he did not much care for hunting, and seldom went with any but the Baron's, as he wished particularly 'to promote Christianity amongst the Jews'.[81]

The Earl of Verulam's younger brother Robert Grimston, an Old Harrovian whose twin passions were hunting and cricket, and who as a bold horseman had a number of very bad falls, was a regular with the Baron's. Lord Clanricarde, statesman and member of the Royal Hunt Club, was an occasional member of the field, as were Viscount Alford, Lord Charles Russell and Captain Robert Boyle, of the Coldstream Guards, a younger son of General the eighth Earl of Cork. Captain Boyle's nephew, the ninth Earl of Cork, married a daughter of Lord Clanricarde and was for three terms Master of the Buckhounds.[82] In March 1843 the 'Gentlemen Hunting with Baron Rothschild's Hounds' gave a dinner to the local farmers at the White Hart Inn at Aylesbury; and that year Richard Dighton produced a portrait of Mayer dressed for hunting.[83]

In a class of his own among the Baron's field, there was Fitz Oldaker, London saddler, horse dealer, hound finder and supplier of gun dogs, whose services were for many years employed by Lionel and his brothers and cousins. 'Rattling away with his nasal twang', Oldaker did not count as a gentleman – could not, for example, 'bestride the pigskin' as a gentleman jockey. When, in April 1846, the Gentlemen hunting with the Baron's entertained Lionel, Anthony and Mayer to dinner at the Clarendon Hotel in London – Captain Boyle presiding – Hall and Cooke were there, alongside Gilpin, Grimston, Lord Alford and others to enjoy 'every delicacy of the season . . . wines of the first-rate quality'; but Fitz Oldaker's presence was not noticed.[84]

Another Londoner who went down to the Vale for the hunting was the artist Francis Grant. Late in life, when thanking his 'dear old friend Baron

Lionel' for a kind message, Grant recalled 'the merry days when we were young & used to gallop together over the green fields of Aylesbury'. Having painted the *Meeting of the Royal Staghounds on Ascot Heath* for Lord Chesterfield, Grant – who became President of the Royal Academy – was later commissioned to paint *Full Cry*, a large oil painting of Lionel and his three brothers (they and their horses to go to Grant's studio) galloping after their hounds across Creslow Great Ground.[85]

12

Competitors

———

IN THE SUMMER of 1814, London had witnessed the gathering of the
Allied Sovereigns to whom Nathan had been channelling British subsidies in the war against Napoleon, and of whom Hannah caught a glimpse
during her day at the races at Egham that June. In Piccadilly, the gardens of
Burlington House were covered with tents and temporary rooms for the
fetes being given in the Sovereigns' honour, and among the throng there
was Miss Amelia Murray, the daughter of a lady-in-waiting, who got a
good view of the visiting royalty.[1]

Miss Murray did not think Tsar Alexander of Russia a handsome man;
'he looked red, and stiff, and square'. His son Nicholas, the future Tsar, she
found to be 'a magnificent young Prince'. The King of Prussia was 'noble-
looking, melancholy and gentlemanlike'. The Prince of Orange was 'not
particularly attractive'. Prince Leopold of Saxe-Coburg, on the other hand,
was 'a handsome young man, not then specially noticed; but very soon it
was discovered that Princess Charlotte preferred him to her former lover
[the Prince of Orange]. Small blame to the Princess!'

Princess Charlotte had become engaged to Prince William of Orange in
December 1813, but the engagement was broken off – to the Princess's
relief – when in 1814 it became clear that William was returning to
Holland. The fixing of Charlotte's affections on Prince Leopold was then
to prove significant to Nathan and his family. As the only child of the
Prince Regent – whose creditors included the Rothschilds – the Princess
was second in line to the throne, then still occupied by her grandfather
George III.[2]

Nathan's nephew Solomon Worms, who arrived to live with his cousins
at New Court in 1814, recalled how one morning the handsome Prince
Leopold, 'who had come to England to pay his addresses to Princess
Charlotte, drove to New Court in a shabby hackney carriage, with letters
of introduction and credit. Nathan severely berated him on the impropri-
ety of driving about London in a hackney, and sent him back to Carlton
House in a glass coach.'[3]

Although Leopold's subsequent marriage to Princess Charlotte in 1816 would prove short-lived – the Princess died after giving birth to a stillborn son the next year – Nathan and his brothers maintained links with Leopold and his family, and the policy was to pay dividends as, one after another, the Saxe-Coburgs married into the powerful ruling families of Europe and ascended new thrones.

The Rothschilds extended banking facilities to the Duke of Kent, the Prince Regent's brother, when he went to Germany to marry Prince Leopold's widowed sister Victoria; and when the new Duchess of Kent gave birth to a daughter, Princess Victoria, in May 1819, Nathan offered the Duke financial advice and the use of his secure and efficient courier service.[4]

Princess Victoria, Leopold's niece, became Queen Victoria and in 1840 married her cousin, Leopold's nephew, Prince Albert of Saxe-Coburg. Leopold, who married, as his second wife, Princess Louise of Orléans, daughter of King Louis Philippe, was by then well established as the first King of the Belgians. Queen Victoria, Prince Albert, the Duchess of Kent and King Leopold all took advantage, in various ways, of services that Lionel and his family were pleased to provide. The Queen, the Prince and the Duchess all made use of the Rothschild courier service for communicating with cousins on the Continent. Prince Albert and his relations borrowed money from the Rothschilds – Lionel and Anthony would go to see the Prince at Buckingham Palace – and the Kingdom of Belgium was in its early years all but dependent on Rothschild credit. And there was social contact, too.[5]

Passing through Brussels on the way to Frankfurt in 1836, Hannah regretted that she and Nathan could not accept King Leopold's invitation to dinner. When visiting relations in Germany, the Duchess of Kent would see the Rothschilds in Frankfurt. In England, Queen Victoria's uncles – the Duke of Sussex, who gave Victoria away at her marriage to Albert, and the Duke of Cambridge – attended Hannah's fetes at Gunnersbury with their wives. The carriage of the Duke of Sussex's friend and equerry Lord Dinorben was among those at Nathan's funeral.[6]

The Duchess of Gloucester, the Queen's aunt, whose presence in Brussels was noted by Hannah in 1836, dined and paid calls at Gunnersbury. When she met Lionel's wife and children there with Hannah – Charlotte found the Princess 'as usual . . . extremely kind and sympathetic' – she asked them to visit her. Even the King of Hanover, who, despite his visit to the Great Synagogue in 1809, was not at all well disposed to the Jews, accepted Rothschild hospitality.[7]

Yet it has often seemed that Queen Victoria herself, until very much later in her reign, was all but socially blind to the Rothschilds. She was not.

From Paris, on 30 April 1842, Nat wrote to his brothers in London: 'I have already attended to yr. costumes for the ball. Fat Bill [Anthony] will be attired in light blue velvet & gold, a white wig & heeled shoes 1½ inch high. He must show his calves which the Queen will fancy . . .' In a postscript to a letter a few days later he wrote: 'Dear Rab [Lionel] . . . the tailor recommends you to have a costume of black velvet made. The Duke de Guise's of the time of Henri 3rd. It wd. hide yr. fat belly & make you look charming.'[8]

On 7 May, Nat informed his brothers: 'Your dresses will be sent off tomorrow. As for a military dress it wd. not have suited you my dear Lionel; it requires a tall fellow like old Tup [Mayer] & not one of our height. You will look very well if you wear the dress I send you, & wishing you all much amusement . . .'[9] Shortly afterwards, he confirmed: 'Your costumes leave by the diligence, everything complete with the exception of Rabbi Leib's [Lionel's] shoes which the Duke of Devonshire takes with him this evening & which you had consequently better send for. I think you will look uncommonly well & be very much admired . . . I wish you much amusement . . .'[10]

Disappointingly, as in the case of the uniform that he had had made for himself in Constantinople, Nat was soon afterwards writing: 'I am sorry your costumes were too small; it is a sign you are grown pretty fat' – and he himself experienced the problem again when he was invited to a concert at the Tuileries: 'a great bore as I shall be obliged to pack my fat body into a tight uniform'.[11]

Fortunately, fancy dress was not compulsory for the ball to which Lionel and Anthony had been invited: Nat had read in the newspapers that 'gentlemen wd. be allowed to go in Court dress or a uniform', and Lionel, for one, as Austrian Consul in succession to Nathan, would obviously have had a court uniform. As a way of amusing Prince Pückler-Muskau after a good dinner one evening, Nathan had tried on various new suits of uniform that had recently been made for him.[12]

It is clear that 'the Queen' referred to by Nat in his letter of 30 April was Queen Victoria. The fancy dress ball to which Lionel and Anthony had been invited was the first of three to be given by Victoria and Albert at Buckingham Palace. It took place on 12 May 1842: Prince Albert was dressed as King Edward III, Victoria as Queen Philippa. Edwin Landseer painted them in their costumes, standing beneath a splendid Gothic canopy in the palace Throne Room.

On Saturday 14 May, *The Times* reported: 'Her Majesty's fancy-dress ball on Thursday night was a scene of such brilliance and magnificence, that since the days of Charles II, with the solitary exception of one fête given in the reign of George IV, there has been nothing at all comparable to it in all the entertainments given at the British Court.' Those whose presence among the 2,000 guests the *Times* reporter considered noteworthy included 'Baron Rothschild'.[13]

Nat would have read the full account of the event when his *Times* of 14 May arrived in Paris, but that day he wrote to ask for 'all details respecting the ball, the costumes, & wot [sic]'. The next day he was 'delighted to hear you were so well amused at the Ball', though disappointed to hear that Lionel had not worn his costume – and sorry that 'fat Bill did not appear in his wig'.[14]

Three years later, when Victoria and Albert were visiting Germany in August 1845, the Frankfurt Rothschilds booked rooms for the royal party at the Hotel de l'Europe in Mainz. A special water closet, 'made in princely style', was installed for the royal visitors, who, when they received Mayer Charles and his uncle Amschel, 'were both extremely gracious, affable & kind: they both talked for almost 20 minutes and no doubt it was a very great honor as nobody else was received, not even Her Majesty's minister or any member of the Corps Diplomatique.'[15] It was felt that the Queen might have accepted an invitation to luncheon in Amschel's garden in Frankfurt 'had not Prince Albert said that the arrangements of the journey would not allow it'. The Lord Steward, Lord Liverpool (half-brother to the late Prime Minister), asked after Hannah and 'was pleased to hear she was going on well'.[16]

Besides booking the hotel rooms in Mainz, the Rothschilds in London and Frankfurt provided Victoria and Albert with foreign currency for their trip: 32,000 thaler, 5,855 gulden, 1,500 Friedrich d'or and 500 Napoleons.[17]

Earlier in the year, writing to Lionel's wife Charlotte, Hannah had observed: 'I perceive the Queen is to hold a drawing room on the 10th. I think you and Lionel should go . . .' And less than two months before the royal visit to Germany, Lionel and Mayer had been to Buckingham Palace for the second *bal costumé*, the suggested dress style for which was early Georgian.[18] Reading a report of 'H.M.'s ball' in *Galignani's English Messenger*, Chilly, in Frankfurt, enjoyed the description of Lionel's 'splendid peach coloured dress with diamond buttons' (ordered from Paris), and supposed that, but for the fact that Lionel had had to shave off his whiskers for the occasion, the ball would now seem like a 'brilliant dream'. Louisa read of the ball too. 'How did you look dear Muffy in your dress of light blue & silver,' she asked Mayer, 'did it not make you look rather stout? And how did you like showing your legs, and shaving off your whiskers [?]' *The Times* reported that invitations to the ball had also been issued to Hannah and Charlotte, as well as to Anthony and Nat and their wives.[19]

By the time Nat was writing to his brothers about their costumes for the first royal fancy dress ball, his presence in Paris was no longer simply for the purposes of work. By then he was only three months away from his marriage to another Charlotte de Rothschild, James and Betty's only daughter.

An early indication that a more than cousinly affection was forming between Nat and Charlotte is contained in a short note that Mayer added to a letter written by Anthony in Switzerland in July 1839. The brothers were visiting James and Betty and their children at Heinrichsbad spa, where James was recovering from the serious illness with which he had been struck down at Naples earlier in the year.

'Anthony has given you an account of the family here. On that point I will not detain you,' Mayer conveniently informed his mother, 'however to a certain young lady I have only said three words & that was when I first arrived who seemed very much disappointed in not meeting with the *right brother* . . .'[20]

On 19 July, Betty also wrote to Hannah from Heinrichsbad. 'We had the pleasure a few days ago to welcome your good sons Anthony and Mayer,' she reported. 'You may imagine, my dear Hannah, the satisfaction we experienced in seeing so dear relations after so many months of separation. Anthony looks very well, and is not changed at all, but Mayer has grown so tall, that I really took him at first for Nat, he has so great a likeness with [him].'[21]

In August, Anselm wrote from Paris to congratulate 'Murphy' (poking fun at the French pronunciation of 'Muffy') 'on his entrée into the Counting House', adding – more in hope than with realism – 'and [I] expect very fine letters from him'. When Anselm wrote to his cousins again in October, he remarked: 'James & Baron Nat are at Ferrieres shooting & riding with the Ladies. Nat gets quite a courtly gentleman . . .'[22]

Towards the end of October, Anthony, also writing from Paris, told his brothers: 'Baron Stag [Nat] leaves tonight, the poor gentleman is so in love that he can hardly leave . . .' In a letter to Nat from Frankfurt a few months later, Chilly asked: 'How is your beloved? Very sweet & tender? Does she grow tall or fat or thin or not at all [?]'[23] On 18 April 1840, Nat himself wrote to his brothers from Paris: 'I have as usual been uncommonly well received and have every reason to be pleased . . . Mrs Salomon has offered me a very nice room in her house which I find much more comfortable than being at an hotel . . .'[24]

Judging by a remark of Betty's that was overheard by the diarist Thomas Raikes, Nat would certainly have been very comfortable staying with his aunt Caroline. A ball that James and Betty gave in rue Laffitte in March 1836 offered, Raikes wrote, 'a display of the most costly furniture and of everything that money could command in its greatest profusion. One of the guests expressed his admiration to the lady of the house at the sumptuous decorations, to which she replied, "If you had seen the hotel of M. Salomon Rothschild (which is next door), you would think our house was only the stables attached to it." '[25]

Nat also informed his brothers: 'My fair young cousin was very pleased to see me again, her Mamma was equally well displeased.' The reason for Betty's displeasure, if she really was displeased, is unclear. Many of Nat's letters contain humorous remarks, though it might be that Betty was saddened by the prospect of her only daughter leaving home. On the other hand, as Nat and Charlotte were going to live in Paris, not London, Betty would not be too much deprived of her daughter's company.[26]

In April 1842, Nat paid a three-week visit to England for his sister Louisa's marriage to Mayer Charles in London. After returning to France, he then moved from the rue Laffitte to stay with James and Betty and their family at Boulogne-sur-Seine, though he did not stay under the same roof as his bride-to-be. 'We are going to reside at Boulogne tomorrow,' he wrote to Hannah on 26 May, 'which for me is not particularly agreeable as I inhabit the Chalet in the vicinity of which is the poultry yard, & whence proceed the cackling of the fowls, ducks & geese which with the crowing of the lusty cocks prevent my sleeping much after 5 o'clock. Early hours are not bad for one's health & I try to console myself with the idea that it is not to last long.

'My house advances famously & in a month the plasterers & bricklayers will I hope take their departure. Then will commence the furnishing, when I shall have recourse to yr. good taste. Anthony knows the things which I want & will have the pleasure of communicating with you on the subject. I only hope my dear Mamma you will excuse the trouble . . .'[27]

Besides his desire to escape the sounds of the poultry at Boulogne in the early hours, there was another reason for Nat to look forward to his approaching nuptials. 'The Baron & all his family have gone to Boulogne,'

Anthony informed Lionel and Mayer in London. 'Nat goes there every night . . . He says the country air has a greater effect upon him than the air of Paris & he is obliged to touch a certain part every minute. He wishes that the month of Aug[ust] was over, as he says he is in great want.'[28]

To cool off, Nat, whom the summer heat reminded of his trip to Greece and Turkey, would go for a swim at six o'clock in the morning. In the evening there was the odd visit to the theatre, on one occasion to see the much admired tragedienne Mlle Rachel (Elisa Félix) in the title role of Thomas Corneille's *Ariane*. The play was not up to much, but it hardly mattered; Rachel was, as Nat's sister Louisa put it, 'completely *the rage* . . . nothing can exceed the enthusiasm she has created . . .'[29]

'It appears,' wrote Anthony in his earthy way, 'that the Prince de Joinville works her up before she plays. They report that he shaged [*sic*] her 24 times in 24 hours. He goes it better *than old Tup*.' James seems to have been interested, too. Joe Montefiore, who judged Rachel 'very handsome', put it to Anthony: 'If Baron James patronised her, I do not think his only aim was the furtherance of theatrical art.' Rumour had it that when the Prince de Joinville heard that Mlle Rachel would welcome a visit, he asked: 'Where? When? How much?'[30]

When Hannah arrived in Paris in August, she reported to Mayer that the house at Boulogne 'though not large' was 'countrified and pleasant'. Otherwise, she observed that the 'table and servants are in the best style; the Bride is as you have heard before, very nice agreeable and ladylike etc. Nathaniel is good spirited and all thank God promises well . . .' To Lionel his future sister-in-law bore a resemblance to Henrietta Montefiore and to Anthony's wife, as well as to his sisters; her head, hair and the upper part of her face reminded him of Hannah Mayer, the lower part of her face made him think of his sister Louisa.[31]

Nat's house, the future marital home, was under construction in the rue Taitbout, a street parallel to the rue Laffitte, leading off the Boulevard des Italiens, with the fashionable Café de Paris – famous for the *veau à la casserole* that Alfred de Musset was said to eat there three times a week – on the corner; and in the months before and after his marriage Nat made preparations for his new establishment at No. 40.[32] In Paris he was 'booby enough' to buy a painting attributed to Rembrandt for 10,000 francs (£400) from the dealer C. J. Nieuwenhuys. 'I am very pleased with my picture,' he told his brothers. '[Count Anatole] Demidoff told the Baron [James] last night he was sorry he was too late & that he had intended buying it.' He also bought a number of fine Sèvres vases, and a green Sèvres service consisting of 106 pieces.[33]

But it was to London that Nat looked for much else; England, as James once remarked to Anthony, was 'the "promised land" where one finds everything'. Nat asked Lionel to enquire about a pair of bay carriage horses (Lionel favoured greys) from a dealer named Dyson, and to check on the progress of a phaeton and a buggy that he had ordered from Tilbury's, the coach builders. He also asked Lionel to pay for some pearl drops and a necklace he had bought from the silversmiths Storr & Mortimer; to enquire about some silver plate he had ordered; and to engage a servant 'to clean the plate, the china & glass, to be out of livery & to be able to wait at table' for not more than £40 a year.[34]

To his mother, he wrote for designs for a sideboard resembling one that she had at Gunnersbury, and requested her to send 'a handsome but plain dinner chair to serve as a model, very comfortable to sit upon, not too small, fit for a broad bottom – also two or three arm chairs. Old Bill knows what I want – but I have only confidence in your taste my dear Mamma.' Anthony was asked to 'send over the drawing of the best livery. You wd. also oblige me by letting me know the price of a dozen plates like the one I selected at Mortlock's for your guidance. It was a white plate with a blue & gold edge.'[35] Mayer was asked to buy 'two very nice riding whips' for James's young sons Alphonse and Gustave. 'They must be as nice as possible but I do not wish them to cost more than 5 @ [to] 10£.'[36]

As his house neared completion, the London shopping list would continue to grow. He asked his brothers to commission Seymour Huffam ('Huff') to find him a sedan chair 'as *light*, cheap & convenient as possible', and to obtain for him 'some nice editions of the English classics & well bound into the bargain'. He also wanted four bottle stands; a dozen silver gilt dessert knives, forks and spoons ('quite plain', from Garrard); sauce-boats; and some carpet patterns.[37]

If it could not be arranged for the dessert items from Garrard to be sent to Paris in a sealed diplomatic bag, Nat was anxious that they should 'appear as if they had been used. If new they pay double duty & gilt things pay 20% more than common silver, therefore try to have them sealed. I wd. sooner wait a little longer & get them in without duty.' He strongly advised his mother against attempting to smuggle the plate through French customs – 'unless it is sealed it is sure to be confiscated' – and in due course the French embassy in London obliged with the bag.[38] When the bottle stands arrived they were found to be too small, and were returned. When the time came to pay for various items, Nat asked his brothers to settle up with Garrard 'as far as possible . . . deducting 7½% which Bill tells me he allows for cash payments'.[39]

In July the date for the wedding was fixed for 17 August. Initially, Lionel was not sure that he would be able to attend, as his Charlotte – who in November 1840 had given birth to their first son, Natty – was nearing the end of another pregnancy. But after Charlotte had been safely delivered of a second son, Alfred, on 20 July, Lionel decided to go. Mayer, with Ben Cohen at his side, was left in charge of affairs at New Court.[40]

James was as keen as Nat that Lionel should be in Paris for the wedding, though not only for personal reasons. Lionel was now head of the most profitable of the five Rothschild banks, and as James and his brothers intended, as always, to combine business with pleasure when they met together in one place – 'to speak about business & the concerns of our own houses', as Nat put it – Lionel's presence was especially desirable.[41] Owing to the heat, Anthony recommended that anyone coming from London should 'travel by night – it is much pleasanter . . . and starting at 4 o'clock [in the afternoon] from Boulogne [the Channel port] with a good courier you [should] get here easily by the next day at 9 o'clock in the morning.'[42]

Several accounts of Nat's wedding exist in the family's correspondence – in Lionel's and Hannah's letters, as well as in a letter to Mayer from Hannah's nephew John Helbert – but the best and fullest account is that contained in Moses Montefiore's diary:

Paris, Hotel Windsor, August 17th – The great day has at length arrived, and, happily, our presents also: they were sent last night to the Bois de Boulogne. Ours was similar to that we gave Baron Charles and Louisa de Rothschild; a large and handsomely-carved ewer and basin, worth £180. We left Paris before twelve o'clock, and on reaching the Bois de Boulogne, found the party already assembled, all the ladies most elegantly dressed. A procession was formed by a number of choristers, led by the *minister officiant*, and preceded by the Grand Rabbin. Then followed the bridegroom with his brother, Baron Lionel de Rothschild, as best man, and on his left Baron James; afterwards Barons Salamon [*sic*], Anthony, and other relatives and friends present. We proceeded to a magnificent canopy of white satin and gold embroidery, erected in the garden: the ground was covered with velvet carpets. The path leading to the canopy was covered with crimson cloth strewn with roses. The choir was singing Hebrew hymns all the time. Then followed the bride, led by her mother and Mrs de Rothschild, the other ladies following. Under the canopy stood the bride and bridegroom, their parents, Barons Anselm, Lionel, and myself. The marriage ceremony was performed by the Grand Rabbin, who delivered an excellent discourse in French. After the ceremony the whole party walked to the Swiss cottage in the garden, where a sumptuous breakfast was laid. No toasts or health were drunk, but grace was said. Afterwards the gentlemen went back to Paris to dress, the ladies being accommodated in the house. We were back again by four o'clock, and now found the ladies most magnificently attired. At seven we entered the banquetting room. It was in a perfect blaze of light: only once, at the Archbishop of Canterbury's [William Howley's] have I seen such splendour. The repast consisted of all the luxuries the world produces. The gardens were brilliantly illuminated. The host and hostess were most attentive. It was past eleven when we left.[43]

Of the various themes to which Nat returns in his daily letters from Paris in the 1840s, the most noticeable in the business sphere – besides never-ending reference to the price of the *rentes* (French government stock) and to political events likely to result in price fluctuations – is de Rothschild Frères' involvement in the financing and construction of France's railways. 'Every day there is a new railroad projected,' he moaned in 1844.[44]

At times the railway projects occupied James, and consequently Nat, as well as Anthony, almost to the exclusion of anything else. 'I did not know that the Baron [James] wrote disagreeable letters to you,' Nat wrote, for example. 'You must not be too touchy my dear Lionel as you do not know how terribly bored he is – from 7 o'clock in the morning till past 5 every day receiving railroad folks & running about from the North to Lyons & then Strasburg. I wd not do it for all the world.'[45]

But as that last remark suggests, it was Nat, not James, who was bored. 'The stinking railroads engross all our attention & for my part I wish his Satanic Majesty had them all,' he wrote in March 1842. 'There has been no business,' he wrote again, 'all our time has been taken up with the railroads, a most disagreeable occupation & you may congratulate yourselves upon having nothing to do with them, and I hope you will always keep out of every concern which is at all foreign to those belonging to regular merchants & bankers.'[46]

While Anthony enjoyed, and was good at dealing with, the practical aspects of the projects, notably of the Chemin de Fer du Nord, as they neared completion – ordering engines and engine drivers from England, visiting the construction sites, keeping up staff morale – he, too, found the business hard-going.[47] 'You cannot have any idea how difficult it is to manage our Railroad,' he wrote of the Nord in its early days. 'I never thought it would be so difficult – a long line, the difficulty of procuring good employees & all the other difficulties in the world. It will take us another year & then please God I hope we shall go on better.'[48] On the other hand, Anthony felt he had a better understanding of the territory than the French did. 'These French frogs,' he said, 'understand Railroads as much as a certain part of mine does.'[49]

Life in Paris, however, had its compensations, as Anselm intimated two years after Nat's – and nearly four years after Anthony's – marriage. Having received a joint letter from his English cousins, Anselm was 'glad to see the Baron Billy in so good spirits. He is now in his element: les Boulevards, le Café de Paris, le Club, & something else which I dare not mention – all things he cannot enjoy nor [sic] at frft nor at London. I wish I were with you not for those objects, but to smoke a good cigar with you, & laugh at every one.'[50] When staying in Paris in 1844, Joe Montefiore asked Anthony to 'send me a good address or two, some old Lady who can procure a young one'; in Spain, Joe said, he had recently found the women (six in all) 'very springy and active'.[51]

Although New Court participated in the French railway projects, in England Lionel kept clear of the railway craze. His mother, who thought it as well that he did, was none the less an early enthusiast for rail travel. 'The expenses in Germany are not exorbitant,' she wrote to Mayer from Mainz in 1842, 'and travelling by steam boat or rail road nothing like posting, the accommodation very good . . .' To Lionel's wife Charlotte, she later ventured: 'There is certainly a luxury in lounging in one's own carriage . . . but the advantages of rail road travelling counterbalance this . . .'[52]

By way of relief from the railways and the *rentes*, another subject to which Nat returned regularly in his letters was the art market, with an emphasis on Old Master paintings. It was an interest he shared not only with Lionel, but also with Anthony and Mayer and, in the wider family, with James and his cousins Anselm and Charles. Their collecting focused on works by the most sought-after artists of the seventeenth-century Low Countries, with the occasional addition of something Spanish, French or English. At 2 Grosvenor Place Houses in London, one of the best pictures was a 'glorious picture by Van Dyck' – a Madonna and Child – that Anthony and Louisa were given by Henrietta Montefiore.[53]

Before buying his Rembrandt from Charles Nieuwenhuys, Nat had been a buyer at the sale in Paris of the Comte de Perregaux's pictures, at the Hôtel Drouot, in December 1841. He had set his heart on a painting by Adrian van de Velde, which he considered to be 'one of the finest pictures by the master' and 'quite worth' 30,000 francs (£1,200); Anselm wrote to congratulate him on his purchase, and to say that Chilly had left a bid on a Greuze in the sale but had failed to secure it.[54]

Lionel purchased works by Aelbert Cuyp and Willem van de Velde from the sale that followed Lord Coventry's death in 1843; and by the time Nat wrote to congratulate him on the purchase of the mystery Piccadilly house that summer, he concluded: 'You will have a beautiful gallery of pictures now my dear Rab' – adding that it would make their uncle James 'quite jealous'.[55]

In 1844, the directors of the British Institution in Pall Mall wrote to Lionel to request the loan of several pictures for their forthcoming exhibition of Old Masters: 'Cattle piece, by Cuyp; Frost piece, by Cuyp; Landscape and figures, by Ruysdael and A. Vandevelde; Landscape, by Decker'. Three years later, Lionel received a request from an American visitor to London 'to see the pictures and decorations at his house in Piccadilly'.[56]

At the sale in Paris of pictures from the estate of the Hispano-French banker Alexandre Aguado (a great friend of Rossini's) in 1843, Nat bought a painting by Velasquez – *Lady with a Fan*, the face 'not a pretty one altho' very well painted' – which he felt sure was worth twice the 12,700 francs (£580) he paid for it. His aunt Caroline bought two Murillos in the Aguado sale, though Nat rated neither of them as good as the one that his mother owned.[57]

At the auction of Jeremiah Harman's pictures in London in May 1844 (Lionel had made a fruitless attempt to see the pictures before they went on view at Christie's), Nat, with Lionel acting on his behalf, bought a painting by the Dutch landscape master Meindert Hobbema, *Peasants crossing a Ford*. He would have liked to have a Willem van de Velde as well – 'but as he [van de Velde] is a master whose middling productions are cold I should only wish for one if it be quite 1st rate in quality like the little one you [Lionel] bought of Lord Coventry'.[58] From other sources Nat acquired works by Philips Wouwerman, David Teniers, Paulus Potter, Ludolf Backhuysen, Nicolaes Berchem and Caspar Netscher.[59]

The four brothers were careful not to compete for the same things. When a London art dealer who acted for Mayer was in Paris, Nat wrote to the 'most amiable and communicative Tupus': 'If you want things you should write to yr humble servt as well as to him because it might happen that unconsciously I might spoil yr market.' And they learned to keep art market intelligence to themselves. When Lionel, on a trip abroad, got wind that Lord Bute was to sell his estate at Luton, he was anxious to know if the Bute pictures might be offered for sale as well. 'Let me know my dear Billy if he will sell some of his pictures,' he wrote to Anthony. 'They are the finest in England & I should like to have some most famously. But keep it to yourself and do not talk about it. Take care that no person goes there before you do.'[60]

'With regard to curiosities,' Lionel would say, 'mystery is absolutely necessary in order not to spoil the market.' Nat had to reprimand Anthony for talking too freely about forthcoming sales; and when James was put out on discovering that Lionel already knew about a sale of which he had only just heard, Nat found himself explaining to his uncle that Lionel had as much right to buy the pictures as anyone. James, for his part, wrote to agents in London about the Coventry sale without telling his nephews; and at the Harman sale he bought works by Willem van de Velde, Cuyp and Teniers.[61]

Competition in the salerooms from non-Rothschild bidders was put up by several extremely rich men. One of them was Count Anatole Demidoff, who would have liked to have the Rembrandt Nat bought from Nieuwenhuys and who in 1830 had gone to London with a letter of introduction from Lionel to Nathan. Married to Jerome Bonaparte's daughter Princess Mathilde, and now bearing the Tuscan title Prince of San Donato, Demidoff derived a vast income from silver mines in the Urals.[62]

A second competitor, following the death of his father in 1842, was the fourth Marquess of Hertford, who lived in Paris at No. 1 rue Laffitte, on the corner with the Boulevard des Italiens. 'He buys up every thing & spoils the market,' Nat wrote of Hertford in 1843. 'I wish he wd. go back to London.' Charles lost courage in the face of 'mighty competitors like Lord Hertford [who] . . . give enormous prices to secure the best lots'. There was competition also from the British millionaire Robert Holford, a brother-in-law of Coutts Lindsay, who was among the buyers at the Harman sale in London – and who with Coutts Lindsay's help rebuilt Dorchester House (where 'Red herrings' Hertford had died) on Park Lane.[63] Lord Hertford's natural son, 'Monsieur Richard' (Richard Wallace, later of Wallace Collection fame), who lived with Lord Hertford's mother and brother in apartments above the Café de Paris, was at the same time a great speculator in *rentes* on the Paris bourse – as also, from time to time, was his mother Mie Mie.[64]

In the spring of 1845, Mayer Charles went to view the pictures to be sold in Rome from the collection of Cardinal Fesch, Napoleon's maternal uncle, following the death in Florence of the Count de Survilliers – Joseph Bonaparte, the former King of Spain – in Florence the previous summer. 'I shall be [only] too happy to attend to your commissions,' Charles wrote to Lionel, 'but I am afraid there will be little chance for it, Ld. Hertford having made his appearance with the full intention of securing all the best pictures . . .'[65]

At the sale at the Palazzo Ricci in March, Charles nevertheless secured one of the late Cardinal's paintings by Greuze for Lionel, and for Nat a Karel Dujardin, which, said Charles, had been admired by everyone who saw it in Rome but none the less was still knocked down to Nat at a favourable price. Indeed, with the exception of a painting by Gabriel Metzu, which went to Lord Hertford for an impressive 86,000 francs (£3,440), Charles told Nat that 'the best pictures have been bought by members of the R family'.[66]

Five years earlier, following Cardinal Fesch's death in 1839, Joseph Bonaparte himself had approached the Rothschilds with a proposal involving his pictures. Nat's opinion had been that 'the sum to be advanced is much too large', and that although it would be 'very well' for James or Lionel or any other family member to buy as many of the pictures as they liked, it was 'not proper to engage in large transactions having pictures as their basis'.[67] That Joseph Bonaparte had been in touch with the Rothschilds was clearly no secret. The King of Württemberg instructed his court bankers to write to New Court indicating that he might like to buy some of the Fesch pictures 'should a sale in part be agreed to at moderate prices'.[68]

As all eyes were on the Fesch sale in Rome, Anselm was about to pull off the Rothschild family's first purchase of a notable picture collection *en bloc*. In June 1845 he bought, in The Hague, the entire collection of the Dutchman Klerk de Reuss – one, the new owner pointed out, no doubt in a spirit of cousinly competition, 'which Lionel knows well'. The collection contained, said Anselm, 'master-pieces[s] of nearly all the first Flemish & Dutch painters [such] as [Jan] Both, C. Dujardin, Teniers, Ostade, Ruysdael, Berghem, Wouwermans, Van de Velde & God knows the name of all those great Gentlemen . . . The Wouwermans & V. de Velde are of the best I have ever seen . . . I have four *Jan Steen* . . . They say that the King of Holland is extremely vexed that these pictures have left the country.'[69]

Naturally, like the King of Württemberg, they all hoped to buy cheaply – pictures 'of the finest quality & not too dear' as Nat said. Prior to the Perregaux sale in 1841, Lionel, Anthony, Nat and Mayer engaged in a long debate as to the value of the whole collection, and as to the most advantageous price at which they might be able to buy it *en bloc* and then divide it up among themselves by lottery.[70] Having viewed the Perregaux collection, which, in addition to the Adrian van de Velde and the Greuze, contained works by Willem van de Velde, Karel Dujardin and Philips Wouwerman, Anthony reported that he would not hesitate to buy them all for 350,000–400,000 francs (£14,000–16,000). 'There are 20 of the very first rate . . . & they are worth at least 20,000fr each on average,' he said. 'Do not mention one word about this to any Person, & particularly *not to Claret* [James's agent] or else we shall get into a bother.'[71]

Prior to the sale, Anthony was then offered 'Perrigaux's [*sic*] Wouwerman & his Van de Velde' for 60,000 francs (£2,400); but his response, which must have confounded the vendor, was that he would give no more than 50,000 francs '& then I would not purchase them'. Having recounted this to his brothers, he added further to the confusion: 'Ask Mamma if she would like to have them at 55,000. They are not dear & I think them well worth it. They would look beautiful in the green Room at Gunnersbury.'[72]

After Nat, accompanied by an adviser named Martini, had been to view the pictures – 'Some of them beautiful & such as you scarcely ever see in the finest collections' – he valued them 'decidedly under the price which I am sure they wd fetch if sold by auction in London and we made them worth 500,000 franks [*sic*] (£20,000) at least & you [Lionel and Mayer] can do the same without incurring any risk'.[73] Yet when he reported the next day that the vendors wanted 505,000 francs, and that there would be a further 2,000–3,000 francs to pay the broker, he recommended making an offer of 450,000 francs (£19,200), while Lionel, having consulted Hannah, appears then to have been unwilling to go above the low end of Anthony's original estimate of 350,000. Although the vendors dropped their price to 480,000, the pictures were left to go to auction – at which, according to the *Gentleman's Magazine*, sixty-nine pictures sold for a total of approximately £17,600.[74]

Later, at Lord Coventry's sale in London, Nat would have liked to have one of the Cuyps 'if not too expensive'; and at the Harman sale, Anthony hoped to buy for his wife 'one of Sir J. Reynolds, if not too dear'. Anselm, crowing over his acquisition of the Klerk de Reuss pictures, considered that he had 'bought the whole collection at a cheap price. I think I could have the double of it in a public sale at London or Paris . . . Old *Reus* [*sic*] is now so sorry to have sold his pictures that he left the Hague for a long journey . . .'[75]

When Nat learned the price at which Lionel had bought the Hobbema for him at the Harman auction – 1,850 guineas, the highest price in the sale – he asked Lionel to try and resell it for him without taking a loss 'as £2,000 is a very large sum for a poor little Jew to spend on a picture', 'too great a sum for a poor Jew like me to invest in an object only affording pleasure to the eyes'.[76] Lionel did as Nat asked, but the man to whom he offered it, a Mr Wheeler, declined, pleading that his wife had already used up his current budget for luxuries.

Fortunately, as it turned out, Nat was delighted with his purchase: 'My Hobbema is a most charming production, in fact I don't think I ever saw one more to my liking & I can not tell you how much obliged I am to you for having purchased it. I wd. not take £500 profit and when once suspended in my red room it will become the greatest favorite in the world.' Anthony – who despite his admiration for the Perregaux pictures had dropped out of the scheme to buy them before the sale – thought Nat's Hobbema 'one of the finest I have ever seen & I am pleased that it is in his house as I can admire it without it costing me my good tin'.[77]

The scope of Rothschild collecting extended from pictures, furniture and porcelain to ivory, silver and silver-gilt items, Renaissance metalwork (cups in particular), *Schatzkammer* objects and majolica. Anthony, on a visit to The Hague in 1842, made 'some good purchases of objets de vertu'; Lionel bought some gold dishes and a unicorn for Nat at the Duke of Sussex's estate sale in 1843; and both Lionel and Anthony collected majolica.[78]

In the mid-1840s, Charles asked Lionel to buy 'anything pretty' coming up in a sale of 'silver things' in London. 'I rely entirely on your taste,' he said, 'and [on] your qualities of chief connaisseur [*sic*] and celebrated judge . . .' Anselm, a *soi-disant* 'amateur of fine things', asked to be sent a catalogue of the same London sale, expressing an interest in 'ivories, cups &c – Cellini as you call them'. In 1842 he already had enough 'bric-a-brac' to attract a visit from the King of Württemberg, who having looked over Anselm's collection stayed to dinner.[79]

By 1849, Lionel had become quite choosy; with a sale of 'some pretty things' coming up in Paris, he asked Anthony to buy 'anything good in Silver or any good Crystal Cups . . . in fact anything you think really first rate. I do not want any China or glass or enamels. I have quite enough of them.'[80]

A third – and constant – preoccupation of Nat's was his and his brothers' sporting interests. 'There is no better fun than hunting & racing & every thing is flat & stale when one has been accustomed to the excitement occasioned by their enjoyment,' he declared in 1842.[81] In the autumn and the winter he wrote wistfully of hunting in 'old England'. 'What magic there is in a pair of leather breeches,' he once exclaimed. 'I have half a mind to put a pair on & gallop round the bois de Boulogne. Old Tup wd. exclaim go it you cockney.' He would plead for 'more detail abt. yr. hunting & let us know all abt. the horses you ride & whether old Tup manages to tumble into the dirty black ditches'. Year round, Nat also wrote extensively about his and his brothers' ups and downs on the Turf.[82]

While hunting was possible from Paris – there was a subscription pack of foxhounds, generously subsidised by the francophile Earl of Pembroke, at Versailles, and royal packs of hounds at Chantilly and Saint-Germain – Nat wrote of 'us poor fellows who can only hunt thro' the columns of Bell's Life'. Opportunities for racing – a pursuit close to the hearts of the governing and affluent classes on both sides of the Channel – were, on the other hand, plentiful.[83]

Looking forward to his mother's arrival from England for his wedding, Nat commented in a letter to Lionel: 'Today there is no business. All the world is at Notre Dame where I did not feel inclined to go . . .' The event Nat missed at Notre Dame (which Anthony did attend) was the funeral of King Louis Philippe's heir, the Duc d'Orléans, who had died, after being thrown from a runaway carriage, on 13 July.[84] Two months after Nat's wedding, on 16 October, Benjamin Disraeli wrote to his sister from Paris: 'Of English here, are the Adrian Hopes (who have arrived from Normandy), Henry Hope, Smythe, Cochrane, Lord Pembroke, Antony [sic] de Rothschild, Mrs Montefiore. Antony succeeds the Duke of Orleans in his patronage of the turf, and gives costly cups, which his horses always win.' (Anthony observed in a letter to London: 'Disraeli and his wife dine with us today.')[85]

Since Anthony had built his stables at La Morlaye in 1839, he had certainly had his fair share of success on the flat. In September 1840 in Paris, for instance, his horse Anatole, ridden by the English jockey Elnathan (Nat) Flatman, beat the Duc d'Orléans' Rocquencourt to first place in the Special Prize, the opening race of the Champs de Mars meeting, winning Anthony 3,000 francs (£120). Nat Flatman – who used to go ratting with Colonel Jonathan Peel, Sir Robert's younger brother – rode regularly for Anthony, and became the first acknowledged champion English jockey, with eighty-one winners accredited to him in 1846.[86]

At the Chantilly meeting in October 1841 – 'the Royal Dukes of Orléans, Nemours, and Aumale were present with their suites, and a few of the most Distingués on both days' – Anatole (Flatman up) beat the Duc d'Orléans' Gyges to first place in the first French St Leger, winning Anthony 4,000 francs (£160), the prize money having been put up by Louis Philippe.[87]

'We unfortunately did not win the French Derby, Muse [another Rothschild racehorse] could not run,' Anthony wrote to Lionel and Mayer eighteen months later. 'Annetta ran an uncommonly true & good little race & was only beaten by a length & ½ coming in 3rd . . . We won another race with Anatole for 5,000 fr [£200]. Till now we have gained about

30,000 fr [£1,200] and I think that we shall gain a good deal more by the end of the year.'[88] As with their farmland, so Anthony and his brothers expected their racehorses to pay their way, to produce at least enough prize money to cover the costs, preferably with some 'pocket money' left over. 'With luck,' as Nat put it, 'a racing establishment seldom pays more than its expenses but if one is out of luck it is dreadful expensive work.'[89]

Betting could be a costly business, too, and for a Rothschild could lead to social complications. Anthony and Nat, whose circle of French friends included the Prince de Beauvau, the Ducs de Mouchy and de Guiche and Count d'Hédouville, belonged to the aristocratic French Jockey Club, where betting, and play for high stakes at cards, was rampant.[90] Owed 50 Napoleons by one man and 25 by another – '& the Lord knows when I shall see the colour of their tin' – Nat complained: 'It's a deuced bad thing betting in this part of the world. I am obliged to pay whilst my friends do not experience the same necessity of discharging their obligations towards me. I shall therefore give up the trade & leave it to others.' A week later, he was 'most happy to say that nobody [at the Jockey Club] has asked me to lend them any money & that is the reason I do not wish to be too intimate with any of them'. Betting, he mused, 'is something like fucking – when one gets into the habit of it one seldom leaves off'.[91]

Besides Anatole, Annetta and Muse, the horses in training in 1842–3 at La Morlaye included Eliezer, The Curé, Donna Isabella, Nautilus, Governor, Drummer and Prospero. At the Paris meeting in October 1844, Flatman landed Drummer the winner, by two lengths, of the 6,000-franc (£240) Royal Prize. After Drummer, Prospero was the best horse in the stable; Donna Isabella was the best mare.[92] By the end of October 1842, Anthony was hoping to 'win one or two more [races] this year, so that our Expenses of next year will all be paid. It would be a famous good thing.'[93]

With Sir Robert Peel's introduction of income tax that year, one might surmise that this became all the more pressing a consideration – especially as Nat and Anthony derived their incomes from New Court. 'I am very sorry to observe that Peel has proposed an income tax. I thought it impossible,' Nat wrote to Lionel and Mayer. 'What can't be cured must be endured and we must not repine if we have a good deal to pay.'[94] Anthony, who did not care to play whist after dinner for fear of losing his 'good tin', wrote with foresight: 'As regards the Income Tax we cannot help it. We must hope that the Tories will not remain in to [sic] long; but I am frightened that it is found such a convenient Tax that it will not be taken off in such a hurry.' The Rothschild brothers' political sympathies were Whig.[95]

In June 1842, Anthony wrote to Lionel and Mayer 'that Annetta won her race most famously & we had the pleasure of beating all the [other] nags – so it appears she can beat them all on a flat. It was a pretty good stake of 8,000 fr [£320] – everything helps – and therefore I hope that we shall win a little more in Sep & before the end of the year. Till now we have won about 37,000 fr [£1,480], which is not a bad thing.'[96]

As a measure of worth, when Nat interviewed a French lady's maid ('the model of a waiting woman, can dress hair to perfection, make dresses . . . ugly enough to frighten your horses') for Anthony's wife Louisa in March 1842, he explained that she would require wages of 600 to 800 francs (£24–32) a year. The Duc d'Orléans' former cook, whom Lionel interviewed – and who appeared to him a 'respectable man' – explained that the late Duke had paid him 2,500 francs (£100) a year, but that if he were to move to London he would require 3,000 francs (£120) (modest enough when one considers Ude's £1,200 salary at Crockford's).[97]

Disraeli's remark to his sister about Anthony giving costly cups which his horses always won, was probably inspired by the Chantilly meeting of early October 1842, when the flags at the racecourse were bound to their poles by black crape in mourning for the Duc d'Orléans. Anthony and Nat both attended the meeting on 1 October, the first day, and had the satisfaction to see a cup they had given, worth 5,000 francs (£200), carried off by Anthony's filly Annetta (Flatman up).[98]

When in 1843 Anthony began planning to move his family back to London, Nat gradually took over the racing operation at La Morlaye, continuing with Thomas Carter as trainer. In 1846, he won the French Derby with Meudon (Flatman up), and in 1852 the French Oaks with Bounty.[99]

While neither Anthony's nor Nat's presence was noted on the opening day of the Paris spring meeting in April 1843, there were a fair number of Englishmen in attendance, among them the Earl of Chesterfield, Lord Somerton (described by Anthony as a friend of Mayer's) and 'Baron L. Rothschild'.[100] Besides maintaining his already 'far-famed pack and stud of hunters' at Hastoe, Lionel had by now made a modest foray into English racing with a chestnut gelding called Consul (by Irish Napoleon), trained by James Messer at Brickwall, near Welwyn. In 1841, Consul won a hunters' stakes worth £65 at Gorhambury, near St Albans, on the racecourse that the Earl of Verulam (brother-in-law to Lord Liverpool, the Prime Minister) had opened there in 1838, so giving Lionel his first taste as a winning owner. Among the 'very large and fashionable' attendance at that Gorhambury meeting were the Dukes of Rutland and Dorset; the Marquesses of Exeter and Angelsea; the Earls of Jersey, Chesterfield and

Uxbridge. The principal steward at the meeting was the Earl of Albemarle, assisted by Robert Grimston.[101]

In 1842, in company with 'the *elite* of the Hunting field from far and near' and crowds of spectators, Lionel watched Consul, ridden by Fitz Oldaker, win the Newport Pagnell Steeplechase by half a length. Tom Ball, in this instance riding for Lord Edward Russell (brother of the seventh Duke of Bedford and of Lord John Russell), came in second on Lord Edward's Lather. That year Consul also won a steeplechase at Hereford, came in 'a dashing third' in the Oxford Handicap; and ran, but was not placed, at Northampton, as well as in the fourth Liverpool Grand National Steeplechase (as it was then known) at Aintree.

In a sweepstakes at Aylesbury in February 1842 – 'no horse qualified to start unless he has been up at the taking of six deer with Baron Rothschild's stag-hounds during the present season' – Lionel (one of the stewards, with Lord Edward Russell) saw his horse Oliver Twist come in first. At Gorhambury that year he had two runners, a black three-year-old filly by Rockingham out of Flight, and a chestnut colt of the same age by Sir Hercules out of Worthless, though neither was successful.

Consul ran again in the Grand National in 1843 – 'Lottery, Peter Simple, The Returned, and Consul were of themselves sufficient to draw a host of admirers of the sport'. Although Lottery and Peter Simple were two of the best-known steeplechasers of the period, neither won. Consul came in fourth. Shortly after Lionel had acquired The Whaler, a son of Lord Jersey's famous Bay Middleton, from Lord George Bentinck (Disraeli's political patron), the horse ran a dead heat for the 1843 Huntingdonshire Stakes with Rooksnest, a horse belonging to Colonel Jonathan Peel.[102]

In 1842 Lionel had registered his first racing colours: amber with lilac sleeves and red cap; but soon afterwards he exchanged them for dark blue and a yellow cap, which from then on served as the Rothschild family racing colours on both sides of the Channel. 'I am in great hopes of seeing Annetta win tomorrow,' Nat wrote from Paris in May 1842. 'If so the little mare will pay nearly all the expenses of the stable for this year . . . I hope to goodness she [Annetta] will win for it's the best fun in the world seeing the blue & yellow come in first. It is quite as good fun as getting first over a big brook & being alone with hounds for ¼ of an hour.'[103]

If Anthony or Nat required a steeplechase horse in Paris, or a horse for a hurdle race, they might ask Lionel to send one over from England; Tiger was one such. Tom Ball sometimes went over to Paris as jockey. But it was flat racing that came to dominate the Rothschild brothers' enthusiasm for racing. 'You have no idea what fun it is having a horse in a good race with a probability of winning,' Nat wrote, 'ten times the excitement of a steeple chase because you see the whole of it.'[104]

In 1846, Lionel had two mares in training with Henry Scott, of the Engelmere training stable, Ascot Heath; and Mayer had three yearlings in training at John Scott's famous Whitewall House stable, near Malton in the Yorkshire wolds – at a cost, per horse, of £2 6s 6d a week, exclusive of blacksmith's and vet's charges and an annual levy of £2 2s for each horse exercised on the wolds.[105]

In July 1842, after a visit to England, the Prince de Beauvau told Nat that Mayer had 'bought a race horse & intends winning the Derby'; and it was soon afterwards that Mayer began to race a filly named Emerald. Initially trained by James Messer, Emerald, by Defence out of Emiliana, ran at Gorhambury in May 1843, and came in third in the One Thousand Guineas in 1844. 'I suppose Tupus has been at Newmarket,' wrote Nat, 'as we have not seen anything of his beautiful handwriting lately.'[106]

Tradition has it that Mayer came by Emerald in 1842, as the result of a lottery held among the staff and partners at New Court; first prize was an emerald worth £300. Mayer won the stone, sold it back to the dealer from whom it had been bought, at a reduction of £60, and with the £240 remaining bought the filly from Fitz Oldaker, who had picked her up cheaply at Tattersall's. Although, in effect, Emerald had cost Mayer nothing, when it came to winning races, she proved a dud.[107]

In May 1844, she ran (John Day junior up), but was not placed, in the Oaks at Epsom; and at the Ascot meeting in June, she came in third in the Great Ascot Produce Stakes. Nat advised Mayer to 'stick to the scarlet coat, instead of the silk jacket, it is more beneficial to the health and less expensive'. But as a brood mare Emerald really showed her worth, providing Mayer with a string of excellent racers who raked in the winnings.[108]

13

Sidonia, or The Curly Forties

————◦∞◦————

ONE MINOR EVENT associated with Rothschild racing interests in the 1840s lends extra credence to a well-established notion – to the identification, in certain respects, of Lionel with a character in Disraeli's novel *Coningsby; or The New Generation*, which was published in 1844. The character is the financier Sidonia, a cosmopolitan Jew whose father had 'made a large fortune by military contracts, and supplying the commissariat of the different armies' during the Napoleonic wars; who had emigrated to England, 'with which he had . . . formed considerable commercial connections'; and who went on to become 'one of the greatest capitalists in Europe'.

Sidonia senior made loans to France, Austria, Prussia and Russia; he became 'one of the most considerable personages in Europe' and 'established a brother, or near relative . . . in most of the principal capitals'. In time he became the 'lord and master of the money-market of the world', but 'in the height of his vast prosperity he suddenly died', leaving 'the greatest fortune in Europe, so great, indeed, that it could only be calculated by millions' to his only son.

The son, like Lionel and his brothers rolled into one, was 'taught from his cradle to be proud of being an Englishman'. As a young man he 'resided some time with his uncle at Naples', 'made a long visit to another of his father's relatives at Frankfort', and for some years lived in Paris.

In England, like Nathan's sons, Sidonia is appreciated for his 'immense wealth' and for 'his devotion to field-sports, which is the safety-valve of his energy'. When staying with Lord Monmouth at Coningsby Castle, he wins a steeplechase for gentleman jockeys in the valley of Coningsby – a country as 'deeply ditched and stiffly fenced' as the Vale of Aylesbury.[1]

As 'every person' was 'as polite as possible' to Anthony and Louisa when they were entertained at Chantilly by the Ducs d'Aumale and de Fitzjames in May 1841, and as then 'All the ladies asked after Baron Nat. All the great beauties were there',[2] so the young Sidonia is 'received in all circles with great distinction', and is 'admired by women'.

Like Lionel from boyhood, Sidonia 'observed everything'; and he is given to 'poignant sarcasm', a characteristic of Lionel's – and of his wife's – that unnerved Anthony's Louisa. As he grows older, Sidonia becomes 'the only man who tells one anything new', which might have as much applied to Lionel as to his father: it was, for example, during a visit to New Court in July 1842 that the Austrian envoy Philipp von Neumann first learned of the Duc d'Orléans' death – on 14 July, the day after the fatal carriage accident.[3]

Hannah, having read *Coningsby* in May–June 1844, was complimentary about Disraeli's presentation of the Jewish concerns that arise in the book (she called the book a 'spiritual production'); but, despite the pointers, she did not remark on the Sidonia–Rothschild parallels. Neither did Joe Montefiore: 'At last Coningsby has made its appearance,' he wrote to his sister Louisa, 'will it be popular? I think not – it is too political to please regular novel readers, too personal to be greatly understood, and too sketchy and undefined to satisfy party spirit.'[4]

Perhaps they felt the Rothschild parallels too obvious to mention and were more struck, as were others, by the points in common between the younger Sidonia's outlook and that of the author himself, even if the character was dressed up as a Rothschild. Joe's phrase 'too personal to be greatly understood' might suggest this. Also, the Jews, for Sidonia, are 'essentially Tories'; and if Nat confessed to 'ultra red-hot conservative' sentiments when it came to French politics, he and his brothers were not Tories. 'A Whig you are and a Whig you must remain,' a friend of Lionel's once wrote to him from the Carlton Club.[5]

In a letter begun at Broadlands on 30 May 1844 and finished in London on 5 June, Lord Palmerston wrote to his brother William Temple, the British Minister at Naples: 'I send you *Coningsby*, Disraeli's novel, well worth reading and admirably written. The characters are, many of them, perfect portraits. You will recognize [J. W.] Croker in Rigby, Lord Hertford [the third Marquess] in Monmouth, Lowther [Lord Lonsdale's heir] in Eskdale . . . Madame Zichy [a daughter of Hertford's mistress] in Lucretia, but not Lady Strachan [Hertford's mistress] in Countess Colonna . . . Sidonia is, I presume, meant as a sort of type of the author himself . . .'[6]

Disraeli would surely have been pleased. Sidonia possesses a 'clear vigorous intellect'; he is a 'great philosopher' and takes a 'comprehensive view of human affairs'. He exhibits a 'very singular freedom from passion and prejudice on every topic'; he possesses 'knowledge of strange and hidden things'; he knows 'everybody as well as everything'. For his 'personal qualities' he is 'immediately cherished'; he 'could please. He could do more, he could astonish'; 'few men were more popular, and none less understood'. Sidonia's roots, moreover, are in Spain, and Disraeli liked to propagate the romantic fantasy that his own family was of ancient Spanish-Jewish descent.[7]

Nevertheless, in a letter of May 1844 to his sister Sarah, Disraeli himself makes it plain that he had borrowed elements for his fictional character from Lionel: 'Lord Ponsonby is so enchanted with "Sidonia" that we are all to dine together at the Lionels' *en petit comité* on Sunday.'[8]

Lord Ponsonby had been Ambassador to the Porte at the time of Nat's visit to Turkey in 1833–4, and the Montefiores had dined with him at Therapia in 1840. (In the course of his 'comprehensive travels', Sidonia, like Moses and Judith, 'visited and examined the Hebrew communities of the world'.) Ponsonby's sister Mary had married Earl Grey, of the Reform Bill, which Lionel had so welcomed in 1831–2 and of which Sidonia, when asked to comment, says: 'I have ever been of the opinion that revolutions are not to be evaded.'[9] When, later, Lord Ponsonby was Ambassador in Vienna (with George Samuel as his private secretary), he was said by Anselm to be 'a good friend of the family'.[10]

That Disraeli had drawn on a Rothschild source for ingredients of Sidonia's make-up might have dawned on Lord Palmerston when he met Lionel at a dinner in Frankfurt, given by Lionel's uncle Amschel, in August 1844. Another guest at the dinner was the Earl of Clarendon, whom, as George Villiers, Lionel had known during his time in Madrid – a city with which Sidonia maintains connections.[11] Subsequently, as Palmerston was laid up in Frankfurt with gout, Lionel paid him and his wife a visit. Besides an interest in political intelligence and gossip, Palmerston, who had been Foreign Secretary in the ministries of Lords Grey and Melbourne, shared other interests with Lionel, too: he was an inveterate horseman and a race-horse owner.[12]

When Coningsby, the hero of Disraeli's novel, first catches sight of Sidonia, lit up by a flash of lightning as he gallops for shelter at an inn in a storm (rather like Lionel at the inn at Metz in 1836), it is the 'remarkable beauty' of Sidonia's horse that attracts Coningsby's particular attention. 'She is not only of pure race,' Sidonia explains later, 'but of the highest and rarest breed in Arabia. Her name is "the Daughter of the Star".' Recalling the tale told by Anthony to Fowell Buxton (and perhaps later to Disraeli too) – that he had 'applied to the emperor of Morocco for a first-rate Arab horse. The emperor sent him a magnificent one . . .' – Sidonia adds of his horse: 'The Pacha of Egypt gave her to me . . .'[13]

Two years after the publication of *Coningsby*, Disraeli – whose next novel *Sybil; or The Two Nations* opens with a scene at Crockford's on the eve of the Derby – accompanied Lionel to the races at Egham in August 1846. One of the runners that day belonged to Lionel: a bay filly by Kremlin out of Evening Star, the latter being a mare that Fitz Oldaker had bought from Lord Westminster and resold to Lionel in 1843. The filly won a small sweepstakes for two-year-olds – and her name was the Daughter of the Star. So it seems as if Lionel enjoyed being linked to Sidonia, though recognition of his contribution to the character was not widespread.[14]

One theory, dating from the 1840s and still current in the 1890s, identified Sidonia with 'Baron A. de Rothschild, of Naples'. Lionel's brother-in-law Adolphe (Dolly) was about twenty at the time Disraeli was writing; and perhaps, as traces of Anthony and Nat may be detected in Sidonia, there is something in the connection. Sidonia belongs to a cadet branch of the noble Medina Sidonias, of Spain, but he has his relations in Naples, and Disraeli seldom missed an opportunity to butter up Charlotte. Moreover, the destructive eruption of Vesuvius in 472, when volcanic ash was carried as far away as Constantinople, was in 474 referred to by Sidonius Apollinaris in one of his epistles – a fact noted in the *Quarterly Review* in 1844, the year of *Coningsby*'s publication.[15]

A possible source of inspiration for the name 'Coningsby' lies on a rather more remote edge of the Rothschild world. Before buying West Drayton in Middlesex, Hubert de Burgh's grandfather, Fysh Coppinger, had sold the manor of Coniston, near Swine in the East Riding of Yorkshire, to Robert Wilberforce, father of the anti-slavery campaigner William Wilberforce. The property – which passed from father to son and remained in the Wilberforce family for generations – incorporated the hamlet of Coniston, which in earlier times was called Coningesbi.[16]

Disraeli was to draw again on the Rothschilds for characters in his later novels. Sidonia reappears, duly aged, in *Tancred; or The New Crusade*, and Charlotte is said to have been an inspiration for Eva Besso; in *Endymion*, Lionel and his wife are cast as the Adrian Neuchatels; and then there are the Hartmanns in *Falconet*. As he became a longstanding friend of the Rothschilds, it seems that they did not object to be made use of in this way, though Lionel himself had died before *Endymion* and the unfinished *Falconet* were published. Doubtless, Disraeli's rich friends were flattered; but, on the other hand, as his political influence grew, the ambitious Disraeli was a useful man to know.[17]

Coningsby does contain one more or less blatant reference to the Rothschilds: the description of a party given at the sumptuous *hôtel* in Paris of 'Madame S. de R—d', a place 'not more distinguished by its profuse decoration, than by the fine taste which has guided the vast expenditure. Its halls of arabesque are almost without a rival . . . The rooms were very crowded; everybody distinguished in Paris was there . . . a sea of sparkling tiaras, brilliant bouquets, glittering stars, and glowing ribbons, many beautiful faces many famous ones . . .'[18]

Looking forward to just such an occasion in January 1845, Charles wrote to his cousins in London: 'To-night Mrs Salomon gives her grand ball & there will be plenty to do for our legs & stomachs. I understand that 900 invitations have been issued & the room will be famously stocked . . .' Although Salomon himself was seldom seen in the evening after half past eight, the day after the party Nat reported: 'We had a most magnificent ball at Made. Salomon's last night & danced away like good ones. We did not go to bed till ½ past 4 o'clock' – to which Charles added: 'The ball yesterday was on a princely scale and everybody talks of it.'[19]

Disraeli may well have drawn on Salomon's Paris residences and hospitality for Coningsby. The year after the book's publication, he and Mary Anne were guests, together with Count Apponyi '& a lot more great guns', at a 'magnificent dinner' given by Salomon and Caroline. Of the 'Dizzys' on that occasion, Nat detected that 'both of them are in love with Baron Lionel & his fair wife'. Disraeli was entertained by James and Betty, too; and when he attended a ball they gave next door to the Salomons' in the rue Laffitte, he marvelled at 'an hotel in decoration surpassing all the palaces of Munich: a greater retinue of servants, and liveries more gorgeous than the Tuileries, and pineapples plentiful as blackberries'.[20]

The setting for the fictional soirée in Coningsby, and also the description of Sidonia's own palatial Parisian hôtel, perhaps also owes something to Disraeli's friendship with the Hopes, the immensely rich Anglo-Dutch banking associates of Barings. Coningsby is dedicated to Henry Hope, whose presence in Paris was noted by Disraeli in the letter to his sister in 1842, and with whom Disraeli was staying in England, at Deepdene, when he was writing the novel in the summer of 1843. A cousin, William Williams Hope, built a house in Paris on the rue Saint-Dominique so huge and luxurious that it was known as little Versailles. It was said to have cost 7.5 million francs, and one of its three dining rooms could seat two hundred.[21]

The Rothschilds knew the Hopes, too. 'I never saw anything so magnificent as Hope's Ball,' Nat told his brothers in February 1843. 'The houses of both our worthy uncles might take a walk in his palace but with all its splendour there are a great many things which wd. shock fat Bill's classic taste.'[22]

In fact the Paris of the 1840s offered a well-connected novelist plenty of material for the description of a splendid ball, dinner or concert – though it was the foreign hosts, like the Rothschilds and the Hopes, who gave the best parties. As Boniface de Castellane – Marshal and Count – once observed: 'It is foreigners who do the honours of Paris.'[23]

If one wished to mix with as varied and influential a crowd as was in attendance at Madame S. de R—d's party in *Coningsby* – to rub shoulders with 'the lady of the Court, the duchess of the Faubourg, the wife of the rich financier, the constitutional Throne, the old Monarchy . . . Marshals of the Empire, Ministers of the Crown, Dukes and Marquesses . . . diplo-matists of all countries, eminent foreigners of all nations, deputies who led sections . . . occasionally a stray poet' – an entrée to the Rothschilds was certainly one of the best bets.[24]

Staying with James and Betty prior to Nat's wedding, Hannah was taken into dinner by François Guizot, Louis Philippe's Prime Minister from 1840, with whom James was in constant contact, and to whom, and to whose policies, Nat continually refers in his letters. Guizot, who had pre-viously been Ambassador in London, was James's guest in the country also, as was his mistress Princess Lieven, whose late husband, Prince Nicholas, had been the Russian ambassador in London. 'Princess Lieven is going to Ferrieres this evening, to remain there a week. There is a go for you,' Nat reported one September. 'Guizot is going on Monday and all the ministers in the course of the week are to make their appearance. It is a great bore.'[25]

Returning to the matter a few days later, Nat reported that Guizot and the Princess – whose former lovers included Prince Metternich – were both installed at Ferrières: 'The old frump was particularly anxious that G should have the bedroom next to hers. What they do I can not say but some sort of fun they must indulge in & of a very nasty description I fancy it must be . . .' Nat was none the less happy enough to be enter-tained by the Princess in Paris, and his wife paid calls on her – at the apartments the Princess rented in a house owned by James in the rue Saint-Florentin.[26]

Members of the royal family were guests at Ferrières, too. On his way to stay there in August 1840, Nat regretted that James 'will not let me shoot in the good places because the Duke of Orleans & all the princes are to have a grand day on the 29th Augst'.[27]

The hospitality was reciprocated. Anthony received invitations from the Duc d'Orléans; and after a ball given by Orléans' younger brother, the Duc de Nemours, Nat, who used to go riding with Nemours at Saint-

Germain, was 'amazingly glad to go to bed as it is no joke to go to a ball at ½ past 8 o'clock & remain there till 2 in a tight uniform & breeches'.[28]

When Anthony dined with Nemours one evening he had 'a most famous bad dinner' but afterwards 'smoked & piped away most famously'. There was 'plenty of play' at cards, but, thinking of his income tax liability, Anthony did not join in. During a spring race meeting at Chantilly, Nat joined the Duc d'Aumale (Louis Philippe's fourth son) and his party at the château; dinner was followed by 'a hop & a smoking which wd have suited old Billy'. The royal parents were approachable too, and in 1845 Nat and his wife were received by Queen Marie Amélie.[29]

'H.M. was exceedingly gracious and asked all sorts of questions,' Nat recounted to his mother afterwards. 'They have a queer way of receiving. The Queen & her ladies sit round a table stiching [sic] away like so many dressmakers, & only leave off when some stranger makes his or her appearance. H.M. then converses with the new comer & then resumes her work. The King goes into another room with the individual whom he wishes to speak to & talks generally for an hour or two which unluckily was the case last Monday. He was en conférence with old Soult when we came & when we left he was talking to the old Maréchal still. We therefore did not see him – something like going to Rome without getting a view of the old Pope. I suppose I shall go there again one day & have a little conversation with Mr Louis Philippe.'[30] Marshal Soult had been Prime Minister in 1839–40. He had resigned – to be succeeded in rapid succession by Adolphe Thiers and then Guizot – because the Chambers had refused to grant a fixed revenue to the Duc de Nemours.

Coningsby's 'diplomatists', 'eminent foreigners' and the old French aristocracy were also well represented in the Rothschild social world. Anthony's friend Count Medem, whose hat and sword Nat had borrowed for his audience with the Sultan in Constantinople, was chargé d'affaires at the Russian embassy in Paris, and after attending a ball given by the family of Count Pozzo di Borgo, the former Russian ambassador in Paris and London, Nat wrote to his brothers at New Court: 'They have got a magnificent house. All the Carlist societé du faubourg St Germn. was there, very fine folks but not particularly amusing. There are parties every night & if you were fond of dancing I should say come here, but hunting is better fun & I wd give 20 hops for a good gallop with the crack pack.'[31]

A soirée given by Madame Apponyi, the Austrian ambassadress and a leading hostess in Paris, Nat 'did not find very amusing'; but, he remarked: 'All Paris was there'. On the other hand, when he and his wife attended a *bal costumé* given by Madame Alexandre Aguado – *Coningsby*'s 'wife of the rich financier' embodied – they happily 'danced away', Nat sporting a 'Louis 14 wig, a very great improvement', Charlotte 'beautifully dressed'.[32]

Of the British diplomats in Paris, until Lord Melbourne's ministry was replaced by Peel's in 1841, there was Lord Granville, serving his second term as ambassador, and Henry Bulwer, a protégé of Palmerston's. The Granvilles dined with James, and James dined with them. Bulwer, who during Granville's absences was chargé d'affaires, dined and played whist at Boulogne and would drop in at the rue Laffitte. Princess Lieven considered him to have 'a thousand times more intelligence than the whole Diplomatic Corps in Paris put together'. In May 1841, Bulwer showed Anthony the letter he had received from London announcing the forthcoming dissolution of Parliament; in August he told Nat that Palmerston had written to say that the Tory Party would shortly be back in office – 'very much to his lordship's disappointment'.[33]

On Lord Granville's departure, the embassy went to Wellington's youngest brother Henry, Lord Cowley. 'There was a most stupid party last night at Lady Cowley's,' Anthony complained in 1842. 'Your friends the Stanhopes are here,' he reported with less feeling the following January. 'I saw them t'other night at Lady Cowley's.' Wilhelmina, the Stanhopes' daughter, was the future Lady Dalmeny and then Duchess of Cleveland who, with her children, was to live next door to Anthony and Louisa in London. As Peel's premiership gave way to that of Lord John Russell in 1846, the Paris embassy was given to Hannah's old friend Lord Normanby.[34]

English visitors to Paris who gravitated in the Rothschilds' direction included Lords Melbourne and Clarendon, Lord Lansdowne, Lord and Lady Londonderry, the Earl and Countess of Jersey (the Earl was Lord Ponsonby's brother-in-law), the Earl and Countess of Wilton, Lord Beauvale (Sir Frederick Lamb, Melbourne's brother), Lord Brougham, who had been Lord Chancellor during the ministry of Lord Grey, and Edward 'Bear' Ellice, Grey's son-in-law, whom Nat found 'generally pretty well informed about home politics' but inclined to be self-important. Lord Beauvale, who had a good nose for stock market movements, would drop in to the rue Laffitte to pick up bourse gossip and to place orders.[35]

'There are a whole host of English here, the Cadogans &cet. Fat Bill has seen them all,' wrote Nat in 1842. When Captain H. J. Rous, 'perpetual Steward' of the English Jockey Club and then manager of the Duke of Bedford's racing stable at Newmarket, was expected in Paris, Nat looked forward to showing him over the stables at La Morlaye. When Henry FitzRoy's friend Lord Castlereagh presented himself, Nat observed that he had 'grown enormously fat from the effects of Anthony's excellent dinners'.[36]

A curiosity among the regular visitors was the Marchioness of Ailesbury, a Tollemache granddaughter of the old Countess of Dysart; like Lord Beauvale, she would talk to the Rothschilds about her investments and the state of the markets. At social gatherings, her dress sense made her a noticeable presence. When she was spotted at a ball in Paris by Henrietta Montefiore, she was wearing, it appeared, 'two of the famous petticoats . . . such a size'.[37] Princess Lieven wrote to Lady Palmerston (Melbourne's sister) of the 'remarkable sight' of Lady Ailesbury's 'extraordinary contours' and 'voluminous clothes'. When Lady Ailesbury entered the Princess's drawing room, the 'most serious-minded guests' were 'hardly able to contain themselves'; Count Molé 'completely lost countenance'. Nor was she very beautiful; Nat said that he 'wd. sooner have a run for 40 minutes across the vale than look at her ugly face without a veil'.[38]

Count Molé, a minister under Napoleon, Louis XVIII and Louis Philippe, was a former lover of Cordélia Greffuhle, who became the wife of Boniface de Castellane and whose brother Jean-Louis Greffuhle, a Protestant banker, had followed King Louis XVIII to Ghent in 1815 and had later been made a Count. The Duc and Duchesse de Berri attended a ball given by the Greffuhles on 12 February 1820, the day before the Duc's assassination – news of which reached Vienna and Berlin by Rothschild courier more than twenty-four hours ahead of the official diplomatic couriers. Anthony knew Count Greffuhle's sons; when they visited England in 1836, he asked Nat to 'be a little polite' to them. 'They are the richest young men of France,' he explained, '& two very good sorts of fellows.' Alfred d'Orsay knew them too.[39]

With the arrival of the Broughams and the Ailesburys in Paris in late 1842, Anthony considered that there were now 'great guns enough to please the Baron [James]'. Lord Ailesbury had an apoplectic fit, but recovered. When the Duke of Devonshire was staying in Paris three years later, James entertained him and 'lots of fine people' to a 'famous good dinner' – though with 'rather too many Truffules [sic]' for Anthony's liking.[40]

Easter generally signalled an influx of English visitors, but if it coincided with Passover the Rothschild family did not entertain them. When the Londonderrys and the Wiltons arrived in the spring of 1847, Nat regretted that it was impossible to 'give them any good dinners on acct of Passover'. Nat missed the good dinners too; he complained that motzers made him feel heavy and sleepy and gave him wind, and that *kosher* food made him feel sick. 'During these holydays we have dined every day at Mrs

Salomon's,' he wrote one April. 'The cooking has always been wretched and the wines still worse if possible.'[41]

One of Salomon's cooks, Adolphe, moved on to the Trois Frères Provençaux, one of the best restaurants in Paris. James would call on his services if planning a private banquet at home, though when Lionel dined at the restaurant in 1861 Adolphe 'did not distinguish himself' and only produced 'a fair dinner'.[42]

Lord Lansdowne, the Normanbys, Lord Brougham and the Jerseys were among those who enjoyed Rothschild hospitality in Frankfurt as well as Paris. Charles relished showing his art treasures to Lord Lansdowne; Anselm gave a dinner for the Jerseys. Granddaughter and heiress of the London banker Robert Child, Lady Jersey was observed by Anselm to be 'in good appetite & very fond of potatoes'. The Jerseys' eldest daughter, Sarah, married Prince Nicholas Esterhazy, son of the long-serving Austrian ambassador in London.[43]

Again, the hospitality was not all one-way. Hannah, Louisa and Charles had stayed with the Normanbys at Mulgrave Castle in 1841; Lionel and his wife joined a house party at Bowood, Lord Lansdowne's seat in Wiltshire, for several days in the New Year of 1843. Nor, as in *Coningsby*, were all the Rothschilds' guests grandees.[44] As Hannah explained to Lionel's Charlotte in 1845: 'At James and Betty's the rooms are well filled with company two or three times a Week . . . Persons of all ranks and *classes* come in. A Whist Table is made up, and others chat, and there is a continuous going in and coming out for about 2 Hours – but no ceremony whatever is made.'[45]

As for the 'stray poet' who might be met with at Madame S de R—d's Parisian *hôtel* in *Coningsby*, the poet Heinrich Heine was a frequent guest of James's – as, too, was Honoré de Balzac, who made James the dedicatee of *Un Homme d'affaires*. During a stroll along the boulevards in 1840, Franz Liszt ran into both Heine and Balzac – as well as Hector Berlioz, who composed a *Chant des Chemins de Fer* for the inauguration of James's Chemin de Fer du Nord in June 1846, and Chopin, who performed at Betty's soirées and dedicated a waltz to Nat's Charlotte, to whom he gave lessons, as he did also to Chilly's very musical daughter Mathilde.[46]

Besides the diplomats and the visitors, there were the semi-permanent British residents who came within the Rothschild orbit. Magnates (and Jockey Club members) such as Lords Hertford, Henry Seymour and Pembroke, found life more congenial in Paris than London. The bachelor Lord Hertford had his illegitimate son Monsieur Richard; and Lord Henry's paternity was a subject for debate. When Lionel was on a visit to Paris, he dined with Lord Hertford – '& a few beaux' – at Nat's.[47]

Lord Pembroke – one of whose sisters married Lord Ailesbury's heir, and another Lord Lansdowne's – had contracted an ill-advised marriage to an Italian princess; the marriage was dissolved, and thereafter Lord Pembroke made do with a mistress. The future Foreign Secretary Lord Malmesbury – who applied to view James's picture collection when he was in Paris – described Lord Pembroke as a 'very handsome man' who lived in Paris 'in great state' and was 'as famous for his cook as for his horses'.[48]

Dividing her time between England and France, there was Lady Tankerville, wife of the Earl of Tankerville and a daughter of the Duc de Gramont, who had married Alfred d'Orsay's sister. When the Tankervilles arrived in Paris in December 1843, Princess Lieven found the Countess 'the same as ever. Gay and friendly.' She was the mother of Lord Ossulston, who supplied Lionel with deer from the park at Chillingham Castle; and when her nephew Agénor, the Duc de Guiche, paid a visit to London, he did so armed with a letter of introduction to Lionel from Nat, who described him as 'a very nice gentlemanlike fellow. I should be very much obliged if you would show him a little politeness, ask him to dinner . . .'[49] Nearly thirty years later, Agénor, by then the tenth Duc de Gramont, became France's Foreign Minister and was in part responsible for the bungling of negotiations that led to the Franco–Prussian war of 1870–71. His son Agénor, Duc de Guiche, was to marry Margaretha de Rothschild, the sixth of Charles and Louisa's seven daughters – and their eldest son Armand in due course married a Greffuhle.

In 1840s Paris there was also Captain Gronow, Jockey Club member and the author of the eponymous *Reminiscences and Recollections*, who would pass on gossip to Nat; and, as well as several resident English doctors, there were the London press correspondents. At a party the Normanbys once gave, Nat 'never saw such a lot of rubbish anywhere – all the trumpery English in Paris such as the newspaper corresponds [*sic*] & their wives'.[50]

But if one preferred not to mingle with such people at a party, acquaintance with them had its advantages. Nat found *The Times*' Paris correspondent, Andrew O'Reilly, an 'obliging sort of man' and would use him to get items through French customs. 'Will you be so good as to send my carriage if possible by Mr O'Reilly the correspondent of the Times,' he wrote to New Court in 1842. 'He will get a courier passport & pass it without duty . . .'[51]

Dealing with a carriage at the Channel ports could be a hazardous affair. Nat heard how 'Lord Pembroke's carriage fell into the sea whilst they were putting it on board at Boulogne & all his things were spoilt. He had 20 new coats & all the most beautiful things that [his tailor] could make.

They say it will cost him near 100,000 fr to have a new wardrobe, but they say his greatest loss was a most magnificent wig, one of a new fashion.'[52] Instead of O'Reilly, it was in the event a Rothschild agent who took charge of Nat's carriage, with an unfortunate outcome: Anthony afterwards requested Lionel to 'be so good as to tell J. Cullen that his donkey of a nephew broke Nat's carriage most famously'. A man from Windus & Co. was sent over from London to inspect the damage, and regretted that he would not be able to fix the carriage 'so as to make it look new'.[53]

More routinely, while O'Reilly might employ the Rothschild pigeon man, Samson – whose practice was to send off six copies of any one pigeon despatch at a time – the Rothschilds had the use of The Times' London courier and carrier pigeons. If O'Reilly wished for information that New Court could provide, Nat would ask his brothers to send it over. And there was the odd bonus for the Times correspondent as well: in 1846 Anthony was able to provide an eyewitness account of an attempt on King Louis Philippe's life; Anthony was 'at the place to hear the music & . . . told it all to O'Reilly'.[54]

Wider benefits of the relationship seem to have accrued to the London Rothschilds in consequence of a note that O'Reilly wrote to Anthony, in Paris, in November 1844, begging 'to be allowed to introduce to you my friend Mr William Delane who (if [it has] not [already been] done by your Brother the Baron Nathaniel) will have the pleasure of explaining the object of the introduction'. The purpose of the introduction is not disclosed, but its significance lies in the introduction itself.[55]

William Delane was then treasurer of The Times, the 'chief proprietor' of which was John Walter, the son of the newspaper's founder, and the editor of which, from 1841, was Delane's son, John Thadeus Delane. William Delane shared the financial management of The Times jointly with Thomas Alsager, who as the newspaper's City correspondent in London from 1819 had known Nathan, and who since 1827 had been a partner in The Times with Walter.

When, in 1842, Anselm wrote to his cousins in London enclosing a new 'regulation which the Prussian Govt. intends issuing about the poor Jews', he considered it desirable that 'articles in favour of the Jews' should appear in the French and English papers to whose criticism the King of Prussia was known to be sensitive. 'As you well know the leading men of The Times,' Anselm continued, 'you will easily obtain from them the insertion of some articles, & I will then send you some German articles [that] you may have translated.'[56]

Of the 'leading men of The Times' to whom Anselm refers, Thomas

Alsager was obviously known to the Rothschilds in 1842; but to whom else the phrase might refer is unclear. Four months after O'Reilly had supplied Delane senior with his letter of introduction to Anthony, in March 1845 Nat wrote to his brothers from Paris: 'I was very pleased with the article in the Times. I am sure it must do good. I recommend you to give a few railroad shares to Delane of that Paper so that he may remain well disposed towards us.' But to which Delane it was that Nat referred is, again, unclear.[57]

Tradition has it that the Rothschilds' connection to the very much more important figure of John Delane − a connection that was to be valued by both sides − commenced when, on a date unrecorded, Lionel and he met at a barber's shop they both patronised in the City. It is not inconceivable that this happened, but it seems unlikely.[58] When, in 1845, Charlotte's brother Adolphe was looking for a valet at the same time as Lionel's man, George Toogood, was looking for a position on the Continent, Nat wrote that 'two essential qualifications were shaving & hairdressing . . . if Twogood [sic] knows how to handle the razor & twist the curling irons, he will do for yr worthy brother in law'. In the unlikely event that Lionel did not employ a servant with these skills, he would surely have summoned a barber to attend to him at New Court or Piccadilly rather than go out to a barber in the City.[59]

If the barber's shop incident did take place, it is likely to have done so after November 1844, and probably after March 1845. It seems implausible that William Delane would have sought an introduction to Nat or Anthony via The Times' Paris correspondent if he or his son had become known to the Rothschilds before, or in the intervening period since Anselm's letter of 1842; and the phrasing of Nat's letter of March 1845 does not suggest that he had in mind more than one Delane: by then he had known or known of William Delane since the previous November.

In all likelihood it was through O'Reilly's introduction of William Delane to Nat and to Anthony in Paris that the Rothschilds, Lionel in particular, became close to John − and that probably as a result of an internal incident at The Times that blew up a few months after Nat's letter of 1845. When John Walter took against William Delane, and also against Alsager, over a misleading statement that Delane senior had prepared concerning the financial position of The Times' printing department, Lionel became involved in resolving the dispute that ensued. In the result, while Lionel helped William Delane to find a berth at Sir John Easthope's liberal Morning Chronicle − where William was then ready to oblige Lionel with the publication of desired items − John Delane, whose position might well have been undermined by the rumpus, continued as editor of *The Times* for a further thirty years, and by mid-1847 had become a trusted ally and adviser of Lionel's.[60]

The only casualty of the dispute was Thomas Alsager, who left *The Times* in October 1846 and the next month died following a botched attempt to cut his own throat. The new financial manager of *The Times*, Mowbray Morris, took to riding to hounds with Baron Rothschild's, as did John Delane.[61]

The context of the article in *The Times* that pleased Nat was the campaign for Jewish civil rights, in particular, at that time, concerning municipal offices. Before turning to the newspaper item, Nat explained: 'D[avid] Salomons showed me the bill which entre nous I find rather shabby as it is confined entirely & solely to municipal offices. You should try to induce yr friend Lord [Chancellor] Lyndhurst to introduce generally all corporate offices . . .'[62]

Since Robert Grant's Bill for the removal of Jewish disabilities had failed to pass the unreformed House of Commons in 1830, the Bill had been tabled anew in 1833, after the Reform Act, and had passed. Lord Brougham, the then Lord Chancellor, had introduced the Bill into the Lords, where it was rejected; and further disabilities relief Bills in 1834 and 1836 had come to nothing.

Otherwise, there had been some modest advances. Since 1831 Jews had ceased to be barred from becoming Freemen of the City of London. After David Salomons had joined the Coopers' Company that year, the Rothschild brothers fanned out into the ranks of the Fishmongers (Lionel), Merchant Taylors (Anthony) and Spectacle Makers (Nat).[63]

In 1835 Lord John Russell's Sheriff's Declaration Bill had passed both Houses of Parliament without opposition, so enabling Salomons to take up the office of Sheriff of London and Middlesex that year, and enabling Moses Montefiore to do so two years later. But when Salomons, by now a member of his livery company's court of assistants, was in 1836 elected alderman for Aldgate ward in the City, he once more found his way blocked by the words 'upon the true faith of a Christian'. The Court of Aldermen declared his election void, and a subsequent appeal to law eventually foundered in the Court of Exchequer Chamber in 1839.

By then there had not only been two Jewish Sheriffs of London. Elsewhere in the country, where returning officers had not enforced the declaration, there were Jewish aldermen in Birmingham and Southampton. Moreover, in October 1838 both Salomons and Joe Montefiore had joined the Sussex Bench as JPs. 'Everything went off very well at Lewes in the oaths which we had to take,' Joe had reported to Lionel. 'The words "upon the true faith of a Christian" were omitted – so that we had no difficulty whatsoever, and nobody even seemed astonished at our swearing with our hats on – so much for the good breeding of the Sussex people.'[64]

A chance to resolve such anomalies came in 1841 when Edward Divett, MP for Exeter, introduced a Bill into the Commons 'For the Relief of Persons of the Jewish Religion elected to Municipal Offices'. After reading a report of the Commons' debate on the Bill in March, Anselm was 'delighted with the manner [in which] Lord J Russell expressed himself in favour of our cause. I hope in one year or two to be able to congratulate one of you on a seat in Parliament, & to admire your eloquent speeches.' Having passed the Commons, however, the Bill was defeated in the Lords.[65]

Anthony was 'so very grumpy about those stinking Lords that I cannot write. Patience. I hope they will all go to Hell.' In August, though, he welcomed the news that a baronetcy had been bestowed on Isaac Goldsmid: 'He is as you say a great Blackguard,' he commented to Lionel, 'but so much the better for the Jews.' He 'should have liked Sir Lionel de R much better' and thought Lionel should have tried to get the honour for himself. But, he concluded: 'It does not matter who got it – the more the better & I hope that in a few years the poor Jews will be able to get everything. It shows that the Queen is very liberal & I only hope that when the Tories come in they will not change her.'[66]

When Peel was sent for by the Queen to form a Ministry that year, Nat hoped 'that he will be liberally inclined towards us poor Jews, & if he emancipates us, he shall have my support, as I find his sentiments . . . most worthy of admiration, I never was much of a Vig [sic] like old Tup & I must say I am now rather more of a Tory than when I was in London.'[67]

Three years later, David Salomons stood again, and was again elected, a City of London alderman, on this occasion for Portsoken ward. 'The time at present suggested for my being called before the Court of Aldermen will be next Tuesday,' he advised Anthony. 'There is however not the *smallest* chance of my being admitted by them . . . It would be most desirable to get a favorable notice in The Times, but I am afraid *in my own case* to go near them. If some friendly hand could suggest it to them, one might have a better chance. Do you know any such?'[68]

As Salomons predicted, his election was again declared void. The situation was by now more inconsistent still: there was a Jewish alderman in Portsmouth; in 1843 Moses Montefiore had been appointed a JP for Kent and for the Cinque Ports; Salomons had by now served as High Sheriff of Kent; there had been a Jewish High Sheriff of Devon; and in July 1844 the Rothschilds entered the frame when Baron Alderson approved Mayer as a 'fit and proper person' to serve as High Sheriff of Buckinghamshire in 1847–8 (and also as a Deputy Lieutenant).[69]

To resolve such anomalies, in 1845, on Peel's directions, Lord Lyndhurst introduced a Bill into the Lords for the Relief of the Jews from Municipal Disabilities. For the Whigs, Lord Lansdowne 'expressed his happiness at seeing this proof of the advance in liberal opinion' and trusted that the Bill would be passed unanimously. Lord Brougham 'entirely concurred', 'rejoiced that the Bill had been brought in' and 'hoped the time would come when a more general Bill would be introduced in favour of his fellow-citizens of the Jewish religion'. The Duke of Cambridge gave the measure his warm support, and the Bill was read a second time without a division.[70]

'You ought to call on the D of Cambridge & thank him for the speech he made in favor of us poor Jews,' wrote Nat. 'I think we may congratulate ourselves on the way the measure has been generally taken up.' Hannah looked forward to her family's participation in 'the good which we so sincerely hope and [en]treat may result to the community we belong to'.[71] Although her sons did not particularly care for David Salomons – Nat once described him as 'the greatest bore I ever had the misfortune to have anything to do with, except I. L. Goldsmid' – Hannah thought it reasonable that Salomons should draw attention to his share of the credit for the Bill's progress.[72]

Subsequently, Peel himself introduced the Bill into the Commons, where it was carried swiftly through all its stages, and in 1847 Salomons entered the Court of Aldermen for Cordwainer ward. Eight years later he became the first Jewish Lord Mayor of London. Lord Lyndhurst remained a friend of the Rothschilds for life.

Other obstacles to the Jews remained in place. While *De Judaismo* remained on the statute book, it was debatable whether Jews could own freehold land. Lord Ellenborough, Lord Chief Justice from 1802 to 1818 and before that Attorney-General, believed that they could: he purchased a freehold property from Benjamin Goldsmid at Roehampton. Otherwise, while a degree from Oxford or Cambridge was still off-limits to Jews, admission to Parliament was the greatest remaining hurdle, and it was here that acquaintance with John Delane of *The Times* was to prove notably useful to the Rothschilds.[73] When the Liberal London Registration Association selected Lionel as one of four Whig parliamentary candidates for the City of London on 29 June 1847, Delane, the sympathetic editor of an influential liberal newspaper (with a daily circulation of some 40,000 copies), was there to help, even to draft Lionel's election addresses.

Following the split in the Tory party caused by Peel's promotion of Corn Law Repeal, Peel had resigned as Prime Minister in late June 1846. The majority of the party, opposed to Peel and his Free Trade supporters (Peelites), formed themselves into a party of Protectionists, led by Lord George Bentinck, supported by Disraeli, in the Commons and by Lord Stanley (later the fourteenth Earl of Derby) in the Lords. In July Lord John Russell became Prime Minister at the head of a Whig ministry that was committed to Free Trade and Corn Law Repeal.

Besides Lord John, several of the incoming ministers were already well known to the Rothschilds: Lord Lansdowne, President of the Council and Leader of the House of Lords; Lord Palmerston, Foreign Secretary; Lord Clarendon, President of the Board of Trade; and Lord Clanricarde, Postmaster-General. The post of Paymaster-General went to Thomas Babington Macaulay, who had spoken in favour of the remission of Jewish disabilities in his maiden speech in 1830.

Since 1841, moreover, Lord John had sat in the Commons as one of the four members for the City. In Paris during the election campaign of 1841, Anthony was pleased to hear that Lionel was 'canvassing with so much zeal for little Lord John' – who scraped home with a majority of just nine votes.[74]

After Lord John became Prime Minister in July 1846, Lionel's old friend John Abel Smith, MP for Chichester, acted as Lord John's informal political manager in the City; and Smith lost no time in encouraging Lionel to stand as a candidate in the general election that was certain to follow the Whigs' return to power. 'I hope dear Lionel you will follow J. A. Smith's advice and stand or state officially you will stand for the city,' Nat wrote in early July. 'You should engage some clever fellow to come & read with you in the evenings for an hour or so, to be a little more at home on the different questions of political economy. Old [J. R.] McCulloch . . . is a very clever fellow & if you had time [it] wd be really a good plan. I don't think there is the least doubt that a Jew if elected for the city of London wd be allowed to take his seat.'[75]

'Can anything be more absurd,' Disraeli makes Sidonia ask in *Coningsby*, 'than that a nation should apply to an individual to maintain its credit, and, with its credit, its existence as an empire, and its comfort as a people; and that individual one to whom its laws deny the proudest rights of citizenship, the privilege of sitting in its senate and of holding land? For though

I have been rash enough to buy several estates, my own opinion is, that, by the existing law of England, an Englishman of Hebrew faith cannot possess the soil.'[76]

The Jewish landowning question was settled by the repeal of *De Judaismo* in 1846; and from the point of view of gaining election to Parliament, the City was a promising proposition. When Robert Grant had introduced his Jewish Disabilities Bill in 1830, Alexander Baring had presented a petition in favour of the Bill signed by 14,000 City merchants, bankers and traders. In 1833, he had presented another, this time signed by 11 bankers, 37 'prominent merchants', 2,600 'other merchants' and 15,000 inhabitants of the City; and the Duke of Sussex had presented a petition in favour signed by 7,000 residents of Westminster. Although no measure for the removal of the words 'upon the true faith of a Christian' from the oath of abjuration had been attempted for a decade, Lionel took Smith's advice.[77]

When Nat wrote again in the summer of 1846, it was to 'congratulate you most sincerely my dear Lionel on the resolution you have taken of standing for the city. You are quite right. Don't be afraid. The more courage you display the better & if you do not succeed you will do good. Eventually success will crown yr efforts & thanks to you in a few years please God we shall all be enabled to add the honorable appendage of M.P. to our respective names.'[78] When Lionel's resolution wavered during the months that followed, Nat wrote to urge him 'most strongly to make up yr mind [to stand] & stand as stiff as a poker'. 'Should you not come in,' he judged, 'it will be something to have been put on the list of candidates by the side of the Prime Minister by his party. It can only do good . . .' Nat was also ready to contribute £3,000 towards Lionel's election expenses.[79]

Whether it was simply the thought of failing to win a seat that caused Lionel to hesitate is unclear. At one point, Nat expressed his 'regret to observe the liberal Party make such difficulty abt yr standing'; and despite Nat's confidence that, if elected, a Jew would be allowed to take his seat in the Commons, Lionel was certainly concerned about the legal bar. He knew where he was with an old friend like John Abel Smith, but seems not to have been so sure about Lord John Russell's intentions for a new Jewish Disabilities Bill. 'Have you seen Lord John [?]' asked Anthony in early 1847. 'Do you think he is as great a humbug as ever – or do you think that he will do something for the poor Jews [?]'[80]

It may be that Lionel's fears on this score were to an extent allayed by a note he received from John Abel Smith in April 1847. 'I saw Lord John yesterday, & had a most satisfactory conversation with him,' Smith assured his friend. 'I am satisfied that fear of defeat in the House of Lords was & is the real reason of the wish for delay. Finally I have Lord John's express consent & approval of the Bill's being brought in *this* year *if* Lord Stanley will support it. He strongly recommends it being brought in first in the Lords . . . The House will be up at the end of June if possible.'[81]

Yet a little more than a fortnight before his nomination for the City was approved by the Registration Association on 29 June, Lionel was still in two minds about allowing his name to go forward. On 13 June, another friend of his, Frank Mills, having sounded out 'the best man the Whigs have in the City', wrote to advise him not to do so. Hoping to see Lionel in person on 15 June, Mills continued: 'I hope you will not decide in the affirmative before that time.' It was Mills' belief that the Whigs wanted Lionel to stand because he would 'pay the whole cost of their expenses . . . But it is not for the money that I speak. I do not believe that you will succeed. I have asked people of all opinions & I cannot get one [single?] voice in favor of the risk . . .'[82]

In the event Lionel decided to go ahead – and by that time his brother Mayer, now serving his term as High Sheriff of Buckinghamshire, had entered the fray as a Whig candidate for Hythe Sandwich in Kent, the seat recently resigned by Stewart Marjoribanks, David Robertson's uncle and once the co-manager, with Harvey Combe, of the Old Berkeley hunt. Prior to Marjoribanks, the seat had for seven years been held for the Whigs by the banker Samuel Jones Loyd.

In the City, four Whig candidates were pitted against a Peelite, three Tories and an Independent for four seats; in Hythe, which returned one MP, there was only one candidate for Mayer to oppose – another Whig, Edward Drake Brockman, who came from a prominent local family.

While Moses Montefiore (by now a baronet) had a small estate at Ramsgate and was a JP for the Cinque Ports (of which Hythe and Sandwich are two), the Rothschilds had long had connections with the Kent coast through their Channel port agents and packet captains. Nathan had even bought a property on Romney Marsh – Burmarsh Farm – which the family retained. So when a disaffected Whig faction in Hythe was scouting for an alternative to Brockman, it was not so surprising that an approach should have been made to New Court. More surprising, perhaps, was that Mayer should have agreed to stand against a Whig contrary to the wishes of the Whig leadership in London. As Lord Marcus Hill put it to Lionel, 'we hope you will give no encouragement to the adoption of so mischievous a course'.[83]

When Mayer went ahead and stood all the same he did so with family support at least. 'I hope Tupus will add M.P. to his name,' wrote Nat. 'It will be quite respectable to see the Squire of Mentmore in the house & I have no doubt if elected by a considerable majority you will be allowed to take yr seats. Don't mind a little trouble – it's quite worth while & afterwards success will recompense you for all yr exertion . . .'[84]

Furthermore, while Lord Marcus Hill's main objection to Mayer's candidacy for Hythe was that the retiring Stewart Marjoribanks 'had made all safe for our present Candidate Mr Brockman', David Robertson wrote to propose that Anthony should stand as a candidate for Berwickshire, his father Sir John Marjoribanks' old seat, although there was already a Whig candidate in place. 'A few thousands properly spent would carry it,' Robertson ventured. 'I should do all I could for you.'[85]

By then, however, it was already mid-July, two weeks away from the election, and the idea was not taken up. Anthony remained in London and gave Lionel a hand with his campaign in the City. 'We had the pleasure of receiving yr kind letter this morning my dear Billy,' Nat acknowledged. 'As for our worthy Brother Lionel we have the satisfaction of reading every day one of his speeches . . . I can well fancy the election gives you bother & trouble enough but please God you will succeed & it will be one of the greatest triumphs for the Family as well as of the greatest advantage to the poor Jews in Germany and all over the world.'[86]

In his speeches Lionel spoke in favour of free trade and freedom of religion. He welcomed the repeal of the Corn Laws; he advocated a reduction in tobacco duty and the abolition of duty on tea; he urged the founding of a London Chamber of Commerce. He commended the cause of Jewish rights, but not – in reference to the controversial grant made by Parliament in 1845 to the Catholic seminary at Maynooth – the notion that anyone should be liable to pay for the upkeep of a religious establishment dedicated to a religion or sect to which he did not belong. He also spoke in favour of extending the franchise; and he declared a dislike of capital punishment.[87]

The result of the City of London election – which was described as 'by far the most closely contested, most interesting, and most important' of the 1847 general election – was declared on 30 July. Three of the four Whig candidates secured seats, Lord John Russell with 7,137 votes, James Pattison with 7,030 and Lionel with 6,792; the fourth seat went to a Peelite named Masterman, who polled 6,722 votes, a majority of three over the fourth Whig candidate, Sir George Larpent. At Hythe, where the electorate numbered a mere 458, Edward Brockman won with 211 votes to Mayer's 189.[88]

Family and friends hastened to congratulate Lionel on his success, the news of which reached Frankfurt in the evening of 1 August. Louisa wrote the next day; she thought the result a 'most important step taken and gained', hoped it would 'work most beneficially for the cause of our co-religionists generally', and trusted 'that but little difficulty will be met with in taking your seat in Parliament'. Her husband Charles (a respecter of rank and dignity) hoped that it would be 'a beginning for future honours and distinctions'. 'My dear M.P.,' wrote Chilly. 'A thousand Congratulations. I cannot tell you, how glad we were to learn your victory.'[89]

Nat's wife hailed the result as 'the beginning of a new era for the Jewish Nation, having a most distinguished champion like you'. Henry FitzRoy was 'very anxious to join my congratulations with those of your friends on your success in the city' and thought it 'a very great blessing that the question is set at rest'. He was also 'very sorry for poor Mayer. He had always wished so much to be in Parlt.'[90]

Lord Beauvale sent Lionel his 'sincere congratulations upon yr success. It has given me the greatest pleasure, and is I trust the prelude to a complete victory.' From Vienna, Salomon wrote that no news could have given him greater happiness, and the next day he forwarded the congratulations of Prince Metternich.[91]

14

The Stinking Lords

BEHIND THE REPEAL of the Corn Laws – the purpose of which had been to subsidise England's rural economy and to prevent cheap foreign imports of corn – lay the prospect of famine in Ireland. Poor wheat harvests in 1845–6 combined with the arrival in Ireland of potato blight to usher in a period of human devastation. In 1845, the country's population stood at about eight million; by 1850, some 775,000 had died of starvation – and a further two million were driven to emigrate.

Lionel's response to the unfolding catastrophe was to help establish, under the chairmanship of Samuel Jones Loyd, a famine relief committee, the British Association for the Relief of the Extreme Distress in the Remote Parishes of Ireland and Scotland, in 1846. After the Queen's subscription of £2,000, the next largest contributions came from Lionel and the Duke of Devonshire, each of whom gave £1,000. From April 1847, the committee met four times a week, on Mondays, Wednesdays, Fridays and Saturdays at South Sea House in the City.[1]

Subsequently, it was stated in the House of Commons that in 1847 Lionel – whose old acquaintance Lord Clarendon went to Dublin as Lord Lieutenant of Ireland that year – not only 'subscribed most largely to the funds of the British Association', but 'devoted his whole time to their proceedings' and 'placed three ships at the disposal of the committee for the carriage of meal'. By the time of the final committee meeting in March 1849, the Association had raised a fund of approximately £470,000.[2]

In addition to the relief committee work, in March 1847 Rothschilds, jointly with Barings, underwrote an £8 million government loan – the Irish Famine Loan – to finance aid to the stricken country; and it was perhaps in connection with the organisation of this, and of the relief work, that in November 1846 Lionel was offered a baronetcy. As his father had turned down a knighthood in 1815, however, Lionel declined the honour, though not because he preferred to remain untitled. In 1838 he had obtained the consent necessary to be known officially in England as Baron Rothschild; his arms, with supporters (a lion and a unicorn), were painted on his carriage doors. Rather, it was that Lionel felt a baronetcy to be, for him, an insufficient mark of distinction. To Prince Albert he is alleged brazenly to have said: 'You have nothing better to offer me?'[3]

Those close to Lionel were not so fastidious; and as James had deprecated Nathan for declining the knighthood thirty years earlier, so when Lionel canvassed his relations about the baronetcy they one and all advised him to accept it. James thanked God 'that your nice Queen has . . . taken such a liking to you' and urged Lionel to accept – 'one must never let such an opportunity pass by'. Anthony was 'glad to see that her Majesty wishes to make you Sir Lionel. Follow my advice & take it, & if you do not wish it for yourself accept it for one of us. These things are always better to be had when one can [get them], & do not refuse it . . .'[4]

Nat was 'delighted to observe that H.M. knows how to discern & reward real merit. She ought to make you a Lord but I am afraid it would be a difficult matter. Nevertheless if I were you I would accept an English Baronetage. It's better than being a German Baron. Old Billy thinks Sir Anthony wd sound very well & if you do not wish it for yourself you might get it for him . . .' Anselm advised Lionel 'to accept without the least hesitation the title of a Baronet which the Govmnt proposes to confer on you.' He also addressed Lionel's particular reservations: 'It is always a great distinction, & it does not at all matter that others not so worthy of it have been favored with it before you. As an Englishman it becomes you much better to be an English Baronet than a foreign one, & therefore I advise you to accept the title offered to you. I shall have much pleasure to address you in future: Sir Lionel, & your good wife Lady Rothschild . . .'[5]

While 'others not so worthy' of a baronetcy are not named, the phrase is surely a reference to Isaac Goldsmid, a baronet since 1841 – and a 'blackguard' in the eyes of the Rothschild brothers. The only other Jew to have received a baronetcy was Moses Montefiore, a baronet (recommended by Peel) since June 1846, and he was unquestionably worthy. Nevertheless, some remarks made by Hannah suggest that Lionel felt that the simple fact that two Jews, worthy or not, had received baronetcies before him diminished the compliment to such an extent that he did not wish for it.

Offering her opinion 'concerning the offer *by her Majesty* of the Barony [*sic*]', Hannah did 'not think it in good taste for you to refuse it [for] as your little friend [Lord John Russell] remarks what [else] can she bestow [?] The Peerage cannot be bestowed at present without taking the Oath and that I suppose you would not do. A Personal Compliment from the Highest Personage should be esteemed and may lead to other advantages but to repudiate it might create anger – and in accepting it you do not do away with your original Title . . . The previous granting to the other two gentlemen I think has nothing to do with yours – and decidedly does not reduce the Compliment – this is my opinion – excuse my candour . . .'[6]

No doubt it was as a result of such family feeling that although Lionel could not bring himself to accept the honour, rather than reject it altogether he did as his brothers suggested and arranged with Lord John for a baronetcy to be given to Anthony, with remainder to his own sons in the event of Anthony producing no male heir. Anthony was duly created a baronet on 12 January 1847. As to the notion that Lionel might receive a peerage – something that Jones Loyd was given, with the title Lord Overstone, in 1849 – the likelihood of that must have looked increasingly remote in the aftermath of his election for the City.

On 13 December 1847, Hannah went to spend a few days with the Duke of Bedford at Woburn. The Duchess had 'tea &c ready' when Hannah arrived and assigned her rooms 'very magnificent [,] well prepared and nicely warmed'; the Duke, too, was 'friendly and hospitable', but exhibited 'some of the cool rigidity that is attributed to His Grace's brother [Lord John]'. At dinner, the conversation was 'general but on no particular subject – Politics avoided – a good table – and the dinner nicely served'. By the time Hannah wrote to Lionel the next day, however, she had been talking politics with another guest, the Earl of Orford: she had 'had a conversation with Lord Orford on the Bill' and had found him to be 'against the Question'.[7]

Two days later, in the evening of 16 December, Lord John brought before the House of Commons that question in a resolution 'That the House should resolve itself into a Committee on the removal of civil and religious disabilities affecting Her Majesty's Jewish subjects' – the stage prior to the Bill that would, if passed by both Houses of Parliament, enable Lionel to take his seat in the Commons.

In contrast to the three million who had benefited by his successful campaign to repeal the Test and Corporation Acts, and to the very large class – including the Irish – affected by Roman Catholic Emancipation, Lord John estimated the country's Jewish community to number about 40,000, a figure amounting to no more than 0.2 per cent of the country's entire population. The question, said Lord John, did not, therefore, affect 'so large a portion of the population'; 'the peace and welfare of the country at large' were not at stake. That being so, Lord John explained, he would address the House on the question of principle involved, not on the ground of political expediency.[8]

He placed the question on the ground – 'simple, and as I think, solid' – 'that every Englishman, born in the country, is entitled to all the honours and advantages of the British constitution'. He believed 'that religious opinions of themselves ought not to be any disqualification or bar to the enjoyment of those advantages', and stated 'with confidence' that the Jews 'stand in the position of persons born in this country, bearing all the burdens imposed by its laws, ready to serve their prince or their country in any capacity in which their service may be required, and therefore entitled to all the privileges which their fellow subjects enjoy'. The merits of the Jews aside, he considered that entitlement to be 'a matter of right'.

His opponents claimed that to admit Jews to the Legislature would be to un-Christianise it, along with the constitution and the country. Yet pronouncement of the words 'on the true faith of a Christian', said Lord John, could hardly be supposed to ensure religious motives in legislators, or religious legislation in Parliament. Was there ever, he asked, a man who sneered more thoroughly at Christianity than Edward Gibbon? And yet Gibbon had taken the oath and sat on the Treasury benches. It was a mistake to imagine that a seven-word formula – 'the postscript of an oath . . . the fag end of a declaration' – could secure Parliament's Christian character.

He went on to show how, in the early seventeenth century, Parliament's intention in inserting the words 'on the true faith of a Christian' into the oath required of all MPs had been 'not to exclude either Jews or infidels, but to give greater sanction to the oath which the Roman Catholic Christian took when he declared himself a faithful and true servant of the Crown'. The intention had been 'to meet the cases of those Roman Catholics who bore true allegiance to the Crown . . . and to separate them from those who declared that their prince might lawfully be murdered'. Lord John warned his opponents not to cite popular prejudice against Jews as an excuse for voting against the resolution. Since Parliament had passed an Act for the naturalisation of the Jews in 1753, and had then, induced by popular feeling, repealed it the next year, he believed that such prejudice had 'greatly subsided'. Indeed, he had recently seen proof of it in Lionel's election for the City.

The resolution was opposed by the ultra-Tory Sir Robert Inglis, Bt, senior of the two members returned by Oxford University and seasoned opponent of the removal of Jewish disabilities since Robert Grant's Bill of 1830. Prior to the debate, Inglis had presented a petition from the University against the resolution (another came from Cambridge); and, once on his feet in the House, he condemned the resolution as one of 'unmixed evil – evil in itself and in its consequences'. In so far as it was brought forward by the Prime Minister himself, the measure was also 'far more alarming' than previous attempts.[9]

Inglis did not deny 'the merits of the Jews who are in England', but did not consider those merits to justify the Jews' admission to Parliament, and thereby the sacrifice of the country's Christian constitution. Admit non-Christians to Parliament and 'Rango Bapogee, the vakeel of the late Rajah of Sattara, might as fitly take his place amongst us as the Jew – or at all events the gentleman with the peaked cap, the Parsee from Bombay'. If the Bill should pass, 'every one will be at liberty, so far as law is concerned, in using his privilege here to the open contempt of Christianity'.

Moreover, the Jews could never be English. They were, said Inglis, a 'separate people', a 'separate nation'; they were 'strangers', some of whose 'very names and titles prove them to be un-English'. Over the last two hundred years, they had come to England 'drop by drop, preserving their own inherent and insoluble character'; they had done so 'for their own profit, for their own convenience'; 'they sought protection, and they found it; they sought the means of wealth, and they obtained it'. But they had no right to any share in the government of Christian England.

Lord Ashley – later the seventh Earl of Shaftesbury, known for his philanthropy – had made 'inquiries throughout the country' on the issue in debate. What he had found supported Lord John's contention that popular prejudice against the Jews had subsided. Attitudes bore 'no resemblance whatever to the personal antipathy and contempt exhibited . . . in the debates of 1753'. The Jews now occupied a far higher position in public regard and, he would add, in the affections of the community. But such considerations were not, for him, material to the point at issue.[10]

Had Lord John convinced him that justice required that Jews be admitted to Parliament, Ashley would have been satisfied; but Lord John had not done so. Was exclusion from Parliament a greater injustice to Jews than to the 'hundred other nations of every language and colour' in the British dominions? Perhaps Lord John intended to admit everybody. Some years ago, the Lords had stood out for a Protestant Parliament. They were quite right to do so, but they had been beaten. Now they stood out for a Christian Parliament. Next they would have to stand out for a white Parliament – and perhaps they would have a final struggle for a male Parliament! According to Lord John's principle, Lord Ashley declared (to cheers), not only Jews would be admitted to Parliament, but 'Mussulmans, Hindoos, and men of every form of faith under the sun in the British dominions'.

He then quoted with approval Dr Thomas Arnold's assertion that the

Jews 'had no plea of justice whatever. They are voluntary strangers here, and have no claim to become citizens but by conforming to our moral law, which is the Gospel.' Let the Jews have the honorary citizenship that the Romans often gave, Dr Arnold had said – the private rights of citizens, but not the public rights.

Lord Ashley did not look upon the Jews, he said, as others did, as 'a degraded, illiterate, money-loving race, fit only for the Stock Exchange or to take care of orange stalls'. Nor did he belong to that class of persons who regarded the Jews as having incurred a penal retribution for the crucifixion of Our Lord. On the contrary, he admired the Jews and revered them for their great qualities – qualities of intellect, cultivation, diligence, and, in many cases, genius. He was 'fully prepared to make every concession that could contribute to their honour and comfort'; but he would not strike from the oath those words that maintained the supremacy of the Gospel.

Nat, having read and reread the text of Ashley's speech, declared that he had 'never read a more Jesuitical one'. 'He talks of his feelings of reverence for the Jews & at the same time says they are only fit to be stock jobbers . . .'[11]

William Gladstone, Peel's protégé and then the junior member for Oxford University – 'a constituency so much connected with the national Church, and comprising so large a number of its ministers', as he put it – supported the motion, despite the petition. No one, he said, believed that it would lead to the presence of anything but an 'extremely small fraction of Jews' in Parliament, and he did not accept that the presence of 'a few solitary Jews' would 'paralyse and nullify the Christianity of all those who sit there'. Unitarians denied Christ's divinity and the doctrine of atonement by his death, but they sat in the Commons. Gladstone was 'unable to detect any practical evil or inconvenience' likely to flow from the motion, and considered Lord John to be 'inviting us to perform an act of justice' – and thus 'one worthy of a Christian Legislature to enact'.[12]

Benjamin Disraeli considered the question of Jews' admission to Parliament to be a religious question, and for him a question of religious truth. The Jews, he said, acknowledged 'the same God as the Christian people of this realm . . . the same divine revelation'; they were, 'humanly speaking, the authors of your religion'. 'Where,' he asked, 'is your Christianity, if you do not believe in their Judaism?' All the early Christians were Jews. The admission of Jews to Parliament, he considered, was 'testimony to our own Christianity'; and the position of the Jew ought not to be mixed up with that of 'a follower of Mahomet or a Pagan'.

Although out of step on the issue with the overwhelming majority of his fellow Protectionists in the Commons, Disraeli declared that he could not, whatever the consequences for the seat he held in the House might be, give a vote that did not accord with what he believed to be 'the true principles of religion'. 'Yes,' he proclaimed, 'it is as a Christian that I will not take upon me the awful responsibility of excluding from the Legislature those who are of the religion in the bosom of which my Lord and Saviour was born. That is the consideration on which I place the question . . .' A majority of the Commons might decide the question on grounds of political justice, expediency and truth; Disraeli would decide it 'on the religious ground, on the religious principle alone'.[13]

As the debate continued into 17 December, Anthony's wife Louisa sat in the Commons Gallery for eight hours with her sister Charlotte Montefiore. While Nat would praise the speeches made by Lord John Russell and by Disraeli, Louisa recorded that what she heard of the debate 'was but indifferent and the only time any enthusiasm was shown was when our opponents screamed out their "noes". Charlotte was dreadfully excited; I cannot say that I was, nor had the violence or ill nature of a few of the enemies of the Bill much effect on me . . . On the whole we were very courteously treated and we could not expect all prejudice, bigotry and dislike to be silent . . .'[14]

When the House divided, the Ayes were 253, the Noes 186 – a majority of 67. Disraeli and Lord George Bentinck were two of only four Protectionists (a third was Tom Baring, of the banking family) to vote for the resolution, and soon afterwards Lord George resigned the leadership of the Protectionists in the Commons.

On 20 December, Lord John brought in the Bill itself and it was read a first time. Colonel Charles Sibthorp, the diehard Tory member for Lincoln, believed that the day was not far off when a 'Mahometan' would be sitting in the House, 'and that at the instance and recommendation of the noble Lord'.

Prior to a further Commons' debate on the Bill in February, Disraeli discreetly undertook some research for Lionel. 'I find that *18* men, now Peers, voted against the Jews in the Commons in 1833,' he reported, '& only *11* in their favor! I agree with you, therefore, that we must be cautious in publishing the lists of the division, & rather give a précis of them, calling attention only to what is in your favor.'[15]

At the end of the Commons' debate on the Bill on 1 February, the House divided by 277 Ayes to 204 Noes. By electing Lionel, Richard Monckton Milnes had said, the citizens of London 'had told the House of Commons distinctly and palpably that they did not approve of this exclusive system of legislature. The people ask the House to remove all those religious restrictions.' No stronger test of the feeling of the people could be offered, said Milnes, than the election by the City of 'Mr' Rothschild – he did not say Baron Rothschild because he would not wish someone to sit in the Commons and use a foreign title – as a representative. Lionel's election was, said Milnes, 'a speaking evidence of the opinion of the people'.[16]

Nat imagined his brothers to be 'greatly delighted with the majority in favor of our bill. One thing is certain – there is infinitely more importance attached to the measure than ever was the case formerly. We must hope for the best.'[17]

During an amendment debate on 3 April, Lord Dudley Stuart drew the House's attention to the fact that the Commons' table had been 'covered with the petitions of the people, praying that the Bill might be passed into a law'. He pointed out that up to 29 March 'there were petitions *against* the removal of Jewish disabilities, signed by 56,000 persons; but the petitions *for* the removal of those disabilities had more than 300,000 signatures'. The latter group included 'petitions from the corporations of almost every important town in the kingdom' – with, so far as Lord Dudley knew, only two exceptions, Jedburgh and Sudbury.[18]

At the third and last reading of the Bill, on 4 May, it was carried by a majority of 61. As before, however, the real obstacle lay ahead in the House of Lords; and in expectation of that – and within a week of Hannah's conversation with Lord Orford at Woburn – Lionel had been considering how to surmount it.

The measures Lionel contemplated would have made complete sense to Lord Monmouth in *Coningsby* – '"You know he has bought all [Lord] Studcaster's horses," said Mr Melton. "I wonder he does not buy Studcaster himself," said Lord Monmouth; "I would if I were he; Sidonia can buy anything."'[19] In the past, Anthony had written frankly, if furtively, of offering bribes to Metternich and to Talleyrand to achieve certain desired ends. Such practice was not uncommon. While David Robertson suggested that a 'few thousands properly spent' might secure Anthony's election for Berwickshire in the election of 1847, Lord Grey informed Lord John Russell that he had heard of Lionel's 'determination to carry his election [for the City] by money', and it looks as if he had heard rightly.[20] When, subsequently, Lionel contemplated standing for re-election for the City, Nat recommended him 'most strongly to abstain from anything *like bribery*. On no account wd I give the most trifling consideration for votes. This time yr friends must do it & not you.' And there is no doubt that Lionel considered taking such an approach to ease the passage of Lord John's Bill through the Upper House.[21]

'I regret much to observe that you think it necessary to use certain means to secure some votes in the House of Lords which are not particularly commendable,' Nat wrote to him in late December 1847. 'I must say I should have preferred to have seen it otherwise . . . To come however to the point, on this occasion our worthy Uncle & yr humble servant are of opinion that we must not be too scrupulous and if it be necessary to ensure the success of the measure we must not mind a sacrifice. We can not fix the amount. You must know better how much is required than we do. I hope that as you say half the sum demanded will suffice. At all events our good Uncle has authorised me to write that he will take it upon himself to satisfy all the Family that whatever you do is for the best and that you may put down the *sum* to the house.

'Of course you will not cash up until the bill passes the Lords, and you must not make any bargain or care about who gets it . . . All we have to do is to give the money in the event of the race being won to the lucky jockey. I think you can not be sufficiently cautious in managing this job & I therefore do not see how you can propose a subscription to yr friends. On what plea? – if merely a trifle it will not be worth while; if on the other hand they will cash up & not ask for particulars of course I wd take their money as they are as much benefited as ourselves.'[22]

Of Lionel's further action in this business there is no record; but by mid-February 1848 Nat was fearful that the Bill would come to grief in the Lords. 'You should now work the Court party,' he advised Lionel, 'get yr friend P. A. [Prince Albert] to use his influence and then perhaps it will go thro'.' Pleased to hear that 'Prince Albert is so favourably disposed towards you and that he will support our bill', Nat urged his brother to 'pay him now & then a visit & coax him a little'. In another letter he was 'delighted that P.A. was so amiable & promised to be useful'.[23]

By early May 1848, however, it seems that such a plan, if acted upon, had not proved worthwhile. Asked for his opinion about a loan of £15,000 to Prince Albert, Nat replied on 10 May that he saw 'not the slightest occasion to consent to it . . . If I do not mistake my dear Brothers he already owes you £5,000 which we paid here [in Paris] to the Bavarian minister . . . There is not the slightest reason to make compliments with him & I am convinced that whether you give the cash or not it will not make the slightest difference to the Jews bill . . . I am decidedly against the advance . . .'[24]

Lord Lansdowne moved the second reading of the Jewish Disabilities

Bill in the House of Lords on 25 May. The next day, Nat was sorry to learn that Lionel had 'so little hope' of the measure passing, and was himself sure it would be voted down 'by the most intolerant of its opponents'. The signals going out from London, though, were mixed.[25] In mid-May, Charles had reported to Lionel from Frankfurt that Baron Stockmar, trusted adviser to Victoria and Albert, 'says that yr bill is sure to pass, & he is not very black'; and from Vienna, on 1 June, Anselm wrote of 'the expected success at the House of Lords'.[26]

Addressing the objection that the admission of Jews would have a serious effect on the Christian character of the Legislature, Lord Lansdowne stated his opinion that it was less dangerous to admit two or three Jews than 'many professing Christians . . . persons believing themselves Christians but who may, at the same time, be not properly and thoroughly acquainted with the truths and principles and doctrines of Christianity. You will find acts of the most objectionable character receiving the sanction of such persons . . .' People who came 'in the garb of Christians' were, to his way of thinking, 'infinitely more dangerous to a Christian Legislature . . . than if they came openly in another avowed character'.

He pointed out that Jews were sitting as members of the Legislature in Canada, Jamaica and Ceylon. 'Yet the Bishops are safe in those colonies; and the religion of each colony is not affected by the fact that a Jew may be a member of the Legislature.' He believed 'that none should be excluded from the pale of the constitution unless disqualified in a political sense'; England's constitution was 'bound up with the predominance of Christianity', but that predominance did 'not require for its support that we should exclude Jews from those rights to which they are entitled by the fundamental rules of the constitution'.

The Earl of Ellenborough, a former Governor-General of India and First Lord of the Admiralty whose father, the Lord Chief Justice, had bought some land from Benjamin Goldsmid, would not have Jews or any non-Christians sit in Parliament. Christianity was 'part and parcel of the common law of the land, identified with and inseparable from the State'. How could the truths of religion be taught, he asked, when in the same breath it was stated that the country's institutions were founded upon Christianity, but that the legislators need not be Christian?[27]

He felt it necessary also to consider other aspects of the Jews than their religion. He readily admitted that many Jews had 'distinguished themselves much by acts of benevolence; but a man who is very rich may appear to be extremely charitable by exercising only a very ordinary extent of charity'. As to 'the social character of the Jew as a citizen', the Jew stood 'one of a nation within a nation, totally distinct from that nation in every characteristic'.

'In the midst of agriculturists and manufacturers,' Lord Ellenborough continued, 'he [the Jew] is neither an agriculturist or manufacturer. The Jew does not labour; the Jew buys and sells at a small profit the fruit of the labour of others. There are few poor amongst them – no paupers. There are a few rich, but some very rich. They cannot intermarry with the people of this country. Except in the higher classes, they mix but little socially with the members of other religious associations. They are citizens of the world rather than citizens of England.' Wherever a Jew might go in the world, 'he finds his own people, his own religion, his own language, and, at the same time, he finds all persons of his nation engaged in transactions similar to himself. I cannot therefore consider that they are, or ever can be identified with the people amongst whom they live.'

Lord Ellenborough then read out a passage from Fowell Buxton's account of the dinner with Nathan at Ham House, Buxton's memoirs having just been published by John Murray. The passage was the one in which Nathan explained how he had left Frankfurt for Manchester after a visiting trader had refused to show him his patterns. 'Such,' said Lord Ellenborough, rather enjoying himself, 'is the origin of the introduction of the great house of Rothschild to this country, and I will say, also, such is the origin of this Bill. It has been observed that Providence often avails itself of mean instruments to effect the greatest objects; and certainly if the effect of this measure should be to unchristianise the Legislature of this country, never was a great event brought about by a meaner instrument than the refusal of a Manchester traveller to show his patterns to a German Jew.'

Jews were now eligible as magistrates, sheriffs or Lord Mayors of London, but Lord Ellenborough did 'not attach great importance to municipal dignities. Some of the most considerable men in every city refuse to hold them.' He wished, though, that Lionel's ambition were 'like that of Caesar, who said he would rather be the first man in the municipality than the second man in Rome'. As Lord Mayor of London, sitting in Dick Whittington's chair, Lionel 'might have proudly reflected that the advantage of the refusal of the patterns had had consequences as memorable as the celebrated adventure of the Cat'. Seriously and above all, however, Lord Ellenborough trusted that the Bill would not be passed, and that 'the desecration of Parliament and the destruction of the exclusive Christian character of the British Legislature' would be avoided.

The Duke of Cambridge, despite his desire to assist the Jews in obtaining all privileges that could be 'safely accorded' them, despite entertaining the 'very highest respect for many individuals of the Jewish persuasion', and despite being president of the Jews' Hospital, none the less felt – one senses a little uncomfortably – that 'as long as the British Government continues to be a Christian Government, we cannot admit Jews to a share in the counsels of State . . . as long as this country is a Christian country it is impossible to admit Jews to sit in the Legislature'.[28]

For Dr John Bird Sumner, the new Archbishop of Canterbury (he had been enthroned on 28 April), the Jews laboured under disabilities that even the House of Lords could not remove; their adherence to the Jewish faith simply disqualified them from taking part in 'the counsels of a Christian nation'. Sumner – an evangelical Old Etonian and former Eton beak (Captain Gronow's 'Crumpety' Sumner) – stated that if a Jew 'acted up to his principles', he would be 'as diametrically hostile to the Christian Church as their Lordships would be to the promotion of Mahometanism'. He acknowledged, though, that if, as had been the case with the Roman Catholics, the Jewish population of the country were larger – say 25 or 30 Jews in every hundred – 'a new element would be introduced into the question, which does not exist at present'.

According to the Archbishop's information – noticeably different from Lord John Russell's – the Bill was 'contemplated with conscientious dislike and anxious dread by a large class of persons . . . who consider it as a sort of insult to the religion which they reverence and honour'. He referred to that 'large class of persons' only in delicate euphemisms – 'the most valuable members of the community', 'the best members of society' – but made it clear that he was not talking about a well-educated or sophisticated class of people, but rather that one which it was 'very undesirable to disgust . . . with the institutions of this country'.

Sumner concluded on a familiar note: 'The same argument which is pleaded in favour of Jewish legislation would scarcely exclude a Mahometan or a Hindoo, or any idolater whatever, whose residence in the land gave him a claim to naturalisation, or whose wealth shall raise him to influence and distinction. If nothing else deterred us from this innovation, I think such an inference as this should prevent us from admitting the principle which leads to it, and determine us to reject the Bill.'[29]

The Bishop of Oxford, Samuel ('Soapy Sam') Wilberforce, son of the slave trade abolitionist, was clear that the Jews had no right to sit in Parliament. They were not Christian; they were a distinct nation; they had been allowed into the country 'on the condition that they would have shelter and kindness, but not political privileges'. The Jews in England were 'like a people who had been shipwrecked, and who had received shelter, and then claimed from those whose hospitality they had enjoyed the full rights of citizenship'. He recognised that 'there might have been in certain cases certain advantages derivable from the election of Jewish representatives' – but he did so only as a preliminary to taking a swipe at Lord John Russell.

Although the Bishop 'knew nothing about the secrets of the late election for the city of London', he was 'not without some knowledge of the public history of that transaction'. It was 'pretty well known', he said, 'that it was because the Prime Minister at the head of the Government, finding himself hard put to it for his election, thought it convenient, in order to secure his success, to connect himself with a firm where one of the partners found the capital and the other the character. Declarations in favour of removing Jewish disabilities might under such circumstances have been found exceedingly convenient.'

It was a 'plain and practical truth', he went on, that to pass the Bill 'must be to un-christianise the Legislature'. By the step now proposed, the Lords were being asked to take 'the greatest step that ever a Christian Legislature was asked to take'. They were being asked to let in those who were 'not only not Christians, but were even haters of Christianity – men either calling themselves Jews, being absolute unbelievers, or really Jews believing that the God whom we worshipped their ancestors betrayed, and justly slew, as a malefactor'.

If the Bill passed, said the Bishop, the Lords would be 'inflicting a wound on the religious feelings of the people of this land which they could never heal'. It had been said in the House that there had been no outcry in the country against the present measure. But the Bishop thought he could 'read the riddle of that silence'; it was 'the crushed silence of great indignation and great apprehension'. He implored their Lordships 'not to change the present absence of tumult, the now comparative quiet, into indignation amongst the population', and to beware lest, 'under the influence of kindly frailty', they 'un-christianise this land'.[30]

Writing in her diary of the Lords' debate, Anthony's wife Louisa declared that the Bishop of Oxford had spoken 'like a fiery, zealous, unscrupulous, *party man*, and not the least like a *clerical* one'. She was 'quite sorry that [William] Wilberforce's son should have made such a display'. Her sister Charlotte thought that the Bishop was 'not good enough for Christian or Jew'.[31]

Dissenting from Bishop Wilberforce's arguments and conclusions, the Earl of St Germans stated that in England all natural-born subjects had the same legal rights. He considered it inconsistent to admit into the

Legislature persons who denied the doctrine of the Trinity (Unitarians), but to refuse such admission to the Jews. He regarded Wilberforce's allusion to the affair of the election for the City of London as 'totally irrelevant', and trusted that their Lordships would, by passing the Bill, 'sweep away that last remnant of a barbarous system of legislation'.[32]

The Earl of Harrowby was against the Bill. It would result, he feared, in an un-Christian Parliament, and 'would also tend to lower the tone of that great assembly'. The Earl of Ellesmere, on the other hand, gave the measure his support; he thought it 'safe to the religious and political interests of the country, and just to the Jews, to give them a share in the making of those laws which they had hitherto obeyed so cheerfully, and in some instances administered so well'.[33]

Lord Stanley, leader of the Tories in the Lords and future Prime Minister as the Earl of Derby, thought that the House should 'at once reject this Bill'. Stanley had heard it said 'that a great constituency has returned a Member of the Jewish persuasion to Parliament, and that the Legislature ought not to resist the wishes of the electors'. But he did not regard constituencies as necessarily 'the best judges of the candidates who can really best represent their proper interests'; nor was he convinced of the right of a constituency 'to fly in the face of the laws of the country, and to elect a person to sit in Parliament who is disqualified by the law from taking his seat, and to insist that the judgment of Parliament should be overruled, and that such a person should have a seat in the Legislature'.

If the City 'had elected a pauper, or a minor, or a female to represent them in Parliament, would it for a single moment be tolerated that that pauper, or minor, or female, should appear at the bar of the House, and claim the right to take his or her seat, because the city of London had so exercised its choice; and, knowing much better than the Legislature as a body, what was good for its own interests, had thought fit to return such a person?' Lord Stanley was 'quite sure that that is an argument which cannot hold for a single moment'.

While Stanley believed 'the educated Jew to be a man honourable, conscientious, charitable, well disposed, and loyal', a Jew was not 'on the footing of any denomination of Christian', nor of other British subjects. The Jews of Britain, he said, 'are not of this country, but are a nation apart'; they had no special British interests any more than they had German or French interests. They had the interests of Jews at heart, not British interests, and 'above all not Christian interests'.

What, Lord Stanley asked, if the Queen were to bestow on Lionel a British barony to replace his foreign title? 'Neither in name, nor in title, nor I believe in undivided interests, is Baron Rothschild to be considered as an English citizen; and I confess I should regret to see him introduced into your Lordships' House, for I think it would materially interfere with the freedom of discussion.' The Christian character of the Legislature must be preserved, and Lord Stanley trusted that their Lordships would 'act in accordance with what I believe to be the general feeling of this great country, and again and again reject the measure'.[34]

Lord Brougham expressed his great satisfaction at 'the temperate, and, generally speaking, fair, candid and charitable spirit' that had prevailed throughout the debate; but he lamented 'that the discussion should not have closed without a great and glaring exception' – the Bishop of Oxford's speech. On the subject of the City election, the Bishop had done nothing but repeat a lot of slanders propagated by the press – slanders which Brougham then dealt with one by one.

As to Lord Stanley's talk of constituencies that flew in the face of the law in choosing a person they knew to be disqualified from Parliament, Lord Brougham said that the citizens of London had a perfect right to elect a Jew – since there was no law to disqualify a Jew from sitting in Parliament. The oath required a declaration on the faith of a Christian, not a declaration that one was a Christian – though Brougham did not deny that a conscientious Jew would feel it impossible to use those words. The effect of the law was thus not to bar non-Christians from Parliament, but 'to keep out the honest man and to let in the knave'.

The doctrine involved in the Bill they had been debating, Lord Brougham explained, was that all the rights and all the privileges to which the King's subjects were entitled, and all the enjoyments of subjects, and all the prerogatives of subjects ought to be accessible to all the King's subjects who were not debarred by personal disability. That was the doctrine of the constitution; and to say that a Jew, because of his religious belief, should be debarred from those rights, was 'one of the flimsiest and grossest fallacies that ever was uttered'.[35]

With Hannah and their aunt Judith, Lionel, Anthony and Mayer watched the closing stages of the House of Lords' debate. The Earl of Malmesbury later recalled that he had never seen the House so full, and that Lionel and one of his brothers 'stood like the elder sons of peers on the steps of the throne, and would not even retire when the division took place'.[36]

The result of the division was the Bill's rejection by a majority of 35 votes (128 for, 163 against). Four bishops and an archbishop (York) were among the Contents; sixteen bishops and two archbishops (Armagh as well as Canterbury) were among the Not-Contents. The Bishop of Durham (for) was paired off with Viscount Lake (against). Lord Orford, as good as his word, was of the Not-Contents.

Lionel's Charlotte, who had been waiting up at home with Louisa, described the state in which her husband and his brothers presented themselves on their return from the House of Lords at half past three in the morning. They arrived, 'Lionel with a smiling face – he always has so much firmness and self-control – Anthony and Mayer crimson in the face . . . they said the speeches were scandalous and I was advised not to read a word of them . . . Apparently, when the result of the vote was declared, a loud, enthusiastic roar of approval resounded . . . throughout the House. Surely we do not deserve so much hatred. I spent all Friday weeping and sobbing out of over-excitement.'[37]

Louisa characterised the speeches against the admission of Jews, during the 'long and violent' debate in the Lords, as 'intolerant and bigoted and calumnious'. The result was a 'severe disappointment' and she felt 'quite ill' the next day. Charlotte Montefiore was 'indignant and pained and excited not at our defeat so much as at some of the speeches', Wilberforce's especially.[38]

With the Bishops all but holding the balance of the Lords' vote in their hands, prior to the introduction of a new Bill into the Commons on 19 February 1849 Lionel was in touch with an Anglican clergyman acquaintance of long standing, the Reverend Thomas John Hussey, Rector of Hayes, in Kent. It was Hussey's mother, Catherine, to whom Lionel's father had offered help when she was defrauded of £50,000. Lionel had become involved in the affair, and since then had occasionally heard from her grateful son.[39]

A High Churchman, Hussey was also high-minded, and some remark that Lionel had made to him drew a sharp response: 'You have such an abominable habit of assigning to anything a money value that you seem to think even principle may be purchased.' How precisely Lionel might have done this, or whose principles he had in his sights, is not explained; but to counter clerical hostility to the Bill by '[a] great section of the High Church Party and the Low Church Party to a man', Hussey recommended Lionel to get one of their journals on side – to 'get one of their organs to fight your battle if you can, for their opposition is a conscientious one'. Offering a glimpse of his own High Church perspective, he went on: 'I came to advocate the rights of the Jewish people because I believe this country stands in need of God's blessing and that blessing is granted only to the nations who uphold his chosen people in this their second dispersion. That is my religious belief, as it is the belief of all the High Churchmen with whom I am identified.'[40] While Hussey was sure that Lionel's 'democratic friends' would laugh at such a stance, what Lionel himself thought of all this can only be guessed at; but he must surely have been somewhat surprised if he mistook Hussey's signature, as at a cursory glance it is easy to do, for that of Lord John Russell.[41]

On 19 February Louisa was again in the Commons to hear the debate. 'Lord John made a very clear, earnest speech, and Mr Gladstone delivered a fine, silvery toned one in our favour. Seven oppositionists attacked it, but not very brilliantly and *Disi* was silent. Mrs Disi was right when she spoke of the changes that Friendships undergo, last year he was our warmest champion and now!'[42] Possibly Louisa was doing Disraeli an injustice, but some months earlier Lionel had asked his wife to find out from Mary Anne Disraeli 'why Mr Dizzy cannot come up to speak with me whenever he sees me. Is there any reason why I should empty the Room always to speak to him [?]' It sounds as if Disraeli did not want to be identified too closely with Lionel in public – did not wish to give credence to any rumour that he had given Lionel covert assistance.[43]

Despite Disraeli's silence in the Commons, there was a majority in favour of 103, and then in May, at the end of the second reading debate – in the course of which Disraeli did, in a brief speech, reaffirm his support for the measure – a majority of 93. Nat was 'most happy to learn that the bill passed the 2nd reading with so large a majority. With a little trouble you might get 100 for the 3rd and then I think the Lords will not venture to throw it out.'[44]

The Bill was read for the last time in the Commons in mid-June. 'The division,' Louisa recorded, 'was not a very brilliant one – majority 66 – and no one seems sanguine about its success in the Lords.' But she went to the House of Lords with her sister for five and a half hours; 'Lord Brougham's was the great speech of the night, alternately witty and grave, he amused and delighted the House, but alas! did not persuade – for we lost by a majority of 25.'[45]

Lionel now resigned his seat in the City to trigger a by-election. This was not a course of action recommended by Nat – not, at least, if it were to entail the substantial outlay of funds. 'If I may be allowed to give you a piece of advice my dear Lionel,' he wrote, 'I should say do not bother yrself with a fresh election. You have enough to do with our own business & I do not think circumstances sanction your spending again large sums for any political purpose. If they like to bring you in tant mieux but I wd not play the same game over again if I were you . . .'[46]

Lionel offered himself for re-election all the same. On 28 June he placed a notice in *The Times* addressed to his electors. 'The contest is now between the House of Lords and yourselves,' he declared. 'They attempt to retain the last remnant of religious intolerance; you desire to remove it . . . I believe that you are prepared to maintain the great constitutional struggle that is before you.'[47]

Dining at Hannah's the evening before, Louisa had enjoyed sitting next to Lord John Manners, younger son of the fifth Duke of Rutland and the model for Lord Henry Sydney in *Coningsby*. In his letter to Lionel of late December 1847, the calculating Disraeli had reported: 'Writing to Ld. John Manners to day, I particularly mentioned the anxiety of the Court that the bill shd pass, as this will be conveyed to the Duke of Rutland, who is a great Courtier.'[48]

Until losing his Commons' seat in the general election of 1847, Manners, a Tory, had represented Newark. A few days after dining at Hannah's in June 1848, he learned that he was to be nominated as the Tory candidate to oppose Lionel in the City by-election. A likeable man (Louisa had 'talked of books, drawings, &c' with him at dinner), Manners hastened to inform Lionel – he thought it 'only due to the private friendship that has subsisted between us' to do so – that he would accept the nomination, 'not shrinking at this crisis from coming forward as the assertor of the rights of the House of Lords. Would that it were otherwise!'[49]

In the result, in early July 1849, Lionel defeated Manners soundly with a majority of 3,203 votes (6,017 votes to 2,814). 'I cannot imagine,' said Lionel's sister Louisa, 'why poor Lord J. Manners was thrust forward to oppose you, when he, of all others, had no chance of success. It is now to be hoped that the Lords will not throw out the Bill next session, and next year I hope that you will be enabled to take your seat where you ought already to have sat two years ago.'[50]

Timothy Curtis, founder director of the Alliance and former Governor of the Bank of England, congratulated Lionel on his triumph and trusted that 'the effect of it will lead to the accomplishment of your wishes & I may say the wishes of all people not bigots and as a Christian I hope that the first vote you give in the House of Commons will be to kick out the Bishops from the House of Lords.'[51] Chilly hoped that 'the stupid old Lords will give way or at least refrain from making active opposition so that next summer you may have the opportunity of displaying your eloquence before all the wise heads of Great Britain . . .'[52]

She was to be disappointed. The next July, having failed to persuade Lord John to introduce a further disabilities relief Bill, Lionel attempted, as he had for some time planned, to take his seat. 'I am glad my dear Lionel that you have such good hopes of success,' Nat had written from Paris in March. 'It will be a glorious thing if you can manage to take yr seat without an appeal to the stinking Lords.' But when the day came in July, on stating his desire to be sworn on the Old Testament, Lionel was directed by the Speaker to withdraw from the Commons chamber, which he did.[53]

In consequence of the debate on the question that followed, he was then asked why he wished to be sworn in this way. He replied that it was 'the form of swearing that I declare to be most binding on my conscience'. A further debate followed, and it was resolved to permit him to be sworn on the Old Testament. Lionel duly reappeared at the Commons' table, but when asked to repeat the words 'upon the true faith of a Christian' in the oath of abjuration he declined to do so. 'I omit those words as not binding upon my conscience,' he said. Again he obeyed the Speaker's direction to withdraw from the chamber and was barred from taking his seat.[54]

A year later, the artist Richard Dighton optimistically sent Lionel a drawing entitled *The Maiden Speech*, but Lionel was to obtain three further City election victories – one in 1852 and two in 1857 – before in 1858, and after a total of fourteen attempts to remove the Jews' parliamentary disabilities, he was finally able to take his seat in the Commons, and then only as a result of a compromise that allowed each House of Parliament to adopt its own form of oath. In 1859 he was joined on the Commons' benches by Mayer, as the Member for Hythe, and by David Salomons, for Greenwich.[55]

15

The Purses Bleed

O F THE ARGUMENTS against the admission of Jews to Parliament, an overwhelming majority, Lord Brougham observed in the House of Lords in May 1848, consisted in saying that the Legislature was a Christian legislature and that the presence of Jews would un-Christianise it. Brougham would not, he said, go so far as to state that the Lords had been 'nauseated', but only that 'nine parts out of ten' of the arguments advanced had consisted in those propositions – which he dismissed.

The popular line of argument had appealed to Lord Ellenborough, who having made his remarks about Lionel and the patterns and Dick Whittington and the cat, abruptly changed gear, portentously warning his fellow peers of the calamities they risked calling down on their heads – calamities that were only waiting to befall them – should they 'deprive themselves of all right to heavenly aid' by passing the Bill and ending the exclusively Christian character of the Legislature.

He spoke of 'the great danger now impending on this country in its foreign and domestic concerns', and of that present 'great crisis of the fate of this country' that it was impossible – 'from what we have witnessed' – to deny. 'We ourselves,' he said, with Ireland and other troubles in mind, 'have received a warning in famine, a warning in general distress, a warning in pestilence, a warning in the divisions amongst our people, still threatening the dismemberment of the Empire.'

Poor harvests, potato blight and famine in Ireland had been compounded by outbreaks of cholera – there was a major epidemic in Britain in 1848–9 – and there had been an upsurge in social unrest. Chartists demanding social and political reforms, including universal male suffrage, were combining, moreover, with Irishmen demanding 'Ireland for the Irish'. The planning of a great rally in London for 10 April had prompted the departure of the Queen and royal family for Osborne on the Isle of Wight – and most likely Archbishop Sumner's reference in the Lords to those whom it was 'very undesirable to disgust . . . with the institutions of this country'. Troops and a vast police force had been placed on alert in the capital.

On the day, however, rather than the expected hundreds of thousands of protesters, a crowd of 20,000 assembled on Kennington Common and, outnumbered by the police, remained peaceful and dispersed. A Chartist petition delivered to the House of Commons bore 1.2 million signatures, many of them said to be fraudulent, when three million signatures had been predicted.[1]

Fears had been greatly fuelled by events on the Continent. 'I hope yr Chartist meeting will pass over without fighting,' Nat wrote from Paris the day before the rally in London. 'Where will it remain quiet if in Engld the workpeople intend playing the same game as here [?]'[2]

It was to the situation abroad that Lord Ellenborough turned next in his speech. 'When we look around us,' he proceeded, 'we see nations convulsed; the most ancient and powerful dynasty of Europe crushed in one day; the great empire of Austria broken to pieces like the potter's vessel; we see the disruption of some of the most ancient combinations of territory; the formation of new combinations . . . all the great landmarks of nations displaced.' Continental society had been 'shaken to its centre'; the 'wildest schemes for its reconstruction' were under way. 'How long are we to remain,' Lord Ellenborough asked, 'separated by a narrow channel, untouched by the contamination of these evils?'

He was speaking of the revolutionary movements that had been sweeping across Europe since January, when a rising by Sicilian artisans in Palermo (news of which the Rothschilds were the first to hear) had induced the Neapolitan King Ferdinand II, on 29 January, to grant a new constitution. 'We have received very bad news about Sicily,' Anselm had written to Lionel from Frankfurt four days later. 'Our good Uncle Charles & Adolf [Adolphe] who both are no great heroes in matters of courage must not be in a pleasant disposition of mind. I hope to God that matters will soon come to an amiable conclusion.' On 6 March, King Ferdinand granted Sicily its own parliament, which, shortly afterwards, deposed him there.[3]

In northern Italy on 11 February, growing hostility to Austrian rule led to the proclamation of a state of siege in Milan, where ten years earlier the Austrian Emperor Ferdinand had been crowned with the famous Iron Crown of Lombardy. To Count Rodolphe Apponyi in Paris, it appeared that Europe was 'on the eve of a general combustion. It can only end in disorder and pillage, it is a war of those who have nothing against those who have something.' When Nat met with 'the whole diplomatique corps' at Princess Lieven's, they were 'all very black and talk of Italy as if it were en feu & en flames & irrevocably lost'.[4]

In France, following an exceptionally poor harvest in 1846, there had been food shortages; high grain prices in 1846–7 provoked rioting in Paris, and there was a growing clamour for social and political – especially electoral – reform. In a speech in the Chamber of Deputies on the day of the proclamation of the new constitution for Sicily in January, Alexis de Toqueville foresaw 'the most redoubtable revolutions . . . at the present time we are sleeping on a volcano'.[5]

During the early weeks of 1848, Nat nevertheless wrote approvingly from Paris that Guizot's ministry – Guizot had by now been in power for eight years – was 'decidedly opposed to all sorts of political reform for the present. They are quite right – they must be very firm otherwise every trumpery fellow to gain a little popularity would be proposing something new . . . a change of any sort wd send things to the deuce . . .'[6]

By the third week in February, though, he was on edge: 'On Tuesday the [reform] banquet is to take place. Every body is afraid of rows & if you were here you wd find good folk speak exactly as they did just before the revolution of 1830. I think a change of ministry wd remedy the evil but in the meantime it is impossible to say what will occur. No one can tell how a French mob will behave . . .'[7]

On 21 February, praying that the reform banquet, planned by radical deputies, would 'pass over quietly', Nat wrote: 'All Paris is most dreadfully frightened, ministers, deputies, conservatives & radicals. The different parties have however gone so far that it is almost impossible for them to withdraw without making a demonstration, otherwise I think the banquet would be adjourned sine die . . . The truth of the story is that at present no one can tell how matters will end . . .'[8]

In the event the government intervened and the banquet was cancelled, but on 22 February crowds of demonstrators began to gather in the Place de la Concorde and the Champs Elysées, near the hall where the banquet was to have been held. Barricades appeared in the streets, students and workers sang the Marseillaise, and there were cries of 'A bas Guizot! Vive la réforme!'[9]

On hearing that Guizot, in response to hostility from the National Guard, had been dismissed by the King on 23 February, Nat hoped that Louis Philippe and Count Molé, for whom the King had sent, would 'between them . . . cook up a good governmt'; but he feared it was 'a dangerous experiment to yield to the wishes of a factious minority and of a turbulent set of national guards'. It was, he felt, 'a most dangerous precedent & by no means favorable to French securities. The rentes are very low . . . I think we ought to hold as little stock of any kind or description as possible . . .'[10]

Molé took soundings, but was unable to form a ministry, and so the next morning, with ugly street scenes and the outbreak of fighting, Louis Philippe sent for the radical Adolphe Thiers. As the rioting grew more violent, not long after midday the 74-year-old King – who had been looking 'old & cut up' and 'did not say anything worth repeating' when Nat had last seen him at Court – lost heart and left Paris.[11]

'We are in the midst of the worse revolution that ever happened,' Nat scribbled in a note to his brothers that day. 'You may perhaps see us shortly after this reaches [you]. Our ladies & children left at 3 o'clock for Havre & London & please God they will reach you safe & sound. We are still deliberating whether we shall leave or no. I think we shall. The King has abdicated – a gouvernmt provisoire . . .'[12]

That night in London, at Grosvenor Place Houses, Anthony's daughter Constance was carried downstairs to see the Rothschild women and children from France, who 'had arrived in a sad state of misery and depression'.[13] Nat and Charlotte now had two little boys, Jimmy, aged three, and Albert, not yet two. James and Betty had four sons, Alphonse, Gustave, Salomon and Edmond.

James and Nat decided to remain behind in Paris, where a republic was proclaimed and the Provisional Government formed. Louis Philippe landed at Newhaven on 2 March, to spend the remainder of his life in exile, almost a forgotten figure.

When Prince Metternich received the news of the French revolution from a Rothschild courier, he is said to have remarked: 'Eh bien, mon cher, tout est fini.' In a Germany 'roused up by the French Revolution', Anselm reported to New Court on 1 March that 'the whole population wants reform; unity of the country, & God knows what else . . . The Govt[s] will be obliged to yield . . . In Baden the Govt [of the Grand Duke] has already granted liberty of the press & other concessions. All depends now on the determination of Austria. If they are wise they will recognise the French Republic, else there will be a general war beginning in Italy.'[14]

On 12 March, Charles wrote to London from Frankfurt: 'Here we are a little quiet, the Elector [of Hesse-Kassel] having given way. But still everybody continues to be very alarmed and fidgety about things which may happen.'[15] Two days later, Anselm reported: 'We are in very bad times here. Germany also is in a state of convulsion. The peasantry burns the houses of the noblemen in the country & commits all sorts of excess.' As in Hesse-Kassel, liberal constitutions were swiftly granted in the grand duchy of Hesse-Darmstadt and in the kingdoms of Württemberg and Hanover.[16]

On 13 March revolution broke out in Vienna. As Anselm wrote to his English cousins the next day, Prince Metternich fled with his family for

England – armed with a credit note from Anselm's father Salomon. Emperor Ferdinand promised a constitution, but on 15 May, ten days before the House of Lords in London was treated to Lord Ellenborough's dramatic survey of events on the Continent, he fled Vienna for Innsbruck.[17]

Elsewhere, on 15 March there was an uprising in Rome, where Adolphe had not liked the look of things during a visit in mid-January. On 17 March, after days of public unrest, Prussian troops sought to contain insurgents on the streets of Berlin and, though Nat rightly dismissed reports that a republic had been established and the King of Prussia and all his ministers arrested, King Frederick William IV appointed new liberal ministers. On 18 March there was full-scale revolt in Milan.[18]

England appeared a haven of peace. 'I only wish we all were on Albion's shore & hope to give you soon better accounts,' Charles wrote again from Frankfurt on 29 March. 'For business nothing is going on as every one thinks of nothing but liberty and republics.'[19] Ten days later he reported that a crowd had 'smashed all Uncle Anselm's [Amschel's] windows and made a devil of a *Charivari* before his house from 10 till midnight'. It was the third time in a month that Amschel and Eva had been subjected to such demonstrations. 'You have no idea how unpleasant it is to be here at present,' Charles went on, '& I would rather be in China than in this beastly place.' In Paris, Salomon's house at Suresnes was ransacked and burned by a mob.[20]

On 4 April Anselm left Frankfurt to see the Prussian Finance Minister in Berlin, thence to make his way to Vienna, where Salomon was sitting out the storm. From the Rhine steamer on his way to Cologne, Anselm wrote to New Court of 'very bad terrible times'. 'You have no idea of the agitation reigning now in Germany. No law, no authority is respected; people speak of the Republic, & publicly damn all the Thrones as you would speak of the most indifferent thing in the world. I wish I could leave that country & business, & live quietly in a village in England.'[21] When news reached the rue Laffitte that King Ludwig I of Bavaria had abdicated in favour of his son, Nat's comment was: 'Much luck to him. Kings & Princes are by no means in an enviable situation and Bankers likewise . . .'[22]

Anselm had left Frankfurt, he confided to Nat, 'with a sorrowful heart'; he had not only received 'desolating' letters from Vienna, but was in fear of a general European war breaking out – the one thing that the Rothschilds, with their Europe-wide interests, feared above all. 'Russia is already concentrating its troops in Poland,' Anselm reported, '& Austria its army at the frontier of Italy to reconquer the Lombardies. It is not very likely that England could remain neutral . . .'[23]

The more Anselm thought about it, the more 'inevitable' it seemed to him that Russia would go to war with Germany and France; but then, he reflected, 'the revolutionary principles will soon find their way in Russia'. On a personal note, with financial markets in disarray all over Germany, Anselm would, he told Lionel, lose 'the greatest part' of his private fortune. Yet he did not lose sight of the bigger picture. 'The only thing we must aim at,' he urged, 'is to maintain our name in honor, & for that purpose, one house must support the other with all its means & power, for the dishonor of one reflects on the other.'[24]

The value of family solidarity became all the more clear as, in the wake of the revolutionary upheavals, two of the five Rothschild banks – Vienna and Paris – were brought to the brink of insolvency, while the Frankfurt house, of which Vienna and Naples were effectively branches, was almost fatally weakened. By an irony, it was in part notions of honour that brought them low. In 1847, a year of monetary crisis in Europe, Nathan's surviving brothers had felt obliged to rescue from collapse a Frankfurt bank that belonged to the Beyfus family, into which two of their sisters had married; and then, acting alone, Salomon had bailed out a bank in Vienna with which he had often worked in partnership in issuing Austrian government bonds.[25]

In Paris, the outbreak of revolution found James holding an enormous quantity of 3 per cent *rentes*, the market value of which, by April 1848, was less than half the price at which in 1847 he had contracted to pay the state for them by 10 million franc monthly instalments over two years. He also owed some 10 million francs to various railway companies – companies that the new French government was expected (wrongly, as it turned out) to take over in return for *rentes* rather than cash.[26]

On top of this, on 4 April an unwelcome letter arrived from the liquidator of the royal *domaines privés*. Under a contract to advance Louis Philippe, by way of a mortgage, four million francs against his forests (which according to Nat were worth six times as much), 500,000 francs was still owing; and the liquidator asked for this to be held at his disposal. 'It is really dreadful to live in such times,' said Nat, 'every day something fresh.'[27]

With little but depreciating or worthless securities to sell, the prospect of meeting such commitments looked bleak. In mid-March, Nat had thought the position of the Paris house 'not bad' and hoped that 'with God's help we shall pull thro''; but at one point in April, James's cash reserve sank to little more than a million francs – and when, briefly, a clerical error made the figure appear to be even less, James had a moment of panic.[28]

In Vienna, Salomon was caught out, in Nat's words, 'up to his neck in stinking securities', industrial stock that he at first would not and then could not sell. It transpired also that Salomon owed £200,000 to the Paris house, £70,000 to New Court and, perilous to the lender, £1.5 million to Frankfurt. 'What can he have done with all the money [?]' Nat wondered. On 10 April, having heard reports that the Austrian Empire was 'on the point of complete dissolution', Nat was still wondering: 'God knows what our good Uncle Saln's position is. I can not think he owes [as] much money there [in Austria] as he owes Fft, us & you . . .' But Nat was wrong.[29]

The full picture emerged after Anselm had arrived in Vienna. In all, including large state loan commitments to Austria and his liabilities arising from bank rescue operations the year before, Salomon's debts amounted to approximately £3.4 million, and none of his assets was at the time realisable. He was, he confessed to his brothers, 'in the most painful situation that ever existed'; now aged seventy-three, he 'envied his blessed brother Nathan'.[30]

'My good father is very depressed and dispirited,' Anselm wrote from Vienna in confidence to Charles, 'I have to do the utmost to be considerate and to strengthen his spirits. He blames himself bitterly for what has been done and what cannot be undone, however prejudicial. Uncle Amschel's severe reproaches [,] not altogether unfounded, augment the depression and make my father unable to attend to business with the necessary peace of mind and energy . . .' Anselm implored Charles 'to induce Uncle Amschel to reserve his judgment and the continuous recriminations, embittering and crushing my father, already torn enough by grief'.[31]

Fortunately, the situation in Naples, as Nat had learned from a Rothschild courier in late March, was 'not so bad as reported'. There had been 'a row in the streets, some severe fighting', but King Ferdinand had 'remained master'. In contrast with Sicily, the revolution in Naples failed, though the King did eventually allow a parliament to assemble. The Rothschild bank there had a tolerably good year, and in April Lionel's father-in-law was in a position to send money to Frankfurt.[32]

On 17 April Anselm wrote from Vienna to Charles: 'Should no further storms arise, the Viennese House, please God, will be able to meet all engagements.' In London a week later, Nat appeared from Paris 'in much better spirits'; according to Anthony's wife, he no longer thought that there would be 'a *sanguinary revolution* – our *purses alone* will bleed . . .'[33]

Notwithstanding that in 1847 New Court had had its worst year ever, with losses of £670,000 (30 per cent of its capital), Lionel was able to provide the Rothschild houses on the Continent with vital support – consignments of silver bullion, much of it obtained in America by August Belmont, the Rothschild agent (and formerly, as Schönberg, a clerk in the Frankfurt house). Not only, moreover, was Lionel able to supply the family banks, but also the needy central banks of Austria and France – the latter service providing his relations with a useful lever in negotiations for the rescheduling of their state loan commitments. 'The position of the [Frankfurt] house is not bad,' Nat was able to report on 9 June. 'They have for about £400,000 specie in the house and have arranged so that till the end of the year they can meet all their engagements, without selling any more stock . . .'[34]

Nat was then writing from Frankfurt itself, having been staying with his wife at the nearby spa town of Ems; and it is noticeable that in spite of the situation in Europe, having once recovered from the initial fright, the Rothschild family's cosmopolitan way of life, for business or pleasure, continued as usual. By 24 March, a month to the day since Nat had found himself 'in the midst of the worst revolution that ever happened', his wife, children and mother-in-law were planning to leave for Ems on 4 April and to meet up there with Anthony's wife, 'the amiable Lady Tony', from England.[35]

At the same time, fear of what the future might hold did not drive out thoughts of all else. Lionel's relations on the Continent followed the progress of the Jewish Disabilities Bill in London with interest; Nat continued to follow events on the English turf. 'I hope your mare is well,' he wrote to Mayer as the day of the Oaks approached. 'If you think very well of her chance I should like to back her for 50 or £100 at 10 @ 1 – but only do so if you are of opinion that it is a good bet. What magnificent weather for Epsom. I should have liked to have paid you a visit but under existing circumstances I can not well leave Paris.'[36]

As things turned out, Betty and Charlotte delayed their departure for Ems until the second half of May, and Nat was with them there in early June. By 9 July, Anthony, who had been in Paris at the beginning of the month, was staying with his wife in Frankfurt, and towards the end of the month returned with Louisa to Paris, where they 'found the Baron [James] very well – but rather grumpy as everything does not go exactly as he wishes'.[37]

It was by then a month since the French capital had been rocked by the most violent episode of the year. Finding the quiet of Ems 'intolerable when one thinks of all that is going on in the capitals of Europe', Nat had sensed that 'a great deal of blood' would be shed before the 'political cholera' infecting the world ran its course. Three weeks later, Paris – 'that Volcano, Paris', as Louisa described it – was in the grip of the *journées*.[38]

Following French national elections held under universal male suffrage in April, the Provisional Government had been replaced by a Constituent Assembly, with Louis Eugène Cavaignac as Minister of War. Faced with a mass worker uprising in Paris on 22 June, General Cavaignac, to whom the executive had resigned its powers, conducted a ferocious and bloody campaign of suppression. Over three days, 23–25 June, 1,600 soldiers and 3,000 civilians were killed; and in the aftermath there were 11,000 arrests and 4,000 summary transportations.[39]

When Anthony arrived in late July, he found Paris – which was to remain under a state of siege until October – 'extremely quiet', but thought 'that things can only remain as they are as long as Paris remains en Etat de Siege'. His elder brother was more hopeful.[40]

Having paid a visit to Paris in late February, Lionel returned in mid-July, a fortnight ahead of Anthony. To his 'Dearest wife' he reported 'a very great improvement with the state of Paris; it has not been so quiet since the Revolution & I think within a short time, the noisy folks of this town will return to their former occupations . . .' Cavaignac was acting President of the Republic, and James, said Lionel, was being treated as 'a great favorite and as there is no other banker or person with money or disposition to come forward, he is actually very much looked up to . . .'[41]

On 7 July Nat had commented on 'the rise in the rentes and shares'; and an air of relative normality had been restored. One evening Lionel dined with 'Bear' Ellice and afterwards played cards until midnight; another evening he dined with the Normanbys 'en famille', returning home at half past nine. With time on his hands one afternoon, he went out for a walk 'to see if there is anything new & to buy a few trifles as I have not yet been into a shop'.[42]

While Nat remained jittery – 'Prudence & caution are more necessary now than ever' – to Lionel the auguries seemed good. 'In another month,' he predicted, 'Paris will be quite another place and in my opinion they will very soon forget the late events.' After a family holiday at Trouville in August, and two days' partridge shooting at Ferrières in early September, on his return to Paris even Nat could sigh with relief: 'Thank God the news is good . . .'[42] At Naples, King Ferdinand had by then reclaimed Sicily. In Paris the name of Louis-Napoleon Bonaparte, who had been living in exile in London, had begun to be bruited as a possible President of the Republic; in September Louis-Napoleon was elected to the Constituent Assembly and returned to Paris.[44]

In the second week of October, having just arrived from London, Anthony found that there had been 'a wonderful change' in Paris. Prices were up; business was on the increase, and the city was 'a great deal gayer'. 'The great affair,' Anthony went on, 'is the President – they think that L. Bonaparte will be elected, but no living person can say. I think that the Republic has greater chances of lasting than before . . .'[45]

In presidential elections held in December, Louis-Napoleon was elected, with 74 per cent of the national vote, for a four-year term, soundly beating General Cavaignac. Nat was by then taking a break of several months in England (in early December he was seen out foxhunting with William Selby Lowndes' hounds near Winslow), but on 16 December his trainer Thomas Carter reported to him from La Morlaye: 'Paris appears very calm and from all I can hear People seem pleased that Louis Napoleon Bonaparte has so great a majority.'[46]

Having returned to Paris in early 1849, Nat did not dissent from Carter's assessment: 'Paris is very quiet and I do not believe there is the slightest fear of disturbances or rows,' he told his brothers. 'There are plenty of fine equipages about & horses are as dear as ever. The coach makers have lots to do. The one I employ told me he had 30 one horse phaetons to make & had 180 workpeople at high wages in his pay . . . There is certainly a very general improvement & if we remain *quiet* there will be no difference between the republic and the monarchy.'[47]

'The president,' he reported, 'is generally liked. He goes about on horse-back, gives balls & dinners, rogers tremendously & leads a very comfortable life . . .' Later, Nat heard that Louis-Napoleon ('a little ugly fellow very much like G. Samuel') had taken a fancy to the daughter of the Greffuhles' gardener – 'She was tupped by the stable boy and since by the town. They say she is very pretty . . .' Anthony, for whom a hard day's work in Paris meant '*no ladies* to pay a visit to in the middle of the day', nevertheless con-sidered the President to be 'too fond of using his Gentleman', and thought it unsuitable that he should have his English mistress, Elizabeth Ann Howard, to live with him at Saint-Cloud.[48]

One Saturday in February, James gave a 'grand dinner' for 'nearly all the govt'. English friends were invited, too: Lady Ailesbury, Lord Newport and the Londonderrys, as well as Henry and Hannah Mayer FitzRoy – long since back in the family fold – on their way to take a cure at Pau. After dinner, they were joined by 'all the Corps diplomatique', so that, as Nat said, 'H.M. and FitzRoy had an opportunity of seeing tout ce qu'il y avait de plus distinguée in French Society.'[49]

Nat attended a concert at the Elysée – 'the President was very polite & shook hands with every body' – and he was asked to join a 'very select party consisting of the principal Carlist families, all sorts of diplomatiques, nearly all the young fellows . . . whom the [Orléans] Princes were so fond of . . .'. The President spoke to Nat; he had seen him in England, he said. The ladies present 'were beautifully dressed with lots of jewels, and when the carriages were called the titles were *not* omitted'.[50]

Louis-Napoleon was already being spoken of as a future Emperor. From

Pau, Henry FitzRoy wrote to Lionel in early January: 'The general anticipation seems to be that Napoleon will not rest until he has made himself Emperor; & that the votes of the Army & the Peasantry combined will be enough to secure his success.' In mid-October, Anthony wrote from Paris to Mayer: 'They are trying what they can to make LN Emperor as they want to get rid of the Republic . . . & should we see an Emp we shall see everything 5% better.' A little more than two years later, in December 1851, the President was to bring off the *coup d'état* – an event foreseen by Lionel in November 1849 – that led to his proclamation as Emperor Napoleon III.[51]

In Vienna, from where in May 1848 Anselm had related how the 'students govern the town, the Ministry & the Crown [and] . . . run about the streets & give charivaris to the persons they dislike', imperial forces restored order, after an artillery bombardment. In October a mob had stormed the Arsenal – 'situated,' Anselm explained, 'only one house from our own'. But by early November there was a garrison of 40,000 troops in Vienna, which Anselm hoped would 'maintain order & tranquillity for the future'. Emperor Ferdinand abdicated in favour of his nephew Franz Josef.[52]

From Frankfurt in December, Charles regretted a 'total eclipse of business', but reported things in general 'very quiet'. His wife Louisa described Frankfurt as 'very gay, there are parties almost every evening'. They went to a dinner given by Lord and Lady Cowley, the new British Minister in Frankfurt and his wife ('very nice people . . . inclined to be friendly'); and they invited the Prince of Leiningen to dinner.[53] Lord Brougham was in Frankfurt at the end of the month, and for New Year's Eve, having received a delivery of good things from England, Charles and Louisa asked him and Lord Cowley 'to come & enjoy themselves as they are both Epicures and there is nothing good to be had in this stinking place'. A fortnight earlier Charles had been looking forward to receive 'a good Stilton cheese & a fine leg of mutton' from his English cousins.[54]

On a visit to Frankfurt for a family conference towards the end of January, Lionel told Mayer that the bank there was 'on a very good position' and, judging 'from what those best conversant in German affairs say', thought 'things rather better than worse and I dare say German funds will rise'. Although the position of the Vienna house appeared 'quite the contrary', Lionel said the details were 'not worth the trouble of writing'; and as Anselm replaced his father in Vienna, and thought 'of nothing else than settling the old affairs as well as possible', the house slowly recovered. In early May, Anselm was much cheered by the arrival in Vienna of the young Emperor Franz Josef.[55]

Lionel's Charlotte, it seemed, had been right in her sentiments when she had written to him during one of his visits to Paris in the revolutionary year that 'it will never do to give up hope of a brighter European and *a Rothschild* future'.[56]

Aside from the consequences of revolution for the Rothschilds' business and for their private fortunes, there had been intermittent worries about personal safety. Amschel's house in Frankfurt had been attacked while he was in residence, and the gunfire during the height of the *journées* seriously unnerved James. Added to that, on returning to France from England in March, James's eldest son Alphonse had been conscripted into the National Guard (No. 4 Company, 2nd Legion), and Gustave was due to be called up.[57]

Fearful for his sons' safety – Alphonse's company received several casualties, killed and wounded at the barricades – James arranged to send his eldest son to America (with some letters of introduction from Joshua Bates, of Barings) and Gustave to Frankfurt. A bonus in the case of Alphonse was that the arrival of a Rothschild on his doorstep in New York served to give Belmont – whom Nat and Anselm viewed as 'that stinking Jew [who] speaks higher [than] the most important man' – an added impetus in organising silver bullion shipments to Europe.[58]

Moreover, when personal loss did befall the family at this time, it was due simply to natural causes. In May 1848, Adolph Herz, whom Lionel had known since his days with Anthony at Göttingen, and whose niece he had married, died in Frankfurt; and in July Amschel's wife Eva passed away. Then the following May Charles wrote to inform his cousins of an event that spelt the end of an even more remarkable link with the past: Mayer Amschel Rothschild's widow Gutle had expired aged ninety-six.[59]

Five years earlier, when Hannah had seen Gutle in Frankfurt, she had noted: 'Gros Mutter [*sic*] is debilitated on account of her great age, but retains all her faculties and is as acute as ever'; now, on 8 May 1849, Charles wrote: 'I hope these lines will find you quite well and in better spirits than we have been for the last week owing to grossmutter's protracted illness and her death which melancholy event took place yesterday morning in the presence of her children & your humble servant. It is a great loss to Uncle Anselm [Amschel] who is deeply affected & I cannot tell you how many wretched hours we have spent lately. I hope to God this will be the last unfortunate event in our family for a long time to come . . .'[60]

After the news of Gutle's death had reached Paris, Nat commented on 'the sad event' in his daily letter to London: 'Poor old Grosmutter [*sic*] she had arrived at a good old age and had had the happiness of seeing all her sons prosper beyond her fondest hopes. God rest her soul & may all of us live as long.' Once Amschel had got over the shock of losing his wife and his mother, he thought of marrying his great-niece – Anselm and Chilly's eldest daughter Julie – but, rather to everyone's relief, the idea came to nothing, and the next year Julie married her cousin Adolphe.[61]

Fearful of risks to the person, members of the family on the Continent had also been concerned for their possessions. 'Direct acts of spoliation would by no means surprise me,' Nat wrote in early April 1848, and that month he sent some of the more valuable of his chattels – pictures, porcelain and plate – to England. Anselm considered doing the same, and both he and Nat took steps to preserve such funds as were held for them and their wives in England. Any money they were able to raise by sales of Continental stock they sent to London for investment in English securities. Nat also scaled down his racing establishment at La Morlaye.[62]

There was also the risk to real property, as the sacking of Salomon's house at Suresnes had too clearly shown. After Betty had returned from England to France in March, she and James paid a visit to Ferrières. Nat thought it 'quite necessary for them to go. It is almost heartbreaking to think of a place where one has had so much enjoyment being taken away from you as will be the case some day or other.'[63]

Besides the town houses in Paris and Frankfurt and James's properties at Ferrières and Boulogne, there were by then numerous Rothschild houses and estates to be concerned about. In 1843, having been granted exceptional permission, as a Jew, to own property in Vienna, Salomon had bought the Hotel zum Römischen Kaiser, as well as the house next door. Having pulled them both down, he had rebuilt a house on the site – and had obtained permission to buy a country estate as well.[64]

'Uncle Salomon has bought an estate in Bohemia,' Anthony informed his brothers in 1844. 'I hope that one of these days we shall have one also in old England. You see that they all are taking good care of themselves & so must we.' The estate Salomon had bought was called Schillersdorf, near Oderberg, in Silesia.[65] Chilly, having stayed there with Anselm and her children for the first time some years later, told Lionel that there were 'more than 20,000 acres of land, magnificent trees, fine views, a large Chateau and all the necessary qualifications for making it even to English ideas a fine place. But it is a long way off, nearly 12 hours by rail from Vienna, & requires much expended to make it really a nice place for a family to reside in.'[66]

At Frankfurt in 1844, Anselm bought some farmland 'in the vicinity of the Neuhof'; and he told Lionel and Nat that their uncle Charles was building a 'most magnificent house, large enough to hold us all' – the Villa

Günthersburg – in 150 acres of gardens and fields that he owned on the north-eastern edge of the city. 'The garden will be pretty,' Anselm ventured, 'but it is a pity that such a large house is not in the middle of 10,000 acres about ten miles from the town.'[67] Three years earlier in Naples, Lionel's father-in-law had bought the Villa Pignatelli – 'a paradise upon earth,' according to Charlotte, 'with a view over the bay and the islands, over the celebrated Mount Vesuvius, the most animated street and the Villa Reale, the Neapolitan Kensington Gardens . . . the garden which surrounds it is by far the most wonderful in the whole world'.[68]

As Charles's house was going up at Günthersburg, Amschel gave Anselm and Chilly four acres in which to build a house on some land he owned on the outskirts of Frankfurt at Grüneburg – 'one of the prettiest spots round ffort,' according to Lionel, 'and Uncle Salomon says he will pay for it'. By the end of that year, Anselm and Chilly had three daughters and three sons between the ages of fourteen years and a few months; one more daughter was to come, and for a 'growing up family' Chilly considered a country house to be 'almost indispensable'.[69]

Anthony was asked to obtain architectural plans and drawings for the house at Grüneburg in England – plans that were to combine, said Lionel, 'some of the Gothic, the Elizabethan and all sorts – not a palace but a good sized house'. To her mother, Chilly wrote that she was 'hesitating between the Elizabethan & Cottage style as it is to be perfectly English'. For her and her sister Louisa, neither of whom ever much cared for life in Frankfurt, England set the standard.[70]

'Bohemia reminded me a little of England,' Chilly wrote to Lionel six months later. 'It is divided into a succession of estates. I have been to see two or three of them & although they contain collections of Armour, china & sometimes good pictures can sustain no comparison with the refined abodes of British Noblemen.' Louisa's house in Frankfurt was arranged 'with a great deal of taste, imitating English fashion as much as possible'; and when Hannah saw the Günthersburg under construction, she thought it would be magnificent, but noted that the grounds and the garden did 'not accord with English taste'.[71]

In the end, Chilly had to settle for a Villa Grüneburg built by a German architect in a confection of Franco-German styles; the plans Anthony sent from England (costing £42) were 'grander & more magnificent', but it would have taken 'years to have them executed & millions to finish them'. Perhaps Salomon jibbed at the cost. In 1845 the Villa's foundations were dug, 100ft long and 60ft wide 'independently of verandas, porticoes &c . . . sufficient for a place to pass the Summer months'.[72]

For country living in England, by contrast, the Rothschild family were still making do with Gunnersbury, where Hannah remained châtelaine, and a modest house on Mayer's land at Mentmore. The FitzRoys had a cottage at Garboldisham in Norfolk, where Lionel and his brothers went for the shooting; and Joe Montefiore would ask his cousins down to shoot with him at Worth in Sussex. But for Lionel's and Anthony's wives – and occasionally for Nat's as well – this situation was far from satisfactory. Lionel's Charlotte did not go to Garboldisham; and none of the sisters-in-law liked staying with Hannah.[73]

'We came here last night,' Louisa wrote in her journal at Gunnersbury in October 1847. 'I felt my usual *chill* creep over me when we advanced through the stately carriage drive to the stately mansion and were received in rather a stately manner by Aunt [Hannah].' As the prospect of staying there the next autumn loomed, she tried to console herself: 'Our stay there will not be very long this year, so let me think only of its advantages – Anthony's presence and my vicinity to C [her sister Charlotte] and greater facility for drawing lessons.'[74]

When Nat was planning to visit England in October 1848, he thought of taking his wife to stay at Leamington or Cheltenham ('rather cockney, but the hunting is good from the former'). He asked Lionel to consult with Mayer, but requested particularly, 'do not say anything on the subject to our good Mamma as she might wish us to stay at Gunnersbury & on no account do I wish to do so, in fact Charlotte wd not go there'.[75]

The prospect of accompanying Hannah to stay with Mayer at Mentmore in 1848 made Lionel's wife unusually peevish. 'You ask, dear husband, if I am going to Mentmore,' she wrote; 'as your mother wishes to go for a few days I have no choice but to go with her. Ever since I became your wife, I have got to do what others want, never what I would like to do. Pray that I shall be compensated in heaven . . . You might take the trouble to write to my mother; once in twelve years is not asking too much . . .'[76]

Writing to Lionel of Charlotte's letters – pages and pages of which streamed daily from her pen (she also wrote 'sermons to children') – Chilly once regretted 'not being gifted with her brilliant imagination and epistolary talents'; Hannah wrote to Lionel of 'the able Pen of One who cannot fail to gratify you in every detail'. Louisa's younger brother Nat Montefiore wrote to his sister of 'Mrs Lionel's known partiality to poetical writing'. While others made mild fun of Charlotte's letter writing behind her back, Louisa found her a challenge in person; and the fact that the two women lived either on one another's doorsteps in London or under their mother-in-law's regime at Gunnersbury was for Louisa hardly ideal.[77]

Having escaped to stay with her own mother at Brighton for a 'quite independent mode of life' in November 1848, Louisa first had her favourite cousin Louisa, Charles's wife, for company, then Lionel and his wife. 'Charlotte and Lionel came down on Friday,' she recorded, 'and remained a couple of days with us – rather slow work. C is clever and amiable and yet how much quicker the hours passed when Louisa was our guest and what a far more agreeable reminiscence did her visit leave behind. I suppose it is her truthfulness and simplicity that render her so attractive and the want of those two qualities that prevent Charlotte from being so . . .'[78]

This may have been harsh, but her cousin also felt uneasy in Charlotte's company. In the summer of 1844, when Lionel and his family were staying in Frankfurt, Charles and Louisa saw a good deal of them. 'Since the arrival of Lionel and Charlotte,' Louisa wrote to her namesake in England, 'we have had family dinners almost every day; on Thursday they all honored us with their presence, and I assure you that I felt nervous at receiving our worthy relations, knowing their propensity for criticising. However, the cook did his best, and it went off satisfactorily.'[79]

Anthony's Louisa got on better with Nat's Charlotte, whom she considered (without a trace of malice) to be 'very pretty, very *grande dame* and very intellectual', but of whom inevitably she saw much less. The prospect of having to find amusing people to meet Nat's wife when she visited London would, on the other hand, fill Lionel's Charlotte with despair.[80]

Despite Nat's assumption that his wife would refuse to go to Gunnersbury, they did spend a few days there together in December 1848. 'Charlotte has been here since Sunday,' Louisa wrote with pleasure. 'We have certainly many feelings in common, more than CL and myself.' The visit also helped Louisa to see the best in Hannah; after Nat and Charlotte had left, she had 'a long tete a tete with Aunt who was kind, mild and gentle. What a pity that faults of temper and education should spoil so much that is intrinsically good and beautiful in her character.'[81]

Relations between Louisa and Lionel's Charlotte seem to have reached a low point over a family matter that had surfaced a few weeks before. 'I hear that Murphy who never honors me with a few words is [to be] the happy bridegroom of Miss Juliana Cohen,' Anselm wrote from Vienna on 5 November. It was true; but Louisa had been expecting Juliana – the daughter of Hannah's brother Isaac, who had died the year before – to marry her brother Joe. As her daughter Constance found when she was going through Louisa's letters years later, Joe 'tried to marry Aunt Juliana, who literally threw him over for Uncle Mayer'.[82]

Two undated letters from Louisa to Charlotte suggest that, to say the least, the sisters-in-law did not see the affair of Mayer and Juliana eye to eye. In the first, Louisa complained that Charlotte had not only 'gratuitously wounded' her feelings but had expressed no regret – 'but what grieved and angered me were your stinging words, your bitter and sarcastic tone & above all your insinuations against those I love most dearly'. In the second letter, by which time Louisa had received a 'kind little note' from her sister-in-law and was calmer, she explained: 'It seemed so very hard to be estranged from you because I *could not* like Juliana. But now dear Charlotte I have forgotten all the painful past & only hope that you will forgive me if I have said anything to displease you.'[83]

Plans for Mayer's marriage to Juliana were not finalised for many months. In January 1849, when Lionel was attending a family conference in Frankfurt and Mayer was holding the fort at New Court, Anthony (standing in for James and Nat in Paris) wrote to his 'dear fat Tupus': 'No hunting this week but you can make it up *by Poking*.' However, in early January 1850 Chilly wrote to 'wish Mayer joy [now] that he has at last commenced courting'.[84]

Two months later, Louisa was still smarting at the turn of events. 'All is at last arranged between Mayer and Juliana,' she noted in her journal on 3 March, 'and I hope we shall now be quiet. I am *as usual* pleased that she is Mayer's and not Joseph's bride and angry at the manner [in which] the Rs have behaved towards Joseph.' Ten days later she was still 'angry about all the matrimonial news – nearly as vexed as Mamma'. By then Joe had also failed to win the hand of Anselm and Chilly's daughter Julie, who – to her father's delight – married her Neapolitan cousin Adolphe instead. When Lionel attempted to take his seat in the House of Commons in July, Louisa felt 'as deeply interested in the cause as ever', but 'less zealous and warm in favour of the representative of that cause'. 'I wish him every success,' she wrote in her journal, 'though I cannot forget.'[85]

Fortunately, relief from the claustrophobic housing arrangements was now at hand. During her engagement a decade earlier Louisa had declared Anthony to be 'quite right in saying that living in the country is quite according to my taste . . . a country life has to me more charms than any other'; and a train of events that began in 1848 was to make this possible.[86]

16

Squires

———⊸◦◦⊷———

T HE WELCOME EXTENDED to Baron Rothschild's Staghounds by local
farmers and such Buckinghamshire landowners as the Dashwoods and
the Harcourts in 1839–40 was for a period in the mid-1840s clouded by the
conduct of the second Duke of Buckingham (the Duke of Agincourt in
Coningsby). According to John Fowler, whose father was the proprietor of
the White Hart Hotel at Aylesbury – a favoured base from which to hunt
with the Baron's, the Buckhounds and three other neighbouring packs –
the cause of the trouble was Corn Law Repeal.[1]

'Bucks,' Fowler recalled, 'was torn to pieces by the discussions which
ensued between the two parties. The Rothschilds were free traders, and
therefore in favour of abolition, while many of the farmers, believing the
repeal would be ruinous to them, became very inimical to the hounds
hunting over their land, and the Duke of Buckingham was not loth to
make political capital out of this discontent, and prepared a notice to warn
the Barons off the land, and obtained the signatures of all his tenants and a
great number of their friends, with several of the local squires, to carry the
notice into effect.

'This was a serious blow to the Rothschilds, as a large portion of the
vale of Aylesbury, including all the best grass country, would be alienated
from them. My father, who had a farm at Broughton, situated between
Aylesbury and Tring, although a staunch Tory, felt very indignant at the
tyrannical conduct of the Duke. He thought the Rothschilds had been
shamefully treated, and got up a counterblast, and wrote to Baron Lionel
inviting him to his farmhouse to breakfast, and to turn out the stag in the
best field on his farm. The Baron readily accepted the invitation, and most
of the independent gentry and farmers of the district were pleased at my
father's pluck, and came in large numbers to the breakfast and the meet.
The Barons Rothschild were delighted at the spirit shown, and for a time
forebore to meet on or near the Duke's estates. This was the prelude to the
well-known hospitality shown for many years afterwards at every farm-
house at which the hounds met.'

Fowler, who succeeded his father at the White Hart, was writing nearly half a century after the repeal of the Corn Laws, and his account of the saga is in some respects open to question. He makes no connection, for example, between the stance taken by his father and the fact that the White Hart benefited from Rothschild patronage, as he describes elsewhere. When High Sheriff, Mayer gave a series of dinners at the White Hart, prepared under the direction of his chef, Chardonnel, at the winter and summer assizes; and the inn regularly received an influx of well-heeled visitors drawn to the Vale by the Staghounds. Other factors also cast doubt on Fowler's presentation of the Duke's behaviour.[2]

There is no doubt that the Duke, a Tory, banned the Rothschild Staghounds from his land. Having received some sporting intelligence in Paris in 1846–7, Anthony wrote to his brothers: 'You would have had a famous long run over to the Duke of Bucclugh [Buccleuch, at Boughton, in Northants]. Did he warn you off like his grace of Buckingham [?]' Yet Corn Law Repeal seems not to have been the only reason – if indeed it was the reason at all – that prompted the Duke and members of his family, aside from anyone else, to declare their land off-limits to the Baron's hounds.[3]

A letter from the Duke's uncle, Lord Nugent of Carlanstown, to Lord Denman, the Lord Chief Justice, indicates that so far as he was concerned the ban on the Baron's hounds had nothing to do with the Corn Laws. In a way this was hardly surprising, since Nugent himself (an Irish peer) was a Whig MP, for Buckingham and then Aylesbury; but he had warned the Staghounds off his land all the same.

To Denman, who seems to have taken on the role of peacemaker, Nugent explained that he had asked Lionel not to turn out a deer on his land near Weedon 'not from any personal feeling disrespectful to him, nor indeed believing that what I felt to be a neglect of ordinary courtesy was chargeable to him', but because he was 'aware that the affairs of the hunt were in other, *rough* hands, which influence I am very glad to find no longer prevails in the management of them'.

Now that things had changed, Nugent continued, he would be 'very glad to see the Baron so often as he may be disposed to come this way. I will only beg him to give me a few days' notice in order that I may, if I can, avail myself of a share in the day's sport, and also that farmers round me, as well as myself, may get the stock out of the fields which the hounds might disturb.' He offered Denman the use of a horse if he cared to come down to Bucks for the hunting.[4]

The letter is undated, but at the beginning of 1846, well before the issue of the Corn Laws reached its culmination in Parliament, an announcement

ull Cry, after Sir Francis Grant, with (*left to right*) Nat, Lionel, Mayer and
.nthony riding to hounds in the Vale of Aylesbury

.ring Park, *c.*1830, when it belonged to William Kay. A dog belonging to one of
.e Rothschilds' servants killed a deer in the park

The Grand Hall, Mentmore, by H. Brewer,
1863. Juliana and Hannah are joined by
Mayer, who filled the house with magnificent
furniture, works of art and pictures

The entrance front of Mentmore Towers, built in the Elizabethan style, with preparations under way for a day's hunting in the Vale of Aylesbury, *c.*1855

Above: A late Victorian photograph of Gunnersbury Park. It was convenient for London, though less convenient for country pursuits

Left: Hannah Mayer, the second of the Rothschild sisters, with her husband Henry FitzRoy. The fact that Henry was not Jewish led to family tensions, but these were soon resolved

Right: Anthony's wife Louisa, *née* Montefiore, in about 1860

Below: Aston Clinton in the late nineteenth century: when bought from Lord Chandos, it was 'not like a fancy place'

Above: Henry Barraud's painting of Lionel, flanked by Lord John Russe[ll] (*left*) and John Abel Smith, entering the House of Commons to take his seat in 1858

Left: Lionel, always hoping to hear some news, in his sixties

Below: Lionel's Charlotte, a tireless correspondent, in the 1860s

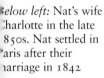

Above: Hyde Park Corner, *c.*1900: No. 148 Piccadilly (to the right of Apsley House) as rebuilt for Lionel; two houses were demolished to make way for it

Left: New Court, as seen from St Swithin's Lane in the 1960s, a century after its redevelopment by Lionel

appeared in the sporting press: 'The Duke of Buckingham has withdrawn his opposition to Baron Rothschild's hounds, and has sent his tenants notices that Lord Lonsdale's (the White Cross Green) harriers and Baron Rothschild's hounds are both to be allowed to hunt over his estates.' So it seems as if Lionel's was not the only hunt to have been warned off; and Lord Lonsdale (the second Earl, and the model for Lord Eskdale in *Coningsby*) was a Tory.[5] Furthermore by mid-May 1846, it had been decided that Bill Roffey – perhaps the '*rough* hands' referred to by Lord Nugent – would give up his position as the Staghounds' huntsman; and at about the same time John Oliver, the groom whose greyhounds had earlier killed the deer in Tring Park, left as well.[6]

Roffey was for two seasons replaced by William Barwick, who came from Lord Fitzwilliam but proved a 'very poor performer in the saddle', and then by Tom Ball. Zach Boxall – and subsequently Harry Jennings, Fred Cox and Mark Howcott – succeeded Ball as whip. George Fountain, and later Joseph Barker (who rode second horse for Mayer), filled Oliver's place as stud-groom. Fred Cox, who had previously been with Thomas Assheton Smith's and the Cottesmore, as well as the Puckeridge, succeeded Ball as huntsman in 1858, when Ball left to run a public house at Leighton Buzzard.[7]

Roffey's departure may also explain the curious fact that the composition of Sir Francis Grant's painting *Full Cry* does not include the Baron's huntsman, as originally it was intended to do. Grant actually got as far as finishing the huntsman's horse, and only required a two-hour sitting from the man himself to make the picture, as he put it to Lionel, 'fit for exhibition in your dining room'; yet the finished picture depicts Lionel and his brothers – Nat out in front on a chestnut, Lionel in the foreground on a grey, then Mayer and Anthony – on their own.[8]

As for Lord Lonsdale, at whose family seat in Westmorland, Lowther Castle, Hannah had lunched in 1841, he kept his horses and a 'menagerie of foxes' in the stables of the Harcourt Arms Hotel near Tring station and his hounds at Grove Place, Tring. His father (the first Earl), a foxhunting and hound-breeding fanatic, had kennelled his hounds in Leicestershire at Cottesmore House, which eventually gave its name to the pack – with which the Rothschild brothers seem to have hunted in the 1830s. In January 1846, and again in early 1847, Nat applauded Lionel's plans to go down to Melton for a few days' hunting in Leicestershire.[9]

Lionel and the younger Lonsdale corresponded about the supply of deer from the fells around Lowther for the Baron's, and in the autumn of 1846 they dined together, Lionel as Lonsdale's guest. And if the Duke of

Buckingham was not exactly a friend, his response was entirely amiable when, in October 1845, Lionel sought permission to take a party over Stowe, the Duke's treasure-filled palace.[10] In residence there at the time, the Duke explained that although as a rule the house was open to visitors twice a week between 1 May and 1 September '*when it is closed*', as 'it will be agreeable to the Baron Rothschild to see it on Tuesday next, I will with pleasure in the present instance, grant the permission'. Having said that he would give directions for Lionel's party to be shown over the house 'on Tuesday at one o'clock!' the Duke concluded: 'I am glad of the opportunity also of obliging you . . .'[11]

Irrespective of the motives behind the temporary opposition to the Rothschild hounds, the very fact of it seems to have made Lionel and his brothers all the more keen to become Bucks landowners themselves. In 1847 Nat announced that he would like 'to lay out in a profitable way £100,000 in Bucks. I'll promise you to let you hunt over my land without sending you a notice. We must all of us become Buckinghamshire squires.'[12]

With the help of Sir Harry Verney (the former Harry Calvert) and his steward at Claydon, and also with the assistance of Thomas Hart, now acting as his land agent, Mayer had for some time been seeking to add to his land at Mentmore, of which he was making very full use.[13] The Baron's hunt kennels, deer paddocks and stables were now established there, and Mayer had set up a hunting stud. At the start of the 1845–6 season, there were more than thirty red deer in the paddocks; and by the summer of 1847 there were thirty-nine horses. Mayer also farmed cattle – shorthorns, including a bull called Railway King – and sheep.[14]

In 1847 Disraeli, who became MP for Buckinghamshire that year (and whose father lived at Bradenham, near High Wycombe), wrote to let Lionel know that Fawley Court, 'one of the finest estates in Bucks', was for sale. Lionel did not buy the place, and earlier had 'blamed' Disraeli for failing to inform him that the 5,000-acre Hampden estate – which was valued for Mayer by an agent of Harry Verney's at £162,000 – was for sale.[15]

Then in 1848 the Duke of Buckingham obliged the Rothschilds not just by letting them see over his house and resume hunting over his land, but by going spectacularly bankrupt, resulting in the 40-day long auction of the contents of Stowe that summer, and also in the sale of large tracts of land in Bucks, much of which the Duke had bought with borrowed money (as Disraeli did with Hughenden that year). And at roughly the same time, during and after Mayer's term as High Sheriff, other farms and estates came up for sale in the county as well.[16] Indeed, Lionel and his brothers became almost spoilt for choice: when in July 1848 Anthony heard that a fine estate in the Vale had been sold to Samuel Jones Loyd, he was 'rather glad that Loyd has bought Aston Abbotts as we did not. I would rather that he did than any other person.' Eighteen months later Mayer tactfully declined to buy a farm at Steeple Claydon in case Harry Verney wished to add it to his estate.[17]

The situation suited the Rothschilds to a tee, not least because they were able to look around for property at the right price. Indeed, at the auction of the larger Buckingham estates that took place in May 1848, they seem to have bought nothing – though in August they did buy items in the Stowe contents sale.

Acting through Israel Russell, a London dealer, Lionel spent £69 12s on a pair of ivory chairs and two 'Raphael' vases, and Hannah spent £315 12s on two pieces of jewellery (one of a horse) and five 'Raphael' salts. Anthony, acting on his own behalf, bought 'a pair of exquisite taper-candlesticks, of agate mounted with silver gilt, with masks, lizards, and insects of the most beautiful work' for £48 16s 6d. As the lot was knocked down to him, 'the manager of a very well-known London house' was heard to remark, 'I made them and sold them for less than half the money' – which prompted the auctioneer, Mr Manson (of Christie's), to offer 'a rather sharp rebuke'.[18] For 235 guineas, Mayer bought what was described as 'a beautiful cabinet of marquetrie of the finest old German work formed as a table supporting a cabinet' – an Augsburg ormolu-mounted *table méchanique* of about 1830, constructed in part from a mid-eighteenth-century writing cabinet. 'Of all the exquisite marquetrie cabinets distributed throughout the mansion,' it was said, 'this was decidedly the most superb.'[19]

Subsequent to the estates auction in May, Mayer negotiated for land purchases with the Duke of Buckingham's son, the Marquess of Chandos, Tory MP for Buckingham, whose manner was both friendly and hospitable. Anthony even contemplated buying Stowe, which, as Nat said, 'if purchased cheap must be a very valuable acquisition' – though Nat thought that the size of the house might be a drawback. At one point their cousin Charles thought of buying Stowe for himself and Louisa; but in the end the house was not sold, and Charles simply bought some of the contents.[20]

In time, Nat resolved that he could not very well buy an estate in England without his wife's approval, and that he must bow to Charlotte's decided preference for living in Paris – '& you know by experience that the ladies always rule the roost'. He also thought it impractical to manage an English estate from France; but he continued to view land as an investment, as did his uncle James.[21]

Regarding some farms for sale in Buckinghamshire in 1851, James and Nat were at one in thinking that 'if they pay 3½% you might buy them for the house if not for one of us or all 4. 3½% is a very good rate of int for land & were I sure of it I should not mind having them for myself.' The next year, for a return of 3½ per cent, Nat alone was ready to invest £200,000 in farms in Gloucestershire.[22]

Now and again, the attraction of life in England also made him waver about a house and estate for himself. Briefly, in 1852, he considered going out on a limb and buying the late Earl of Shrewsbury's remarkable house in Staffordshire, Alton Towers, though it seems that he had not appreciated the size of it. 'I don't think it will suit if the house is as large as Chatsworth,' he said after his brothers had made some enquiries.[23]

Three estates in Buckinghamshire that his brothers did buy, however, provided a solid basis for the kind of country life that they had long contemplated. As before, it was Mayer who led the way, and in comparison to Nat's notions he was not extravagant.

Mayer had been coveting William Harcourt's small estate at Mentmore, which incorporated the manor of Mentmore, since 1843, when it was valued for him 'as an investment' at £12,250, and by Harcourt's agent at £19,000. It comprised rather more than 200 acres. Two years later, Harry Verney, who wished to see Mayer established as 'a Bucks County Gentleman', doubted that Harcourt would dispose of the estate, by exchange or sale, during the lifetime of his mother, the Marquise d'Harcourt, an English Harcourt who had married a French cousin and whose father had previously owned the property. But following the Marquise's death, and the resolution of legal difficulties, in 1850 Mayer bought the estate for £12,400. His uncle Charles was soon calling him, in polyglot style, 'der Duc of Mentmore'.[24]

The manor of Mentmore came with the advowson, the right of presentation to the local church benefice. A decade earlier, Lionel and his brothers had received a strong letter from a local incumbent, complaining of 'the *most indecent conduct* of some parties who followed your hounds on Thursday last'. The gate of the churchyard had been unlocked to admit a funeral procession – 'and but a very little time before that procession came up, and the grave being open near the churchyard gate, several persons on horseback, and one if not more in scarlet coats, galloped through the churchyard, and leaped the fence on the other side'.[25] Having heard that Mayer was intending to buy the Harcourt estate at Mentmore, Anthony suggested that when he had done so he might like to 'give the Parson a kick in his B'.[26]

The second estate they acquired had belonged to the Dashwoods. 'I recommend you strongly to buy Halton & a few farms,' Nat urged his brothers in October 1850. 'They can not hurt. You must get me in [as MP] for Aylesbury & then I shall be able to pass a few months every year in yr amiable society.' In mid-November, he was 'glad that you think yr offer for Halton will be accepted. I fancy it will want a great deal doing to it. This will however be an amusement for the worthy Bart Sir Anthony. I hope he will occupy himself with it & get up the shooting famously so that when one comes to pay you a visit one may have a little fun . . .' Six days later, Nat remarked, seemingly to Lionel: 'I congratulate you my Ld of Halton.' The estate comprised 1,400 acres and, as with Mentmore, the advowson.[27]

The third property, an estate of 1,050 acres with a small brick-built and stuccoed 'sporting residence' at Aston Clinton, was purchased from Lord Chandos. Located about three miles from Tring and four from Aylesbury, just south of Halton at the foot of the Chiltern Hills, the Aston Clinton estate had previously been sold to the Duke of Buckingham in 1838 by Viscount Lake, who, as a Not-Content, paired off with the Bishop of Durham, a Content, in the division at the end of the Jewish Disabilities debate in the Lords in 1848.[28]

Having been withdrawn from one of the Buckingham estates sales in 1848, Aston Clinton was offered for sale in July 1849 and, after Thomas Hart had looked over the property for Mayer in August, Lionel suggested that if it could 'be had to pay clear 3½–¾ I should not be sorry to have it, but I should like it better if it paid 4%.' The next day he proposed offering £25,000 (the original sale estimate) 'and if they will not take it to let us know the lowest price and wait a week for our answer'.[29]

Hart had told Mayer that Aston Clinton was 'not a favorite spot' of his, and that he did not consider the estate 'truly desirable'. Likewise, Lionel, a week after suggesting an offer of £25,000, wrote to Mayer: 'If you think that the Aston Clinton estate is worth 26,000 I have no objection to yr offering it, but I think we ought always to be able to rely on 3½ clear of all charges. It is not like a fancy place. You must consider it entirely as an investment.'[30]

It seems that the purchase of Aston Clinton would have had a stronger appeal for the Rothschild brothers had it been possible at the same time to acquire an adjoining estate, Rookery Park. Owned by George Minshull, a well-known Bow Street magistrate, until his death in 1840, Rookery Park had passed to his daughter, the Comtesse de Broc.[31] When Nat went to see the Comtesse on the subject in Paris in 1851, she told him that she would 'put every thing down in writing & send you an order to view her estate'.

But she would only sell, she told Nat, 'if her income is thereby increased & as she must reinvest her money in the English funds I am afraid it will be a dear purchase . . . I was mighty civil to her & she said she preferred selling to us than to anyone else . . .'[32]

As Nat came to realise that he was getting nowhere with the Comtesse – 'When she thinks you want to buy her farms she will stick it on the price & perhaps not sell at all' – his brothers sent James James, their Aylesbury solicitor, to Paris to see if he could do any better. But James, who had without difficulty presented the necessary court application prior to Mayer's appointment as High Sheriff, was not much more successful than Nat with the Comtesse de Broc.[33] 'James told me yesterday he expected to buy Mde de Broc's property for £16,000 & at that price it wd bring in 2½%,' Nat wrote. But apparently such a deal was unattractive: a decade later Rookery Park remained in the Comtesse's hands.[34]

However, the Rothschild brothers went ahead and bought the Aston Clinton estate, though which of them did so, or in what combination they put up the money, is not clear. Having recommended his brothers to buy Halton, in late 1850 Nat declared that he would 'willingly take ¼ share in Aston Clinton as well as in the former [Halton]. I hope Sir Anthony will look well after it & get the rentes [sic] paid as well as the shooting up. Our land in Kent [Burmarsh] does not pay well but I trust it will not be so in Bucks.'[35]

Having failed to secure Rookery Park – though an agreement to rent some of the Comtesse de Broc's land at Aston Clinton seems to have been struck – Lionel bought the manor of Bierton, together with its large estate and the advowson of Hulcott, to the north-east of Aylesbury. Further properties fell into Rothschild ownership, and as the 1850s advanced, locals dubbed the neighbourhood 'Judaea'. Sir Philip Pauncefoot-Duncombe, Bt, of Great Brickhill, Fenny Stratford, jested that the hill on which his house stood was the only one in the area that did not belong to a Jew.[36]

The quip Nat had made about getting in for Aylesbury was, he said later, 'more a joke than anything else'; but the political aspect of land purchase weighed with Lionel all the same. In 1849 he wrote to Mayer: 'Also with regard to Aston Clinton I should go as far as 25,000. If you like to give a little more I should not hesitate, if you think one of these days Sir J Dashwood's place [Halton] is likely to be sold. It would give a little interest in the Aylesbury Election which is also worth something.'[37]

The next year, Lionel was proved right. When, in December 1850, Harry Verney's younger brother, Frederick Calvert, stood as the Whig candidate for Aylesbury, Mayer campaigned for him – with 'persuasive eloquence', so Nat heard. Having won the seat, Calvert lost no time in writing to thank Mayer for his 'effective assistance' in the election, and he added: 'All those voters who are desirous of promoting your wishes, I believe, without exception gave me their vote.' When advising the Rothschild brothers on further local land purchases, for example at Bierton, over the coming years, James James would bear their political interests in mind.[38]

Although Anthony himself was no crack shot – in the Great Derby Pigeon Stakes at Hornsey Wood House shooting ground one year, he failed to bring down any of his six birds – he did, as Nat hoped, get up the shooting (pheasant and partridge) at Halton. Moreover, as things worked out, Anthony also took on Aston Clinton and Bierton, making Aston Clinton, where he extended the house, his and Louisa's country base. That it was not Lionel and Charlotte who did so may perhaps be explained in part by the fact that in 1850 their circumstances were unexpectedly changed.[39]

For a period the previous summer Hannah had been very unwell, with symptoms that suggested cholera; but she had recovered and in late September, after convalescence on the Continent, had gone to Frankfurt, where Lionel and Charlotte were staying with their children. She was installed at Chilly's new house at the Grüneburg ('very Comfortable', according to Lionel), and liked it very much. 'She is a little thin,' Lionel told Mayer, 'but that was to have been expected.'[40]

The purpose of Hannah's visit to Frankfurt, and of Lionel's and his family's, was to attend the wedding of Chilly's daughter Mathilde (Matty) to Charlotte's younger brother Willy, which, after a long delay caused by jockeying for control of £25,000 belonging to the bride-to-be, finally took place in late November. Afterwards, 'being so well lodged &c among my Friends here', Hannah remained in Frankfurt until the end of January, staying with Louisa and Charles.[41]

By mid-December, she was obviously feeling more her old self. Lionel, having returned to London, heard from Charles: 'Your excellent mother who is very fond of society goes out every night and seems to be delighted with people's attentions.' Hannah would have liked to borrow Amschel's villa to give a party herself, but as her brother-in-law 'did not much relish the prospect' she gave up the idea. On 19 December, she wrote to Mayer: 'The Season for Visiting is at its Height at present here. Dinners and Evening Parties every Evening.'[42]

In January, while she appeared to Chilly 'infinitely better than last year', Hannah was still at times subject to 'slight returns of her former pains'.

These, however, said Chilly, 'seldom deprive her mixing in that society and sociability such as this town can afford. In the evening she often has her game of Whist, goes to the theatre or accompanies Louisa into society.' But having returned to England, and having had the satisfaction of seeing Mayer marry Juliana in the early summer, on 5 September 1850 Hannah died.[43]

She had been ill for about ten days; according to Charlotte, it was on 25 August, Leonora's and Evy's joint birthday, that Hannah 'met with the accident that brought on her last fatal illness'. On 4 September, Charlotte had been planning to dress her girls in new outfits, 'that poor Aunt might be pleased with their appearance at breakfast. She never saw them – the new dresses they wore were black.' The children, Charlotte recorded, were taken to pay their last respects to their grandmother on her deathbed – 'they kissed her hands when she was no more. All the children did except Leo. We told him she was an angel in heaven; he remembered Jacob's dream and the ladder, and thought she had walked up as those celestial messengers did.'[44]

As Hannah had left no will, Lionel was appointed administrator of her estate – which included jewellery valued by Hunt & Roskell (formerly Storr & Mortimer) at £9,006 for 'mercantile' purposes and at £11,695 for the 'possessor'. The most valuable item was 'A fine Brilliant Necklace consisting of 36 brilliants, estimated weight 437grs or 109¼ carats: £2,819 in the one list, £3,750 in the other.'[45]

'As far as I am concerned,' Louisa Charles wrote to Lionel from Frankfurt, 'it would give me pleasure to receive something that belonged to our beloved Parent and that she wore. The jewels themselves of course I care little about. You know how many I have and how few opportunities I have of wearing them. I think I should like to have one of her large diamond studs, should this choice not interfere with that of any of my Brothers or Sisters.' Chattels aside, Louisa's share in her mother's estate amounted to £7,624 5s 9d, which was placed on account for her at New Court.[46]

Hannah's death had greater material consequences for her sons and their families. As Mayer and Juliana made 107 Piccadilly their town house, Gunnersbury passed to Lionel and Charlotte; and in these circumstances it no doubt made sense to them that Anthony and Louisa should take on Aston Clinton. Land purchases at Gunnersbury had resulted in an estate of several hundred acres; horses, Hereford cattle and sheep – as well as the odd alpaca – grazed the meadows.[47]

Hannah died while Mayer and Juliana were away on their 'wedding tour', the first stage of which, after a spell at Gunnersbury and prior to a tour on the Continent, they spent in England, of which, ever since his boyhood, Mayer had always been keen to see more.[48]

On the way home from the Perthshire grouse moor in 1843, Mayer and his uncle James had parted company from Lionel to return to London at a more leisurely pace. They visited Carlisle, Liverpool and Manchester (where Mayer was 'almost stifled with the smoke'); and they went to see the Leger run at Doncaster, where everyone they met, said Mayer, was 'excessively polite' and where they were invited to dinner – 'There is an honor' – by Lady Chesterfield.[49] Mayer and James had also made a brief tour together on the way down to Perthshire, before joining Lionel in Yorkshire for Castle Howard. On 8 August they visited Hardwick Hall (the Duke of Devonshire's), which Mayer found to be 'an old place really worth seeing', and they made arrangements to see Belvoir Castle (the Duke of Rutland's) the next day.[50]

Mayer's thirst for this kind of tour remained unquenched. On honeymoon in 1850, after visiting Cheltenham ('another Leamington on a grander scale'), Mayer and Juliana stayed at Ross, in Herefordshire, from where, at the urging of Lionel and Anthony, they visited Berkeley Castle. The house – Grantley Berkeley's ancestral home – was to Mayer's eyes 'very antient, one of the best specimens of the middle ages I have seen in this country, almost superior to Warwick; but the interior is fitted up in very bad taste . . .'[51]

He could not have had a better companion than Juliana. 'I was very pleased to find that my better ½ did not object [to] visiting the kennels,' he went on, '& she almost took as great an interest in the pack as my worthy eldest brother himself. They have 94 couples of working hounds; but have none to spare . . .'

As Lionel, when a young man on tour in Europe, had felt himself to be a connoisseur in matters of art, so Mayer, at the same stage, earned his mother's respect when it came to houses. As the decoration of Gunnersbury was nearing completion in May 1838, Hannah wrote to him at Cambridge (at Trinity after Magdalene had made a fuss about chapel attendance): 'You, my dear Mayer, will know if the state is good having seen many of the best finished houses.'[52]

As it seems doubtful that Mayer would have visited any more grand London houses than his brothers by then, presumably Hannah had in mind his experience of country houses, beginning with his stay at Gordon Castle. Whoever his friends were at Cambridge the likelihood is that some of them came from families with big country houses. Then, or later, he obviously became familiar with Warwick Castle; and after marrying Juliana he lost no time in building a very large country seat of his own.

According to one great expert on the Victorian country house, for the majority of mid-Victorian country house owners and builders the desired 'Old English' style was either Elizabethan or Gothic. 'The choice depended on the tastes of the person building; if he saw himself as an English gentleman he would tend to build Elizabethan, if as a Christian English gentleman, Gothic . . .' Hence the style preferred by the pious Roman Catholic Lord Shrewsbury for Alton Towers, and by his fellow Catholic Lord Beaumont for Carlton Towers, was Gothic, while that selected by Mayer for Mentmore Towers was Elizabethan.[53]

When he had written to his brothers on 8 August 1843, Mayer had asked them to direct the next day's post to Grantham; and later, in 1850, he and his brothers expressed an interest in buying an estate 'near Grantham' that came on the market. To the west of Grantham, Nottingham is the next large town, and just outside Nottingham stands Wollaton Hall. There does not appear to be any record of Mayer having visited the place, but he might easily have done so; and it was Wollaton, an Elizabethan house by Robert Smythson, that was to provide the model for Mentmore, the first stone of which was laid by Mayer's infant daughter Hannah on 31 December 1851.[54]

The result of Charles Barry's extensive remodelling, for Lord Pembroke's kinsman the third Earl of Carnarvon, of Highclere Castle in Hampshire (where work began in 1842), is reminiscent of Wollaton. The main block of Mentmore, on the other hand, is closely based on Wollaton, a symmetrical house, its walls 'gridded with glass which turns the solid masonry into an airy palace'. Where Wollaton has above its centre a high 'Prospect Room', though, Mentmore was instead given a plate glass ceiling over its 40ft-high 'grand hall'. The service blocks were built in matching Wollaton style.[55]

The architect Mayer chose was Sir Joseph Paxton, whose Great Stove Hannah had seen on her visit to Chatsworth in 1841, and whose then employer (and friend), the Duke of Devonshire, the Rothschilds knew. Further to recommend Paxton was that he had recently designed and in 1851 constructed the sensational Crystal Palace in Hyde Park, to house Prince Albert's Great Exhibition, for which Mayer sat on one of the committees and of which Lionel was a treasurer. Paxton designed Mentmore with his son-in-law, George Stokes, and the builder employed was George Myers, of Lambeth, who built churches for A. W. Pugin. Stokes and Myers also worked for Anthony at Aston Clinton.[56]

'I am glad my dear Tup that you have bought such fine Limoges [enamel] cups,' Nat wrote to Mayer in November 1851. 'Mentmore Towers will soon arise & decorated with all the splendors of antiquity & modern times will astonish the admiring multitude. I hope dear Tupus to be able to accept yr invitation next year & am sure the towers, bowers, & flowers will surpass my expectations.' The contract price for the house itself was £15,400, and altogether the project was to cost approximately £38,000.[57]

Approaching Mentmore in early 1854, a visitor found his attention 'attracted to a large pile of buildings, evidently in course of construction, and as evidently intended for the residence of a wealthy and princely inhabitant'. The house was about eighteen months away from completion. 'Situated on an eminence, though by no means an exposed one,' the man continued, 'the house commands extensive views of the surrounding country, the celebrated Vale of Aylesbury being delightfully conspicuous.'[58]

The site selected for Mayer's house was a low hilltop overlooking the Vale, with views to the Dunstable Downs and the Chiltern Hills. The finished result was to be a magnificent, if not cosy, 80-room mansion, faced in golden Ancaster stone and with acres of glass, which Mayer proceeded to fill with the finest furniture – including many pieces by the best *ébénistes* of eighteenth-century France – and paintings and works of art of all kinds. The house was also fitted with such modern conveniences as under-floor central heating, hot and cold running water, a ventilation system and flush lavatories. A supply of gas came from a gas works erected in the grounds.

Mayer and Juliana invited family and friends to the consecration of the house towards the end of December 1855. The ceremony was performed by Rabbi Kalisch, who for many years filled the role of non-resident family chaplain to Mayer and his brothers, and who gave religious instruction to the children, as Mr Levy had done years before at Stamford Hill. 'Dr Kalisch read prayers, also several psalms, and affixed mezuzas or phylacteries to the doors,' Moses Montefiore noted in his diary. 'A splendid breakfast and dinner followed the ceremony.'[59]

By then, Mentmore had already made such an impression on Mayer's uncle James that in 1854 Paxton had been commissioned to rebuild James's château at Ferrières along the same lines, but on a larger and grander scale. When Lionel's Charlotte visited the new Ferrières for the first time three years later, though, she liked it 'infinitely less than Mentmore Towers'. Both house and setting seemed to her 'very much inferior to Mentmore & its architectural advantages & real beauty of position. The woods & the villages are not to be compared with Halton & Aston Clinton.' James complained that the English people who had built Ferrières for him were 'thieves and pickpockets'.[60]

Of the four Rothschild brothers, Mayer spent the least time abroad. 'The good folks here,' Hannah once wrote to him mischievously from Paris, 'wonder at your Apathy, and at your want of Enthusiasm at not coming to this place, the Centre of all *that can boast* of the beauties of Nature and Art in their Own Imagination.' Alphonse, having once missed Mayer's presence at a family gathering in Paris, wrote to say how sorry he was not to have seen his cousin Muffy – 'But you are such a staunch Englishman that you do not like to leave Old England.'[61]

Another characteristic of Mayer's that was a subject for frequent comment was his disinclination for letter writing, a boyhood trait that remained with him in adult life. Anthony and Nat make regular reference to the scarcity of 'lazy Tup's handwriting'. They presume that he is either too busy 'tupping' some girl – here Anselm joined in the joshing – or that he has gone off hunting or racing. The references are usually humorous, occasionally censorious and often tinged with envy. 'I give you my word that it is a very fine thing to be a great man and to be at the head of all that is going on in the way of business,' Nat wrote from Paris in 1843, 'but for my part I think it is a great bore & wd. prefer a little more quiet & a great deal less agitation. One enjoys nothing. Old Tup is the lucky boy.'[62]

Mayer would make fun of himself. Scouring the country for horses in 1849, he wrote to Lionel from Shrewsbury (which on market day made him fancy that he was 'most exactly in Old England'): 'If any body were to read this epistle they would fancy it scribbled by a horse dealer instead of a city merchant.'[63]

That Mayer led the life of an English gentleman of sporting tastes has become a cliché in accounts of his family. He makes a routine appearance – usually rather brief – as a bluff, good-natured, pleasure-loving individual who enjoyed his wealth, bought some fine things, built a big house, and spent the greater part of his life in a barely intelligible world of rich, unpraiseworthy sporting types who were no more likely to be found doing anything useful at a desk in the City than he was. Every now and again he surfaces to fight, and to win, a seat in Parliament, which he attends but where he never makes a speech. The caricature contains grains of substance; yet Mayer was a partner with his brothers in New Court, and one might wonder why his way of living, in particular his inattention to banking, was borne.

Part of the explanation seems to be that Mayer was not such a rare bird at New Court – or, for that matter, on the Continent – after all. 'The more I see,' he wrote to Lionel from Germany in 1846, 'I am convinced the more, there is no place like our old New Court; where would all the rubbishy French shares be if we did not support them [?] I think we may give ourselves a few airs & be as great men as others.' Nat, having once remarked that 'that old rogue Tup gets all the hunting & other good things all to himself', proceeded to complain that Mayer 'can not write a line except to communicate the variations of Stock'; and when in 1849 Mayer wrote to Lionel from Shrewsbury, when he was on the point of leaving for Chester, he ended his letter: 'If I am wanted in town, I can always be back in 12 hours after the receipt of your letter so you can write me word.'[64]

By the early 1850s, alongside Lionel and Anthony, Mayer was a recognised figure in the City on Change – though not on the same Change of which Nathan had been such a fixture at his pillar in Jews' Walk. Having gone up in flames in early 1838, the Royal Exchange had been rebuilt and, though the signs bearing the names of the old walks were done away with, from 1844 – 'notwithstanding we have lost the great Rothschild and a few other ancient faces' – business carried on as before. Transactions involving foreign exchange continued to be concluded, by regulation, on Tuesdays and Fridays – which were still foreign post days at New Court – between 3.30 and 4.30 p.m. The three Rothschild brothers were known to make their appearance by 3.45 and to position themselves by a pillar on the south side of Change, near to the spot where Nathan had stood. There, as the 'great Rothschild' had done before them, they took contracts for bills on foreign places, their weekly dealings in foreign exchange being estimated at in excess of £100,000.[65]

'Since the death of their father, the sons have carried on the business with great success,' a City commentator observed. 'They are three in number, and usually attend Change together; always two of them, if not three, are at their accustomed place . . . Once having seen the father, there is no mistaking the sons, the same peculiarity of Hebrew visage and heaviness of physiognomy, the same rotundity of person, the same apparent aptitude for business, mark the family, their race, and dealing.'

Mayer's absences from the City, on the other hand, seem likely to have been tolerated, if not encouraged, by Lionel and Anthony because, from the point of view of furthering and consolidating their interests in Buckinghamshire and beyond, they could have found no better representative than their brother. For one thing, people warmed to him. In 1851, Nat reported an English friend's comment 'that the Squire of Mentmore was the beau ideal of a Buck'shire farmer, 20 stone & as hard as nails. It does one good to look at his beautiful face.' To another, Mayer was 'the jolly, happy-looking Baron, the perfect model of a Buckinghamshire squire'.[66]

Friendly, he also had a good sense of humour. At the Baron's annual meet at Hardwick Rectory, the Reverend Kit Erle would have a breakfast laid out, always with a fine ham at the centre of the table. Time and again, Erle would press the ham on Mayer – assuring him that it was a *mutton* ham. 'The Jews,' Erle used to say, 'like being chaffed.' On the other hand, when William Selby Lowndes enquired about hunting his foxhounds over the Baron's country on a Saturday in the 1860s, Mayer regretted that 'the Foxes would be at Synagogue'.[67]

As the ailing Nathan had made jokes at Lionel's wedding in Frankfurt in 1836, so Mayer's niece Matty hoped that her 'Dear Uncle Muffy' would add some cheer at her marriage to Willy in Frankfurt in 1849. 'Your jovial presence would enliven the solemnity of the scene,' Matty wrote. 'I am sure in the midst of the sermon I should hear your voice exclaim: How d'you do Matty, so that bon gré, mal gré I shall be obliged to smile. Pray come dear uncle Muffie & do not let our [*kosher*] dinner be a drawback on your good intentions.'[68]

To some English Rothschild eyes Willy was 'too Caucasian [Jewish] in looks to be ornamental', though Lionel's wife considered 'his gait and manner and mode of speech' to be more typically Jewish than his features. In habits, Willy was a stickler for orthodox Jewish practices. Five years before Matty became engaged to him, Hannah wrote of his 'enthusiasm in observing all the strictest duties of the Jewish religion', though she doubted 'that his religious devotion will be followed by Fanaticism'. Mayer, in contrast, when he was at Cambridge, was particularly asked by his mother to avoid 'infringing upon our religious duties', in particular to 'abstain from those indulgences such as riding on horseback on Saturdays'. Her injunction seems to have struck home; writing from Shrewsbury on a Sunday, Mayer told Lionel that 'like a good Hebrew yesterday I only walked about the town'.[69]

For a landowner who farmed in Buckinghamshire – where whilst Disraeli was recalled as 'always particularly anxious to pose as the British farmer', Mayer was remembered as a 'practical farmer' who liked to trudge over his farms in the early morning – sporting predilections were unquestionably an asset. And as Lionel found it increasingly less easy to get down regularly for the hunting in the 1850s, Mayer – a Deputy Lieutenant for the county as well as a magistrate – was there to become effective, and resident,

Master of the Baron's Staghounds, though Lionel still paid the bills. The annual cost of an average foxhunting establishment in 3-day-a-week country was estimated at £1,348 14s.[70]

By then Mayer had served as High Sheriff of Buckinghamshire, which had been an honour as well as a milestone for him and his family; but in a mid-Victorian ranking of 'The County' it was the Master of Foxhounds and the agricultural landlords who ranked immediately after the Lord Lieutenant. Only after them came the Bishop, the Chairman of Quarter Sessions, the Colonel of the Yeomanry and the Member of Parliament (in the case of Buckinghamshire Disraeli, the county member). The office of High Sheriff, held only for a year, did not even enter the reckoning.[71]

In this context, the Rothschild pack counted as foxhounds. The country hunted by the Baron Rothschild's Staghounds is delineated as clearly as any other hunt country on foxhunting maps of the period; and, as had been the case with the harriers that Lionel had bought from Adamson, the Baron's hunted foxes as well as carted deer. In a similar way, Lord Lonsdale's hunted foxhounds on Tuesdays and Saturdays, harriers on Fridays – so combining with the Baron's meets on Mondays and Thursdays to offer hunting in the neighbourhood six days a week.[72]

As sporting interests could bolster status, they also gave a boost to local life. In the early 1850s, two rich Londoners, Cheslyn Hall and Samuel Baker, who had already hunted with the Baron's for some years, built loose boxes and all appurtenances for twenty hunters at Aylesbury – where John Oliver seems to have found a berth as stud-groom. They installed themselves at the White Hart, where they also took rooms for Robert Grimston and for 'the immortal' Jem Mason, who since hunting with Hubert de Burgh's staghounds in his youth had become the most famous steeplechase rider of his days.[73] John Fowler remembered how Hall and Baker and their guests 'lived luxuriously on rare viands and the most noted vintage wines', but also that Hall and Baker were 'at the head of every subscription for promoting sport, agricultural shows, charitable or other useful works in the neighbourhood'.[74]

Such popular actions could pay dividends, as Mayer well knew. For instance, although he failed to win Hythe Sandwich in the 1847 general election, he kept in touch with his supporters in the constituency. 'It is renowned at Folkestone,' his agent there reported to him in the spring of 1849, 'that you have undertaken to send a Horse to the Steeple Chase and to present the Stakes to the Charities of the Town if you should win them. This would be a very popular Act on your part . . .'[75]

In Buckinghamshire, Mayer instituted a spring steeplechase at Mentmore, over four miles of country, for horses belonging to farmers who lived within the limits of the country hunted by the Baron's and Lord Lonsdale's hounds. This was said to have 'excited much local interest', not least because there was a plate of 40 sovereigns to be won.[76]

Mayer and Juliana also gave prizes at local shows. Mayer awarded a silver cup to the breeder, being a farmer or tradesman, of the best yearling colt or filly. Juliana presented a silver teapot to the exhibitor of the four best pens of poultry ('preference being given to the most useful sorts') and gave a prize of £5 to the dairymaid who had lived for the longest period on the same farm. Mayer also provided, free of charge, the services of a good thoroughbred stallion for the use of mares belonging to the farmers over whose land the Staghounds hunted; and he was always careful to compensate the farmers for any damage done to their property by his hounds.[77]

There were now eighteen hunters at Mentmore, besides those for the huntsman and whipper-in, for the exclusive use of Mayer and his brothers, all of them up to carrying 'very great weights'. This might sound extravagant, but given that the Rothschild brothers were no featherweights, and that a second horse was in any case all but essential for a hard day's staghunting, it was not excessive if three of them wished to hunt together on consecutive days. Staying in Paris in October 1849, Anthony wrote to Mayer that he looked forward to returning to England, with Nat, in November when, he said: 'You & Nat can go & hunt 5 days a week & I 2.'[78]

In addition to the hunters, twelve or thirteen brood mares had been selected 'with the most scrupulous regard to power, soundness, constitution, action, and all the other desiderata for breeding valuable weight-carrying hunters'. The hunt kennel contained twenty-eight and a half couple of hounds, described as 'particularly handsome'; Dairymaid, Patience, Feudal, Prodigal, Playful, Darling and Trouncer were considered near faultless.[79]

Mayer also devoted much time and thought to the Turf, the then widespread enthusiasm for which it would be hard to overestimate; and from the outset, his approach to the business was shrewd – very definitely not that of a rich dimwit indulging his fancy. In 1853, on a farm he owned at Crafton, he set up a racing stud, with Charles Markham as stud-groom and manager. Dissatisfied with John Scott's Whitewall House stable at Malton (he suspected Scott of cheating him), he put his racehorses in training with William King, previously Scott's head lad, and Joseph Hayhoe, who had also been with Scott for some years, at Russley Park, near Lambourn, in Berkshire. Success was instantaneous.[80]

In that first year, 1853, Mayer's Hungerford (by John o'Gaunt) won the Nottinghamshire Handicap, the Great Yorkshire Handicap and the Doncaster Cup (beating Lord Exeter's Ilex), besides plates at Brighton and Leicester. Mayer's Hyacinth (by Bay Middleton) brought home the Windsor Town Plate from Ascot; his Orestes (by Orlando) won the Eglinton Stakes at Doncaster; and at Newmarket his Mentmore Lass (by Melbourne) beat Lord Zetland's Comfit (Flatman up) to first place in the One Thousand Guineas, Mayer's first classic. Johnny Charlton was jockey in every case. In 1855 Mayer's Baroncino (by the Emperor out of Geneviève de Brabant) won the Goodwood Cup (Fordham up).[81]

William King, too fond of the bottle, faded from the picture in 1854–5 (he became landlord of the Salutation at Doncaster) and in 1856 Mayer moved the training operation, under Joe Hayhoe, to Newmarket. Markham was to manage the stud at Crafton for twenty-five years, and Mayer was set on course to become one of the most successful racehorse owners in the country – thanks, in no small part, to an inspired purchase.[82]

Bred in 1851, King Tom (by Harkaway out of Pocahontas), a bright bay more than 16 hands high, was acquired by Mayer in 1853 from Captain Thellusson for a hefty £2,000. The next year King Tom (Charlton up) finished second to Andover in the Derby – 'Had the Baron's horse been quite fit, it is just on the cards that he would have won'. Subsequently, he did not win Mayer much prize money; of the six races he ran, he won three. But from 1857, when he was put to stud, King Tom sired a string of successful and valuable progeny. Of the 170 foals he sired from 1857 to 1863, for example, 56 turned out winners, with 24 two-year-old winners. Outstanding among the two-year-olds was Mayer's colt North Lincoln, who excelled at trials before the Criterion Stakes of 1858.[83]

During the season of 1864 Mayer scooped £11,320 in prize money, second only to William I'Anson, the owner whose Derby victory with Blair Athol that year took his prize winnings to £15,686. It was noted that Mayer's winnings were 'made up entirely by King Tom'; and that twenty-eight of that season's winners – 'not only of the highest quality, but also of the best stakes' – were by King Tom. A year later, having been to inspect Mayer's racing stud, a visitor described Mayer's stallion as 'the most powerful thorough-bred horse alive', and King Tom's foals 'as near perfection as is possible to arrive at'. Mentmore was even dubbed 'the seat of King Tom'.[84]

Three of many winners under the Rothschild colours that King Tom sired were Tomato (out of Mincemeat, a mare purchased by Mayer), who won the One Thousand Guineas and the Ascot Stakes in 1864; Hippia, a filly out of Lionel's Daughter of the Star (a mare that Nat always fancied), who won the Oaks (Johnny Daley up) in 1867; and Restitution, who in 1869 won the Goodwood Cup (Daley up, and 'very easy' according to Mayer), as well as the Brighton Cup. The latter trophy was described in the press as 'decidedly the handsomest racing prize ever given in this country', and Mayer had a special train waiting to take it up to London. The Goodwood Cup trophy, though, struck Mayer as 'an ugly piece of plate, like a public house pot', and he noted that the Duke of Richmond's party had backed the favourite and lost.[85]

Hippia belonged to Lionel, and when Charlotte, who disapproved strongly of racing and betting, heard of the Oaks victory in 1867, she was racked by the thought that someone outside the family might learn the true identity of Hippia's owner, who, she insisted fancifully, 'has nothing on earth to do with racing, thank God for it'. Lionel in fact had a small racing stud at Gunnersbury, and by 1851 had at least three horses – two colts and a filly – in training with John Scott at Whitewall House. Lionel's colt Middlesex (by Melbourne, out of Evening Star) ran, but was not placed, in the Derby that King Tom lost to Andover; and his Gunnersbury, a son of Hippia, proved a valuable sire. After 1853, Lionel would now and again send his horses down to Crafton, and thence to Newmarket for training with Hayhoe.[86]

Like King Tom, Emerald, the filly Mayer had bought with the proceeds of his lottery win at New Court, did not win her owner many prizes, but as a brood mare she proved an excellent investment. Mentmore Lass, winner of the One Thousand Guineas in 1853, was a daughter of Emerald, as was Hannah (by King Tom), who in a single season was to win the One Thousand Guineas, the Oaks and the Leger, Charlie Maidment up in all three. Mayer considered it 'a great thing to win a Leger & quite as difficult as to effect a Derby'. A third of Emerald's daughters was Corisande (a sister to Sidonia), who in Hannah's great season was ridden to victory by Maidment in the Cesarewitch. From Zephyr, Hannah's sister, Mayer bred Favonius (by Parmesan), reckoned to be 'perhaps the most valuable horse in the world', who was to win the Goodwood Cup and the Derby.[87]

Race victories aside, Mayer chalked up another first when he became the first Jew to be elected to the Jockey Club, where it was almost impossible not to be on terms with the rich and the influential. 'Look at the Jockey Club and Private Stand,' it was exclaimed one Derby Day, 'on which you may discern Cabinet Ministers, great Diplomatists, able Chief Justices, learned judges, warriors, statesmen . . .' Lord Palmerston was a member of the Jockey Club, and in 1863 both he and Mayer had horses running in the Derby. Beforehand, Palmerston was overheard to josh Mayer for starting 'such a camel' as King of the Vale; Mayer riposted that his horse would beat Palmerston's 'scrubby little chestnut' Baldwin to a certainty. Palmerston got the best of it when King of the Vale tumbled over Saccharometer.[88]

Added to the shrewdness he demonstrated with racing, Mayer possessed other sterling qualities that impressed his uncle James. When preparing to send Alphonse to America in 1848, James was concerned that his son was too young to go on his own, and proposed that 'someone as resolute and efficient as Mayer ought to accompany him'. Mayer did not go; but from his few letters he emerges as someone with a sharper mind than Anthony, and also as one who was much less of a worrier than either Anthony, who was prone to headaches and illness under pressure, or Nat, who quickly became nervous, depressed and short-sighted in adverse conditions. During a period of concern about events on the Continent in the 1860s, Lionel's wife observed to one of their children: 'Uncle Mayer is cheerful, Uncle Anthony in a state of restlessness and dear Papa calm.'[89]

So Lionel had no qualms about leaving Mayer in charge of New Court, as he had done when attending Nat's wedding in Paris; and there is nothing to suggest that Mayer felt in any way flustered by the responsibility. If Hannah were available, he liked to discuss the state of the markets with her; otherwise, he could always consult his uncle Ben Cohen, to whom Lionel assumed that Mayer would in any case show the incoming daily correspondence.[90]

For four months in 1849, while Lionel was on the Continent with his family, Mayer, with Ben to hand, deputised for him. His sister Louisa hoped that Mayer was 'not too much bored by close attendance at the counting house'; his cousin Adolphe supposed that he 'must have plenty to do being alone in the Shop'. Anthony, helping out in Paris for several months, suggested cheerily: 'Be a good Jew & do not tup too much.' He also recommended Mayer to call on Prince Albert, in case the Prince had any news worth hearing.[91]

Preferring the country air, Mayer commuted daily from Mentmore to London by train. 'I assure you,' Anthony wrote to him from Paris, 'that I do not amuse myself but work so hard that all my hair tumbles off & the little gentleman does not stand.' But at New Court, where at times he found himself 'under an extraordinary press of business', Mayer made no such fuss. 'You write such short letters,' Lionel remarked to him, 'that you must expect short answers.'[92]

Whenever James was away from Paris, he always wished, said Nat, 'to direct the House as if he were at his Bureau'. Lionel, by contrast, believed that day-to-day decisions in business should be left to the man on the spot, so while he offered Mayer advice, he did not give instructions; and, thanks to what Hannah referred to as Mayer's 'arduous but satisfactory applications', all went well. 'I dare say, dear Mayer,' his mother wrote to him in November, '[that] you look forward to some release from your occupations but still you must be pleased and gratified at having gone through all the business for some time which you have done with so much satisfaction which I assure you I have heard expressed many times.'[93]

Hannah was even able to report to Mayer that his uncle Amschel, who was forever complaining about the attitude of the London and Paris houses to Frankfurt, was 'much satisfied with your business like employment and says he sees with much pleasure that you proceed in the same manner as your Friends to become a great Man of Business'.[94]

This was not so surprising. As his remark in the letter from Shrewsbury makes plain, Mayer regarded himself as a 'city merchant'. If anyone needed reminding of what he was, it was Anthony, not Mayer. When Anthony was left in charge at New Court in October 1851, Lionel wrote to him (with an echo of Nathan's advice to young Edward Buxton at Ham House): 'You will say I write to you all about things which you know just as well, but . . . I assure you, as long as one is in business, the only way is to attend very closely to it and not to neglect anything. One can never do two things – and you may be sure that it is only the business we do which makes us of importance . . .' Mayer took over from Anthony at New Court in November and December that year.[95]

It was Lionel, as senior partner, who as a rule directed affairs at New Court. He would sound out his brothers for their opinions, but it was he who made the decisions and looked after their interests. For example, he judged that the gathering of their uncles in Frankfurt for Matty's marriage to Willy would 'be a very good opportunity to speak about our money affairs and to ask for more. Let me know yr opinion and I will try to do everything you like.' For added support in London he had his uncle Ben and several dozen New Court clerks (who were paid from £50 to £550 a year).[96]

Anthony, as when he had worked on railway projects in France, was best suited to the role of a manager; he was, as his daughter Constance put it, 'of a naturally bright and cheerful disposition, ready to make the best of everything, satisfied with his round of daily duties'. A useful role, beyond signing papers on behalf of New Court, was found for him in London when, in the wake of the gold discoveries in Australia and California, in 1852 the bank took a long lease (signed by Anthony) on the Royal Mint Refinery, the running of which he oversaw, and which was very profitable. In its first year the refinery processed more than 300,000 ounces of Australian gold, and 450,000 ounces of Californian.[97]

In 1858, when Lionel finally took his seat in the Commons, Anthony also took his elder brother's place as Austrian Consul in London, a post for which Lionel had never shown much enthusiasm. In such circumstances, Mayer, though well able to pick up the reins at New Court when required, could under normal circumstances be deployed to further his family's interests beyond the Square Mile.

17

Most Painful of Complaints

A<small>T THE</small> HÔTEL he shared with his mother on the corner of the rue Taitbout and the Boulevard des Italiens in Paris, Lord Henry Seymour – an exceptionally fine fencer and boxer, as well as a great name in French racing – founded a gymnasium and fencing school. Nat, whose tutor Fritz Schlemmer had fenced and boxed, lived at rue Taitbout No. 40 and it seems as if in the early part of 1845 he may have paid Lord Henry's establishment a visit.[1] 'I have not heard from you for a very long time,' his cousin Charles wrote to him from Frankfurt in May, 'and hope to be soon favored with a line from your Lordship informing me that you are all quite well again and that your success on the turf has vastly contributed to brighten your spirits, and to make you forget all the ennui & uneasiness which the unhappy result of your fencing lesson has caused.'[2]

In March, Nat had had leeches applied to his temples and behind his ears on account of what his mother described as a 'severe cold' in the eyes. In early April, he was finding it hard to write and was unable to work; he was 'very nervous and indisposed', 'suffering considerably', and his eyes 'affected in an extraordinary manner'. In consequence, he was 'physicked & blistered', which, he volunteered, was 'no joke'. His French medical advisers, in whom he felt less confidence than in doctors in England, now attributed his trouble to 'rheumatism' and said, not very encouragingly, that they had 'had patients afflicted in this manner who have recovered'. The problem was most acute in the right eye.[3]

'With the right eye, wherein the affliction is I see double,' Nat told Lionel. 'When I shut either eye I see perfectly with the other but when I look to the right I see double & in order to see properly I am obliged to incline my head to the right. It is a very disagreeable thing. They tell me here there is no danger in it [,] that however it generally lasts 2 or 3 months.' Whether this trouble had been caused, or triggered, by the fencing lesson, or whether Nat's already poor vision had led to the mishap, or whether in fact the two were unrelated, is hard to discern. When he asked

Lionel to pass on his description of the ailment to William Lawrence, the British eye specialist, Nat did not attempt to assign the problem to any cause. Whatever the true facts of the case, the problem did not go away.[4]

In mid-April, confined to his room, Nat was obliged to dictate his letters to Charlotte: 'My good wife is kind enough to serve as secretary . . . I for my part pass all my days in my room listening to my good wife while she reads the papers, take my physic, and try to digest my vegetable fare.' By the end of the month he was 'going on a little better', but was 'not able as yet to write'. Having seen Nat a fortnight later, Anthony reported: 'His eyes are in a better state, his spirits are much better . . . He has got thin, but I don't attach any importance to that & please God with a change of air & some good English Roast Beef & a little of the Mentmore air he will certainly soon come round.' By then Nat had been visited by an English doctor, who considered that he would be well again 'in a very short time'.[5]

On 12 May, Nat wrote, in his own hand, to say that his eyes were 'very weak still', but that he was very pleased with 'old Drummer's performance yesterday. The old nag is a regular trump.' With Drummer (Flatman up), Nat had secured his first flat-racing victory of the season, a useful prize of 4,000 francs at the Champs de Mars meeting in Paris – the 'success on the turf' that his cousin Charles had hoped would brighten his spirits. A week later, on the point of escorting Nat and his wife to England, Anthony found his brother 'pretty well, but [he] still requires a great deal of care & cannot support the least draught & still requires to be very careful'.[6]

Fourteen months later, in July 1846, Nat's overall physical state had improved, but still his eyes were not right. 'I am thank God very well,' he wrote to Anthony, '& my eyes will I trust be better but as yet there is not much difference.' He was now writing from Wildbad, the spa town near Frankfurt, where he was undergoing a course of twenty-one baths – the side effects of which, at least, were making some difference. 'These waters have a wonderful effect and you my dear Billy if you were to take 21 would require a whole seraglio,' he reported. 'You have no idea of the vigor these waters infuse into one's blood – & the worst is the Doctors strictly prohibit bleeding one's monkey.'[7]

Having completed the water cure, he paid a visit to Professor Chelius in Heidelberg. 'Old Chelius found me better,' he told Lionel. 'I do not *see* much difference. He says however the benefit of the Wildbad waters is only visible some weeks after one has taken them.' Whether or not as a result of the Wildbad regime, by the late summer of 1846 Nat was obviously better. Shooting with him at Ferrières, Mayer found that he 'really knocks the birds over in very good style. He is as much excited about it as if he were shooting a wager.' A year later, Nat shot forty-five partridges in one day, his record bag for a day's partridge shooting.[8]

In early 1848, though, Nat had again a 'bad inflammation' in his eyes, serious enough to deter him from leaving Paris for a time. In July, made even more nervous by revolutionary events, he announced that he had 'lost all inclination for important affairs'. Later in the year he found that the 'shaking' of rail travel made him ache 'so terribly' that he did not like to undertake a long train journey. William Lawrence seems to have recommended that he should either spend the winter in Italy or by the sea; but as Nat did not like the look of the political state of Italy, and as the seaside did not suit his wife, they went to England – where by then his brothers were in indifferent health too.[9]

Shooting at Ferrières in 1846 Mayer had noticed that Anthony, in contrast to Nat, 'takes it more coolly. He can no longer walk. I think if he were to use his pegs a little more he would soon regain his perambulatory powers.' The following September, after shooting at Ferrières again, Anthony wrote to Lionel that he was 'in as bad condition as you are & could hardly walk'; and in the autumn of 1848, Nat regretted to hear that Lionel had 'walked so badly out shooting with H. FitzRoy'. Anthony recovered, but not Lionel; in December 1848 Louisa wrote to her eldest brother that she was 'very sorry to perceive by the last that you still suffered from your tiresome *tendency*, and that you are not so satisfied with the state of your health'. Louisa suggested he take some 'sea baths'; Lionel's doctors prescribed 'rhubarb powders'.[10]

One of Lionel's afflictions was gout, 'the complaint that attacks the limbs of grandees' as his wife defined it; or at any rate in the autumn he had had a swollen big toe. Nat attributed this to the consumption of too much turtle soup at Fishmongers' Hall, and he and his family were certainly aware that a simple diet had its advantages. When Lionel confessed to having eaten 'nearly a whole Strasburg pie' after a day's hunting, Nat was not surprised to hear that his brother was feeling 'an occasional tickling' in his big toe. But resisting rich fare did not come easily.[11]

James, whose guests were regaled with barrels of English turtle soup and oysters, was quite prepared to put up with 'a few hours' martyrdom' for the pleasure of 'devouring mountains of truffles and fresh foie gras, and bathing the repast in streams of champagne and Bordeaux'. Once, after he had been feeling off-colour for a few days, James was discovered by Lionel's wife lunching in his office in the rue Laffitte on 'first beefsteak with potatoes and then an enormous helping of lobster'. 'One must be well or nearly so,' Charlotte reflected, 'to venture upon such a heavy diet.'[12]

Anthony – who was considered by James to be a 'connoisseur in the art of cooking' and the most dependable judge of a chef – got away with eating what he liked longer than most; he had twinges of gout, but ploughed on, keenly interested in the fare prepared by his chef Caniret. 'Fat Bill is the luckiest fellow,' an envious Nat declared in 1849. 'He can tuck in as many truffles as he likes & drink as much Champagne & Claret whilst we poor devils must live upon rhubarb & soda water.'[13]

After a Davidson cousin from London had dined with Charles and Louisa in Frankfurt, he wrote to Anthony that he had eaten some *quenelles de volaille aux champignons* 'worthy of 2 Grosvenor Place'. On hearing that Anthony's friend the Duke of Cambridge had been invited to a Rothschild dinner in London, from Paris Nat sent a consignment of asparagus and 'fat poulards'. Anthony employed a cheeseman, Brown, and a Viennese confectioner – 'a celebrity' according to Charlotte – who, when he was on the point of leaving Europe to work for the ill-starred Emperor Maximilian of Mexico, had a last-minute change of mind and entered Anthony's service instead.[14]

At a 'grandissimo dinner' given by Chilly in Frankfurt in 1849, Lionel regretted that he did not have Anthony's 'good digestion' – 'or I should have tucked into a famous truffled turkey and a Strasburg pie'. Cutting out certain foods, though, did not mean cutting down. While Charlotte advised Lionel to stick to the 'plainest fare', she, and his doctors, liked to see him eat three 'simple but substantial' meals a day – a day that began with an early morning cup of chicken broth, followed by a breakfast of grilled sole, fried chicken, eggs, toast and tea.[15]

Under chefs Potel, Brie and Dolabelle the menu for dinner featured a variety of seasonal game: venison, hare, partridge and pheasant, grouse (to which Anthony was particularly partial), woodcock and snipe (Lionel's favourite game bird), ruffs and reeves, and ortolan buntings. 'I do not believe that Solomon in all his glory ever feasted upon *Ortolans farcis à la Talleyrand*,' Lord Macaulay ventured after dining at the Lionels' shortly before his death. 'I may observe in passing that the little birds were accompanied by some Johannisberg which was beyond all praise.'[16]

Larks, if desired, were obtainable from Dunstable, and wheatears (caught in turf traps) from the Sussex Downs. After Sir Joseph Paxton had 'feasted upon plovers' eggs' with Lionel and Charlotte one Sunday, he was given several dozen more to take home with him. Anthony bred peafowl for the garden – in 1864 he provided some for the gardens of Buckingham Palace, which he could see from the upstairs windows of his house in Grosvenor Place – and also for the table, though the more orthodox among his co-religionists would not eat it. In respect of one of Anthony's birds, which had been received and roasted by friends, the Chief Rabbi pronounced that although King Solomon sent peacocks to the Queen of Sheba, they tear their food and therefore should not be eaten – and so the roasted bird was disposed of, to the consternation of the younger members of the family.[17]

Vegetables and herbs of all kinds were grown in Gunnersbury's kitchen garden, under the supervision of head gardener William Forsyth, and fruit – grapes, peaches, pineapples and so on – in the hothouses.[18]

Lionel's swollen toe may well have been gout, but numerous ailments were in those days described as either gout or rheumatism. On hearing that Mayer was suffering from what Lionel described as gout in October 1849, the elder brother advised the younger to look after himself, and not to eat 'too many good things nor drink too much wine' and reminded him: 'You know my gout began with a stiff back &c . . .' And as Nat's 'cold in the eyes' was described by the French doctors as rheumatism, when Hannah wrote to Mayer in November 1849 it was to commiserate with him for falling prey to 'some attack of Rheumatism'; she could, she said, 'speak from experience of that Most Painful of Complaints'.[19]

Anselm, at that time, was suffering from what Anthony called 'the gout in his hands'. In 1850–51 Hannah Mayer had what Nat described as a 'gouty leg' – a swollen knee that Hannah Mayer herself attributed to 'rheumatism', and on account of which she could 'hardly move but for an occasional hobble'. In early 1852, Anthony reported from Paris that Chilly had had 'the gout in her stomach'; and in late 1852 Nat reported that Anselm had had 'a severe attack of gout in the eyes' – brought on by 'catarre [sic] in the bladder'. In the 1860s, Mayer was said by Lionel's wife to have 'gout flying about him, gout in the limbs, gout in the lungs, gout in the head'; by 1867 he had named one of his racehorses 'Water Cure'.[20]

By the time of the contest with Lord John Manners in the City by-election in 1849, Lionel's 'gout' was no longer confined to his big toe. Wishing her brother every success in the City, and referring to the great '*anxiety*' it was causing him, Hannah Mayer thought it 'no wonder' that Lionel's health had been affected. Chilly, after congratulating Lionel on his subsequent victory, added: 'But now I trust you will do something for the recovery of your health otherwise my dear Brother you will not be able to remain on your legs.'[21]

Following the by-election, Lionel, now with swollen knees and hands, went briefly to take a cure at Bath – the waters 'very soft & nice', the doctor 'talking rather fine', the cooking 'middling', 'very little to be seen' in the town – and then left with Charlotte and their children for Wildbad, where they met James, fit and sprightly, at the end of July. 'My gout is much the same,' Lionel told Anthony a fortnight later. 'I suffer a good deal about the shoulders and am very stiff but the Dr says the waters always bring out the pains & in a few weeks I shall be better.'[22]

Charlotte's account of his condition was more vivid. 'If we spent the whole day at home,' she told Anthony's wife in mid-August, 'I might sometimes forget to consider my husband in the light of an invalid, it is only out walking that he and I are inconveniently, sometimes painfully reminded of his infirmities; we walk along like tortoises . . .' They were still in Germany two months later, Lionel having been advised to consult a doctor at Gräfenberg, the hill spa above Freiwalden, near Wroclaw in Silesia. The doctor, Charlotte told Louisa, 'actually said that unless Lionel submitted patiently to the hardships and horrors of the water-cure in Silesia, he would ere long lose the use of his hands and feet, become hopelessly crippled, and never, during the whole period of his existence, be able to leave his armchair any more . . .'[23]

Nat and his Charlotte had been at Gräfenberg since June, and from his brother Lionel had already heard that 'the worst part of the job is the hardship of it'. Nat was wrapped up in wet sheets twice, rising to four times, a day for fifteen minutes; then came a bath in a 'huge tub the water cold as ice', then a walk, then a douche – 'the force of which you can not form an idea' – and finally a rub down. In a frugal diet, from which tea, wine and beer were excluded, bread and butter and cold milk featured prominently. The regime made Nat feel stronger, he said, but its effect was 'to bring out boils & pimples which in the technical language of the place are termed crises. I have already had an immense boil and have been generally complimented on the fortunate event. They tell me I am to have at least a dozen more. It may be good for the health but it is decidedly unpleasant.'[24] When James had been unwell three years before, he had 'had a dozen leeches put on his bottom' to suck out 'all the bad blood'. The boils and pimples that Nat experienced were similarly considered necessary, so Lionel was informed, to 'clear the blood'.[25]

When Lionel saw his brother at Gräfenberg in October, Nat had 'just had on his thigh a famous Boil nearly as big as an egg'. Heavily bearded and dressed in a short coat, he appeared to Lionel like 'a Hungarian Rebel'; but, though he walked with a stick, Nat seemed well. However, despite the doctor's dire warning reported by Charlotte, and notwithstanding the sobering prognosis that if he did not act soon he would in ten years' time be crippled 'like Lord Lichfield', Lionel was not prepared to submit to the

Gräfenberg ordeal himself – 'very hard work and by no means agreeable' – until he had consulted his doctors in London and had seen how he got on in the hunting field that winter.[26]

Ten days later, having rejoined his wife in Frankfurt, he had 'a regular attack of gout in the hand', the pain of which kept him awake at night. In London, Benjamin Travers prescribed a medicine containing colchicum to be taken in the form of powders (mixed by Messrs Allen & Co., of St James's) three times a day. Taken in conjunction with 'a pill' on alternate nights, this, Travers believed, would relieve the pain; but it was in 1849 that Lionel gave up shooting, and from then on his days spent hunting in the Vale were few in number. The Gräfenberg cure might possibly have brought him temporary relief, but it had a bad effect on Nat.[27]

When, after a whole six months at the spa, Nat returned to Paris towards the end of December 1849, he was 'very much out of sorts', 'not in the best of humors' and – as 'a great enemy of locomotion' – wanted 'more than anything else a little quiet and repose'. He felt 'completely useless', and was 'not up to the mark for a hunting trip' to England, a surer sign than anything that he was low. 'I have not occupied myself much with business since I have been here,' he wrote to his brothers on 1 January 1850. 'When one has been away so long & one's spirits [are] so depressed one does not feel much inclined to sit down by one's desk drawing little men & women on one's blotting paper & with nothing else to do.' When Edward Ellice's niece Marion, a family friend, saw Nat, she found him 'dreadfully altered'; he looked, she told Anthony's wife, 'as if he was just out of a long and painful illness'.[28]

The fact that Nat's presence at his desk in the rue Laffitte was now barely required can hardly have helped to lift his low spirits; and as Marion Ellice commented to Louisa, '*quel* rôle les nerfs jouent in all his ailments'. At the start of 1850 James's son Alphonse was twenty-two, and he had returned from America, Lionel noted, 'more of a man than when he left & [he] thinks a little more of himself'. So when in February 1850, Alphonse's brother, Gustave, attained the age of twenty-one, James had two sons, both of them fit and capable, to work alongside him. That Nat had been able to spend six months at Gräfenberg indicates that his presence in Paris was hardly essential; and, as if to confirm that, in mid-October 1850 James wrote to let him know that he was intending to change the name of the Paris house from de Rothschild Frères to 'J de R & Sons'. Nat saw nothing wrong with the idea and, although the plan was dropped, the notion was a clear expression of the changed circumstances. On 17 October, Marion Ellice reported that Nat looked 'well in health, but very melancholy'.[29]

Feeling fitter, Nat now planned a sporting trip to England: 'Mind I am to ride Voltigeur dear Billy the first day we hunt this year,' he wrote to Anthony. 'You must get up the shooting at Halton.' But on 30 November, on his return to the rue Taitbout from a visit to Ferrières, he found that the younger of his two sons, Albert, aged four, was 'very poorly'. Ten days later, having appeared to improve, the child had a sudden relapse. Nat was now 'much too uneasy to think of business', and Anthony – 'the best fellow in the world' – arrived shortly afterwards from London.[30]

On 17 December, the doctors were 'more satisfied with their little patient', but two days later, the one thing that they had been dreading took place: 'the water rushed to the brain'. Albert, wrote Anthony, was 'exactly in the same state as poor Mamma was the day before she was taken from this world. How long this child can last I do not know . . .' Three days later, on 22 December, Albert died – almost exactly seven years since Nat and Charlotte had lost an infant daughter, Nathalie, their first child, at the age of a few months, on 21 December 1843. 'Poor little Albert,' wrote Nat on Christmas Day. 'God's will be done. We must do our best to submit without murmuring.'[31]

Charlotte was then expecting her and Nat's fourth child, who was born on 28 March 1851. 'The little Arthur is a good big fellow, God bless him and protect him,' Nat told 'dear Mrs Lionel' three days later, '& is like all babies but the likeness finders say he resembles his Papa.' Lionel's wife sent 'a magnificent enamelled fish' as a gift for the baby boy; and both Arthur and his elder brother Jimmy were to survive well into adult life. A 'most magnificent boy' by the time he reached the age of ten, Arthur was affectionately compared by his close family to a 'mastodon'.[32]

Nat's brothers and their wives were spared the experience of infant mortality, and late 1851 found Lionel on a carefree holiday with his children. Leonora, the eldest, was now fourteen; Leo, the youngest, nearly six. They were staying with Charlotte's parents at Hemsbach, near Heidelberg, where Charles and Adelheid owned a house and some land. The house was beautifully situated, Lionel told Nat, the surrounding country very pretty and the air good. They pottered about, ate well and laughed. The children 'were very merry, danced and sang & all members of the family [were] in good spirits'. Lionel passed two days, he wrote to Nat, 'as pleasantly as one can, when there is no shooting nor hunting'.[33]

Nat, yearning for life in England, picked up on the latter theme a week later. 'Had I merely to cater for my own amusement,' he declared, 'I should like to establish myself at Aston Clinton with the great Baron's stud & show you the way.' He dreamt of owning an English estate, and thought of buying Alton Towers; yet had he been able to persuade his wife to live in England, a country life would not have suited them for long. London, as Lionel's wife once put it, 'offers more resources for an invalid than the country, which is bright and gay, but more suited to those who can walk and ride and pass the greater part of the day in the open air'.[34]

It was a view that Charlotte came to form with Lionel in mind, but the considerations applied no less to Nat. 'We all of us are no longer Chickens,' Lionel observed to a poorly Anthony in November 1851, 'and cannot do what we used ten years ago. I cough every now & then just like an old man, good for nothing.' And when Anthony saw their brother in Paris on New Year's day 1852, he reported to Lionel and Mayer: 'Nat does not look better.'[35]

Nat and Charlotte spent the months of July and August 1852 at Bad Gastein, where James, hoping to cure a bad knee, joined them. They had not been to Gastein before, but Nat had been told that the Gastein waters were 'stronger' than those at Wildbad. Now something of an expert on the comparative advantages of the various Continental spas, on hearing that Anthony had developed a 'nasty boil', from Gastein Nat wrote to recommend his brother to spend a few weeks at Homburg or Bad Kissingen, to the east of Frankfurt. And against the quality of the waters, there were other factors to be weighed in selecting a spa.[36]

Prior to fixing on Gräfenberg in 1849, Nat had pondered going to Wildbad, and Bad Homburg, both of them within easy reach of Frankfurt. Wildbad, in Lionel's estimation, was 'a very nice place for anyone who wishes to pass a few weeks in a beautiful country, to enjoy the most agreeable fresh air and to try what the Baths can do'. At Homburg, on the way to Wildbad, on the other hand, he 'met several old faces and many persons with whom one would not like to be very intimate anywhere else . . . so many wornout doubtfuls and gamblers, that however good the Baths may be I could not remain there'. Mayer, paying a flying visit to Homburg during his honeymoon in 1850, found the place 'very full of second rate people & there was nothing distinguished or pleasing'; the main hall was 'very crowded with ugly people & the breezes were none of the most refreshing'. James and Anthony liked it, nevertheless: in the 1860s the Kursaal restaurant was run by Chenet, a chef who was compared to Soyer, and not everyone who went to Homburg was so second rate.[37]

Staying there with his family one summer (and experiencing a bad attack of gout in his arms), Anthony welcomed the arrival of the Duke of Cambridge, who appeared with 'a little gout & most famous red nose'; the Prince of Wales arrived a few days later. The decoration of some of James's apartments in the rue Laffitte reminded Lionel's wife of Homburg's gambling rooms – 'the gold & glaring colours on the walls & ceilings positively hurt my eyes'.[38]

A drawback to Gastein, Nat concluded, was that its remoteness from any 'civilised places' meant that he only received his post at irregular intervals; he felt as if he were staying 'in the mountains of the moon'. Gastein was, he said, 'the most beautifully romantic picturesque place in the world', but at the same time 'most boring', the 'dullest of watering places'. His stay there was also blighted by a brief frenzy of anxiety about his sight; having jabbed himself in the eye with a comb, he feared losing the sight of that eye. A further frustration was that, as at Wildbad, he found the Gastein water cure made 'one's prick stand most infernally' and that, again, it was 'strictly forbidden to make use of the old gentleman'.[39]

From Gastein, he and his wife migrated to Brighton, where for September and October they put up at the Bedford Hotel. Hannah Mayer and Henry were staying nearby, Henry complaining of liver trouble and 'looking very unwell . . . as yellow as saffron'. Nat, however, felt fit enough to go out with a local pack of harriers. He had a 'capital gallop'; but when out for a ride the next day he was thrown from his horse – somersaulted clear over the horse's head – when jumping a 'trumpery little hedge'. He picked himself up, and afterwards felt none the worse for it; but the incident, he confessed to Lionel, did not encourage him to attempt staghunting – 'the muscles of my thighs & seat of honor are sadly out of order'.[40]

It may be that this incident lies behind the theory advanced in the past that Nat's health problems began with either a riding or a hunting accident. Over the years he had a fair number of bruising falls from his horse, as did Mayer. 'Baron Nathaniel cared nothing for falls,' it was said in the sporting press, 'and twice in one season he swam the canal between Tring and Aylesbury.' Yet neither Nat's nor any of his brothers' letters suggest that he suffered any serious long-term effects. Lionel's infirmities were attributed by an acquaintance to the fact of his having too often remained for too long in damp clothes as he inspected his hounds after a day's hunting, but this seems to be no more than guesswork.[41]

In November 1852, having returned to Paris, Nat was going to the office 'merely to read the private letters & enquire how the rentes are & read the papers &cet'. He could think of almost nothing but his health: 'I only wish I cd get well.' Having looked forward to 'an immense destruction of pheasants & hares' at Ferrières, when it came to it he did not enjoy the shooting at all; indeed, he said that he did not intend to go out again.

'Alphonse will write you about business as I follow yr advice & bother my head very little about it,' he wrote to his brothers as the end of the year neared. 'I think of beginning with another water cure tomorrow which is not very agreeable but I can not remain as I am & do nothing but take Watson's acid medicine.'[42]

The cure now in prospect was in Paris, at Bellevue, to which Nat could go from home twice a day. 'I hope you spent yr Xmas day merrily & consumed plenty of turkey & plum pudding,' he wrote on 26 December. 'Here I lead the most monotonous life in the world & tomorrow my water cure will begin to hose me famously as I shall have to go morning and evening to Bellevue.' At the end of December 1852, having informed his brothers that he did not wish to pursue the idea of buying Alton Towers, he went on: 'To tell you the truth in my present state of health a country seat wd be of little advantage to me.'[43]

Having given up the idea of an estate in England, in 1853 Nat instead bought a vineyard in the Médoc – Château Brane-Mouton, near Pauillac, which he renamed Mouton-Rothschild. Like his brothers and cousins, he had as much of a taste for fine wine, and for good cigars (Anthony's cigars were manufactured to his specification in Havannah), as he had for rich food.[44]

In Brighton the year before, having already made 'a great hole' in Lionel's cellar, Nat had asked his brother to arrange to send down some champagne and hock; and for Paris he ordered butts of sherry from London (to be declared as Madeira, not sherry, at French customs). German wines could be obtained from the family in Frankfurt. From Anselm, Mayer received a supply of Steinberger for his cellar at Mentmore in 1846; and in 1852 Charles sent his London cousins four dozen bottles (two dozen for Lionel, a dozen each for Anthony and Mayer) of 1846-vintage Johannisberg – 'the best Johannisberg there is' – and a further fifty bottles that had been requested by Ben Cohen. But claret was the wine of most interest.[45]

Volunteering to help Mayer stock his cellar at Mentmore in 1847, James sent his nephew fifty bottles of a good Château Lafite; and before he bought Brane-Mouton (one of Lafite's neighbours in the Pauillac commune) Nat would send Mayer at least six dozen bottles of Lafite a year, possibly hoping to drink some of it himself. '25 minutes on Voltigeur across the Vale wd do me as much good as a dozen bottles of claret,' he wrote in early 1852. 'I make a great consumption of that sort of wine, just 1½ bottles a day.' Mayer went in for mulled claret as well, and was noted for his fondness for champagne.[46]

Nat's acquisition of Brane-Mouton was part fulfilment of a long-held family ambition. His uncle Charles had expressed an interest in acquiring Château Lafite in 1830. On hearing, via James, that the vineyard was to come on the market, Charles explained to Anthony that he wanted 'an Estate which will give me better interest than other placements now that money is abundant & public securities dear'. Anthony, having developed a taste for Margaux, had hoped that one of his uncles would buy the Château Margaux estate in 1842; and James finally bought Château Lafite (which became Lafite-Rothschild) in 1868, a year after Lionel – who kept his cellar at Gunnersbury well stocked with Margaux – had been alerted to the forthcoming sale of the Saint-Estèphe vineyard of Cos-d'Estournel.[47]

Lionel did not proceed with Cos-d'Estournel, but Nat had no cause for regret in respect of Mouton. As well as a source of good wine for family drinking, Mouton-Rothschild turned out a profitable investment. A decade after acquiring the estate, for which it was later reported that he had paid 1.2 million francs (James paid 4.14 million francs for Lafite), in November 1864 Nat calculated that, after deduction of all expenses, sales of Mouton wine that year would leave him with 'about 250,000 francs clear' – especially useful at a time when the foundations were being dug for an immense new house he was building in the rue du Faubourg Saint-Honoré (No. 33), for which he imagined he would have 'plenty more to pay'. Six years later, the Mouton-Rothschild estate was valued at 2.5 million francs.[48]

Lionel paid a visit to Nat's vineyard in September 1859. Charlotte, who was holidaying on the Isle of Wight, heard that all the talk had been of 'important questions of vintage, and also the respective merits of rival clarets', and that the garden of Nat's agent at Mouton was 'full of pomegranate and fig trees, and fat little ortolans fluttering about among the crimson flowers, and the honeyed fruit'. Despite such attractions, however, there is no record of Nat himself ever having visited his property in Bordeaux. When Lionel's wife saw him in Paris in August 1857, the state of his hands was making it difficult for him to eat, and the condition of his legs made it hard for him to stand; he had become 'the poor invalid'.[49]

In the public arena, two accomplishments contributed to enhance Lionel's standing in the 1850s. First, in 1855–6 New Court raised loans for Britain, France and Turkey totalling more than £66 million – approximately £30 million each for the British and French governments – to pay for the Crimean War. From the British angle, this was the first major loan to be issued by the government since the loan to compensate the slave-owners, raised by Nathan, in 1835. Secondly, in July 1858, flanked by John Abel Smith and Lord John Russell, Lionel finally took his seat in the Commons – where neither he nor Mayer, who joined him there the next year, ever spoke.[50]

On the private side, in the second half of the decade Lionel commissioned a gigantic new house in Piccadilly, to make way for which his own house and the house next door (No. 147) were pulled down; and he and Charlotte saw their eldest daughter married off to the most eligible male Rothschild.

Leonora's marriage to Alphonse took place at Gunnersbury in March 1857. After the religious ceremony, which was conducted by Dr Nathan Adler, Solomon Hirschel's successor as Chief Rabbi, there was a banquet, with music provided by the band of the First Life Guards. Count Persigny, the French ambassador, proposed the toast to the bride; Benjamin Disraeli, by now a former Chancellor of the Exchequer, proposed a toast to the health of James and Betty; Lord John Russell proposed the health of Lionel and Charlotte. A ball followed, Alphonse and Leonora departed for Mentmore, and the festivities were detailed effusively in the pages of the *Illustrated London News*, the alliance of the young couple being described as 'one which may not inaptly be said to have an European interest'. The Ministers of Hanover and Belgium, the Duchesses of Bedford and Wellington, Lord and Lady Lyndhurst, John Abel Smith and J. T. Delane were among the guests whose presence was noted alongside 'the various members of the illustrious house of Rothschild'.[51]

Anthony, Nat and Mayer and their wives were all present, as were Hannah Mayer and Henry FitzRoy, Hannah Mayer being seated at the top table. Eight of the sixteen bridesmaids were Rothschilds: Leonora's sister Evelina, Anthony's daughters Constance and Annie, Mayer's daughter Hannah and four cousins from Frankfurt. Representatives of the elder generation of the family, however, were few in number: James's brothers Amschel, Salomon and Charles had all died in 1855, as had Charles's wife Adelheid in 1853 and Salomon's wife Caroline in 1854. Anselm now ran the Rothschild bank in Vienna; Charles was at the helm in Frankfurt; and until 1863, when at his request he was bought out of the bank partnership and the branch closed, Adolphe filled his father's place in Naples.[52]

Leonora was nineteen when she married, but the idea of a union with Alphonse had been in her mother's mind for some time. 'Among us Jews,' Charlotte wrote in one of her journals in early 1854, 'I have seen no one, heard of no one superior, or even equal to Alphonse.' She found her future son-in-law more 'gentlemanlike looking' than handsome; he had a 'clever' face, and she liked the look of his mouth and the sound of his voice; he was well informed ('does not hide his knowledge under a bushel'); his conversation was 'natural, lively, varied and interesting'. What Charlotte did not like was what she perceived to be Alphonse's indifference to Leonora – but then, she reflected, 'the man whose passions are dead, whose feelings have lost all freshness, all depth, is likely to prove a safe husband and the wife will probably find happiness in the discharge, in the fulfilling of her duties. Her disenchantment will be bitter, but not lasting. Telle est la vie.'[53]

It is difficult not to suppose that Charlotte was drawing on her own experience of marriage, though Lionel's letters to her are full of expressions of love and affection for his 'dearest darling wife'. Six years into marriage he wrote from Paris that he hoped 'within twenty four hours after the arrival of this to have you in my arms and to tell you verbally how dear you are to me and how you are loved by your L. A kiss to all the chicks.' A year later, he asked Charlotte to 'kiss the children tenderly for me and very shortly you shall have a good many more from your ever loving husband L'. From Paris again in the summer of 1848, he concluded: 'Good bye dearest wife. I send you a thousand kisses & am your most *faithful* husband LR.' Yet such expressions of tenderness did not strike home; indeed, they were met with a kind of stubborn resistance.[54]

'Happiness,' Charlotte declared after almost eighteen years of marriage, 'such happiness as is independent of outward events & circumstances, can only be enjoyed by the scrupulous fulfilment of duty, and by the power of occupying every hour of the day with useful pursuits. In prosperity and adversity such power is invaluable. I hope I may be able to develop it to the utmost limits in my children. Worldliness & inordinate love of society spring in many cases from the inability of finding occupations for the whole day & every day of one's life. I thank God that such is not the case with me.' Leo, when aged fifteen and enjoying himself at Mentmore for the New Year of 1861, received a letter of good wishes from his mother, but not without an injunction to 'shake off any assault of that dangerous enemy idleness, and endeavour to earn a place in the cheerful ranks of the industrious and painstaking'.[55]

Rather than lower her defences to Lionel, Charlotte immersed herself in a life of earnest activity. A useful day was one spent 'vibrating between my kitchen for the poor and the [Jews'] Free School', with perhaps a visit to the Jews' Free Hospital at Sydenham. She collected money for charity, went to charity bazaars, and dealt with a deluge of begging letters, sometimes as many as fifty a day. Her average weekly post-bag in the mid-1860s amounted, she estimated, to more than 100 letters.[56]

Besides supervising the running of two houses, each of them with a butler and housekeeper (Getliffe and Mrs Cobham in London, Newman and Mrs Parkin at Gunnersbury), and when not writing to family members – in tones fond, concerned, disapproving, admonitory, indignant, gossipy, gushing, waspish, self-critical, self-sacrificing and dramatic – she worked diligently on her 'sermons to children'. These ('my poor sermons') were composed for the benefit of the pupils of the Jews' Free School, of which Anthony was the president and Matthew Arnold the school inspector; but they reached the ears of other children too. A niece of Charlotte's to whom one of the sermons was read every Saturday in Frankfurt, found them 'rather too high-flown and extensive for the purpose they are written for' and supposed that 'the poor children from the free school could hardly understand such brilliant and high language'.[57]

No matter how busy Charlotte kept, though, she was haunted by a sense of her 'insignificance and uselessness' – something that other Rothschild women had perhaps more concrete reason to feel. Salomon was an unfaithful husband, and for much of his marriage he and Caroline spent long periods apart, he in Austria, she in France. Anthony chased after women in Paris. Anselm, during the last decade of his marriage to Chilly, who died in 1859, lived mostly in Vienna, leaving his wife and children in Frankfurt; and earlier he had had an affair with Jane Digby, during the Munich phase of her enterprising romantic career. Divorced by Lord Ellenborough, the pompous opponent of Jewish disabilities relief, in 1830, and then deserted by Prince Felix Schwarzenberg, in Munich Jane became the mistress of King Ludwig I and married Baron Venningen, finding time for Anselm as well. After taking up with a Greek count, and finally settling down in Syria with a Bedouin sheikh, Jane long remained an object of fascination for Anselm.[58]

One thing that served to draw the discontented Charlotte closer to Lionel, for whom she never hinted at anything but admiration and affection in her letters to their children, was the ever more crippling effects of his 'rheumatic gout'. Severe attacks in the knees in the early 1860s necessitated his being carried up and down stairs; a lift was installed at his new house in Piccadilly, but sometimes he could not walk at all. Paying a visit to Paris in 1863, he declined to be carried up the stairs to see Nat, who, 'much shrunk and wasted', could not get down; but when Charlotte saw Lionel 'struggle through the room without any help at all' at the Bristol Hotel, she found it 'by no means a pleasant sight'.[59]

As Nat lost his sight and the use of his legs – by late 1861 he was already 'cut off from all the enjoyments of life which those who see and move can partake of' – his wife spent long spells away from him on expeditions, accompanied by drawing and music masters, to Germany, Switzerland, the South of France, Austria and Italy (sometimes for the whole winter). As her embonpoint steadily increased – she would crave almond puddings from London – she took cures at a succession of spas (Vichy with her mother, Homburg with the Duchess of Manchester, Marienbad with the Queen of Holland) in a somewhat half-hearted struggle to lose weight.[60]

Nat was relieved to think that she was keeping herself amused (when at home she tended to complain about her health), and in her absence had for company a succession of well-educated young Englishmen whom he retained as private secretaries. As Lionel observed to Mayer, Nat was always 'delighted to talk about everything English'.[61]

Considered by Lionel's wife to be a 'good, but fastidious judge' of people, in 1863 Nat engaged the services of the 'lively and talkative' Robert Romer, who had just left Cambridge as senior wrangler. A future professor of mathematics, Fellow of the Royal Society and distinguished Chancery barrister, Romer would rise to be a Lord Justice of Appeal. Having married Betty Lemon, daughter of Mark Lemon, the founding editor of *Punch*, before leaving Nat's service in 1865 Romer arranged for his brother Frank, from the War Office in London, to take his place.[62]

Lionel's wife, in contrast to Nat's, was constantly at hand to attend to her husband's welfare and needs; except for visits to Paris for the birth of Leonora's children, she seldom left Lionel's side. At Gunnersbury and in London she monitored his regime of 'exhausting baths' and massage sessions ('shampooings' and 'rubbings', bearable to the patient if administered by a Swedish masseuse); and she accompanied him during lengthy sojourns at the English seaside, to which Lionel was sent for the saltwater baths, the coastal climate and the sea air. Although Charlotte found the seaside 'distasteful and disagreeable', she was determined to be selfless, and went so far as to regret that 'all the aches and pains of the family' had not been visited on her. 'I could have borne them so well,' she said to Leo, 'and I should have been so delighted to see Papa free from suffering.'[63]

With the railway, Brighton was even more convenient than in Nathan's day, and in the 1860s Lionel and Charlotte were regular patrons, during the autumn and winter months, of the Bedford Hotel, from which an attendant would wheel Lionel off in a bath chair to inspect the 'excursionists' and to pass the time of day with friends down from London.[64]

But with the growth of the railways, other seaside resorts were within easy reach too. After illness had kept him away from New Court for most of July 1862, from late August to mid-October Lionel took Charlotte,

Evelina and Alfred to stay at Folkestone, at the Pavilion Hotel, where Mayer and Juliana were staying in 'the grand rooms' with Hannah, who had an abscess in one of her legs. Alfred, who was convalescing after an operation to have an abscess drained, travelled down from London Bridge station in a special 'invalid carriage' that had been added to the train.[65]

Saddle horses from London went with them, and in mid-September Lionel managed a ride along the beach to Saltwood Castle and back – after which Charlotte sent for chestnut oil to rub into his knees. By early October swollen legs made it impossible for Lionel to pull on his boots; and as Charlotte considered a railway journey in slippers to be 'out of the question', they stayed on at Folkestone, confined to the hotel, listening to music from a band that played beneath their windows and receiving visitors.[66]

Lady Lyndhurst and her daughter called to see them; they reported that Lord Lyndhurst was 'better than he has been for a long time' (he died the next year), and passed on some Society gossip. William Makepeace Thackeray and his two daughters dropped by, Thackeray 'out of spirits' and bemoaning that 'the gingerbread of life has lost its gilding for him'. The Thackerays were particular friends of Anthony's family, and in *Pendennis* there appears a charming pen portrait of Louisa, despite the author's jaundiced views on Jews in general. Other friends and relations came and went. Matty, Willy's wife, offered to visit them provided that she would be able to find *kosher* food; Charlotte advised that there were no Jews in Folkestone 'but plenty at Dover, who will be delighted to cover the table of the pious Jewess with the choicest delicacies'. Once assured of being fed, Matty arranged to spend a fortnight at Folkestone, sharing a house with the Prince and Princess of Schleswig-Holstein, family friends of long standing in Frankfurt.[67]

When James arrived by the Boulogne steamer to see them for a few days, he was proud to report that of the 130 passengers on board he was the only one not to have been seasick. Lionel found him to be 'as active as ever'; but even the indefatigable James had begun to experience periodic bouts of 'gout in the eyes' that made him sensitive to light and required poultices and bandages to be applied. When Evelina visited Ferrières two years later, James had been 'suffering from great pain' and was being 'wheeled about in a little chair, ditto Aunt Betty, & they each had three attendants a piece to carry the bread & chestnuts for their deer, fish and birds'.[68]

Thinking of something to write about in a letter from Folkestone posed a challenge. One day Lionel was driven to report that Evelina had been eating too many walnuts. 'Once or twice one may commit an excess,' he advised Leo, 'but it will not do every day.'[69]

From Folkestone the party, joined for a time by Leonora, moved down to Torquay, for November, December and January, occupying rooms at Webb's Royal Hotel. For five weeks, stiff joints and swollen knees obliged Lionel to be carried up and down the hotel stairs. He and his family read the newspapers, went for little walks if feasible and, when the weather was fine, drove along the coast and about the surrounding country in pony-phaetons. Leonora and Evelina, both of them keen riders and drivers, had a day out with a local pack of harriers, though no hare was to be seen; when Alfred had a singing lesson, his teacher, 'Maestro' Campana, pro-nounced the pupil's 'natural organ' to be 'very fine indeed'.[70]

'The inhabitants of Torquay and the visitors here,' Charlotte was sorry to observe, 'have no particle of the loveliness which distinguishes the population of Folkestone.' But the Rothschilds' servants – menservants, ladies' maids (Charlotte's Augusta, Evy's Edwardes) and a groom (George) who brought the horses down from London – liked the place and found people they knew in the town: a French cook and a schoolmaster, an English butler, a hotel landlady from Frankfurt and an enterprising Turk from Paris who had opened a local shop. Charlotte thought that the Turk would have been better off opening a shop in Brighton.[71]

At a private villa with views out to sea – which struck Charlotte pleas-antly as 'perfectly Italian' – there was a lunch with the bank heiress and philanthropist Angela Burdett-Coutts, who in London occupied the house in Piccadilly previously owned by her grandfather Coutts and Harriot St Albans. On a visit to Miss Coutts one afternoon, Charlotte met 'three very prim and very silent old maids, with traces of tears and disappointments and regrets marking otherwise good features', and discovered that they were the daughters of Colonel Bradyll, who as a boy had sat to Sir Joshua Reynolds for a portrait – *Portrait of Master Bradyll* – that Lionel had bought at auction in 1846.[72]

A social evening entailed dinner and a rubber of whist with London friends, Lord Wicklow one evening, the Willoughby de Eresbys another. Asked if he had any Torquay news, Lord Willoughby replied that he had none, 'only that there is no one here'; but he offered to take Leonora and Evelina out fishing in the bay in his boat. When Anthony sent down some pheasants, Charlotte made a present of them to Lady Willoughby – who 'had not tasted Bohemian pheasants for forty years' but pronounced Anthony's to be even more delicious.[73]

Such periods spent by the sea were hardly exciting; but then, as Lionel resignedly conceded, one went there 'for one's health and not for amusement'. In 1863 one of his medical attendants, Dr Ferguson, predicted that he would be 'a rheumatic man all his life', but for Lionel there was at least the chance of some temporary relief from physical discomfort – something for which Nat, and soon Hannah Mayer, were obliged to give up hope altogether.[74]

A widow since Henry's early death in 1859, Hannah Mayer now lived alone in London, in Upper Grosvenor Street, with her daughter Blanche; after suffering from what Nat called 'scrofula', and following an exceptionally hard fall from his pony, her son Arthur had died an invalid, at the age of fifteen, in 1858. Further tribulation now followed.[75]

In late January 1863, Charlotte wrote to Leo from Torquay that Hannah Mayer had been 'suffering dreadfully from Rheumatism, not from her abscesses'. Well enough to make a trip to the Continent with Blanche in the summer, in November Hannah Mayer then spent a happy few days at Mentmore; she had 'never seen anyone so good tempered as Mayer', even though he was suffering from twinges of gout. By early 1864, however, Hannah Mayer had developed what Charlotte described as 'a large hump on her back as prominent as the hump of a camel, not a mere swelling, but a gathering'. While Lionel experienced 'coldness of limbs' and 'depression of spirits', in late February his sister's hump was 'perfectly enormous and quite hot'; Hannah Mayer was 'shivering and trembling with pain'.[76]

She was at the same time desperate to see Blanche married to a 'good husband' and to head off various suitors, Lords Loughborough and Courtenay among them, whom she thought undesirable and whom Charlotte considered to be no more than fortune-hunters. So she was greatly relieved when Blanche received a proposal from Sir Coutts Lindsay, Bt, grandson and heir of Sir Coutts Trotter. At thirty-nine, Coutts was twenty years older than Blanche, but he had a fine estate and £10,000 a year. He and his sister, Mrs Robert Holford, of Dorchester House, as well as his cousin, Lady Somers, were people to whom Lionel (Blanche's trustee) had no special objection, though Charlotte felt that the two women had 'sedulously fanned the flame' of attachment that led to the acceptance of Coutts' proposal by the 'affected and namby pamby' Blanche.[77]

As the wedding approached in June, Hannah Mayer was dangerously ill, unable to walk. She lay at home awaiting 'four necessary, but fatiguing evils, a lawyer, an apothecary, a surgeon and a physician'. The doctors pronounced her case to be 'not at all a hopeless one', though there was 'a piece of dead bone, a portion of rib, that must come away ere she can recover'. If she were ever to walk again, it was feared she would be 'very crooked'.[78]

Lionel, in the meantime, went to Garrard's to select plate as wedding presents from himself and from Nat; Evelina went with him and to look for a 'handsome ornament', perhaps a locket, to be given to Blanche by Nat's wife. James sent Alfred £150 to buy whatever he thought best for the bride. 'Every thing has become fearfully expensive,' Charlotte complained, 'and nothing seems to produce any effect – but we must do our best.'[79]

The wedding over, Hannah Mayer began to sleep her days away; codeine was prescribed to relieve her pain. By early October her condition was such that only on a good day could she sit up in an armchair, which she was able to do when receiving a visit from her sister Louisa. Towards the end of the month, now weak and exhausted, Hannah Mayer was 'delighted' and 'overjoyed' to see Louisa again; but so affected was Louisa by her sister's noticeable decline that she burst into floods of uncontrollable tears.[80]

By the end of November, Hannah Mayer had been suffering so much that Lionel was 'prepared for the worst'; Charlotte hoped that the 'chain of uninterrupted sorrow and suffering' would not be prolonged. For several weeks the doctors had been expecting death to strike at any time, and on 2 December Hannah Mayer finally faded away. 'Poor H.M., she had not a happy life, and suffered a good deal,' Lionel reflected. 'She like a good many others will soon be forgotten.'[81]

18

Follow the Baron

'I DO NOT KNOW whether Natty will be able to attend the Lord Mayor's banquet today, as poor Mr Solomon Cohen was not expected to live through the day.' Charlotte was writing to Leo from Brighton on 9 November 1864. 'It is true,' she went on, 'that your brother has never even seen him – but he is the eldest member of the Cohen family and the Lord Mayor's Feast is a public entertainment. Uncle Mayer, however, does not put off his expected guests.' The next day Charlotte wrote again: 'About midday dear Papa received the announcement of poor Mr Cohen's death, and that event sent Natty to Mentmore.'[1]

On 8 November Natty had celebrated his twenty-fourth birthday. That he had never met Solomon Cohen is an indication of the distance that had opened up between his family and its less consequential English connection. 'Tomorrow the Helberts dine with us,' Lionel had written to Leo a year earlier. 'Mamma thought it necessary to ask them once. We have invited 3 or 4 young men, our usual friends to meet them, no one particular.' Lionel Helbert, a first cousin on the Cohen side, acted as a broker to New Court; he talked 'rather fine', affected 'fine, grand manners' and so, while a brother and a sister of his lived in poverty, was dubbed the 'Prince of Stockbrokers'. To Charlotte he was 'perfectly insufferable', and to the Lionel de Rothschilds the Lionel Helberts were known as 'the Cockies'.[2]

When the brothers Gabriel and Maurice Worms, cousins through both Nathan and Hannah, returned to England in 1865 after twenty-five years in Ceylon, tea planting on an estate they named 'Rothschild', Lionel, Natty and Alfred were 'much startled' by their arrival. Nat, on whom the pair had called in Paris a few days before, had found them 'very funny fellows – the eldest one talks at railroad speed'. Charlotte was amused by Gabriel's non-stop conversation, but found him to be 'scarcely civilized in his appearance'; and as to his and his unmarried brother's prospects of matrimony, she could only wonder who would marry 'such old, hideous anglo-caucasian [Anglo-Jewish] Indians'.[3]

Later, Gabriel Worms returned with news of the Samuels, from whom, as from Solomon Cohen, the Rothschilds had drifted apart. 'He condemns the whole Samuel family,' Charlotte told Leo. 'You hardly know the individuals, but he says no one can have a conception of their stinginess – that they live more like dogs than human beings.' George Samuel remained a friend nevertheless, though when he arrived in Brighton to stay at the Bedford Hotel in the mid-1860s, Lionel, then in residence, had not seen him for some time. George, who had brought with him a 'whole cargo' of women, seemed to Lionel to have 'grown quite an old boy & [a] real made up dandy'.[4]

Cousins who did not bear the name of Rothschild had their place, but at the same time were expected to know their station. In May 1864, during a visit to Henrietta Montefiore at her house in Great Stanhope Street, Charlotte met a German relative (through one of her Rothschild aunts), Gustave Sichel, whose sister was now married to Joe Montefiore. 'What his object can be in coming to England beyond the very legitimate one of paying a visit to his sister I know not,' she commented to Leo. 'I hope he is not so completely deficient in judgment as to aspire to a Rothschild hand, and that Mrs Joe, to whom Uncle Anthony keeps complaining that his daughters are not yet married, is not weakminded enough to suppose that the Baronet could have thought of the said Gustave as a son-in-law. Aunt Lou was exceedingly cold to him; indeed she did not take any notice whatsoever of him, and today at a charitable meeting she said: "he is extremely ugly".'[5]

Yet a sense of obligation to non-Rothschild relations persisted; the Lionel Helberts were invited to dinner because 'relatives expect civilities', and the obligation went further than hospitality. The day after the Lord Mayor's feast in November 1865, Charlotte explained to Leo that although the list published of those present at the event contained 'the names of all the Rothschilds', not one of them had been there. The reason for this was the suicide, following ruinous financial speculation, of David Davidson, a cousin on the Cohen side. On hearing the news, Lionel had contacted John Delane at *The Times*, and Delane had undertaken to 'take care that the feelings of his relatives are not unnecessarily shocked' – adding: 'If his poor widow would like to get rid of her house in James Street, I should be very glad to take it off her hands.'[6]

Moses Montefiore's stern response to the Davidson tragedy made him seem a remote and archaic figure. 'Sir Moses, in a very religious frame of mind,' Charlotte recounted, 'was heard to declare that the unfortunate man, by cutting himself from life cut himself away from all claims on the affection, mourning, or regret of the family – but that is a view of the case which I could not adopt.' Anthony would go to the trouble of having pheasants 'sacrificed in the orthodox way for the table of his revered relative' (now in his eighties), but by the late 1860s he was weary of Sir Moses' 'old-fashioned punctilious politeness'.[7]

That it was the surname of Rothschild that counted had been made clear at the banquet following Leonora's marriage to Alphonse at Gunnersbury. As Evelina's marriage to her cousin Ferdinand approached in 1865, the bride's mother, finding it 'a great bore to be obliged to ask all the family, whom one never sees on ordinary occasions', was troubled that whereas at Gunnersbury, for Leonora, 'the non-Rothschildian relatives were in the further room', at the new house in Piccadilly, the setting chosen for Evy's wedding, those relatives would 'be in view, and they are not fascinating'.[8]

Cousins not blessed with the Rothschild name were inclined to trade on the family connection. When Baron Henry de Worms (later Lord Pirbright), a son of Nathan's nephew Solomon Worms and his wife Henrietta Samuel, was reported to be giving 'grand entertainments' at Cowes in August 1871, Natty heard that de Worms and his wife 'as usual have aired their relationship to the House of Rothschild'. No connection, however tenuous, went unadvertised. When Clarissa Bischoffsheim, whose husband Henri was to make a fortune from banking, put it about that her sister was engaged to a cousin of the Rothschilds, the claim was far-fetched. The prospective bridegroom's father, Charlotte pointed out, was 'first cousin to our third cousin [Hermann Goldschmidt], who is chief clerk in the Vienna house. It seems there are people who think an immense deal of our name.'[9]

Lionel heard that 'the sister of Mrs Bisch intended for our Goldsmid [sic] is not the pretty one'; and had Mrs Bischoffsheim been aware of Charles de Rothschild's views on Jewish clerks she might well have kept quiet about the whole thing. 'You have no idea how disagreeable it is when every moment one of the clerks leaves the House, either to become the manager of a bank or for the sake of establishing himself on his own account,' Charles wrote to his London cousins from Frankfurt in the 1870s. 'Jews with their terrible ambition are the worst employees . . . they merely want to poke their nose everywhere and try to find out as much as they can to cut their stick when it suits their purpose. There is not a good clerk to be had and I assure you it is a perfect nuisance.'[10]

A sense of their own importance on the part of Lionel, Anthony and Mayer was apparent in their dealings beyond the family. The same bystander who observed their presence on Change on Tuesdays and Fridays in the early 1850s gave a cautious airing to the notion that in their business dealings there might perhaps be 'a little more show of "proud imperiousness" than was customary with the father', and that that might be explained by 'their consciousness of wealth'. Qualifying his remarks carefully, he went on: 'The father was, in great part, the constructor of his own fortune, and therefore had not imbibed the prejudice of persons born with over-flooding riches; which is precisely the reverse of the case with the sons. This is stated of them in some quarters, but there may be no solid foundation for the assertion, and envy may have raised the rumour for the gratification of a certain picque.'

A remark once made by Ferdinand suggests, though, that Lionel's attitude to business could certainly appear grand, even if it was in fact governed by nothing but good sense. 'As far as my opinion is concerned,' Ferdinand wrote when a state loan was in prospect, 'I know that you are not fond of dealing with such small states as Portugal . . .' The grandiose social tastes and attitudes of the younger generation of Rothschilds, on the other hand, made an impression even on Lionel and his brothers.[11]

In February 1864 Mayer 'quizzed Alfy respecting his presumed adoration of Duchesses, and declared the Mentmore parties were not sufficiently "swell" to win the honor of his presence'. In July, Lionel noted that Alfred and Evy had enjoyed a dinner given by the Duchess of Montrose, followed by a ball given by the Duchess of Sutherland. 'They go to such crack parties,' he said, 'that they get quite spoilt and only like the cream of the cream.' Five days later Natty and Alfred, who had both been up at Trinity, Cambridge, with the Prince of Wales and had got to know him there, joined the Sutherlands at Chiswick for a party at which the Prince was expected. So blasé did the younger generation become, though, that at times even the prospect of the cream of the cream could not stir them.[12]

In February 1865, when Natty and Alfred were asked to a small dance in honour of the Prince and Princess of Wales given by the Marchioness of Ely, Lady of the Bedchamber to Queen Victoria, Evy and Ferdinand were asked as well; but while Evy telegraphed to Paris for 'a snow-white dress from Worth', Ferdinand announced that he would only go to the dance for an hour. And in May 1865, when Natty, Alfred, Evy and Ferdinand were all due to attend a party given by the exiled French royal family for the Waleses at Orleans House, Alfred alone could summon up the energy to go. 'Ferdy is tired,' Charlotte told Leo, 'Natty equally so, consequently Evy will not go, and Alfred will be the only representative of the Lionel branch of the R family; but Sir Anthony takes his young ladies, and it is always an advantage that some of the Rothschilds should be seen.'[13]

The elder Rothschilds' staple social round was comparatively modest. In London or at Gunnersbury, family dinners would frequently be augmented by the presence of one or more members of a small group of intimates – John Delane ('JD'), 'the great editor'; the statesman Charles Pelham Villiers ('CPV'), Lord Clarendon's younger brother and, according to Charlotte, Lionel's 'best friend'; the liberal politician Bernal Osborne ('BO'), 'the great wit', who considered Lionel to be his best friend; the engaging homeopathic physician Frederic Quin, 'a good-natured old tuft hunter and humbug', who attended on the Duchess of Cambridge; John Abel Smith, and the Disraelis. They were all people from whom Lionel, now mostly confined to a wheelchair, hoped to hear something. 'Tonight CPV and JD dine with us,' he wrote in November 1863, 'so we shall hear all the news.' But inevitably he was sometimes disappointed. 'We had a little dinner yesterday,' he told Leo that December; 'it was like all parties, they ate & drank famously but said nothing new.'[14]

With or without anything to report, though, the intimate friends were made welcome. For Evy's birthday dinner on 25 August 1864, Delane, Villiers and Quin were invited to join the family circle. Delane and the Disraelis had attended a small Rothschild dinner on 2 August; Delane and Osborne had been to dine on 9 August. And should they have no intelligence to communicate, such friends could at least keep their hosts amused. 'Last night we had our usual two guests to dine with us CPV & BO,' Lionel recounted during the aftermath of the Reform Act of 1867; 'the former talked a good deal and after dinner amused us by going on against the Aristocracy who have had a most famous slap in the face, which they will never forget.'[15]

Members of the group of intimates were almost as likely to be found dining, or staying, with Anthony or Mayer as with Lionel. Present at the first dinner party given by Anthony and Louisa at 2 Grosvenor Place Houses were Charles Villiers ('in high form') and Bernal Osborne (who 'ranted'). Villiers, Disraeli, Delane and Smith all subsequently became regular recipients of Anthony's hospitality in London and the country. The Disraelis were invited to stay at Mentmore in January 1863; and having paid a visit to the Lionels at Brighton in the autumn of 1864, Osborne set off to stay with Anthony at Aston Clinton, with plans to move on to Mentmore the following week.[16]

The high standard of hospitality that Anthony dispensed in London was a subject for talk beyond the close circle. When the Queen learned that Lady Ely was going to dine with Anthony at Grosvenor Place one evening in 1864, she remarked that her ladyship could 'be sure of having an excellent and most enjoyable repast'. Mayer's table, and the company to be found around it, had less allure – though the table itself might be adorned with 'the finest Sevres' and 'flowers enshrined in the marvellous china [that] would have made a garden of Eden sweet and brilliant without any ornament'. After Quin had once dined at 107 Piccadilly, he pronounced the dinner, so Charlotte reported to Leo, 'to have been excellent and delightful, although as a rule he thinks that Uncle Mayer's repasts are the least successful of the "Trois freres"'. In 1867, Andalusia Molesworth, the socialite widow of the liberal politician Sir William Molesworth, Bt, reportedly met 'such non-attractive guests at 107 that she does not believe herself obliged to return good for evil, charming society for ugly unpleasant company'.[17]

A reliably glamorous assemblage, sprinkled with the close friends, gathered at the larger dinners that Lionel and Charlotte regularly gave, when parties of twenty-six were the norm. After two Jewish women had once complained to Charlotte that it was difficult to be admitted into 'London society', Charlotte replied: 'Not at all . . . whoever wishes to appear in the world must either get into parliament, or give twenty-five grand dinners in the course of a year.' Dukes and duchesses featured quite as much at such dinners given by Lionel and Charlotte in the 1860s as they did in the Rothschild children's social lives of the period.[18]

Those accepting the parents' hospitality included the Duke of Cambridge; the Duke and Duchess of Manchester; the Duke and Duchess of Buccleuch; the Duchess of Sutherland; the Duchess of Newcastle; the Duchess of St Albans, her son the Duke (who had been at Cambridge with Natty and who married Bernal Osborne's daughter) and his sister Lady Diana (a friend of Evy's); and the Duc and Duchesse d'Aumale. Lord and Lady Clarendon were occasional guests, as were the Marquess of Hartington (politician and heir to the Duke of Devonshire); the Earls of Sefton and Cork (whose French was not up to scratch); Lady Mary Craven; Sir Robert and Lady Emily Peel; General Jonathan and Lady Alice Peel; the Gladstones; Prince and Princess Edward of Saxe-Weimar; Countess Wittgenstein; Count Apponyi; Count Nesselrode (who was 'violently sick after dinner') and a host of other aristocrats, ambassadors, diplomatists and politicians – as well as the socially adept Roman Catholic Archbishop of Westminster, Dr Henry Manning.[19]

Of the duchesses, the Duchess of Manchester was noted for her outstanding good looks. 'No one knows,' Vicary Gibbs wrote of her, 'how gloriously beautiful a woman can be who did not see the Duchess when she was thirty.' Towards the end of a state visit to London in 1867, the

Sultan of Turkey was asked which of England's ladies he admired the most; 'the Duchess of Manchester and the Queen' was his unhesitating reply. The Duchess of Sutherland was beautiful too. As hostess at a dinner in 1864, Charlotte observed how John Delane 'flirted the whole evening with the Duchess of Sutherland, taking no notice of any other ladies – a proof, if any be needed, that a combination of high rank and beauty is sure to exercise great power, even over the wisest of men, for the Duchess is not clever'. Anthony and Mayer had an especially soft spot for Lady Mary Craven (a beauty but no blue stocking), whom they enjoyed entertaining to lunch at New Court.[20]

Having accompanied the Grand Duke Vladimir of Russia and his suite to a dinner given by Lionel and Charlotte in 1871, Colonel Arthur Hardinge reported to his friend Colonel Ponsonby that among the thirty-six guests who 'sat down to an interminable banquet . . . the Darwinian principle of selection was perfectly developed in a matchless cluster of English beauty'.[21]

Qualities of a quite different order were manifested in the racehorse-owning, deer-stalking, homburg-wearing Caroline Montrose, who eschewed make-up, raced under the name of 'Mr Manton' and continued to style herself Duchess throughout two marriages (one to a man forty-six years her junior) subsequent to the Duke's death in 1874. Known as 'Carrie Red' for her red hair (and 'Six Mile Bottom' for her ample figure), the Duchess of Montrose stood no nonsense from jockeys or clergymen; but she was appreciated by Charlotte for her 'clear, soft, joyous voice' and for the fact that she was 'very domestic and maternal in all her sayings'.[22]

Neither a pleasure to look at nor to listen to, but borne for the sake of their husbands, were Disraeli's wife ('his decidedly worst half') and the wife of the liberal politician, and *Times* leader writer, Robert Lowe. Mary Anne Disraeli was variously 'an immense bore', 'ill-dressed', 'in boastful humour' and 'perfectly odious'. Georgiana Lowe – 'the formidable and dreadful Mrs Lowe . . . wrapt up in a flowing white opera mantle and carrying a flower garden of royal lilies, and an orchard of cherries on her head' – never tired of the sound of her own piercing voice; and as Mary Anne Disraeli chattered away, Charlotte 'wished her not at the bottom of the sea but in her own drawing room'.[23]

As with the intimate friends, so many of the guests who were invited to join a large dinner party given by one of the Rothschild brothers in London could expect to receive invitations, on other occasions, from the other two. 'I really think,' Charlotte confessed in 1865, 'that more than two

Rothschild banquets each week would be impossible as the same people would be constantly asked – and repetitions are not pleasant.'[24]

On the other side of the coin, returning hospitality that was acceptable to Anthony or to Mayer (Lionel seldom dined out) was not easy. 'Uncle Mayer did not like Lord Wilton's party,' Charlotte told Leo in 1867, 'he thought it was full – and that the dinner was not superabundant or even abundant enough. He bears his disappointment well.' The year before, Lady Molesworth's hospitality had been found wanting by both brothers. Anthony, satisfied with nothing less than 'first rate eating', was, said Charlotte, 'only half-satisfied with the entertainment which his hostess had prepared'. Mayer went further; he was 'so irate with the hospitable Andalusia for having asked him last season to a dreary party of the dullest, most tiresome people in London, that he has refused her ladyship's invitation for this evening . . . Uncle Mayer says he dines at Buckingham Palace today, prepared, of course, to find fault with every thing.'[25]

While short rations at a dinner party, as at Lord Wilton's, might spoil the evening for him, Mayer cannot very often have gone hungry. 'Last night we drove over to Aston Clinton,' Natty wrote to his parents in January 1863. 'I know not the respective weight of Juliana and Uncle Muffy, but I suppose together they must weigh 30 stone or more, suffice it to say the springs of Peter's contract Brougham broke and we had the most uncomfortable drive I ever had in my life.'[26]

From 1859 to 1864, during the construction of their new London residence ('Piccadilly House' to Lionel, 'Piccadilly Palace' to Anthony), Lionel and Charlotte gave their dinner parties principally at Kingston House, Knightsbridge, which they were renting from the Earl of Listowel. The house and its extensive grounds were later to be developed as Ennismore Gardens, named for one of Lord Listowel's subsidiary titles, Viscount Ennismore. A move to Ellesmere House, in Belgrave Square, was briefly contemplated in 1862, but in the event Lionel and Charlotte remained Listowel's tenants for five years. It was at Kingston House that in 1859 Lord Macaulay marvelled at the exquisite stuffed ortolans and Johannisberg.[27]

Building works at Piccadilly were nearing completion in the autumn of 1863. When Evy gave the Willoughby de Eresbys a tour of the site in October, they 'expressed themselves delighted with all they saw'. Although still unfinished internally (months of plastering lay ahead), the house was ready for part occupation in early May 1864; Lionel and Charlotte spent their first Sabbath there on 7 May. 'We have been very quiet till now at Piccadilly,' Lionel wrote to Leo, 'and have not yet had any friends to dine with us.' Friends, however, were soon dropping by. The orientalist Sir

Henry Rawlinson, translator of the cuneiform inscriptions at Behistun (Bisitun), admired the Persian carpets; the Duke of Somerset, 'though not an expansive man, thought the house beautiful'. One Saturday, forty-five callers 'came staggering in'.[28]

A six-storey Portland stone structure, designed by Nelson & Innes, of Whitehall, and built by George Myers, the house (since demolished) was 90ft deep and had a 67ft-wide Piccadilly frontage. On the ground floor a dining room and a library, each 36ft by 20ft, overlooked a terrace garden to the rear; a reception room on the first floor occupied the whole of the Piccadilly front; at the centre of the house an 8ft-wide white marble stair-case led up to the first landing and thence, dividing to right and left, by two further flights to the principal first-floor landing, all of marble.[29]

The house was equipped with gas lights, though Lionel found that 'the white marble looks so well at night that it hardly wants any lighting'. The staircase balustrade, which took three months to install, was made of silver; the dining room was gold. For daily dining, Charlotte preferred to use the library, reserving 'the somewhat sparkling room for festive occasions only' – one of the first and the happiest of which took place on 7 July 1865.[30]

Evy's marriage to Ferdinand was a match that combined true love with family approbation. Earl Cadogan wrote to say that he had heard the news of the engagement from Lady Ely, who had heard it from the 'happy couple' themselves. Lady Clarendon, who had recently had Leo to stay at The Grove, wrote to Charlotte: 'From what we have heard this marriage meets with your and the Baron's entire approval.' Lady Carrington judged that 'one thing must make it very agreeable to you & the Baron, & that is that you keep your dear child with [you] in this country'. Anselm simply deplored the fact that there was not an Evy for each of his three sons.[31]

While Leonora was admired for her looks – Queen Victoria was much struck by her appearance when she was presented at Court, and to her proud father she looked, *en grande tenue*, 'quite a Princess of Israel' – her younger sister was not so striking; but Evy was adored by her family, friends and future husband for her vivacity, sense of fun and good nature. Evy, said Charlotte in 1863, 'always enjoys admirable spirits; she is like the best Champagne, quite as exhilarating, but wholesome instead of pernicious'. When Evy and Leonora returned to the Bedford Hotel after a day's hunting near Brighton in late 1864, their mother observed: 'Laurie enjoys the fun more than Evy, but the latter never fails to bring home many little anecdotes to amuse dear Papa.'[32]

Thanks to Anselm's generosity, Ferdinand was able to shower Evy with jewels – a diamond riviere, a diamond tiara and a collection of pearl drops stood high on the list – and to buy a house in Piccadilly (No. 143) as the marital home. Her mother gave Evy an emerald parure; from her aunt Juliana came a cabochon brooch; the Duchess of Sutherland produced a ring mounted with a diamond and an emerald, each in the shape of a heart, surmounted by a ducal coronet.[33]

A flurry of family parties preceded the wedding. When Anthony became anxious that his entertainments, which included a ball, might clash with Lionel's, Evy thought that it might be just as well if they did clash, 'as it is utterly impossible to invite all the Rothschilds at one table without giving up hope of asking any strangers to meet them'. Although confident in the success of the Grosvenor Place ball (Anthony's arrangements being 'always so brilliant and so perfect'), Charlotte could not help but reflect on the misfortune that 'we Rothschilds are obliged to ask a great many non-ornamental people'.[34]

Disraeli, now First Lord of the Admiralty, the French and Austrian ambassadors and the Duke of Cambridge were among the guests who attended a dinner and a ball at 148 Piccadilly following the marriage. After the wedding, as Leonora and Alphonse had done before, the bridal couple left for Mentmore, where Charlotte paid them a visit ten days later. She found Evy 'as happy and cheerful as usual, talking of every body and every thing with the same unflagging interest . . . Baroness Ferdinand is just like Miss Rothschild, without a grain of selfishness.'[35]

In the course of a Continental tour that followed, Ferdinand and Evy spent several weeks in the autumn with Anselm at Schillersdorf; and by the time Ferdinand returned there alone a year later to visit his sick father, Evy was on the point of giving birth to their first child. On 22 November 1866, Charlotte observed Evy to be 'as merry as a cricket'. Four days later she wrote to Leo from Piccadilly: 'Ferdinanda dined here last evening, and was in wonderful spirits; so blithe and merry was she that dear Papa prophesied the infant would be ushered into the world between two peals of laughter.' But on 4 December calamity struck: Evy died in giving birth to a stillborn child, and her family was plunged into grief.[36]

'Sadder even than the day before,' Constance wrote in her diary on 5 December. 'Coming up to London and reading that terrible message in the paper. It was enough to arrive all trembling with fear and anguish. The house, all dark and shut up, confirmed our unhappy fear. And then, the sight of the mourners – oh, it went to my heart. Saw the bedroom, that gay, bright room with the motionless form on the bed, with the poor, tiny baby on the sofa. Oh, what a sight.'[37]

*

Two years earlier, James's third son, Salomon, a likeable, popular and promising young man who was known for his uncanny good luck on the horses, had dropped dead at the age of twenty-nine. His grief-stricken widow, Adèle, the eldest of Charles and Louisa's seven daughters, was so shocked that she could not cry; she felt that Salomon had been 'too good to live'. When Natty and Alfred arrived in Paris for the funeral, which Charlotte heard was attended by 3,000 people, James 'burst into tears . . . and sobbed convulsively'. A year later Adèle lost her much loved sister Clemmy, aged twenty, to tuberculosis.[38]

Less poignant, but more public, was the loss suffered by the family in 1868. In May, James wrote to his nephews that his health was 'very much changed' and that his doctor had forbidden him to travel; in August he was 'getting weaker every day' and could no longer write; in November, suffering from a bout of jaundice from which his doctor breezily predicted he would recover, he succumbed, aged seventy-six. Natty, Alfred and Leo attended the funeral.[39]

'I never saw such an assembly of people as came to the Rue Laffitte this morning,' Natty reported to his parents. '4,000 people passed through the Drawing room, they say there were 6,000 people in the courtyard and from the Rue Laffitte to Pere la Chaise the streets were lined 5 deep on both sides and not a carriage was to be seen.' For Alfred, James's funeral was 'more like that of an Emperor than of a private individual'. Nine months later, Leo found Alphonse 'delighted with the wonderful results of the last five years as during that time the Paris House have made over four millions sterling'.[40]

In December 1862 James and Betty had feted Emperor Napoleon III at Ferrières; salutes were fired, 900 pheasants were shot, and the chorus of the Paris Opéra sang under the direction of Rossini. In May 1868, prevented from travelling, James particularly regretted being unable to get to London for a dinner that Anthony was to give for the Prince of Wales. It would, James vouched, 'have been a great satisfaction for me, as his Royal Highness was always so very kind and amiable towards us'. Two months earlier, on 5 March, the Prince had gone down to Mentmore for a breakfast with Mayer and Juliana and a day's hunting in the Vale of Aylesbury with Baron Rothschild's Staghounds.[41]

Natty travelled down from London with the Prince and his party in the Duke of Sutherland's private saloon coach, which had been attached to the nine o'clock train from Euston. Mayer and Anthony met them at Cheddington station, and from there conducted them to Mentmore for a breakfast 'of all the delicacies of and out of season' – which, Natty observed, the Prince ate 'as if he did not mean to go out hunting'.[42]

When lunching with the Prince at Madingley during their time together at Cambridge, Natty had once been asked what a first-rate hunter up to 13 stone ought to cost. When he said £300, he was told that the Prince's three hunters 'cost exactly that amount' and so was not surprised that the Prince was always falling off. But for his visit to the Vale in March 1868 the Prince was decently mounted, on a chestnut called Paddy, and he went very well – 'and considering,' Natty wrote to his mother, 'that the pace was terrific and the best riders fell on every side, he was very lucky to escape without any accident at all'.[43]

From Aston Abbotts, where they were laid on the scent of the deer (one from Lord Petre's herd in Essex), the Baron's hounds 'flew away, up wind, like a flock of pigeons', with a field of more than two hundred horsemen in pursuit. After a run of an hour and three quarters, with a brief pause, to Ludgershall, 'having crossed the entire county of Buckingham', out of the two hundred riders 'the Prince and eleven others only were with hounds when the deer was run into, although some others scrambled up before he was finally taken'. Having heard how the Prince had ridden 'very forward through all the jumps', Lionel commented to Leo that 'it seldom happens that anyone going down into that part of the country for the first time where there are so many large doubles, escapes without one little fall. But all passed off well; it was an excellent breakfast and [a] first rate run & no crowd which the Prince was afraid of.'[44]

Present among the large field that day were 'cheery Sir Anthony Rothschild going best pace on his favourite Peacock', and Ferdinand's unmarried sister Alice, who, following Evy's death, had settled in England to be near her brother, taking the house next door to his in Piccadilly. Alice, Lionel was told, 'lost her hat at the first fence and rode all the day without one, racing & jumping over everything'.[45]

At the Epsom race meeting in May 1864, Mayer had shared his 'cake, mayonnaise and Champagne' with the Prince of Wales; in October 1868, he and Juliana entertained Disraeli, by now Prime Minister, at Newmarket. Leo, a great favourite with his uncle and aunt, was there too, and provided his parents with a brief sketch. 'The Premier,' he wrote, 'was in very good spirits and brought forth reminiscences of the turf & pleased all his racing listeners. Mrs D slumbered in a corner & then woke up rather silent. Dolabelle's dinner might have been better . . . The Heath was not so animated as usual, but all the turf magnates rushed round Diz and[,] mounted on the cob with leather gaiters . . . the noble chief was certainly worthy of admiration.' On 6 October they all watched Mayer's horse Restitution come a disappointing second in the Cesarewitch.[46]

Life at Aston Clinton and Mentmore was less crowded with the stars of the social and political firmaments of London. Bachelor clergymen from the surrounding parishes – men viewed by both Anthony and Mayer as desirable, and safe, society for their daughters – were much in evidence. After a dinner at Mentmore in November 1863, 'the guests played at a variety of "jeux innocens" – four vicars and four young maidens thought of each other and had to guess one another's thoughts, so there were peals of merriment'. Having spent a week at Aston Clinton in 1866, a Mrs Coleman, a friend of Betty's from Paris, declared herself to have been 'enchanted' by the visit. Of Constance and Annie, Mrs Coleman's aunt, a Mrs Finch, of Berkhamsted, had 'spoken volumes in favour of their goodness and popularity, adding – they are the most innocent and guileless young girls in the wide world – they walk, ride, drive, pay visits, drink tea over the entire length and breadth of two counties, chaperoned by youthful curates, and fascinating incumbents'.[47]

That the clergymen were as ready to accommodate one Rothschild household as the other could lead to bad feeling. When a county neighbour, a Mrs Bright, gave a small dance to please Constance and Annie, the girls and their mother went escorted by Maynard Currie, the Rector of Mentmore; Lionel Dawson Damer, the Rector of Cheddington, and Damer's young resident pupil, the Marquess of Huntly. Mayer, who had presented Currie to the Mentmore benefice and was very fond of him, complained crossly of Louisa and her daughters: 'They always take my clergymen.' Charlotte put this down to the 'childish jealousy of the Mentmorians with regard to their friends, whom they cease to like whenever they show the least particularity for any other member of the R family'. Mayer learned to keep the details of his Mentmore guest lists and house parties to himself.[48]

Louisa, like Charlotte, helped to teach the children at the Jews' Free School in London, and there she made a friend of Matthew Arnold, the school's inspector. Arnold and other men of letters, including Thackeray and G. J. Whyte-Melville (who, like Anthony Trollope, rode to hounds with the Baron's), were as welcome at Aston Clinton as were members of the core group of family friends from London. And such, at Aston Clinton, was the penchant for clergymen – and the interest in matters of religion, as well as literature – that even Samuel Wilberforce, the Bishop of Oxford, once excoriated for his remarks against the Jews made in the House of Lords, became an admired and honoured guest.[49]

Of a piece with the society they gathered around them, Louisa and her daughters took an active interest in local education, poor relief and good causes; but there was a limit to the familiarity they were inclined to encourage with the less fortunate. During a Scottish tour in 1866, they were all three 'somewhat shocked at the extreme condescension of the Prince and Princess of Wales, who not only gave balls to their stalwart bare-kneed pipers, but danced all night honoring with the touch of their royal hands the hard ungloved fingers of ghillies and red-haired serving lasses'.[50]

Anthony, possessing a *joie de vivre* and bonhomie that his wife lacked, was less staid – as his daughters became as they grew up. Leaving Louisa at home, in December 1869 Anthony took Constance and Annie to stay with the Earl and Countess of Leicester at Holkham, in Norfolk, where they joined a house party that included the Prince and Princess of Wales and the Duke and Duchess of St Albans. Although Anthony was disappointed by the food ('Eating *very* bad,' he was grieved to report), he was quick to enter into the spirit of the party, notably during dances after dinner. 'The Princess is the heart & soul of these dances,' he explained to Lionel and Mayer, '& the more noise & gayer that you are the more the Prince & Princess like it. As she thought that I made the most noise she chose me for her Partner.'[51]

Annie, who waltzed with the Prince, observed that her father 'was very frisky, and danced so well that the Princess invited him to dance the lancers with her; and under the royal tuition got on very well'. Constance, having put her experience in Scotland behind her, now looked forward excitedly to the Holkham servants' ball – not least because everybody was predicting that her pretty maid, Morrell, would 'have a great success with His Royal Highness'.[52]

Thackeray and Matthew Arnold were occasional guests of Mayer's and Juliana's at Mentmore, as were Caroline Norton and Whyte-Melville, the latter bridging the worlds of letters and sport. Of hunting with the Baron's, Whyte-Melville considered that 'a sportsman must indeed be prejudiced who will not admit that "ten mile points" over grass with one of the handsomest packs of hounds in the world, are most enjoyable; the object of the chase, when the fun is over, returning to Mentmore, like a gentleman, in his own carriage, notwithstanding'. In his novel *Satanella*, the company on the way down to the country for a day's hunting by the nine o'clock from Euston – 'soldiers, sailors, diplomatists, bankers, lawyers, artists, authors, men of pleasure, and men of business' – owed its composition to the very company with which Whyte-Melville would travel down from Euston to the Vale in the saloon carriage of the nine o'clock express.[53]

Dinner at Mentmore would be followed by a tour of inspection of

Mayer's ever expanding collection of treasures. 'After dinner, the works of art were as a matter of course looked at and admired,' Natty once wrote, 'and then we attempted to play a rubber, but Juliana's loquacity interfered very much with the game.' Conversation at Mentmore naturally turned also to racing – and probably never more so than in 1871, which went down in Turf history as 'The Baron's Year'. By then the owner of the Palace House stable at Newmarket, where Hayhoe continued as trainer, Mayer had an astounding run of good luck. While he himself was known never to lay out his money in backing anyone's horses but his own, as the 1871 season advanced backers everywhere took up as their motto: 'Follow the Baron'.[54]

It was in 1871 that Mayer's filly Hannah pulled off her remarkable treble – the One Thousand Guineas, the Oaks and the Leger, Charlie Maidment up in all three. Two days before the Oaks, Mayer won the Derby (£5,125), with his colt Favonius (Tom French up), and he finished the season by winning the Cesarewitch with Corisande. Only three times before had both the Derby and the Oaks been won in one year by the same owner, most recently by William I'Anson in 1857. In honour of Hannah's victories, Mayer gave the New Court clerks a dinner at Richmond. 'The luck of the Baron has been certainly extraordinary,' declared the racing correspondent of *Baily's Magazine* in November, 'but he is grudged it by none, and his cheery face makes no secret how proud he is to see his horses – all, with scarcely an exception, not only themselves, but also their sires and dams, bred by himself – win. All honour to such a noble sportsman! It would be well for the best interests of the Turf if all raced as he.'[55]

Nat did not survive to share in Mayer's triumph. By mid-1868 his condition was such that he was visiting the rue Laffitte for only fifteen minutes a day, and then did not even get out of his carriage. Seriously ill towards the end of 1869, he was confined to his room at 33 rue du Faubourg Saint-Honoré; his voice was very weak, he had pains in his chest when he talked, and for days at a time he did not eat. A slight improvement took place in early 1870: on 4 January he had a mutton chop for lunch, some colour returned to his face, and he went on to have a good night's sleep. His doctors' anxiety faded and his manservant, Joseph, so devoted that he was judged to know more about Nat's condition than anyone else, seemed reassured.[56]

By mid-February, having recovered his voice, and with his mental faculties as sharp as ever, Nat supposed, according to Natty, that 'he had taken on a new lease of life'; he talked to Alphonse about the state of the markets, and had details of the sensational Mordaunt case ('too disgusting' for Lionel's taste) read out to him from the newspapers. Yet Natty observed that his uncle 'was not aware of the great change which had taken place in himself'; and in the early hours of 19 February, looking forward to an early morning cup of tea and to having the papers read to him, Nat died.[57]

The last of his English private secretaries, John Cay, telegraphed the news to Lionel in London. 'The exact moment at which your brother passed away is not known,' Cay wrote again later that day, 'but at 20 minutes to 3 this morning he asked what o'clock it was and also to be raised a little in bed. As he appeared to fall asleep his attendant returned to his armchair, but after half an hour not hearing the usual restlessness returned to look at him when he found him motionless. He at once gave the alarm when it was found his suspicions were only too true. It will be satisfactory to you to know that he died without any pain & looks perhaps more peaceful in death than he did in life.'

'It is needless perhaps for me to say how universally he is regretted,' Cay continued, 'but I am sure there is not a person who ever came in contact with him who does [not] bear an affectionate remembrance of his kindness & thoughtfulness for others, and the courage with which for 18 years he has fought against what to others would have been an insupportable illness. For myself I must add that he has been always the kindest of masters and has treated me with a kindness and consideration I never deserved or expected.'[58]

Nat was fifty-seven at the time of his death; when Mayer died in 1874 he was only fifty-five. Illness struck in the summer of 1873. Swellings led to spasms of pain that could only be alleviated with morphine, without which Mayer found it difficult to sleep. Unable to walk, in the autumn he none the less managed the journey from London down to Mentmore, and seemed to enjoy the fresh country air on his way home from the railway station. James James arrived to help Mayer finish his will, and afterwards wrote to Lionel of his brother that 'the fortitude with which he bears his sufferings is certainly accorded of high minded courage'.[59]

Whether or not cancer was the cause of these sufferings is not clear. Certainly, the word cancer itself was not used, which from Mayer's point of view was perhaps as well. Writing from Frankfurt in 1868, Natty had described the 'newly discovered cure for cancer' that was then in vogue there: 'A peculiar kind of yellow bug with red eyes which abounds in this neighbourhood is intoxicated with Spirits of Wine after which process they are like leeches applied to the cancer which they suck up.' Spared such treatment at least, Mayer died on 6 February 1874.[60]

The obituary of Mayer published by *Baily's Magazine* in March ran to more than five pages. Entitled 'A Model Sportsman', the piece paid unqualified tribute to Mayer's shrewdness, practical knowledge and experience in racing matters, and noted also that he had been 'content to accept the smiles or frowns of Fortune without running further risks by coquetting with Chance'. To his jockeys, and to everyone connected with his stables, it was stated, Mayer 'always showed himself a steady and consistent friend, not peevishly seeking better luck in constant changes, nor dismissing any one he believed to be an honest servant at the mere hint of incapacity . . . He was generous to the extreme in making allowances, and giving credit for services performed to the best of his jockeys' powers; and once to be taken in hand by the Baron was no small compliment paid to ability and integrity in the rider.'

Further as to character, Mayer was perceived to have possessed 'those qualities of head and heart which endeared him, not only to a large and united family, but also to that more extensive circle of society which could appreciate his splendid hospitality, his lavish patronage of art, and the munificence of his well-directed charity. Courteous, cheery, affable and sincere, he loved to gather round him in social intercourse all that talent, distinction and worth could contribute from the cosmopolitan sphere in which he moved as a distinguished member of the greatest financial race in Europe. Mentmore was more like the palace of some Italian merchant prince, in the palmiest days of Genoa or Florence, than the country residence of an English gentleman devoted to out-door sports, and never so happy as when in the paddock or on the flags.'

Anthony survived Mayer by less than two years, having spent the greater part of his last decade leading the life of a country gentleman or attending to his duties at the refinery. As Natty, Alfred and Leo successively joined their father at New Court (Natty, like Lionel, being temperamentally the best suited to the work), Anthony's presence there seems barely to have been expected, even if his absence might sometimes be resented. 'As you say I am grumpy,' Lionel wrote to him from Brighton one winter, 'I will not contradict you – and so would you be if you could not run after yr birds & feed yr pigs &c or pass day after day looking at yr nags & amusing yrself . . . I hope you got plenty of stuff for yr refinery.'[61]

He spent holidays at home and abroad with his wife and daughters, and had plenty of time for what Constance described as 'the enjoyments that his love of social life and his country pursuits brought him'. In social terms he neared the very top of the ladder, staying as a guest at Sandringham in 1871, though the regime there did not really suit him. 'You can have no idea what a life they lead here,' he told his brothers, 'nothing but amusement from the time they get up till they go to bed . . . As regards Politics, no person speaks a word, but our party is not political and the Prince does not know much.' The house itself he thought 'not worthy of the Prince of W', and although the Prince and Princess 'cannot be more amiable to their guests', the food, as so often, was not good: 'Alfred knows what sort of dinners they give – nothing very wonderful.'[62]

Subsequently in 1873 Anthony entertained the Prince quietly at Aston Clinton, and then the next year welcomed the Prince's younger brother, the Duke of Edinburgh, and the Tsarevich (the Princess's brother-in-law) to a shoot there. Louisa found the Duke to be 'in high spirits and full of fun', but in her estimation he was 'not *princely* in mind or manner'. As for the Tsarevich, he was 'an extremely good natured, natural and amenable young man', but there was 'no royal prestige about him either'; Louisa did 'not see *why* he should be the Emperor of all the Russias. Such princes, amiable and friendly as they are, might well furnish arguments to republicans!'[63]

Having borne the disappointment of seeing his daughter Annie marry a Christian, Eliot Yorke, in February 1873 (Constance was to follow suit and marry Cyril Flower in 1877), in May, as Mayer approached the onset of illness, Anthony was in Vienna for the Universal Exhibition, for which he was a member, with Sir Richard Wallace and others, of the British commission. Dressed, on the advice of the Prince of Wales (and to the consternation of the British ambassador), in his Austrian Consul's uniform, Anthony attended the inaugural dinner given by Emperor Franz Josef.[64]

The room in which the dinner was held – to the strains of Strauss's band – seemed to Anthony like 'the Egyptian Hall at the Mansion House but nothing near so fine . . . The tables were very shabbily decorated, & did not look more Imperial than the tables which are set out at Richmond.' After dinner, the Prince of Wales presented him to the Emperor, and also to the Crown Prince of Prussia, who pretended to know him well. One thing that impressed Anthony was the appearance of the Austrian Empress, who was 'looking magnificent – covered with an immense quantity of Diamonds & a lilac dress & looked an Empress in every respect'. On his way back to London, Anthony put up for a few days at Homburg, from where he paid a brief visit to Frankfurt – there to go 'to the Juden Gasse to see the Old House'.[65]

Not long before he died, Mayer had bought a steam yacht, *Czarina*, in which in 1872 he and Juliana had been joined for a short cruise off the coast of Cornwall by the Prince Imperial, heir to Napoleon III but with no throne in prospect since France's defeat in the Franco-Prussian war. As Anthony entered a period of physical decline in the summer of 1875 – 'swellings' were accompanied by 'violent pains' – and found the summer heat hard to bear, he had a fancy for life on board ship, and so removed to a large chartered steamer in Southampton Water. Annie and her husband, and also her father-in-law, the Earl of Hardwicke, had houses nearby, and Anthony took another one for Louisa and Constance. The change seemed to do Anthony good; the sea air agreed with him, and he enjoyed being on the deck of his steamer watching the ships and boats sail by. But his condition worsened, and on 3 January 1876 he died.

'Heard last night of the death of my dear old friend, Sir Anthony Rothschild, after much suffering,' the Duke of Cambridge recorded in his journal the next day. 'It grieves me sadly, for he was a dear old fellow, and the kindest of friends to me.' Lamenting the passing of yet another of Nathan's sons – 'one more of that band of brothers' – an obituary writer recalled Anthony's face 'beaming with good-humour', the 'genial manners' that had made him 'popular with all', the hospitality that he had dispensed 'with no niggard hand', the table he had kept 'which could not be surpassed', and the charitable giving 'as well managed as it was munificent'. In sum, declared the author: 'Extreme good-nature was his great characteristic'. Louisa was left to endure a long widowhood of thirty-four years.[67]

The last decade of Lionel's life opened with his being turned down for a peerage by Queen Victoria in 1869. The royal objection, as expressed to Lord Granville, leader of the Liberals in the Lords, was twofold: first the Queen was dismayed by 'the *very* large number of Peers as well as Baronets proposed to be made' and was not prepared to create more than four new peers at a time; secondly, she declared that 'to make a *Jew* a Peer is a step she cd. *not* consent to.' That the proposal for Lionel's ennoblement had been made by Gladstone, whose capacity to irritate the Queen was almost boundless, was perhaps an added factor – although in 1885 the Queen accepted Gladstone's nomination of Natty.[68]

Judging by Lionel's reaction when it was rumoured that he might receive a peerage in 1868, it seems doubtful that he would have cared much about not getting one the next year. On 8 March 1868, less than a month after Disraeli had succeeded Lord Derby as Prime Minister, Charles Villiers turned up for dinner with Lionel (Charlotte was away) at Piccadilly. Just prior to dinner, Villiers, Lionel told Charlotte the next day, 'had been paying Lady Palmerston a long visit, where it appears they had been talking a good deal about your humble servant'. Villiers, 'famously intrigued about the paragraph in the papers respecting my being raised to the Peerage', had been baffled to hear that Lionel would not accept one from the Tory government. 'They all fancy Dis is under great obligations to us,' Lionel went on, 'so the best thing is to hold my tongue and let them think what they like. It is only amusing to hear all this nonsense.'[69]

By the time Natty was elevated to the House of Lords, twenty years had passed since he had first taken his seat in the Commons, as MP for Aylesbury, and eighteen since he had married his cousin Emma, a daughter of Charles and Louisa. In 1874, with their six-year-old son, Walter, the future zoologist, and their infant daughter Evelina, Natty and Emma had taken over Tring Park, which Lionel had bought for them two years before. Lionel's grandchildren could not have grown up in a place of greater contrasts to his father's childhood home in the Judengasse.[70]

'I went first to Tring to embrace the children,' Charlotte wrote after a visit to the Vale of Aylesbury in August 1874, 'and there the house felt cool and the gardens looked bright with flowers and birds. Walter, who was lively, talkative and very active, insisted upon showing me his favorites. It was delightful to see the little boy so pleased and happy, feeding the tame partridges and pheasants that are being brought up on the lawn, stroking the white parrots that are swinging in round iron rings and half-hoops under the large elm tree, and helping – en amateur – the attendant to prepare the daily puddings of rice, currants, potatoes and eggs for the more delicate birds in the temple, and in the aviaries of the conservatory.'[71]

Lionel paid a hefty £230,000 for Tring Park and its 4,000 acres in 1872. In the same year, for his own enjoyment, he paid £25,000 for fifty-seven Old Master paintings that had formed the collection of the late Frederick de Heusch, of The Chestnuts, Wimbledon. Richard Dawes, of the solicitors Dawes & Chatfield (still, as in Nathan's day, of 9 Angel Court, Throgmorton Street), handled the payment and, with Leo's help, supervised the collection of the pictures from Wimbledon for Lionel – 'trusting you may be spared many years to enjoy your new acquisition'.[72]

Such considerable sums paled in comparison to the size of the transaction masterminded by Lionel in late 1875: the raising of the funds required, on a few days' notice, to enable the British government (under Disraeli's premiership) to buy the Khedive of Egypt's shares in the Suez Canal Company. By three stages, on 1 and 15 December 1875 and 1 January 1876, New Court advanced to the British government, to be held at the disposal of the government of Egypt, a shade less than £4 million, and charged £150,000 for the three-month term of the loan. Agreement to the deal in principle had been struck at the now palatial premises of New Court, which Lionel had had demolished and redeveloped a decade earlier.[73]

Away from the City, Lionel pulled off two further notable coups. In 1878 – the year in which Mayer's daughter Hannah married Lord Rosebery – Lionel purchased more than eighty Dutch and Flemish Old Masters from the heirs of a Dutch collector, Willem van Loon; and on 28 May 1879 he won the centenary Derby with his brown colt Sir Bevys, at odds of 20–1. Among the few racegoers who backed Sir Bevys that day was Alfred Tennyson, the Poet Laureate, who laid out £5 'because Sir Bevys was the hero of one of my early poems'. Racing under the name of 'Mr Acton', Lionel in fact had two Derby runners in 1879, Sir Bevys and Squirrel (both of them sons of Favonius); but it was Sir Bevys (George Fordham up) who took the lead a hundred yards from home and brought in the prize money – £7,025.[74]

Following his triumph at Epsom, Lionel received a visit from a clergyman acquaintance, William Rogers, the incumbent of a City parish, who called to offer his congratulations. Although still at his desk in New Court, Lionel, now seventy, was far from well; a weak heart compounded his other crippling afflictions. Indeed, although Rogers found him very cheerful . . . in better health', he none the less supposed that death might carry him off 'at any moment'. On Friday 30 May Lionel left New Court to spend the weekend at Gunnersbury, and then on Sunday returned to the house in Piccadilly. On Monday he felt much more poorly than usual, quite unfit to attend to business in the City. His doctors were summoned, and word spread that he was nearing his end. When Edward Wagg, of stockbrokers Helbert, Wagg, received an urgent summons to 148 Piccadilly, he wondered wildly if he might have earned a favourable mention in Lionel's will, and that perhaps it was of this that the ailing man wished to speak to him. Having put on his best clothes and silk hat and hurried round, Wagg was shown into Lionel's room – though only to be told that Lionel had detected an arithmetical error in the fortnightly account submitted to him by Wagg's firm. Within hours Lionel suffered a stroke and fell into unconsciousness, and early in the morning of Tuesday 3 June he died.[75]

The greater part of the obituary published in *The Times* the next day was devoted to Lionel's role in obtaining the political emancipation of the Jews, and thus with the history of his eleven-year campaign to take his seat in Parliament. Tribute was paid to the combination of firmness, patience and wide-ranging ability that had enabled him 'to conduct the business of one of the greatest and most delicate of commercial undertakings, to win one of the foremost positions in English society, and by means of these two influences together to vindicate the rights of a race long the victims of bigotry and injustice'. In Thursday's *Times*, a letter to the editor reminded readers of the prominent and active part played by Lionel – 'indefatigable in his exertions' – in organising relief for the victims of the Irish Famine; and a notice announced that his funeral cortège would leave 148 Piccadilly at 10 a.m. on Friday, bound for the Jewish cemetery at Willesden.

Prior to its removal from Piccadilly, the plain coffin containing Lionel's remains lay in a ground-floor room, 'covered,' it was reported, 'with wreaths of blush roses, pale noisettes, white stephanotis, and gardenia, with leaves of lilies of the valley'. While some of the flowers had come from Gunnersbury, 'the largest wreaths had been sent by ladies of the family from Paris or Ferrières'.

On Friday the funeral procession began exactly on time, although it was forty minutes before the last of forty mourning carriages finally left Hyde Park Corner for Willesden. Disraeli, Prime Minister and now the Earl of Beaconsfield, sent his carriage; ambassadors and other heads of diplomatic missions sent theirs; so, too, did the Duke of Wellington, the Duke of Manchester, the Duke of St Albans, the Duchess of Somerset, Lady Molesworth, Lady Emily Peel and the Lord Mayor of London. Among other carriages joining the procession were Charlotte's and Louisa's, women being excluded from the funeral by religious custom. The first coach contained Natty and Alphonse, the second coach Alfred and Leo. All along the route, the shutters of shops belonging to Jewish shopkeepers were closed as the procession passed, and in the Uxbridge Road it was observed that the omnibus drivers all wore black crape. 'His ambition seems to have been,' it was remarked, 'to be regarded as a useful English gentleman, and as such he was regarded by all classes of society in this country.'[76]

At Willesden, Lionel's body was interred in a plot not far from the graves of Anthony and Mayer – Anthony's 'already bordered with thick ivy' – in a burial ground that was then set 'in the midst of rural scenery, with lilacs and laburnums in its garden, and surrounded by rich meadows sown with buttercups and daisies'.

Nathan's dying wish, expressed in his will, that his four sons 'should always act together in union and peace' had been fulfilled, and that Lionel had seen the sound sense of it he made plain in his own will. He urged that his sons 'be mindful of their duties towards God and towards all about them and that they will not forget the family union and friendship which has so much contributed towards placing us in the honourable position we now hold'. As Lionel and his brothers had also been mindful of Nathan's wish that they carry on the banking business he had established in London, so

Natty and his brothers would maintain the New Court partnership to hand on to future generations.[77]

'Vague and immeasurable conceptions of the wealth of the house of Rothschild seem to possess the popular mind,' *The Times* declared on Lionel's death, 'but they are, probably, great exaggerations of the reality.' Notwithstanding, while Mayer and Anthony had, respectively, left property valued for probate at £2.1 and £1.8 million, Lionel left an estate of £2.7 million. Following Juliana's death on board the yacht *Czarina* at Nice in March 1877, her daughter Hannah had become the greatest heiress in England. 'Poor Papa,' Nat had once written to his brothers, 'he never said a truer thing than that it is ten times more difficult to keep one's money than to make money.' Yet added to the estate left by Nat (whose widow survived until 1899), the collective value of all four of Nathan's sons' estates at death amounted to £8.4 million, a sum that exceeded the worth of any other family in England of the day.[78]

As with Mayer and Anthony, so with Lionel the obituary writers made note of his charitable giving. 'In his benevolence there was no ostentation,' wrote one. 'His was not the mind to find gratification in praise for paraded acts of charity, for almsgiving proclaimed to all the world. Only those who knew him intimately are aware how universal and constant were his good deeds . . . It mattered not of what creed or nationality were those who sought his aid . . . Whether relief was needed by the burnt-out inhabitants of some wooden town in Poland, or boots required for the boys at an English free school, an appeal to the Baron was sure to be successful.' In his will Lionel bequeathed £15,000 to charity, two thirds of it to go to the Jewish charities of London, one third to the Christian.[79]

Lionel's Charlotte lived on, out of the public eye and at times in a state of bewilderment, for a further five years. She died at Gunnersbury in 1884, three months short of her sixty-fifth birthday, and was buried beside Lionel at Willesden.

Notes

The following abbreviations appear *passim*. Published sources are given in full in the Bibliography.

RAL	The Rothschild Archive, London
SM	*The Sporting Magazine*
NSM	*The New Sporting Magazine*
BM	*Baily's Magazine*

A	Anthony	LA	Louisa Anthony
CA	Charlotte Anselm (Chilly)	LMC	Louisa Mayer Charles
CL	Charlotte Lionel	M	Mayer
H	Hannah	MC	Mayer Charles
HM	Hannah Mayer	N	Nat
L	Lionel	NM	Nathan

PROLOGUE

1 Howitt, *German Experiences*, p. 60.
2 Ibid., pp. 84, 85.

1: THE IMPORTANCE OF THE INDIVIDUAL

1 RAL, 000/13/102, L to N, Frankfurt, 1 May 1836.
2 RAL, 000/13/103, L to H, Frankfurt, 15 May 1836.
3 RAL, 000/13/105, L to N, Frankfurt, 18 May 1836.
4 RAL, 000/13/106, L to A, Frankfurt, 1 June 1836.
5 RAL, 000/10/54, H to N, Calais, 1 June 1836.
6 RAL, 000/10/55, H to N, Brussels, 3 June 1836.
7 RAL, 000/10/57, Louisa in PS to H to N, Frankfurt, (undated, early June) 1836; Weinstock, *Rossini*, p. 192.
8 RAL, 000/10/56, H to N, Brussels, 4 June 1836.
9 RAL, 000/13/115, L to A, Frankfurt, 5 June 1836.
10 RAL, 000/13/110, L to N, Frankfurt, 11 June 1836.
11 RAL, 000/10/57, H to N, Frankfurt, (undated, early June) 1836.
12 RAL, XI/109/27/4/77 (box for 1832), Charles Aston Key to H, (undated).

13 RAL, 000/13/109, L to N, Frankfurt, 10/11 June (1836); RAL, 000/10/61, H to N, Frankfurt, (undated, early) June 1836.

14 RAL, 000/13/112, L to A & N, Frankfurt, 13 June 1836.

15 RAL, 000/13/108, L to N, Frankfurt, 9 June (1836); Ferguson, *Rothschild*, vol. I, p. 283.

16 RAL, 000/10/60, H to A, Frankfurt, 14 June 1836.

17 Mendelssohn Bartholdy (eds), *Mendelssohn letters*, pp. 118, 120.

18 RAL, 000/13/114, L to A & N, Frankfurt, 15 June 1836.

19 RAL, XI/109/34/1/6, T23/80, Fritz Schlemmer to N (German), Frankfurt, 16 June 1836.

20 RAL, 000/10/62, H to N, Frankfurt, 16 June 1836.

21 RAL, XI/109/34/1/6, Fritz Schlemmer to N (German), Frankfurt, 16 June 1836; RAL, 000/13/116, L to A & N, Frankfurt, 17 June 1836.

22 RAL, 000/184, B17Anth 1836/13, A to N, (Paris, undated, June 1836).

23 RAL, 000/184, B17 Anth 1836/15, A to N, (Paris) 21 June (1836); RAL, 000/13/116, L to A & N, Frankfurt, 17 June 1836.

24 RAL, 000/13/117, L to A & N, Frankfurt, 22 June 1836.

25 See RAL, 000/10/66, H to A, Frankfurt, Thursday (25 June) 1836; RAL, 000/10/61, H to N, Frankfurt, Wednesday (undated) June 1836; RAL, 000/10/64, H to A, Frankfurt, Friday (?10 July) 1836; RAL, 000/10/57, H to N, Frankfurt, (undated, early June) 1836.

26 RAL, 000/10/65, H to N, Frankfurt, 27 June 1836; RAL, 000/10/64, H to A, Frankfurt, Friday (?10 July) 1836.

27 RAL, 000/13/119, L to A & N, Frankfurt, 26 June 1836.

28 RAL, XI/109/34/1/1, HM to N, Frankfurt, Friday (undated, June 1836).

29 RAL, 000/10/65, H to N, Frankfurt, 27 June 1836; RAL, XI/109/34/1/1, HM to N, Frankfurt, Friday (undated, June 1836).

30 Quoted in Ferguson, *Rothschild*, vol. I, p. 294.

31 RAL, 000/13/122, L to A & N, Frankfurt, 29 June 1836; RAL, 000/13/125, L to A & N, Frankfurt, 1 July 1836.

32 RAL, 000/10/67, H to A & N, Frankfurt, Friday 1 July 1836.

33 RAL, 000/13/128, L to A & N, Frankfurt, 7 July 1836.

34 RAL, 000/13/130, L to A & N, Frankfurt, 9 July 1836.

35 RAL, 000/13/131, L to A & N, Frankfurt, 11 July 1836.

36 RAL, XI/109/34/1/11, Fritz Schlemmer to N (German), Frankfurt, 2 July 1836.

37 RAL, 000/13/132, L to A & N, Frankfurt, 12 July 1836.

38 RAL, 000/13/137, L to A & N, Frankfurt, 14 July 1836.

39 RAL, 000/13/138, L to N, Frankfurt, 14 July 1836; RAL, 000/13/136, L to A & N, Frankfurt, 15 July 1836.

40 RAL, 000/13/140, L to A & N, Frankfurt, 17 July 1836.

41 RAL, 000/13/144, L to A & N, Frankfurt, 20 July 1836; RAL, 000/13/145, L to A & N, Frankfurt, 21 July 1836.

42 RAL, 000/13/146, L to A & N, Frankfurt, 22 July 1836.

43 RAL, 000/13/148, L to N, Frankfurt, 25 July 1836.

44 RAL, 000/13/149, L to N, Frankfurt, 26 July 1836.

45 Loewe (ed.), *Montefiore diaries*, vol. 1, p. 103.

46 Rothschild, *Shadow of a Great Man*, pp. 49–50.

47 Thornbury, *Old and New London*, p. 491.

48 RAL, XI/109/68A/1/234, Sir George Grey to L, Whitehall, 27 July 1848.

49 Wolf, *Montefiore*, p. 23.

50 *Observer*, 7 Aug 1836; Kynaston, *City of London*, p. 105.

51 *Annual Biography and Obituary*, p. 61.

52 Loewe (ed.), *Montefiore diaries*, vol. 1, p. 104.

53 *Annual Biography and Obituary*, p. 63.

54 RAL, XI/104/1/6/163, Anselm to cousins, Frankfurt, 28 Dec 1841; RAL, XI/109/58/27, T24/63, MC to L, 11 July 1844; RAL, XI/109/57/4/7, N to L, (Frankfurt, undated, 1846); RAL, XI/109/57/4/35, N to A, (Wildbad, undated, 1846); RAL, XI/109/57/4/64, N to L, (Ostende/Dieppe, undated, 1846).

55 *Gentleman's Magazine*, ns, vol. vi, 1836 (July–Dec), p. 328.

56 RAL, XI/109/37/3/1, Benjamin Travers to 'My dear Sir' (L), Bruton Street, 4 March 1839.

57 Rothschild, *Shadow of a Great Man*, p. 49.

2: DINNER AT UPTON

1 RAL, 000/924, 'Souvenirs du Docteur Schlemmer' (Schlemmer).

2 RAL, 000/924, Schlemmer, p. 20.

3 See, e.g., RAL, XI/109/29/1/83, H to NM, Brighton, 23 Jan (1833).

4 Gray and Aspey (eds), *Life and Times of NMR*, 'Manchester, 1799 to 1809', p. 88.

5 Picciotto, *Sketches*, p. 344.

6 Buxton (ed.), *Buxton memoirs*, p. 161; Gray, 'An off-hand man', in Gray and Aspey (eds), *Life and Times of NMR*, p. 14; Rothschild, *Shadow of a Great Man*, p. 2.

7 Anderson, *Northrepps Grandchildren*, p. 19; Battersea, *Reminiscences*, p. 336.

8 Bermant, *Cousinhood*, p. 60.

9 Anon., *The Black Book*, 1835, p. 261.

10 Emden, *Quakers*, p. 7.

11 Ibid., pp. 16–17; Picciotto, *Sketches*, p. 124.

12 Kynaston, *City of London*, p. 62.

13 Wright and Fayle, *Lloyd's*, p. 135; Cottrell, 'The Businessman and Financier', p. 34.

14 Bermant, *Cousinhood*, p. 60.

15 Loewe (ed.), *Montefiore diaries*, vol. 1, p. 61; RAL, 000/184, B17Anth 1836/77, A to bros, (Paris, undated, 1836).

16 Loewe (ed.), *Montefiore diaries*, vol. 1, p. 65.

17 Ayer, *A Century of Finance*, pp. 38–9.

18 Emden, *Quakers*, p. 120.

19 Hare, *Gurneys of Earlham*, vol. I, pp. 223–4.

20 Quoted in Battersea, *Reminiscences*, p. 336.

21 See, e.g., RAL, XI/112/87, 1828, Overend, Gurney to NM, 1 July 1828.

22 Corti, *House of Rothschild*, vol. 1, p. 206; Ferguson, *Rothschild*, vol. I, p. 198.

23 Buxton (ed.), *Buxton memoirs*, pp. 343–5.

24 Ferguson, *Rothschild*, vol. I, pp. 304, 482; Roth (ed.), *Essays in Jewish History by Lucien Wolf*, 'A Memoir', p. 31.

25 Wolf, 'Rothschildiana', pp. 263–5.

26 Emden, *Jews*, p. 175.

27 Wolf, 'Lady Montefiore's Honeymoon', p. 235.

28 Roth (ed.), *Essays in Jewish History by Lucien Wolf*, 'A Memoir', p. 31.

29 Aspey, 'Mrs Rothschild', p. 61; Beresford Chancellor, *Neumann diary*, vol. II, p. 222.

30 Slugg, *Reminiscences*, p. 191.

31 Baines, *Lancaster*, vol. II, pp. 134–5.

32 Harper, *Manchester & Glasgow Road*, p. 20; Bovill, *Country Life*, p. 133; Harper, *Great North Road*, vol. I, p. 20; Margetson, *Journey by Stages*, pp. 100–101; Wolf, 'Lady Montefiore's Honeymoon', p. 247; Baines, *Lancaster*, pp. 397–8; RAL, XI/109/17/1/17 (box for 1830), M to NM, second page missing, unsigned, Manchester, 28 Nov (1831).

33 Slugg, *Reminiscences*, p. 191; Williams, *Manchester Jewry*, p.19 (quoting Aiken, *Description*, p. 205, and citing *Manchester Exchange Herald*, 18 Nov 1809 to 24 Feb 1810: advert for the sale of NM's house and warehouse).

34 Aston, *Picture of Manchester*, p. 220.

35 Gray and Aspey (eds), *Life and Times of NMR*, 'Manchester 1799 to 1809', p. 92.

36 Ibid., pp. 88, 89; Aspey, 'Mrs Rothschild', p. 61.

37 Gray and Aspey (eds), *Life and Times of NMR*, 'Manchester 1799 to 1809', p. 91; Battersea, *Reminiscences*, p. 7.

38 Nightingale, *Beauties*, p. 164.

39 Hugo, *Bishopsgate*, p. 21.

40 Liedtke, 'Nathan Rothschild and London Jewry', p. 50; Picciotto, *Sketches*, p. 148 (quoting Charles Wesley).

41 Ibid., p. 265.

42 Nightingale, *Beauties*, p. 156.

43 Cohen, *Changing Faces*, p. 27; Picciotto, *Sketches*, pp. 267–8.

44 Ibid., p. 285; Wolf, 'The Queen's Jewry', p. 312.

45 Thornbury, *Old and New London*, p. 490.

46 Wolf, 'Rothschildiana', p. 271; RAL, XI/109/52A/2/12, George Henry Crocker to 'Dear Sir' (L), 25 Felix Terrace, Islington, 2 May 1845.

47 Wolf, 'Rothschildiana', p. 272.

48 Ferguson, *Rothschild*, vol. II, p. xxii.

49 Quoted in ibid., vol. I, p. 89.

50 RAL, T20/J, 109/2/3, Amschel to NM, Frankfurt, 12 Jan 1815.

51 Ferguson, *Rothschild*, vol. II, p. xxiii; ibid., vol. I, p. 167 (quoting James, 1816).

52 See Wolf, 'The News of Waterloo'; RAL, XI/104/0, 1840, 86/299, Isaac Cohen to L, Boulogne, 8 Sept 1840; Thornbury, *Old and New London*, p. 491.

53 Wolf, *Montefiore*, pp. 23–4.

54 Gallatin (ed.), *Gallatin diary*, p. 76.

55 Jennings (ed.), *Croker Papers*, vol. I, pp. 59–60.

56 Margoliouth, *Jews*, vol. II, p. 198; RAL, XI/109/74/2, M. Angel, Headmaster, Jews' Free School, to A, Bell Lane, Spitalfields, 4 Feb 1850.

57 Battersea, *Reminiscences*, p. 3.

58 RAL, T6/113, MBKN to NM (German), 15 Oct 183?; Wolf, 'Anglo-Jewish Families', p. 213; RAL, XI/82/7/6/5, T5/101, NM to brother Carl, London, July 1815.

59 Wolf, 'Lady Montefiore's Honeymoon', pp. 241–52.

60 RAL, 000/10/117, H to NM, (Paris, undated, ?Sept 1830).

61 Quoted in Davis, *English Rothschilds*, p. 37 (quoting RAL, 109/4/1/5, NM to bros, 2 Jan 1816).

62 Ferguson, *Rothschild*, vol. I, p. 168.

63 Anon., *Albion*, vol. I, p. 92.

64 Barman, 'Rothschild and Brazil', p. 38.

65 Chateaubriand, *Memoirs*, vol. iv, p. 71.

66 Shuttleworth, *Woodbine Parish*, pp. 200–202.
67 Corti, *House of Rothschild*, vol. 1, p. 214; Gille, *Maison Rothschild*, vol. 1, p. 67.
68 Kynaston *City of London*, p. 50.
69 See RAL, XI/112/81 (1827), RAL, XI/112/104 (1832), RAL, XI/112/115 (1834), also RAL, XI/112/100, RAL, XI/82/6/1/25; Gallatin (ed.), *Gallatin diary*, p. 104.
70 Spohr, *Autobiography*, vol. II, p. 78.
71 RAL, XI/109/30/2/12, HM (& H) to NM, Paris, 29 Sept (1833); Mansel, *Paris*, p. 325.
72 Quoted in Dowling, *Exchanges of London*, pp. 4–5.
73 Ibid., p. 5; Kynaston, *City of London*, p. 91.
74 *Gentleman's Magazine*, ns, vol. vi, 1836 (July–Dec), p. 328.

3: STAMFORD HILL

1 See Davis, *English Rothschilds*, p. 26; Battersea, *Reminiscences*, pp. 27–8.
2 Loewe (ed.), *Montefiore diaries*, vol. 1, pp. 60–61.
3 Aspey, 'Mrs Rothschild', p. 60.
4 Roth, *Provincial Jewry*, p. 45; Picciotto, *Sketches*, p. 285.
5 RAL, 000/10/146, H to A, 17 June (1827).
6 Cohen, *Changing Faces*, p. 12.
7 Ibid., pp. 26, 12–13.
8 Ibid., pp. 12, 36; Brinson, *European Ballet*, p. 156.
9 RAL, XI/109/32/1/28, T22/575, L to H, Paris, 24 May 1834; Jerdan, *Autobiography*, vol. IV, p. 71; Disraeli, *Correspondence with His Sister*, p. 7.
10 Ibid., p. 10; Chapman, *Austen letters*, vol. II, no. 111, p. 425 and no. 117, p. 437.
11 Ibid., vol. II, no. 87, p. 351.
12 Quoted in Wolf, 'Lady Montefiore's Honeymoon', pp. 243–4.
13 Gilbert, *Brighton*, p. 18.
14 Quoted in Wolf, 'Lady Montefiore's Honeymoon', p. 249.
15 Quoted in ibid., p. 250.
16 Loewe (ed.), *Montefiore diaries*, vol. 1, p. 20; RAL, XI/109/10/2/6, CA to H, Brighton, 10 Oct 1819.
17 Cohen, *Changing Faces*, pp. 9–10.
18 Quoted in Gilbert, *Brighton*, p. 18.
19 Battersea, *Reminiscences*, p. 336.
20 RAL, 000/924, Schlemmer, p. 5; RAL, XI/109/43A/4/34, Thos Hawkins to L, 12 Dec 1842.
21 Roth, *Anglo-Jewish Letters*, p. 264; Wolf, 'Lady Montefiore's Honeymoon', p. 256.
22 Roth, *Wolf essays*, 'A Memoir', p. 31.
23 RAL, XI/109/43A/4/33, Carl Holzer to L, 16 Nov 1842; RAL, XI/109/17/2/1–30 (box for 1830), Miss M. Andrews to H, with PS from CA, continuation sheet, (Frankfurt, undated, 1824).
24 Endelman, *Jews*, p. 56.
25 Sprigge and Napier (transs), *Geijer, Impressions*, pp. 82, 113–14.
26 Wolf, 'Rothschildiana', pp. 272–3.
27 Loewe (ed.), *Montefiore diaries*, vol. 1, p. 22.
28 Ibid., p. 16.
29 Ibid., p. 23; RAL, 000/848 (Lydia Cohen's will).

30 Murray, *High Society*, p. 101; Loewe (ed.), *Montefiore diaries*, vol. 1, p. 20.

31 RAL, 000/10/188, H to James, (?24 June) 1814.

32 Picciotto, *Sketches*, p. 250; RAL, XI/109/5, List of missing or broken items 'in Mr Boddington's House, Clapton, late in the occupation of N. Rothschild Esqre', 17 Dec 1816.

33 Picciotto, *Sketches*, p. 251.

34 RAL, XII/158/OA, Bill from Dawes & Chatfield to N. M. Rothschild Esq 'respecting a purchase made by him of Mr Taylor's House at Stamford Hill', April 1819; Thorne, *History of Parliament*, vol. V, p. 339; Brown, 'Jews of Hackney', p. 81.

35 Chateaubriand, *Memoirs*, vol. iv, p. 71, note.

36 Spohr, *Autobiography*, vol. II, p. 78; Baker (ed.), *Victoria County History: Middlesex*, vol. viii, p. 187.

37 Hensel, *Mendelssohn Family*, vol. I, p. 191.

38 RAL, 000/1380.

39 Baker (ed.), *Victoria County History: Middlesex*, vol. viii, p. 142; RAL, XI/109/106/3, John Brock to 'Baron Rothschild' (L), St John's Road, Hoxton, 24 July (1871).

40 Wolf, *Montefiore*, pp. 19, 6; *Notes and Queries*, July–Dec 1914, p. 287; Roth (ed.), *Wolf essays*, 'A Memoir', p. 32.

41 Baker (ed.), *Victoria County History: Middlesex*, vol. viii, pp. 165, 169.

42 RAL, 000/924, Schlemmer, p. 7; and RAL, XI/109/43A/4/33, Carl Holzer to L, 16 Nov 1842.

43 Allen, *Poe*, vol. I, pp. 77–85.

44 RAL, 000/10/80, H to Lady Carmarthen, Stamford Hill, 24 Sept (?1830).

45 Brown, 'Jews of Hackney', pp. 81, 83; Cohen, *Changing Faces*, pp. 37, 3.

46 RAL, XI/109/17/2/1–30 (box for 1830), Miss M. Andrews to H, with PS from CA, continuation sheet (Frankfurt, undated, 1824); Wolf, 'Lady Montefiore's Honeymoon', p. 245.

47 RAL, XI/109/27/4/53, William Babington to H, 15 Devonshire St, Portland Place, 31 Dec 1832; Wolf, *Montefiore*, p. 27.

48 RAL, 000/924, Schlemmer, p. 4; RAL, XI/109/27/3/13, CA to LMC, Paris, 11 Nov (?1832); Roth (ed.), *Wolf essays*, 'A Memoir', p. 31.

49 Bamford and Wellington (eds), *Arbuthnot journal*, vol. I, p. 304; RAL, XI/109/11/9/2, NM to Mr Allason (dictated), 10 Aug 1826.

50 Sundry box RAL, XI/112/92, D. Campbell to 'NMR Esq' at New Court, Regent Street, 3 Nov 1830; RAL, 000/10/116, H to NM, (Paris, undated).

51 RAL, XI/109/22/1/49, HM to NM (continuation sheet missing), Paris, 11 Sept 1831; RAL, XI/109/17/1/24, CA to H, Paris, Tuesday (undated, 1830); RAL, XI/109/12/1/24, Richard Sheppard to L, The Ridge, Nr Uley, Glos., 11 June 1829.

52 RAL, 000/924, Schlemmer, p. 4.

53 Blessington, *Idler*, vol. II, p. 473.

54 Baines, *Lancaster*, p. 259; RAL, XI/112/122/2, Fritz Schlemmer to N, Heidelberg, 16 Nov 1836.

55 Buxton (ed.), *Buxton memoirs*, p. 344.

56 Baron-Wilson, *St Albans memoirs*, vol. II, p. 265.

57 Ibid., vol. II, pp. 125–6.

58 Page (ed.), *Victoria County History: Middlesex*, vol. 2, pp. 193–5; RAL, XI/109/50/13, Windus & Co. estimate for building a Clarence Coach (1844, 7th box); RAL, XI/109/76/2, Eric Windus to A, Stamford Hill, (no day) Aug 1850.

59 Emden, *Jews*, p. 178; Cohen, *Changing Faces*, pp. 4–5.

60 Pückler-Muskau, *Letters*, vol. III, p. 62.

61 RAL, XI/109/25/3/29, Lady Stepney to 'Baroness de Rothschild, 107 Piccadilly' (H), an invitation for 28–29 March (1832); Bessborough (ed.), *Guest journal*, p. 29; Coleridge (trans. & ed.), *Moscheles*, vol. I, pp. 58–9.

62 Beresford Chancellor (ed.), *Neumann diary*, vol. I, p. 63.

63 Spohr, *Autobiography*, vol. II, p. 132; Storck (ed.), *Schumann letters*, p. 61.

64 Roth (ed.), *Wolf essays*, 'A Memoir', p. 31.

65 Leveson Gower (ed.), *Granville letters*, vol. I, p. 243.

66 RAL, 000/10/156, H to NM, Paris, 17 Oct 1833; RAL, XI/109/30/2/13, LMC (& HM) to NM, Paris, Thursday (undated, autumn 1833).

67 RAL, XI/109/33/1/15, L to A, Madrid, 8 April 1835.

68 Pückler-Muskau, *Letters*, vol. III, pp. 165–7.

69 RAL, 000/924, Schlemmer, p. 4.

70 Ibid., p. 16; Margoliouth, *Jews*, vol. II, p. 189.

71 RAL, XI/109/18/1/44, CA to H, Frankfurt, 28 Nov 1831.

72 RAL, T30/49/2, James to H, 26 Aug 1815; RAL, 000/848, H to NM, (Paris, undated, late 1824); RAL, 000/848, H to L & A at Göttingen, London, 7 Jan 1826.

73 RAL, XI/109/23/1/21, LMC to NM, (Paris, undated, Sept 1831).

74 RAL, 000/848, L. A. Lowdham to NM, Leicester, 31 Aug 1824; Loewe (ed.), *Montefiore diaries,* vol. I, p. 65.

75 RAL, 000/848, L. A. Lowdham to NM, Leicester, 31 Aug 1824.

4: MONARCHS OF THE GOLDEN BAGS

1 RAL, XI/109/48/2/42, N to A & M, (Paris) 4 Sept (1844); RAL, XI/109/89/1, Ferdinand to L, Scarborough, 15 Aug 1866; RAL, XI/101/2, James to N, 29 June and 16 July 1839; Ferguson, *Rothschild*, vol. I, p. 188.

2 RAL, XI/109/17/2/1–30 (box for 1830), Miss M. Andrews to H, with PS from CA, continuation sheet, (Frankfurt, undated, summer 1824).

3 RAL, 000/924, Schlemmer, p. 2.

4 Wolf, *Montefiore*, pp. 29–33.

5 Wolf, 'Rothschildiana', p. 266.

6 Londonderry, *Steam Voyage*, vol. I, pp. 11–12; RAL, 000/848, H to NM, Brussels, postmarked 28 June 1824.

7 Leveson Gower (ed.), *Granville letters*, vol. I, p. 259.

8 RAL, 000/848, H to NM, Brussels, postmarked 28 June 1824; Healey, *Coutts*, pp. 160–61; Baron-Wilson, *St Albans memoirs*, vol. II, p. 174.

9 RAL, 000/848, H to NM, Brussels, postmarked 28 June 1824.

10 Dod, *Autumn Near the Rhine*, pp. 14, 15.

11 Ibid., p. 68.

12 Irving (ed.), *Washington Irving*, vol. II, p. 79.

13 Brownlow, *Eve of Victorianism*, p. 3.

14 Reeks, *Mother of Goethe*, p. 276.

15 Brimley Johnson (ed.), *Fry*, pp. 96–7.

16 Battersea, *Reminiscences*, p. 64.

17 RAL, 000/848, H to NM, Frankfurt, Sunday 8 July 1824.

18 RAL, 000/848, A to NM, Frankfurt, 5 July 1824; RAL, 000/848, L to NM, Frankfurt, 5 July 1824.

19 RAL, XI/109/11/9, CA to H, Geneva, 22 Oct 1827.

20 RAL, 000/848, H to NM, Frankfurt, 8 July 1824.

21 RAL, 000/848, PS from CA in H to NM, Frankfurt, 8 July 1824.

22 RAL, 000/848, H to NM, (Paris, undated, spring 1825).

23 Coleridge (trans. & ed.), *Moscheles*, vol. I, pp. 40–41; Beresford Chancellor (ed.), *Neumann diary*, vol. I, p. 78.

24 Leveson Gower (ed.), *Granville letters*, vol. I, pp. 322, 342.

25 Beresford Chancellor (ed.), *Neumann diary*, vol. I, p. 186; Murray, *High Society*, p. 171; Kelly, *Carême*, p. 202.

26 RAL, XI/103/0/53, A to N, Paris, 21/26 Aug (1839).

27 RAL, 000/848, H to NM, (Paris, undated, spring 1825).

28 Russell, *Tour in Germany*, p. 244.

29 Kellner, *Humboldt*, p. 11; Wolf, 'The Queen's Jewry', p. 312.

30 Russell, *Tour in Germany*, pp. 250–51.

31 Joshua, 'Rothschild at Göttingen', p. 3; Russell, *Tour in Germany*, p. 263.

32 Joshua, 'Rothschild at Göttingen', p. 1.

33 RAL, XI/109/11/8/49, A to H, Strasbourg, 3 Feb (1827); Joshua, 'Rothschild at Göttingen', p. 3.

34 RAL, 000/848, A to NM, Göttingen, 4 Dec 1825.

35 RAL, XI/109/18/1/46 (box for 1831), CA to H, Paris, 6 Nov (1825).

36 Joshua, 'Rothschild at Göttingen', pp. 1, 3, 10 and 4.

37 RAL, 000/848, H to L & A at Göttingen, London, 7 Jan 1826; RAL, 000/848, H to A at Göttingen, (London) 21 March 1826.

38 RAL, 000/848, H to L & A at Göttingen, London, 7 Jan 1826.

39 RAL, 000/848, L to N at Stamford Hill, Frankfurt, 2 Jan 1826.

40 Quoted in Ferguson, *Rothschild*, vol. I, p. 137.

41 Rothschild, *Shadow of a Great Man*, p. 41.

42 Quoted in Forster, *Marianne Thornton*, p. 122.

43 Davis, *Buckinghamshire Study*, p. 60.

44 Ziegler, *Barings*, p. 90.

45 Quoted in Forster, *Marianne Thornton*, p. 123.

46 RAL, 000/848, H to L & A at Göttingen, London, 7 Jan 1826.

47 Ibid.

48 RAL, XI/109/72/1, J. Berridge to 'Baron Rothschild' (L), 22 St Swithin's Lane, 16 July 1849.

49 Jennings (ed.), *Croker Papers*, vol. I, p. 371.

50 Ibid., vol. I, pp. 239–41; Mansel, *Paris*, p. 156.

51 Nevill, *Romantic London*, p. 76.

52 Ziegler, *Barings*, p. 88.

53 *Survey of London*, vol. 29, 'The Pulteney Estate', pp. 26–8; RAL, XI/109/72/2, payments made on a/c of L, Aug 1849.

54 Wheatley, *Piccadilly*, p. 213.

55 Wolf, 'Lady Montefiore's Honeymoon', p. 252.

56 RAL, XI/109/28/1/27, L to H, Paris, 22 Sept 1832; RAL, XI/109/29/1/88 (box for 1833), CA to H, second sheet only, (Paris, undated).

57 RAL, 000/848, H to A at Göttingen, (London) 21 March 1826.

58 Loewe (ed.), *Montefiore diaries*, vol. 1, p. 34.

59 Murray, *High Society*, pp. 149–50.

60 Loewe (ed.), *Montefiore diaries*, vol. I, p. 74.

61 Ibid., p. 61; RAL, XI/109/14/3/11, Duke of St Albans to H, 1 Stratton St, London, 4 Jan 1830.

62 Bamford and Wellington (ed.), *Arbuthnot journal*, vol. I, p. 408; Baron-Wilson, *St Albans memoirs*, vol. II, p. 185.

63 Ibid., vol. I, p. 207; Dasent, *Piccadilly*, pp. 69–70; Beresford Chancellor (ed.), *Neumann diary*, vol. I, p. 212; Ferguson, *Rothschild*, vol. I, p. 305.

64 RAL, 000/10/146, H to A in Vienna, 17 June (1827).

65 Pückler-Muskau, *Letters*, vol. IV, p. 37.

66 RAL, XI/112/70, 1825, David Jacques to NM, Hanover, 14 Dec 1825.

67 Loewe (ed.), *Montefiore diaries*, vol. 1, p. 61.

68 Battersea, *Reminiscences*, p. 54; Coleridge (trans. & ed.), *Moscheles*, vol. I, p. 21; RAL, XI/109/58A/2/2, Louisa Dulcken to 'Dear Madam!' (H), 80 Harley St, 1 Nov 1846.

69 Coleridge (trans. & ed.), *Moscheles*, vol. I, p. 222.

70 RAL, XI/109/21/1/8, L to H, Paris, 14 May 1831; Coleridge (trans. & ed.), *Moscheles*, vol. I, p. 252.

71 RAL, XI/109/86B, (Trinidad) Huerta to L, London, 22 June 1865.

72 RAL, XI/109/11/8/48, A to H, Strasbourg, 6 Jan 1828.

73 RAL, T6/87, Henry Abbott to NM, Havre, 20 June 1828; Barman, 'Rothschild and Brazil', p. 38; RAL, XI/109/43A/2/11, A to bros, (Paris) 29 Oct 1842; RAL, XI/109/43A/2/12, A to bros, (Paris) 9 Nov 1842; RAL, XI/109/73/1, A to M, (Paris) 11 Oct (1849); RAL, XI/109/43A/2/11, A to bros, (Paris) 29 Oct 1842.

74 Pückler-Muskau, *Letters*, vol. III, pp. 165–7; Roberts, *Beechey*, p. 257.

75 RAL, XI/109/64A/2/111, Richard Dighton to 'Sir', 10 Stafford Place, Pimlico, 15 Nov 1847; Margoliouth, *Jews*, vol. II, pp. 172–3.

76 RAL, XI/109/33/4/18, J. D. Herrmann to NM, 11 Sept 1833.

5: ENGLISHMEN ABROAD

1 RAL, 0000/239, L's 'Journal through Germany'.

2 RAL, XI/109/27/3/13, CA to L, Paris, 11 Nov (1832).

3 Spohr, *Autobiography*, vol. I, p. 102.

4 Quoted in Ferguson, *Rothschild*, vol. I, pp. 141–2.

5 Passavant, *Tour*, vol. I, p. 59.

6 Ibid., vol. I, pp. 148, 122.

7 RAL, XI/109/52B/1/81, Messrs Smith to L, 137 New Bond Street, 14 June 1845.

8 Bamford and Wellington (eds), *Arbuthnot journal*, vol. I, p. 27; Passavant, *Tour*, vol. I, p. 61.

9 Spohr, *Autobiography*, vol. I, p. 284.

10 RAL, XI/109/11/9/9, A to H, Vienna, 6 June 1827; Russell, *Tour in Germany*, vol. II, p. 233.

11 See Cowles, *Rothschilds*, p. 63, and Wilson, *Rothschild*, pp. 76–7.

12 RAL, XI/109/11/9/9, A to H, Vienna, 6 June 1827.

13 RAL, 000/10/146, H to A (in Vienna), London, 17 June (1827).

14 RAL, 000/10/147, H to A in Vienna, (London) 23 June (1827).

15 Russell, *Tour in Germany*, vol. II, pp. 1–2.

16 Bovill, *English Country Life*, p. 129.

17 RAL, XI/109/28/1/48, CA to H, Strasbourg, 5 Dec 1832.

18 Russell, *Tour in Germany*, vol. II, p. 14.

19 RAL, XI/109/11/9/7, A to H, Strasbourg, 30 Dec 1827.

20 RAL, XI/109/11/8/48, A to H, Strasbourg, 6 Jan 1828.

21 RAL, XI/109/11/8/49, A to H, Strasbourg, 3 Feb 1828.

22 RAL, T10/215, Alphonse to cousins, (Paris) 3 Sept 1870.

23 RAL, XI/109/11/8/43, Amschel to L & Ben Cohen, Frankfurt, 23 Aug 1828; RAL, 000/10/73, H to L, Frankfurt, 18 Aug 1828.

24 RAL, 000/10/72, H to L, (Frankfurt) Wednesday (Aug 1828).

25 RAL, T6/94, Abraham Crailsheim to NM, (Frankfurt) 8 Jan 1829.

26 RAL, XI/109/12/1/59, A to NM, Frankfurt, 27 July 1829.

27 RAL, XI/109/18/1/42, CA to NM, Paris, 4 Dec (1829).

28 RAL, XI/109/12/1/62, A to H, Frankfurt, 24 Nov 1829.

29 Loewe (ed.), *Montefiore diaries*, vol. 1, p. 76.

30 RAL, 000/924, Schlemmer, pp. 7–8; RAL, XI/109/34/1/16, Fritz Schlemmer to N (German), Leipzig, 24 July 1836.

31 RAL, XI/109/18/1/42, CA to NM, Paris, 4 Dec (1829).

32 See Leveson Gower (ed.), *Granville letters*, vol. I, pp. 296–7.

33 Whitwell Wilson (ed.), *Greville Diary*, vol. I, p. 206; Ferguson, *Rothschild*, vol. I, p. 215.

34 RAL, XI/109/15/1/25, L to NM, Calais, 25 July 1830; RAL, XI/109/16/1/3, L to NM & H, Paris, 27 July (1830).

35 RAL, XI/109/16/1/3, L to NM & H, Paris, 27 July 1830; Ferguson, *Rothschild*, vol. I, p. 218.

36 Ibid., vol. I, pp. 210 ff.; Mansel, *Paris*, pp. 237 ff.

37 RAL, XI/109/15/1/1, L to NM & H, Paris, 30 July 1830.

38 RAL, XI/109/27/1/1, L to NM & H, Paris, 31 July 1830.

39 RAL, XI/109/48/2/47, N to bros, (Paris) 17 Sept (1844).

40 RAL, XI/109/18/1/39, N to H, Coire, 2 Oct, postmarked 1830; RAL, XI/109/17/1/19, N to CA at 15 rue d'Artois, Milan, 9 Oct (1830).

41 RAL, 000/924, Schlemmer, pp. 8–9.

42 RAL, XI/109/19/1/22, N to NM, Naples, 4 Feb (1831); Richard, *Guide*, p. 373.

43 RAL, XI/109/19/1/21, N to NM, Naples, 3 Feb (1831).

44 RAL, XI/109/19/1/23, N to NM, Naples, 7 Feb (1831).

45 RAL, XI/109/19/1/25, N to L in Paris, Naples, 13 Feb (1831).

46 Whitwell Wilson (ed.), *Greville Diary*, vol. I, p. 204.

47 RAL, XI/109/19/1/26, N to NM, Naples, 26 Feb (1831).

48 RAL, XI/82/6/1/1, N to NM, Naples, 13 March (1831).

49 RAL, XI/109/20/1/40, N to NM, Naples, 17 March (1831); RAL, XI/82/6/1/2, N to NM, Naples, 21 April (1831).

50 Blessington, *Idler*, pp. 206–7.

51 RAL, XI/109/19/1/22, N to NM, Naples, 4 Feb (1831); RAL, XI/109/19/1/25, N to L, Naples, 13 Feb (1831).

52 RAL, 000/924, Schlemmer, pp. 10–11.

53 Loewe (ed.), *Montefiore diaries*, vol. 1, p. 74.

54 Ibid., p. 52; Gatty, *Morrison*, p. 94.

55 RAL, XI/109/31/1/68, Henrietta Montefiore to H, Naples, 25 Jan 1834.

56 Richard, *Guide*, p. 373.

57 RAL, XI/109/20/1/40, N to NM, 17 March (1831).

58 Wolf, *Montefiore*, p. 67.

59 RAL, XI/109/25/1/43 (box for 1832), N to NM & H, Naples, 26 March (1831).

60 RAL, XI/109/31/1/70 (box for 1834), N to NM, Naples, 16 April (1831); RAL, XI/109/21/1/34, N to L, Naples, 17 April (1831).

61 Jamieson, *Diary of an Ennuyée*, p. 273; Selden-Goth (ed.), *Mendelssohn letters*, p. 130.

62 RAL, XI/109/20/1/42, N to NM, Naples, 26 April (1831); RAL, XI/82/6/1/6, N to NM, Naples, 3 May (1831).

63 RAL, XI/109/21/1/35, N to H, Paris, 4 June (1831); RAL, James's letters to NM translated from Judendeutsch, J to NM, Paris, 4 June 1831.

6: CULT OF THE HORSE

1 RAL, XI/82/6/1/17, L to H, Paris, May 28 1831.

2 RAL, XI/109/52B/1/92, W. H. Schwabe to 'Sir', (The) Rectory, Throwleigh, near Exeter, 16 June 1845.

3 Emden, *Jews*, p. 116.

4 UCL student register; RAL, XI/109/57/1/53, N to bros, Wildbad, 8 July (1846).

5 RAL, XI/109/22/1/46, CA to H, Frankfurt, 17 July (1831).

6 RAL, 000/924, Schlemmer, pp. 13–14.

7 RAL, XI/109/20/1/42, L to H, Paris, 27 April (1831).

8 RAL, XI/109/20/1/31, L to NM & H, Paris, 25 April 1831.

9 RAL, XI/109/23/3/7, CA to H, Suresnes, 6 Oct 1831.

10 RAL, XI/109/24/1/24, CA to H, (Paris) 9 Dec (1831).

11 RAL, XI/109/21/1/37, L to NM, Paris, 11 Sept 1831; RAL, XI/109/18/1/44, CA to H, Frankfurt, 28 Nov 1831.

12 RAL, XI/109/24/1/24, CA to H, 9 Dec (1831).

13 RAL, XI/109/17/1/17 (box for 1830), M to NM, second page missing, unsigned, Manchester, 28 Nov (1831).

14 Ward Jones, *Mendelssohns on Honeymoon*, p. xvi; Williams, *Manchester Jewry*, p. 169.

15 Bovill, *Nimrod and Surtees*, p. 155 note and ill. XIII, opp. p. 146.

16 See RAL, XI/109/61/1/95, (Lord) A. Marcus Hill to L, House of Commons, 17 June (1847).

17 RAL, 000/184, B17Anth 1836/25, A to N; RAL, 000/184, B17Anth 1836/44, A to N, (undated, 1836); Battersea, *Reminiscences*, p. 27.

18 Kynaston, *City of London*, p. 59; RAL, XI/109/104/3, David Robertson (ex Marjoribanks) to L, New Club, Edinburgh, 16 Aug 1871; RAL, XI/109/103/1, David Robertson (ex Marjoribanks) to L, Ladykirk, Berwickshire, 15 Oct 1870.

19 RAL, XI/109/26/3/23, David Marjoribanks (later Robertson) to N, (undated, 1832).

20 *SM*, Aug 1827, pp. 262–3.

21 Bovill, *Nimrod and Surtees*, p. 3.

22 Buxton (ed.), *Buxton memoirs*, p. 345.

23 Ibid., p. 193.

24 RAL, XI/109/31/2/30, Hy[?] of [sic] Wertheimstein to N, Vienna, 21 May 1834; Gronow, *Reminiscences*, vol. 1, pp. 122–3.

25 *SM*, vol. 13, ns, Dec 1823, p. 106.

26 *SM*, vol. 8, 2nd series, Jan 1834, No. XLV, p. 273.

27 *The Field*, 4 Dec 1858. In the 1930s, Nubar Gulbenkian hunted with the Old

Berkeley. When an outbreak of foot and mouth had obliged the neighbouring Whaddon Chase to suspend hunting, Lord Rosebery, Master of the Whaddon Chase (and Mayer de Rothschild's grandson), remarked to him of the Old Berkeley: 'They're all right – after all they can draw the Zoo if they like – it's in their country': Gulbenkian, *Pantaraxia*, p. 153.

28 RAL, XI/109/27/3/6, N to A, Paris, 11 Dec (1831).

29 *BM*, vol. 34, 1879, p. 147; Letter from 'A Member of the Burton Hunt', *SM*, vol. 18, ns, Feb 1826, No. CI; *Annual Biography and Obituary*, p. 64.

30 *BM*, vol. 25, 1874, pp. 216–18; Page (ed.), *Victoria County History: Hertfordshire*, vol. i, pp. 364–6.

31 Ibid., p. 365; *Army List, 1830*, p. 146; RAL, 000/84, CL to Leo & Leonora, Folkestone, 3 Sept 1862; *SM*, vol. 20, 2nd series, 1830, No. VIII, p. 152.

32 *SM*, vol. 20, ns, 1827, No. CXIX; Berry, *Puckeridge*, pp. 30, 37.

33 Page (ed.), *Victoria County History: Hertfordshire*, vol. i, p. 353; Dixon, *Scott and Sebright*, p. 351; Anderson, *Northrepps Grandchildren*, p. 113.

34 Dixon, *Scott and Sebright*, p. 352; Bovill, *Nimrod and Surtees*, p. 83.

35 Quoted in Berry, *Puckeridge*, p. 30.

36 Berry, *Puckeridge*, pp. 21, 30.

37 Albemarle, *Fifty Years*, vol. II, pp. 8, 71.

38 RAL, XI/109/37/2/10, John Abel Smith (to L), Sacombe Park, nr Ware, 24 Dec 1839.

39 RAL, 000/10/73, PS from N in H to L, Frankfurt, 18 Aug 1828; Leveson Gower (ed.), *Granville letters*, vol. I, p. 46 (4 Jan 1813).

40 Loewe (ed.), *Montefiore diaries*, vol. 1, p. 65; RAL, XI/109/25/3/6, L. A. Lowdham to NM, Nottingham, 8 Jan 1832.

41 RAL, XI/109/32/5/40, Matthias Prime Lucas to N, Wateringbury, 29 Aug 1834.

42 RAL, XI/109/15/1/4, L to NM, Paris, 5 Sept 1830.

43 RAL, XI/109/22/1/39, L to NM, Paris, 4 Sept 1831.

44 RAL, XI/109/18/(1)/31, L to NM & H, Paris, Sept 1832.

45 Garrick Club candidates book, 1832.

46 RAL, XI/109/27/4/55, David Marjoribanks to N, Melton, 9 Dec 1832.

47 Carr, *Fox Hunting*, p. 72.

48 RAL, XI/109/30/4/20, Fritz Schlemmer to A (German), Coldstream, 17 Oct (1833).

49 RAL, XI/109/33/1/47 (box for 1835), A to N, Frankfurt, 24 Oct (1832).

50 RAL, XI/109/36B (box for 1838), Stultz & Housley, Clifford Street, Mayfair, invoice to N.

51 Bovill, *Nimrod and Surtees*, p. 89; RAL, XI/109/78/1, (Messrs) Anderson & Son to L, 52 South Audley Street, Grosvenor Square, 1 Jan 1851.

52 RAL, XI/109/27/2/7, A to L, Frankfurt, 28 Oct 1832.

53 Berry, *Puckeridge*, pp. 40–41; RAL, XI/109/30/4/20, Fritz Schlemmer to A (German), Coldstream, 17 Oct (1833).

54 RAL, XI/109/47/1/160, N to bros, (Paris, undated, 1844).

55 *SM*, vol. 9, 2nd series, 1834, p. 114; Beresford Chancellor (ed.), *Neumann diary*, vol. I, p. 107; *SM*, vol. 16, ns, 1825, pp. 24–5.

56 *BM*, vol. 25, 1874, p. 218; Berkeley, *Reminiscences*, pp. 56–7.

57 *SM*, vol. 25, ns, Nov 1829; *SM*, vol. 25, ns, Jan 1830.

58 RAL, XI/109/42A/4/33, Charles James Apperley ('Nimrod') to The Baron Rothschild (L), 14 April 1842.

59 *SM*, vol. 8, 2nd series, April 1834.

60 Berry, *Puckeridge*, p. 31.

61 *SM*, vol. 6, 2nd series, Feb 1833.

62 RAL, T File ref XI/109/27/5/22, T22/323, Note to N (German), (undated, 1832 sequence); Beresford Chancellor (ed.), *Neumann diary*, vol. I, p. 107.

7: A SNUFFBOX FROM THE SULTAN

1 RAL, 000/924, Schlemmer, pp. 11–12.

2 Loewe (ed.), *Montefiore diaries*, vol. 1, p. 74.

3 Auldjo, *Journal*, p. 53.

4 RAL, XI/109/29/1/53, N to NM & H, Paris, 27 April 1833.

5 RAL, XI/109/26/1/12 (box for 1832), N to NM & H, Paris, 15 May (1833).

6 RAL, XI/109/29/1/59, N to H, Paris, 18 May 1833.

7 Ayer, *A Century of Finance*, pp. 36–7.

8 RAL, XI/109/29/1/59, N to H, Paris, 18 May 1833; Londonderry, *Steam Voyage*, vol. 1, p. 275.

9 RAL, XI/109/30/1/2, L to H, Paris, 26 May 1833.

10 Kelly, *Carême*, p. 202.

11 RAL, XI/109/30/1/2, L to H, Paris, 26 May 1833; RAL, XI/109/30/2/26, N to NM & H, Hotel Quillacq, Calais, 4 June 1833 – dated 4 May by N, but postmarked Calais 5 June 1833.

12 RAL, XI/82/6/1/17, L to H, Paris, 28 May 1831; RAL, XI/109/101/1, John F. Cay to L, 33 Faubourg St-Honoré, Paris, 5 Jan 1870.

13 RAL, XI/109/30/2/28, N to NM & H, Paris, 9 June (1833); RAL, XI/109/29/1/23, L to NM & H, Paris, 20 June 1833; RAL, XI/109/29/1/22, L to NM & H, Paris, 19 June 1833; RAL, XI/109/30/1/2, L to H, Paris, 26 May 1833.

14 RAL, XI/109/30/2/29, N to NM & H, Frankfurt, 2 July (1833).

15 RAL, XI/109/30/1/8, N to NM & H, Frankfurt, 31 June (1833).

16 RAL, XI/109/30/2/31, N to NM & H, Frankfurt, 10 July 1833.

17 RAL, XI/109/30/2/29, N to NM & H, Frankfurt, 2 July (1833); RAL, XI/109/30/2/30, N to NM & H, Frankfurt, 5 July (1833).

18 RAL, XI/109/30/2/32, N to NM & H, Frankfurt, 17 July 1833; RAL, XI/109/30/1/14, L to A, Paris, 21 July 1833.

19 RAL, XI/109/22/1/34 (box for 1831), N to A, Aix, 18 Aug (1833).

20 RAL, XI/109/30/2/33, N to NM & H, Milan, 24 Aug (1833).

21 RAL, XI/109/30/1/35, L to NM & H, Paris, 21 Sept 1833.

22 Auldjo, *Journal*, pp. 15–16; Slade, *Turkey, etc*, vol. I, p. 187.

23 Ibid., vol. I, pp. 188–9; Murray, *Handbook for Greece*, p. 272.

24 Auldjo, *Journal*, p. 17.

25 RAL, XI/109/32/2/25 (box for 1834), N to NM & H, Nauplia, 24 Sept (1833).

26 RAL, XI/109/32/2/26 (box for 1834), N to H, Nauplia, 26 Sept (1833).

27 Auldjo, *Journal*, p. 18; Slade, *Turkey, etc.* vol. I, p. 188.

28 Ibid., vol. I, pp. 188–9.

29 RAL, XI/109/31/1/73, N to NM & H, Constantinople, 25 Nov 1834 (but 1833).

30 Slade, *Turkey, etc*, vol. II, pp. 263–5.

31 Ibid., vol. I, p. 281.

32 Ibid., vol. I, pp. 283–4.

33 Ibid., vol. I, pp. 286–7.

34 Ibid., vol. II, p. 37; RAL, XI/109/31/1/73, N to NM & H, Constantinople, 25 Nov 1834 (but 1833).

35 Slade, *Turkey, etc*, vol. I, p. 416.

36 Auldjo, *Journal*, pp. 50, 51; RAL, XI/115/5A, 1835–7, section C Misc., copy of a letter from John Cartwright to 'Sir', Constantinople, 18 March 1835; Henrey, *Century Between*, p. 62.

37 Auldjo, *Journal*, pp. 76–7; Henrey, *Century Between*, pp. 59, 61.

38 Auldjo, *Journal*, p. 50; Slade, *Turkey, etc*, vol. I, p. 461.

39 Kinglake, *Eothen*, p. 40; Henrey, *Century Between*, pp. 55–6; Londonderry, *Steam Voyage*, vol. I, p. 165.

40 Slade, *Turkey, etc*, vol. I, p. 448; Auldjo, *Journal*, p. 51; Londonderry, *Steam Voyage*, vol. I, p. 325; RAL, XI/109/31/1/74, N to NM & H, (undated, Constantinople, March–April 1834).

41 RAL, XI/109/31/1/73, N to NM & H, Constantinople, 25 Nov 1834 (but 1833).

42 Ponsonby, *Ponsonby Family*, pp. 75, 80; Loftus, *Diplomatic Reminiscences*, vol. I, pp. 129–30; RAL, XI/109/79/3, CA to L, Vienna, 11 Sept 1851.

43 Slade, *Turkey, etc*, vol. I, p. 411.

44 Cohen, *Lady de Rothschild*, p. 24; Slade, *Turkey, etc*, vol. II, p. 271.

45 Ibid., vol. II, p. 266; ibid., vol. I, p. 363; Cohen, *Lady de Rothschild*, p. 25.

46 Slade, *Turkey, etc*, vol. I, p. 411; Londonderry, *Steam Voyage*, vol. I, p. 188.

47 Slade, *Turkey, etc*, vol. I, p. 412.

48 Murray, *Handbook for Turkey*, p. 34.

49 RAL, XI/109/31/1/69, N to H, Constantinople, 14 Jan 1834.

50 Albemarle, *Fifty Years*, vol. II, p. 275; Londonderry, *Steam Voyage*, vol. I, p. 230.

51 Ibid., pp. 228–30.

52 RAL, XI/109/31/1/69, N to H, Constantinople, 14 Jan 1834.

53 Beresford Chancellor (ed.), *Neumann diary*, vol. II, p. 20; Sudley (ed.), *Lieven–Palmerston Correspondence*, pp. 63, 66, 173; Loewe (ed.), *Montefiore diaries*, vol. 1, p. 261; Barnett, 'A Diary That Survived: Damascus 1840', p. 163.

54 Auldjo, *Journal*, pp. 97–8.

55 RAL, XI/109/32/2/23, N to NM & H, Constantinople, 4 March 1834.

56 Londonderry, *Steam Voyage*, vol. I, p. 211; RAL, XI/109/32/2/23.

57 Slade, *Records*, p. 239.

58 Auldjo, *Journal*, p. 64.

59 Londonderry, *Steam Voyage*, vol. I, p. 271.

60 RAL, XI/109/31/1/74, N to NM & H, (undated, Constantinople, March–April 1834).

61 Slade, *Turkey, etc*, vol. II, p. 381 note; Slade, *Records*, p. 245 note.

62 Walsh, *Residence at Constantinople*, vol. II, p. 297.

63 RAL, XI/109/31/1/69, N to H, Constantinople, 14 Jan 1834.

64 RAL, XI/109/32/2/27, N to NM & H, (undated, Constantinople, March–April 1834).

65 RAL, XI/109/31/1/74, N to NM & H, (undated, Constantinople, March–April 1834).

66 Murray, *Handbook for Turkey*, p. 131; Kinglake, *Eothen*, pp. 1–2.

67 RAL, XI/109/31/1/71, N to NM & H, Vienna, 19 April 1834; RAL, XI/109/31/1/72, N to NM & H, Vienna, 22 April 1834.

68 RAL, XI/109/31/1/72, N to NM & H, Vienna, 22 April 1834.

69 RAL, XI/109/32/2/24, N to NM & H, Frankfurt, 7 May 1834.
70 RAL, XI/109/32/1/52, L to NM & H, Paris, 2 July 1834.

8: GUNNERSBURY PARK

1 RAL, XI/109/29/1/85, HM to L, Brighton, 5 Feb 1833.
2 Loftus, *Diplomatic Reminiscences*, p. 2; *SM*, vol. 9, 2nd series, 1834, p. 116; *NSM*, vol. 14, 1838, pp. 176 & 181.
3 Roth, *Provincial Jewry*, pp. 36, 38.
4 RAL, XI/109/49/1/179, R. Stuckey(?) to Baron Rothschild, (The) Albion (Hotel), Brighton (undated); RAL, XI/109/12/1/25, Benjamin Cohen to NM, New Court, Saturday, 3 o'clock (undated).
5 Roth, *Provincial Jewry*, p. 92; Roth (ed.), *Wolf essays*, 'The Queen's Jewry', p. 312; RAL, XI/109/55/2/125, N to bros, (Paris) 22 March (1846).
6 RAL, 000/10/133, H to A, Paris, 11 Aug 1831.
7 Murray, *High Society*, p. 117; RAL, XI/109/29/1/53, T22/382, H to NM in PS to N to NM, (Brighton) 31 Jan 1833.
8 Baron-Wilson, *St Albans memoirs*, vol. II, pp. 243, 217.
9 RAL, 000/10/148, H to NM, Brighton, 5 Feb 1833.
10 RAL, 000/10/80, H to Lady Carmarthen, 24 Sept (?1830); Bamford and Wellington (eds), *Arbuthnot journal*, vol. I, p. 421, note.
11 Ibid., vol. II, pp. 213, 280; Jennings (ed.), *Croker Papers*, vol. II, p. 311.
12 RAL, XI/109/29/1/85, HM to L, Brighton, 5 Feb 1833.
13 RAL, XI/109/29/1/83, HM, with others, to NM, Brighton, 23 Jan (1833); RAL, XI/109/29/1/86, HM to NM, Brighton, 7 Feb 1833.
14 RAL, XI/109/29/1/82, H, HM & L to NM, Brighton, 9 Jan 1833.
15 RAL, XI/109/17/2/1–30 (box for 1830), Miss M. Andrews to H (continuation sheet), (undated, Frankfurt, 1823–4); RAL, XI/109/29/1/82, H, HM & L to NM, Brighton, 9 Jan 1833.
16 RAL, XI/109/29/1/86, HM, with others, to NM, Brighton, 7 Feb 1833.
17 Boyd, *Reminiscences*, p. 94.
18 RAL, XI/109/30/2/24, M to NM, Coldstream, Oct 1833.
19 RAL, XI/109/30/4/20, Fritz Schlemmer to A (German), The Lees, Coldstream, 17 Oct (1833).
20 Bovill, *Nimrod and Surtees*, p. 68; Carr, *Fox Hunting*, pp. 82, 41.
21 Harper, *Great North Road*, pp. 48–9.
22 RAL, XI/109/30/2/25, M to NM, Edinburgh, 21 Oct (1833).
23 Baron-Wilson, *St Albans memoirs*, vol. II, pp. 194–5.
24 RAL, XI/109/30/4/20, Fritz Schlemmer to A (German), The Lees, Coldstream, 17 Oct (1833).
25 RAL, XI/109/18/1/46 (box for 1831), CA to H, Paris, Monday, 6 Nov (1825).
26 RAL, XI/112/54, Abraham Montefiore to 'My Dear Friends', Clifton, 27 Feb 1821; Leveson Gower (ed.), *Granville letters*, vol. I, p. 143 (letter to Lady M, dated Bolton Abbey, 28 Aug 1819).
27 RAL, 000/239, L's 'Journal through Germany'.
28 RAL, 000/924, Schlemmer, p. 14.
29 *Complete Peerage*, vol. vi, p. 7, note (a).
30 Wheatley, *Piccadilly*, p. 259.

31 Gallatin (ed.), *Gallatin diary*, pp. 108, 52 note, 56.

32 Margoliouth, *Jews*, vol. II, p. 122; Picciotto, *Sketches*, p. 185.

33 Margoliouth, *Jews*, vol. II, p. 123; Picciotto, *Sketches*, p. 186; Roth, *Anglo-Jewish Letters*, p. 200.

34 RAL, 000/924, Schlemmer, pp. 14–15; Harper, *Great North Road*, p. 49.

35 *Gentleman's Magazine*, May 1844, pp. 541–2.

36 Ziegler, *Barings*, pp. 49–51; Ferguson, *Rothschild*, vol. II, p. xxv.

37 Hansard, *Parliamentary Debates*, 3rd series, lxxxvi (1846), pp. 86–7, quoted in Mordaunt Crook, *Nouveaux Riches*, p. 216.

38 RAL, 000/848, Henry Harrison to H, 31 Park St, Grosvenor Square, 1 July 1835; RAL, 000/848, Mr Rainy, of solicitors White, Blake & Houseman (Alexander Copland's executors), to H, Essex Street, Strand, London, 1 July 1835.

39 RAL, 000/848 (particulars on Gunnersbury).

40 RAL, XI/82/6/1/95, L to H, Paris, 7 Aug 1832.

41 RAL, 000/10/142, HM to NM, St Leonard's, 27 Jan (1832); RAL, XI/109/30/2/12, HM & H to NM, Paris, 29 Sept (1833).

42 RAL, XI/109/30/2/15, H to Mr (Thomas) Allason (at Alliance Office, Bartholomew's Lane), Stamford Hill, Thursday 21 Nov 1833.

43 *Boyle's Court Guide, for January 1836.*

44 RAL, 000/13/130, L to A & N, Frankfurt, 9 July 1836.

45 RAL, 000/10/68, H to N, Frankfurt, 17 July 1836.

9: COURTSHIP AND MARRIAGE

1 RAL, XI/109/22/1/46, CA to H, Frankfurt, 17 July (1831).

2 RAL, XI/109/18/1/44, CA to H, Frankfurt, 28 Nov 1831; RAL, XI/109/23/1/24, CA to H, Frankfurt, 9 Dec (1831).

3 RAL, XI/109/26/1/43, Henrietta Montefiore to H, (undated, Frankfurt, 1832).

4 RAL, XI/109/27/2/4, A to NM & H, Frankfurt, 18 Oct 1832; RAL, XI/109/27/2/23, A to H, Frankfurt, 4 Dec 1832.

5 RAL, 000/297/B, LA to LMC, Naples, 25 March 1834.

6 RAL, XI/109/31/1/66, CA to H, (Frankfurt) 27 April (1834).

7 Ferguson, *Rothschild*, vol. I, p. 385.

8 RAL, XI/109/32/1/24, L to NM & H, Paris, 19 May 1834.

9 RAL, XI/109/32/1/86, L to A (in Paris), Madrid, 30 Nov 1834.

10 RAL, XI/109/32/1/89, L to A, continuation sheet, (undated, Madrid, 1834).

11 RAL, XI/82/5/1/14 & 16 (box XI/109/82), L to A (in Paris), Madrid, 13 Dec 1834; RAL, XI/109/33/1/2, L to A (in Paris), Madrid, 15 Feb 1835.

12 RAL, XI/109/86B, (Trinidad) Huerta to L, London, 22 June 1865; RAL, XI/109/68A/1/289, Lionel Helbert to M, Madrid, 10 April 1848.

13 RAL, XI/109/33/1/6, L to A (in Paris), Madrid, 21 March 1835.

14 RAL, 000/10/1, H to CL, London, 29 Sept 1835.

15 RAL, 000/10/2, H to CL, London, 24 Oct 1835.

16 RAL, 000/13/2, L to CL, Metz, Monday night (Jan 1836).

17 RAL, 000/13/5, L to CL, Paris, 7 Jan 1836.

18 RAL, 000/848, nos. 1–13, CL to L, Frankfurt, 8 Jan 1836.

19 Battersea, *Reminiscences*, p. 23; RAL, XI/109/71/2, W. Howe to 'Baron', 154 New Bond Street, London, 1 May (1849).

20 RAL, 000/13/6, L to CL, Paris, 13 Jan 1836.

21 RAL, 000/13/3, L to CL, (Paris) undated (Jan 1836); RAL, 000/13/4, L to CL, Paris, 7 Jan 1836.

22 RAL, 000/13/5, L to CL, Paris, 7 Jan 1836.

23 RAL, 000/13/7, L to CL, (Paris) 16 Jan (1836).

24 RAL, 000/13/8, L to CL, Paris, 17 Jan 1836.

25 See, e.g., RAL, 000/13/11, L to CL, London, 27 Jan 1836; RAL, 000/13/9, L to CL, London, 22 Jan 1836.

26 RAL, 000/13/11, L to CL, London, 27 Jan 1836; RAL, 000/13/100, L to CL, London (undated, 1836).

27 RAL, 000/184, B17Anth 1836/7, A to N, (Paris) 1 June (1836); RAL, 000/184, B17Anth 1836/65, A to N, (Paris, undated, 1836).

28 RAL, 000/13/13, L to CL, London, 6 Feb 1836.

29 RAL, 000/13/19, L to CL, London, 19 Feb 1836; RAL, 000/10/3, H to CL, London, 23 Feb 1836.

30 RAL, 000/13/21, L to CL, London, 27 Feb 1836.

31 Annual Biography and Obituary, p. 64; RAL, 000/13/26, L to CL, London, 12 March (1836); Boyle's Court Guide, for January 1838, p. 122.

32 Ferguson, Rothschild, vol. I, pp. 299–300.

33 Rosebery Papers, Dalmeny House (transcript RAL), H to M, Roehampton, 11 Oct 1836.

34 RAL, 000/184, B17Anth 1836/69, A to bros, Paris, 31 Dec 1836.

35 Ferguson, Rothschild, vol. I, pp. 295, 370.

36 RAL, 000/1067, Leonora.

37 RAL, XI/109/36/1/6, Adelheid to H, Frankfurt, 25 Sept 1838.

38 RAL, 000/1067, Evelina.

39 RAL, XI/103/0, 1839, no. 54, A to L, Paris, 28 Aug (1839).

40 RAL, XI/104/0, no. 168, James to nephews (at New Court), (Paris, undated, 1840); RAL, XI/109/72/2, L to M, Wildbad, 7 Aug 1849.

41 RAL, XI/103/0/12, A to bros, Paris, (undated, early 1839).

42 RAL, XI/109/37/2/4, Moses Montefiore to Messrs R, London, with PS from Judith M, Naples, 19 March 1839.

43 RAL, XI/109/37/1/1, Alphonse to L, (Paris) 8 April 1839; RAL, XI/109/37/3/30, Alexander Philp to 'Rothschild Esq' at St Swithun's (sic) Lane, 3 Brown's Buildings, St Mary Axe, Thursday Morng (undated, 1839).

44 RAL, XI/103/0/11, A to N, (Paris) 23 April (1839).

45 Battersea, Reminiscences, p. 54; RAL, XI/109/72/1, J(?) Sheard(?) to L, 4 St John's Road, Oxford, 28 July 1849; Henrey, Century Between, pp. 11–12.

46 RAL, XI/109/72/1, J(?) Sheard(?) to L, 4 St John's Road, Oxford, 28 July 1849.

47 RAL, XI/103/0/40(a), A to bros, Heinrichsbad, 17 July (1839).

48 RAL, XI/101/2, James to N (Judendeutsch), 29 June and 16 July 1839.

49 Henrey, Century Between, pp. 21–2.

50 Ibid., p. 26.

51 Ibid., pp. 36, 44.

52 Annual Biography and Obituary, pp. 64–5.

53 RAL, XI/109/66/1/41, N to bros, (Paris) Tuesday 4 April (1848).

54 Bamford and Wellington (eds), Arbuthnot journal, vol. II, p. 324; Fowler, Echoes, p. 4.

55 RAL, XI/101/2, James to N (Judendeutsch), 16 July 1839.

56 RAL, XI/103/0, biro ref. 40, T7/9, A to N & L, (Heinrichsbad) 17 July 1839.

57 RAL, 000/10/83, H to N, (Paris) Sunday 19 May (1839); RAL, 000/136, LA to A, 18 Jan (1840); RAL, XI/104/1/91, A to bros, (Frankfurt, undated, July 1841); *SM*, vol. 1, 3rd series, 1843, pp. 184–93.

58 RAL, XI/109/55/140, T24/270, Anselm to cousins, Frankfurt, 14 Aug 1843; RAL, XI/109/50, undated folder, ref. 129, N to bros, (Paris, undated, 1844); RAL, XI/109/47/1/140, N to bros, (Paris, undated, 1844).

10: THE CRACK PACK

1 RAL, 000/239, L's 'Journal through Germany'; RAL, XI/109/27/3/11, CA to H, Frankfurt, 17 Oct (1832).

2 RAL, 000/924, Schlemmer, pp. 16–17.

3 Ibid. pp. 17–18.

4 Storck (ed.), *Schumann letters*, p. 103.

5 Ward Jones (trans. & ed.), *Mendelssohns on Honeymoon*, p. 35, fig. 1; RAL, XI/109/34/1/16, Fritz Schlemmer to N (German), Leipzig, 24 July 1836.

6 Howitt, *German Experiences*, p. 65.

7 RAL, XI/112/122/3, Fritz Schlemmer to N (German), Leipzig, 16 Dec 1836; Rosebery Papers, Dalmeny House (transcript RAL), H to M, 15 Nov 1836; Davis, *English Rothschilds*, p. 54.

8 Rosebery Papers, Dalmeny House (transcript RAL), H to M, Roehampton, 9 Nov 1836.

9 RAL, XI/112/122/2, Fritz Schlemmer to N (German), 16 Nov 1836; Davis, *English Rothschilds*, p. 51.

10 Quoted in Cohen, *Changing Faces*, pp. 24–5.

11 RAL, XI/109/36/1/1 (box for 1838), L to N, Paris, 27 Dec 18(37?).

12 Loewe (ed.), *Montefiore diaries*, vol. 1, pp. 114, 115, 131.

13 Cohen, *Changing Faces*, p. 25.

14 Battersea, *Reminiscences*, p. 229; RAL 000/1373, 'The History of the Firm' by A. R. Wagg (typescript).

15 Kessler, 'Rothschilds and Disraeli', p. 13; Bamford and Wellington (eds), *Arbuthnot journal*, vol. I, ill. opp. p. 412; ibid., vol. I, pp. 374, 213–14 note, 409.

16 Disraeli, *Correspondence with His Sister*, pp. 94–5.

17 Bermant, *Cousinhood*, pp. 59–60; Disraeli, *Correspondence with His Sister*, p. 106; Loewe (ed.), *Montefiore diaries*, vol. 1, p. 142; *Court Gazette*, 21 July 1838, quoted in Bermant, *Cousinhood*, p. 60.

18 Loewe (ed.), *Montefiore diaries*, vol. 1, p. 142.

19 Bessborough (ed.), *Guest journal*, p. 72.

20 Loewe (ed.), *Montefiore diaries*, vol. 1, p. 142.

21 Baron-Wilson, *St Albans memoirs*, vol. II, pp. 265–70; Loewe (ed.), *Montefiore diaries*, vol. 1, p. 143.

22 Mordaunt Crook, *Nouveaux Riches*, p. 52, quoting from Disraeli's *Falconet* (1881; Bradenham edition, 1927).

23 Beresford Chancellor (ed.), *Neumann diary*, vol. II, p. 136.

24 RAL, XI/109/33/2/13, George Samuel to N, Lisbon, 4 April 1835.

25 Page (ed.), *Victoria County History: Middlesex*, vol. 3, p. 192.

26 *NSM*, vol. 12, 1837, pp. 182–3.

27 *SM*, vol. 18, 1838–9, p. 174; Loewe (ed.), *Montefiore diaries*, vol. 1, p. 65.

28 *SM*, vol. 16, 1837–8, p. 469; *NSM*, vol. 14, 1838, pp. 267–8.

29 *The Field*, 4 Dec 1858, 'Mr Harvey Combe' (obituary); Battersea, *Reminiscences*, p. 27.

30 *SM*, vol. 21, 1840, p. 348.

31 RAL, 000/184, B17Anth 1836/65, A to N (in London), (Paris, undated, 1836); RAL, 000/184, B17Anth 1836/25, A to N (in London), (Paris) 13 July (1836); RAL, 000/184, B17Anth 1836/44, A to N (in London), (Paris, undated, 1836).

32 RAL, XI/109/78/7, Seymour Huffam to M, Newmarket, Monday Evg (undated, Jan–June 1851); *SM*, vol. 26, 3rd series, 1855, 'Turf Register', p. 93.

33 RAL, XI/109/36/1/23, Joe Montefiore to L, Sunday, postmarked Crawley 21 Oct 1838.

34 RAL, XI/109/36/1/1, L to N, Paris, 27 Dec (1838).

35 RAL, XI/103/0, 1839, no. 57, A to bros, (Paris) 20 Sept (1839).

36 RAL, XI/109/37/6/1–68, Joseph Anderson to N, Piccadilly, 3 Jan 1839.

37 Berkeley, *Reminiscences*, p. 24; Dixon, *Scott and Sebright*, p. 287.

38 RAL, XI/109/37/3/20, William Herring to N at New Court, London, 25 Sept 1839.

39 RAL, XI/109/37/3/25, Thomas Hart to 'BR' at Tring House, Ascott, 22 Nov 1839; RAL, XI/109/37/3/28, Henry Charles Sawyer to Fitz Oldaker, postmarked 23 Nov 1839.

40 RAL, XI/109/38/3/3, John Glenister to L, Tring, 3 Feb 1840; RAL, XI/109/37/3/26, John Field to N, 224 Oxford Street, 22 Nov 1839; *BM*, vol. 18, 1870, p. 107.

41 RAL, XI/109/39/3/10, 8 Aug 1840; Rothschild, *Dear Lord Rothschild*, p. 4; Kessler, 'Rothschilds and Disraeli', p. 8.

42 Rothschild, *Dear Lord Rothschild*, p. 4.

43 Kitching (ed.), *Crewe journals*, pp. 42–3.

44 Austen Leigh, *Memoir*, pp. 47, 61, 49, 71–2.

45 Baron-Wilson, *St Albans memoirs*, vol. II, p. 141; RAL, XI/104/1/5/117, A to bros, (Frankfurt) 27 Aug 1841.

46 RAL, XI/109/25/3/40, L. A. Lowdham to NM, 13 Lin[coln's] Inn Fields, Monday (undated, box for 1832); RAL, XI/109/25/3/2, Mr Ward to NM, Customs, Dover, 2 Jan 1832.

47 RAL, XI/109/40/1/3, John Glenister to L, Tring Park, 7 Jan 1841.

48 RAL, XI/109/37/3/29, Major Henniker to 'de Rothschild', Friday 23 (1839).

49 RAL, XI/109/38/3/10, Mr Dashwood to Baron Rothschild at Hastoe Kenel (*sic*), West Wycombe, 14 March 1840.

50 Kessler, 'Rothschilds and Disraeli', pp. 12–13; Davis, *English Rothschilds*, p. 93; Ferguson, *Rothschild*, vol. I, p. 339; RAL, XI/104/0, 129/368, N to bros, Paris, 21 Nov (1840).

51 Berkeley, *Reminiscences*, p. 56.

52 *NSM*, vol. 14, 1838, pp. 180–82; *SM*, vol. 41, 1863, p. 108.

53 RAL, XI/109/39/3/25, Charles Davis to L, Ascot, 24 Oct 1840; RAL, XI/109/51B/197, R. B. Davis to Baron de Rothschild (L), 9 Bedford Place, Kensington, 25 March 1845.

54 *BM*, vol. 9, 1864–5, 1864, p. 63; Gash, *Surtees*, pp. 32–3; Cowen, *Victorian Jews*, p. 4 (ill.).

55 Gash, *Surtees*, pp. 29, 32; Surtees, *Ask Mamma, passim*; id., *Plain or Ringlets*, pp. 81–2, 114.

56 RAL, 000/24, CL to Leo, London, 7 Oct 1862; RAL, XI/109/44/1/37, Charles

James Apperley to 'the Baron Rothschild', 20 Upper Belgrave Place, 10 April 1843; *SM*, vol. 16, 1825, p. 241.

57 Liedtke, 'Nathan Rothschild and London Jewry', p. 50; Salbstein, *Emancipation*, p. 37.

58 *SM*, vol. 11, 1848, pp. 165–6; RAL, XI/109/78/3, Henry Poole to M, London, 4 March 1851; Fowler, *Echoes*, p. 4.

59 RAL, XI/109/42A/2/17, N to bros, Paris, 4 March (1842); RAL, XI/109/43A/2/160, N to bros, Sunday (Paris, undated, 1842); RAL, XI/109/57/4/64, N to L, (Ostende/Dieppe, undated, 1846); Willoughby de Broke, *Passing Years*, p. 163.

60 RAL, XI/103/0/10, A to N, (Paris) 18 April (1839); RAL, XI/103/0/11, A to N, (Paris) 23 April (1839); Lejeune, *Gentlemen's Clubs*, p. 105; Gallatin (ed.), *Gallatin diary*, p. 265.

61 Gronow, *Reminiscences*, vol. 2, p. 83; RAL, XI/109/57/1/53, N to bros, Wildbad, 8 July (1846).

62 Gronow, *Reminiscences*, vol. 1, p. 278; RAL, XI/104/0, 53/222, N to bros, Paris, 2 June 1840.

63 RAL, XI/109/38/3/14, N from (?Initials) Hampton, Secretary of the Windham Club, 2 May 1840; RAL, 000/13/61, L to CL, Evy & Natty, London, 30 July 1860; Eeles and Spencer, *Brooks's*, p. 62.

64 *SM*, vol. 20, 1827, p. 9.

65 RAL, XI/104/0, 1840, 128/367, N to bros, Paris, 20 Nov (1840); RAL, XI/104/1/6, 1841, N to bros, (Paris, undated, 1841).

66 *BM*, vol. 18, 1870, p. 107.

67 *SM*, vol. 24, 1841–2, p. 199; *BM*, vol. 34, Aug 1879, p. 147.; *SM*, vol. 24, 1841–2, pp. 199–200.

68 Brooks's Club candidates' books, 1841–2, 1850; *BM*, vol. 23, 1873, p. 252.

11: TOWN AND COUNTRY

1 *Gentleman's Magazine*, vol. 8, 1837, p. 425; *Boyle's Court Guide, for January 1840*.

2 RAL, XI/109/43A/1/62, 'Estimates of improvements at No. 148 Piccadilly for the Baron Lionel de Rothschild, by W. Cubitt', October 1842.

3 RAL, XI/109/50/1/16, John Tollemache to L, 2 Dec 1844; RAL, XI/109/55/106, T24/236, CA in PS to Anselm to cousins, Scheveningen, 13 June (1843); RAL, XI/109/45B/6/131, N to bros, (Paris) Sunday (undated, 1843).

4 RAL, 000/13/39, L to CL, Edinburgh, Thursday morning (undated, mid-Aug 1843); RAL, XI/109/56/73, T24/351, Anselm to L, Frankfurt, 17 March (1844).

5 RAL, XI/109/51B/2/27, N to bros, (Paris, undated, early 1845); RAL, XI/109/64A/1/199, L to Mr Myddleton Biddulph at the Clarendon Hotel (draft), 25 Oct 1847; RAL, XI/109/46/2/9, note from Mary Cobham on behalf of CL, (undated, Jan–Feb 1844); RAL, XI/109/73/3, Mary Cobham to no addressee, 148 Piccadilly, 8 Dec 1849.

6 RAL, T6/139; RAL, XI/109/64B/1/61, Edmund Antrobus to L, 11 Dec 1847.

7 Bamford and Wellington (eds), *Arbuthnot journal*, vol. II, p. 321.

8 RAL, XI/109/54B/2/81, N to bros, (Paris, undated, Oct–Dec 1845); RAL, XI/109/51A/2/144, Michael L—? to L, 22 Henrietta St, Cavendish Square, 12 March (1845); RAL, XI/109/51A/2/194, Lord Rosebery to L, Piccadilly, 24 March (1845); RAL, XI/109/51A/2/196, B(?) Yelland(?) to L, 55 Mount St, Grosvenor Square, 25 March (1845).

9 Kauffmann, *Wellington Museum*, p. 10; Jennings (ed.), *Croker Papers*, vol. I, p. 426.

10 RAL, 000/13/6, L to CL, 13 Jan 1836.

11 RAL, XI/104/0 (1840; ink no. 47, pencil no. 196), N to bros, (Paris) Friday (undated).

12 RAL, XI/109/20/1/42, L to H, Paris, 27 April (1831).

13 RAL, XI/82/6/1/89, L to H, Paris, 31 July 1832.

14 Wilson, *English Country House*, p. 143; Bamford and Wellington (eds), *Arbuthnot journal*, vol. I, p. 53 (14 Nov 1820).

15 Sotheby's Mentmore sale catalogue (1977), vol. I, lot 905, pp. 298–300.

16 RAL, 000/848, N to bros, Paris, 8 Oct 184(?).

17 RAL, XI/109/32/1/86, L to A, Madrid, 30 Nov 1834; RAL, XI/82/5/1/7?, L to A, Madrid, 10 June 1835.

18 RAL, XI/109/36/4/22, Dr Taylor Gordon to 'The Baron Rothschild, London' (L), Lymington, Tuesday, postmarked 18 April 1838.

19 *Gentleman's Magazine*, vol. 13, ns, 1840, p. 624.

20 RAL, XI/104/0 (1840; no. 190), James to A, Paris, 12 May 1840.

21 Dasent, *Piccadilly*, p. 121.

22 RAL, 000/184, B17Anth 1836/68, A to bros, (Paris, undated, 1836–7).

23 RAL, XI/109/53A/2/97, D/Dr A. Reubens to L, 46 Greek Street, Soho, 14 Aug 1845; RAL, XI/109/76/4, M to bros, Ross (Herefordshire), Wednesday (undated, July–Sept 1850); RAL, XI/103/0/10, A to N, (Paris) 18 April (1839).

24 *SM*, vol. 19, 1839, pp. 177–9.

25 RAL, XI/109/37/1/2, L to N, Suresnes, Sunday 19 May (1839).

26 *SM*, vol. 20, 1840, p. 308.

27 Onslow, *Headquarters*, pp. 74, 75.

28 *NSM*, vol. 11, 1837, p. 458; RAL, XI/109/42A/2/42, N to bros, (Paris) 7 May (1842).

29 RAL, XI/103/0, M to bros, Baden-Baden, 7 July (1839).

30 RAL, XI/103/0 (no. 38; T7/8), A to bros, (Baden-Baden) Friday 11 July (1839).

31 Disraeli, *Correspondence with His Sister*, p. 73.

32 Battersea, *Reminiscences*, p. 3; RAL, XI/109/61/2/100, N to bros, (Paris, undated, 1847).

33 Quoted in Kass, 'Friends and Philanthropists: Montefiore and Dr Hodgkin', pp. 72, 75–6, 78.

34 RAL, XI/103/0, Anselm to cousins, Paris, 14 Nov 1839; RAL, XI/103/0, Anselm to cousins, Paris, 22 Nov 1839.

35 RAL, 000/136, LA to A, 7 Jan 1840.

36 RAL, XI/109/37/1/7, CA to H, (Paris) Thursday (undated, Nov–Dec 1839).

37 RAL, 000/136, LA to A, postmarked 31 Dec 1839.

38 RAL, XI/104/0/136, A to bros, (undated, early April 1840).

39 Battersea, *Reminiscences*, p. 62.

40 RAL, XI/109/43A/2/7, A to bros, (Paris) 15 Sept 1842; RAL, XI/109/43A/2/83, A to bros, (Paris) 25 J(?) (no year).

41 Walsh, '19/20 Grosvenor Place', Part 1; Battersea, *Reminiscences*, p. 336.

42 Ibid. pp. 51–2.

43 RAL, XI/109/45A/1/12, A to bros, (Paris) 11 Aug 1843; RAL, XI/109/48A/216, Philip Nowell to A, Pimlico, 17 Sept 1844; Battersea, *Reminiscences*, p. 10.

44 Ibid., p. 16, 17; Cohen, *Lady de Rothschild*, pp. 31, 32.

45 Mordaunt Crook, *Nouveaux Riches*, p. 39.

46 RAL, 000/10/4, H to L & M, Derby, 29 Sept 1841.

47 RAL, 000/10/5, H to CL, York, 5 Oct 1841.

48 RAL, 000/10/7, H to L & M, Mulgrave Castle, (?)12 Oct 1841.

49 RAL, 000/10/11, H to L, Dumfries, 30 Oct 1841.

50 RAL, 000/10/12, H to CL, Lancaster, 3 Nov 1841.

51 RAL, 000/13/40, L to CL, Thirsk, Aug 1843.

52 RAL, 000/13/36, L to CL, Alnwick, Tuesday morning (undated, Aug 1843).

53 RAL, 000/13/39, L to CL, Edinburgh, Thursday morning (undated, Aug 1843).

54 RAL, XI/109/58B/1/158, Bot(?) of Dixon & Douglas, French & Italian Warehouse, 81 George Street, Edinburgh, to Edward Turner, 2 New Court, 4 Jan 1847.

55 RAL, 000/13/42, L to CL, Crieff, 19 Aug 1843.

56 RAL, 000/13/42, L to CL, Crieff, 19 Aug 1843; RAL, 000/13/44, L to CL, Crieff, 23 Aug 1843.

57 RAL, 000/13/45, L to CL, Crieff, 25 Aug 1843; RAL, XI/109/55/1/171, T7/122, Alphonse to M, Paris, 31 Jan (1844).

58 RAL, 000/13/43, L to CL, Crieff, 22 Aug 1843; RAL, 000/13/42, L to CL, Crieff, 19 Aug 1843.

59 Ferguson, *Rothschild*, vol. I, p. 192; RAL, 000/10/67, H to M, postmarked Paris 2 Sept 1842.

60 *SM*, vol. 1, 3rd series, 1843, pp. 144–5.

61 RAL, XI/104/0 (1840; ink no. 76, pencil no. 279), N to bros, Paris (undated).

62 RAL, XI/109/39/3/9, Sarah Norwood to Baron R, Rose & Crown, Tring, 8 Aug 1840.

63 RAL, XI/109/37/3/3, J. R. Glenister to L, Tring, 2 April 1839; RAL, XI/109/37/2/12, John Abel Smith to L (undated); RAL, XI/109/37/3/13, Fairbrothers, solicitors, to Rothschild, 14 Aug 1839.

64 RAL, XI/109/41/1/30, Thos Marshall to L, Amersham, 4 Nov 1841.

65 RAL, XI/104/0 (1840; ink no. 62, pencil no. 245), N to bros, Paris (undated); RAL, XI/109/47/2/51A, Anselm to A & N (in Paris), (Frankfurt) 17 June/July (1844); RAL, XI/109/0 (1840; ink no. 133, pencil no. 374), A to cousins, Frankfurt, 25 Nov 1840.

66 RAL, XI/104/0 (1840; 34/167), N to bros, Paris, 24 April 1840.

67 RAL, XI/104/0 (1840; 62/245), N to bros, Paris (undated, 1840); RAL, XI/104/0 (1840, 49/198), N to bros, Paris, 21 May (1840).

68 RAL, XI/109/38/3/18, W. Brown to Baron M. Rothschild (M) at New Court, Tring, 14 May 1840; RAL, XI/109/39/3/4, W. Brown to Baron Rothschild (M) at New Court, Tring, 1 July 1840; RAL, XI/109/39/3/20, Mr Gordon, on behalf of A, to 'Sir H. S. Blane, Bart, Moor Place', Stocks, Hemel Hempstead, 10 Oct 1840, and RAL, XI/109/39/3/22, Recipient of XI/109/39/3/20 to A, Mount St, 13 Oct 1840.

69 RAL, XI/104/0 (1840, 46/194), N to bros, Paris, 18 May (1840); RAL, XI/104/0 (1840, 53/222), N to bros, Paris, 2 June 1840.

70 RAL, XI/109/43A/1/61, ?W. Brown to 'Baron Rothschild' at New Court, Tring, 26 Oct 1842; RAL, XI/109/49/1/15, L to bros, Paris, 3 Oct 1844; RAL, XI/109/49/1/163, Thos Hart to 'Baron Rothschild', Ascott, 29 Oct 1844; RAL, XI/109/43A/1/54, Messrs David Smith & Son, Waterloo Place, Pall Mall, to A, 29 Aug 1842.

71 RAL, XI/109/43A/1/55, Richard Dawes to M, Angel Court, Throgmorton Street, 7 Sept 1842; RAL, XI/109/43A/1/60, Richard Dawes to M, Angel Court,

Throgmorton Street, 15 Oct 1842; RAL, XI/109/45A/3/13, M to bros, Carlisle, Saturday morning (undated, postmarked Carlisle (?date) 1843); RAL, XI/109/43A/2/43, A to bros, (Paris, undated, late Oct 1842).

72 RAL, XI/104/1/5/106 (1841), A to bros, (Frankfurt) 8 Aug 1841; and RAL, XI/109/41/1/24, A to L, Tring, 28 Oct 1841; *SM*, vol. 1, 3rd series, 1843, p. 185.

73 RAL, XI/109/43A/4/31, John Harris to L, (undated, indistinct postmark, 1842).

74 RAL, XI/109/44A/1/36, John Cole, Park Keeper, Chillingham, to L at 148 Piccadilly, Chillingham, 9 April 1843; RAL, XI/109/44A/1/35, (Lord) Ossulston to 'Dear Rothschild' (L), London, 3 April 1843; RAL, XI/109/49/1/23, G. M. Palmer, Park Keeper to Earl Fitzwilliam, to M at 107 Piccadilly, Wood North, Wentworth Park, near Rotherham, 4 Oct 1844; RAL, XI/109/50/unreferenced folder/91 (1844, 7th box), valuation of late Charles Stuart Wortley's red deer; RAL, XI/109/52A/2/110, James S. Wortley to 'Dear Sir', 19 Lower Grosvenor Street, 17 May 1845; *SM*, vol. 5, 3rd series, ns, 1845, p. 67.

75 *SM*, vol. 1, 3rd series, 1843, p. 192; RAL, XI/109/52B/1/83, L to no addressee (draft), London, 14 June 1845.

76 *BM*, vol. 12, 1867, p. 342; ibid., vol. 34, 1879, p. 147.

77 RAL, XI/109/44A/1/66, Major Richard Gilpin to 'My dear Baron' (L), Hockcliffe Grange, 9 Feb 1843; RAL, XI/109/43A/2/160, N to bros, (Paris) Sunday (undated, 1842).

78 *SM*, vol. 1, 3rd series, 1843, p. 192; RAL, XI/109/50 (box for 1844, undated folder, ref. 57), L to A, Mentmore, Wednesday Evng (undated, 1844), and ref. 73, GC to L, Winslow, Monday (undated, 1844).

79 *BM*, vol. 20, 1871, p. 8; RAL, XI/109/45B/6/116, N to bros, (Paris, undated, 1843); *SM*, vol. 38, 3rd series, 1861, pp. 451–3.

80 RAL, XI/109/45A/3/40, Capt. Richard Howard Vyse to 'My dear R', 25 Dec 1843; RAL, XI/109/44A/1/66, Richard Gilpin to 'My dear Baron' (L), Hockcliffe Grange, 9 Feb 1843, and see *Army List for 1839*, p. 488; RAL, XI/109/64B/1/87, H to L, (Woburn) 14 Dec 1847.

81 Fowler, *Echoes*, p. 98.

82 *BM*, vol. 20, 1871, pp. 8, 12.

83 RAL, XI/109/44A/1/34, J. Sherriff to no addressee, Aylesbury, 13 March 1843; RAL, XI/109/45A/3/23, Richard Dighton to 'Dear Sir', 13 Severn Terrace, Worcester, 26 Dec 1843.

84 RAL, XI/109/42A/2/20, N to bros, (Paris, undated, 1842); RAL, XI/109/73/1, Adolphe to Fitz Oldaker, (Naples, undated, Oct 1849); RAL, XI/109/82/4, Adolphe to L, (undated, July–Sept 1852); *SM*, vol. 38, 3rd series, 1861, pp. 451–3; RAL, XI/109/42A/2/19, N to bros, Paris, 8 March (1842); RAL, XI/109/56/1/84, invitation to 'BR'; *SM*, vol. 7, 3rd series, 1846, p. 346; *BM*, vol. 20, 1871, p. 8.

85 RAL, 000/924, Francis Grant to CL, 27 Sussex Place, Regent's Park, 4 Jan (1860s?); RAL, XI/109/70/3, March 1849, Francis Grant to L, Sussex Villa, Regent's Park, 26 March (1849).

12: COMPETITORS

1 Murray, *Recollections*, p. 48.
2 Ferguson, *Rothschild*, vol. I, pp. 155–6.
3 Wolf, 'Rothschildiana', p. 273.

4 Ferguson, *Rothschild*, vol. I, p. 157.

5 RAL, XI/109/38/3/31, T23/145, F. Schenk to Messrs von Rothschild, Buckingham Palace, 19 March 1840; RAL, XI/109/61/1/49, G. Anson to 'My Dear Baron', Buckingham Palace, 9 June 1847; RAL, XI/109/77/2, Baron Stockmar to L, Windsor Castle, 19 Nov 1850; RAL, XI/109/60/2/104, Dr Meyer to L, Buckingham Palace, 12 May 1844; Ferguson, *Rothschild*, vol. I, p. 387.

6 RAL, XI/109/52B/1/147, MC to cousins, Frankfurt, 24 June 1845; Loewe (ed.), *Montefiore diaries*, vol. 1, p. 142.

7 Beresford Chancellor (ed.), *Neumann diary*, vol. II, p. 267; RAL, T8/72, XI/109/69b/2/66, CL to L in Paris, Gunnersbury, 3 Oct (1848?); Loewe (ed.), *Montefiore diaries*, vol. 1, p. 317.

8 RAL, XI/109/42A/2/39, N to bros, (Paris) 30 April (1842); RAL, XI/109/42A/2/43, N to bros, (Paris, undated, 1842).

9 RAL, XI/109/42A/2/42, N to bros, (Paris) 7 May (1842).

10 RAL, XI/109/42A/2/47, N to bros, (Paris, undated, 1842).

11 RAL, XI/109/42A/2/45, N to bros, (Paris, undated, 1842); RAL, XI/109/47/1/125, N to bros, (Paris, undated, 1844).

12 RAL, XI/109/42A/2/41, N to bros, (Paris) 4 May (1842).

13 *The Times*, Saturday 14 May 1843, pp. 6–7.

14 RAL, XI/109/42A/2/48, N to bros, (Paris) 14 May (1842); RAL, XI/109/42A/2/49, N to bros, (Paris) 15 May (1842).

15 RAL, XI/109/53A/1/176, MC to cousins, (Frankfurt) 28 July 1845; RAL, XI/109/53A/2/46, MC to cousins, (Frankfurt) 6 Aug 1845; RAL, XI/109/53A/2/119, MC to L, Mainz, 17 Aug 1845.

16 RAL, XI/109/53A/2, between 115 & 116, Anselm to cousins, (Frankfurt) 17 Aug 1845; RAL, XI/109/53A/2/119, MC to L, Mainz, 17 Aug 1845.

17 RAL, XI/109/53B/1/70, G. Anson to L, Osborne House, 20 Sept 1845.

18 RAL, 000/10/44, H to CL, Paris (undated) 1845.

19 RAL, XI/109/52B/1/63, CA to L, Frankfurt, 11 June (1845); RAL, XI/109/52B/1/77, LMC to M, Frankfurt, 13 June 1845; *The Times*, Monday 9 June 1845, p. 6.

20 RAL, XI/109/37/1/8 (box for 1839), A & M to H, (Heinrichsbad, undated, 1839).

21 RAL, XI/109/37/1/3, Betty to H, Heinrichsbad, 19 July (1839).

22 RAL, XI/103/0/2, Anselm to cousins, Paris, 12 Aug 1839; RAL, XI/103/0, Anselm to cousins, Paris, ?14 Oct 1839.

23 RAL, XI/103/0 (1839; no. 57), A to bros, (Paris, undated, late Oct 1839); RAL, XI/104/0 (1840; 143/389), CA to N, Frankfurt, Monday (undated).

24 RAL, XI/104/0 (1840; 23/163), N to bros, Paris, 18 April 1840.

25 Raikes, *Journal*, vol. II, p. 335.

26 RAL, XI/109/42A/2/36, N to bros, Paris, 31 March (1842).

27 RAL, XI/109/42A/2/38, N to bros, Paris, 20 April (1842); RAL, XI/109/42A/2/54, N to H, (Paris) 26 May (1842).

28 RAL, XI/109/42A/2/8, A to bros, (Paris, undated, 1842).

29 RAL, XI/109/42A/2/61, N to bros, Paris, 11 June 1842; RAL, XI/109/42A/2/63, N to bros, (Paris, undated, 1842); RAL, XI/109/42A/2/57, N to bros, (Paris, undated, 1842); Cohen, *Lady de Rothschild*, p. 23.

30 RAL, XI/109/42A/2/10, A to bros, (Paris, undated, 1842); Cohen, *Lady de Rothschild*, p. 22; Mansel, *Paris*, p. 293.

31 RAL, 000/10/17, H to M, (undated, August) 1842; RAL, 000/13/28, L to CL (Paris, undated, Aug 1842).

32 See, e.g., RAL, XI/109/46A/1/62, N to bros, (Paris) 17 Feb (1844); Mansel, *Paris*, p. 366.

33 RAL, XI/109/42A/2/29, N to bros, (Paris, undated, 1842); RAL, XI/109/42A/2/77, N to bros, (Paris, undated, 1842); RAL, XI/109/42A/2/1, A to bros, (Paris) 23 May (1842); RAL, XI/109/43A/2/154, N to bros, 24 Dec 1842, and RAL, XI/109/46A/1/80, N to bros (PS to A), (Paris, undated, box for 1844).

34 RAL, XI/109/94/1, James to A, Paris, 7 May 1868; RAL, XI/109/94/3, H. R. Phillips to L, Albert Gate, Knightsbridge, SW, London, 8 April 1868; RAL, XI/109/42A/2/15, N to bros, (Paris, undated, 1842); RAL, XI/109/42A/2/48, N to bros, (Paris) 14 May (1842); RAL, XI/109/43A/2/110, N to L, (Paris) 30 Sept (1842).

35 RAL, XI/109/42A/2/65, N to bros, (Paris, undated, 1842); RAL, XI/109/42A/2/53, N to bros, Paris, 23 June 1842.

36 RAL, XI/109/43A/2/138, N to L (Paris, undated).

37 RAL, XI/109/43A/2/116, N to bros, Paris, 9 Nov (1842); RAL, XI/109/43A/2/117, N to bros, (Paris) 13 Nov (1842); RAL, XI/109/43A/2/118, N to bros, (Paris) 15 Nov (1842); RAL, XI/109/43A/2/128, N to bros, Paris, 24 Dec 1842.

38 RAL, XI/109/43A/2/128, N to bros, Paris, 24 Dec 1842; RAL, XI/109/43A/2/137, N to L, (Paris, undated, 1842); RAL, XI/109/45/6/5, N to bros, Paris, 17 Jan (1843).

39 RAL, XI/109/45A/1/27, A to bros (PS from N), (Paris, undated, early 1843); RAL, XI/109/45B/6/191, N to bros, (Paris, undated, 1843).

40 RAL, XI/109/43A/2/135, N to bros, (Paris, undated, 1842).

41 RAL, XI/109/43A/2/108, N to L, (Paris) 4 August (1842).

42 RAL, XI/109/43A/2/20, A to bros, (Paris, undated, 1842).

43 RAL, XI/109/4A/4/45, John Helbert to M, (Paris, undated, 1842); Loewe (ed.), *Montefiore diaries*, vol. 1, p. 309.

44 RAL, XI/109/47/1/146, N to bros, (Paris, undated, 1844).

45 RAL, XI/109/57/4/43, N to bros, (Paris, undated, 1846).

46 RAL, XI/109/42A/2/24, N to bros, (Paris) 17 March (1842); RAL, XI/109/42A/2/77, N to bros, (Paris, undated, 1842).

47 RAL, XI/109/59A/2/15, N to bros, Paris, 3 Feb (1847); RAL, XI/109/57/4/15, A to bros, (Paris, undated, 1846); RAL, XI/109/57/4/64, N to L, (Ostende/Dieppe, undated, 1846).

48 RAL, XI/109/59B/2/33, A to bros, (Paris, undated, early 1847).

49 RAL, XI/109/57/1/4, A to bros, (Paris) 1 July (1846).

50 RAL, XI/109/48A/1/51A, Anselm to A & N in Paris, (Frankfurt) 17 June/July (1844).

51 RAL, XI/109/48A/2/230, Joe Montefiore to A, postmarked Paris (undated, 1844).

52 RAL, 000/10/40, H to L, East Cliff Lodge, 28 July 1844.; RAL, 000/10/23, H to M, Mainz, 26 Sept 1842; RAL, 000/10/36, H to CL, Paris, 14 June 1844.

53 Battersea, *Reminiscences*, p. 10.

54 RAL, XI/109/42A/2/29, N to bros, (Paris, undated, 1842); RAL, XI/104/1, N to bros, (Paris, undated, Dec 1841).

55 RAL, XI/109/45B/6/51, N to bros, Paris, 9 June (1843); RAL, XI/109/45B/6/56, N to bros, Paris, 22 June (1843); RAL, XI/109/45B/6/132, N to bros, (Paris, undated, 1843); XI/109/47/1/147, N to bros, (Paris) Sunday (undated, 1844); RAL, XI/109/45B/6/131, N to bros, (Paris) Sunday (undated, 1843).

56 RAL, XI/109/47/2/105, British Institution, Pall Mall, to 'Baron Rothschild', 23

April 1844; RAL, XI/109/64A/2/25, The Revd J. Huntington to L, 2 Montague Street, Russell Square, 2 Nov 1847.

57 RAL, XI/109/45B/6/22, N to bros, Paris, 15/16 March (1843); RAL, XI/109/55/52, T18/78–80, N to bros, (Paris, undated, 1843); RAL, XI/109/45B/6/119, N to bros, (Paris, undated, 1843).

58 RAL, XI/109/47/2/2, D. Mildred to L, Nicholas Lane, 11 April 1844; RAL, XI/109/47/1/147, N to bros, (Paris) Sunday (undated, 1844); RAL, XI/109/47/1/128, N to bros, (Paris, undated, 1844); *Gentleman's Magazine*, vol. 21, ns, 1844, June, p. 632; RAL, XI/109/47/1/123, N to bros, (Paris, undated, 1844); RAL, XI/109/47/1/147, N to bros, (Paris) Sunday (undated, 1844).

59 RAL, XI/109/47/1/95, N to bros, Paris, 14 April (1844); RAL, XI/109/54B/2/78, N to bros, (Paris, undated, 1845); RAL, XI/109/54B/2/99, N to bros, (Paris, undated, 1845); RAL, XI/109/59B/2/95, N to bros, (Paris, undated, 1847); RAL, XI/109/59B/2/96, N to bros, (Paris, undated, 1847); RAL, XI/109/70/4, N to bros, (Paris, undated, Jan–March 1849).

60 RAL, XI/109/75/2, N to bros, (Paris), 30 May (1850); RAL, XI/109/45B/6/187, N to bros, (Paris, undated, 1843); RAL, XI/109/49/1/15, L to bros, Paris, 3 Oct 1844.

61 RAL, 000/84, CL to Leo, Gunnersbury, 18 Nov 1865; RAL, XI/109/43A/ 2/160, N to bros, (Paris) Sunday (undated, 1842); RAL, XI/109/45B/6/187, N to bros, (Paris, undated, 1843); RAL, XI/109/47/1/128, N to bros, (Paris, undated, 1844).

62 RAL, XI/109/15/1/4, L to NM, 5 Sept 1830.

63 RAL, XI/109/45B/6/117, N to bros, (Paris, undated, 1843); RAL, XI/109/74/1, MC to L, Frankfurt, 3 Jan 1850; see also, for Sebastiani sale, RAL, XI/109/79/5, N to bros, Paris, 26 Nov (1851).

64 RAL, XI/109/45B/6/127, N to bros, (Paris, undated, 1843); RAL, XI/109/74/1, N to bros, (Paris) 15 Jan (1850).

65 XI/109/51B/226, MC to L, Vienna, 28 March 1845.

66 RAL, XI/109/54B/2/78, N to bros, (Paris, undated, 1845); RAL, XI/109/52A/ 2/174, MC to cousins, Paris, 28 May 1845; RAL, XI/109/52B/1/116, MC to L, Frankfurt, 19 June 1845; RAL, XI/109/52B/1/147, MC to cousins, Frankfurt, 24 June 1845; RAL, XI/109/52B/2/15, no. 2, MC to N, (undated, April–June 1845); RAL, XI/109/52B/2/15, no. 3, MC to N, (undated, April–June 1845).

67 RAL, XI/104/0, 61/244, N to bros, Paris, 24 June 1840.

68 RAL, T6/157, Württemberg Court Bank to NMR, Stuttgart, 21 May 1841(?).

69 RAL, XI/109/52B/1/31, Anselm to A, Frankfurt, 6 June 1845. Some of the paintings that Anselm bought from Klerk de Reuss were inherited by his son Ferdinand and may now be seen at Waddesdon Manor, Buckinghamshire, the house built for Ferdinand in the 1870s.

70 RAL, XI/109/45B/6/113, N to bros, (Paris, undated, 1843); RAL, XI/109/47/1/123, N to bros, (Paris, undated, 1844); RAL, XI/104/1/5/121, N to L & M, (Paris) 2 Sept (1841).

71 RAL, XI/104/1/5/121, N to L & M, (Paris) 2 Sept (1841); RAL, XI/104/1/5/114, A to N, Frankfurt, 25 Aug (1841).

72 RAL, XI/109/43A/2/11, A to bros, (Paris) 29 Oct 1842.

73 RAL, XI/104/1/5/121, N to L & M, (Paris) 2 Sept (1841).

74 RAL, XI/104/1/5/122.121a, N to L, (Paris) 3 Sept (1841); RAL, XI/104/ 1/5/126, A to L, Frankfurt, 6 Sept 1841; RAL, XI/104/1/5/140a, A to bros, (Paris, undated, 1841); *Gentleman's Magazine*, vol. 17, ns, 1842, March, p. 296.

75 RAL, XI/109/45B/6/51, N to bros, Paris, 9 June (1843); RAL, XI/109/57/50, T18/334–7, A to bros, (Frankfurt) 12 May (1844); RAL, XI/109/52B/1/31, Anselm to A, Frankfurt, 6 June 1845.

76 RAL, XI/109/47/2/107, sale advice from Christie's to Baron Rothschild, 28 May 1844, for lot 114, 17 May 1844: £1,942 10s; RAL, XI/109/47/1/154, N to bros, (Paris, undated, 1844); RAL, XI/109/47/1/155, N to bros, (Paris, undated, 1844).

77 RAL, XI/109/47/2/110, S. Wheeler to L, 67 Cadogan Place; RAL, XI/109/47/1/128, N to bros, (Paris, undated, 1844); RAL, XI/104/1/5/140a, A to bros, (Paris, undated, 1841).

78 RAL, XI/109/48A/1/2, A to bros, (Paris, undated, 1844); RAL, XI/109/42A/3/18, T23/331, Anselm to cousins, The Hague, 10 May (1842); RAL, XI/109/45/6/1/212, N to bros, (Paris, undated, 1843); RAL, XI/109/75/3, N to bros, Paris, 4 June (1850); RAL, XI/109/78/7, N to bros, (Paris, undated, Jan–June 1851); RAL, 000/13/53, L to CL, Piccadilly, 4 Feb 1859.

79 RAL, XI/109/56/1/79, MC to L, (Frankfurt) 14 April 1846; RAL, XI/109/42A/3/18, T23/331, Anselm to cousins, The Hague, 10 May (1842); RAL, XI/109/56/1/125, A to cousins, Frankfurt, 22 April 1846; RAL, XI/109/43A/1/42, T23/411, Anselm to A & N, (undated, 1842).

80 RAL, XI/109/72/1, L to A in Paris, Wildbad, 31 July 1849.

81 RAL, XI/109/43A/2/160, N to bros, (Paris) Sunday (undated, 1842).

82 See, e.g., RAL, XI/109/43A/2/161, N to bros, (Paris, undated, 1842); RAL, XI/109/43A/2/160, N to bros, (Paris) Sunday (undated, 1842).

83 NSM, vol. 11, 1837, p. 464; RAL, XI/109/43A/2/160, N to bros, (Paris) Sunday (undated, 1842).

84 RAL, XI/109/43A/2/138, N to L, (Paris, undated, 1842).

85 Disraeli, Correspondence with His Sister, p. 181; RAL, XI/109/43A/2/55, A to bros, (Paris, undated, autumn 1842).

86 SM, vol. 22, 2nd series, 1841: Nov 1840 issue, no. 127, p. 39; Onslow, Headquarters, p. 80.

87 SM, Nov 1840 issue, p. 40.

88 RAL, XI/109/42A/2/1, A to bros, (Paris) 23 May (1842).

89 RAL, XI/109/45B/6/220, N to bros, (Paris) Sunday (undated, 1843).

90 RAL, XI/109/59B/2/58, N to bros, (Paris, undated, early 1847); RAL, XI/109/43A/2/130, N to bros, (Paris, undated, 1842); RAL, XI/109/43A/2/101, N to bros, Paris, 22 July 1842; RAL, XI/109/45B/6/78, N to bros, Paris, 20 Sept (1843).

91 RAL, XI/109/45B/6/41, N to bros, Paris, 20 May (1843); RAL, XI/109/45B/6/42, N to bros, Paris, 27 May (1843); RAL, XI/109/47/95, N to bros, Paris, 14 April (1844).

92 RAL, XI/109/42A/2/68, N to bros, (Paris, undated, 1842); RAL, XI/109/45A/3/33, Thomas Carter to A, Paris, 8 May 1843; RAL, XI/109/45B/6/35, N to bros, Paris, 8 May (1843); RAL, XI/109/45B/6/41, N to bros, Paris, 20 May (1843); SM, vol. 4, 3rd series, ns, 1844, p. 305; RAL, XI/109/45B/6/30, N to bros, Paris, 12 April (1843).

93 RAL, XI/109/43A/2/43, A to bros, (Paris, undated, late Oct 1842).

94 RAL, XI/109/42A/2/28, N to bros, (Paris) Sunday (undated, 1842).

95 RAL, XI/109/42A/2/10, A to bros, (Paris, undated); RAL, XI/109/43A/2/35, A to bros, (Paris, undated, 1842).

96 RAL, XI/109/42A/2/4, A to bros, (Paris) 6 June 1842.

97 RAL, XI/109/42A/2/26, N to bros, Paris, 21 March 1842; RAL, 000/13/33, L to CL, Paris, 18 Aug (1842).

98 *SM*, vol. 25, 2nd series, 1842: Nov issue, no. 151, p. 550.

99 RAL, XI/109/45/6/9, N to bros, Paris, 4 Feb (1843); *BM*, vol. 12, 1867, p. 204; RAL, XI/109/81/2, N to bros, Paris, 15 May (1852).

100 *SM*, vol. 1, 3rd series, ns, 1843: issue no. 3, p. 389; RAL, XI/109/43A/2/53, A to bros, (Paris, undated, 1842).

101 RAL, XI/109/51B/103, James Messer to 'Dear Sir', 14 March 1845; *BM*, vol. 34, 1879, pp. 146–50.

102 Ibid.; RAL, XI/109/45B/6/241, N to bros, (Paris, undated, 1843); *BM*, vol. 34, 1879, p. 148.

103 RAL, XI/109/42A/2/41, N to bros, (Paris) 4 May (1842).

104 RAL, XI/109/42A/2/39, N to bros, (Paris) 30 April (1842); RAL, XI/109/51B/106, N to bros, (Paris) 14 March (1845); RAL, XI/109/45B/6/40, N to bros, Paris, 16 May (1843); RAL, XI/109/51B/2/27, N to bros, (Paris, undated, Jan–March 1845); RAL, XI/109/42A/2/50, N to bros, (Paris, undated, 1842).

105 RAL, XI/109/55A/2/9, Henry Scott to L, Engelmere Training Stable, Ascot Heath, 2 Feb 1846; RAL, XI/109/58A/2/51, John H. Peart to M, Whitewall House, near Malton, 8 Nov 1846; RAL, XI/109/58A/2/154, N to bros, Paris, 24 Nov (1846); RAL, XI/109/57/2/33, John H. Peart to 'BR' (M), Whitewall House, near Malton, 15 Aug 1846.

106 RAL, XI/109/43A/2/102, N to bros, Paris, 5 July 1842; RAL, XI/109/45B/6/66, N to bros, Paris, 19 July (1843); RAL, XI/109/45B/6/175, N to bros, (Paris) 24 May (1843); RAL, XI/109/47/94, N to bros, (Paris) 12 April (1844).

107 Suffolk and Berkshire, *Racing and Steeple-chasing*, p. 190; Dixon, *Gladiateur to Persimmon*, p. 232.

108 See RAL, XI/109/47/1/49, A to bros, (Frankfurt) 27 May (1844); RAL, XI/109/57/68, T24/17, N to bros, (Paris) Sunday 26 May (1844).

13: SIDONIA, OR THE CURLY FORTIES

1 Disraeli, *Coningsby*, pp. 235, 236, 237, 243, 265–7, 263.

2 RAL, XI/104/1/49, A to bros, (Paris) 17 May 1841.

3 Disraeli, *Coningsby*, pp. 238, 143, 230; Beresford Chancellor (ed.), *Neumann diary*, vol. II, p. 188.

4 RAL, 000/10/35, H to CL, Soden, Monday 3 June 1844; RAL, 000/297/B, Joe Montefiore to L, Southampton, 20 May 1844.

5 Disraeli, *Coningsby*, p. 271; RAL, XI/109/43A/2/105, N to bros, Paris, 9 July 1842; RAL, XI/109/71/2, Thomas John Hussey to L, Carlton Club, Tuesday (undated, May 1849).

6 Dalling and Bulwer, *Palmerston*, vol. 3, pp. 138–9.

7 Disraeli, *Coningsby*, pp. 243, 241, 143, 242, 232.

8 Disraeli, *Correspondence with His Sister*, p. 201; Monypenny, *Disraeli*, p. 225.

9 Disraeli, *Coningsby*, pp. 242, 245.

10 RAL, XI/109/71/1, Anselm to cousins, Vienna, 24 April 1849.

11 RAL, XI/109/48/2/9, L to N (in Paris), Frankfurt, 31 Aug 1844; Disraeli, *Coningsby*, p. 360.

12 RAL, XI/109/48/2/17, L to bros, Frankfurt, 5 Sept 1844.

13 Disraeli, *Coningsby*, pp. 140, 146.

14 Dixon, *Gladiateur to Persimmon*, pp. 209–10; *BM*, vol. 34, 1879, p. 148; RAL,

XI/109/57/4/13, A & N to L, (Paris, undated, summer 1846).

15 *Notes and Queries*, 8th series, vol. 3, 1893 (Jan–June), p. 363, col. 1; Disraeli, *Coningsby*, p. 235; *Quarterly Review*, vol. 74, 1844 (June–Oct), p. 297.

16 Kent (ed.), *Victoria County History: Yorkshire, East Riding*, vol. vii, pp. 138–40.

17 Battersea, *Reminiscences*, p. 232.

18 Disraeli, *Coningsby*, pp. 332–3.

19 RAL, XI/109/51B/2/41, MC in PS to N to bros, (Paris, undated, Jan–March 1845); RAL, XI/109/52A/1/76, H to CL, Paris, 10/16 April (1845); RAL, XI/109/51A/1/108, N to bros, Paris, 18 Jan (1845).

20 RAL, XI/109/54B/2/87, N to bros, (Paris, undated, 1845); Monypenny, *Disraeli*, vol. 2, p. 159.

21 Disraeli, *Coningsby*, pp. 357–8, 360–61; Mansel, *Paris*, p. 338.

22 RAL, XI/109/45B/6/11, N to bros, Paris, 12 Feb (1843).

23 Mansel, *Paris*, p. 338.

24 Disraeli, *Coningsby*, pp. 332–3.

25 RAL, XI/109/63/1/159, N to bros, (Paris) 25 Sept (1847).

26 Mansel, *Paris*, p. 333; RAL, XI/109/63/1/204, N to bros, (Paris) 30 Sept (1847); RAL, XI/109/43A/2/145, N to bros, (Paris, undated, 1842); RAL, XI/109/45B/6/71, N to bros, Paris, 4 Aug (1843); Muhlstein, *Baron James*, p. 175.

27 RAL, XI/104/0, 76/279, N to bros, Paris (undated, Aug 1840).

28 RAL, XI/104/0, 8/54, A to bros, (Paris, undated 1840); RAL, XI/109/51B/2/40, N to bros, (Paris, undated, Jan–March 1845); RAL, XI/109/50 (box for 1844, undated folder, ref. 44), N to bros, (Paris, undated).

29 RAL, XI/109/52A/2/120, A to bros, (Paris) 19 May (1845); RAL, XI/109/61/2/52, N to bros, (Paris, undated, spring 1847).

30 RAL, XI/109/51B/2/65, N to H, (Paris, undated, Jan–March 1845).

31 Sudley (ed.), *Lieven–Palmerston Correspondence*, p. 173; RAL, XI/109/51A/1/56, N to bros, Paris, 9 Jan (1845).

32 RAL, XI/104/0, 47/196, N to bros, (Paris) Friday (undated, 1840); RAL, XI/109/59B/294, N to bros, (Paris, undated, 1847).

33 RAL, XI/104/0, 50/199, N to bros, Paris, 25 May (1840); RAL, XI/104/0, 137/381, N to bros, (Paris, undated, 1840); Sudley (ed.), *Lieven–Palmerston Correspondence*, p. 173; RAL, XI/104/1/52, A to bros, (Paris) 22 May 1841; RAL, XI/104/1/109c, N to bros, (Paris) 19 Aug (1841).

34 RAL, XI/109/43A/2/85, A to bros, Paris (undated) 1842; RAL, XI/109/ 43A/2/83, A to bros, (Paris) 25 J(an) (1843).

35 RAL, XI/104/0, 32/163, N to bros, Paris, 18 April 1840; RAL, XI/109/78/7, N to bros, (Paris, undated, Jan–June 1851).

36 RAL, XI/109/43A/2/54, N to bros, (Paris, undated, late 1842); Bird, *Rous*, pp. 52, 54; RAL, XI/109/61/2/160, N to bros, (Paris, undated, 1847); RAL, XI/109/57/4, T24/359, N to bros, Paris, 3 April 1844.

37 Cohen, *Lady de Rothschild*, p. 21.

38 Sudley (ed.), *Lieven–Palmerston Correspondence*, pp. 241, 243; RAL, XI/109/43A/2/158, N to bros, (Paris, undated, late 1842).

39 Mansel, *Paris*, pp. 206, 207, 187; RAL, 000/184, B17Anth 1836/no. 5, A to NM & H, (Paris) 29 May (1836); RAL, XI/103/0/10, A to N, (Paris) 18 April (1839).

40 RAL, XI/109/43A/2/68, A to bros, (Paris, undated, late 1842); Sudley (ed.), *Lieven–Palmerston Correspondence*, p. 243; RAL, XI/109/52A/2/102, A to bros, (Paris) 15 May (1845).

41 RAL, XI/109/61/2/130, N to bros, (Paris, undated, 1847); RAL, XI/109/78/7, N to bros, (Paris, undated, Jan–June 1851); RAL, T24/359, 109/57/4, N to bros, Paris, 3 April 1844; RAL, XI/104/0, 34/167, N to bros, Paris, 24 April 1840.

42 RAL, 000/84, CL to Natty & Leo, Hotel Bristol, Paris, 27 Sept 1863; RAL, 000/13/58, L to CL & Alfred & Leo, Paris, 7 April 1861.

43 RAL, XI/109/48/2/47, CL to H, Frankfurt, Friday 13 Sept (1844); RAL, XI/109/45A/1/77, MC to A (in Paris), Frankfurt, 19 Sept 1843; RAL, XI/109/69B/1/238, MC to cousins (PS to Judendeutsch letter), Frankfurt, 31 Dec (1848); RAL, XI/109/55/142, T24/272, Anselm to N, Frankfurt, 26 Aug 1843.

44 RAL, XI/109/46A/1/98, N to bros, (Paris, undated, box for 1844, but 1843); RAL, XI/109/45A/1/5, L to A, Thursday, Bowood, postmarked Calne 5 Jan 1843; RAL, XI/109/44/1/87, T24/169, M to L at Bowood, 6 Jan 1843.

45 RAL, XI/109/52A/1/76, H to CL, Paris, 10/16 April (1845).

46 Muhlstein, Baron James, p. 154; Mansel, Paris, pp. 366, 386; RAL, XI/109/63/1/179, James & M to H, Paris, 27 Sept 1847; RAL, XI/109/63/1/180, CA to H, Paris, Monday 27 (Sept 1847).

47 RAL, XI/109/64B/1/74, N to bros, (Paris, undated, 1847); RAL, XI/109/79/5, L to bros, Paris, 30 Nov (1851).

48 RAL, XI/109/75/4, N to bros, (Paris, undated, April–June 1850); Malmesbury, Autobiography, vol. 1, p. 78.

49 Sudley (ed.), Lieven–Palmerston Correspondence, p. 243; RAL, XI/109/43A/2/130, N to bros, (Paris, undated, 1842).

50 RAL, XI/104/0, 52/220, N to bros, Paris, 1 June 1840; RAL, XI/109/61/2/160, N to bros, (Paris, 1847).

51 RAL, XI/109/42A/2/74, N to bros, (Paris, undated, 1842).

52 RAL, XI/109/43A/2/84, A to bros, (Paris, undated, 1842).

53 RAL, XI/109/43A/2/36, A to bros, (Paris, undated, July 1842); RAL, XI/109/43A/2/26, A to bros, (Paris, undated, Sept–Oct 1842).

54 RAL, XI/109/61/2/93, N to bros, (Paris, undated, 1847); RAL, XI/109/59B/2/83, N to bros, (Paris, undated, Jan–March 1847); RAL, XI/104/1/147, A to bros, (Paris, undated, 1841); RAL, XI/104/1, N to bros, (Paris, undated, 1841); RAL, XI/109/59B/2/75, N to bros, (Paris, undated, 1847); RAL, XI/104/0, 58/234, N to bros, Paris, 13 June 1840; RAL, XI/109/57/4/29–30, A to L, (Paris, undated, 1846).

55 RAL, XI/109/49/2/166, A. O'Reilly to A (in Paris), Paris, 25 Nov 1844.

56 Quoted in Ferguson, Rothschild, vol. I, p. 288.

57 RAL, XI/109/51B/106, N to bros, (Paris) 14 March (1845).

58 See, e.g., Booth, London Town, p. 262.

59 RAL, XI/109/51B/2/27, N to bros, (Paris, undated, 1845).

60 RAL, XI/109/69A/2/198, W. Delane to L, Morning Chronicle Office, 24 Nov 1848; RAL, XI/109/69B/1/157, A. O'Reilly to N, Paris, 19 Dec 1848.

61 Fowler, Echoes, p. 4; RAL, XI/109/87/2, John T. Delane to L, (London) 8 Nov (1865).

62 RAL, XI/109/51B/106, N to bros, (Paris) 14 March (1845).

63 RAL, XI/109/62/1/149, W. B. Towse[?] to L, Fishmongers Hall, 23 July 1847; RAL, XI/109/62/1/79, Jno[?] Alliston[?] to A, (Merchant Taylors) 3 Warnford[?] Court, 15 July 1847; RAL, XI/109/42/5/35, T23/275 (Spectacle Makers).

64 Salbstein, Emancipation, p. 131; RAL, XI/109/36B/1/23, Joe Montefiore to L, Sunday, postmarked Crawley 21 Oct 1838.

65 Salbstein, *Emancipation*, p. 129; RAL, XI/104/1/2/37, Anselm to cousins, Frankfurt, 21 March (1841).

66 RAL, XI/104/1/3, A to bros, Paris, 14 June 1841; RAL, XI/104/1/5/119, A to bros, (Frankfurt) 29 Aug (1841); RAL, XI/104/1/5/111, A to N, (Frankfurt) 29 Aug (1841).

67 RAL, XI/104/1/5/118, N to L, (Paris, undated, 1841).

68 RAL, XI/109/48A/2/232, David Salomons to A, Tuesday morning (undated, 1844).

69 Salbstein, *Emancipation*, p. 131; RAL, XI/109/48A/1/134, James James to M, Aylesbury, 14 July 1844.

70 Hansard, *Parliamentary Debates*, vol. lxxviii, cols. 524–5.

71 RAL, XI/109/52B/2/25, N to bros, (Paris, undated, 1845); RAL, 000/10/44, H to CL, Paris (undated) 1845.

72 RAL, XI/109/45B/6/117, N to bros, (Paris, undated, 1843); RAL, 000/10/44, H to CL, Paris (undated) 1845.

73 Salbstein, *Emancipation*, p. 48.

74 RAL, XI/104/1/61 (no. 4), A to bros, (Paris, undated, 1841); *Annual Register*, 1841, 'Chronicle', p. 65.

75 RAL, XI/109/57/1/53, N to bros, Wildbad, 8 July (1846).

76 Disraeli, *Coningsby*, p. 270.

77 Margoliouth, *Jews*, vol. II, p. 234; Hansard, *Parliamentary Debates*, vol. xcvi, col. 471; Margoliouth, *Jews*, vol. I, p. 92.

78 RAL, XI/109/57/4/7, N to L, (Frankfurt, undated, summer 1846).

79 RAL, XI/109/63/2/72, N to bros, (Paris, undated, 1847); RAL, XI/109/61/2/119, N to bros, (Paris, undated, 1847); RAL, XI/109/63/2/53, N to bros, (Paris, undated, 1847).

80 RAL, XI/109/63/2/68, N to bros, (Paris, undated, 1847); RAL, XI/109/59B/2/16, A to bros, (Paris, undated, early 1847).

81 RAL, XI/109/60/1/33, John Abel Smith to L, Belgrave Square, 7 April (1847).

82 RAL, XI/109/61/1/72, Frank Mills to L, Sunday Evng, 13 June (1847).

83 RAL, XI/109/74/1, 'Dear Jeffrey' (Cullen?) from unsigned (letter incomplete), Ingles, 9 Jan 1850; RAL, XI/109/61/1/95, (Lord) A. Marcus Hill to L, House of Commons, 17 June (1847).

84 RAL, XI/109/63/2/48, Henry FitzRoy to L, Garboldisham, Harling, Friday (undated, 1847); RAL, XI/109/63/2/72, N to bros, (Paris, undated, 1847).

85 RAL, XI/109/61/1/95, (Lord) A. Marcus Hill to L, House of Commons, 17 June (1847); RAL, XI/109/62/1/91, David Robertson (ex Marjoribanks) to 'My dear Rothschild' (L), Ladykirk, near Berwick, 16 July 1847.

86 RAL, XI/109/63/2/87, N to bros, (Paris, undated 1847).

87 Salbstein, *Emancipation*, pp. 142, 143.

88 *Annual Register*, 1847, 'Chronicle', p. 95; Salbstein, *Emancipation*, p. 144; Hanham (ed.), *Electoral Facts*, pp. 151–2.

89 RAL, XI/109/62/2/14, LMC to L, Frankfurt, 2 Aug 1847; RAL, XI/109/ 62/2/13, MC to L, Frankfurt, 2 Aug 1847; RAL, XI/109/64B/2/109, CA to L, (undated, Aug 1847).

90 RAL, T7/129, 109/63–1, Charlotte Nat in PS to letter from Betty to L (French, T7/128); RAL, XI/109/63/2/48, Henry FitzRoy to L, Garboldisham, Harling, Friday (undated, 1847).

91 RAL, XI/109/63/2/15, Lord Beauvale to L, Melbourne Hall, Derby, '?6th' (Aug 1847); RAL, XI/109/63/2/48, Henry FitzRoy to L, Garboldisham, Harling, Friday

(undated, 1847); RAL, XI/109/62/2/36, T7/99, Salomon to L (German), Vienna, 4 Aug 1847; RAL, XI/109/62/2/51, T7/100, Salomon to Anselm/nephews (?) (German), Vienna, 5 Aug 1847.

14: THE STINKING LORDS

1 *The Times*, Thursday 5 June 1879, p. 8; Ferguson, *Rothschild*, vol. I, p. 443; RAL, XI/109/60/1/82, memo on paper headed British Relief Association, Committee Room, South Sea House, 14 April 1847.

2 Hansard, *Parliamentary Debates*, 3rd series, vol. xcvi, col. 237; RAL, XI/109/70/3, British Relief Association to L, 14 March 1849; Ferguson, *Rothschild*, vol. I, p. 443.

3 RAL, XI/109/55/1/146, Anselm to L, Paris, 28 Jan 1846.

4 Quoted in Ferguson, *Rothschild*, vol. II, p. 25; RAL, XI/109/58B/2/115, A to bros, (Paris, undated, late 1846).

5 RAL, XI/109/58B/2/58, N to bros, (Paris, undated, late 1846); RAL, XI/109/58A/2/156, Anselm to L, Frankfurt, 24 Nov 1846.

6 RAL, 000/10/99, H to L, Frankfurt, Monday (undated, Nov 1846).

7 RAL, XI/109/64B/1/87, H to L, 14 Dec 1847.

8 Hansard, *Parliamentary Debates*, 3rd series, vol. xcv, cols. 1234–49 (Lord John Russell); Salbstein, *Emancipation*, p. 124.

9 Hansard, *Parliamentary Debates*, 3rd series, vol. xcv, cols. 1249–65 (Sir Robert Inglis).

10 Ibid., cols. 1272–82 (Lord Ashley).

11 RAL, XI/109/64B/1/138, N to bros, (Paris) 21 Dec (1847).

12 Hansard, *Parliamentary Debates*, 3rd series, vol. xcv, cols. 1282–1304 (W. E. Gladstone).

13 Ibid., cols. 1321–30 (Benjamin Disraeli).

14 RAL, 000/297, LA's journal, 19 Dec 1847.

15 RAL, 000/848, Disraeli to L, Bradenham, High Wycombe, 26 Dec 1847.

16 Hansard, *Parliamentary Debates*, 3rd series, vol. xcvi, cols. 242–8 (Richard Monckton Milnes).

17 RAL, XI/109/65B/2/19, N to bros, (Paris, undated, Jan–March 1848).

18 Hansard, *Parliamentary Debates*, 3rd series, vol. xcvii, cols. 1235–6 (Lord Dudley Stuart).

19 Disraeli, *Coningsby*, p. 230.

20 RAL, XI/109/33/1/35, A to NM & H, Paris, 4 April 1835; RAL, XI/109/33/1/43, A to NM & H, Paris, 1 June (1835); RAL, XI/109/62/1/91, David Robertson (ex Marjoribanks) to 'My dear Rothschild' (L), Ladykirk, near Berwick, 16 July 1847; Salbstein, *Emancipation*, p. 144.

21 RAL, XI/109/67/2/69, N to bros, (Paris, undated, ?June 1848).

22 RAL, XI/109/64B/1/153, N to bros, Paris, 23 Dec (1847).

23 RAL, XI/109/65A/2/79, N to bros, (Paris) 14 Feb (1848); RAL, XI/109/65B/2/56, N to bros, (Paris, undated, Jan–March 1848); RAL, XI/109/64B/2/99, N to bros, (Paris, undated).

24 RAL, XI/109/66/2/81, N to bros, (Paris) 10 May (1848).

25 Hansard, *Parliamentary Debates*, 3rd series, vol. xcviii, cols. 1330–40 (Marquess of Lansdowne); RAL, XI/109/66/2/238, N to bros, (Paris) 26 May (1848).

26 RAL, XI/109/66/2/124, MC to L, (Frankfurt) 15 May 1848; RAL, XI/109/67/1/3, Anselm to cousins, Vienna, 1 June 1848.

27 Hansard, *Parliamentary Debates*, 3rd series, 1847–8, vol. xcviii, cols. 1340–45 (Earl of Ellenborough).

28 Ibid., cols. 1345–6 (Duke of Cambridge).

29 Ibid., cols. 1349–52 (Archbishop of Canterbury).

30 Ibid., cols. 1371–82 (Bishop of Oxford).

31 Cohen, *Lady de Rothschild*, p. 41.

32 Hansard, *Parliamentary Debates*, 3rd series, vol. xcviii, cols. 1382–3 (Earl of St Germans).

33 Ibid., col. 1387 (Earl of Harrowby), cols. 1387–90 (Earl of Ellesmere).

34 Ibid., cols. 1390–98 (Lord Stanley).

35 Ibid., cols. 1398–1405 (Lord Brougham).

36 Malmesbury *Autobiography*, vol. 1, pp. 230–31.

37 Quoted in Ferguson, *Rothschild*, vol. II, p. 35.

38 Cohen, *Lady de Rothschild*, p. 41.

39 RAL, XI/109/39/3/26, Thomas Hussey to 'Baron Rothschild' (L), Rose Cottage, near Henley on Thames, 17 Dec 1840.

40 RAL, XI/109/70/2, Thomas John Hussey to 'Baron Rothschild' (L), (The) Rectory, Hayes, Kent, 18 Feb (1849).

41 Ferguson, *Rothschild*, vol. II, p. 38.

42 Cohen, *Lady de Rothschild*, p. 42.

43 RAL, 000/13/49, L to CL, Paris, Sunday morning (undated, postmarked Boulogne 16 July 1848).

44 RAL, XI/109/71/4, N to bros, (Paris, undated, April–June 1849).

45 Cohen, *Lady de Rothschild*, pp. 42–3.

46 RAL, XI/109/66/1/238, N to bros, (Paris) 26 May (1848).

47 Salbstein, *Emancipation*, p. 176.

48 Cohen, *Lady de Rothschild*, p. 43; RAL, 000/848, Disraeli to L, Bradenham, High Wycombe, 26 Dec 1847.

49 RAL, 000/848, Lord John Manners to L, Carlton Club, Saturday, 6 o'clock (undated, June 1850).

50 RAL, XI/109/72/1, LMC to L, Frankfurt, 6 July (1849).

51 RAL, XI/109/72/1, T. A. Curtis to L, Liverpool, 5 July 1849.

52 RAL, XI/109/72/1, CA to L, Frankfurt, Friday 6 July (1849).

53 RAL, XI/109/74/3, N to bros, Paris, 12 March 1850.

54 Salbstein, *Emancipation*, p. 178.

55 RAL, XI/109/78/5, Richard Dighton to L, 5 Hugh Street West, Eccleston Square, 12 May 1851,

15: THE PURSES BLEED

1 Wilson, *Victorians*, p. 120.

2 RAL, XI/109/66/1/95, N to bros, (Paris) 9 April (1848).

3 Ferguson, *Rothschild*, vol. I, pp. 450, 454; RAL, XI/109/65B/2/27, N to bros, (Paris, undated, Jan–March 1848); Mansel, *Paris*, p. 398; RAL, XI/109/65A/2/10, Anselm to L, Frankfurt, 2 Feb 1848.

4 Mansel, *Paris*, p. 398; RAL, XI/109/65B/2/53, N to bros, (Paris, undated, Jan–March 1848).

5 Quoted in Mansel, *Paris*, p. 397.

6 RAL, XI/109/65B/2/55, N to bros, (Paris, undated, Jan–March 1848).

7 RAL, XI/109/65B/2/12, N to bros, (Paris) Sunday (undated, Jan–March 1848).

8 RAL, XI/109/65A/2/114, N to bros, (Paris) 21 Feb (1848).

9 Mansel, *Paris*, p. 399.

10 RAL, XI/109/65A/2/124, N to bros, (Paris) 23 Feb (1848).

11 RAL, XI/109/65B/2/44, N to bros, (Paris, undated, Jan–March 1848).

12 RAL, XI/109/65A/1/130, N to bros, postmarked Paris 24 Feb 1848, Boulogne 25 Feb.

13 Battersea, *Reminiscences*, p. 75.

14 Ferguson, *Rothschild*, vol. I, p. 453; RAL, XI/109/65B/1/4, Anselm to cousins, Frankfurt, 1 March (1848).

15 RAL, XI/109/65B/1/84, MC to cousins, (Frankfurt) 12 March 1848.

16 RAL, XI/109/65B/1/94, Anselm to cousins, PS to Judendeutsch letter, Frankfurt, 14 March 1848; Ferguson, *Rothschild*, vol. I, pp. 453–4.

17 Ibid., vol. I, p. 453.

18 RAL, XI/109/65A/1/77, N to bros, (Paris) 16 Jan (1848); RAL, XI/109/65A/1/173, N to bros, (Paris) 24 March (1848); Mansel, *Paris*, p. 408.

19 RAL, XI/109/65B/1/234, MC to cousins, (Frankfurt) 29 March 1848.

20 RAL, XI/109/66/1/86/i, MC to cousins, (Frankfurt) 9 April 1848.

21 Ferguson, *Rothschild*, vol. I, p. 459; RAL, XI/109/66/1/86/47/i, Anselm to cousins, 5 April 1848.

22 RAL, XI/109/65B/2/31, N to bros, (Paris, undated, Jan–March 1848).

23 RAL, XI/109/66/1/39, Anselm to N, (Frankfurt) 4 April (1848); RAL, XI/109/66/1/10, Anselm to L, (Frankfurt) 2 April (1848).

24 RAL, XI/109/66/1/47/i, Anselm to cousins, 5 April 1848; RAL, XI/109/66/1/10, Anselm to L, (Frankfurt) 2 April (1848).

25 Ferguson, *Rothschild*, vol. I, p. 464, 445.

26 Ibid., vol. I, p. 462.

27 RAL, XI/109/66/1/41, N to bros, (Paris) Tuesday 4 April (1848).

28 RAL, XI/109/65B/2/14, N to bros, (Paris, undated, Jan–March 1848) in conjunction with RAL, XI/109/65B/1/94, Anselm to cousins, PS to Judendeutsch letter, Frankfurt, 14 March 1848; Ferguson, *Rothschild*, vol. I, p. 463.

29 RAL, XI/109/65B/2/17/i, N to bros, (Paris, undated, Jan–March 1848); RAL, XI/109/65B/2/30, N to bros, (Paris, undated, Jan–March 1848); RAL, XI/109/66/1/106, N to bros, (Paris) 10 April (1848).

30 Ferguson, *Rothschild*, vol. I, p. 463; RAL, XI/109/48A/37, L to bros, postmarked Frankfurt 9 Sept 1844.

31 RAL, T8/46, XI/109/66/1/166, Anselm to MC (German), Vienna, 17 April 1848.

32 RAL, XI/109/65B/1/174, N to bros, Paris, 24 March (1848); Ferguson, *Rothschild*, vol. I, p. 465.

33 RAL, T8/46, XI/109/66/1/166, Anselm to MC (German), Vienna, 17 April 1848; Cohen, *Lady de Rothschild*, p. 52.

34 Ferguson, *Rothschild*, vol. I, pp. 465, 467–8; RAL, XI/109/66/1/146A, MC to cousins, (Frankfurt) 18 April (1848); RAL, XI/109/66/2/46, MC to L, (Frankfurt) 5 May 1848; RAL, XI/109/67/1/17, N to bros, Frankfurt, 9 June (1848).

35 RAL, XI/109/65A/1/174, N to bros, Paris, 24 March (1848).

36 RAL, XI/109/65A/1/174, N to bros, Paris, 24 March (1848); RAL, XI/109/66/2/181, N to bros, (Paris) 20 May (1848).

37 RAL, XI/109/66/2/125, MC to N, (Frankfurt) 15 May 1848; Cohen, *Lady de*

Rothschild, p. 53; RAL, XI/109/68A/1/62, A to bros, (Frankfurt) Wednesday 9 July (1848); RAL, XI/109/68A/1/258, A to bros, (Paris) 29 July (1848).

38 RAL, XI/109/67/1/17, N to bros, Ems, 4 June (1848).

39 Mansel, *Paris*, p. 412.

40 RAL, XI/109/68A/1/258, A to bros, (Paris) 29 July (1848).

41 RAL, 000/13/49, L to CL, Paris, Sunday morning, 16 July (1848); Mansel, *Paris*, p. 412.

42 RAL, XI/109/68A/1/52, N to bros, (Paris) 7 July (1848); RAL, 000/13/49, L to CL, Paris, Sunday morning, 16 July (1848), and RAL, 000/13/50, L to CL, Paris, 18 July 1848.

43 RAL, XI/109/68A/1/52, N to bros, (Paris) 7 July (1848); RAL, 000/13/50, L to CL, Paris, 18 July 1848; RAL, XI/109/68A/2/150, N to L, Trouville, 16 Aug (1848); RAL, XI/109/68B/1/59, N to bros, Paris, 8 Sept (1848).

44 Mansel, *Paris*, p. 414.

45 RAL, XI/109/69A/1/87, A to bros, (Paris) 11 Oct (1848).

46 Mansel, *Paris*, p. 414; *NSM*, ns, vol. 17, 1849, p. 93; RAL, XI/109/69B/1/133, Thomas Carter to N, La Morlaye, 16 Dec 1848.

47 RAL, XI/109/70/4, N to bros, (Paris, undated, Jan–March 1849).

48 RAL, XI/109/78/6, N to bros, (Paris) 12 June (1851); RAL, XI/109/72/2, A to M, (Paris) 29 Aug (1849).

49 RAL, XI/109/70/4, N to bros, (Paris, undated, Jan–March 1849).

50 Ibid.

51 RAL, XI/109/70/1, Henry FitzRoy to L, Pau, 2 Jan 1849; RAL, XI/109/73/1, A to M, (Paris) 17 Oct (1849); RAL, XI/109/73/2, L to M, (Paris) 6 Nov 1849.

52 RAL, XI/109/66/2/32, Anselm to cousins, Vienna, 4 May (1848); RAL, XI/109/69A/2/49, Anselm to L & A, nr Vienna, 5 Nov (1848).

53 RAL, XI/109/69B/1/30, MC to cousins, PS to Judendeutsch letter, Frankfurt, 5 Dec (1848); RAL, XI/109/69B/1/128, LMC to L, Frankfurt, 15 Dec (1848); RAL, XI/109/69B/1/111, MC to cousins, (Frankfurt) 13 Dec 1848.

54 RAL, XI/109/69B/1/238, MC to cousins, PS to Judendeutsch letter, Frankfurt, 31 Dec 1848; RAL, XI/109/69B/1/111, MC to cousins, (Frankfurt) 13 Dec 1848.

55 See RAL, XI/109/70/1, L to M, ('London', but Frankfurt) 24 Jan 1849; RAL, XI/109/70/4, L to A in Paris, (Frankfurt, undated, Jan–March 1849); RAL, XI/109/71/2, Anselm to N, Vienna, 24 May 1849; RAL, XI/109/71/2, Anselm to cousins, Vienna, 5 May 1849.

56 RAL, XI/109/67/2/33, T8/69, CL to L (in Paris) (German), (London, undated, 1848).

57 RAL, XI/109/67/2/57, N to bros, (Paris) Friday 2 o'clock (April–June 1848); Muhlstein, *Baron James*, p. 184.

58 RAL, XI/109/67/2/57, N to bros, (Paris) Friday 2 o'clock (April–June 1848); RAL, XI/109/69A/2/84, Joshua Bates to L, Bishopsgate Street, 9 Nov 1848; Muhlstein, *Baron James*, pp. 184–5; RAL, XI/109/70/1, Anselm to L, Frankfurt, 11 Jan 1849.

59 RAL, XI/109/66/2/188, MC to L, (Frankfurt) 21 May 1848; RAL, 000/13/50, L to CL, Paris, 18 July 1848.

60 RAL, XI/109/47/1/102, H to L, (Frankfurt) 14 May (1844); RAL, XI/109/71/2, MC to cousins, (Frankfurt) 8 May 1849.

61 RAL, XI/109/71/4, N to bros, (Paris, undated, April–June 1849); RAL, XI/109/72/2, L to M, (Wildbad, Aug 1849, continuation sheet).

62 RAL, XI/109/66/1/41, N to bros, (Paris) Tuesday 4 April (1848); RAL,

XI/109/66/1/84, N to A, (Paris) 18 April (1848); RAL, XI/109/66/1/47/i, Anselm to cousins, 5 April 1848; RAL, XI/109/65B/1/163, Anselm to L & A, Frankfurt, 23 March (1848); RAL, XI/109/66/1/41, N to bros, (Paris) Tuesday 4 April (1848); RAL, XI/109/67/2/73, N to bros, (Paris, undated, April–June 1848); RAL, XI/109/66/2/238, N to bros, (Paris) 26 May (1848).

63 RAL, XI/109/65B/2/16, N to bros, (Paris, undated, Jan–March 1848).

64 Ferguson, *Rothschild*, vol. I, p. 333.

65 RAL, XI/109/48A/5, A to bros, (Paris, undated, July–Sept 1844).

66 RAL, XI/109/79/3, CA to L, Vienna, 11 Sept 1851.

67 RAL, XI/109/48A/51A, Anselm to A & N in Paris, (Frankfurt) 24 July 1844; RAL, XI/109/48A/61, Anselm to L & N in Paris, Frankfurt, 15 Aug (1844).

68 RAL, 000/84, CL to Leo, Gunnersbury, 25 Jan 1867; Ferguson, *Rothschild*, vol. I, p. 333.

69 RAL, XI/109/48A/2/19, L to bros, Frankfurt, 9 Sept 1844; RAL, XI/109/48A/2/96, CA to H, Frankfurt, Friday 13 Sept (1844).

70 RAL, XI/109/50/1/31, N to A, (Paris, undated, Dec 1844); RAL, XI/109/48A/2/19, L to bros, Frankfurt, 9 Sept 1844; RAL, XI/109/48A/2/96, CA to H, Frankfurt, Friday 13 Sept (1844).

71 RAL, XI/109/52B/1/189, CA to L, Franzensbad, 29 June 1845; RAL, XI/109/43A/1/23, T24/150, CA to one of her bros, Frankfurt, Thursday 22 Dec (1842); RAL, XI/109/57/54, T18/338–9, H to L, (Frankfurt, undated).

72 RAL, XI/109/55/4/17, page torn from an account book; RAL, XI/109/52A/2/121, CA to bros, Frankfurt, Monday 19 (May 1845).

73 RAL, XI/109/63/2/48, Henry FitzRoy to L, Garboldisham, Harling, Friday (undated, Sept 1847); RAL, XI/109/68B/1/158, HM to L, Garboldisham, Thursday 21 Sept (1848); RAL, XI/109/69B/2/21, N to bros, (Paris, undated, Oct–Dec 1848); RAL, XI/109/79/3, N to bros, Paris, 6 Sept (1851); RAL, XI/109/79/7, N to bros, Paris (undated, July–Dec 1851); RAL, XI/109/69A/2/220, Joe Montefiore to A, (undated, Nov 1848); RAL, XI/109/63/2/48, Henry FitzRoy to L, Garboldisham, Harling, Friday (undated, Sept 1847).

74 RAL, 000/297, LA's journal, 29 Oct 1847, and 19 Nov 1848.

75 RAL, XI/109/68B/1/146, N to L, 20 Sept (1848).

76 RAL, T8/74, XI/109/69b/2/68, CL to L (German), (undated, 1848).

77 RAL, XI/109/74/1, CA to L, Frankfurt, 9 Jan 1850; RAL, 000/848, H to L, Gunnersbury, August (undated, late 1840s); RAL, 000/297/B, Nat Montefiore to LA, (Naples) Tuesday 24 (?) 1844.

78 RAL, 000/297, LA's journal, 1 Dec 1848, 5 May 1852, and 19 Nov 1848.

79 RAL, 000/297/B, LMC to LA, Frankfurt, 11 Aug 1844.

80 RAL, 000/297, LA's journal, 3 March 1849; RAL, 000/84, CL to Leo, 148 Piccadilly, 29 May 1866.

81 RAL, 000/297, LA's journal, 13 Dec 1848, and 16 Dec 1848.

82 RAL, XI/109/69A/2/49, Anselm to L & A, nr Vienna, 5 Nov 1848; RAL, XI/109/61/2/79, N to bros, (Paris, undated, April–June 1847); Cohen, *Lady de Rothschild*, p. 5.

83 RAL, 000/136/75, LA to CL (undated); 000/136/76, LA to CL, (undated).

84 RAL, XI/109/70/1, A to M, (Paris) 21 Jan (1849); RAL, XI/109/74/1, CA to L, Frankfurt, 9 Jan (1850).

85 RAL, 000/297, LA's journal, 3 March 1850, and 12 March 1850; RAL, XI/109/73/3, MC to L, (Frankfurt) 9 Dec 1849; Cohen, *Lady de Rothschild*, p. 5; RAL,

XI/109/74/1, Anselm to L & A, Frankfurt, 21 Jan 1850; RAL, 000/297, LA's journal, 26 July 1850.

86 RAL, 000/136, LA to A, 21 Jan (1840).

16: SQUIRES

1 *NSM*, ns, vol. 30, 1855, pp. 253–4; Fowler, *Recollections*, pp. 167–9.

2 Ibid., p. 94.

3 RAL, XI/109/59B/2/18, A to bros, (Paris, undated, Jan–March 1847).

4 RAL, XI/109/43A/1/75, Lord Nugent to Lord Denman, Lilies, Tuesday (undated).

5 *SM*, vol. 7, 3rd series, ns, 1846, p. 125.

6 RAL, XI/109/56/2/79, W(?) Metcalfe to M, 14 May 1846; RAL, XI/109/56/3/147, Evelyn Denison to 'Baron Rothschild', 28 June (1846).

7 RAL, XI/109/59B/1/75, William Barwick to no addressee, Mentmore, 12 March 1847; *BM*, vol. 11, Jan 1866, p. 51; *BM*, vol. 34, 1879, p. 147; *BM*, vol. 12, 1867, p. 345; *BM*, vol. 18, 1870, p. 156; *BM*, vol. 20, 1871, p. 8; RAL, XI/109/54B/1/166, George Fountain to no addressee, Mentmore, 29 Oct 1845; RAL, XI/109/69A/1/213, George Fountain to L, Mentmore, 28 Oct 1848; *SM*, vol. 38, 3rd series, 1861, pp. 451–3; *BM*, vol. 35, 1880, p. 388; *BM*, vol. 20, 1871, p. 7.

8 RAL, XI/109/70/3 (March 1849), Francis Grant to L, Sussex Villa, Regent's Park, 26 March (1849).

9 *SM*, vol. 38, 3rd series, 1861, pp. 451–3; Fowler, *Echoes*, p. 188; *BM*, vol. 11, 1861, p. 72; RAL, XI/109/55/1/6, N to bros, (Paris) 1 Jan 1846; RAL, XI/109/61/2/83, N to bros, (Paris, undated, early 1847).

10 RAL, XI/109/47/2/24, Lord Lonsdale to L, 17 April 1844; RAL, XI/109/58B/2/42, N to bros, (Paris, undated, Oct–Dec 1846).

11 RAL, XI/109/54B/1/20, Duke of Buckingham and Chandos to L, Stowe, 5 Oct (1845).

12 RAL, XI/109/61/2/110, N to bros, (Paris, undated, 1847).

13 See, e.g., RAL, XI/109/72/2, Thomas Hart to M, Ascott, 7 Aug 1849; RAL, XI/109/48A/1/57, L to M, (Frankfurt, undated, Aug 1844); RAL, XI/109/52A/2/42, (Sir) Harry Verney (ex Calvert) to M, Claydon House, Bucks, 6 May 1845; RAL, XI/109/52B/1/151, (Sir) Harry Verney to M, Claydon, 24 June 1845.

14 RAL, XI/109/60/2/233, George Fountain to M, Mentmore, 31 May 1847; RAL, XI/109/62/1/169, George Fountain to M, Mentmore, 26 July 1847; RAL, XI/109/70/2, Thos Brooks to 'Dear Sir' (M), nr Caistor, Lincs, 18 Feb 1849.

15 RAL, XI/109/60/1/30, Alex Fraser (for Harry Verney) to M, Claydon, Winslow, Bucks, 6 April 1847; RAL, 000/848, Disraeli to L, Grosvenor Gate, 10 March 1847.

16 RAL, XI/109/72/2, statement of Mayer's Sheriff's account, 7 Aug 1849.

17 RAL, XI/109/68A/1/258, A to bros, (Paris) 29 July (1848); RAL, XI/109/74/1, (Sir) Harry Verney to M, Claydon House, Bucks, Saturday 5 Jan 1850.

18 RAL, XI/109/68A/2/161, Israel Russell to L, Swan & Castle, Buckingham, 17 Aug 1848; RAL, XI/109/68A/2/192, Israel Russell to L, same address, postmarked 22 Aug 1848; Forster, *Stowe Catalogue*.

19 Sotheby's Mentmore sale catalogue (1977), vol. 1, lot 904, p. 297 note.

20 RAL, XI/109/72/3, L to M, Frankfurt, 27 Sept 1849; RAL, XI/109/78/2, (Lord) Chandos to 'My dear Sir' (M), Wotton, 3 Feb 1851; RAL, XI/109/81/3, N to bros,

Paris, 23 June 1852; RAL, XI/109/68A/1/62, A to bros, (Frankfurt?) Wednesday 9 July (1848).

21 RAL, XI/109/69B/2/12, N to bros, (Paris, undated, Oct–Dec 1848); RAL, XI/109/75/2, N to bros, (Paris) 11 May (1850).

22 RAL, XI/109/78/1, N to bros, Paris, 9 Jan (1851); RAL, XI/109/83/3, N to bros, Paris, 30 Dec (1852).

23 RAL, XI/109/83/3, N to bros, Paris, 30 Dec (1852).

24 Rosebery Papers, Dalmeny House (transcript RAL), C. P. Beurdeley to M, Piazza Hotel, Covent Garden, 21 June 1843; RAL, XI/109/53A/2/153, (Sir) Harry Verney to M, Claydon House, Bucks, 23 Aug 1845; RAL, XI/109/52A/2/42, (Sir) Harry Verney to M, Claydon House, Bucks, 6 May 1845; RAL, XI/109/80/3, Carl to nephews (German), Naples, 24 March 1851.

25 RAL, XI/109/40/1/7, John Fereday(?) to 'Baron Rothschild', Aston Abbotts Vicarage, 1 Feb 1841.

26 RAL, XI/109/72/2, A to M, (Paris) 8 Aug (1849).

27 RAL, XI/109/77/1, N to bros, (Paris) 19 Oct (1850); RAL, XI/109/77/2, N to bros, (Paris) 13 Nov (1850); RAL, XI/109/77/2, N to bros, Paris, 19 Nov (1850); Kessler, 'Rothschilds and Disraeli', p. 22.

28 Gulland, 'Aston Clinton', p. 33.

29 Ibid., p. 34; RAL, XI/109/72/2, Thomas Hart to M, Ascott, 7 Aug 1849; RAL, XI/109/72/3, L to A (in Paris), Frankfurt, 15 Sept (1849); RAL, XI/109/72/3, L to M (in London), Frankfurt, 16 Sept 1849.

30 RAL, XI/109/72/2, Thomas Hart to M, Ascott, 7 Aug 1849; RAL, XI/109/72/3, L to M, Frankfurt, 23 Sept 1849.

31 Sheahan, *Buckinghamshire*, pp. 86, 88.

32 RAL, XI/109/79/1, N to bros, Paris, 1 July (1851).

33 RAL, XI/109/79/1, N to bros, Paris, 5 July 1851; RAL, XI/109/79/1, N to bros, Paris, 28 July (1851); RAL, XI/109/48A/1/134, James James to M, Aylesbury, 14 July 1844.

34 RAL, XI/109/79/7, N to bros, Paris (undated, July–Dec 1851); Sheahan, *Buckinghamshire*, p. 86.

35 RAL, XI/109/77/4, N to bros, (Paris, undated, Oct–Dec 1850).

36 RAL, XI/109/91B/2, A to Alfred, Paris, 24 Sept (1867); Sheahan, *Buckinghamshire*, p. 95; Kessler, 'Rothschilds and Disraeli', p. 8.

37 RAL, XI/109/77/2, N to bros, Paris, 20 Nov (1850); RAL, XI/109/72/2, L to M, Wildbad, 11 Aug 1849.

38 RAL, XI/109/78/4, N to bros, Paris, 13 April (1851); RAL, XI/109/77/3, Frederick Calvert to M, Claydon, Winslow, 20 Dec 1850; RAL, XI/109/107, James James to A, Halton, Tring, Monday 9 Oct 1871.

39 *SM*, vol. 36, 3rd series, 1860, p. 119; Sheahan, *Buckinghamshire*, p. 95.

40 RAL, XI/109/72/3, LMC to HM, Ostend, 10 Sept 1849; RAL, XI/109/72/3, L to A, Frankfurt, 23 Sept 1849.

41 RAL, XI/109/73/4, H to M, Frankfurt, Monday (undated, Oct–Dec 1849); RAL, XI/109/73/3, H to L, Frankfurt, 3 Dec 1849; RAL, XI/109/74/1, LMC to L, Frankfurt, 30 Jan (1850); RAL, XI/109/73/3, H to CL, Frankfurt, 14 Dec (1849).

42 RAL, XI/109/73/3, MC to L, (Frankfurt) 23 Dec 1849; RAL, XI/109/73/3, H to CL, Frankfurt, 14 Dec (1849); RAL, XI/109/73/3, H to M, Frankfurt, 19 Dec (1849).

43 RAL, XI/109/74/1, CA to L, Frankfurt, 9 Jan (1850); Aspey, 'Mrs Rothschild', p. 67.

44 RAL, 000/1067, Leonora, pp. 59, 60.

45 See RAL, XI/109/78/4, LMC to L, (Frankfurt, 20 April 1851); RAL, XI/109/77/2, Jno Hunt, of Hunt & Roskell, Late Storr, Mortimer & Hunt, Jewellers, Goldsmiths & Silversmiths To The Queen, to A, 156 New Bond Street, 27 Nov 1850.

46 RAL, XI/109/77/2, LMC to L, Frankfurt, 8 Nov 1850; RAL, XI/109/78/4, LMC to L, (Frankfurt) 20 April 1851.

47 RAL, XI/109/108/2, Alfred Slater to L, 9 & 10 High Street, Kensington, London, 15 Jan 1872; RAL, XI/109/77/4, N to bros, (Paris, undated, Oct–Dec 1850); RAL, XI/109/47/2/35, W. Herring, Importer of Red and Fallow Deer (etc), to 'Baron Rothschild', 21 June 1844; RAL, XI/109/48/1/99, William Walton to 'Baron Rothschild' (L), 9 Fitzroy Street, Fitzroy Square, 1 Aug (1844); RAL, XI/109/48/2/182, A. Herring to L, 21 New Road, 10 July 1844.

48 Battersea, *Reminiscences*, p. 28.

49 RAL, XI/109/45A/3/12, M to bros, Monday afternoon (undated, postmarked Manchester 11 Sept 1843); RAL, XI/109/45A/3/13, M to bros, Carlisle, Saturday morning (undated, postmarked Carlisle ? Sept 1843); RAL, XI/109/45A/3/11, M to bros, Doncaster, 12 Sept 1843.

50 RAL, XI/109/45A/3/14, M to bros, paper headed 'North-Midland Railway', Chesterfield (undated, postmarked 8 Aug 1843).

51 RAL, XI/109/74/3, M to L & A, Cheltenham, Monday (undated, on honeymoon, 1850).

52 Rosebery Papers, Dalmeny House (transcript RAL), H to M, 10 May 1838.

53 Girouard, *Victorian Country House*, p. 53.

54 RAL, XI/109/45A/3/14, M to bros, paper headed 'North-Midland Railway', Chesterfield (undated, postmarked 8 Aug 1843); RAL, XI/109/75/1, N to bros, (Paris) 22 April (1850); RAL, XI/109/75/4, N to bros, (Paris, undated, April–June 1850).

55 Girouard, *Victorian Country House*, p. 132; Cook, *English Country House*, p. 83.

56 Kessler, 'Rothschilds and Disraeli', p. 21; Gulland, 'Aston Clinton', p. 34.

57 RAL, XI/109/79/5, N to bros, Paris, 27 Nov (1851).

58 *NSM*, ns, vol. 27, 1854, p. 365.

59 Loewe (ed.), *Montefiore diaries*, vol. 2, pp. 57–8.

60 RAL, 000/848, no. 26, CL to L, Paris, 9 Aug 1857; RAL, 000/84, CL to L, Natty & Alfred, Hotel Bristol, Paris, 18 Sept 1854.

61 RAL, XI/109/51B/2/4, H to M, (Paris, undated, March 1845); RAL, XI/109/ 73/4, A to M, (Paris, undated, Oct–Dec 1849), with PS from Alphonse.

62 RAL, XI/109/45B/6/106, N to bros, (Paris, undated, 1843).

63 RAL, XI/109/71/4, M to L, Shrewsbury, Friday Evng (undated, April–June 1849); RAL, XI/109/71/1, M to L, Shrewsbury, Sunday morng (undated, April 1849).

64 RAL, XI/109/57/4/34, M to L, Wildbad, Sunday (undated, July–Sept 1846); RAL, XI/109/45B/6/232, N to bros, (Paris, undated, 1843); RAL, XI/109/71/1, M to L, Shrewsbury, Sunday morng (undated, April 1849).

65 Battersea, *Reminiscences*, p. 231; Evans, *City Men and Manners*, pp. 99–102.

66 RAL, XI/109/78/3, N to bros, (Paris) 9 March (1851); *SM*, vol. 38, 3rd series, 1861, pp. 451–3.

67 Fowler, *Echoes*, p. 100; *BM*, vol. 20, 1871, p. 12; RAL, XI/109/100/1, M to L, Mentmore, Leighton Buzzard (undated, Oct–Dec 1869, dated in pencil: 13 Nov 1869).

68 RAL, XI/109/68B/1/109, Matilda to M, Frankfurt, 14 (?Sept) (box for 1848, but should be 1849).

69 RAL, 000/84, CL to Leo, Gunnersbury, 4 Feb 1867; RAL, XI/109/47/1/102, H to L, (Frankfurt) 14 May (1844); Rosebery Papers, Dalmeny House (transcript RAL); RAL, XI/109/71/1, M to L, Shrewsbury, Sunday morng (undated, April 1849).

70 Fowler, *Echoes*, p. 53; *BM*, vol. 25, 1874, p. 62; *BM*, vol. 34, 1879, p. 147.

71 Willoughby de Broke, *Passing Years*, p. 57.

72 RAL, XI/109/70/4, N to bros, (Paris, undated, Jan–March 1849); RAL, XI/109/72/4, A to M, (Paris, undated, July–Sept 1849); *BM*, vol. 11, 1861, p. 72.

73 Fowler, *Echoes*, pp. 7–8; *NSM*, vol. 27, ns, 1854, p. 368; *SM*, vol. 38, 3rd series, 1861, pp. 451–3; *BM*, vol. 12, 1866–7, p. 230.

74 Fowler, *Echoes*, pp. 7–8.

75 RAL, XI/109/70/3, R. Hart to M, London, 2 March 1849.

76 *NSM*, vol. 27, ns, 1854, p. 370.

77 Ibid.; *SM*, vol. 38, 3rd series, 1861, pp. 451–3.

78 *NSM*, vol. 27, ns, 1854, p. 366; RAL, XI/109/73/1, A to M, (Paris) 16 Oct (1849).

79 *NSM*, vol. 27, ns, 1854, pp. 366–7; *BM*, vol. 11, 1866, pp. 342–3.

80 Sheahan, *Buckinghamshire*, p. 715; RAL, XI/109/72/3, L to M, Frankfurt, 23 Sept 1849; RAL, XI/109/79/3, N to bros, Paris, 20 Sept (1851); *NSM*, vol. 28, ns, 1854, p. 376; *SM*, vol. 40, 3rd series, 1862, p. 94; *NSM*, vol. 30, ns, 1855, p. 155.

81 *NSM*, vol. 27, ns, 1854, 'Turf Register', pp. 82, 127–8, 130, 92, 136, 53, 129, 25–6; *NSM*, vol. 30, ns, 1855, 'Turf Register', p. 93.

82 Onslow, *Headquarters*, p. 97; *BM*, vol. 31, 1877–8, p. 20.

83 Dixon, *Gladiateur to Persimmon*, p. 209; *BM*, vol. 7, 1864, pp. 241, 242; *SM*, vol. 30, 3rd series, 1857, p. 17; Suffolk and Berkshire, *Racing and Steeple-chasing*, p. 139.

84 *BM*, vol. 9, 1864–5, pp. 150–51, 242; *BM*, vol. 11, 1866, pp. 47, 106.

85 RAL, XI/109/86B, N to bros (dictated, Paris), Wednesday 8 June 1864; *BM*, vol. 13, 1867, pp. 212, 263; *BM*, vol. 17, 1869–70, pp. 162, 163; RAL, XI/109/99/1, M to L, Thursday Evng (27 July 1869).

86 RAL, 000/84, CL to Leo, Kingston House, 30 Oct 1863, and CL to Leo & Leonora, 148 Piccadilly, 5 Aug 1867; RAL, 000/84, CL to Leo at Cambridge, 148 Piccadilly, 25 May 1867; RAL, 000/84, CL to Leo, Bedford Hotel, Brighton, 27 Oct 1864; RAL, 000/924, Leo to L & CL, Mentmore, Sunday (undated, 1860s); RAL, XI/109/77/3, John Scott to L, Whitewall House, 11 Dec 1850.

87 RAL, XI/109/106/1, M to Natty, Doncaster, Tuesday (undated, July–Sept 1871); *BM*, vol. 29, Aug 1875, p. 242; *BM*, vol. 31, 1877–8, p. 20.

88 *BM*, vol. 20, 1871, p. 183; *SM*, vol. 46, 3rd series, 1865, pp. 317–18.

89 Quoted in Muhlstein, *Baron James*, p. 185; RAL, XI/109/72/2, L to A (in Paris), Wildbad, 27 Aug 1849; RAL, XI/109/72/3, A to M, (Paris) 22 Sept (1849); RAL, 000/84, CL to Leo, 148 Piccadilly, 11 July 1866.

90 RAL, XI/109/70/4, M to H, (New Court, undated, Jan–March 1849); RAL, XI/109/72/1, L to M, Wildbad, 7 Aug 1849.

91 RAL, XI/109/72/1, L to M, Wildbad, 7 Aug 1849; RAL, XI/109/72/3, H to M, postmarked Lille 8 Sept 1849; RAL, XI/109/72/3, Adolphe to M, (Naples) 17 Sept (1849); RAL, XI/109/72/3, A to M, (Paris) 15 Sept (1849); RAL, XI/109/73/1, A to M, (Paris) 6 Oct (1849).

92 RAL, XI/109/72/3, HM to M, Garboldisham, 9 Sept (1849); RAL, XI/109/73/4, A to M, (Paris, undated, Oct–Dec 1849); RAL, XI/109/73/2, Lionel Davidson to M, Paris, Monday 19 Nov 1849; RAL, XI/109/73/4, L to M, (Paris, undated, Oct–Dec 1849).

93 RAL, XI/109/86B/2, N to bros (dictated, Paris), Thursday 7 July 1864; RAL, XI/109/72/1, L to M (in London), Wildbad, 31 July 1849; RAL, XI/109/73/4, H to A (in Paris), (Frankfurt) Friday (undated, Oct–Dec 1849); RAL, XI/109/73/4, H to M, Frankfurt, Monday (undated, Oct–Dec 1849).

94 RAL, XI/109/72/3, H to M, Frankfurt, 27 Sept (says Dec) 1849.

95 RAL, XI/109/79/4, L to bros, Frankfurt, 19 Oct 1851; RAL, XI/109/79/5, L to bros, Paris, 30 Nov (1851); RAL, XI/109/79/5, A to M, (Paris) 4 Dec 1851.

96 RAL, XI/109/73/2, L to bros, Paris, 9 Nov 1849; RAL, XI/109/72/2, L to M, Wildbad (undated, Aug 1849); RAL, XI/109/59B/1/12, unsigned letter to Jas Campbell Esq, Assistant Secretary, GPO, New Court 3 March 1847.

97 Battersea, *Reminiscences*, p. 9; Ferguson, *Rothschild*, vol. II, p. 70.

17: MOST PAINFUL OF COMPLAINTS

1 Mansel, *Paris*, p. 158.

2 RAL, XI/109/52B/2/15 (no. 2), MC to N, (Frankfurt, undated, April–June 1845); RAL, XI/109/52A/2/74, Note from N in A to bros, Paris, 12 May (1845).

3 RAL, XI/109/51B/2/4, H to M, (Paris, undated, but March 1845); RAL, XI/109/51B/2/30, N to bros, (Paris, undated, Jan–March 1845); RAL, XI/109/52A/1/39, H to sons, Paris, 6 (April 1845); RAL, XI/109/52A/1/76, H to CL, Paris, 10/16 April (1845); RAL, XI/109/52A/1/36, extract from RAL, XI/109/52A/1/37, N to bros, (Paris) Sunday 6 April (1845), copied out by L; RAL, XI/109/52A/1/75, H to A, Paris, 10 April (1845).

4 RAL, XI/109/52A/1/37, N to bros, (Paris) Sunday 6 April (1845); RAL, XI/109/52A/1/36, extract from RAL, XI/109/52A/1/37, N to bros, (Paris) Sunday 6 April (1845), copied out by L.

5 RAL, XI/109/52B/2/30, N to bros (dictated to Charlotte Nat), (Paris, undated, April 1845); RAL, XI/109/52A/1/163, N to bros, Paris, 28 April (1845); RAL, XI/109/52A/2/131, A to bros, (Paris) 10 May (1845).

6 RAL, XI/109/52A/2/74, PS from N in A to bros, Paris, 12 May (1845); *SM*, vol. 5, 3rd series, 1845, p. 410; RAL, XI/109/52A/2/120, A to bros, (Paris) 19 May (1845).

7 RAL, XI/109/57/4/32, N to A, Wildbad, 8 July (1846); RAL, XI/109/57/4/35, N to A, Wildbad (undated, July–Sept 1846).

8 RAL, XI/109/57/4/7, N to L, (Frankfurt, undated, July–Sept 1846); RAL, XI/109/57/4/36, M to L, (Paris, undated, July–Sept 1846); RAL, XI/109/63/2/77, N to bros, (Paris, undated, Aug–Sept 1847).

9 RAL, XI/109/65B/2/18, N to bros, (Paris, undated, Jan–March 1848); RAL, XI/109/68A/1/52, N to bros, (Paris) 7 July (1848); RAL, XI/109/69B/2/12, N to bros, (Paris, undated, Oct–Dec 1848); RAL, XI/ 109/69A/1/20, N to bros, (Paris) 3 Oct (1848).

10 RAL, XI/109/57/4/36, M to L, (Paris, undated, July–Sept 1846); RAL, XI/109/63/2/32, A to bros, (Paris, undated, Sept 1847); RAL, XI/109/69B/2/21, N to bros, (Paris, undated, Oct–Dec 1848); RAL, XI/109/69B/1/128, LMC to L, Frankfurt, 15 Dec (1848); RAL, XI/109/71/4, N to bros, (Paris, undated, April–June 1849).

11 RAL, 000/84, CL to Leo, 27 Sept 1859(?); RAL, XI/109/69B/2/36, N to bros, (Paris, undated, Oct–Dec 1848); RAL, XI/109/83/4, N to bros (Paris), Sunday (undated, Oct–Dec 1852).

12 RAL, 000/84, CL to Leo, Torquay, 5 Dec 1862; RAL, 000/84, CL to Leo, Paris, 23 Oct 1861; RAL, 000/84, CL to L & Natty & Alfred, Hotel Bristol, 25 Sept 1864.

13 RAL, T7/152, XI/109/61/1/3, Alphonse to A (French), Paris, 2 June (1847); RAL, 000/84, CL to Leo, Bedford Hotel, Brighton, 10 Nov 1864; RAL, XI/109/71/4, N to bros, (Paris, undated, April–June 1849).

14 RAL, XI/109/72/3, Lionel Davidson to A, Frankfurt, 25 Sept 1849; RAL, XI/109/45B/6/121, N to bros, (Paris, undated, 1843); RAL, 000/84, CL to Leo, Kingston House, 6 Feb 1864; RAL, 000/84, CL to L, Kingston House, 5 April 1864.

15 RAL, XI/109/70/4, L to A, (Frankfurt, undated, Jan–March 1849); RAL, 000/848, CL to L letters, Gunnersbury, 23 Oct 1852; RAL, 000/84, CL to Leo & Leonora, 31 July 1862; RAL, 000/84, CL to Leo & Leonora, Kingston House, 28 July 1862.

16 RAL, 000/13/230, L to Leo, London, 20 Oct 1863; RAL, 000/84, CL to Leo, Gunnersbury, 18 Aug 1864, and 1 Oct 1866; RAL, XI/109/106/3, David Robertson to L, Ladykirk, Berwickshire, 6 Sept 1871; RAL, XI/109/72/3, A to M, (Paris) 21 Sept (1849); RAL, XI/109/103/1, Bernal Osborne to L, (Ireland) 12 Dec 1870; RAL, 000/84, CL to Leo, 29 April 1864, and 148 Piccadilly, 8 May 1864; RAL, XI/109/72/4, CL to M, Brussels, Tuesday evening (undated, July–Sept 1849); RAL, 000/13/191, L to Leo & Leonora, 11 Aug 1862; Pinney (ed.), *Macaulay letters*, vol. vi, p. 228.

17 Bovill, *English Country Life*, p. 111; RAL, 000/84, CL to Leo, 148 Piccadilly, 8 May 1864; RAL, 000/84, CL to Leo, Bedford Hotel, Brighton, 11 Dec 1864; RAL, 000/924, Hannah (M's daughter) to L, Bedford Hotel, Brighton, Thursday (undated).

18 RAL, XI/109/90/2, William Forsyth to L, 7 June (1867); RAL, 000/13/77, L to CL, Piccadilly, 7 July 1867.

19 RAL, XI/109/73/1, L to M, 31 Oct 1849; RAL, XI/109/73/2, H to M, (Frankfurt) 14 Nov 1849.

20 RAL, XI/109/73/1, A to M, (Paris) 29 Oct (1849); RAL, XI/109/77/3, N to bros, 4 Dec (1850); RAL, XI/109/78/1, HM to L, 109 Marine Parade, Brighton, 29 Jan (1851); RAL, XI/109/80/1, A to bros, (Paris) 1 Jan 1852; RAL, XI/109/83/2, N to bros, Paris, 27 Dec (1852); RAL, XI/109/83/4, N to bros, (Paris) Sunday (undated, Oct–Dec 1852); RAL, 000/84, CL to Leo, Gunnersbury, 21 Jan 1867; RAL, XI/109/92/1, M to L, Newmarket, Sunday (undated, Oct–Dec 1867).

21 RAL, XI/109/70/2, HM to L, Pau, 13 Feb 1849; RAL, XI/109/72/1, CA to L, Frankfurt, Friday 6 July (1849).

22 RAL, XI/109/72/2, CL to H, Wildbad, Aug 1849; RAL, XI/109/72/1, L to A, Bath, 12 July 1849; RAL, 000/84, CL to LA, Wildbad, 1 Aug 1849; RAL, XI/109/72/1, L to A (in Paris), Wildbad, 31 July 1849; RAL, XI/109/72/2, L to A, Wildbad, 15 Aug 1849.

23 RAL, 000/84, CL to LA, Wildbad, 14 Aug 1849; RAL, 000/84, CL to LA, Frankfurt, 18 Oct 1849.

24 RAL, T8/152, N to bros, Gräfenberg-Freiwalden, 28 June (1849); RAL, XI/109/72/1, N to bros, Gräfenberg, 7 July (1849); RAL, T8/152, N to bros, Gräfenberg-Freiwalden, 28 June (1849).

25 RAL, XI/109/58A/2/154, N to bros, Paris, 24 Nov (1846); RAL, XI/109/73/1, L to M, Freiwalden, 9 Oct 1849.

26 RAL, XI/109/73/1, L to M, Freiwalden, 9 Oct 1849; RAL, XI/109/73/1, L to James & A (in Paris), Berlin, 13 Oct 1849.

27 RAL, XI/109/73/1, Lionel Davidson to M, Frankfurt, Friday 26 Oct 1849; RAL,

XI/109/75/4, Benjamin Travers to L, Athenaeum Club, Monday Evening (undated, April–June 1850); RAL, 000/84, CL to Leo, Kingston House, 14 Sept 1859.

28 RAL, XI/109/73/3, N to bros, (Paris) 30 Dec (1849); RAL, XI/109/74/1, N to bros, (Paris) 1 Jan (1850); RAL, 000/297/B, Family Letters, Marion Ellice to LA, Paris, 9 Jan 1850.

29 RAL, XI/109/72/2, L to A, Wildbad, 15 Aug 1849; RAL, XI/109/77/1, N to bros, (Paris) 19 Oct (1850); RAL, 000/297/B, Family Letters, Marion Ellice to LA, Paris, 17 Oct 1850.

30 RAL, XI/109/77/4, N to bros, (Paris, undated, Oct–Dec 1850); RAL, XI/109/77/2, N to bros, Paris, 30 Nov (1850); RAL, XI/109/77/3, N to bros, Paris, 10 Dec 1850; RAL, XI/109/77/3, N to bros, (Paris) Tuesday 17 Dec (1850).

31 RAL, XI/109/77/3, A to bros, (Paris) 19 Dec (1850); RAL, XI/109/77/3, N to bros, Paris, 25 Dec (1850).

32 RAL, XI/109/78/3, N to bros, with a PS to CL, 31 March (1851); RAL, XI/109/78/4, N to bros, Paris, 2 April (1851); RAL, 000/84, CL to Leo, Paris, 18 Oct 1861.

33 RAL, XI/109/79/4, L to bros, Frankfurt, 23 Oct 1851; RAL, XI/109/79/4, L to N, Frankfurt, 24 Oct 1851.

34 RAL, XI/109/79/4, N to bros, (Paris) 31 Oct 1851; RAL, 000/84, C to Leo, Kingston House, 21 Oct 1863.

35 RAL, XI/109/79/5, L to bros, Berlin, 12 Nov 1851; RAL, XI/109/80/1, A to bros, (Paris) 1 Jan 1852.

36 RAL, XI/109/82/1, N to bros, Gastein, 9 July 1852; RAL, XI/109/82/1, N to L, Gastein, 6 July (1852); RAL, XI/109/82/2, N to bros, Gastein, 2 Aug (1852).

37 RAL, XI/109/71/4, N to bros, (Paris, undated, April–June 1849); RAL, XI/109/72/1, L to M (in London), Wildbad, 31 July 1849; RAL, XI/109/76/4, M to bros, Frankfurt, Thursday (undated, July–Sept 1850); BM, vol. 8, 1865, p. 158.

38 RAL, XI/109/99/1, A to 'L & Gents', Homburg, 13 Aug (1869); RAL, XI/109/99/1, A to bros '& Gents', Homburg, 18 Aug (1869); RAL, 000/848, CL to L letters, no. 23, Paris, 5 Aug 1857.

39 RAL, XI/109/82/2, N to bros, Gastein, 2 Aug (1852); RAL, XI/109/82/1, N to bros, Gastein, 3 July (1852); RAL, XI/109/82/2, N to bros, Gastein, 2 Aug (1852); RAL, XI/109/82/1, N to bros, (Gastein) 13 July (1852).

40 RAL, XI/109/82/3, N to bros, Brighton, 21 Sept (1852); RAL, XI/109/83/4, N to L, (Brighton, undated, Oct–Dec 1852).

41 Kessler, 'Rothschilds and Disraeli', p. 22; Battersea, Reminiscences, p. 79; RAL, XI/103/0, H to L & N in PS to letter from A, (Paris) 22 May (1839); RAL, 000/10, H to N, Suresnes (undated, 1839); BM, vol. 18, 1870, p. 107; BM, vol. 34, 1879, p. 147.

42 RAL, XI/109/83/4, N to bros, (Paris, undated, Oct–Dec 1852); RAL, XI/109/83/2, N to bros, Paris, 19 Nov (1852); RAL, XI/109/83/4, N to bros, (Paris, undated, Oct–Dec 1852); RAL, XI/109/83/2, N to bros, Paris, 29 Nov (1852); RAL, XI/109/83/2, N to bros, (Paris) 21 Dec (1852).

43 RAL, XI/109/83/2, N to bros, Paris, 26 Dec (1852); RAL, XI/109/83/3, N to bros, Paris, 30 Dec (1852).

44 Ferguson, Rothschild, vol. II, p. 46; BM, vol. 28, 1876, p. 182.

45 RAL, XI/109/83/4, N to L, (Brighton, undated, Oct–Dec 1852); RAL, XI/109/91B/2, N to bros, (Paris, undated, July–Sept 1867); RAL, XI/109/56/1/124, Anselm to M, Frankfurt, 22 April 1846; RAL, XI/109/81/3, MC to cousins, Frankfurt, 4 June 1852.

46 RAL, T7/151, XI/109/60/1/211, James to M (French), Paris, 30 April 1847; RAL, XI/109/71/4, N to bros, (Paris, undated, April–June 1848); RAL, XI/109/80/1, N to bros, Paris, 13 Jan (1852); RAL, XI/109/71/3, N to bros, Freiwalden, 27 June (1849).

47 RAL, XI/109/14/1/22, MC to A, Frankfurt, 22/25 March 1830; RAL, XI/109/43A/2/11, A to bros, (Paris) 29 Oct 1842; Ferguson, *Rothschild*, vol. II, p. 46; RAL, XI/109/106/1, A to bros, Paris, Thursday (undated, July–Sept 1871); RAL, XI/109/90/1, Howard & Son to 'Baron', 26 & 27 Berners Street, London W, 30 April 1867.

48 RAL, XI/109/110/1, Alfred to L & CL, Paris, 2 Oct 1872; Muhlstein, *Baron James*, p. 211; RAL, XI/109/86B/2, N to bros, (Paris) Tuesday 22 Nov 1864; RAL, XI/109/86B/2, N to bros, Paris (undated, Jan–Dec 1864).

49 RAL, 000/84, CL to Leo, Isle of Wight, 24 Sept 1859; RAL, 000/848, CL to L letters, no. 23, Paris, 5 Aug 1857.

50 Ferguson, *Rothschild*, vol. II, p. 76; ibid., vol. I, pp. 379–80.

51 *Illustrated London News*, 7 March 1857.

52 RAL, 000/13/220, L to Natty & Leo, Paris, 22 Sept 1863.

53 RAL, 000/1067, Leonora, p. 101.

54 RAL, 000/13/39, L to C, Edinburgh, Thursday morning (Aug 1843); RAL, 000/13/35, L to CL, Paris, Saturday evening (undated, Aug 1842); RAL, 000/13/43, L to CL, Crieff, 22 Aug 1843; RAL, 000/13/50, L to CL, Paris, 18 July 1848.

55 RAL, 000/1067, Evelina, p. 42; RAL, 000/84, CL to Leo, Gunnersbury, 31 Dec 1861.

56 RAL, 000/84, CL to Leo, New Court, 28 Nov 1865; RAL, 000/84, CL to Leo, 148 Piccadilly, 2 Aug 1864, and Gunnersbury, 12 Sept 1871; RAL, 000/84, CL to Leo, Gunnersbury, 11 Nov 1865; RAL, 000/84, CL to Leo, 148 Piccadilly, 23 July 1866.

57 RAL, 000/84, CL to Leo, 148 Piccadilly, 17 July 1866; RAL, 000/297/B, Family Letters, 1834–89, Adele to Constance, Frankfurt, 16 Feb 1859.

58 RAL, 000/84, CL to Leo, Gunnersbury, 24 Aug 1864; RAL, T11/27, Anselm to Ferdinand (German), Vienna (undated, 1873).

59 RAL, 000/84, CL to Leo, Torquay, 27 Jan 1863; RAL, 000/84, CL to Leo, Kingston House, 24 Nov 1863; RAL, 000/84, CL to Natty & Leo, 7 Sept 1863; RAL, 000/84, CL to Natty & Leo, 9 Sept 1863.

60 RAL, 000/84, CL to Leo, Paris, 8 Nov 1861; RAL, 000/84, CL to Leo, 184 Piccadilly, 6 Sept 1866; RAL, 000/84, CL to Leo, London, 11 Nov 1861; RAL, 000/84, CL to Leo, Bedford Hotel, Brighton, 9 Dec 1864; RAL, 000/84, CL to L, Natty & Alfred, Paris, 16 Sept 1864; RAL, 000/84, CL to Leo, 148 Piccadilly, 29 Aug 1871; RAL, 000/84, CL to Leo, Gunnersbury, 30 Aug 1866; RAL, 000/84, CL to Leo & Leonora, Paris, 7 Aug 1874.

61 RAL, 000/84, CL to Leo, Bedford Hotel, Brighton, 8 Dec 1864; RAL, XI/109/99/1, L to M & Natty, (Paris) Wednesday (undated, July–Sept 1869).

62 RAL, 000/84, CL to Natty & Leo, Paris, 14 Sept 1863; RAL, 000/84, CL to Leo, Kingston House, 27 Oct 1863; RAL, 000/84, CL to Leo, 148 Piccadilly, 11 March 1865; RAL, XI/109/87/2, Frank Romer to 'Gentlemen', (Paris, undated, July–Dec 1865).

63 RAL, 000/84, CL to Leo, Gunnersbury, 16 Sept 1865; RAL, 000/84, CL to Leo, 148 Piccadilly, 2 May 1865, and CL to Leo, London, 4 March 1865; RAL, 000/84, CL to Leo, Bedford Hotel, Brighton, 13 Dec 1864; RAL, 000/84, CL to Leo, Bedford Hotel, Brighton, 16 Oct 1864.

64 RAL, 000/84, CL to Leo, Bedford Hotel, Brighton, 1 Oct 1864; RAL, 000/84, CL to Leo, 148 Piccadilly, 3 Oct 1864.

65 RAL, 000/84, CL to Leo & Leonora, Kingston House, 3/4 Aug 1862; RAL, 000/13/194, L to Leonora, Alphonse & Leo, Folkestone, 29 Aug 1862; RAL, 000/84, CL to Natty & Leo, Pavilion Hotel, Folkestone, 30 Sept 1862; RAL, 000/84, CL to Leo & Leonora, Kingston House, 14 Aug 1862, and Folkestone, 27 Aug & 29 Aug 1862.

66 RAL, 000/84, CL to Leo & Evelina, Folkestone, 15 Sept 1862; RAL, 000/84, CL to Leo, Folkestone, 2 Oct 1862; RAL, 000/13/198, L to Leo, Folkestone, 15 Oct 1862.

67 RAL, 000/13/197, L to Leo, Folkestone, 14 Oct 1862; RAL, 000/84, CL to Leo & Leonora, Folkestone, 29 Aug 1862; Battersea, *Reminiscences*, pp. 60–62; RAL, 000/84, CL to Leo & Leonora, Pavilion Hotel, Folkestone, 31 Aug 1862; RAL, 000/84, CL to Leo & Leonora, Folkestone, 3 Sept 1862.

68 RAL, 000/84, CL to Leo & Leonora, Pavilion Hotel, Folkestone, 28 Aug 1862; RAL, 000/13/194, L to Leonora, Alphonse & Leo, Folkestone, 29 Aug 1862; RAL, 000/13/174, L to Leo, Paris, 6 Nov 1861, and 000/13/180, L to Leo, Paris, 13 Nov 1861; RAL, 000/84, CL to Leo, Paris, 8 Nov 1861; RAL, XI/109/86B/2, Evelina to L, Paris, Monday morning (undated, July–Dec 1864).

69 RAL, 000/13/198, L to Leo, Folkestone, 15 Oct 1862.

70 RAL, 000/84, CL to Leo, Webb's Royal Hotel, Torquay, 30 Nov 1862; RAL, 000/84, CL to Leo, Torquay, 27 Jan 1863; RAL, 000/13/201, L to Leo, Torquay, 1 Dec 1862; RAL, 000/13/202, L to Leo, Torquay, 2 Dec 1862.

71 RAL, 000/84, CL to Leo, Torquay, 27 Nov 1862; RAL, 000/13/212, L to Leo, Torquay, 25 Jan 1863; RAL, 000/84, CL to Leo, Torquay, 5 Dec 1862.

72 RAL, 000/84, CL to Leo, Torquay, 2 Dec 1862; RAL, 000/13/202, L to Leo, Torquay, 2 Dec 1862, and RAL, 000/84, CL to Leo, Torquay, 1 & 2 Dec 1862; RAL, 000/84, CL to Leo, Torquay, 7 Dec 1862, and Ferguson, *Rothschild*, vol. I, p. 342.

73 RAL, 000/13/206, L to Leo, Torquay, 9 Dec 1862; RAL, 000/84, CL to Leo, Torquay, 27 Jan 1863; RAL, 000/13/199, L to Leo, Torquay, 28 Nov 1862; RAL, 000/84, CL to Leo, Torquay, 15 Jan 1863.

74 RAL, 000/13/199, L to Leo, Torquay, 28 Nov 1862; RAL, 000/84, CL to Leo, Kingston House, 10 Nov 1863.

75 RAL, XI/109/72/1, N to bros, Gräfenberg, 7 July (1849); Battersea, *Reminiscences*, p. 54.

76 RAL, 000/84, CL to Leo, 27 Jan 1863; RAL, 000/84, CL to Leo, Kingston House, 24 Feb 1864; RAL, 000/84, CL to Leo, Kingston House, 10 Nov 1863; RAL, .000/84, CL to Leo, Kingston House, 11 Feb 1864; RAL, 000/84, CL to Leo, London, 12 May 1865.

77 RAL, 000/84, CL to Leo, Kingston House, 24 Feb 1864; RAL, 000/84, CL to Leo, Kingston House, 11 Feb 1864; RAL, 000/84, CL to Leo, Kingston House, 11 April 1864; Battersea, *Reminiscences*, p. 55; RAL, 000/84, CL to Leo, Kingston House, 9 May (1864); CL to Leo, 148 Piccadilly, 16 July 1864.

78 RAL, 000/84, CL to Leo, 148 Piccadilly, 4 June 1864; RAL, 000/84, CL to Leo, 148 Piccadilly, 6 June 1864.

79 RAL, 000/84, CL to Leo, 148 Piccadilly, 9 June 1864.

80 RAL, 000/84, CL to Leo, 148 Piccadilly, 19 July 1864; RAL, 000/84, CL to Leo, Bedford Hotel, Brighton, 9 Oct 1864; RAL, 000/84, CL to Leo, Bedford Hotel, Brighton, 27 Oct 1864.

81 RAL, XI/109/86B/2, L to bros & Natty & Alfred, (Brighton, undated, Nov–Dec 1864); RAL, 000/84, CL to Leo, Bedford Hotel, Brighton, 15 Nov 1864; RAL, XI/109/86B/2, L to bros & Natty & Alfred, Friday morning (Brighton, undated, Dec 1864).

18: FOLLOW THE BARON

1 RAL, 000/84, CL to Leo, Bedford Hotel, Brighton, 9 Nov 1864; RAL, 000/84, CL to Leo, Bedford Hotel, Brighton, 10 Nov 1864.

2 RAL, 000/13/247, L to Leo, London, 24 Nov 1863; RAL, XI/109/72/1, L to A, Bath, 12 July 1849; RAL, 000/84, CL to Leo, 148 Piccadilly, 3 Feb 1865, and CL to Leo, 148 Piccadilly, 8 Feb 1865; RAL, 000/13/248, L to Leo, (London) 25 Nov 1863.

3 RAL, XI/109/87/1, N to bros (dictated), (Paris, undated, July–Dec 1865); RAL, 000/84, CL to Leo, Gunnersbury, 24 Oct 1865.

4 RAL, 000/84, CL to Leo, Gunnersbury, 17 Feb 1867; RAL, 000/13/380, L to Leo (Leonora's hand), Brighton, Monday 12 Dec (no year).

5 RAL, 000/84, CL to Leo, 4 May 1864.

6 RAL, 000/84, CL to Leo, Kingston House, 24 Nov 1863; RAL, 000/84, CL to Leo, 148 Piccadilly, 11 Nov 1865; RAL, XI/109/87/2, J. T. Delane to L, (London) 8 Nov (1865).

7 RAL, 000/84, CL to Leo, 148 Piccadilly, 11 Nov 1865; RAL, 000/84, CL to Leo, Gunnersbury, 6 Jan 1867.

8 RAL, 000/84, CL to Leo, 148 Piccadilly, 15 May 1865.

9 RAL, XI/109/106/1, Natty to L & CL, Birnam, 30 Aug (1871); RAL, 000/84, CL to Leo, 148 Piccadilly, 24 July 1867.

10 RAL, 000/13/78, L to CL, New Court, 9 July 1867; RAL, T11/29, MC to cousins and nephews, Frankfurt, 13 Jan 1873.

11 RAL, XI/109/95/2, Ferdinand to L & cousins, Vienna, 7 Sept 1868.

12 RAL, 000/84, CL to Leo, Kingston House, 6 Feb 1864; RAL, 000/13/263, L to Leo, New Court, 7 July 1864; RAL, 000/13/263, L to Leo, New Court, 12 (July 1864).

13 RAL, 000/84, CL to Leo, 148 Piccadilly, 8 Feb 1865; RAL, 000/84, CL to Leo, London, 25 May 1865.

14 RAL, 000/84, CL to Leo, 13 Aug 1866; RAL, 000/84, CL to Leo, Bedford Hotel, Brighton, 13 Nov 1864; RAL, 000/848, Bernal Osborne to Natty, Reform Club, 7 June 1879; RAL, 000/84, CL to Leo, 26 Aug 1864; RAL, 000/84, CL to Leo, Gunnersbury, 1 Oct 1866; RAL, 000/13/244, L to Leo, London, 18 Nov 1863; RAL, 000/13/252, L to Leo, London, 3 Dec 1863.

15 RAL, 000/84, CL to Leo, Gunnersbury, 23 Aug 1864; RAL, 000/84, CL to Leo, 148 Piccadilly, 3 Aug 1864; RAL, 000/13/275, L to Leo, New Court, 9 Aug 1864; RAL, 000/13/89, L to CL & Leo, New Court, 3 March 1868.

16 Cohen, *Lady de Rothschild*, p. 32; Battersea, *Reminiscences*, pp. 106, 233; RAL, 000/12/29, Natty to L & CL, Mentmore, 18 Jan 1863; RAL, 000/[?]/29, Natty to L & CL (at Torquay), New Court, 16 Jan (1863); RAL, 000/84, CL to Leo, Bedford Hotel, Brighton, 31 Oct 1864.

17 RAL, 000/84, CL to Leo, 148 Piccadilly, 7 July 1864; RAL, 000/84, CL to Leo, 148 Piccadilly, 10 March 1866; RAL, 000/84, CL to Leo, 148 Piccadilly, 19 May 1870; RAL, 000/84, CL to Leo, 148 Piccadilly, 3 June 1867.

18 RAL, 000/13/272, L to Leo, London, 30 July 1864; RAL, 000/84, CL to Leo, 148 Piccadilly, 12 July 1866.

19 RAL, 000/84, CL to Leo, London, 29 May 1865; RAL, 000/13/263, L to Leo, New Court, 12 (July 1864); RAL, 000/84, CL to Leo, London, 29 May 1865; RAL, 000/13/272, L to Leo, London, 30 July 1864.; RAL, 000/84, CL to Leo, Kingston House, 28 Feb 1864; RAL, 000/84, CL to Natty & Leo, Kingston House, 23 Dec 1860; RAL, 000/84, CL to Leo, 148 Piccadilly, 12 July 1864; RAL, 000/84, CL to Leo, 148 Piccadilly, 19 July 1866; RAL, 000/84, CL to Leo, 13 Aug 1866; RAL, 000/84, CL to Leo, Gunnersbury, 4 Nov 1866; RAL, 000/84, CL to Leo, 19 Nov 1866.

20 RAL, 000/84, CL to Leo, 148 Piccadilly, 24 July 1867; RAL, 000/84, CL to Leo, Kingston House, 28 Feb 1864; RAL, 000/84, CL to Leo, 148 Piccadilly, 7 June 1866.

21 Ponsonby, *Sidelights*, p. 76.

22 RAL, 000/84, CL to Leo, 148 Piccadilly, 3 Aug 1864.

23 RAL, 000/84, CL to Leo, Kingston House, 13 March 1864; RAL, 000/84, CL to Leo, 148 Piccadilly, 3 Aug 1864; RAL, 000/84, CL to Leo, London, 20 March 1865; RAL, 000/84, CL to Leo, 148 Piccadilly, Monday 18 July 1864; RAL, 000/84, CL to Leo, London, 6 March 1865; RAL, 000/84, CL to Leo, Kingston House, 22 Feb 1864

24 RAL, 000/84, CL to Leo, 148 Piccadilly, 2 May 1865.

25 RAL, 000/84, CL to Leo, 148 Piccadilly, 22 May 1867; RAL, 000/13/93, L to CL, New Court, 9 March 1868; RAL, 000/84, CL to Leo, 148 Piccadilly, 17 July 1866; RAL, 000/84, CL to Leo, 148 Piccadilly, 3 June 1867.

26 RAL, 000/12/29, Natty to L & CL (at Torquay), Mentmore, 18 Jan 1863.

27 RAL, 000/13/204, L to Leo, Torquay, 5 Dec 1862; RAL, 000/13/240, L to Leo, New Court, 10 Nov 1863; RAL, XI/109/100/1, A to bros, (Paris) Sunday (28 Oct 1869); RAL, 000/13/196, L to Leo, Folkestone, 1 Oct 1862.

28 RAL, 000/84, CL to Leo, Kingston House, 27 Oct 1863; RAL, 000/84, CL to Leo, 148 Piccadilly, Sunday 8 May 1864; RAL, 000/13/260, L to Leo, New Court, 8 ?Feb 1864; RAL, 000/84, CL to Leo, 148 Piccadilly, 30 May 1864; RAL, 000/84, CL to Leo, 148 Piccadilly, Monday 18 July 1864.

29 *Illustrated London News*, 6 Sept 1862.

30 RAL, 000/13/240, L to Leo, New Court, 10 Nov 1863; RAL, 000/13/276, L to Leo, London, 27 Aug 1864; RAL, 000/84, CL to Leo, 148 Piccadilly, 8 May 1864; RAL, 000/84, CL to Leo, 3 May 1864.

31 RAL, 000/924, Lord Cadogan to CL, 28 Lowndes Street, SW, 21 Jan 1865; RAL, 000/924, Lady Clarendon to CL, Grosvenor Crescent, 26 Jan 1865; RAL, 000/924, Lady Carrington to CL, 142 Piccadilly (undated); RAL, 000/84, CL to Leo, 148 Piccadilly, 3 Feb 1865.

32 RAL, 000/84, CL to Natty & Leo, Hotel Bristol, Paris, 9 Sept 1863; RAL, 000/84, CL to Leo, Bedford Hotel, Brighton, 21 Dec 1864.

33 RAL, 000/84, CL to Leo, 148 Piccadilly, 3 Feb 1865; RAL, 000/84, CL to Leo, 148 Piccadilly, 8 Feb 1865 (no. 2); RAL, 000/84, CL to Leo, London, 28 Feb 1865.

34 RAL, 000/84, CL to Leo, London, 6 May 1865; RAL, 000/84, CL to Leo, London, 25 May 1865.

35 Ferguson, *Rothschild*, vol. II, p. 242; RAL, 000/84, CL to Leo, 16 June (but July) 1865.

36 RAL, 000/84, CL to Leo, Gunnersbury, 2 Nov 1865, and 5 Dec 1865; RAL, 000/84, CL to Leo, 148 Piccadilly, 22 Nov 1866; RAL, 000/84, CL to Leo, 148 Piccadilly, 26 Nov 1866.

37 Cohen, *Lady de Rothschild*, p. 126.

38 RAL, 000/84, CL to Leo, 148 Piccadilly, 17 May 1864; RAL, 000/84, CL to Natty & Leo, Hotel Bristol, Paris, 28 Sept 1863; RAL, 000/84, CL to Leo, 19 May 1864.

39 RAL, XI/109/94/1, James to A, Paris, 7 May 1868; RAL, XI/109/95/1, James to nephews (dictated), Paris, 5 Aug 1868; RAL, XI/109/96/1, N to bros (dictated), Paris, 26 Oct 1868.

40 RAL, XI/109/96/1, Natty to L & CL, (Paris, undated, Nov 1868); RAL, XI/109/96/1, Alfred to L & CL, Paris, Wednesday (undated, Nov 1868); RAL, XI/109/99/1, Leo to M & Natty, Paris, 30 Aug 1869.

41 Muhlstein, *Baron James*, p. 210; RAL, XI/109/94/1, James to A, Paris, 7 May 1868; *BM*, vol. 15, 1868, p. 361.

42 RAL, 000/12/50, Natty to CL, 6 March 1868.

43 RAL, 000/12/8, Natty to L & CL, Cambridge, Thursday (no day) Dec 1861; *BM*, vol. 15, 1868, p. 362; RAL, 000/12/50, Natty to CL, 6 March 1868.

44 *BM*, vol. 15, 1868, pp. 361, 362; RAL, 000/12/50, Natty to CL, 6 March 1868; RAL, 000/13/92, L to CL & Leo, New Court, 6 March 1868.

45 Ibid.

46 RAL, 000/84, CL to Leo, 148 Piccadilly, 25 May 1864; *BM*, vol. 15, 1868, p. 370; RAL, 000/84, CL to Leo, Gunnersbury, 19 Sept 1865; RAL, 000/924, Leo to L & CL, Newmarket, 6 Oct (1868).

47 RAL, 000/84, CL to Leo, Kingston House, 13 Nov 1863; RAL, 000/84, CL to Leo, Gunnersbury, 9 Nov 1866.

48 RAL, 000/84, CL to Leo, Kingston House, 10 Feb 1864; Battersea, *Reminiscences*, pp. 124, 126; RAL, 000/84, CL to Leo, Kingston House, 10 Feb 1864; RAL, 000/84, CL to Leo, Kingston House, (Saturday) 14 Nov 1863; RAL, 000/84, CL to Leo, Kingston House, 2 Feb 1864.

49 Trollope, *Autobiography*, p. 222; Battersea, *Reminiscences*, p. 129.

50 RAL, 000/84, CL to Leo, Gunnersbury, 25 Sept 1866.

51 Cohen, *Lady de Rothschild*, p. 75; RAL, XI/109/100/1, A to bros, Holkham, Tuesday (28 Dec 1869); Cohen, *Lady de Rothschild*, pp. 136–40; RAL, XI/109/100/1, A to bros, Holkham, Wednesday (29 Dec 1869).

52 Cohen, *Lady de Rothschild*, pp. 138, 140.

53 Battersea, *Reminiscences*, p. 49; RAL, 000/12/48, Natty to CL, London, 28 Feb 1868; Whyte-Melville, *Riding Recollections*, p. 211; id., *Satanella*, pp. 288, 289; *BM*, vol. 22, 1872, p. 179.

54 RAL, 000/12/29, Natty to L & CL (at Torquay), New Court, 16 Jan (1863); *BM*, vol. 25, 1874, p. 18.

55 'Thormanby', *Kings of the Turf*, p. 305; RAL, 000/13/355, L to Leo, New Court, Wednesday (undated, 1871); *BM*, vol. 21, 1871, p. 36.

56 RAL, XI/109/95/1, John F. Cay to L, A & M, Paris, 6 July 1868; RAL, XI/109/101/1, John F. Cay to L, 33 Faubourg St-Honoré, Paris, 5 Jan 1870.

57 RAL, XI/109/101/1, Natty to L & CL, 2 rue St-Florentin (Paris, 21 Feb 1870); RAL, 000/13/353, L to Leo (Alfred's hand), 24 Feb 1870.

58 RAL, XI/109/101/1, John F. Cay to L, 33 Faubourg St-Honoré, Paris, 19 Feb 1870.

59 RAL, 000/13/413, L to Leo, (London, undated); RAL, XI/109/114A/1, M to L, Mentmore, Leighton Buzzard, Thursday p.m. (Oct–Dec 1873); RAL, XI/109/114A/1, Hannah (M's daughter) to L, Mentmore, Leighton Buzzard, Monday (Oct–Dec 1873); RAL, XI/109/114B/2, James James to L, Mentmore, Leighton Buzzard, Monday, 5 p.m. (Oct–Dec 1873).

60 RAL, XI/109/95/2, Natty to L & CL, Frankfurt, 2 Aug (1868).

61 RAL, XI/109/86B/2, L to A, (Bedford Hotel, Brighton, undated, Nov 1864).

62 Battersea, *Reminiscences*, p. 9; RAL, XI/109/104/1, A to bros, Sandringham, King's Lynn, Thursday (undated, Jan–March 1871); RAL, XI/109/104/1, A to bros & nephews, Sandringham, King's Lynn, Tuesday (undated, Jan–March 1871).

63 RAL, 000/297, LA's journal, 12 Nov 1874; Cohen, *Lady de Rothschild*, p. 163.

64 RAL, XI/109/112/1, A to bros, Vienna, 1 May (1873).

65 RAL, XI/109/112/1, A to bros, Vienna, 3 May (1873); RAL, XI/109/113/1, A to bros, Frankfurt, 22 Aug (1873).

66 RAL, XI/109/109/1, Juliana to L, *Czarina* (Cornish coast, probably Falmouth, undated, July–Sept 1872); Filon, *Prince Imperial*, p. 96; RAL, 000/84, CL to Leo, 148 Piccadilly, 28 July 1875; RAL, 000/13/384, L to Leo (in pencil), (London, undated); RAL, 000/13/384, L to Leo, (London, undated); Cohen, *Lady de Rothschild*, p. 166.

67 Sheppard (ed.), *Duke of Cambridge memoir*, vol. 2, p. 40; *BM*, vol. 28, 1876, p. 182.

68 Ferguson, *Rothschild*, vol. II, p. 253.

69 RAL, 000/13/93, L to CL & children, 9 March 1868.

70 RAL, XI/109/108/2, ?J. Sheppard to L, 12 Old Jewry Chambers, Old Jewry, EC, 9 May 1872.

71 RAL, 000/84, CL to Leo & Leonora, 148 Piccadilly, 7 Aug 1874.

72 Rothschild, *Dear Lord Rothschild*, p. 5; RAL, XI/109/109/1, Richard Dawes to L, 9 Angel Court, Throgmorton Street, London, 3 July 1872.

73 Ferguson, *Rothschild*, vol. II, p. 299.

74 Quoted in Mortimer, *Derby Stakes*, p. 262.

75 RAL, 000/848, William Rogers to Natty, Rectory House, Bishopsgate, 3 June (1879); RAL, 000/924, 'The History of the Firm' by A. R. Wagg (typescript).

76 *BM*, vol. 34, 1879, p. 150; *Annual Register*, 1879, 'Obituary', p. 199.

77 RAL, 000/176/4, L's will.

78 RAL, XI/109/78/7, N to bros (Paris, undated, Jan–June 1851); Ferguson, *Rothschild*, vol. I, p. 482.

79 *BM*, vol. 34, 1879, pp. 149–50.

Bibliography

Aiken, John, *A Description of the Country from Thirty to Forty Miles around Manchester* (Manchester, 1795)

Albemarle, George Thomas, Earl of, *Fifty Years of My Life, by George Thomas, Earl of Albemarle*, 2 vols (London, 1876)

Allen, Hervey, *Israfel: The Life and Times of Edgar Allan Poe*, 2 vols (London, 1927)

Anderson, Verily, *The Northrepps Grandchildren* (London, 1968)

The Annual Biography and Obituary, vol. 21, 1837 (London, 1837), 'Nathan Meyer [*sic*] Rothschild, Esq.', pp. 54–68

The Annual Register, 1836 (London, 1837); 1841 (London, 1842); 1847 (London, 1848); 1879 (London, 1880)

Anonymous, *Letters from Albion to a Friend on the Continent, written in the years 1810, 1811, 1812 & 1813*, 2 vols (London, 1814)

Anonymous (ed.), *The Black Book: An Exposition of Abuses in Church and State, Courts of Law, Municipal Corporations, and Public Companies; with a précis of the House of Commons, Past, Present, and to Come* (new edition, London, 1835)

Aspey, Melanie, 'Mrs Rothschild', in Victor Gray and Melanie Aspey (eds), *The Life and Times of N. M. Rothschild 1777–1836* (London, 1998), pp. 58–67

Aston, Joseph, *A Picture of Manchester* (Manchester, 1816)

Auldjo, John, *Journal of a Visit to Constantinople, and some of the Greek Islands, in the Spring and Summer of 1833* (London, 1835)

Austen Leigh, Mary Augusta, *James Edward Austen Leigh: A Memoir by his Daughter Mary Augusta Austen Leigh* (for private circulation, 1911)

Axon, William E. A. (ed.), *The Annals of Manchester: A chronological record from the earliest times to the end of 1885* (Manchester and London, 1886)

Ayer, Jules, *A Century of Finance, 1804 to 1904: The London House of Rothschild* (London, 1905)

Baines, Edward, *History, Directory, and Gazetteer, of the County Palatine of Lancaster [etc]*, 2 vols (Liverpool, 1825)

Baker, T. F. T. (ed.), *The Victoria History of the County of Middlesex*, vol. viii (1985)

Bamford, Francis, and the Duke of Wellington (eds), *The Journal of Mrs Arbuthnot 1820–1832*, 2 vols (London, 1950)

Barman, Roderick J., 'Nathan Mayer Rothschild and Brazil: the role of Samuel Phillips & Co.', in *The Rothschild Archive Review of the Year April 2002–March 2003*, pp. 38–45

Barnett, Richard David, 'A Diary That Survived: Damascus 1840', in Sonia and Vivian D. Lipman (eds), *The Century of Moses Montefiore* (Oxford, 1985), pp. 149–70

Baron-Wilson, Mrs Cornwell, *Memoirs of Harriot, Duchess of St Albans*, 2 vols (second edition, London, 1840)

Battersea, Constance, Lady, *Reminiscences* (London, 1922)

Beresford Chancellor, E. (trans. and ed.), *The Diary of Philipp von Neumann 1819 to 1850*, 2 vols (London, 1928)

Berkeley, G. C. Grantley F., *Reminiscences of a Huntsman* (London, 1854)

Bermant, Chaim, *The Cousinhood: the Anglo-Jewish Gentry* (London, 1971)

Berry, Michael F., *A History of the Puckeridge Hunt* (London, 1950)

Bessborough, Earl of (ed.), *Lady Charlotte Guest, Extracts from her Journal 1833–1852* (London, 1950)

Bird, T. H., *Admiral Rous and the English Turf* (London, 1939)

Blessington, Marguerite Gardiner, Countess of, *The Idler in Italy*, 2 vols (London, 1839–40)

Booth, J. B., *London Town* (London, 1929)

Bovill, E. W., *The England of Nimrod and Surtees 1815–1854* (London, 1959)

——, *English Country Life 1780–1830* (London, 1962)

Boyd, Mark, *Reminiscences of Fifty Years* (London, 1871)

Boyle's Court Guide, for April 1828

——, *for January 1836*

——, *for January 1838*

——, *for January 1840*

Brimley Johnson, R. (ed.), *Elizabeth Fry's Journeys on the Continent 1840–1841* (London, 1931)

Brinson, Peter, *Background to European Ballet: A Notebook from its Archives* (Leyden, 1966)

Brown, Malcolm, 'The Jews of Hackney before 1840', in *Transactions of the Jewish Historical Society of England*, vol. 30 (1987–8), paper delivered to the Society on 20 Feb 1986, pp. 71–89

Brownlow, Emma Sophia, Countess, *The Eve of Victorianism* (London, 1940)

Buxton, Charles (ed.), *Memoirs of Sir Thomas Fowell Buxton, Baronet, with selections from his correspondence* (London, 1848)

Carr, Raymond, *English Fox Hunting, A History* (London, 1976)

Chapman, R. W. (ed.), *Jane Austen's Letters to Her Sister Cassandra and others*, 2 vols (Oxford, 1932)

Chateaubriand, François René, Vicomte de, *The Memoirs of François René Vicomte de Chateaubriand, sometime Ambassador to England* (translated from the French by Alexander Teixeira de Mattos), 6 vols (London, 1902)

Cohen, Hannah F., *Changing Faces, A memoir of Louisa Lady Cohen* (London, 1937)

Cohen, Lucy, *Lady de Rothschild and her daughters 1821–1931* (London, 1935)

Coleridge, A. D. (trans. and ed.), *Life of Moscheles, with Selections from his Diaries and Correspondence, by his wife, adapted from the original German*, 2 vols (London, 1873)

The Complete Peerage or a History of the House of Lords and all its members from the earliest times by G. E. C[okayne], revised and enlarged by the Hon. Vicary Gibbs, now edited by H. A. Doubleday, Duncan Warrand and Lord Howard de Walden, vol. VI, *Gordon to Hurstpierpoint* (London, 1926)

Cook, Olive, *The English Country House, an art and a way of life* (London, 1974)

Corti, Count Egon, *The Rise of the House of Rothschld*, 2 vols (London, 1938)

Cottrell, P. L., 'The Businessman and Financier', in Sonia and Vivian D. Lipman (eds), *The Century of Moses Montefiore* (Oxford, 1985), pp. 23–44

Cowen, Anne, and Roger Cowen, *Victorian Jews Through British Eyes* (London, 1998)

Cowles, Virginia, *The Rothschilds: a family of fortune* (London, 1973)

Dalling and Bulwer, Sir Henry Lytton Bulwer, Lord, *Life of Henry John Temple, Viscount Palmerston*, ed. the Hon. Evelyn Ashley, MP, vol. 3 (1874)

Dasent, Arthur Irwin, *Piccadilly in Three Centuries, with some account of Berkeley Square and the Haymarket* (London, 1920)

Davis, Richard, *Political Change and Continuity, 1760–1885: A Buckinghamshire Study* (1972)

——, *The English Rothschilds* (London, 1983)

Disraeli, Benjamin, *Coningsby, or the New Generation* (1844, Penguin Classics edition, 1989)

——, *Lord Beaconsfield's Correspondence with His Sister 1832–1852* (London, 1886)

Dixon, Henry Hall ('The Druid'), *Scott and Sebright* (London, 1862)

Dixon, H. Sydenham, *From Gladiateur to Persimmon, Turf Memories of Thirty Years* (London, 1901)

Dod, C. E., *An Autumn Near the Rhine, or Sketches of Courts, Society and Scenery in Germany, with a Tour in the Taunus Mountains in 1820* (second edition, London, 1821)

Dowling, S. W., *The Exchanges of London* (London, 1929)

Eeles, Henry S., and Earl Spencer, *Brooks's 1764–1964* (London, 1964)

Emden, Paul H., *Quakers in Commerce: A Record of Business Achievement* (London, 1940)

——, *Jews of Britain: A Series of Biographies* (London, 1944)

Endelman, Tod M., *The Jews of Britain 1650 to 2000* (London, 2002)

Evans, David Morier, *City Men and Manners* (London, 1845; updated edition, 1851)

Ferguson, Niall, *The World's Banker: The History of the House of Rothschild*, 2 vols (Penguin edition, 2000)

Filon, Augustin (trans.), *Memoirs of the Prince Imperial (1856–1879)* (London, 1913)

Forster, E. M., *Marianne Thornton 1797–1887, A Domestic Biography* (London, 1956)

Forster, Henry Rumsey, *The Stowe Catalogue Priced and Annotated* (London, 1848)

Fowler, John Kersley, *Echoes of Old Country Life, being recollections of sport, politics and farming in the good old times* (London, 1892)

——, *Recollections of Old Country Life, social, political, sporting and agricultural* (London, 1894)

Gallatin, Count (ed.), *A Great Peace Maker, The Diary of James Gallatin, secretary to Albert Gallatin, US envoy to France and England 1813–1827 [etc]* (London, 1914)

Gash, Norman, *Robert Surtees and Early Victorian Society* (Oxford, 1993; R. S. Surtees Society edition, 1996)

Gatty, Richard, *Portrait of a Merchant Prince: James Morrison 1789–1857* (Northallerton, 1977)

The Gentleman's Magazine, ns, vol. vi, 1836, July to December inclusive (London, 1837), 'N. M. Rothschild, Esq', pp. 325–30

Gilbert, Edmund W., *Brighton: Old Ocean's Bauble* (London, 1954)

Gille, Bertrand, *Histoire de la Maison Rothschild*, 2 vols (Geneva, 1965)

Girouard, Mark, *The Victorian Country House* (revised and enlarged edition, London, 1979)

Gray, Victor, 'An off-hand man: The character of Nathan Rothschild', in Victor Gray and Melanie Aspey (eds), *The Life and Times of N. M. Rothschild 1777–1836* (London, 1998), pp. 14–21

Gray, Victor, and Melanie Aspey (eds), *The Life and Times of N. M. Rothschild 1777–1836* (London, 1998)

Gronow, R. H., *The Reminiscences and Recollections of Captain Gronow [etc], 1810–1860*, 2 vols (London, 1892 edition)

Gulbenkian, Nubar, *Pantaraxia: The Autobiography of Nubar Gulbenkian* (London, 1965)

Gulland, Diana, 'Aston Clinton House, Buckinghamshire', in *The Rothschild Archive Review of the Year April 2002–March 2003*, pp. 32–7

Hanham, H. J. (ed.), *Electoral Facts from 1832 to 1853 Impartially Stated, by Charles R. Dod* (1972)

Hansard, *Parliamentary Debates*, vol. lxxviii (London, 1845)

Hansard, *Parliamentary Debates*, 3rd series, vols xcv, xcvi, xcvii, xcviii (London, 1848)

Hare, Augustus J., *The Gurneys of Earlham*, 2 vols (London, 1895)

Harper, Charles G., *The Great North Road, The Old Mail Road to Scotland*, 2 vols (London, 1901)

——, *The Manchester & Glasgow Road: London to Manchester* (London, 1924)

Harte, Negley, *The University of London 1836–1986: An illustrated history* (London, 1986)

Healey, Edna, *Coutts & Co. 1692–1992: The Portrait of a Private Bank* (London, 1992)

Henrey, Robert, *A Century Between* (London, 1937)

Hensel, Sebastian, *The Mendelssohn Family (1729–1847), from letters and journals*, 2 vols (second edition, London, 1882)

Howitt, William, *German Experiences: addressed to the English; both stayers at home, and goers abroad* (London, 1844)

Hugo, Thomas, *An Illustrated Itinerary of the Ward of Bishopsgate, in the City of London* (London, 1862)

Irving, Pierre M. (ed.), *The Life and Letters of Washington Irving*, 3 vols (London, 1862)

Jamieson, Anna, *Diary of an Ennuyée* (new edition, London, 1826)

Jennings, Louis J. (ed.), *The Croker Papers: The Correspondence and Diaries of the late Right Honourable John Wilson Croker, Secretary to the Admiralty from 1809 to 1830*, 3 vols (London, 1884–5)

Jerdan, William, *The Autobiography of William Jerdan*, 4 vols (London, 1852 and 1853)

Joshua, Essaka, 'Lionel and Anthony von Rothschild at Göttingen University', in *The Thomas Lovell Beddoes Society Newsletter*, vol. 11 (2005)

Kass, Amalie M., 'Friends and Philanthropists: Montefiore and Dr Hodgkin', in Sonia and Vivian D. Lipman (eds), *The Century of Moses Montefiore* (Oxford, 1985), pp. 71–103

Kauffmann, C. M., *Catalogue of Paintings in the Wellington Museum* (London, 1982)

Kellner, L., *Alexander von Humboldt* (London, 1963)

Kelly, Ian, *Cooking for Kings: The Life of Antonin Carême, the first celebrity chef* (London, 2003)

Kent, G. H. R. (ed.), *The Victoria County History: Yorkshire, East Riding*, vol. vii (2002)

Kessler, David, 'The Rothschilds and Disraeli in Buckinghamshire, An Essay' (Rothschild Waddesdon Ltd, 1996; originally published in *Transactions of the Jewish Historical Society of England*, vol. 29 (1982–6), pp. 231–53)

Kinglake, A. W., *Eothen, or traces of travel brought home from the East* (London, 1844)

Kitching, Colin (ed.), *Squire of Calke Abbey, The Journals of Sir George Crewe 1815–1834* (1995)

Kynaston, David, *The City of London, Volume I, A World of Its Own 1815–1890* (London, 1994; Pimlico edition, 1995)

Lejeune, Anthony, *The Gentlemen's Clubs of London* (London, 1979; 1984 edition)

Leveson Gower, F., *Letters of Harriet Countess Granville 1810–1845*, 2 vols (second edition, London, 1894)

Liedtke, Rainer, 'Nathan Rothschild and London Jewry', in Victor Gray and Melanie Aspey (eds), *The Life and Times of N. M. Rothschild 1777–1836* (London, 1998), pp. 50–57

Lipman, Sonia and Vivian D. Lipman (eds), *The Century of Moses Montefiore* (Oxford, 1985)

Loewe, Louis (ed.), *Diaries of Sir Moses and Lady Montefiore*, 2 vols (London, 1890)

Loftus, Lord Augustus, *Diplomatic Reminiscences, 1837–1862*, 2 vols (London, 1892)

Londonderry, C. W. Vane, 3rd Marquess of, *A Steam Voyage to Constantinople, by the Rhine and the Danube, in 1840–41, and to Portugal, Spain, &c, in 1839*, 2 vols (London, 1842)

Malmesbury, J. H. Harris, 3rd Earl of, *Memoirs of an Ex-Minister: An Autobiography*, 2 vols (second edition, London, 1884)

Mansel, Philip, *Paris Between the Empires, 1814–1852* (London, 2001)

Margetson, Stella, *Journey by Stages, Some Account of the People who Travelled by Stage-Coach and Mail in the Years between 1660 and 1840* (London, 1967)

Margoliouth, Moses, *The History of the Jews in Great Britain*, 3 vols (London, 1851)

Mendelssohn Bartholdy, Paul, and Carl Mendelssohn Bartholdy (eds), and Lady Wallace (trans.), *Letters of Felix Mendelssohn Bartholdy, from 1833 to 1847* (London, 1863)

Monypenny, William Flavelle, *The Life of Benjamin Disraeli, Earl of Beaconsfield*, vol. 2 (London, 1912)

Mordaunt Crook, J., *The Rise of the Nouveaux Riches: Style and Status in Victorian and Edwardian Architecture* (London, 1999)

Mortimer, Roger, *The History of the Derby Stakes* (London, 1962)

Muhlstein, Anka, *Baron James: The Rise of the French Rothschilds* (London, 1983)

Murray, the Hon. Amelia, *Recollections from 1803 to 1837, with a conclusion in 1868* (London, 1868)

A Handbook for Travellers in Greece [etc], fourth edition, John Murray, London, 1872

A Handbook for Travellers in Turkey, third edition, John Murray, London, 1854

Murray, Venetia, *High Society, A Social History of the Regency Period, 1788–1830* (London, 1998)

Nevill, Ralph, *Romantic London* (London, 1928)

Nightingale, the Revd Joseph, *The Beauties of England and Wales: or, Original Delineations, Topographical, Historical, and Descriptive, of Each County* (vol. x, part iii, London, 1815)

Notes and Queries, 11th Series, vol. x, July to December 1914

Onslow, Richard, *Headquarters, A History of Newmarket and its Racing* (1983)

Page, William (ed.), *The Victoria History of the County of Hertford*, vol. 1 (London, 1902)

——, *The Victoria History of the County of Middlesex*, vol. 2 (London, 1911)

Passavant, M. J. D., *Tour of a German Artist in England, with notices of private galleries, and remarks on the state of art*, 2 vols (London, 1836)

Picciotto, James, *Sketches of Anglo-Jewish History* (London, 1875)

Pinney, Thomas (ed.), *The Letters of Thomas Babington Macaulay*, vol. 6 (Cambridge, 1981)

Ponsonby, Sir Frederick, *Sidelights on Queen Victoria* (London, 1930)

Ponsonby, Major-General Sir John, *The Ponsonby Family* (London, 1929)

Pückler-Muskau, Prince Hermann von, *Tour in Germany, Holland and England in the Years 1826, 1827 & 1828, with remarks on the manners and customs of the inhabitants, and anecdotes of distinguished public characters, in a series of letters, by a German Prince*, 4 vols (London, 1832)

Raikes, Thomas, *A Portion of the Journal kept by Thomas Raikes, Esq, from 1831 to 1847*, 4 vols (London, 1857)

Reeks, Margaret, *The Mother of Goethe, 'Frau Aja'* (London, 1911)

Richard, J. B., and Mariana Starke, *Guide du Voyageur en Italie* (sixth edition, Paris, 1833–4)

Roberts, W., *Sir William Beechey, R.A.* (London, 1907)

Roth, Cecil, *A History of the Jews in England* (Oxford, 1949)

——, *The Rise of Provincial Jewry* (London, 1950)

—— (ed.), *Essays in Jewish History by Lucien Wolf, with a Memoir* (London, 1934), 'A Memoir', pp. 3–34

—— (ed.), *Anglo-Jewish Letters (1158–1917)* (London, 1938)

Rothschild, the Hon. Miriam, *Dear Lord Rothschild: Birds, Butterflies and History* (London, 1983)

Rothschild, Lord (Victor), *The Shadow of a Great Man* (London, 1982)

Russell, George W. E., *Lady Victoria Buxton, a memoir with some account of her husband* (London, 1919)

Russell, John, *A Tour in Germany and Some of the Provinces of the Austrian Empire in 1820, 1821 and 1822*, 2 vols (new edition, Edinburgh, 1828)

Salbstein, M. C. N., *The Emancipation of the Jews in Britain: The Question of the Admission of the Jews to Parliament, 1828–1860* (London, 1982)

Schooling, Sir William, *Alliance Assurance 1824–1924* (London, 1924)

Selden-Goth, G. (ed.), *Felix Mendelssohn: Letters* (London, 1946)

Sheahan, James Joseph, *History and Topography of Buckinghamshire Comprising a General Survey of the County, preceded by an Epitome of the Early History of Great Britain* (London, 1862)

Sheppard, Edgar (ed.), *George Duke of Cambridge: A memoir of his private life based on the journals and correspondence of His Royal Highness*, 2 vols (London, 1907)

Shuttleworth, the Hon. Nina L. Kay, *A Life of Sir Woodbine Parish, KCH, FRS (1796–1882)* (London, 1910)

Slade, Adolphus, *Records of Travel in the East* (London, 1833; new edition 1854)

——, *Turkey, Greece and Malta*, 2 vols (London, 1837)

Slugg, J. T., *Reminiscences of Manchester Fifty Years Ago* (Manchester, 1881)

Sotheby's, Mentmore sale catalogue, 1977, vol. 1, French and Continental Furniture, Tapestries and Clocks

Spohr, Louis, *Louis Spohr's Autobiography*, translated from the German, 2 vols (London, 1865)

Sprigge, Elizabeth, and Claude Napier (transs), *Erik Gustav Geijer, Impressions of England 1809–1810, compiled from his letters and diaries* (London, 1932)

Storck, Karl (ed.), and Hannah Bryant (trans.), *The Letters of Robert Schumann* (London, 1907)

Sudley, Lord (trans. and ed.), *The Lieven–Palmerston Correspondence 1828–1856* (London, 1943)

Suffolk and Berkshire, Earl of, and W. G. Craven (and others), *Racing and Steeple-chasing – The Badminton Library* (London, 1886)

Surtees, Robert Smith, *Ask Mamma* (London, 1858; R. S. Surtees Society edition, 1983)

——, *Plain or Ringlets* (London, 1860; R. S. Surtees Society edition, 1986)

'Thormanby', *Kings of the Turf* (London, 1898)

Thornbury, George Walter, *Old and New London: A Narrative of its History, its People, and its Places*, vol. I (London, n.d., pre-1874)

Thorne, R. G., *The History of Parliament. The History of the House of Commons, 1790–1820*, vol. V (London, 1986)

Trollope, Anthony, *An Autobiography* (1883, edited with an introduction by David Skilton, Penguin Classics edition, 1996)

Walsh, Edward, '19/20 Grosvenor Place: The Buildings and Occupancy', Part 1, in *The Penspen Review*, No. 29, October 1987

Walsh, the Revd R., *A Residence at Constantinople during a period including the commencement, progress, and termination of the Greek and Turkish revolutions*, 2 vols (London, 1836)

Wansell, Geoffrey, *The Garrick Club, A History* (London, 2004)

Ward Jones, Peter (trans. and ed.), *The Mendelssohns on Honeymoon: The 1837 Diary of Felix and Cécile Mendelssohn Bartholdy Together with Letters to their Families* (Oxford, 1997)

Weinstock, Herbert, *Rossini: A Biography* (London, 1968)

Wheatley, Henry B., *Round About Piccadilly and Pall Mall; or a Ramble from the Haymarket to Hyde Park* (London, 1870)

Whitwell Wilson, Philip (ed.), *The Greville Diary, Including Passages Hitherto Withheld from Publication*, 2 vols (London, 1927)

Whyte-Melville, G. J., *Satanella, A Story of Punchestown* (London, 1872)

——, *Riding Recollections* (London, 1878)

Williams, Bill, *The Making of Manchester Jewry 1740–1875* (Manchester, 1976)

Willoughby de Broke, Lord, *The Passing Years* (London, 1924)

Wilson, A. N., *The Victorians* (London, 2002)

Wilson, Derek, *Rothschild: a story of wealth and power* (London, 1988)

Wilson, Michael I., *The English Country House and its furnishings* (London, 1977)

Wolf, Lucien, *Sir Moses Montefiore: A Centennial Biography, with extracts from letters and journals* (London, 1884)

——, 'The News of Waterloo: how it reached the Rothschilds', in the *Daily Graphic*, 15 April 1903

——, 'Old Anglo-Jewish Families', in Cecil Roth (ed.), *Essays in Jewish History by Lucien Wolf* (London, 1934), pp. 205–29

——, 'Lady Montefiore's Honeymoon', in ibid., pp. 233–58

——, 'Rothschildiana', in ibid., pp. 261–308

——, 'The Queen's Jewry', in ibid., pp. 311–62

Wright, Charles, and C. Ernest Fayle, *A History of Lloyd's* (London, 1928)

Ziegler, Philip, *The Sixth Great Power, Barings 1762–1929* (London, 1988)

Index